The Interpretation of
St. Paul's Epistles to the Galatians
to the Ephesians
and to the Philippians

By
R. C. H. LENSKI

AUGSBURG PUBLISHING HOUSE
Minneapolis, Minnesota

ABBREVIATIONS

R. = A Grammar of the Greek New Testament in the Light of Historical Research, by A. T. Robertson, fourth edition.

B.-D. = Friedrich Blass' Grammatik des neutestamentlichen Griechisch, vierte, voellig neu-gearbeitete Auflage besorgt von Albert Debrunner.

C.-K. = Biblisch-theologisches Woerterbuch der Neutestament-lichen Graezitaet von D. Dr. Hermann Cremer, zehnte, etc., Auflage, herausgegeben von D. Dr. Julius Koegel.

B.-P. = Griechisch-Deutsches Woerterbuch zu den Schriften des Neuen Testaments, etc., von D. Walter Bauer, zweite, etc., Auflage zu Erwin Preuschens Vollstaendigem Griechisch-Deutschem Handwoerterbuch, etc.

M.-M. = The Vocabulary of the Greek Testament, Illustrated from the Papyri and other Non-Literary Sources, by James Hope Moulton and George Milligan.

R., W. P. = Word Pictures in the New Testament by Archibald Thomas Robertson.

INTRODUCTION

Saint Paul's Epistle to the Galatians has always been famous; Luther's use of it, together with his commentary on it, have increased this fame. The Reformer prized its doctrinal contents, its mighty defense of justification by faith alone, and its glorious vindication of liberty from the law. Galatians is the impregnable citadel, a very Gibraltar, against any attack on the heart of the gospel. This epistle is the grand arsenal which is stocked with the weapons that assure victory in the ceaseless battle for the central truths of the gospel.

Romans, too, has its militant side. Romans 2 is the annihilation of the greatest foe of justification by faith alone, of the moralism, pagan (Rom. 2:1-17) as well as Jewish (Rom. 2:18-29), which proposes to save the sinner by means of law and moral reform, by which every moralist condemns himself and his following the more by his reliance on moralism. See the writer's interpretation of this great chapter. Aside from that chapter Romans is thetical and not polemical. Galatians is polemical and militant throughout. Luther loved this short letter because he had to fight Paul's battle over again. He fought with the same joy and the same assurance of victory. We range ourselves behind Paul as Luther once did. Galatians is our love as it was his.

Only a letter of six short chapters, written almost 2,000 years ago, but a document of such power as has never been duplicated! Immortal victory is set upon its brow. It is not Paul whom we admire; he, indeed, penned these lines, but the Holy Spirit speaks in them, speaks to this day. The supreme proof of Inspiration is its product. Galatians, read in this light, leaves nothing to be desired.

More recent scholarship has busied itself with the historical side of the letter, a task that was neglected until these latter times but is now accomplished with thoroughness. The epistle itself contains most valuable historical data. Failure to apprehend what they convey, as well as any misunderstanding of their content and their bearing would mean great loss. Dispute is, of course, still rife. Whatever ardor may be developed in this part of exegetical polemics must not be allowed to supersede our ardor for the supreme contents of this epistle, the blessed, saving, glorious doctrines which it defends. All the historical data only support the main thesis: their great value lies in this fact.

Many introductions compile all the available information about Paul and his two great missionary journeys and often include what lies beyond. In addition to this fact, in their introductions many writers discuss the bulk of the details found in the epistle itself and thus duplicate the exegesis they offer. This fills many pages and creates bulk. Is it necessary? We confine ourselves to the essentials. In the interpretation of Acts Paul's missionary journeys are fully treated in a manner which is impossible in an introduction to Galatians. The careful student must necessarily delve into Acts. This is true also with regard to the historical material embedded in Galatians. Any adequate study of the material offered can best be made on the basis of the epistle itself by treating each item fully in the context where it occurs. This is the really satisfactory method.

*   *   *

Every present-day student is compelled to face the question: "Who were the Galatians?" Is the word Γαλάται used in the original ethnographic sense as denoting nationality, or is it to be understood in the geographic sense as designating the inhabitants of the Roman province that was called Γαλατία in Paul's time? If the latter is correct, then we must ask further: "Were the churches addressed by Paul located in the great stretch of northern Galatia, in the widely separated cities Pessinus, Ancyra, and Tavium, or in the smaller area of southern Galatia, in the cities that were more closely contiguous, which we know so well from Acts: Antioch, Iconium, Lystra, and Derbe?" We note two answers: 1) congregations in Upper Galatia; 2) congregations in Lower Galatia. Please examine the map.

The name Γαλάται is only a later modification of the original name Κέλτοι or Κέλται, who were Celtic tribes of ancient Gaul, in particular the Τρόκμοι and Τολιστοβόγοι, combined with the Germanic Tectosages (from Toulouse). These tribes invaded Greece and pillaged Delphi in 280 B. C., established a kingdom in Thrace which was called Thyle, and then appeared on the shores of the Hellespont. They crossed into Asia on the invitation of Nikomedes I, king of Bithynia, to aid him in a civil war. Once established in Asia Minor, these warlike tribes extended their ravages far and wide. During the following years they were repressed and finally conquered, and in the final wars, which established the power of the Romans in their territory, they were subdued by Manlius, the Roman consul, in 189 B. C., and appear as a subject kingdom, at first under a tetrarch and then under a king of their own. The boundaries of the territory they inhabited varied from time to time. They retained their language and their customs for many years.

After the death of Amyntus, the last king of the Galatian tribes, in 25 B. C., the Roman province of Galatia was formed by adding to the northern territory, over which these Celts had spread, certain southern sections, the greater part of the Pisidian region, Isauria, Lycaonia, and portions of eastern Phrygia, the whole province as thus formed being called Galatia.

A valuable observation is this, when Luke speaks of Asia Minor and of other districts he employs the old ethnographic names without regard to the boundaries of the Roman provinces; Paul, however, employs the names of the Roman provinces regardless of the nationalities inhabiting them. Part of the confusion of the commentators is due to failure to note this fact. We need not again compile the proof from Luke and from Paul. Suffice it to say that the province of Galatia is not identical with the old kingdom ruled over by the descendants of the Celtic tribes. The province included the added southern sections which incorporated the descendants of other ethnographic stocks. In Lystra, for instance, the natives were Lycaonians who still clung to their ancient language. Acts 14:11. The southern parts of the province were not made up of a Celtic population.

All this, however, does not yet locate within the province the churches addressed by Paul as "Galatians." They might still be located in either Upper or Lower Galatia, possibly even in both parts of the province. Yet so much is already assured that "Galatians" does not necessarily mean Celts; it may refer to any of the inhabitants of the Roman province irrespective of their extraction, including even Jews, certainly also Greeks and Latins, living anywhere in the province.

*   *   *

Luke describes Paul's missionary journeys very accurately by taking us from place to place without leaving a gap. In the whole of Acts there is not a word about a visit of Paul's to Upper Galatia. The only time, according to Luke's account, when Paul might have entered Upper Galatia, his mind was set on Bithynia, but the Spirit directed him away from that province to the city of Troas and after he reached that place led him to cross into Europe to the province of Macedonia. Acts 16:6-10. After visiting the churches already founded in Southern Galatia, no work was done on this second missionary journey until Paul reached Philippi in Macedonia. Now the epistle not only presupposes that Paul founded the congregations to which it is addressed but that, after founding them, he had visited them and had spent some time in their midst on this second visit. If these were churches in Upper Galatia, time and occasion must be found when Paul could have founded and afterward visited churches in this locality. Attempts to find these are unsatisfactory.

On the other hand, we know all about the churches in Southern Galatia. We have the full story of their founding, also the account of Paul's visit to them on his second missionary journey when he brought them the letter from the convention held at Jerusalem and thereby confirmed these churches and increased their membership. Acts 15:23-29; 16:4, 5. All this agrees with the epistle. Also the fact that all was well with these churches when Paul visited them as Luke reports. No Judaizers had appeared in their midst. The invasion came later, after Paul had left, possibly some weeks later.

This, then, is the situation: Paul's letter fits exactly all that we know about the churches in Southern Galatia, not a single point can be urged to the contrary; on the other hand, the very existence of churches in Northern Galatia is hypothetical, we do not have the name of one city and, of course, not a word about number, size, or character of the members. If we accept the view that our epistle is addressed to cities in Upper Galatia, all we are able to do is to transfer to them whatever we may gather from the epistle and ignore the southern churches. We ought, then, also to reconstruct Luke's record of Paul's journey so as to make room for two periods of gospel work in Upper Galatia on the part of Paul. We therefore conclude that the epistle was addressed to churches in Lower Galatia.

Yet the commentators of an early date and also most of the moderns, Lightfoot being prominent among the latter, advocate what is called the northern theory. Smith's *Bible Dictionary,* for instance, under "Galatians" merely quotes Lightfoot at length and does not even mention another view. Those of the ancients who touch upon this subject wrote after 350 A. D., and were probably misled by the fact that since 297 A. D. Galatia had again been reduced to the old territory that was once dominated by the Celtic tribes.

* * *

The following may be added. If Paul had worked in Upper Galatia, he would have encountered language difficulties since Greek culture and Greek speech were not dominant in these regions. Again, if Paul desired to name the churches of Phrygia, Pamphylia, and Lycaonia in Lower Galatia with *one* name, that name could have been only "Galatians." In the same way he speaks of "Macedonians" although different nationalities were represented in these European churches. Even in Upper Galatia the churches would have been of a mixed population, could not have been Celtic alone or even predominantly Celtic.

A good deal is usually made of Paul's remark in 1:6 that the Galatians so quickly gave up their faith. It is supposed that the bulk of these congregations were made up of Celts, and that therefore Cæsar's estimate of the Gallic Celts is reflected in Paul's remark: "The infirmity of the Gauls is, that they are fickle in their resolves, fond of change, and not to be trusted." Thierry: "Frank, impetuous, impressible, eminently intelligent, fond of show, but extremely inconstant, the fruit of excessive vanity." This invites to pertinent homiletical application, which few resist. But it is evident that these characterizations apply to Paul's words only if the bulk of the churches were made up of actual Celts. Any congregation even in Upper Galatia would include a mixed population and probably have but few real Celts. Paul's words are such as fit any church in which heresies had secured a hold in a comparatively brief time. Moreover, the epistle itself shows that the conclusion is unwarranted that these churches had turned away from Paul's teaching in fickleness of mind; they had not as yet turned away. Paul also expects to keep them true to his teaching. This connects with the following points.

*　　*　　*

Throughout the entire epistle Paul proves himself fully informed as to the situation in the Galatian churches. He knows even the details of the arguments used by the Judaizers. Yet nowhere does he mention the sources of his information — not as though he were concealing the sources, but quite the contrary, he takes it for granted that his readers know these sources. We get the impression that Paul's information has not come from a letter that was sent to him by the churches. Private letters and news through private persons are also excluded; First Corinthians shows us that when Paul uses information of this kind he says so in all frankness. Only one assumption satisfies us regarding Paul's complete information and the lack of necessity for stating its source: a delegation must have been sent to Paul by the Galatian churches, a committee that was duly commissioned by the Galatian churches, a committee that was duly commissioned by the Galatians themselves and was thus known to all. This also explains why Paul does not need to refer to this commission in the epistle since these men will receive this epistle and will bear it to Galatia.

Paul offers no excuse as to why he does not repair to the Galatians in person. In some of his other letters he tells what detains him or what prevents his personal coming at that time. He does not plan to come to Galatia in the near future in order to follow up any good effect his epistle may produce. His whole reliance is placed on the curative effect of the epistle itself. To this we add 1:2: "all the brethren with me," which undoubtedly includes the brethren of the Galatian commission. Paul had completely convinced them of the mistake the Galatians were making by having anything whatever to do with the Judaizers who had invaded their churches. Their conviction would support Paul's epistle.

All this has its bearing on determining the place where Paul wrote the epistle. The older assumption that this place was Ephesus, and that the time of writing was Paul's stay of two years in Ephesus, becomes improbable. This assumption is based on the idea that the churches were located in Upper Galatia. If they were, Paul could have made a quick trip from Ephesus to Upper Galatia and attended in person to the danger that was threatening. He could have made such a trip to Lower Galatia even more easily. The fact that he contemplates nothing of the kind implies that he was much farther away and in the midst of work that could not be interrupted by a journey to Galatia.

Other points must be added. We know that Paul usually dictated his letters to an amanuensis. This epistle he writes with his own hand. He must, then, have been alone. He sends no greetings from Timothy or from Silas or from any of his assistants. This again makes the impression that he was alone. He names as being associated with him in writing "all the brethren with him." This includes those of the committee from Galatia plus a number of other believers. He sends no greetings from a church.

Taking all these points together, where do they place Paul, and at what time do they place him after his second tour through Galatia? Certainly not in Ephesus nor at so late a time. The time and the place that match these data is Corinth a short time after Paul first began to work there, probably before Silas and Timothy joined him (Acts 18:5). Then Paul was alone, far from Galatia, in southern Europe where the Lord had given him specific orders to work, in Corinth where the Lord directed him to stay on, at the time when a church had not yet been formed, when only the first converts had been won.

This is the most likely time and the most likely place. Then, however, Galatians is the *first* Pauline epistle we have. Then First Thessalonians must have been written a little later. These conclusions are not absolute, but they do agree with *all* the data available. The only uncertainty is whether Corinth is the place. Might it, perhaps, have been Athens? It was written at some place near this time, and Corinth is by all odds the likeliest locality.

Corinth appeals to others, who, however, think of the much later stay of Paul in this city, of his stay of three months during the winter just before he accompanied the delegation that bore the great collection to Jerusalem. This is entirely too late, to say nothing more. It would project the journey of the Galatian delegation into the winter. Then shipping ceased. Then the delegation would have traveled by land. This supposition places the date of Galatians close to that of Romans. But Romans in no way hints that it was composed near the date of the epistle to the Galatians. When Paul wrote Romans he was not alone and was in a congregation that had been established for some years, whose greetings he would send when writing to other churches. The collection was about to be sent to Jerusalem at this time. Romans speaks of it. The Galatians were participating in it. Not a word of this appears in Paul's epistle to them. This epistle must be dated at a far earlier time. The old subscription: "Sent to the Galatians from Rome," (A. V.) is spurious.

*   *   *

The Judaizers who had invaded the Galatian churches were of the kind that at one time came to Antioch in Syria and then received their answer at the great convention held at Jerusalem (Acts 15). We hear nothing further about Judaizers until this time. What they were must be gathered from Acts 15 and from our epistle, to which we may add II Cor. 12. In brief, they were Jews who accepted the gospel but combined it with Jewish legalism. What they had of Christ and the gospel was thus no more than a sham. Their claim that they had the real, original, full gospel was a fiction but appealed to many when they represented Paul's gospel as an emasculation, a false liberalization. Did Christ not observe the whole Jewish law? Did the Twelve whom the Judaizers represented as the only true apostles, not continue to live in the Jewish fashion like all the members of the mother church in Jerusalem? We do not know all the details regarding the activity of these Judaizers, especially how they came to invade the Galatian churches, and how they afterward appeared in Corinth. They started no churches of their own but appear as fanatic proselyters in Paul's churches.

In order to gain adherents they attacked the apostleship of Paul and made the highest claims for themselves. In Galatia they came out openly with their false gospel. Those who afterward appeared in Corinth kept their real teaching under cover and assailed not only the apostleship of Paul but also his personal character and the mode of his work. That explains Paul's defense and his attack in II Cor. 10-13, which does not center on their false gospel as does our epistle.

After the convention at Jerusalem, where the Judaizers lost out completely, Paul returned to the Galatian churches and then went on into Europe. It seems that a few of the rabid Judaizers, who had only been silenced at Jerusalem, followed Paul and broke into his Galatian churches after he had gone on to Europe. They found the coast clear and set to work by energetically sowing their evil seed. Paul's epistle shows that this invasion greatly disturbed the Galatian churches and was making headway. Yet, while the danger was great, these churches had not fallen away. If the conjecture of a commission is correct, they did not intend to change without first communicating directly with Paul and hearing him. This was a hopeful sign. The commission returned to Galatia thoroughly enlightened and convinced and also brought Paul's great epistle. This settled the matter. Later references to Galatia show no further trace of disturbance, nor do we again hear of Judaizers until the interval between First and Second Corinthians. Their effort in Corinth again ended in complete defeat although the struggle lasted a little longer.

The most acceptable date to which we are able to assign Galatians is near April in the year 53 while Paul was at Corinth. The whole subject is involved in much controversy, in which both German and English commentators are divided. The data here presented have produced conviction in the writer. We may add, for the sake of completeness, that some have altered the Upper Galatian theory from a reference to the northern cities Pessinus, Ancyra, and Tavium to towns that are just a little north of Iconium, north enough to be able to say they were in Upper Galatia.

*   *   *

Attacks on the genuineness and integrity of our epistle may be dated from the year 1888. Since then assaults have been made on Galatians which involve also Acts, Romans, and other epistles. The very center of the so-called *Corpus Paulinum* has been attacked. But on the base of hypotheses. The historical facts offered by the New Testament are first denied. After these have been removed, theories are substituted which place these epistles in the second century. We are left with no genuine letters of Paul to study or to interpret. Of late, however, critical scholarship is returning to more conservative views.

CHAPTER I

THE GREETING, 1:1-5

"Paul — to the churches of Galatia — grace and peace!" The writer's name in the nominative, the recipients of the letter in the dative, the words of greeting exclamatory nominatives. It is the ancient form for beginning a letter but has two impressive Christian nouns instead of the secular χαίρειν. While it is so common when we compare Paul's other letters, this greeting arrests attention because of the modifiers that are added to the first and to the third member and because of the lack of these in the case of the second member. The thoughts and the feelings of the writer reveal themselves with clearness in this greeting. It foreshadows the contents as well as the character and the tone of all that the epistle contains. The greeting is made of the same steel as the entire epistle. It is admirable in the highest degree.

Paul, an apostle not from men nor by means of man but by means of Jesus Christ and God the Father who raised him from the dead, and all the brethren with me:

To the churches of Galatia:

Grace to you and peace from God the Father and our Lord Jesus Christ, who gave himself for our sins that thus he might deliver us for himself from the present eon (which is) **wicked according to the will of our God and Father: to whom** (belongs) **the glory for the eon of the eons. Amen.**

Printed thus, the unmodified character of the second member of the greeting strikes the eye with full force. Place no comma after "apostle" and make no parenthesis of the following phrases, for these phrases modify "apostle" most closely and directly. The force of the apposition is not that Paul is an apostle but that he is *this kind* of an apostle. The whole impact lies in the phrases. They meet a challenge, meet it head on. They are not an incidental, parenthetical appendix.

Paul's father, strict Pharisee that he was, named his boy "Saul" after the one king that his tribe of Benjamin produced for Israel. This name was used in the old Jewish circles. As a Roman citizen of Tarsus the father gave the boy who was born into this citizenship a second, a Roman name, such as every Roman citizen bore: Παῦλος, "Paul." The idea that at a later time Paul took this name, took it from Sergius Paulus mentioned in Acts 13:9, is probably incorrect. When as a lad Paul played in the streets of Tarsus, his father, when calling him home, shouted: "Saul, Saul!" but the Greek boys on the streets called him "Paul." When Paul's mission work among the Gentiles began in earnest, when in his travels far and wide his Roman citizenship became a valuable asset for him, the sensible thing for him to do was to confine himself to the use of his Roman name, which he also did.

When Paul calls himself "an apostle of Jesus Christ" in a letter heading, perhaps adds, "by the will of God," he would indicate only that he writes officially, that he specifies his office as being ambassadorial and by direct divine appointment. Ἀπόστολος = one commissioned and sent. Paul says more here. Two unexpected negative phrases meet us at the very first glance, against which a double positive phrase is set in strongest contrast. To find this opposition and negation in a letter heading in connection with the writer's own title is startling. There must be a reason for its use. There is. The Judaizers had attacked Paul's apostleship, had denied its direct origin from Christ. Their method was shrewd. In regard to one who is commissioned everything depends on *who* commissioned him. The value of what he brings is no greater than the power of him in whose name he is entitled to speak.

Paul is probably quoting the phrases of the Judaizers who maintained that, whatever his apostleship was, it was either altogether only "from men" or at best had come to him only "through man." Whatever office he claimed he had was either altogether human or divine only in a secondary and thus more or less doubtful sense. Paul might claim what he pleased, the Judaizers pretended to have the facts in Paul's case, and these facts, they maintained, proved that Paul's gospel was not the genuine, original gospel, but one that had been highly modified, not indeed by Paul, but already at the source from which Paul had drawn it. They, the Judaizers, were bringing the genuine article to the Galatians.

Paul's first drop of ink is a decisive, challenging contradiction: "Paul, an apostle *not* from men *nor* by means of man." Men did not send and commission him. He is not the ambassador or representative of men. What he utters is not the word and the wisdom of men. The authority back of him and his message is not human.

We at once see that the Judaizers referred to the church at Antioch in Syria which sent forth Paul and Barnabas on that first missionary journey, in the course of which these two reached Galatia (Acts 13:1-4). At the end of the tour Paul and Barnabas also returned to Antioch and made report to the church that had sent them out (Acts 14:26-28). How easy it was to suppress the fact that the church at Antioch had acted only on direct orders from the Holy Ghost; to suppress also the direct call of Jesus at the time of the very conversion of Paul (Acts 26:16-18). How easy it was to make it appear that only one of the churches had sent Paul, that he was ἀπό only from a church, and that that was not even the old mother church at Jerusalem but an inferior Gentile church which had altered the genuine gospel by removing the ancient legal requirements just in order to attract the Gentiles. Paul, they said, was an emissary of this erring church at Antioch — men had sent him and not Christ.

"By means of man" is only a variation. The ἀπό phrase refers to the ἀπό in ἀπόστολος: sent *from* men, from a body of men, having only a human commission and message. Διά expresses medium. Paul might have obtained his commission from Christ through some human intermediary. In passing to Paul through that human medium the genuine gospel, the Judaizers claimed, was altered, adulterated, falsified. Paul had not gone to the source, he had dipped from the stream lower down where it was already contaminated and impure. He thought he had the pure article and the real office but he was sadly mistaken.

The unarticulated singular does not mean: "through some man," i. e., an individual man. Some think of Barnabas who twice did much for Paul (Acts 9:27; 11:25). But even if this phrase could be referred to an individual, Barnabas could not be considered because he and Paul had worked together in Galatia, where Paul was the leader. It is unwarranted to think that the Judaizers even knew what Acts 9:27 and 11:25 contain; and if they did they could not claim that Paul was made an apostle "through Barnabas."

The noun is generic; "by means of man" = "by means of human agency." It is properly singular after the plural "men." Paul regularly uses plurals and singulars in this way. One could be sent "from men" (some body of men) or "through man" (human agency of some kind). Οὐδέ does not make the phrases exclu-

sive of each other. The stress is on the prepositions as
alternatives and not on the nouns and their number,
plural and singular. One could look at a human commission in two ways; as emanating "from men" (whoever they might be) or as mediated "through man"
(whatever the human medium might be). Both
phrases refer to Acts 13:3. They include both ways
of looking at Paul's commission when trying to make
it human. The two phrases in Paul's denial are used
to indicate completeness.

In flat contradiction Paul asserts that he is an
apostle *in toto* only "by means of Jesus Christ and God
the Father who raised him from the dead." Although
it is only one phrase that has two objects, this phrase
is of the highest possible importance. Paul uses only
the second, διά, of the two previously employed prepositions. "Yes," Paul says, "I did receive my apostolate through a certain mediation." But he names the
two divine persons themselves as the one medium. He
purposely uses διά and not ἀπό nor ὑπό. For there is no
one who is higher than these two persons who could
use these persons as his medium. He could have said,
"an apostle *from* or *by* Christ and the Father." This
would have left a loophole, namely the question: "by
what means," on which there might then have been
quibbling. This is excluded by the use of διά, the lower
preposition "through," "by means of."

"By means of Jesus Christ" refers to Acts 26:16-
18, Paul's original commissioning. He uses the ordinary designation for the person and his office. And
lest someone think that another used Christ as a medium, he names "God the Father" as the joint medium
with Christ. Both are thus placed on the same absolutely supreme level with no higher one remaining
"by" (ὑπό) or "from" (ἀπό) whom Paul was commissioned; and at the same time with no lower one

"through" (διά) whom Paul was or could have been commissioned. Masterly is this διά! Subordinationists claim that Paul really means: *through* Christ and *from* the Father. They invent the meaning they want and then substitute it for the plain meaning Paul himself sets down.

Θεὸς Πατήρ, "God Father," is a unit name exactly like "Jesus Christ"; neither term needs an article in the Greek. In the holy Trinity the first person is distinguished by the term "Father." But was not Paul commissioned at Antioch by the Spirit (Acts 13:2, 4)? Undoubtedly. All the *opera ad extra sunt indivisa aut communa.* For Paul's purpose, to contradict any and all allegations that his apostleship was merely a human and faulty thing, it was enough to name Christ and the Father as proof that his office was wholly divine.

The participial modifier attached to "God the Father" is highly significant: "he who raised him from the dead" (apposition). This connects the two. More than this: it is the risen and glorified Christ who commissioned Paul, the same risen Christ who commissioned all the other apostles. He appeared to Paul even more gloriously than he appeared to the other apostles during the forty days. He made Paul a witness of his resurrection and his glory equal to that of the others. It was, indeed, only Christ who appeared to Paul on the road outside of Damascus, changed his whole life, and appointed him an apostle, but the Father had raised Christ from the dead, and thus in Christ the Father was active in Paul's call. Regarding ἐκ νεκρῶν, regarding the absence of the article, and regarding the misuse which is made of this absence, see Matt. 17:10; Mark 9:9; Luke 9:7; John 2:22; Acts 3:16.

2) In other epistles one or more of Paul's assistants are named as joint writers with Paul; only in this epistle we have "Paul . . . and all the brethren

with me," not μετά, "in my company," but σύν "with," in the sense of supporting me. The idea is not that these brethren are joint writers who help to compose this epistle. We see that Paul alone writes; "I" runs through the letter. All these brethren are at Paul's side, all of them know about the situation in Galatia, all of them know what Paul is writing, all of them agree with him and support him in all that he is writing. The Galatians are not to suppose that Paul is alone and writing by himself in a sort of private way. Nay, all the brethren with him, down to the last one, and "all" implies a goodly number, are backing Paul. It is usually supposed that this refers to Paul's assistants. Then "all" is too strong. If any assistants are included, those known to the Galatians (Silas, Timothy) are excluded, for Paul would have inserted their names.

"All the brethren with me" denotes Christian believers. If the deduction is correct that the Galatians had sent a delegation to Paul, Zahn is right, this delegation itself is included (see the introduction). Paul had fully and completely satisfied this delegation. These Galatians themselves subscribed to all Paul says in this epistle. When they go back with it they will support it and will tell that all the others who are with Paul give it the same support. Paul is happy to point the Galatians to this unanimity of all those with him.

May we not conclude one thing more? Paul's assistants, at least those known to the Galatians, were not with Paul at the moment but were busy with their work. Paul says, "all the brethren with me," and does not name a church at the place where he is writing; he also sends no greetings from a church. Does this not make the impression that he was in the early stages of his work at the place of writing? He had made converts, but a fully established church had not as yet been formed. If Corinth is the place of writing, the time must have been during the first weeks of his work there. Ephesus and Paul's second stay at Corinth are excluded already for the reason that at least greetings would have been sent from the church at either place.

In sharp contrast with the first member of the letter heading is the second, the unmodified dative: "To the churches of Galatia." Not one word more. No predicate of honor or esteem. No other epistle of Paul's shows a phenomenon similar to this. Paul is not a hypocrite. He does not lower himself by pretending. The words of praise and esteem found in other epistles are not cheapened and made hollow by bestowal where none is deserved. Paul's was not a case of personal feeling in a private matter; nor was what we might call his official pride wounded. Paul's concern is Christ and his gospel. His displeasure is due to the treatment the Galatians had begun to bestow upon the Lord who had commissioned him and upon the gospel which formed the burden of his commission. Paul would have been recreant to both if he had not used sternness.

See the introduction regarding "the churches of Galatia." "Of Galatia" was the only term available to designate the churches in Lower Galatia.

3) Luther is right regarding the third member of the heading: "See how he here turns all his words against the own righteousness (of man). Are they not all nothing but thunder crashes down from heaven against all men's own righteousness and piety of all kinds?" Here there is no stinting. Paul wishes the churches of Galatia all that they so greatly need in order to be freed from the errors of the Judaizers who had gained a hold among them. "Grace to you and peace from God the Father and our Lord Jesus Christ" is the same greeting that is found in other epistles, but in this instance it conveys the thought to the Galatians that grace and peace come to them from the two persons from whom Paul's apostleship came. As an apos-

tle of Christ and the Father he prays grace and peace
from the Father and Christ for them. Paul is the
apostle of this grace and this peace; all the brethren
with him are recipients of this grace and this peace.
The Father and Christ dispense these two fundamental
gifts through the apostles they have called and not
through the Judaizers who are false apostles.

"Grace" is fundamental, "peace" is its result. This
order is never reversed. The grammars supply *εἴη*, the
optative of wish: "May grace and peace be with you."
We prefer to supply nothing and regard the statement
as an exclamation: "Grace to you and peace!" Χάρις
is the undeserved *favor Dei* by which alone sinners are
received and cleansed from sin and guilt. Its connotation is free, gratuitous pardon. When it is again
and again bestowed upon those who already have this
grace (John 1:16), it is still the undeserved pardoning
favor which constantly frees us from sin but includes
all the gifts of this favor which we need in order to
build up our spiritual life. "Grace to you!" = "All the
abundant spiritual gifts of grace to you in one ceaseless stream!"

Εἰρήνη is the Hebrew *shalom* in the sense of the German *Heil,* the condition of well-being when God is our
friend and all is well with us. The condition of peace
is objective, the peace established by God through
Christ, but it produces also the corresponding subjective realization of peace, the rest, satisfaction, and
happiness that flow from the possession of peace.

"From" conveys the idea that grace and peace flow
down upon us. Here the names of the divine givers
are chiastically reversed, the Father is named first,
Christ, second, both are again equal, both together are
the joint source. As the natural order in the calling of
Paul was Christ and the Father, so now in the bestowal
of grace and peace it is from the Father and Christ.
The slight variants in the reading do not affect the

meaning. We note only that the soteriological title "our Lord" is added to the name "Jesus Christ" used in v. 1. This is the full designation, which is full of solemnity, that is so frequently used. "Our Lord" is a confession: we belong to him, are wholly dependent on him. He has purchased and won us and made us his own (I Cor. 7:23) ; he directs us in all things.

4) The apposition: "he who gave himself for our sins," etc., refers to the expiatory self-sacrifice of him who is now our Lord Jesus Christ. The substantivized aorist participle denotes the historical fact as such. "He gave" means by a voluntary act; "himself" is his own person and no less, and that means his life. The readings vary between ὑπέρ and περί, "in behalf of" and "concerning"; the difference is small, and the variation in reading appears in other similar statements. In what way our sins required this giving of himself is not stated, but it is perfectly clear from all Paul's teaching. In the LXX περὶ ἁμαρτίας regularly denotes the expiation and removal of sins; and this is what the phrase means here. The reason that Paul attaches this apposition is plain. Nothing removes sin save the self-sacrifice of Christ on the cross; through that sacrifice alone grace and peace are ours. The Galatians were listening to a different doctrine. The Judaizers could not make Christ's expiation the sole fountain of grace and peace.

The addition of the purpose clause emphasizes the point still more: "that thus he might deliver us for himself from the present eon (which is) wicked," etc. Ἵνα expresses simple purpose; ὅπως, purpose and manner combined, the manner being indicated in the governing clause. Christ's purpose is that in the manner just mentioned, namely by giving himself for our sins, he might deliver us, etc. Note the middle voice of the aorist subjunctive (ἐξαιρέω) : "take us out for himself," i. e., to be his own. We should not think of the future deliverance at the end of the world or at the moment of our death. When the Scriptures speak of this they refer to the resurrection of Christ or to his exaltation. The deliverance connected with Christ's expiation is the one effected now, in this life. The aorist is effective, it is an actual deliverance.

A greeting is not the place to expand and to teach in detail how Christ's death accomplishes this purpose for us. This purpose was not accomplished already in the instant when Christ died. Paul writes of himself as an apostle, as one who preaches the gospel in order that men may be brought to faith and justification. All this is included in the accomplishment of the purpose of Christ's death. The reconciling death involves the Word of this reconciliation, its proclamation, and the personal reconciliation of all those who are delivered by Christ (II Cor. 5:18-21). "Might deliver us for himself," is an effective aorist and at the same time constative. Each person is individually delivered, and with "us" Paul takes them all together and thus speaks of the act as being one. That is sufficient; we need not think of "us" as including all the saved of all the ages until the last day.

The great point that the Galatians are to note is the fact that grace and peace are ours through the merits of Christ's self-sacrifice alone. All is due to his death for our sins. We are able to add nothing by any work of ours. We are not delivered by any observance of law. The whole epistle is aimed at this error; the foundation is laid already in the greeting.

Paul writes: might deliver us "from the present eon (which is) evil." The idea of time in αἰών remains but is advancced to include what transpires during this eon of time, what thus marks and distinguishes the great era. Thus a modifier is added, here the predicative adjective: "(which is) wicked," πονηρός, actively and viciously evil. We may use "world" in place of "eon" but only in the sense indicated. Instead of "the present eon" we sometimes have "this eon"; both are in contrast with ὁ αἰὼν μέλλων, "the eon about to come," i. e., that of the blessed eternity. Ἐνεστώς is the perfect participle which is always used in the present sense. The "present" eon is the one which began with Christ's death and is thus now present; it is the final eon of the world which is to be followed by eternity. Satan rules it so that it is "wicked" through and through.

Our one hope is that Christ take us out of it for himself, and this he does by means of his death for our sins. These sins tie us to this world age. Being wicked, all of them, they hold us to this wicked world. Freed from them, we are delivered "out of" this eon. For the time being we, indeed, live in this world, but we are no longer of this world. Christ has made us his own. Our life in Christ separates us from this eon or world, in particular from all that is "wicked" in it. The Galatians were in danger of being drawn back into this present wicked eon by losing the deliverance of Christ, by trusting in the law and in works of their own.

The κατά phrase modifies the entire apposition "he who gave," etc., plus the purpose clause. All this is "according to the will of our God and Father." Θέλημα does not mean the act of willing but what God willed. When Christ gave himself he did what God wanted; when he delivered us he again did what God wanted. This is God's good and gracious will (Luther). One article combines the two names "our God and Father" and designates one person. But in this combination "God" brings out all his greatness and his majesty, "Father" all his love and his tenderness to us who are delivered by Christ. "Our" modifies both nouns: he who in all his majesty and in all his love is ours in order to bless us for evermore. In v. 1 and v. 3 "Father" indicates the trinitarian relation which as such is already soteriological; for God revealed himself as triune only in order to show us how all three persons work out our salvation. Here in v. 4 "Father" with the possessive "our" is likewise soteriological but at the same time confessional as in the Lord's Prayer.

5) The fact that Paul adds a doxology at the end of a greeting is exceptional in the highest degree and thus significant. The greeting is usually followed by a word of thanks to God for the good accomplished in the readers. But what can Paul say about the Galatians who had begun to forsake the gospel? Instead of adding a word of acknowledgment and appreciation regarding their faith and their faithfulness Paul looks up to God and praises him for his gracious purpose and will as much as to say to the Galatians: "Praise him with me by allowing that will and purpose to have full sway among you also!"

The copula is usually omitted in these doxologies, when it is written it is ἐστίν and not εἴη. Moreover, δόξα is often combined with other terms that denote actual possessions of God and not merely something that we bestow on him. So we do not translate *Ehre* but use the objective *Herrlichkeit*. Paul is not thinking of men's bestowing glory and honor upon God but of God in his own eternal glory, the manifestation of his infinite attributes, especially as they shine forth in Christ's death and the saving purpose connected therewith. Ἐστίν with the dative is one of the common ways of indicating possession; the relative used in doxologies is demonstrative: "he, he alone, to whom (belongs) the glory," the sum of the divine attributes in their manifestation.

"For the eon of the eons" is a Hebraistic circumscription for eternity, the grandest of all found in the Greek, which multiplies the idea of "eon" indefinitely. How anyone can think of earthly eras is difficult to understand. In human language terms that denote time must necessarily be used to express what is in reality the opposite of time. "Eternity" is itself a term that designates time. We have no others. The Scriptures condescend to use such terms. Our minds are so tied to time and to space that even the philosophers cannot rise beyond them, cannot even form the concepts timelessness and spacelessnes except in a vague, negative approach.

'Aμήν is only the Hebrew noun for "truth" or "verity" written with Greek letters; call it an adverbial accusative. It has been taken over into other languages unchanged. At the end of a statement, a doxology, or a prayer it solemnly confirms; it is like the affixing of a sacred seal. Jesus alone doubled it and used it as an introduction to his statements as is evident in John's Gospel.

INTRODUCTION

The Denunciation, 1:6-10

6) Instead of saying that he is delighted with this or that in the Galatians when he begins the body of his letter, Paul declares that he is shocked at what the Galatians are on the point of doing. The very first paragraph is stunning. Soft Melanchthonian methods are not in place; heroic measures are demanded. Here there is no error in life; the heart of Christendom is assailed. The foe is deadly. A cancer threatens the vitals; palliatives would be a fatal mistake, the remedy must destroy the ailment to the very roots.

The apostle not from men or by means of man but from Christ and God speaks, speaks in the power of Christ and of God. His words have a conquering ring. He speaks to the churches of Galatia who as churches are bound to hear and to heed every word unless they intend to cease being churches. The voice they hear is

fearless and scorns to please men. This is the voice of
the slave of Christ, the slave who knows only one obedience, that to his heavenly Master alone. This voice
rings with divine authority and power.

The tone of this section is tense and dramatic. Paul
is not swept away by passion. He writes with perfect
self-control. He knows the weight of every sentence.
Every statement is deliberate and straight to the point.
The very first sentence reveals the fact that he is completely informed; all hesitation of uncertainty is absent. We have only one explanation for this decisive-
ness: not a mere report that has at last reached Paul,
not a letter from Galatia that brought a certain amount
of information, but a delegation from the churches,
men whom Paul had questioned on all points and who
had told him all the facts as they actually were. These
facts the apostle meets with incisiveness.

The issue is nothing less than the gospel itself.
That issue Paul states at once. **I marvel that so
quickly you are making a change away from him
who called you in grace, (namely) Christ, to a different gospel which is not (even) another except
in the sense that there are certain ones who are
disturbing you and want to pervert the gospel of
Christ.**

"So quickly." That is the fact that causes Paul
astonishment; he would not have believed it possible if
it were not for the complete information that he has.
The two adverbs are heavily reproving for the Galatians. The statement contains no point from which to
reckon; hence we cannot translate "so soon" (A. V.)
but must translate "so quickly" (R. V.). Paul had
given the Galatians credit for more solidity and more
fidelity. He is deeply pained and hurt. His confidence
has been misplaced. A conclusion is involved, namely
the fact that when Paul last visited the Galatians, all
was well with them. Then came the Judaizers, and

instead of being promptly escorted to the door, all these churches began to listen to them and to find something attractive in their false gospel. This is what happened "so quickly."

The middle μετατίθεσθαι is regularly used to express what the Germans call *uebertreten,* to change from one political party or from one philosophic school to another and thus from one religious conviction to another. There is nothing in the context that points to this being the passive voice, hence we regard it as the middle; to make a change of this kind is a voluntary act. Here we have a case in which the tense is vital. An aorist would mean that the change had been actually made; the present tense states only that the change had begun, is in progress but not yet completed. The cause is not yet lost although there is no time to lose. Paul is stepping in strenuously.

The defection in progress is "away from him who called you in grace." Paul makes the charge personal by naming the person who had called the Galatians and not merely the gospel by which they had been called. At the same time he brings out the full aggravation of this unfaithfulness: the Galatians had been called "in grace." The phrase has no article and is thus to be understood in the sense of "graciously," i. e., without deserving it, yea, deserving the very opposite. "Into the grace" (A. V.) is incorrect. The aorist participle states the past fact.

In the epistles καλεῖν is always used with regard to the successful call and never only with reference to the *invitatio* which one has rejected. Whether the genitive Χριστοῦ is textually genuine or not, he who called the Galatians is Christ. The statement that it is always ὁ Θεός who calls is unwarranted. Paul himself was called by Christ; Rom. 1:6 names the Christians as "called of Jesus Christ." Here the gospel by which the Galatians were called is designated as "the gospel of

Christ." Χριστοῦ is in apposition to the substantivized participle; it does not modify χάριτι.

Nothing in the world should ever make the Galatians change away from him who had called them in grace and at the price of his death delivered them from this present world which was wicked and doomed (v. 4). They should have resisted the most powerful and the most persistent efforts to the last breath. Yet they are quickly beginning their apostasy! Paul might have used a stronger word than "I marvel." He names the deadly thing the Galatians had begun to do: change away from Christ. The Galatians themselves would disavow this. They intended to stay with Christ; the Judaizers themselves taught Christ, yea, came as the genuine apostles of Christ (II Cor. 11:13, 14). Why, the Galatians were now getting Christ better than they ever got him! Any plea of that kind is silenced by the next phrase: "to a different gospel which is not (even) another" but so different as to be no gospel at all.

The point to be noted is that Paul does not say: away from *Christ* — to a different *Savior*. No other person exists who could be placed beside Christ. He says: away from *Christ* — to a *gospel* that is no gospel at all. By forsaking the true gospel and by accepting a substituted fake gospel the Galatians are losing the one Savior there is. That is the dreadful danger toward which they are verging.

The emphasis is placed on this fake gospel, on the adjectives which declare it a fake: "different — not another." The A. V. confuses this: "another — not another." The words ἕτερος and ἄλλος at times amount to the same thing; but here ἕτερον = οὐκ ἄλλο. This gospel is "different" because it is "*not* another." A gospel might be "different" only because it is "another," is couched only in "other" words but leaves the substance the same. But when it is "different" because it is "*not* another," the very substance is changed; such a gospel is a fake, a mere pretense or sham. Its proponents call it a gospel only to gain its acceptance as brass is sold for gold; those who buy are cheated. This is the charge Paul launches. See R. 747. The genuineness of the gospel is so vital because the true gospel is the one and only means by which Christ calls us, transmits his grace to us, in a word, delivers us from this wicked world (v. 4). The substitution of a fake gospel loses us this call, grace, deliverance, does so whether we are aware of the fact or not.

The deception practiced on the Galatians has been repeated to this very day. A "different" gospel is offered which is "*not* another." It is even the same adulteration that is offered. Yes, the name "gospel" is retained, the "Christ" or at least "Jesus" are preached, but for pure grace in his atoning death there is substituted the law, the requirement of works as the means of salvation. The multitude applauds and, like the Galatians, is so quickly and easily deceived.

7) The relative ὅ refers to ἕτερον εὐαγγέλιον, and the relative clause states that this "different" gospel is not another gospel in any sense. Ὅ does not refer to the whole previous statement: "which" in the sense of "your changing to another gospel" is nothing but that some are troubling you. This thought would require ἄλλο τι or οὐδὲν ἄλλο ἐστίν. With εἰ μή, "except," Paul qualifies the clause "which is not another." One might understand this clause to mean that what the Galatians were changing to is totally unrelated to the true gospel and in that sense "not another." Then the matter would be easy, indeed; then the Galatians would scarcely have been deceived. There is an exception to the broad "not another." Paul states what the exception is. This "different gospel" does bear a relation to Christ's true gospel. Right there is where the terrible danger lies; not another "except in the sense that (εἰ

μή) there are certain ones who are disturbing you and want to pervert the gospel of Christ," not another except that its advocates pretend that it is "another," in fact, the genuine article itself.

It is not another except in the sense of a most dangerous perversion. Paul scornfully calls its advocates "certain ones." Substantivized participles must have the article even when they are used as predicates; here, moreover, subject and predicate are identical and interchangeable (R. 768). "Who are disturbing you" is the preliminary, minor description of these perverters. They have come to the Galatians and have made this their business. The present participle says only that they have begun their disturbing work. The main statement is found in the second participle: "and want to pervert the gospel of Christ." Note that Paul does not use the participle μεταστρέφοντες, much less the aorist participle. He does not say that they *are* perverting Christ's gospel or that they have already succeeded in doing so. He says only that they "are wanting" to succeed in this nefarious work. They have only the vicious will.

When Paul writes, "to pervert (aorist, actually to pervert) the gospel of Christ," he is not thinking of what these perverters actually teach. That is an actual and a complete perversion and not merely a willingness to pervert. Paul is thinking of the gospel of Christ which the Galatians had received from him. This gospel these perverters wanted to upset in the hearts of the Galatians so that the Galatians should no longer believe it. Yet thus far they only wanted to do this damnable thing, they had not yet succeeded. Paul is writing in order to prevent their success.

It is well to note that in "the gospel of Christ" the genitive denotes the author. It is the gospel which emanates from Christ, which he has entrusted to his apostle. This is not the objective genitive: the gospel "about" Christ. The Judaizers, too, had much to say about Christ when they converted him into another Moses. But theirs was not Christ's own gospel which he himself had preached, which he then commissioned his apostles to preach, which also the Galatians had received from Paul. This genitive of source and authorship shows the correctness of the interpretation that Christ is the one referred to when it is said that he called the Galatians (v. 6).

8) After thus in the most direct way stating the vital point at issue with the perversion of Christ's gospel to which the Galatians had begun to give ear, Paul utters a solemn malediction on anyone who would dare to pervert this gospel. **But even if we or an angel from heaven shall preach gospel to you contrary to what we preached to you, let him be accursed! As we have said before, also now again say I: If anyone preaches gospel to you contrary to the one you received, let him be accursed!**

'Aλλά is adversative, it takes direct issue with τινές: there are people of this kind, "but" whoever they may be, they are accursed. Note the difference in the conditional clauses: καὶ ἐάν vividly supposes a case; εἰ in v. 9 takes up the real case that is now occurring in Galatia. What is said of the supposed case lends greater justification and strength to what is equally said about the real case. This is augmented by making the supposed case deal with the highest persons, with even an angel, and the real case with lower persons, thus securing the argumentative weight of a *conclusio a majori ad minus*.

"Even if" is concessive: suppose that such a thing should occur, that we ourselves or, still worse, an angel from heaven should so preach. The more improbable, yea impossible the supposition, the more justified the verdict of damnation. Paul intends to state a rhetorical extreme (R. 1026). How could those who had preached the real gospel turn around and preach its contrary? Or how could an angel from heaven do such a thing? The fact that ἡμεῖς and the "we" in the verbs "we preached" and "we have said" cannot be literary plurals and refer to Paul alone and not to Paul and his assistants, is plain from the latter, for there occur together, "*we* have said," and, "*I* now again say." No writer uses "we" and "I" with reference to himself in the same breath; to assume that Paul does this here is untenable.

Paul puts "we" first because he would in no way spare himself and his own best friends and assistants if they should ever falsify the gospel; he also gains a climax by adding "or an angel from heaven." He must add "from heaven," for Satan is able to masquerade as an angel of light (II Cor. 11:14). The reading ὑμῖν (a few texts have ὑμᾶς as in v. 9) is textually well attested. If it is omitted, the proposition is more general; but if it is retained, the sentence is a more personal reference to the Galatians. The Greek idiom for the English "contrary to" is παρά, literally "beside" (R. 313) ; so here and again in v. 9: "contrary to what we preached to you" — "contrary to what you received (from us)," v. 9. These two relative clauses (both are object clauses) define what Paul means by "a different gospel which is not another," namely a gospel "contrary to" the true one which Paul and his assistants preached and the Galatians received.

The verb εὐαγγελίζομαι means to proclaim good news and is generally used in the New Testament to indicate the preaching of the gospel. We use it in the missionary sense of "to evangelize." Here it is first used with the dative and then with the accusative of the persons to whom the gospel is preached; the sense is the same. Note the tenses: two aorists in v. 8: "if . . . shall actually preach as gospel" — "contrary to what we

actually did preach to you"; then the present in v. 9:
"if anyone ever preaches as gospel." One might use
the absolute "gospelize." In the present connection
the verb is used with reference to both false and true
gospelizing as the context makes plain. The correlative idea is always faith in what is proclaimed as good
news; in v. 9 it is expressed by the verb λαμβάνω, "to
receive." Such faith and reception are wrought by the
gospel itself. The enormity of refusing the glad tidings of salvation in unbelief is at once apparent; it
brands this news as a lie.

The most damnable thing, however, is to proclaim
as the true gospel something that is contrary to that
gospel; yea, to induce people who have received the
true gospel to cast this aside and to accept something
contrary in its stead as though this contrary were the
genuine, true gospel. Bad enough for his own soul for
anyone to make this exchange but infinitely worse to
make it one's business to delude others into making
this exchange. The divine gospel is branded as a lie,
the lying gospel is offered as the truth; the double
falsehood leads souls to destruction. Whoever is guilty
of this crime, "let him be accursed!" even if it be one
of us, Paul says, *yea,* an angel out of heaven itself.

The Hebrew *cherem* = something that is removed
from the possession or use of men and set aside for
God, either as an object upon which God's wrath rests
or as an object that is dedicated to God as a gift. Hellenic Greek used ἀνάθεμα for the former in the sense of
"accursed," ἀνάθημα for the latter. The later ecclesiastical "anathema" found in the Decrees of the Council
of Trent is the continuation of "accursed." It is not
known whether anathema was used in excommunication from the synagogue. Any late ecclesiastical use
of this word sheds no light on our passage. Paul is
not acting as a human court nor is he calling on the
Galatian churches to act as a court by pronouncing an

anathema. An angel would not be subject to a human court. The view that Paul is exercising the right of excommunication is not substantiated but answered by I Cor. 5:3-5. Paul had no such right, did not pretend to have it.

As the apostle and representative of Christ and the Father Paul pronounces the verdict: "Let him be anathema!" He repeats the verdict which Jesus himself uttered against the Pharisees in Matt. 23:13-39 (note v. 15 and 33). Anyone who promulgates a different and contrary gospel is *eo ipso* "accursed," not because we say so, but because Christ has said so, and we only repeat his judgment. This includes the devil himself. (I Cor. 6:3; II Cor. 11:14). The *damnamus* found in the Confessions is fully justified. In a ministerial conference a Lutheran was challenged: "You certainly would not damn a Jew?" He replied: "Christ has already done that!" R. 939 states that the imperative crowded out the classical optative of wish; the untenableness of that view is the fact that Paul is here not expressing a wish but a verdict.

9) This is not a new verdict nor one that is pronounced by Paul alone. The Galatians have heard it from him and from his associates before: "As we have said before." Paul is now merely repeating it: "also now again say I." Whether this is a reference to the first missionary journey when Barnabas was Paul's associate and these uttered an advance warning against any falsification of the gospel, or to the second visit in Galatia when Judaizers had already appeared in Syrian Antioch and then in Jerusalem, no one can say. The latter seems more probable. Of course, what was then said to the Galatians does not need to agree verbatim with the denunciation as it is now worded with the repeated anathema. Then the Galatians were told about what might occur, now Paul speaks of what has occurred: "If anyone preaches gospel to you con-

trary to the one you received (from us), let him be
anathema!" Παρ᾽ ὅ has the same force in both verses;
in both cases the relative is not indefinite: "contrary
to what," but refers to the εὐαγγέλιον embedded in the
verb. But note the advance: "contrary to the one we
preached to you" (v. 8) points to the bringing of the
gospel to the Galatians; "contrary to the one you
received" completes the bringing by noting the reception in true faith. This also fits the condition of reality now employed; the Galatians had in fact received
the true gospel.

As certainly as what the Galatians "did receive"
was the divine gospel and that alone, so certainly it
was most damnable to seek to subvert that gospel and
to supplant it by a sham gospel. But were the
Judaizers not sincere? The devil is even more sincere in promulgating the false gospel in order to
crowd out the true. Vicious sincerity never escapes
the anathema.

Perhaps they were unconscious of their sin, acted
ignorantly and not intelligently? The answer to this
then as now is the one Jesus gave to the Pharisees in
John 9:41: "If ye were blind, ye should have no sin:
but now ye say: 'We see!' therefore your sin remaineth." The truth is not that the Judaizers never knew
the true gospel. It is not even only the fact that, when
the true gospel came to them, they did not believe it
(Mark 16:16b). The fact is that the Judaizers had
the true gospel before them and determined to destroy
it, and that not by open opposition and persecution but
by the insidious substitution of a fake gospel, than
which no more devilish means exists. They were worse
than the Pharisees who claimed: "We see!" and thus
refused the truth; they were like those mentioned in
Matt. 23:15, who made their proselytes twofold more
the children of hell than themselves; yea, even worse
than these, for these operated with proselytes from

paganism to Judaism while the Judaizers proselyted true believers.

10) Two startling questions close the double denunciation: they are followed by Paul's own decisive answer. **Indeed, am I now trying to get the approval of men or of God? or am I seeking to curry favor with men? If I were yet currying favor with men I would not be a slave of Christ!**

In this instance γάρ cannot mean "for" (our versions) as either stating a reason or offering an explanation. The insertion of "now," which repeats the "now" of v. 9, restricts us to the thought of what Paul is doing with these startling verdicts. It is as plain as day that he is neither seeking the approval of men nor trying to curry favor with men. Γάρ is but the confirmatory adverb which is here used in a question in order to point to what the previous statements make decidedly plain and thus make the question more urgent and the desired answer more inevitable (Zahn).

Like a flash the questions reveal the charges the Judaizers had launched against Paul in order to discredit him and his gospel. They alleged that Paul toned down the rigorous legal requirements of the original gospel in order to gain the approval of Gentiles, to make the gospel palatable to them, to curry favor with them. In his ambition to build churches and to gain a great following he had emasculated the gospel and stripped it of essential parts. The Judaizers came to Galatia in order to restore the gospel to its true content. Paul's gospel of liberty was a piece of conscienceless accommodation to Gentile reluctance in accepting the Jewish law. O yes, the Judaizers also preached Christ, but in the full legal setting without which the Galatians could not be saved!

Paul meets all this with sudden, smashing questions. Indeed, does anybody who is trying to please men approach them with anathemas? The present tense is conative: "Am I now trying to get the approval of men — seeking to curry favor with men?" If at any time before I have spoken softly, is this now soft language? And have we not before, when we were with you Galatians, spoken in the same uncompromising way (v. 9)?

The force of both πείθω and ἀρέσκειν lies in the personal objects. The former does not mean "persuade," for God cannot be persuaded. It means trying to secure the approval of someone. The second verb is used only regarding men and not regarding God and thus means "to please" in the sense of "to curry favor." The second question thus makes the first clearer; "or" is not adversative and exclusive but conjunctive. Paul puts the questions in such a way that the Galatians will have to answer *no* if they are still honest. Only a man whose sole aim it is to have the divine approval will write as Paul now writes even as he and his assistants have in the same way spoken face to face with the Galatians.

This refutation of the slander spread among the Galatians may well open their eyes to the character of the Judaizers and to the base means with which they work. What the Galatians have found Paul to be before, they will also find him now, a man without fear or favor, with his eye on God and on Christ alone. He is an apostle, not from men or by man, but through Christ and God alone (v. 1). The interpretation that "now" refers to Paul's whole Christian life in contrast with his former Judaism disregards the context and the close connection with the preceding "now" (v. 9); both refer to the present moment.

Paul answers his own question with a conditional sentence that expresses present unreality (εἰ with the imperfect — the imperfect with ἄν): "If I were yet currying favor with men I would not be Christ's slave." This is the verdict under which Paul would then rest.

Not a slave of Christ = a mere slave of men (I Cor.
7:23). The point of δοῦλος or "slave" is not hard labor
done for a master; it is absolute obedience which
knows no will but that of the master. Ἔτι, "yet." If
at this late time in his apostleship Paul did not yet
serve Christ as his supreme Master, then the Galatians
might, indeed, turn away from him. Paul would rather
alienate all the Galatian churches from himself than
reduce in a single point the gospel committed unto him
by Christ to please them or anybody else.

PART 1

The Apostle of Christian Liberty Received His Gospel by Revelation Alone.
1:11-2:21

In the body of this letter Paul first thoroughly silences the plea of his Judaizing opponents that, because he was not one of the Twelve who had been in the school of Jesus, his gospel was therefore unreliable since he had obtained it from men, who themselves, perhaps, understood it wrongly, or whose doctrine Paul modified to suit himself. This plea, which Paul overthrows, includes the claim that the leaders in Jerusalem taught a different doctrine, one in which the old law was still made binding. In fact, it was claimed that Paul himself occasionally observed the old legal requirements. By discrediting him the Judaizers hoped to discredit his gospel so as to substitute their own.

These false claims Paul overthrows by means of three replies, all of which are historical in substance. The first is the fact that he received his gospel directly from Christ by revelation alone and not at secondhand from the other apostles (1:11-24). The second, that the other apostles fully acknowledged Paul's gospel (2:1-10). The third, that on one occasion Paul was obliged to correct Peter himself regarding this very point of complete liberty from the law, and that Peter accepted the correction (2:11-21). This reply, consisting of clear facts, is at once complete and convincing in every respect.

I. *How Paul Obtained His Gospel, 1:11-24*

11) With perfect calmness Paul presents the detailed facts regarding the manner in which he received his gospel. Only one question is to be answered: "What

are the facts?" They and they alone are decisive. Paul presents them to the Galatians whom he clearly distinguishes from the Judaistic teachers. On these latter he has pronounced his anathema, but the Galatians he addressed as his brethren throughout. Paul writes as one who is confident that the truth will prevail; the note of defeat is foreign to him.

For I inform you, brethren, in regard to the gospel preached as gospel by me, that it is not in human style (at all). **For also, as far as I am concerned, I did not receive it from man and was not taught; on the contrary,** (I received it) **through Jesus Christ's revelation.**

These opening statements present the whole matter in a nutshell. No human agency of any kind was employed in transmitting the gospel to Paul, to equip him for preaching it as an apostle who was on a par with the Twelve. The means employed was direct, immediate revelation by no less a person than Jesus Christ himself, the same Jesus Christ who equipped the Twelve in the same way.

"For" at the beginning of the whole paragraph is explanatory in a broad way: "so that you may understand this whole matter aright." "For" does not intend to prove that Paul is "Christ's slave," for it does much more. Of course, it elucidates all that precedes in v. 1-10, but even this is not enough. The elucidation focuses on the great point as to how Paul got his gospel; after this is clear, all will see that this is Christ's very own gospel, and that any "different" gospel cannot come from Christ and must, therefore, be false, a human invention, a vicious substitute. Further elaboration takes care of the details and furnishes the strongest support for the proposition laid down at the start.

The address "brethren" conveys a good deal. The Galatians had been disturbed (v. 7) by the Judaizers, their certainty was not as strong as it had been before, they were in great danger, but they were still "brethren," to whose rescue Paul comes. The Galatians are "brethren," not so the Judaizers whom Paul repudiates utterly. These "brethren" are to listen to Paul who writes to them as their true "brother"; and as "brethren" they will be certain and even glad to do so.

"Brother" has been cheapened by many. Some unionists call anybody "brother," would have called the Judaizers by this name. In the New Testament "brother" and "brethren" are terms that are applied to those only who believe and confess the true gospel and never to those who have become guilty of a repudiation of any part of that gospel. Such "brethren" may need help to maintain the gospel; they then get that help in fullest measure.

"I inform you, brethren," sounds formal and impressive, and for that very reason is tinged with irony. To "brethren" one would expect a brother to say: "You know, brethren," not, "I inform you," unless he were telling something new. The fact "that the gospel gospelized by Paul" is not κατὰ ἄνθρωπον, "in human style," was certainly not news to the Galatians; for if it were news, why had it not been told them at the start? And if Paul withheld this information until this time when he is challenged, how could he suppose that this late telling would make any impression on the Galatians? The effectiveness of Paul's "I inform you" lies in the very fact that Paul has to tell the Galatians, as though it were a piece of entirely new information, what he had told them when he first gave them the gospel. He might have exclaimed because of their forgetfulness or have stirred them to remembrance in some other way; he chose a way that was telling, indeed.

The aorist passive participle indicates the past fact: "gospeled by me." The entire stress rests on the last phrase: κατὰ ἄνθρωπον, "according to or after man," *menschengemaess,* normated in a human way. We are able to give only the general sense: it is not a gospel "in human style." The phrase is broad and does not specify. The points about which Paul is here concerned follow with an explanatory "for." These, however, do not exhaust the phrase, for it covers just about everything in the gospel. In all respects it shows its non-human, its divine nature, quality, power, effect, etc. How strange that this must again be told to the Galatians as though it were news — shame on them!

12) The readings vary. The easier ones are οὔτε — οὔτε and οὐδέ — οὐδέ. We might adopt the latter: "neither — nor." We then get a contrast. The trouble with this reading is the fact that to receive the gospel from man (a human being) and to be taught is not a contrast that fits "neither — nor." For how can one receive the gospel from man except by being taught? If "nor was I taught" means that Paul was not taught even by Christ, the phrase "by Christ" should be in the text. The more one studies the statement, the more the difficult and unusual reading: οὐδέ — οὔτε seems correct, the former specifying, the latter merely adding a point of the one specification: "For also (B.-D. 462, 3 on Rom. 8:7; B.-P. 949: *denn auch nicht*), as far as I am concerned, I (emphatic ἐγώ, subject of both verbs) did not receive it from man and was not taught." This is the one decisive point here at issue. If Paul had received his gospel from man he, of course, was taught by man. In this vital point his gospel would then be "according to man." He would be on the same level with true Christians in general and with the Galatians in particular and not on a level with the Twelve.

"On the contrary (ἀλλά after negations), (I received it) through or by means of Jesus Christ's revelation" exactly like the Twelve. We cannot supply both verbs: "I received and was taught by means of revelation," for, to say the least, it would be peculiar to state that revelation conducts a course of instruction. Revelation reveals instanter, to be taught is a different process. This, too, indicates that οὔτε is correct, and that the two negatives describe the ordinary human reception of the gospel.

What seems to confuse some is the fact that the Twelve were taught by Jesus. But that teaching never enabled them to act as apostles. Much of it they failed to understand; after three years they deserted Jesus and fled. Jesus promised them the Spirit (John 14:26; 16:13, 14). That means revelation, exactly the same thing that Paul received. Before his call to the apostleship Paul knew many things about Jesus, not, indeed, nearly as much as the Twelve; but they as well as Paul needed direct, divine revelation. It and it alone supplied every lack. The least lack was intellectual grasp, the supreme need was power (Acts 1:8). The revelation which supplied the greater need certainly did not fail in the smaller.

"Of Jesus Christ" is the subjective genitive; he is the revealer. The fact that Christ revealed by the Spirit in no way discounts this act as being his. No one is able to say whether the revelation was one act or a succession of acts, nor is this point vital in any way. The veil was withdrawn from Paul's soul, and by a miraculous intervention of the Christ who called him the entire gospel was put into his possession for his office as an apostle. When did this occur? We do now know. The main point is that it did occur.

We meet a peculiar reluctance to admit that Paul received the entire gospel exactly as he here says he received it. Some hold the view that Paul had after all to learn the story of Jesus from Christians who knew it and could teach him. The decisive answer to

this is the fact that the revelation which gave Paul
the main substance of the gospel would certainly not
stop short in regard to the minor things. If Christ had
in a way made Paul dependent upon men, he would
have placed Paul below the apostolic plane. The fact
that Christ did nothing of the kind is the very point
here settled once for all.

We cannot accept the view which has the Judaizers
claim only that Paul's gospel was one κατὰ ἄνθρωπον, of
human type, a perversion that was due to Paul who
ambitiously wanted to get a great following among
the Gentiles, but excepts from the Judaizers' claims
the thought that Paul got his gospel from man and
allows that he obtained it from Christ. Their claim
included what v. 1 intimates, that he was an apostle
from men, by means of man, not from Christ and
God; thus certainly also that his gospel was according,
received from man or man's teaching and not by means
of Christ's revelation. The correspondence between
v. 1 and v. 11, 12 is too great to admit of any other
view. The Judaizers did not need to specify the man
or the men from whom Paul derived either his alleged
apostleship or his alleged gospel.

It is incorrect to say that Paul was made the first
man who taught Christian liberty for the church. Syrian Antioch stands out in this respect. Paul's missionary journeys had started from there. While one
must be careful when he extracts the charges against
Paul from his defense, there is no reason for striking
out the items that he had his gospel, not from Christ,
but from men. The fact that Paul himself then further altered his gospel in order to make it still freer
for the Gentiles may be admitted as an additional
charge against him on the part of the Judaizers.

13) With "for" Paul explains still further. **For
you have heard of my own mode of life at one time**

in Judaism, that beyond measure I continued persecuting the church of God and ravaging it. And
I kept advancing in Judaism beyond many as old as
I in my race, being more exceedingly a zealot for my
ancestral traditions.

"You heard," aorist, is sufficient to the Greek who
cares to mark only the past time; our "have heard"
marks the relation of the action to the present. It is
an old story, long known to the Galatians. For this
very reason Paul refers to it now in order to remind
the Galatians how rather impossible it was for one
who had been what he had been even to be converted
by the agency of man, to say nothing of being made
an apostle. The longer the Galatians have known
what a frightful Jew Paul once was, the more effect
Paul's recalling it will have upon them in the present
connection. He needs to touch only the worst points.

We note ἐμήν which is stronger than the enclitic
"my," for Paul's conduct in life was an exception. "In
Judaism" has the article, like the German *in dem Juda-
ismus,* whereas we do without it; the term itself does
not refer to the Jewish religion (our versions) except
as this is the main thing in Judaism. Paul at once
states the worst: "that I continued persecuting the
church of God and kept ravaging it." He was the
supreme Jewish fanatic of his time. The two verbs
used do not exaggerate in the least. As imperfects
they describe the persecuting and the ravaging. Πορθεῖν
is used with reference to devastating a city with fire
and sword; it is the word found in Acts 9:21. The
enormity of Paul's criminal course is expressed by the
adverbial "beyond measure" and by the formulation
of the object "the church of God." Is there a greater
crime in all the world than to *devastate* — and that
beyond all measure — *God's* own church? "God's" is
the proper possessive, for the word itself denotes
deity; "Christ's" would do that to a lesser degree.

14) In v. 13 Paul lets his former acts speak, now he adds the animus that drove him to these and to other fanatic acts. He says that he cut ahead (προ-κόπτω) in Judaism beyond many of his own age, left many young men as old as he was far behind. As is so often the case in the Greek, the participial clause presents the main point: being more excessively than the other young Jews of his age "a zealot for my paternal traditions." The word used means that he literally burned with zeal that demanded action against anything that was opposed to the Jewish traditions; it recalls the name that was applied to the Jewish sect of the Zealots who preached the sacred duty of revolt against Rome.

Paul was of the same fanatical type, but his zeal was "for my ancestral traditions" (objective genitive). Πατρικός is the adjective formed from the genitive τοῦ πατρός and refers to one's father, grandfather, etc., and not, like πατρῷος or πάτριος, to national ancestry. Paul's father was a strict Pharisee and had trained his son to be even stricter. The adjective makes the impression that this Pharisaism was a trait of long standing in the family. Its proudest and most militant member was Saul.

By "my ancestral traditions" Paul refers to the traditions of the Pharisees, that whole hedge of 613 human commandments which the rabbis had built around the law, and which the Pharisees made it the business of their party to maintain at all costs. Here we should recall all the virulent clashes of Jesus with the Pharisees, for instance, the climax in Matt. 23:13, etc. Paul's violence against the Christians was so excessive because the church meant the death of Pharisaism. A converted Jew and Pharisee might live in the old Jewish way and freely choose to observe parts of the Mosaic law; but he would certainly give up the traditions of the elders as being mere useless and dan-

gerous "commandments of men." These very traditions were the apple of Paul's eye; for them he wished
to tear the church of God to pieces.

What Paul conveys is the idea that he was more
than a defender of the Mosaic law, more than a Pharisee who saw the glory of Judaism in that law. He saw
the crown of Judaism in the traditions. The church
had to be crushed so that these traditions, built to
support the Mosaic law, might be maintained. The
point in all this is not that Paul could not be converted
as many other Pharisees were converted. Although
they believed, some of these still thought that parts
of the Mosaic law were binding (Acts 15:5), but not,
of course, the rabbinical traditions.

Paul was utterly extreme. On the one hand, he
raged for the traditions and went far beyond the Mosaic law; on the other hand, he now stood for complete
liberty even from the Mosaic law and was the very
apostle of this liberty. Once the supreme protagonist
of the traditions, now the very apostle of Christian
liberty! Let the Galatians visualize the gulf that lay
between these extremes. How was it possible that
such a fanatic traditionalist should now be the apostle
of perfect Christian liberty? If he was converted at
all *he* should have been a Judaizer like those referred
to in Acts 15:5. But we already have the full answer:
"Jesus Christ's revelation," v. 12.

15) This concise answer is now amplified. **But
when is pleased God, who separated me from my
mother's womb and called me by means of his grace,
to reveal his Son in me in order that I may preach
the good news of him among the Gentiles, immediately I conferred not with flesh and blood, nor did
I go to Jerusalem to those** (who were) **apostles before me but I went off into Arabia and again I returned to Damascus.**

This is the full account of the revelation which converted the zealot for the rabbinical traditions into the apostle of Christ and of gospel liberty. God did this by an act of revelation, did it completely without the aid of any man, without in any way employing any man as a means in his hand.

It was due to God's pleasure, his εὐδοκία, which is here expressed by the verb εὐδόκησεν. God "had the good pleasure." The word conveys the idea that God was moved only by what is in himself and not by any merit or worthiness in Paul. It also contains the thought of grace and kindness so that all arbitrariness and determinism are excluded. The "good pleasure" of God is the free will whose content is something good (C.-K. 354). This term is used in connection with the bestowal of salvation, cf., Eph. 1:5. It is one of the lovely terms applied to God in the Scriptures. What God did in his good pleasure is stated by the infinitive: "to reveal his Son in me." Distinct from this act are two others which are not connected with the infinitive but made descriptions of the subject: "God who separated and called" (note the article which makes the participles attributive).

"Who separated me from my mother's womb" means more than that God ushered Paul into this life as he does every child that is safely born. Not only does "it pleased God" precede, but a second participle, "called," follows. We are reminded of Jer. 1:5 and may think of Luke 1:15. The intentions of God's good pleasure are not conceived at the time of their execution but long before, so long in advance that he shapes and directs all things toward the good end he has in view. How the divine and the human factors are combined in attaining the good outcome is beyond mortal insight. Speculations are generally unsatisfactory. The point which we should note is the full stress Paul lays on the divine agency which made him the apostle that he was. No one would have believed that the babe born away off in heathen Tarsus, the child of the strictest Pharisees, would come to be the apostle who fought this Pharisaism so mightily.

The Hebrew *pharush*, Aramaic *pherisha'*, "Pharisee," is the Greek ἀφωρισμένος, one separated. Because Paul here uses the aorist participle of this verb, the supposition is advanced that Paul means that God in his good pleasure made him "a separated one," i. e., a *pharush* or Pharisee in a higher (Christian) sense. Even in Rom. 1:1, where we do have the perfect participle, this idea is too superficial to be entertained. It is more so here because of its modifier: "who separated me from my mother's womb."

"Called me by means of his grace" takes us to Damascus. The purpose God had already at the time of his birth came to its fulfillment in the call of grace. While all that intervened between the birth and the call seemed so contradictory to God's good pleasure regarding Paul, it in reality served the divine purpose. What a triumph of grace! What an effect upon the Jews themselves! The Pharisaic career of Paul, once it crashed before grace, made pure grace stand out in its supreme effectiveness in Paul's own experience. When Paul writes, "called me by means of his grace," all the wonders of grace rise before our minds. Yes, this is grace with its connotation of utter guilt in the recipient who ought to be damned, with its implication of absolutely unmerited favor. In the epistles "to call" always denotes the successful call (see v. 6). Here, as in v. 6, Paul has in mind the call that made him a Christian. It is true enough that the same grace called him to be an apostle, and even that both calls were united in one grand act; yet here Paul distinguishes and lets the infinitive say how he was made an apostle.

16) The main statement, which is vital for Paul's object, is that God pleased "to reveal his Son in

me." What is meant is at once shown by the addition
of the purpose of this revelation: "in order that I may
preach him as good news among the Gentiles." This
revelation was to make Paul the apostle to the Gentiles.
The infinitive is an aorist, it denotes a complete and an
effective revelation. Paul does not say, "to reveal
Jesus Christ," but "his Son," Jesus Christ in his deity,
in all that his deity means for the contents of gospel
preaching. Subtract the deity, and all that remains is
hollow sound.

The claim is made that Paul never calls Jesus "God's
Son." Here we have one of the numerous places where
he does so. The fact that "his Son" makes Christ equal
with the Father, makes Christ the second person of the
Trinity, we have seen in v. 1 and 3, where this equality is beyond question. "In me" is stronger than the
mere dative "to me." R. 587 and *W. P.* translates "in
my case" — a strange idea: "to reveal in my case."
"In me" is even more than "in my experience." This
revelation was not intended for the senses of Paul but
was vastly more. It filled his very heart, soul, and
spirit so as to abide with him forever.

In v. 12 Jesus Christ is the revelator, here the revelator is God. This fact may be stated either way. God
ever reveals his Son, the Son ever reveals God. Whatever this revelation did for Paul's personal faith as a
believer — here it is regarded as making him the apostle to the Gentiles. This revelation made Paul the
equal of the Twelve as we have already brought out.
One hesitates to say whether it included more than took
place on the road to Damascus. Its absolute sufficiency
for Paul's apostleship is beyond question. Paul was
made an apostle to the Gentiles from the start. The
strange fact that years passed before he actually
worked among the Gentiles does not change God's appointment. Like Moses, Paul had to await God's own
time.

Paul did not confer with flesh and blood. This verb is regularly used in this sense (M.-M. 546) : to consult with someone in order to obtain advice, to get someone's judgment so as to arrive at a decision. "Flesh and blood" is often thought to refer to Paul himself, i. e., to his own natural inclinations, with the idea that he did not let these speak in the matter. It is claimed that the analogy of Scripture supports this view. Yet in Eph. 6 :12 "flesh and blood" denotes earthly opponents, and in general σὰρξ καὶ αἶμα, *basar w^edam*, derives its meaning from the context. Here Paul has in mind fallible men in general; he uses the highly descriptive abstract expression in place of a concrete term. "Flesh and blood" is in contrast to "God who separated me," etc. Paul in no way referred God's revelation and appointment to the apostleship among the Gentiles to earthly judges before accepting it.

We might think that Paul's emphatic "immediately" refers back to his bloodthirsty ravaging of the church and thus stresses the suddenness of the change in him : one moment tearing the church to pieces, the next going forth with the commission to gospelize even the heathen. But "immediately" is to be construed with two peculiar negative statements. These read like refutations of lying reports; as though Paul had learned from the Galatian delegation that the Judaizers claimed that he did at first listen to others and seek their guidance and then afterward broke away and adopted the wrong course of discarding all the Jewish legal requirements. That was a cunning way of winning the Galatians away from Paul's present teaching, his opponents pretending that theirs was the original doctrine that was held by Paul himself when he at first listened to others. Paul never consulted any man. To have done so would have discredited God himself, the all-sufficiency of God's own revelation.

17) "Nor did I go up to Jerusalem to those (who were) apostles before me" singles out the Twelve as the ones who were worthy of being consulted more than any others. The higher the Twelve stood, the more one must remember that they, too, were only "flesh and blood" as compared with God. "Immediately" is to be construed also with this clause. Paul did not hurry to Jerusalem to get anything, whether information and instruction or corroboration and approval, from any of the Twelve. Paul's action was not a reflection on the Twelve as though he cared nothing about a judgment of theirs. Quite the contrary. He acknowledges them as "the apostles" exactly as God had made him such a one. He also acknowledges the one point in which they outranked him: they were the apostles "before me." God had appointed Paul as the last apostle.

It would have been wrong for Paul to have consulted the Twelve or any number of them whom he might have found in Jerusalem. It will not do to say that they would undoubtedly have approved. They would have rebuked Paul for trying to consult them regarding God's own revelation. Not one of them would have ventured a word where God himself had spoken. Were they higher than God? By his revelation God had not only made Paul an apostle but had equipped him in every respect exactly as he had equipped them, the Twelve, on Pentecost.

Over against the double negation and in order the more to down the false reports the Judaizers were spreading Paul states the facts regarding what he did do in the early days: "on the contrary (ἀλλά after negatives), I went off into Arabia and again I returned to Damascus." We at once see that Paul is writing to people who know where he was called and received God's revelation. Whether they also knew about his trip to Arabia must remain an open question; they did know that he eventually left Damascus never to return there. The point of importance is that there was no apostle in Damascus either at the time of Paul's conversion or when he returned; and in Arabia there certainly was no one with whom it was possible to confer.

But for this mention of Arabia we should not know that Paul had ever been there. Luke says nothing about it although we have no difficulty in fitting Paul's visit to Arabia into Acts 9:20-27. How long Paul remained in Arabia, how long a second time in Damascus, no one knows. Why did he choose Arabia, and what did he do there? Our curiosity is keen, various guesses are ventured, but no one knows more than this brief statement contains.

18)   Now we learn when Paul first came to Jerusalem, what his purpose was in coming, and whom he found there.   **Thereupon, after three years, I went up to Jerusalem to become acquainted with Cephas and remained with him for fifteen days.   But another of the apostles I did not see save James, the brother of the Lord.**

We regard "thereupon," ἔπειτα, as meaning after the return from Arabia, and "after three years" as being in contrast with "immediately" (v. 16), hence three years after Paul's conversion and not three years after his return to Damascus from Arabia.   The latter would hang in the air, since the length of time between Paul's call and his return from Arabia is not mentioned.   Nor is any reason apparent why the return from Arabia and three years from that indefinite date are of importance.   But the fact that Paul waited three years after his conversion before going to Jerusalem is exact and to the point; also that during these three years he had taken a long journey, but *not* to Jerusalem; also that he returned to the place of his call, namely Damascus.   So three years went by since Paul was called.

And since so long a time had elapsed, any idea of consulting the apostles about his revelation was rather late. Paul now tells the Galatians why he went to Jerusalem: "to become acquainted with Cephas." Why only Cephas? Paul could scarcely expect to find all of the Twelve in Jerusalem. We must conjecture that he had learned from traveling Christians that Cephas was making a stay in Jerusalem and hastened to make the acquaintance of this leader among the Twelve.

Here Paul writes "Cephas," the old Aramaic name of Peter; in 2:7, 8, where Jewish opponents are not so prominently in mind, "Peter" is used. Paul remained πρὸς αὐτόν, in reciprocal contact with Cephas, only fifteen days, a trifle over two weeks. This is the extent of Paul's first contact with any apostle. Ἱστορέω = "to visit" for the purpose of learning to know, to become acquainted with, B.-P. 596, not "to inquire of," to get information from.

19) During these brief days Paul did not even see another of the apostles. They were evidently absent from Jerusalem and in other cities. When he adds: "save James, the brother of the Lord," we should at once see that, having just denied seeing a single other apostle, his meaning cannot be that he after all saw another apostle, namely this James, but that Paul feels that he must name the one other person of special importance whom he saw although without really getting acquainted with him. This was not one of the Twelve as Paul makes plain, but one whom he must name since the Judaizers might claim him in support of their teaching. There is not a conflict with Acts 9:27, where Luke says that Barnabas brought Paul "to the apostles" (plural); for Luke calls Barnabas, too, an apostle (Acts 14:14) and could well consider James an apostle in this wider sense of the term.

At this time the church at Jerusalem was no longer under the direct management of the Twelve but had its own elders, chief among whom was James. We know him as a man of great importance; Acts 15 is enough to establish this fact. He is called "the brother of the Lord" in order to distinguish him from James, the brother of John, and probably from James, the son of Alphæus. He came to faith after the resurrection of Jesus. We have shown in connection with Acts 1:14 that the "brothers of Jesus" were not sons of Mary (see that passage); whether they were stepbrothers or cousins is an open question. The writer does not accept the more recent claims which rest their contention on ἀδελφοί as if this settled the question that sons who were born to Joseph of Mary after Jesus are referred to. Acts 1:14 is an impediment in their way, and there are other obstructions that are not removed by this word.

20) This is the whole of that visit of fifteen days three years after Paul's call as an apostle: acquaintance with Peter, seeing James, no conference on Paul's revelation, no passing of his call through any man's hands, nothing to lower Paul's apostleship in any way. **Now as regards what I am writing to you, lo, before God, I am not lying!**

This solemn assurance is called forth by the insinuations and falsifications of the Judaizers who used all that they had heard about Paul in order to discredit him. Some of the Galatians might ask: "Is that really all there was to that visit in Jerusalem?" Paul gives the most solemn answer as if he were before God's own judgment seat. He is writing them the facts, the entire truth without a falsehood. Paul's gospel had its own convincing and faith-working power. Outward proofs add nothing whatever to that; but they do remove barriers which would otherwise block acceptance of the truth such as plausible and cunningly twisted allegations about the apostle himself.

"What I am writing to you" may be regarded as a pendent nominative. Ἰδού is an interjection as the accent shows and has no object; but the formula of solemn assurance: "lo, before God," has adverbial force and thus has the ὅτι clause as its subject, "that I am not lying."

21) What about the time after those fifteen days? That, too, is highly significant. **Thereupon I went into the regions of Syria and Cilicia.** Acts 9:27-30 briefly tells the story of the fifteen days and how the threat of persecution drove Paul from Jerusalem. Paul touches upon only his contact with Peter and with James because the Judaistic falsifications tried to make capital of that. Brought from Jerusalem to Caesarea, Paul went to Tarsus. What made him leave Jerusalem was really a communication from the Lord himself (Acts 22:17-21). He could go by either sea or land. If he went by land, he would go first to Syria and then to Cilicia. It is sometimes supposed that he went by sea and that he here reverses the names and writes Syria first because it adjoins Palestine and then Cilicia because it adjoins Syria. The fact is that after years spent in Tarsus, Barnabas brought him back to Antioch in Syria where they worked together. Paul may mention Syria first because he did not work in Cilicia but finally did considerable work in Antioch.

The remarkable thing is that Paul spent eight years in Tarsus, his native city. They are a blank for us. It is only a guess when one reads of missionary work done during these years in Tarsus and Cilicia. This is impossible. Luke has many silences due to his plan of Acts; but he could not have been silent regarding any work done in Cilicia, for this would have been Paul's *first* great work among the Gentiles, the very work Luke records in Acts. No; Paul was inactive, in retirement. Christ did not as yet deem him ready; like Moses, Paul had to wait. But all this belongs to a consideration of Acts; the point to be noted here is the fact that after fifteen brief days Paul for so many years went far away from any contact with the Twelve. This fact speaks volumes against the Judaistic falsifications.

22) **Moreover, I was not known by sight to the churches in Judea which are in Christ.** Because of the lack of an adjective such as "Christian" we have the phrase "in Christ" added attributively. The Judean churches had never even seen Paul, and he had now been absent from them for years. This does not, of course, include Jerusalem where during those fifteen days Paul went in and out among the brethren and even disputed with the Hellenistic Jews who then tried to kill him (Acts 9:28, 29).

23) **Only they continued to hear: He who was once persecuting us is now preaching the faith which he was once ravaging; and they went on glorifying God in me.**

Note the periphrastic imperfects in v. 22, 23, both stress continuation: "continuing unknown — continuing only to hear." It is easy to see how the Judean churches again and again heard about the man they had never seen. They heard when they came to Jerusalem, or when someone from Jerusalem came to them. Many, no doubt, wondered what had become of Paul. He was certainly not forgotten.

What was said about him in all these churches? Anything derogatory? Any criticism of his gospel, of his apostleship, of his relation to the other apostles? Not a word. On the contrary, everybody got to hear this astounding news that their one-time persecutor is now preaching the very faith he at one time tried to wreck. Note the direct discourse, the sharp contrast "once — now," and again "once" and the significant final clause. All these churches heard not only that Paul was gospelizing but that he was gospelizing the faith he once sought to wipe out. What faith was that? The one the Twelve preached — no other. In Jerusalem, the mother church, whither the Twelve often returned, and in all the Judean churches Paul's gospel was acknowledged as the one original faith. What do the Judaizers mean with their falsifications? Here there is another plain example of ἡ πίστις used in the objective sense: "the faith" = the gospel = the doctrine, which contradicts the statement of C.-K. that this word is never used objectively.

24) Instead of running down Paul as the Judaizers in Galatia did all these churches went on glorifying God "in connection with me," ἐν ἐμοί. All these, mark it, were Jewish churches who also had received all their news about Paul from Jerusalem itself, the very seat of the Twelve. What more can the Galatians ask?

Thus by a simple recounting of the historical facts Paul sets before the Galatians what they should never have allowed anyone to make them doubt: he had his gospel directly from God and Christ, by revelation and not at secondhand, the identical gospel of all the other apostles, of all the churches in Judea.

CHAPTER II

2. *How the Other Apostles Acknowledged Paul's Gospel, 2:1-10*

1) Root and branch Paul destroys the allegation of the Judaizers that his gospel is not the original gospel but that of the other apostles, and that he is not a genuine apostle, sent by the Lord like the Twelve, but has come from or through men only. He continues to let the facts speak their crushing language. In chapter 1 the facts reveal that Paul had his gospel by revelation, that during a long period of time he had only fifteen days' contact with Peter and slight contact with James, but that Jerusalem and all the Judean churches glorified God because he preached the very faith he had once persecuted. So much for *the source.*

Now he presents *the contents* of his gospel regarding the very point assailed by the Judaizers, Christian liberty and circumcision in particular. Paul advances to the time of the great apostolic convention at Jerusalem when he came into fullest contact with the other apostles, yea, with all the leaders and with the church officially assembled. This was the decisive occasion when the first Judaizers were publicly and officially discredited and their Judaistic claims rejected. *They* were disowned, *Paul* was most fully acknowledged. Not that he needed such endorsement — he had never needed it. But if anything was wrong with either Paul's apostleship or his gospel of Christian liberty, this wrong would most certainly have been exposed at this convention in Jerusalem, regarding which Paul now presents the pertinent facts.

The Galatians know all about this convention. For, some time after it took place, Paul started on his sec-

ond missionary journey and began it by visiting the
Galatian churches he had founded and delivered to all
of them the resolution adopted at the great conference.
See the resolution sent out to the Gentile churches,
Acts 15:23-29; Paul delivered it in Galatia, Acts
16:4, 5. When he recalls this convention to the minds
of the Galatians, Paul needs only to touch the points he
deems vital; he does not need to tell the whole story
over again. It certainly was preposterous that not so
long after the whole Judaistic contention had been
utterly repudiated by the apostles and the church as
such right in Jerusalem, Judaizers should creep into
Galatia and try to make the Galatians believe that Paul
and his gospel were repudiated, that the Judaizers were
endorsed, that the Twelve themselves were Judaizers.

**Thereupon, with an interval of fourteen years, I
went up again to Jerusalem in company with Barnabas, taking along with me also Titus.**

This is the third "thereupon," and, as in the case
of the first in 1:18, a phrase expressing time follows.
Διά with the genitive indicates an interval (R. 581)
and counts from the time indicated in 1:18, 21, Paul's
fifteen-day visit in Jerusalem. Fourteen years after
that visit means seventeen years after Paul's conversion. These fourteen years include the eight Paul spent
in Tarsus, regarding which we know nothing definite;
the years spent in Syrian Antioch, working there with
Barnabas in the great church which was chiefly Gentile;
the period of the first missionary journey when Paul
and Barnabas founded the Galatian churches; their
return to Antioch and Paul's further stay in that city
until he went to attend the Jerusalem conference.

The supposition that Paul is speaking of the visit
which he and Barnabas paid to Jerusalem to bring the
relief gathered in Antioch for the poor (Acts 11:27-30;
12:25) is chronologically untenable. This visit antedates the founding of the Galatian churches. At that

time the situation in Jerusalem was distressing; James, the brother of John, had been killed by Herod, Peter had fled, Paul and Barnabas saw no apostle. The visit of which Paul speaks here cannot be identified with the one mentioned in Acts 11:30.

Some interpreters count the fourteen years from the time of Paul's conversion on the plea that this is the dominating date for the reckoning of time. It is; but it dominates just as strongly when the fourteen years follow the three as when they include the three. If they include the three, the conversion of Paul is moved forward three years, which upsets the entire chronology. The date of Herod's frightful death (Acts 12:23) is known independently of the Scriptures: the summer of the year 44. Paul is speaking of the time of the convention (Acts 15). All is in order when we accept this date, the beginning of the year 52. But this is not a matter of dates; what happened on this visit of Paul's and Barnabas' to Jerusalem cannot be assigned to a time when it could not have happened.

We see no reason for questioning the force of πάλιν; whether it is retained in the text or not, this was "again" a visit to Jerusalem. The fact that Paul and Barnabas had brought relief to Jerusalem in the fall of the year 44 need not be mentioned because this visit to Jerusalem had no bearing on Paul's gospel. The claim that Paul could not have ignored a mention of this visit is untenable.

We should note the marked difference with which Barnabas and Titus are named. Paul went up "in company with" Barnabas (μετά), with him as his chief associate. They were the two main members of the commission who were sent from Antioch to the Jerusalem conference (Acts 15:2). The Galatians knew all about this; Paul himself had visited them and had brought them the resolution of the conference, which was to be brought to all the Gentile churches.

Paul names Barnabas because Barnabas had helped to found the Galatian churches. Another reason is that Barnabas had stood with Paul in what Paul now tells about the happenings at the time of this conference. This is of importance because the Judaizers were in reality demanding that the Galatians should turn from both founders of their churches. Titus was not a member of the Antioch commission. Paul took him along. We know Titus as being Paul's assistant in the period following the conference. He is mentioned because of what follows; his became a test case at the conference.

2) **Moreover, I went up in accord with a revelation, and I laid before them the gospel which I am preaching among the Gentiles, and in private before those in repute, whether I am running or did run in vain.**

The church in Antioch elected Paul as one of the commission that was to go to Jerusalem for the conference regarding the issue the Judaizers had raised. In Acts 15 Luke reports only that Paul went along. From Paul we now learn more, namely that the Lord bade him go in a revelation. It seems that, although he was duly elected to go, he had some reluctance about accepting. The Lord himself removed his scruples, and he went.

Δέ adds this for the sake of the Galatians. They are to understand that he did not go of his own accord even after being elected; the Lord himself bade him go. The Galatians must not get the impression that Paul was obliged to lay his gospel before others for their approval, or that the church at Antioch perhaps obligated him to do so, or that he at least felt that he ought to do so. The idea that the Lord, who had called Paul as an apostle, wanted him to get the approval of the men at Jerusalem is, of course, preposterous. The Lord's acts are not subject to any man's approval. As his own approved apostle the Lord wanted Paul present at Jerusalem in order to help with the deliberations just as Paul did help.

Nothing is gained by asking whether the Lord gave the revelation to Paul himself or to one of the other prophets in Antioch. The Lord gave so many revelations to Paul that such a question should not be raised. Paul went with the Lord's own assurance that his going would in no way harm his own apostolic standing. He, of course, does not recite the whole story of that conference. The Galatians knew that; Paul and Silas had made a full report to them. Silas was one of the two who were especially commissioned by the conference to carry the written resolution of the conference to the Gentile churches (Acts 15:27). He was Paul's chosen assistant for the second missionary journey (Acts 15:40) and thus officially informed the Galatians of the conference resolution (Acts 16:4, 5).

Paul here presents the test case that was made of Titus and of circumcision. This actual case shatters the whole contention of the Judaizers, shatters it right at Jerusalem to which the Judaizers constantly appealed, and reveals the fact that the other apostles and the whole church stood with Paul.

It was at the first public meeting at Jerusalem that Paul "laid before them (the entire assembly) the gospel which I am preaching among the Gentiles" as also Luke records in Acts 15:4. Luke speaks of "all the things God had done" through Paul and Barnabas; Paul speaks of the means by which all these things were done. We know that the means, namely the gospel Paul preached, was the subject for calling the conference. Means and results naturally go together. In the assembly at Jerusalem the Antioch delegation told the story of the great work that had been done in their city. Paul and Barnabas had their share in that. Then these two told of their first missionary tour to Cyprus

and to Galatia. Paul words it well: "the gospel
which I am preaching among the Gentiles." It was
entirely a story of the gospel which founded the Galatian churches, of the gospel Paul is still preaching.
From Antioch it had extended to Galatia and now at
the time of Paul's writing was extending still farther.
Jesus had ordered the apostles to carry this gospel to
"all the ἔθνη" ("nations" or Gentiles).

Paul adds information that is perhaps new to the
Galatians, that he laid this gospel of his "in private
(δέ, also) before those in repute," the leaders in Jerusalem. This was not in any way a secret conclave; it
furnished direct personal opportunity for the leaders
to learn from Paul all they might desire to know; we
take it that Paul had Barnabas with him. Paul was
very glad to tell everything, and, no doubt, James,
Peter, and John were equally glad to hear all they could
from Paul and from Barnabas. It was a rare opportunity of which all concerned made the most. Whether
any others of the elders of Jerusalem were present at
this private meeting we cannot determine; it is possible.

Paul calls those with whom he conferred οἱ δοκοῦντες
and repeats this expression four times and plays on it
in a pointed manner. In v. 6 and 9 he amplifies the
designation. The sense is the same throughout. It
might be either they who *think themselves* something;
or they who *seem* to be something *to others* — the latter with or without the idea of justification. The context determines just what is meant. Here it must be
"they who seem to be something to others," they who
are considered to be somebody, more briefly, "those in
repute."

The very repetition of this designation shows that
Paul is quoting it from the lips of the Judaizers in
Galatia. "Who," they said, "is Paul when compared
with men like James, Peter, and John? These are the
men of standing who are considered so in the church."

Paul rubs the word in by his repetitions. The irony of that procedure is directed against the Judaizers. *They* were the ones who thought that repute was the main thing and that it settled everything against Paul. If *they* denied standing and repute to Paul, then Paul counted for nothing, and, of course, the Galatians would accept what *they*, these Judaizers, were pleased to say.

Now Paul is the last man to deny the high repute of James, Peter, and John, or of anybody else. He is also the last man to be jealous of his own repute. All repute among men, whether his own or that of others in the church, is secondary entirely; the essential is something far higher, namely what *the Lord* makes of any man. The business of the church is to consider that and to make its repute correspond to that. That Paul himself held James, Peter, and John in the highest repute is evidenced by the fact that he laid his gospel before these men. He could not have done so if he thought that they did not fully deserve this high repute. He would be a fool for telling the Galatians how he laid his gospel before these men if he at the same time intends to say that in his own estimation these men were nothing.

But the laying of his gospel before James, etc., does *not* mean that he and his gospel were dependent on the verdict of these men because of their repute. Verse 6 leaves nothing to be desired regarding that. Paul is not afraid of laying his gospel before anybody, least of all before these high men of whose great repute the Judaizers sought to make capital against him. Paul's gospel was from God, so was theirs. It was and had ever been one and the same. Any and every time a proper examination is made, this would appear. Paul's repute thus took care of itself. God was back of it as he was back of any true repute that James, etc., enjoyed in the church.

It was solely because of the Judaizers who had appeared in Antioch and with others were now making themselves obnoxious in Jerusalem that Paul (and Barnabas) got together with James, Peter, and John, in order by means of the true gospel, which they all unitedly preached, to crush the Judaistic error most effectively and completely. When the Judaizers of Jerusalem laid their perversion of the gospel (Acts 15:5) before the conference, Peter gave them a crushing reply in his address (Acts 15:7-11). Paul and Barnabas did the same (Acts 15:12), and it was James, who, presiding at this conference, formulated the resolution which the whole conference adopted, put in writing, and sent out to all the Gentile churches (Acts 15:13-32). In this resolution the whole contention of the Judaizers was repudiated. What a farce for any Judaizers now to come to the Galatians with talk of "those in repute" and thereby to throw dust in the eyes of the Galatians! Why are these Judaizers not telling the truth?

Read μή πως as an indirect question: "whether I am running or did run (the English prefers the perfect: have been running) in vain." The implied answer is: "Certainly not!" Both verbs are naturally indicatives, all is grammatically simple. This question does not express a doubt on Paul's part; even πως, "in some way," "perhaps," leaves him without doubt. This question was raised by the Judaizers in Jerusalem; *they* either said outright that all Paul's work was in vain or implied as much. In fact, Paul *was* running in vain if the gospel of the Judaizers was the true gospel. Then all Paul's work was εἰς κενόν, "for emptiness," empty, hollow; it would all have to be done over again. In this indirect question Paul lays the Judaistic contention before the private meeting. James, Peter, and John would have to declare regarding their own work

that it has all been in vain if they pronounced this verdict on Paul's work.

Our versions translate: "Lest by any means I
should be running or had run in vain." R. 988 thinks
that this expresses purpose, "purely final." Let us say
that purpose is not acceptable. B.-D. 370, 2 finds a
feeling of concern in the main verb: Paul laid his gospel before these men with a feeling of concern "lest he
be running," etc. This is not tenable: Paul had a feeling of perfect certainty which rested on God's own
direct revelation. Can any man have greater objective or subjective certainty? As the purpose, so the
feeling of concern is untenable. R. W. P., regards
τρέχω as being subjunctive and explains the aorist indicative ἔδραμον as a sort of afterthought or retrospect
and in his grammar adds that in such final clauses the
classics expressed unreality by the indicative. R.
admires Paul for thus implying that he had *not* run in
vain. B.-D. 361 contradicts this: this indicative is
"not unreal." This question regarding the modes becomes clear the moment we see that this is an indirect
question, one that was precipitated by the Judaizers,
the answer to which was beyond a shadow of doubt to
men such as James, Peter, and John.

3)   So crushingly was the question answered to
the complete overthrow of the Judaizers that Paul
writes: **But not even Titus, the one with me,
although he was a Greek, was compelled to be circumcised even on account of the pseudo-brethren
sneakingly brought in, such as sneakingly came in
to spy out our liberty which we have in Christ Jesus
in order that they might completely enslave us; to
whom we yielded no, not for an hour by way of the
submission** (they demanded) **in order that the truth
of the gospel might continue on for you.**

The Judaizers failed utterly and completely in their
contention at Jerusalem. The Galatians have the ver-

dict, the resolution worded by James and formally adopted by the assembly (Acts 15:13, etc.) ; the failure of the Judaizers was even more complete as we see from the test case of Titus. This was an actual case which occurred right there in the conference. Facts speak even louder than words.

The indirect question asked in v. 2 embodies the verdict of the Judaizers: "Paul had run, was still running in vain!" 'Αλλά is set squarely against this: "On the contrary," and on the contrary to this extent: "not even Titus was compelled to be circumcised." Paul had purposely taken Titus along (v. 1) ; "the one with me" emphasizes this fact. Paul made Titus an open challenge to the Judaizers. They might have allowed other Gentiles who were living in distant places to remain uncircumcised; they dared not permit this regarding Titus right in the conference itself now that he was thrown into their faces as a challenge by Paul himself. He was a Greek, both of his parents were Gentiles. Paul had never had him circumcised and never circumcised him even later on. His case was entirely different from that of Timothy, whose mother was a Jewess and whom Paul intended to use for mission work among the Jews.

Circumcision was a complete adiaphoron to Paul: it was nothing either way (I Cor. 7:19). He performed it with regard to Timothy because it would prove a help in the work. Since Titus was a Greek, it would prove no help in his case, Jews would always be suspicious of him. Titus was just the man with whom to challenge the Judaizers. When they demanded his circumcision, Paul absolutely refused. He had to. The moment any adiaphoron is demanded as being necessary to salvation, it ceases to be an adiaphoron, it becomes a vital issue on which we dare not yield. *C. Tr.* 1059, etc., elaborates this subject on which so many are confused to the detriment of real Christian liberty.

In the person of Titus the whole gospel as it was preached by Paul, by Peter (Acts 11:1-18; 15:7-11), and by all the apostles came to be embodied. That gospel would have crumbled and fallen if this man would have been circumcised at the demand of the Judaizers. That is why he was *not* circumcised, not even for minor, secondary, innocent reasons. Once the Judaizers made their demand regarding Titus, they destroyed all reasons for his ever being circumcised.

Among the exegetical curiosities we list the one which has Paul say the opposite of what he does say, namely that Titus was circumcised, yet not under constraint but by voluntary action on Paul's part. The emphasis is placed on ἠναγκάσθη, and οὐδέ is regarded as modifying only this verb: Titus "was not even forced" to be circumcised. Even if Paul intended to say this, he would not have put it in the words which he here used. The emphasis is on "not even Titus," and it cannot be shifted to "was forced." "Not even Titus" = he with whom Paul made the challenge, not even he, to say nothing about others who were not made a test case.

4) Δέ emphasizes the διά phrase and does not start a new sentence. Δέ calls on the reader to bear in mind that not even Titus was compelled to be circumcised, compelled "on account of the pseudo-brethren," etc., the very men who so strenuously tried to force his circumcision. We do not have an anacoluthon; this view is due to the claim that δέ is metabatic and starts a new sentence. Zahn removes the anacoluthon by cancelling οἷς οὐδέ from v. 5. The texts, however, are against this procedure, especially regarding οὐδέ.

Zahn's concern is to get another thought; the matter of the anacoluthon is only incidental. We are told that Paul *did yield* for a moment with due subjection

in order to conserve the gospel. To whom? To the
pseudo-brethren, the Judaizers? That is unthinkable. Some suggest, to the resolution framed by James
(Acts 15:13, etc.). But Paul did not yield to that, that
was his own hearty conviction; to say that he yielded
to it only "for an hour" is unacceptable. Well, then,
Paul yielded to the authorities in Jerusalem by laying
the clash with the Judaizers in Antioch before these
authorities in due submission. This is Zahn's answer.

Aside from the alteration of the text involved, this
answer itself is unsatisfactory. It bids us jump from
v. 5 to v. 1 and forget about Titus. No reader does
that; no writer could expect it. When one says in a
preamble that certain men tried to enslave him and
then adds that he yielded, every ordinary reader will
understand that he yielded to these men — he *must* so
understand. Textually and in every other way the
negative stands: "I did *not* yield for one moment!"
Add to this the fact that Paul was *not* subject to any
authorities in Jerusalem, that he repudiates this assumption throughout, most decidedly in v. 6. He was
subject only to God and to Christ, was on a perfect
equality with the Twelve. To make Paul subject to
James is unwarranted.

Paul says that what set everybody against circum-
cising Titus for any reason was the attitude of "the
pseudo-brethren," a term that is like "pseudo-apostle"
found in II Cor. 11:13. In forming our estimate of
them we should not forget Acts 15:5 and paint them
too black. Luke calls them "Pharisees who believed"
yet demanded "that it was needful to circumcise them
and to command them to keep the law of Moses." They
were not *dis*believers but *mis*believers, errorists, but
such as had become fixed in their error. They accepted
Christ yet added the Mosaic law to Christ and thus
falsified Christ. From Paul we learn more. First the
adjective "brought in on the side," surreptitiously,

sneakingly. They should never have been brought into
the church as members. Somebody was to blame for
bringing them in; who is not said, but it surely was not
any of the apostles.

"Such as came in on the side," sneakingly, adds the
thought that they were of this type. The real blame
lay on them; they deceived those who brought them
in. This is evidenced by what they proved to be, not
brethren whose aim it was to let go their Pharisaism
and to accept the free gospel wholeheartedly, but men
who were determined to cling to their Pharisaism, set
on "spying" out our liberty which we have in Christ
Jesus."

They are not to be identified with the Judaizers
who appeared in Antioch and first caused the Judaistic
question to be raised. They were not the same men,
for we must conclude from Luke's account that the
Judaizers in Antioch did not send a delegation to Jerusalem at the time of the conference. The pseudo-
brethren in the mother church made it their special
business to pry out whether one or the other of the delegation that came from the church in Antioch was perhaps uncircumcised. Of course, they soon found Titus
and centered their general demand for circumcision
(Acts 15:5) on him. It was entirely a matter of liberty
whether a Christian man wanted to remain uncircumcised or not. Paul writes *"our* liberty," for the matter
concerned the entire delegation from Antioch irrespective of how many were or were not circumcised. "Which
we have in Christ Jesus" declares this to be the true
Christian and gospel liberty.

Paul adds that the purpose of the spying out was
"that they might completely enslave us," κατά in κατα-
δουλώσουσιν, a future indicative after ἵνα (R. 984), the
verb itself being causative (R. 802). "Enslave"
matches "liberty." Acts 15:5 accords with what Paul
says here. It would be the worst kind of spiritual slav-

ery again to be forced under the old Jewish Mosaic ceremonial regulations. With these again in control, works and outward observance would destroy the doctrine of "by faith alone." And that would mean loss of justification and salvation. Even on account of these men, who, in their Pharisaic zeal, surely made the most strenuous efforts, Titus was not compelled to be circumcised. James, Peter, John, and the great body of the church were not moved an inch.

5) Οἷς, like other relatives that are attached at the end of a longer statement, has demonstrative force, cf., Rom. 1:25; 3:8, 30. It is like saying: "These fellows to whom we yielded no, not for an hour by way of the submission" (i. e., the one they demanded). "We" refers to the entire delegation from Antioch (Acts 15:2). "The submission" was not "the submission which Paul and the delegation owed to James," etc. Τῇ ὑποταγῇ is the dative of mode, and the article refers to the submission or obedience in question. Not for a moment did we yield "by way of *the* (demanded) submission" to the enslavement proposed by the pseudobrethren and give up our liberty in Christ Jesus.

Paul states why "we did not yield for an hour (we say: for a moment)." He and Barnabas together with their fellow delegates thought of the Galatians to whom they had brought the truth of the gospel. If they had yielded, that truth would have been lost to the Galatians. Paul and Barnabas would have had to go back to Galatia and undo all that they had done. They stood solid "in order that the truth of the gospel (its verity and reality) might continue on (on through, διά) for you." Πρὸς ὑμᾶς is not "with you"; it is the face-to-face preposition: the truth of the gospel facing the Galatians, they facing the truth. "For you" is a most effective touch when Paul now writes to the Galatians. We can almost see Paul and Barnabas at the convention talking about their Galatian congregations and showing how the point at issue regarding Titus affected them all, and, of course, any other Gentile congregations yet to be founded.

It was only the circumcision of Titus — many shortsighted and weak-kneed preachers would have yielded and then perhaps justified themselves by a reference to their love. But Paul and Barnabas and their associates saw that in this one case "the truth of the gospel" itself was at stake, its very heart was at stake. If the pseudo-brethren gained their point, "by faith alone" would be overthrown right in the mother church in Jerusalem. What was that bound to do to all the other churches?

We add that if οὐδέ is cancelled, if Paul says that he did yield, the purpose clause: "in order that the truth of the gospel might be conserved for you," becomes unintelligible. The idea that Paul submitted to the authorities in Jerusalem in order to secure a favorable verdict, in order that the Galatians might keep the gospel truth, is strangely involved, and the main point is introduced from the outside. Such an exegesis will not meet universal approval.

The situation obtaining at the conference in Jerusalem is a kind of parallel to the one now obtaining in Galatia. There, as here, the Judaizers tried to destroy the liberty of the gospel with their legalism; there, as here, Paul yields not an inch. We may add that there the truth of the gospel was maintained against all legalism. Would that we could say: "It has always been so maintained." Alas, there are many legalists today. Paul's fears that he expressed in Acts 20:29, 30 have become reality. His warning uttered in Rom. 16:17, 18 is not heeded. But note: if the Judaizers in Galatia who opposed Paul's doctrine claimed the support of the apostles and of the mother church, the very opposite was the fact: all of the latter stood solidly behind Paul in the test case of Titus. The force of this truth must have been powerful, indeed, for the Galatians.

6) Paul has facts in connection with the confer- ence, both negative and positive, that are so powerful as doubly to close any Judaizer's mouth. No change in the work of Paul was proposed; on the contrary, James, Peter, and John gave Paul and Barnabas the right hand of fellowship, each acknowledging the other. No right hand of fellowship for the Judaizers! This is what happened at that notable conference.

Moreover, from those reputed to be something (whatever kind they were makes no difference to me — God does not accept a man's face) — before me, then, those in repute placed nothing; on the con- trary, the very opposite, etc.

Here we, indeed, have an anacoluthon, and a beau- tiful one at that. In the middle of the sentence Paul changes from the expected passive ("there was placed before me") to the unexpected active ("they placed before me"). Why did Paul write an anacoluthon, and why did he retain it? It was not due to the rapidity of his mind. That very rapidity saw where he was going when he began the sentence. R. 438 states that the parenthesis led Paul to change the construction. But that view is unsatisfactory. Paul uses the anacoluthon as a legitimate form of expression; it is as "regular" as what the grammarians call regular.

That is the formal side. The material is more im- portant. Paul's anacoluthon is used for a reason: to express what would otherwise not be expressed, what would otherwise require several statements. In the present instance this is quite apparent. The literary beauty of this anacoluthon shows the mastery of Paul in fitting language to thought. We shall explain.

"From those reputed to be something" repeats the designation that was used by the Judaizers when they pitted James and the Twelve against Paul, see v. 2. He now amplifies the designation as the Judaizers themselves did who said that these men really amounted to something while Paul amounted to nothing. To be sure, these men did amount to something, for which reason Paul also laid his whole gospel and his work before them. But if Paul amounted to nothing in comparison with these men, then they would, no doubt, point out to him certain things that he had overlooked, certain mistakes that he ought to correct, errors that he must avoid, in particular that he must insist on circumcision and on the legal regulations of Moses (Acts 15:5). What are the facts? The very contrary. These authorities that enjoyed this high repute laid absolutely nothing before Paul, not a thing regarding those mentioned, and not a thing concerning other, even lesser, matters. This is only the negative side, but it speaks volumes. It declares that in the finding of these very authorities, of whom the Judaizers made so extravagantly much, Paul's gospel and his work were in literally every respect as perfect as their own.

But it is now time to add a remark or two on the designation used so pointedly by the Judaizers: "those reputed to be something." Paul does it in only two brief, parenthetical remarks; no more is necessary: "whatever kind they (actually) were makes no difference to me — God does not accept a man's face." Ὁποῖοί ποτε should not be separated (B.-D. 303: *welcherlei Leute immer*), "whatever kind," R. 732; the adverb merely makes the adjective indefinite. It, of course, made no difference to Paul (*verschlaegt mir nichts*) what high repute James, etc., enjoyed; they might have enjoyed a still greater repute. Paul had received his gospel from far higher authority, from God himself. It is necessary to remind the Galatians of the fact that human repute does not count and did not count at the Jerusalem convention in the case of Paul.

But such a limited statement may seem derogatory to James and to the Twelve as though Paul cared nothing for them or their standing. It is not intended in this way. Paul does not wish to detract from them in the least, for is he not telling the Galatians that these men acknowledged him and his gospel? So he adds a second parenthetical statement: "God does not accept a man's face or person." The emphasis is on πρόσωπον and then on "God" and "man's," which are placed in contrasting juxtaposition: With *God man's* face does not count. The fact that Paul was only Paul, once a persecutor of the church, an abortion when he was called to be an apostle (I Cor. 15:8, 9), was of no consequence to God in comparison with Peter and John and others who followed Jesus from the beginning. God is able to make an apostle of whomever he will. Faces, names, persons are not decisive for him. Any wrong deductions that might be made from the first part of the parenthesis are thus removed.

Paul has begun as if he intends to say, "From them I on my part received nothing." But if he had finished thus, it might sound as though these men of repute tried to impart something to him. Yet they assumed no superior airs toward him, they did not even attempt to lay anything before him which, in their opinion, he ought to accept. He wants to deny both ideas. Most skilfully and with great delicacy he achieves this double denial by using an anacoluthon. The thought that they might possibly have wanted to lay something before him is thereby left only as a mild implication. It is kept down to that by the phrase: "from those reputed to be something," i. e., who might feel they had a right to dictate to me. By leaving this incomplete he brushes away the implication. The anacoluthon, starting the sentence anew with a nominative: "before me, then, those in repute," etc., constitutes only an easy turn in the construction, especially after the two parenthetical insertions.

This is made still easier by placing the dative forward: " — before me on my part 'those in repute' placed nothing." Count my repute what you will — such as I was and still am, these men in high repute, according to the phraseology of the Judaizers, strange as they may deem the fact, "before *me* they placed nothing" that I should accept. The aorist states the fact as a fact. Thus two birds are killed with one stone: the suggestion that "from them" something at least in the way of correction should surely have been placed before Paul; and the cold, solid fact that they did nothing of the kind.   Verily, anacolutha are excellent means for expressing thought if, like Paul and other good writers, one knows how to use them.

Γάρ is another delicate touch.   It connects the new turn of the sentence with the parenthesis by implying that those in repute fully deserved their repute far beyond what the Judaizers realized.   These men in repute understood perfectly what Paul here says, that with God there is no respect of persons. They never dreamed of letting Paul feel their authority by putting at least something before him.   That is what men in repute so generally like to do.   They want all others to feel that they *are* in repute; hence they insist on something even if it be only a triviality in order to have their authority noted.   James, etc., were far above that. Catch this effect from the way in which "those in repute" is once more inserted — they truly deserved to be in repute! We translate: "Before me, then." "I say" (R. V.) is not so good; "for" in the A. V. is better. Προσανέθεντο has the dative as in 1:16: to lay something before another either in the way of counselling with him (thus in 1:16) or in order to have him accept it (so here).

7) Beside the negative, which already says so much, is placed the still stronger positive: **on the contrary, the very opposite, having seen that I have been entrusted with the gospel for the foreskin even as Peter** (with the gospel) **for the circumcision (for he who wrought for Peter with regard to an apostolate for the circumcision wrought also for me with regard to the Gentiles), and having realized this grace given to me, James and Cephas and John, those reputed to be pillars, gave to me and Barnabas the right hand of fellowship that we on our part** (go) **to the Gentiles, and they on theirs to the circumcision, only the poor, that we keep remembering them — the very thing I also hastened to do.**

How mightily the facts do speak! The whole is one grand sentence. While after a negation ἀλλά means "on the contrary" and might thus suffice, here it is reenforced, for this contrary is the direct opposite. Those in repute did the complete opposite of making any demand on Paul, they endorsed him by a solemn public act and agreement. Can anything that is more crushing to the Judaizers be imagined?

The construction is simple: "having seen — and having realized — they gave." Here, for once, Paul's whole teaching and his work were fully examined and competently compared with those of the other apostles. Hitherto no occasion for such a comparison had arisen. Now that the occasion had come, these men saw what was so apparent, that Paul had been entrusted with the gospel for the foreskin just as Peter had been entrusted with the gospel for the circumcision.

The abstracts "foreskin" and "circumcision" generalize and in this sense stand for Gentiles and for Jews. We regard the two genitives as objective: "for the foreskin," etc. God entrusted the one as he did the other. The perfect refers to a past act with continuous effect: the trust given remained. This passive is not intransitive although the active is (R. 816) ; hence it takes the accusative like other transitive passives.

This does not indicate a difference in the contents of the gospel. It is identical for all nations and all times. The idea that our modern times need a different gospel, or that in mission work the gospel should be changed for this or that nation is unwarranted. Any change loses the gospel to the extent of the change attempted. The gospel is fixed and permanent in the Scriptures, in particular in the New Testament. These men naturally had nothing whatever to lay before Paul just as he had nothing to lay before them.

The remarkable thing is that Paul and Peter are placed on a par. John is not mentioned in the statement. This is scarcely due to the fact that the Judaizers claimed Peter as their patron; for the term Paul borrows from their lips is a plural: "those in repute." Peter is not named with the idea of excluding the eleven but as representing them. The division of territory can also not be meant in an exclusive sense. Paul always began his work in the synagogue; Peter preached to Cornelius and to other Gentiles in Caesarea. *A fortiori fit denominatio;* the distinction and the division of work was made on broad lines. In Acts 23:11 the Lord orders Paul to do the great mission work among the Jews that was waiting to be done in Rome. Yet, beginning with Paul's original appointment, especially he was to be the apostle of the Gentiles (Acts 26:17, 18). This is what the men saw at Jerusalem.

8) They compared what God had done. Paul adds this in explanation by means of γάρ; by placing it in a parenthesis the statement is made the more objective: "for he who wrought for Peter with regard to an apostolate for the circumcision wrought also for me with regard to the Gentiles." The two are closely paralleled. As Peter was placed in the Jewish work by God, so

Paul was placed in the Gentile work. The datives are indirect objects (R. V.) and are not due to the ἐν in the verb; "in Peter — in me" (A. V.) The place referred to by this verb is indicated by an ἐν phrase. "Also for me with regard to the Gentiles" is only a briefer form of expression that uses the concrete "Gentiles" instead of the abstract "foreskin." How God wrought is not stated. The fact that he wrought the same miracles for both apostles seems too narrow a conception; also that he bestowed the charismata of the Spirit equally on converted Jews and Gentiles (Acts 15:8 , 9). God wrought alike for Peter and for Paul by grace and by providence in the widest sense so that one came to work mostly among the Jews, the other among Gentiles. The credit for what was done by each is given wholly to God. Regarding himself Paul says in I Cor. 15:10: "Yet not I, but the grace of God which was with me."

9) The men at Jerusalem *saw* what the facts were and then also *realized* what these facts involved regarding Paul, namely, "the grace given to him" by God. Here it is again best to take this grace in its widest sense as including Paul's office, his ability, and his marked success. Although the participle already has its subject, "those in repute," Paul now names "James and Cephas and John" and adds "those reputed to be pillars." The latter is the most specific designation which the Judaizers employed. A few others are perhaps to be included in those of repute. It is immaterial. No other apostles at least were present at this conference, for they would either be named as Cephas and John are or be indicated in some plain manner. The figure suggested by "pillars" states outright what being "something" means in v. 6: columns that support the οἰκοδομή of the church, that are at once essential and ornamental. If they are broken, the building would be wrecked. The men named were pillars indeed although

the Judaizers used the expression to deny such importance to Paul.

James we meet already in 1:19. He is rightly named first although he is not an apostle; he presided at the conference (Acts 15:13). Cephas is next because, aside from all else, he was most prominent at the conference (Acts 15:7). The fact that John was present we know only from what Paul states here. Yet we are not surprised to find Peter and John together also on this occasion. Though each had a brother, we find Peter and John together in John 20:2, etc.; 21:20, etc.; Acts 3:1; 8:14. The two were evidently most intimately attached to one another. The three named here were certainly the foremost pillars of the Jerusalem church; although at the time of the conference they were absent from Jerusalem because of the work, also the rest of the Twelve deserved to be called pillars.

Behold, what these three did! "They gave to me and Barnabas the right hand of fellowship." And this was not merely fraternal fellowship such as is extended to brethren in the faith; κοινωνίας is placed last in order that ἵνα may define it: "of fellowship, that we on our part (go, the verb understood) to the Gentiles, and they on theirs to the circumcision." This was the fellowship of the apostles, the fellowship of the apostolic work. Three pillars acknowledge two others. This is what James, Peter, and John did at the great conference; behold what the Judaizers were trying to do in Galatia!

This giving of the right hand must have been a public act, one that was performed before the entire conference. The most likely moment must have been after the resolution offered by James was adopted. Note that the drafted resolution which was to be sent out to all the Gentile churches contains the words: "our beloved Barnabas and Paul, men that have hazarded their lives for the name of our Lord Jesus Christ," Acts 15:25, 26. That this giving of the hand occurred only at the private consultation is highly improbable. In the Greek the first person is named first, in English last; hence here: "to me and Barnabas." As James is concerned in this, so also is Barnabas. Paul and he were the ones who had gone out from Antioch on the first great missionary journey among Gentiles; they were the heads of the delegation sent to the conference from Antioch (Acts 15:2); they were the ones who would lead in the continuance of this work. The Spirit named Barnabas in Acts 13:2.

Regard both ἵνα clauses as subfinal, as defining the terms of the fellowship here solemnly published. R. 1000 thinks that the first ἵνα = "on condition that," and that the second is an expletive with a voluntative subjunctive (933). Both are alike, the second is added to the first, and neither denotes purpose.

The first stipulation was in regard to fields of work, the Gentile field was assigned to Paul and Barnabas, but not as being just a human arrangement, no, as one that was most plainly indicated by God himself. This implied the fullest endorsement of the work done in Galatia, of all the liberty of the gospel Paul had been and was preaching, and complete repudiation of all the contentions of the Judaizers. What more could Paul's soul desire?

10) In the second ἵνα clause: "only that," etc., the genitive object is placed first: "only the poor, that we keep remembering them." This prolepsis is used for the purpose of emphasis and occurs frequently in connection with ἵνα. These are the poor among the Palestinian churches to whom already on a previous occasion Antioch had sent help by the hands of Barnabas and Saul (Acts 11:30). Zahn rightly says that the pillar-apostles were not begging, nor were they using this

great occasion for begging. The fellowship in the division of labor included the fellowship of love and of loving aid.

When Paul adds: "the very thing I also hastened to do," i. e., carry out, this must refer to collections he took up during the year immediately following the conference; for it was at the end of this year that he wrote this epistle in Corinth. We know nothing further about these alms. The great collection which he later gathered in all his Gentile churches can thus not be referred to here. But we see how Paul got the idea of such a great collection, the object of which was not merely most materially to help the poor but also to cement the "fellowship" between all his Gentile churches and the mother church in Jerusalem from which the gospel had first gone forth into the world.

3. *How Paul Corrected even Peter, and how*
Peter Accepted this Correction, 2:11-21

11) *Ad summa venit argumentum.* This is, in-indeed, the climax. Paul corrects no less a man than Peter himself, and Peter accepts the correction! Is it possible? It was done in public before scores of witnesses. Again Paul lets only the facts, the straight historical facts speak. The secret of all his work is that he is a theologian of fact. He meets the Judaizing movement in its attack upon his person and his apostleship by a few facts, incontrovertible facts. This part of the attack is thereby literally crushed.

When did this episode occur? Before or after the public acknowledgment mentioned in v. 9? No indication of time appears. Such a temporal particle ought to appear if this happened earlier. Otherwise the natural thing to do is to follow the previous narrative where one episode succeeds the other in time, and to understand this last as likewise occurring later than the preceding. Yet, starting with Augustine, a few writers assume that this event antedates the one mentioned in v. 1-10. They tell us that Peter came to Antioch, then the strict Jewish Christians from James, then the pseudo-brethren who made the Jerusalem conference necessary. This is thought to make the case against Peter and for Paul much stronger. But the reverse is true; for then the matter was still subject to a final decision on the part of the church. Summary: Paul follows the chronological order up to 2:10, the natural expectation is that he continues thus in the final episode. If Paul now reversed the order of time, this would necessitate an indication to this effect. Besides all this, it is incomprehensible that Paul could use this episode regarding Peter as the climax of his historical proof if it had occurred at an earlier date. Then, most assuredly, the conference would form the climax.

Now when Cephas came to Antioch, I withstood him to his face because he (already) **stood condemned.**

Δέ is transitional. The terse way in which Paul states the fact that he withstood Peter shows that the Galatians had already heard of this affair, that Paul is now merely recalling it to their minds and emphasizing the features that bear on the present issue in Galatia. It is also probable that the Judaizers made capital of this incident and twisted the facts so as to make it appear that Paul turned against Peter, forsook the old, original gospel that Peter preached together with its legal requirements, and was swept into his liberalism so that he might please the Gentiles. The exact reverse was true.

There is no need to say what brought Peter to Antioch for this visit. In the absence of all information it is gratuitous to say that he had no business there. The apostles did not run around where they had no business. Nor is it necessary to try to save Peter's reputation by assuming this Cephas to be some other man who had this Hebrew name. Paul has been speaking of the Cephas who is Peter and is reputed to be one of the pillars. The main point is stated at once: "I withstood him to his face." That must have occurred in public as also the following shows. It occurred in connection with the agape, before the whole congregation at Antioch. Picture the scene; it was surely dramatic in the highest degree. We know of no other case after Pentecost when one apostle corrected another. The aorist is significant and implies that Paul withstood successfully, that Peter had no defense, that he yielded. Think how this smashed the Judaistic contention which would have Peter correct Paul and never Paul correct the great Peter.

What makes the statement about Peter so severe is the clause: "because he stood condemned." Peter himself stood so by his own act. Anybody could stand against him, and Peter had no defense. Paul did it in Antioch; we shall see why Barnabas failed. R., *W. P.*, regards the verb as a paraphrastic past perfect passive. C.-K. 259, and others consider the perfect participle the predicate of the imperfect ἦν; it does then not mean, "because he had been pronounced against," but, "he was a person who had a pronouncement standing against him," one that had been made some time ago and was still in force (perfect tense). Paul says that Peter was in this unfortunate position. We shall see that this was due to Peter's own act. The term Paul employs is legal, in the active it means *wider jemand erkennen,* so that nothing is left but the fixing of the penalty by the judge. Outside of that the case had been closed. All that Paul did was to point out this fact.

This verb never means "to accuse" in Biblical Greek. When it is used in this sense in secular Greek, the charges are always added. The mere accusation of

Peter would leave the question open as to whether he was guilty or not. Accusation would also call for a competent judge to try Peter; the judge might find him innocent. Paul does not use κατακρίνειν, for that would imply that Peter had had an adverse trial; he uses καταγινώσκειν: an adverse judicial pronouncement stood against Peter.

This fits the situation exactly. It was the pronouncement made by the Jerusalem conference in Acts 15:13, etc. Peter himself had helped greatly in making that pronouncement. If this affair at Antioch preceded that pronouncement, we are left to imagine some pronouncement against which Peter was now sinning and to invent some proper authority who could have so pronounced. All is clear if the conference preceded. For this reason, too, Paul does not need to name the court here involved; it was the conference and its finding against all Judaizers. Here at Antioch, Peter placed himself among these already condemned Judaizers. The moment he did that he stood condemned, condemned by the pronouncement he himself had helped to issue. All defense and even the right to enter a defense had been removed.

Barnabas and all the others at Antioch who acted as Peter did were certainly under the same verdict. Paul took Peter to task, not because he intended to leave out these others, but because Peter was the great apostle, the one who was blameworthy in this instance. When he was convicted, all those who stood with him were convicted. Peter misled even a man like Barnabas. We see at a glance what a calamity was threatening because of Peter's act of Judaizing. It was a God's blessing that Paul was there and withstood Peter to his face.

We see why Peter made no defense. It would have been preposterous for him to make even the attempt. To deny or to contradict the finding of the conference

would have included a denial of the central part of the
gospel. Peter was erring. But his greatness is evident: he accepted public rebuke in all humility, he
mended his ways. How many men, high in the church,
have done the same when they were in the wrong?

Do not ask how a man like Peter could have done
what he did. Just ask yourself how you at times can
and do sin even against better knowledge. That is
the answer. Peter's erring at Antioch has been mentioned in connection with his inspiration. Instead of
hurting the inerrancy of inspiration, Peter's erring
helps to establish the inerrancy. Save for inspiration
errors such as that of Peter here at Antioch would have
spoiled many a page of Scripture. The assumption
that every holy writer was constantly under inspiration in every word he uttered down to "Good morn-
ing!" and "How are you?" was infallible also in every
act and movement, is contradicted right here. Inspiration is that act of God's when he speaks through the
voice or through the pen of chosen men (see Matt.
1:22). This is the Biblical definition. God spoke "at
sundry times" (Heb. 1:1) ; *then* there was inspiration,
then only. And then error was excluded, for *God*
spoke "through" (διά) his human instrument.

12)   Paul explains what Peter did so as to make
him stand condemned. **For before certain ones
came from James he went on eating in company with
the Gentiles, but when they came, he began to draw
back and to separate himself, fearing those of the
circumcision. And there acted the hypocrite with
him also the rest of the Jews, so that even Barnabas
was carried away in their hypocrisy.**

Here we have a graphic description of the situation brought about by the wrong action on the part of
Peter. How long a time elapsed until certain ones
from James arrived in Antioch we do not know, yet
it was long enough to justify the imperfect: "he went

on eating in company with the Gentiles," i. e., the Gentile Christians. This occurred at the agape where the congregation dined together. All the members save the poor brought their own food. They dined in groups, families together with friends, many groups in natural formations. Until those from James arrived, Peter ate regularly with Gentile groups.

To understand this aright we must remember that these Gentile Christians had joyfully received the resolution of the Jerusalem conference (Acts 15:30-32) and brought no meat that had been a part of the sacrifices to idols, or had been taken from strangled animals, or food that was made with blood (*Blutwurst*). Their food was not kosher, but it complied with the omissions the conference asked in order to keep harmony between Jewish and Gentile church members. In their groups the Jewish Christians brought only kosher food such as they had always eaten. They, too, did this in entire Christian liberty, condemned no Gentile Christian for eating other kinds of food. Some Jewish groups perhaps also gave up kosher eating; some Jews and Gentiles ate together in certain groups just as Peter did.

All went well until some came to Antioch from James. "From James" is scarcely the same as "from Jerusalem." These people were not sent by James, did not represent him. They were from the circle about James, in close association with him. When they came to the agape they naturally ate kosher as many Jewish Christians at Antioch did, which was their privilege. Paul hints at no disturbance that they made about Peter's eating in Gentile groups. Paul pictures them as the innocent cause of Peter's wrong action, for he says: "When they came," Peter changed. He "began to draw back" from all Gentile groups, "began to separate himself" from these groups.

The inchoative imperfects are also descriptive; at the same time they point forward to the outcome mentioned in v. 14, to the aorist used there. Peter's change was marked; all noted the reversal in his conduct. If he had eaten in Jewish groups in the first place as was his privilege, all would have been well; if at first he had only occasionally eaten with Gentile groups, it would not have been so bad. But to eat so long a time with Gentiles and then, the moment a few from the circle of James arrived, to eat only with Jews — that was bad.

What was the matter with Peter? He "feared those of the circumcision." Peter turned coward. Fear made him act against his own better convictions. "Those of (the) circumcision" is a specific designation. It might refer to any Jewish Christian, Peter, Paul, Barnabas being among them. It is far narrower here and signifies the Judaizers, those at Jerusalem. Yet "certain ones from James" were not Judaizers; the very phrase "from James" forbids this idea. For James presided at the conference and himself formulated the conference resolution which was adopted in order to disown the Judaizers, and which, when it was sent out, pleased the Gentile church at Antioch and all others exceedingly. Peter's fear was that, on returning to Jerusalem, these friends of James' might report that he ate steadily with the Gentile Christians in Antioch, that the Judaizers would get to hear of it and be enflamed against him. This was the brave Peter who was thrown into a panic in the courtyard at the time of the trial of Jesus. "They that were of the circumcision" (the same designation as here) had assailed him in Jerusalem after he had eaten with Cornelius (Acts 11:2, 3). At that time he had successfully defended his action.

One wonders why he should now be afraid of such Judaizers. Did he now intend to act prudently, to use his Christian liberty first in one way by eating with the Gentile Christians in Antioch and then in another way by eating only with the Jewish Christians? That was false prudence which was dictated by fear and not at all Paul's principle of love (I Cor. 9:19-23) but wretched concern for self. Fear produces strange actions. Calm reason must declare that Peter was wrong, totally wrong. Many wrong acts are devoid of a sensible, reasonable explanation. So it is with Peter's action on this occasion. The fact that an apostle like Peter should become guilty of a grave wrong at this time of his career should be a grave warning to us all (I Cor. 10:12). It is a wonder that he did not lose his apostleship.

13) The worst feature of his action was the evil effect it produced at Antioch. Why did Peter not fear that? He thought only of himself and of possible attacks from already completely discredited Judaizers. The position he held caused the other Jewish Christians, of whom there was a large number in Antioch, to act the hypocrite with him, i. e., to herd off by themselves at the agape and eat only kosher food. An evil rent was being made in the church. The whole question which had been settled at much pains in the Jerusalem conference, threatened to be opened again in a way that was worse than before. What must have pained Paul especially was the fact that even staunch Barnabas who, with Paul, had founded the Galatian congregations, who had been his fellow delegate to the conference, to whom he had been a bosom friend since Barnabas called him from Tarsus to Antioch, that even he should be carried away with the hypocrisy of all the rest (dative of means, R. 532, and not just after σύν in the verb). "Ωστε with the indicative is one of the two instances of this classic construction found in the New Testament to indicate actual result.

Peter, of course, did not set out to act the hypocrite, nor did the Jewish Christians of Antioch, nor did Barnabas. But Peter and those Christians did so act.

Paul states the cold fact. He is more considerate with regard to Barnabas: their hypocrisy carried him away; he should have remained firm like his friend Paul. But that is the sad result when high and revered men head into a wrong course: they often sweep most excellent lesser men along with them. Barnabas is a warning to us. The church is full of great names that are still constantly quoted in support of some false doctrine, false practice, false principle, false interpretation. Their very names stop lesser men from testing what they advocate, and so they, like Barnabas, are carried away.

But is Paul not too severe when he labels their acts hypocrisy? Note that he deliberately uses the word twice, once the verb (an aorist at that!) and then the noun. This duplication serves notice that Paul means just what he says. These men acted as if they believed one thing when at heart they believed another. They all believed as Paul did, that all outward observances were unimportant as far as Christianity is concerned, but here they acted as if, after all, outward observances in regard to meat and drink were an essential, at least a very important thing in Christianity. Both verb and noun are used with reference to show acting; the ancient actors wore masks. These men were playing a part: their action was done for effect, it was thoroughly insincere.

But could Paul look into their hearts? He did not need to do that. At Jerusalem, Peter and Barnabas and the rest of the Antioch delegation had solemnly subscribed to the *modus vivendi* established for Gentile and for Jewish Christians; but here all of them were by their actions denying what they had solemnly affirmed and what the whole church at Antioch had heartily accepted. They acted as if eating with Gentile Christians was defiling and yet knew it was nothing of the kind, such a thing as ceremonial defilement no longer existed for them. Indeed, hypocrisy is the proper term. How could they stoop to it? All sins against better knowledge lack a rational explanation; they are committed against right reason, are irrational.

14) Paul now states how he withstood Peter to his face. **But when I saw that they did not walk uprightly with regard to the truth of the gospel I said to Cephas in the presence of all: If thou who art a Jew livest Gentile-like and not Jew-like, how compellest thou the Gentiles to eat Jew-like?**

Paul did not act hastily; he waited until he saw things clearly. He had just stated when this moment came, namely when even Barnabas was carried away with the hypocrisy. Then it was, indeed, plain "that they are not walking uprightly." The Greek does not change the present tense of the direct discourse to the past as we do after a main verb in the past. The verb is derived from ὀρθόπους, one with straight feet, who is able to stand and to walk accordingly. Πρός, face-to-face with the truth of the gospel, has the idea of comparison and of a reciprocity in this regard: their conduct did not match the truth of the gospel, nor did that truth match their conduct. The two were out of line, badly so. "The truth" of the gospel is its substance, the divine reality it embodies. This is one grand unit. Peter was in conflict with that truth and was putting others into danger.

Then Paul acted and did so effectively. He rebuked Peter, the one who was chiefly guilty, "in the presence of all." Should he not have gone to Peter privately? We have found that men who have committed some grave error are very particular not to have those who rebuke them commit the least error in the place and in the manner of the rebuke otherwise they become the guilty ones and the errorists persecuted martyrs. Well, Paul gave Peter a public rebuke, public not as a deserved punishment for him but so that all might hear it for

their own good. Even Pelagius says: *Publicum scan-
dalum non poterat privatim curari.* Augustine, otherwise his opponent, agrees: *Non enim utile erat error-
em, qui palam noceret, in secreto emendare.* A public
wrong is not to be corrected in private. We certainly
do not hang our dirty linen in the front yard. It was
Peter who sinned as a public man in a public way; *he*
forced the public rebuke from Paul, *he* made it necessary that all should hear.

Paul puts his rebuke into the form of a question. He
throws the onus of the answer on Peter himself. No
legitimate answer can be given save one by which
Peter condemns himself. Peter stood as having been
condemned (v. 11), not by Paul and by what Paul now
says, but by the Jerusalem conference in which Peter
had taken a leading part. Paul merely asks Peter
whether that is not the fact. The moment he asked
this, Peter saw it, had to see it, and all the rest who
were present likewise saw it.

It was masterly in every respect to use the question.
But the point of importance in this epistle is the fact
that Peter deflected from the gospel truth and not Paul.
This the Galatians are to see. The Judaizers of Galatia
tried to play Peter against Paul; such a procedure was
farcical in view of what happened at Antioch. All
Judaistic falsehoods which tried to use Peter as a shield
are exposed by the episode at Antioch as they are
already by what Peter did in conjunction with James
and John at the Jerusalem conference (v. 9, 10). Here
perishes the Catholic contention that Peter was the
first pope, on which much more may be said.

Peter was a Jew by birth but had lived in Gentile
fashion when, on first coming to Antioch, he had steadily eaten with the Gentile Christians. The present
tense, "livest Gentile-like and not Jewish-like," describes Peter's conduct without reference to time. It
was not the first time Peter had done this; he had done

it years before this at Caesarea after that special revelation at Joppa when he remained at the house of the Gentile Cornelius. How often Peter had repeated this we do not know; he must have done so on a number of other occasions.

In the apodosis, which is put into the form of a question, the deduction to be drawn from the "if" clause at once advances to the ultimate deduction. Paul does not stop and ask, "How, then, canst thou now so significantly separate thyself from the Gentile Christians?" He leaps to the conclusion which this wrong conduct involves for all Gentile Christians: "How compellest thou the Gentiles to act Jew-like?" for that was what Peter was really doing.

Peter may not at this time have realized that his action involved so much; but it is undeniable when Paul now points this out to him. It often happens so: the judgment is beclouded in erring conduct. The decisive things which should be seen at once to make us recoil from such conduct are not seen or are placed into a false light. Then, too, many refuse to see when the true light is brought to bear upon them. Paul was right in speaking out publicly. If Peter did not now see, many, if not all the rest, would see. All the Gentile Christians who beheld Peter's marked withdrawal, which was followed by that of the other Jewish Christians at Antioch, including even their pastor Barnabas, could not help but conclude that they, too, in order to be Christians in the full sense of the word, should henceforth, like Peter, stop living Gentile-like and live Jew-like. "Art compelling" refers to silent, moral compulsion which was, however, effective.

The wrong which Peter perpetrated was not that he at one time lived Gentile-like and at another time Jew-like. That was a matter of liberty. The revelation which he had received at Joppa did not imply that he was henceforth to live only Gentile-like. Paul became a Jew to the Jews, but note, only in order that he might gain the Jews, gain them for this truth of the gospel and its liberty (I Cor. 9:20); he also did the same and for the same purpose with regard to the Gentiles. What the revelation granted him at Joppa made a wrong for Peter was any conduct that cast reflection on Gentile-like living. Of that conduct Peter had made himself guilty here at Antioch. "Those from James" were not guilty, nor does Paul in the least imply this. They exercised their liberty by eating kosher and thereby cast no reflection on Gentile Christians for eating otherwise.

15) Is the section, v. 15-21, the continuation of the rebuke administered at Antioch or some reflections on that incident which Paul now adds as he writes about it? In support of the latter view we are told that σύ or ἡμεῖς do not occur in these verses. But the very first word is a plain "we" which is followed by an emphatic ἐγώ. The absence of a connective is to be expected. Paul paused after stating his question, and when Peter offered no answer as he, indeed, could not, Paul continued to speak.

The assertion that "stood condemned" in v. 11 requires no more than the pointed question of v. 14, is not convincing; all ordinary readers expect more, for Paul surely did say more. The fact that Paul reproduces at length what he said to Peter is certainly exceptional; but this entire incident is exceptional, in fact, this whole part of the epistle is so, for it is entirely historical. Just because it is historical, an extended discourse may be reproduced in it; histories abound in such discourses.

At Antioch, Paul stated the doctrinal principles on which his rebuke rested. Peter needed reminding, but so did all others. These principles were the main factor, "the truth of the gospel." The fact that Paul did not interrogate Peter beyond that first painful question shows his consideration and his tact; yet in a fine way he includes Peter in ἡμεῖς, and when he uses ἐγώ he does it so as to voice what must be the conviction also of Peter and of every Jewish Christian.

Paul's reproduction of just what he said at Antioch is admirably suited to the Galatians; this is just what they want to hear. Paul could not tell them anything that would be more necessary, for what Paul said to Peter contains the very gospel that both he and Peter preached, for which Paul was assailed among the Galatians. Finally, the reproduction of the address delivered at Antioch is a perfect transition to the next part of the letter, which is entirely doctrinal.

First a solemn and a complete statement to which every truly believing Jew assents. **We, by nature Jews and not sinners from the Gentiles, yet having come to know that a man is not declared righteous in consequence of work of law but only by means of faith in Jesus Christ, even we came to believe in Christ Jesus in order that we might get to be declared righteous in consequence of faith in Christ and not in consequence of works of law; because no flesh will be declared righteous in consequence of works of law.**

We do not divide this sentence by supplying "are" with the first "we" and letting the second "we" begin a new sentence. The second "we" emphatically takes up the first one: "we — even we."

"We on our part, by nature Jews," characterizes Paul, Peter, and the other Jewish Christians according to their nationality. The apposition makes them "by nature Jews" (R. 532 dative of means) who were born so, trained so. Paul adds the contrast: "and not sinners from the Gentiles." He uses the expression that was current among Jews who denominated all Gentiles ἁμαρτωλοί, "open, plain sinners." The idea contained in this expression was the thought that the Jews strove after righteousness, something that did not occur to Gentiles. The Jews had their νόμος or law and labored to produce "works of law" in order thereby to become righteous; the Gentiles were ἄνομοι, devoid of this law. Paul is simply using Jewish language. He is not calling Jews saints and Gentiles sinners; he is not saying Jews are righteous, Gentiles not. Who is righteous before God he says in the next breath. All he says is that we native Jews are not like the common run of Gentiles who are called "sinners" by Jews because they are not Jews.

16)   Δέ marks a contrast and singles out one class of native Jews, the believing, Christian Jews who "came to know that a man is not declared righteous ἐξ ἔργων νόμου, in consequence (as a result) of works of law but only by means of faith in Jesus Christ." The participle is the ingressive aorist: they got to the point where they knew this. The gospel brought them to this point. Jews though they were who throughout their entire lives banked on the Mosaic law and on works of law as the source (ἐκ) from which to obtain true righteousness before God, they finally discovered their terrible mistake, namely, "that a man is never pronounced righteous (by God) as a result of works of law," no matter how many of such works he may muster; they discovered that a man is not declared righteous thus "but only by means of faith in Jesus Christ." In a succinct statement Paul formulates the old Jewish error which was so fatal to his nation and the simple gospel truth. "A man" is universal: be he Jew or Gentile, it is the German *man*. The Greek keeps the negative with the verb, a construction which we can imitate in English although our common idiom is: "no man (*niemand*) is justified."

Here would be the place for a full discussion of δικαιοῦν and its cognates, which, however, would require many pages. We must refer the student to the

best and the richest source: C.-K. 296 (δίκαιος), 311
(δικαιοσύνη), 317 (δικαιόω). See the author on Rom. 1:17.
We content ourselves with a summary. The passive δικαιοῦται has God as the agent. The
verb, the noun, and the adjective are always forensic;
so are the opposites; so are the synonyms, in Hebrew,
in Greek, in the Old Testament, in the Apocrypha, in
the New Testament. The sense is, "to *declare* righteous" and never, "to *make* righteous." This is the
sense in even secular statements. Always a judge is
involved who pronounces a verdict. When the judge
is God, the verdict establishes a relation to God and
to his judgment, to his δίκη or norm of right. A δίκαιος
is "righteous" because God so declares in his judicial
verdict. Δικαιοσύνη is the quality of "righteousness" possessed by him whom the heavenly Judge pronounces
righteous. The passive is to be understood in the same
sense: "to be pronounced righteous," and is never converted into the middle "to become righteous." True,
some passive forms found in the Koine are to be
understood in a middle sense; a few German commentators translate the passive *gerecht werden* and quote
Luther in support of their translation. When certain
modern interpreters translate δικαιοσύνη "uprightness"
or "goodness," or employ a term that denotes a virtue
to be found in us and not a forensic relation established
by God as the Judge in a verdict pronounced by him,
they depart from the Scriptural use of this term and
eliminate the central doctrine of Scripture.

Ἐκ pictures God's verdict as arising out of works
of law so that these would call forth the verdict in
the court of God. In "works of law" neither noun has
the article, which makes the quality of each stand out;
the two are a practical compound, *Gesetzeswerke*. Paul
is speaking of Jews, hence he has in mind the law of
Moses and the corresponding works. Yet "works of
law" is general, any law and any works of any law

are included as being completely barren in eliciting a declaration of righteousness from God. The Jews of whom Paul speaks, "we," including himself, have discovered this fact, hence no argument is necessary, and none is appended.

'Εὰν μή is elliptical and is really a case of brachylogy (R. 1204) because it follows a negation. It states how alone a man is justified. The sense is offered by the translation of the American Committee of the R. V.: "but (or: but only) by faith." The genitive is objective: "by faith in Jesus Christ." Διά denotes the subjective means. Πίστις is a correlative term that involves the object on which faith or trust rests, which is here "Jesus Christ," his person as the Savior together with his office and his redemptive work.

It should not be necessary to say that "faith in Jesus Christ" is wrought entirely by him who kindles this confidence by coming in contact with us through the gospel. The only means by which we may obtain the divine verdict in our favor is faith, *fiducia*, in Jesus Christ. He who comes before the judgment seat of God with Jesus Christ is instantly pronounced righteous. "We," Paul says, "have come to know this." Hence he adds no more.

What Paul has stated as a truth that he and the others came to realize he now restates in other words; in fact, he states the negative side two additional times: "not in consequence of works of law — not in consequence of works of law," driving this fact in deeply. "Even we" emphasizes the thought that we Jews, we who once thought we had righteousness by works of law, became exactly like the sinners from the Gentiles who never knew anything about such works of law. "Even we," just as they, "came to believe in Christ Jesus in order that we might be declared righteous in consequence of faith in Christ Jesus and not in consequence of works of law."

"Came or got to believe" is the ingressive aorist and marks the first instant of faith; we may say the same regarding the aorist passive: "might get to be declared righteous." In the former instance Paul used "faith" but now he uses the verb "we believed." He turns his expressions over and over in order to make them register the more. "Once," Paul says, "our trust rested in our own works of law, now all our trust has come to be utterly removed from all such works and rests only in Christ Jesus. Such Jews are we now."

He even changes the phrase διὰ πίστεως to ἐκ πίστεως and thus makes it the exact opposite of the repeated phrase ἐξ ἔργων νόμου. See the exposition in Rom. 1:17. "Faith" is both means and source of justification. The latter should not be more startling than the former unless we still have a synergistic conception of faith. It is ever the contents of faith that justifies and saves, and never faith apart from its contents. It is the Christ in the faith and not the faith devoid of Christ. All the believing in the world secures nothing but damnation from the Judge, but the tiniest believing in Christ secures acquittal on the instant. The Scriptures attribute everything to faith because they know only a faith that is filled with Christ, only a faith that is wrought by Christ. Now Paul writes "Christ Jesus," office and person, the sense is the same.

So faith in Christ Jesus is the opposite of all works of law; they exclude each other: to be justified "as the result of faith" = to be justified *not* "as a result of works of law." The two will not mingle. He who would put one foot on faith and the other on such works plunges into the gulf. Make Christ the bridge, all save the last inch, use works of law for that, and the bridge crashes the moment you step upon it.

Enough has been said, and yet Paul repeats once more as though enough cannot be said. Διότι = *denn*

(B.-P. 310) : "because (this fact stands forever) no
flesh will be declared righteous in consequence of works
of law." This negative is so important because of
Peter's dangerous action. For the third time "works
of law" are excluded; for the third time we have the
verb "to declare righteous." In all three instances
the passive is used with God as the agent. The road
to righteousness by way of works is triply barred.

The future "shall not be declared righteous" means
that no case of this kind will ever occur although blind
fools refuse to be convinced and try again and again.
Instead of the previously used ἄνθρωπος we now have
πᾶσα σάρξ, which has the same sense but is more emphatic and emphasizes man's frailty; we may translate
"every mortal." The Greek idiom construes the negative with the verb: "every flesh shall not be justified";
we negative the subject: "no flesh, no mortal shall be
justified." The negation in οὐ — πᾶς is absolute (R.
752). Is Paul quoting Ps. 143:2: "In thy sight shall
no man living be justified"? He has no formula of
quotation, and the words are not identical. It is
enough to assume an allusion just as we also often use
expressions that are more or less Scriptural.

We are perfectly satisfied to let Paul write: "Having gotten to know — we got to believe — in order that
we might be justified." That succession and that order
are correct. In the case of adults it is always thus.
We gain nothing by philosophizing, by letting Paul look
back over his past life and by asking how and why he
came to faith; for even then he is telling us his exact
experience: knowledge — faith — purpose of the
faith. No adult arrives at faith except through knowledge of the very fact here emphasized by Paul. And
no adult believes except for the one purpose that he
may be justified. To say that Paul speaks so but does
not mean so is to employ dangerous language. True

knowledge merges into faith, and faith's vital intent is justification.

17) In v. 15, 16 Paul states what we Jews discovered about works of law and about Christ; what we did, we left the works of law and believed in Christ. Why? So as to be justified, since no mortal can possibly be justified by works of law. Now there follows a thrust at Peter's action and at that of Barnabas and the other Jews who followed their lead: If after all this we only dropped to the level of sinners like the Gentiles and now still have to go back to works of law, must we not then say this blasphemous thing that Christ has ministered nothing but sin to us? Do not Peter and the rest see that their present action necessitates this conclusion?

But if by (our) seeking to be declared righteous in connection (only) with Christ also we on our part came to be found (nothing but) **sinners (after all), is Christ a minister of sin? Perish the thought!**

The condition of reality argues the matter as though it were a fact although, of course, it is not. To put it thus makes the point clearer and stronger. The participle "seeking to be declared righteous in connection with Christ" repeats the preceding purpose clause: our believing "in order that we may be declared righteous in consequence of faith in Christ and not in consequence of works of law." That was our purpose, that was what we were seeking. Paul has said that we were sure we should be righteous in that way by simply believing, by giving up all work of law.

But if, after all, we were mistaken, if our purpose was not attained, if our seeking did not bring us what we sought, if our connection with Christ (ἐν, by faith) did not get us declared righteous by God, if despite this our seeking "we were also ourselves found (nothing

but) sinners," we who once were Jews but had given
up Jewish works of law and thus sank to the level of
"the sinners from the Gentiles": — what good, then,
is Christ to us? "Is he (only) a minister of sin?" Is
that all he amounts to? The very idea is blasphemous.
"Perish the thought!" But this conclusion that Christ
is only a minister of sin automatically follows if the
action of Peter and of these other Jewish Christians
is right, their action of separating themselves from the
Gentile Christians who do not eat kosher and of eating
only with those Jewish Christians who do. Then
kosher eating and, of course, other Jewish observances have to be added in order that we may escape
being such "sinners," in order to be declared truly
righteous by God. What a reflection on Christ! See
what it makes of him! And we Jews believed that
faith in him would get us the declaration of righteousness from God!

Most of the manuscript have the reading ἆρα, the
interrogative particle; some have the reading ἄρα,
"then" which marks a natural conclusion. The thought
is the same; the question is more dramatic. The genitive in "a minister of sin" is objective. It does not
imply that Christ ministers to sin as his master
(διακονεῖν τινί) but that he produces sin (διακονεῖν τι) with
his ministry. The thought is that he makes us do nothing but drop law and works of law so that we are "sinners" who are on the same level with the Gentile sinners who are called ἁμαρτωλοί by all Jews. We must
construe together "sinners from the Gentiles" (v. 15)
— "ourselves also sinners" ("also" like the Gentiles)
— "of sin."

Paul's question is directed straight at Peter and
those whom he was misleading, at what their action
involved: that faith in Christ would not give them
the righteousness they sought, would only make them
the same as Gentile sinners, would turn Christ into

a minister of sin. Here we have another instance in which Paul's thought does not halt halfway but advances to the end, to Christ, to what Peter's action makes of Christ.

We are told that this interpretation is wrong. From v. 15 onward Paul is writing in general terms; these verses do not contain what he said to Peter and to the rest at Antioch; if Paul is addressing anybody, the Judaizers are referred to. But Paul never stoops to argue with the Judaizers, he denounces them. That all of this belongs to Paul's address at Antioch we have shown in v. 15. More serious is the assumption that Paul is speaking of what Jesus makes of every Jew *before* his justification, namely that he reduces all Jews to sinners like the rest of mankind. But then Paul ought to exclaim: "Thank God!" not: "Perish the thought!" If this makes Jesus "a minister of sin" in this general sense of revealing all men and thus also all Jews as sinners, Paul could not be shocked at the thought, in fact, he could not use the expression: "Perish the thought!"

In addition to this, by making Jews sinners in the general sense of the term sinners Jesus would bring them to salvation; for God justifies every contrite and believing sinner. No, no; Paul here speaks of believing Jews. If *after* believing in Christ they are found sinners, not merely sinning daily as Christians still commit sins that must be pardoned daily by God, but "sinners" as the Jews called all Gentiles "sinners" because they had no works of law: then, indeed, the awful conclusion follows that Christ is a minister of sin, that he reduces law-abiding Jews to the low level on which the Jews placed all Gentiles.

This question of Paul's rests on Peter's action in turning from all the Gentile Christians to live in Jewish fashion. If that is necessary, then all believing Jews are not justified, are only Gentile "sinners" until they do what Peter now did; and Christ would be nothing but "a minister of sin" who aided sin — frightful thought. In μὴ γένοιτο we have the optative of wish, one of the few optatives left in the Koine: "May it not be!" in our idiom: "God forbid!" or "Perish the thought!"

18) Paul explains with γάρ by stating the matter in a different way. Peter's action would make all believing Jews nothing but Gentile sinners and Christ a minister of sin. But see what it would make of every apostle if Peter's action is right, if every apostle should do likewise.

For if these very things which I tore down I start building again I prove mine own self a transgressor. For I on my part by means of law died to law in order that I might become alive to God.

"I" is unemphatic, being found only in the verb suffix; no contrast with another person or persons is intended. Paul uses the first person to soften the rebuke to Peter; hence he also uses the conditional form. The singular "I," it seems, refers especially to an apostle, for his was the special work of tearing down and of building up. The condition is again one of assumed reality even as Peter was actually doing what is here stated. What is said fits Peter so accurately that Paul must be writing what he said at Antioch.

When Peter ate regularly with the Gentile Christians in Antioch he certainly tore down works of law, the conception that any Christian needed anything whatever besides faith in Christ for his justification by God; he held true to what v. 15, 16 say of all Jewish Christians when they came to faith. But when Peter turned back, separated himself so markedly from all Gentile Christians, and began to live strictly Jew-like (v. 14), he started to build up again (inchoative present tense) the identical things he had torn down.

Actions speak louder than words. They spoke to the
entire congregation at Antioch. Peter contradicted
all that he had heretofore taught and done. He acted
as though he had undergone a second conversion. His
action proclaimed that some Jewish ceremonial works
were after all necessary — of course, also for Gentile
Christians (v. 14b). Paul loves the figure of building
and uses it aptly here.

Συνίστημι (some texts read συνιστάνω) = *ich stelle dar,*
yet not in order to reveal what one really is or has in
mind but to present and thus to prove and to establish
what is otherwise doubtful or hidden. "I prove mine
own self a transgressor," i. e., of the law, means a
guilty transgressor in all my previous action of tearing
down. My present building it up again is proof
positive of my past transgression. I should never have
torn down, should never have relied on faith alone.
Although Paul softens the rebuke by predicating it
of himself, he nevertheless aimes it squarely at Peter.
And Peter understood. If Peter now continued the
course of conduct he had entered upon, he would be a
Judaizer. If he was afraid of the Judaizers (to be
afraid of whom was foolish), Paul here points him
to something of which to be afraid. "So," Paul says,
"thou now standest forth as having been a miserable
transgressor of the law during all these past years
and art now just coming out of thy long transgression! So this is the kind of apostolic builder thou
art!"

19) With the emphatic ἐγώ Paul now refers to
himself. He for his part had not become a transgressor of the law in the sense in which Peter was
now proving himself one. "For" adds as an explanation how he had used the law in order to be forever
done with the law. The reference is to the three
phrases used in v. 16: "not in consequence of works
of law." Paul states what he does with regard to him-

self, but every true Jewish Christian will second this
as being equally true of himself. "I on my part by
means of law died to law." This is purposely paradoxical: "by means of law to law I died." The thought
is at the same time concentrated. Paul used law in
order to be forever rid of law. Peter is not done with
law, he has started to go back to it as though he had
been a bad transgressor because he ever left it. Paul
writes "law" without the article; R. 796 thinks that
this refers to the Mosaic law. Anarthrous νόμος
includes everything that is "law," Mosaic or otherwise.

The right, the first and foremost use of law is to
use it so as never to respond to it again, so as to die
to it. Let law bring you to the realization of sin (Rom.
3:20), to despair that any and all work of law can
ever do even the least toward securing God's verdict
of righteousness. Let law make you a sinner indeed
and not merely in the sense of the self-righteous Jews
who called Gentiles "sinners." Let law make you give
up all hope in law and by faith place all your hope in
Christ Jesus. The moment you do that you are rid
of law forever unless you blindly return to it as Peter
was doing. You are dead to law. You are like a
corpse, at which law can thunder with all its might
and get in response not even the stirring of a finger
or the flicker of an eyelash. Why? Because you have
found the righteousness of faith. Believing in Christ,
you are justified, "justified from all things from which
you could not be justified (even) by the law of Moses"
(Acts 13:39). There is no verdict of condemnation
against those in Christ Jesus (Rom. 8:1). The servitude "under law" is ended. No master is able to give
orders to a dead slave.

Of course, this is only the negative side which is
never without the positive. Paul utters both in one
breath: "Died to law in order to become alive to God."

His statement is again a paradox but gloriously true. This death makes alive. But note that the subjunctive is an aorist, punctiliar, to designate the moment in which the life enters. It is the moment of God's acquittal, and that is the moment of faith, and that faith is life, spiritual life. Once kindled, that life goes on unless, like Peter, we again endanger it. "Alive to God" means in Christ Jesus, responsive to all God's grace, children, sons in his household, etc.

20) Paul adds only the main part of it. Verse 20 is an expanded and elucidative parallel to v.19. **With Christ have I been crucified; and there is living no longer I, but there lives in me Christ.** Moreover, **what I am now living in flesh, in faith I am living, the** (faith) **in the Son of God who did love me and did give himself up in my stead.** In this way Paul died to law to become alive to God.

The first two sentences are phrased in mystical language, especially the first: "With Christ have I been crucified." Symbolical language is something different. What occurred in a physical way in the case of Christ, Paul predicates of himself in whom it occurred in a spiritual way. We have no figure, no symbol, no verbal beauty, but concentrated facts.

Paul says more than that Christ was crucified for him, and that Christ's crucifixion is regarded as though Paul himself had been crucified, or even as if all the benefits of Christ's crucifixion were personally made Paul's own. The spiritual effect produced in Paul is at once included: "crucified together with." The interval of time is disregarded. Yet this difference remains: Christ's crucifixion was sacrificial, vicarious; Paul's crucifixion spiritual only, escape from law and sin and from the dominion of both. This concentrated predication rests only on the verity of this difference. Of course, the next step follows, the joint life. See Rom. 6:4 and the following mystical

statements: entombed with, died with, living in. Note
the force of the perfect tense "I have been crucified":
having been once crucified, Paul remains so, the effect
is permanent. This state of crucifixion is the state of death Paul
entered when he died to law. Only by being crucified
with Christ does one die to law. It is the one avenue
of escape. Otherwise law has us by the throat and
will destroy us. Σύν in the verb denotes faith, for
it alone joins us to Christ crucified to be crucified
"with" him.

Paul might have continued to use the same completely mystical language: "and with him have I been
raised up." He uses modified mystical expressions:
"and there is living no longer I, but there lives in
me Christ." The first δέ is not adversative (our versions: "yet"), for this living is the normal effect
of being crucified with Christ and not its opposite.
The verbs are placed first, subjects last, both are
emphasized. "And there lives no longer I"; Rom.
6:6: "our old man was crucified with him." Paul
was dead, his old personality was in the bonds of sin,
vainly striving for righteousness by means of works
of law.

It was the same Paul and yet not the same, the
same being, yet one that was utterly changed. "No
longer I" is true. Elsewhere the change is called the
new birth, regeneration; here Paul says: "there lives
in me Christ." Christ, the Life, lives in Paul. By
faith Christ fills Paul's heart, soul, being. That means,
first of all, Christ as Paul's righteousness. His expiation on the cross became Paul's own when he was
crucified with Christ, and this expiation gave him
God's verdict of acquittal. Thus Christ lived in him.
Secondly, Christ lives in him so that his mind and
will ever respond to Christ in thought, word, and
deed. The former is justification, this latter is sancti-

fication, the two are never separated just as life and
its manifestations always occur together and are inseparable.

"No longer I, but Christ in me," is correct. "In
me" is mystical. Hence he adds the further (δέ)
entirely literal statement: "Moreover, what I am
now living in flesh, in faith I am living," etc. Paul is
speaking of his life in the body since he was first crucified with Christ. The neuter "what I am living" is
the whole of this life as it manifests itself day by day.
The Greek needs no article with phrases such as "in
flesh." "Flesh" is used much as it was in v. 16, to
denote our frail, mortal nature and earthly form of existence; here the word is not to be understood in the
ethical sense. Paul's whole present life is "in faith,"
in this blessed sphere of trust. He thinks and acts
as faith ever guides and controls him. At one time
this was the case; at one time he was dominated by
law and works of law, his whole life was vain and
empty.

The article adds the object of faith attributively:
"the (faith) in the Son of God," etc., the genitive
being objective as in v. 16. The emphasis is first placed
on the phrase "in faith" and secondly on "the Son of
God," etc. Here the wonderfulness of justifying faith
becomes evident. This lies entirely in its object. We
have had this named as "Jesus Christ" — "Christ
Jesus" — and then "Christ." Now his deity is added:
"the Son of God." Again and again Paul calls Jesus
"the Son of God."

Two participles are added with one article, thus
indicating that the two acts belong closely together.
The whole is thus a unit designation: who he really is
and what he did. It was the Son of God, he that loved
me and gave himself up in my stead. The all-sufficiency
of his loving expiation is assured by the deity of
his person. Both participles are aorists. The great,

supreme act of his love is referred to when he gave himself over into death. Compare 1:4: "he who gave himself for our sins," etc. The motive and the deed are combined.

'Aγαπᾶν denotes the love of intelligence and comprehension coupled with corresponding purpose, the love with which God loved the world, John 3:16. This love sees the sinner in his doom and resolves to deliver him. It passes all human understanding. It moved God's own Son to give himself up for us on the cross. This God's Son did after he had become incarnate in our human nature. Here he is named according to his deity alone, and yet his dying on the cross is predicated of him, an act that became possible only by means of his human nature. The Scriptures often speak thus. Without Matt. 1 and Luke 1 and 2 all these and other statements become incomprehensible. Yet some think that if Matt. 1 and Luke 1 and 2 can be discredited, the incarnation would be removed. It is woven clear through the New Testament and appears even in the Old. Remove those chapters from Matthew and from Luke, and we should have to supply their main substance from the rest of Scripture. Παραδίδωμι is the verb that is regularly used to designate this act of the Son's self-sacrifice.

Here we have one of the numerous cases in which ὑπέρ plainly denotes substitution: "instead of me." Translate, if you wish, "for me," "in my behalf," these phrases convey and must convey vicariousness, substitution. Linguistically this is settled by R. 632 and his *The Minister and his Greek New Testament* with its chapter on this preposition. In many connections an act cannot be *for me* or *for my benefit* unless it is so by being done *in my stead*. The statement that this latter thought must be expressed by ἀντί is unwarranted; in fact, the Greek prefers ὑπέρ although it may

use either. Those who deny Christ's substitutionary
act do so in the face of ὑπέρ.

When Paul writes: who loved "me" and gave himself up "in my stead" he voices his own faith which
appropriates to him personally this love and sacrifice.
This is the very function of your faith and of mine. He
loved *me*, he gave himself instead of *me*! This faith is
forever done with the intolerable and hopeless burden
of works of law; it rejoices in the certainty of justification and righteousness which is assured to it through
Christ's loving self-sacrifice.

21)   The closing statement clinches all that precedes. **Not nullifying am I the grace of God. For
if by means of law** (there is) **righteousness, then did
Christ die for nothing.**

Who is nullifying the grace of God, setting it aside,
that grace which gave us the Son to die for us so that
by faith in him we might be declared righteous? Who?
Not Paul! We know who: Peter and those who were
following his lead were beginning to make God's grace
void. Paul is not answering a charge made against
himself; nobody in Antioch is charging anything
against him. Paul is washing his hands of what Peter
is doing. The stress is not on "I," for which we have
only the verbal ending, but on this nullifying: *none* of
it for Paul.

The reason is mighty, indeed. If by means of any
law whatever the quality of righteousness could in any
way be obtained in a divine pronouncement and verdict, then (inferential ἄρα) Christ died for nothing, his
death and sacrifice were unnecessary. Since the grace
of God climaxes in the sacrificial death of his Son, if
his death were for nothing, this grace would be
abolished with a vengeance. That is what Peter was
starting. That is what the Judaizers had finished.
Either God's grace is all, or it is nothing. Either

Christ's death is all, or it is for nothing. If the verdict that one is righteous is gained by means of law, then law and works of law are the means and not Christ and his death. Paul states this thought in the negative. We may add the positive: Christ did die. It is impossible to believe that God's Son should die for nothing. He died because no law could gain God's acquitting verdict. God's grace is forever established by Christ's death. Amen and Amen!

Paul says nothing about the effect produced by his action in opposing Peter face to face. He does not need to. Peter dropped his wrong course. His mistake was one of the moment, one of conduct and not one of principle. If Peter had rebelled, Paul would be compelled to say so. Paul is not lowering Peter's standing in the eyes of the Galatians. But he *is* proving that he has the old, genuine gospel, proving it by showing that he had at one time to maintain it even against the Peter whom the Judaizers tried to make their patron. Now Judaizers, men who on principle nullified grace and Christ's death, were trying to sweep the Galatians away to join in this nullification. Peter swiftly recovered from the first step in his wrong course. The Galatians would surely do the same.

PART II

CHAPTER III

The Gospel of Christian Liberty Unfolded Anew for the Galatians, 3:1-5:12

Paul has brought the Galatians the true gospel which was given to him by revelation, acknowledged by the Jerusalem conference, attested in correcting Peter himself. This precious gospel Paul now unfolds anew for the Galatians in such a way as to destroy the Judaistic error that was creeping in among them. The body of this letter consists of doctrinal exposition which is shot through with dramatic application to the Galatians. It covers 3:1-5:12; some stop at the end of chapter 4. There are three circles of thought in this main body of the epistle.

In the first place, like Abraham, the Galatians were declared righteous by faith and not by law, 3:1-14.

In the second place, this becomes very clear when the relation of faith and law is understood, 3:15-4:7.

In the third place, the Galatians are earnestly admonished not to return to law, 4:8-5:12.

---

1. *Like Abraham, the Galatians Were Justified by Faith and not by Law, 3:1-14.*

O foolish Galatians, ask yourselves a few things!

Expression and thought show that a new section begins at this point. Paul pours out a flood of questions upon the Galatians, questions they should have

asked, should now ask, the answers to which would
certainly help to open their eyes.
First, the question of shocked surprise. **O thoughtless Galatians, who bewitched you, you for whom,
plain to the eye, Jesus Christ was publicly placarded
as having been crucified?**
The address fits the question; "brethren" would
not do so. Paul's feeling is the same as that which
is in evidence in 1:6. It is almost unbelievable that,
having Christ crucified before their eyes, the Galatians should start to Judaize. The Greek is sparing
in its use of "O" with vocatives, which makes it more
effective when it is used. Paul says "Galatians" much
as he uses "Galatia" in 1:2. It is a general term that
is taken from the Roman province and includes all the
members of the churches of whatever nationality they
may be, Phrygians, Lycaonians, Roman colonists, or
Jews. This word was a convenient term when only
these people as such were addressed. Paul calls them
ἀνόητοι, "thoughtless" or "foolish" people who were not
using their νοῦς or mind, who were not stopping to
think. The relative clause states of what they should
at once have thought, namely of Christ crucified.
Where were their minds?

"Thoughtless" cannot be understood as a reference
to a national characteristic of the Celts as though
these Galatians were for the greater part Celtic. A few
ancients describe the Celts as being fickle and easily
moved. If these Galatians were predominantly Celts,
and if Paul intended to score them for their national
failing, he should have written: "O thoughtless or
fickle or unstable Celts!" While "Galatians" is
derived from Κέλτοι, Galatia and Galatians designate
the Roman province and any or all of its inhabitants
irrespective of their extraction. All these Christians in Galatia were acting thoughtlessly, pheno-
menally so.

The church has known such waves of thoughtlessness in its history from time to time. People are just swept along. Those who do think are cried down and ignored. People seem to have a spell cast over them. "Who bewitched you?" uses this figure. The question is rhetorical, exclamatory, and asks for no answer. It is like our: "What has gotten into you?" The verb is to be taken in the general sense although some think of the evil eye; the idea of envy does not apply here (R. 473). The point to be noted is that when well-instructed Christians go wrong, they act unreasonably. They need a severe jolt to start them thinking sanely again. Paul supplies the jolt and even the right thoughts to which the Galatians must return.

This does not imply that Paul "believed in witchcraft," i. e., that it produces supernatural effects. The Bible condemns witchcraft; every form of it is devilish, and all its forms run back to paganism in their roots. The devilishness lies in the deception; the devil deceives all who resort to witchcraft. No miraculous effects are produced by it. It is the delusion that such effects are and can be produced that keeps these occult arts alive. Churchmen have ignorantly, sometimes learnedly, held this view and have thus supported the practice of witchcraft. Those who do so today will challenge what is said here. Let them know that the writer does not speak hastily; he speaks after a long and thorough investigation of the entire subject.

The relative clause states that the Galatians should have been the last persons to allow themselves to be deceived. Textual authority is against the insertion of "not to obey the truth" and ἐν ὑμῖν. Sometimes the latter is still retained because of its difficulty, and because its insertion is hard to explain. The clause is sometimes divided: "before whose eyes Jesus Christ was? — He was painted among you," etc. Few will agree to do this. Difficult readings are not *eo ipso* correct, nor is inability to explain a variant a cause for its retention. The relative οἷς is emphatic: "you for whom," etc. The κατά phrase is also emphatic, the sense of which is: "plain to the eye." It would fit the context well to translate: "was painted before your eyes"; but while the simplex is used with regard to depicting, the compound is never so used. It is common as a designation for posting placards (M.-M. 538), for instance, a father posts a proclamation that he will no longer be responsible for his son's debts. We need not think that Paul refers to writings which he had sent to the Galatians. The term is figurative for all Paul's public preaching in Galatia, Barnabas helping him. All of it was like public placards, plain to the eyes, announcing "Jesus Christ" and him "as having been crucified."

In I Cor. 2:2 Paul uses the expression: "Jesus Christ and him crucified" which has the same perfect passive participle. The tense points to the enduring effect of Christ's crucifixion. As for the Galatians, so for us to this day every gospel sermon placards Jesus Christ as the One crucified. Read Paul's placard in 2:20, where the word occurs, and in 2:21 where again, plain to the eye, he writes, "Christ died." In that one perfect participle which is here predicative the entire gospel is concentrated as abolishing all salvation by law or works of law. This participle destroys all Judaistic teaching; it does so today with regard to all the modern forms of this teaching.

This is the indictment against the Galatians: all this placarding was so plain to the eye, and yet they acted as though they could not see, had no sense to read, could not think what this meant. "Crucified — crucified — crucified!" — even a little thinking should

suffice to turn the Galatians against all Judaizers. The
entire Scriptures are so placarded, yet men even preach
on them and see nothing in the cross except noble
martyrdom. II Cor. 4:3, 4.

2) The first question is asked regarding the objective substance, Jesus Christ crucified; now Paul asks
questions regarding the great subjective effects produced in the Galatians. He pours out question upon
question. He wants no answer for himself, *he* needs
none; the Galatians need them for themselves. It is
high time they did a little plain Christian thinking.

**This alone do I want to learn from you: Was
it from works of law that you received the Spirit or
from the hearing of faith?**

"Think for a moment," Paul says, "look back at
your own selves! I want to learn just one thing from
you because it is decisive, must be decisive for you.
You are all Christians, you all received the Spirit, when
he entered your hearts you became Christians." On
this there is no question; it is the basis of Paul's questioning. The question is: *"Whence* did you get the
Spirit? From what source (ἐκ)? Was the source
'works of law' or was it 'hearing of faith'?" It requires
practically no thinking on the part of a Christian to
give the answer.

The majority of the Galatians had been Gentiles
and thus ἄνομοι, people who paid no attention to law as
a source of salvation. Paul's question does not imply that
they at one time relied on works of law. Paul refers
to his own preaching in company with Barnabas. They
were not Judaizers, they brought no "works of law,"
they brought the very opposite, namely "hearing of
faith." Through that the Galatians received the Spirit.
So did the Jews among them who, while they were in
their Judaism, had practiced works of law, but had
failed utterly to receive the Spirit until Paul brought

them to the hearing of faith. The gospel is true apart from our experience; yet all Christian experience corroborates its truth.

On the phrase "from works of law" see 2:16 where it is used three times. Some interpreters think that receiving the Spirit refers to the reception of charismata, wonderful charismatic gifts. They point to λαμβάνειν as the verb that is used in connection with such gifts and refer to Pentecost. But at Pentecost the 3,000 received no such charismata; the 3,000 did not speak with tongues. I Cor. 12:8-10 and Rom. 12:6, etc., list as "gifts" abilities that are devoid of miraculous powers, especially Romans 12. Thousands of Christians in Galatia and elsewhere possessed no miraculous charismata.

Paul addresses all the Galatian Christians; they had received the Spirit when they came to saving faith in the gospel. The reception here referred to occurs at the moment when the Spirit enters the heart by faith and regeneration henceforth to control heart and life. Paul's question is one that every Christian must answer to this day. Regarding the question of miracles in Galatia see v. 5. They should not be introduced at this point. But every Galatian knew that the Spirit had entered his heart with saving power.

"Works of law" and "hearing of faith" are exclusive opposites; neither tolerates the other. "Works" are such as *we* do, and they are many so that no man can know whether he has done enough of them. The opposite is ἀκοή, but not in the active sense, the *actus audiendi*, but as C.-K. 106, etc., shows, in the passive sense: "being made to hear" what *God* wants us to hear.

The genitives are also opposites: "of law" — "of faith," but both are possessive: "works which belong with law" — "a being made to hear which belongs to faith." Both expressions are practical compounds. Yet

we question the view of C.-K. when he has ἀκοή =
κήρυγμα but adds the exception that the former is also
subjective: *Kunde vom Glauben* (objective genitive);
R. V. margin has "message" about faith. Also when,
despite the few times the word is used, ἀκοή is made a
technical term. The genitives are alike. "Being made
to hear" involves the thing God brings to our ears
(Christ crucified, v. 1). This belongs to faith in the
sense of being intended for us to believe. When God
speaks and makes us hear he wants us to believe. As
law calls for works, so our being made to hear calls
for faith. Compare Rom. 1:16, 17; also Heb. 4:2.

God made the Galatians hear about Christ crucified
so that they came to faith, and thus, thus alone, they
received the Spirit and became the Christians they
have been.

**3) So thoughtless are you? Having begun with
spirit, are you now finishing up for yourselves with
flesh?**

More surprising thoughtlessness. The double question is in reality one. There is nothing in v. 2 to which
οὕτως can refer, it points forward. So foolish as to
try to complete in a fleshly way what you began in a
spiritual way? In v. 2 Paul refers to the beginning,
to the time when the Galatians first received the Spirit,
and asks from what source this came; now he refers
to the ending the Galatians are proposing to make. One
may begin well but end ill. The Galatians had, indeed,
begun well (v. 2), but what about now ending altogether otherwise? That would be folly, indeed!

The two datives of means πνεύματι and σαρκί are
paired opposites, hence the former cannot be the Holy
Spirit (our versions). If he were referred to, the
article would be necessary. Both datives lack the article, both stress the quality expressed: "with spirit," in
a truly spiritual manner — "with flesh," in a fleshly
manner. Note also the analogy of Scripture: the Holy

Spirit is never said to be the means which *we* use. Again, the Holy Spirit, this divine Person, is never and can never be paired with an opposite such as flesh.

Paul advances the thought from our reception of the Holy Spirit mentioned in v. 2 to the true spirit that animates our hearts and our lives, the spirit wrought in us by the Holy Spirit. The word "spirit" refers to "faith" mentioned in v. 2, and "flesh" to "works." The latter is not to be taken in the ethical sense: the sinful nature of man, but far more concretely: the outward deeds which belong to the bodily nature of man. For all works of law have to do with physical, bodily matters, circumcision, kosher eating, Sabbath resting, and all manner of ceremonial observances.

Pray, what are you Galatians thinking to start in one way and to conclude in the exactly opposite way, to start in the right and most blessed way and to end in the utterly wrong and ruinous way? This is not even sane thinking. But note that, while the participle is the aorist to indicate the beginning made, the main verb is the present tense, the concluding has not yet been completed, it has only begun. The damage can still be corrected; Paul is doing his utmost to prevent this present tense from becoming a fixed and final aorist.

Is the verb middle or passive? One might say passive because the Judaizers were working on the Galatians; but the middle is very good, for by listening to the Judaizers the Galatians were doing the concluding for themselves. If they actually ended wrongly they could not shift the blame. Ἐπιτελέω = to bring to an end, to finish or complete.

4) First we have a question as to how the Galatians began (v. 2), next a question as to how they propose to finish (v. 3), now a question as to what lies between. **So much, did you suffer it in vain?**

if, indeed, also (as I cannot believe) **in vain!** Again the question and its appendix are exclamatory. "So much" is placed emphatically forward and marks either greatness or quantity. Those who think that these were northern Galatians assume that they, too, suffered persecution; but regarding the southern Galatian churches we know what Paul suffered when he and Barnabas founded them (Acts 13:50, etc.; 14:2, 5, 19, 22: II Tim. 3:11). Acts 14:2 states that "the brethren" were involved. They would naturally be so in every instance. We cannot say positively whether the Galatians were made to suffer more later on; yet we know that in Acts 14:22 Paul tells them they must expect as much.

Do they now intend to say that all of that suffering was in vain, a great mistake, all to no purpose? But he himself adds that he can scarcely believe that they now think so. Εἰ is strengthened by γε: "if, indeed"; but καί is not to be construed with εἰ because γε intervenes, nor is it to be construed with the adverb "in vain." The thought is not that this is something bad enough, namely "in vain," beyond which lies something worse, namely actually falling from the faith. Such an idea is remote from those sufferings. At times Paul uses καί to intimate a contrary supposition that is in his own mind, here one that is indicated by the "if" clause itself: *wenn denn doch wirklich vergeblich,* which is something Paul cannot bring himself to believe. "If, indeed, in vain" already expresses the doubt about its all being in vain, and καί increases this: Paul will not even think of it until he must. He will think only that the Galatians will answer: "No, no; it was and is not in vain!"

5) The sufferings were terrible experiences; beside them Paul places the most glorious works. He introduces the new question with οὖν and rests it on the preceding ones, especially on v. 2, since he repeats

some of the terms there used. **He, accordingly, who furnishes you the Spirit and works works of power among you,** (does he do it) **from works of law or from the hearing of faith?**
Instead of using verbs in the sentence: "Does God furnish and work," etc., Paul substitutes participial descriptions of God and thus elides the verbs and makes the question far more effective. Both present participles are qualitative in the durative sense. They refer to any and every furnishing and giving, whether it occurred at the time when the Galatians were converted or since then. Little is gained by saying that these are imperfect participles, i. e., the present doing duty for the imperfect since it has no participles of its own. We may translate: the Furnisher — the Worker and reproduce the exact sense.

It is Paul's habit to round out and to amplify what he begins. He does this here: first, by adding to the idea of receiving the Spirit on the part of the Galatians (v. 2) the correlative idea of bestowing or furnishing the Spirit on the part of God; secondly, by adding to the first essential reception (v. 2) of the Spirit (v. 2), by which spiritual life was kindled in the Galatians, the further idea of working mighty works of power by the Spirit. Like the simplex, the verb ἐπιχορέω means, "to stand the expense of bringing out a chorus" at some public festival and thus in general "to furnish," "to supply," but always with the strong connotation of great, free generosity. The patron paid the entire expenses of the training, the costuming, and the staging of the chorus, which called for a lavish hand. So God bestowed his Spirit upon the Galatians in full measure. But this is said by way of preamble to the manifestation of the Spirit which the Galatians had witnessed, namely the working of works of power. The term occurs regularly as a designation for miracles in which omnipotent power shows itself operative in a special degree.

This δυνάμεις does not signify any and all of the charismata. Paul does not say: "signs, wonders, and works of power." If he had "charismata" in general in mind he would have used that word. With the specific term "works of power" he thinks back of the time when he labored among the Galatians, when the Lord "gave testimony unto the Word of his grace and granted signs and wonders to be done by their hands" (Paul and Barnabas), Acts 14:3. In v. 8, etc., Luke reports one of the works of power, the healing of the lame man at Lystra.

Ἐν ὑμῖν = "among you"; works of power were never wrought in the hearts of men. In the miracles wrought by Paul and by Barnabas in Galatia the Galatians had the overwhelming evidence of the presence of the Spirit. Luke says that these miracles attested "the Word of the Lord's grace." Paul now puts this very point into his question: "Was all that due to, the result of (ἐκ), works of law or was it the result of the hearing of faith?" See v. 2: Was the source "what you were made to hear as belonging to faith"? Who ever knew a Judaizer to whom the Lord granted a single work of power? But wherever the apostles went, these works followed, yea, in abundance, granted lavishly by God (Acts 14:3). The view that such works continued indefinitely, and that any or all Christians wrought them, is untenable. A few works of power were granted by way of addition, but this occurred very seldom. Paul is not referring to these by his question.

These questions are to stir the thoughtless Galatians into doing some mighty necessary thinking. Let them wake up! A few proper questions will make them throw out the Judaizers. The same treatment ought to be accorded the deceivers of our time. Oh, if

only all of us would think! Put the Word and true
Christian experience with the Word into simple honest
questions and answers like a catechism, and you are
armed and proof against deceit.

* * *

The all-decisive case of Abraham

6) When Paul introduces the case of Abraham he
introduces the greatest Scriptural evidence. When he
writes καθώς, "even as," he parallels the Galatians and
Abraham and does so regarding the essential point of
faith and faith alone. All Judaizers are disowned by
Abraham and by the Scriptures which speak of Abraham, and if these Judaizers try to annex Abraham,
they can do so only by falsification, which is not an-
nexation.

But the parallel is at once intensified. Those who
are like Abraham in the faith of Abraham are sons of
Abraham — no less. That means that all who trust in
works of law are aliens to Abraham; the Scriptures
make them such. More than this. From the very beginning the Scriptures included the ἔθνη, the believing
Gentiles, in this Abrahamitic sonship. This includes
the Gentile Christians in Galatia. Their faith includes
them, their faith alone. This flatly contradicts the
Judaizers who demand that all such Gentiles must also
become Jews by submitting to circumcision and the
Jewish ceremonial works of law. Abraham is the
father of believers, Gentile as well as Jewish believers;
faith alone makes them his sons. The Scriptures say
so. Let the Galatians think of that and rejoice! The
moment they do they will cast out all Judaizers.

**Even as Abraham believed God, and it was
reckoned unto him for righteousness. Realize, then,
that they** (whose characterization is derived) **from
faith, these** (these alone) **are sons of Abraham.**

Verses 6-9 epitomize Romans 4. The conclusion that Galatians and Romans must therefore have been written at about the same time disregards the fact that this exposition of Gen. 15:6 and of the whole Old Testament account of Abraham goes back through the entire ministry of Paul. For him as a former Jew in all his apostolic contact with Jews Abraham and what the Scriptures said about his faith were vital. This was true already in the case of the Baptist (Matt. 3:9).

Paul uses Gen. 15:6 without quoting it: "Abraham believed God," etc. The dative does not mean, "in or on God," but believed what God said, the promise God made to him in Gen. 15:4, 5. He believed the promise about the Heir (Christ) who was to come out of his bowels via Isaac who was as yet unborn; he believed that through this Heir his (spiritual) seed would be in number like the stars of heaven. Abraham believed in Christ (John 8:56), in the gospel. The genuineness of his faith shone out when he held fast to this promise despite God's command to offer Isaac as a burnt offering, accounting in his faith that God was able to raise Isaac (from whom the Heir was to descend) even from the dead, Heb. 11:19. Behold the faith for which Abraham was pronounced righteous!

Moses writes regarding it: "And it was reckoned to him for righteousness," which is only another way of saying: "Through (διά) or as a result of it (ἐκ) God declared him righteous." When did God so reckon? Did he wait until Abraham had proved his faith by proceeding to sacrifice Isaac? Abraham's justification is recorded in Genesis 15 before Isaac's birth and not in Genesis 22. The moment he believed God reckoned him righteous.

Was his believing a good *work* that was of such a value to God as to *make* Abraham righteous, so that God's reckoning was merely computing this value? Moses says the opposite. Λογίζομαί τι εἰς τι == "to reckon

something for something": "Something is transferred
to the subject (person) in question and reckoned as
his which he for himself does not have, . . . it is fig-
ured in for the person *per substitutionem;* the object
present (faith) takes the place of what it counts for
(righteousness), is substituted for it." C.-K. 681.
When Abraham believed he was in himself no more
righteous than before he believed, but God counted his
faith as righteousness for him. God's accounting did
not *make* him righteous, it did not change Abraham's
person, it changed his *status* with God. Although he
was not himself righteous, God regarded him as being
righteous.

Do you ask how God can do so? Any suspicion
of arbitrariness or of lack of strict justice is due only
to our own crooked minds. The justice of the act is
perfect. We know *a priori* that unjustness and injustice are impossible in the case of God. But we ourselves see it when our dogmaticians point out that this
is not an analytic but a synthetic pronouncement of
God. There is no virtue or merit either in the believer
or in his act of believing, nothing of the kind to the end
of his life (analytic).

Here there is something else entirely, more than
the believing, namely the object believed, Christ, his
expiation ("crucified" v. 1), his merit. The faith that
holds to these, for the sake of these and these only
(synthetic) is reckoned for righteousness. The substitution is the perfection of justice. Christ's merit
and his righteousness are his own, but he wants them
to be ours, makes them ours by faith, even himself
kindles that faith; and in the instant of faith this
faith, because of the object it holds, secures the verdict
of righteousness.

The expression used by Moses and by Paul is most
exact: faith for righteousness. When God came with
his grace and his glorious promise, Abraham trusted

that grace and promise and had them as his very own, and they constituted his righteousness, the quality that is due to God's own verdict on all who have his grace and his promise. Abraham did not produce his faith nor any part thereof. "Abraham believed God" is plain as to that. God came to Abraham, and not he to God. God made a glorious promise to Abraham, made that promise shine into Abraham's heart with all its divine power of light, grace, and blessedness. So was he brought to believe. Abraham, indeed, believed, but God's Word and his promise moved him to believe. Nothing else and nothing less could do so.

Nor was there a possibility that Abraham himself might add a little. There was no need to add anything, the promise and the grace were all-sufficient (*gratia sufficiens*). God left nothing to be added for the simple reason that Abraham had nothing he could possibly have added. There is only one preparation for faith, and that, too, God makes and alone can make when, by his law, he brings home to us our utter sin and need of his grace. So Abraham believed, so justifying faith is wrought by God.

7) From the incontestable fact laid down by the Scriptural ἐπίστευσε, "he believed," Paul at once draws an equally incontestable conclusion with the illative ἄρα. He states it imperatively: "Realize, then," etc. The imperative fits the context much better than an indicative would. The tense is the present; the realization is to be enduring and ever renewed. It pertains to the Galatians and to all believers: "these (whose characteristic mark is derived) from faith, these (these alone) are sons of Abraham." Here again ἐκ appears (v. 2, 5), its opposite occurs in 2:12, "they (whose mark is) from circumcision." The demonstrative "these" = these, decidedly these alone, and none who are without faith. Faith makes them like Abraham in his faith, joins them to him inwardly, spiritually for-

ever. Thus they are "sons of Abraham." A great gulf
lies between them and all who are marked by "works
of law." Can the Galatians help seeing that gulf and
remain on the right side of it?

Abraham's "sons" is the proper terms (not, "children," A. V.). Τέκνα suggests the idea of descent, υἱοί
that of *Zugehoerigkeit,* belonging to, as in "sons of the
prophets." C.-K. 1082. So also "sons" marks their
standing: they stand with Abraham. Again, "sons" is
used to mark the fact that they stand with a father,
stand for what their father stands. In all these senses
also all Gentile believers are allied with Abraham as
his true "sons."

8)   Continuative δέ adds another vital statement
in regard to Abraham and his real sons and brings
the matter down to the time of Paul and the Galatians. **Now the Scripture, having foreseen that God
declares the Gentiles righteous in consequence of
faith, proclaimed as good news in advance to Abraham: There shall be blessed in connection with thee
all the Gentiles.**

What God did with Abraham by declaring him
righteous in consequence of faith alone is in the most
vital way connected with what he is now doing as Paul
writes; it is all of one piece.   It is shown to be so, not
by a deduction that Paul now makes, but by what God
himself declared to Abraham ages ago.

"Having foreseen, the Scripture proclaims," etc.,
reverses participle and subject and thereby emphasizes
both. To say that the Scripture foresaw is not a mere
personification. That would be only a rhetorical figure,
but the Scripture is actually the Word of God as it was
expressed by himself in permanent form by means of
inspiration. It is thus that "the Scripture" and "God"
are identified; in fact, the two cannot be separated as
is done by those who deny or reduce inspiration. God
is in the Scripture, and thus the Scripture foresaw.

The aorist refers to the time of Abraham. The word that God spoke to him at that time was put into writing by Moses at a much later time. The foresight is found in the Scripture because the Writer who used Moses spoke with that foresight when he addressed Abraham. Paul is content to speak of the periods of time involved, the age of Abraham and the time in which Paul was living. In reality, all God's works are known to him from all eternity, timelessly, and all his counsels and his plans go back before the founding of the world.

Paul says that the Scripture foresaw "that God declares the Gentiles righteous in consequence of faith," ἐκ, as a result of faith. This is usually regarded as indirect discourse; hence our versions translate, "would justify." But Paul states the simple fact in his own language as he sees it day by day with his own eyes: "God justifies the Gentiles out of faith." That is why he writes "God" does this, i. e., does it now; and thereby he in no way makes "the Scripture" one who looks at "God" as being another. But this he does say, that what God is now doing is not a thing that is new, novel, at all strange for the Scripture. The very first book of Scripture saw it many centuries ago, saw it with all the clarity with which Paul and the Galatians now see it, in the same actuality.

Subject and verb are reversed in order to obtain emphasis on each, and the phrase is placed forward in order to secure the chief emphasis for it. "From faith," from faith God's verdict flows. Nor is it at all marvelous that God now does this with the Gentiles; it is the same thing God did with Abraham before the first Scripture was ever written. There was ever even as there is now but one way in which God pronounces a sinner righteous.

Hence the first book of Scripture proclaimed in advance as good news to Abraham: "There shall be

blessed in connection with thee all the Gentiles." But
how can Paul say that the Scripture proclaimed to
Abraham when the Scripture was not written until
long after Abraham's time? Here the identification of
the Scripture with God is still stronger than it was in
the participle. But the real point to be noted is that
what God spoke directly and in person to Abraham,
that is what all nations were to read as good news, the
same good news that it was to Abraham. Abraham
did not receive it in the form of writing, he received
the substance without which there would never have
been inspired writing. Abraham heard it πρό, "in advance" of the time when the Gentiles were to be so
blessed. On the augment in the verb see B.-D. 69, 4.
"In advance" is to be construed with the future "shall
be blessed."

He heard it as good news. We are told by some
interpreters that this was not "the gospel," and that
our versions should not translate thus. That is an incorrect contention; it is the very sum and substance of
the gospel. On this statement made to Abraham rested
Abraham's faith, the faith by which he was declared
righteous, the faith that was reckoned to him for righteousness. That is the same gospel we have today, save
that now the promise has become fulfillment.

Another incorrect view is that "shall be blessed"
does not include justification. The term is wider than
"shall be justified," but justification is the central
blessing without which no spiritual blessings other
than this come to anybody. In this very sentence we
have the statement "that God *justifies* the Gentiles
from faith" as the thing the Scriptures foresaw and
by God's own mouth told Abraham in advance in the
words: "There shall be blessed," etc. See Gen. 12:3
and 18:18; also 22:18. Subject and verb are again
transposed, each is thus made emphatic. In v. 2 the

reception of the Spirit, the greatest and the most comprehensive blessing, includes justification as its chief factor. Note that the future tense "shall be blessed" is the assured fact, the yea and amen of God. That is why Paul writes: "God (now) justifies the Gentiles." The agent in the passive is God; "shall be blessed" = "I myself will bless."

Ἐν σοί is "in thee" in the sense of "in union or connection with thee." The circle drawn by the preposition has within it, first of all, Abraham himself, and as it is drawn around him by God it is drawn also around all the Gentiles. It is one and the same circle of blessing. The neuter plural subject here has the plural verb in the Greek as it may have when persons are referred to. While Abraham is the forefather of the Jews, when he received this promise he was as much a Gentile as the Gentile Galatians themselves. He was still uncircumcised, a point which Paul drives home so forcibly in Rom. 4:10-12. The astonishing thing to him was not "Gentiles" but the vast number, "all the Gentiles."

But "in thee" contains vastly more. This means Isaac over against Ishmael. This does not imply that Ishmael could not share in the blessing but that Isaac would be the progenitor of the Messiah, and that the line would continue through Jacob (not Esau), Judah, David, etc. "In thee" speaks of the Messiah, of the Messianic blessing. This world-wide blessing in the Seed of Abraham (v. 16), in Christ, was put in the form of promise for Abraham, for him to believe it. Every promise aims at faith, intends to produce faith. It can be received in no other way. This promise set Christ before Abraham. Abraham "believed" (v. 6). "Abraham rejoiced to see my day: and he saw it, and was glad" (John 8:56). Thus was Abraham justified.

"In thee — all the nations" = first, that Christ would be the fount of blessing for all the Gentiles the world over; secondly, that they would appropriate this blessing as Abraham appropriated it, by faith alone. The Hebrew has "all families of the earth"; LXX, "all the tribes of the earth"; Paul, "all the Gentiles," or as we may render, "all the nations." After a fashion the latter is better, for when the promise was spoken, no Jewish nation existed, and this nation was to be included in the circle as were the rest. Still here the whole point rests on non-Jews, on Gentiles. By faith alone they enter the Abrahamic circle as "sons of Abraham" (v. 7).

9) This is stated directly. **Consequently those** (whose characteristic mark is derived) **from faith are blessed with believing Abraham.** The blessing is for all, but to each one it comes ἐκ πίστεως, out of faith as the fount and source. In v. 7 οἱ ἐκ πίστεως are the "sons of Abraham"; here they are blessed σύν, in association with, Abraham. And Abraham himself is called πιστός, which cannot mean "faithful" (our versions), reliable, trustworthy (in the passive sense), but must have the same meaning as ὁ ἐκ πίστεως, "believing" (active), C.-K. 869. Note the plural used in Eph. 1:1: "to the saints and believers." C.-K. calls this the standard Jewish designation for Abraham. Paul, however, uses it in a pointed way, where the decisive thing is that Abraham "believed" (v. 6), that his "faith" was reckoned for righteousness, that "faith" makes sons of Abraham. The clinching statement is that "those of faith" are with Abraham as πιστός, a man marked by faith.

"They are blessed." This changes the future tense used in the promise into the constant present: ever and ever blessed; the passive again makes God the agent. The essential blessing for all these believers is the fact that, like Abraham, their faith is reckoned for righteousness or, as Paul puts it in his own words: "God declares them righteous." With justification there go all the other spiritual blessings that are described at length in Romans 5 to 8. Note that ὥστε is paratactic, it occurs in a sentence by itself and for this reason has the indicative (R. 999).

The case of Abraham is all-decisive. Faith alone obtains justification and all resultant blessings. The Scriptures so declare not only regarding Abraham himself but regarding all other men who believe as Abraham did and are thus joined to him as his sons. This is the positive side; now the negative is stated which is equally decisive as, of course, it must be.

The all-decisive exclusion of works of law

10) **For as many as are** (people whose characteristic mark is derived) **from works of law are under a curse.**

This is the simple fact concerning the entire class of workers with law and γάρ offers it as the negative proof for justification by faith alone. Two classes of men stand in absolute opposition: οἱ ἐκ πίστεως — ὅσοι ἐξ ἔργων νόμου, those marked by faith — those marked by works of law. All of the former are of the same type; the latter, "as many as," are of various types; but despite their variety they are one, alike in "works of law" (see 2:16). The Scriptures declare the one class blessed, the other cursed. "Under a curse" means first, under a divine verdict of curse; secondly, under the power which works out and finally completes the curse.

As he did in the case of the blessing, so Paul now does in that of the curse: he offers the Galatians no assertion of his own, apostle though he was, but, as Jesus so often did, brings the clearest passages of Scripture as proof. **For it has been written: Accursed everyone who does not abide in all the things that have been written in the Book of the Law to do them!**

This is the sword of Damocles which hangs over the head of all workers with law. Paul quotes the LXX

of Deut. 27:26 with a slight change. The Hebrew is:
"Cursed he that confirmeth not the words of this law
to do them," i. e., confirms them by doing them without
fail. This curse is, indeed, conditional. One may
escape it by abiding in all the things written in the
Book of the Law (Torah) by doing them. The aorist
infinitive denotes complete doing, and "all the things"
excludes exceptions. Paul does not prove that no man
can possibly keep the law; how self-evident that is he
shows in the next verses. Besides, who among the Galatians would claim that *he* had kept the entire law?
Most of them had been Gentiles, pagans, who were
guilty of the most frightful transgressions of the law.

In the expressions, "it has been written," "all the
things that have been written," the perfect tenses
have the force: once written and thus now on record,
permanently so for all time. The former is the regular
formula for introducing Scripture passages and contains the very idea of ἡ γραφή, the Scripture, with its
divine and thus final authority. The point of note in
biblion is this, that the very roll or scroll (βίβλος =
papyrus plant from which papyrus sheets or "paper"
were made) on which the divine law is written bears
this curse for all workers with law. Let all the Galatians who are listening to the Judaizers mark it well.
Every one of these Judaizers is under this curse. Will
the Galatians, too, allow themselves to be drawn under
it? "Accursed" means to be under the divine ὀργή or
wrath, awaiting the final ἀπώλεια or destruction. The
infinitive with τοῦ is epexegetical (R. 1086) and not
final.

11) To make the matter perfectly clear Paul
adds (δέ) that the law was never designed by God to
produce the verdict of justification, that God designed faith (the gospel) for this purpose. He has
already pointed to Abraham and to all the sons of
Abraham who are justified by faith alone. Here is

the inner, the basic reason for that fact. **Now that in connection with law** (no article, any kind of law) **no one is declared righteous with God is plain because, The righteous — from faith shall he live.** It is a fact, in connection with law no one is ever declared righteous with God (παρά in the sense of "in God's judgment," B.-P. 973). This is so plain "because" God has said in most simple words how a man receives the verdict of righteousness, namely "in consequence of faith."

Paul might have said that no one is justified in connection with law because no one is able to meet the demands of the law and have brought proof for that fact. This would limit the whole elucidation to law alone, i. e., to negation. It is simpler and better at once to advance to the opposite affirmation, to God's own declaration as to how a person *is* declared righteous with God. For this is the main thing: How am I justified? The other: How am I *not* justified? is only corollary. When I know the one right way I will discard any proposed wrong way.

'Εν, "in connection with" law, of course, means the connection indicated by "law" itself: law *demands*, demands constant, flawless, complete doing on my part, i. e., works, "works of law." But every connection which any sinner is able to make with law, or the law itself makes with him, damns him from the very start. He goes down before every single demand of the law.

Not the connection with law and any attempt to meet its demands by our doing does God declare to be the way to obtain his verdict of righteousness and consequent life. In Hab. 2:4, which Paul simply repeats as being well known to all his readers, the prophet says: "The righteous — from faith shall he live." Some would construe together "the one righteous from (out of, due to) faith" and leave as the predicate only the verb "shall live." But in the Hebrew the phrase "from faith" is marked by the tiphcha to indicate that it bears the emphasis and is thus to be construed with the verb. In English we should underscore the phrase: "The righteous — *from faith* he shall live." "From faith" is exactly what Paul means.

Nor is it correct to say that we have two thoughts: 1) the righteous shall live; 2) his living shall be due to faith. The thought is a unit: By faith alone shall the righteous live. Again it is not the thought of the prophet that a man is pronounced righteous by God, and that he *then* gets faith, and that he *then* lives. All three occur simultaneously: the pronouncement — faith — life. No man is righteous for even a second before he has faith, or has faith even a second before God declares him righteous; the same is true with regard to his being alive. The prophet and Paul with him emphasize faith. Righteousness and life are inseparable from it. Nor is the gospel omitted; faith is ever the product only of the gospel, and the gospel is ever the contents of faith.

Here, as in Rom. 1:17, Paul corrects the LXX who translate, "out of *my* faith," i. e., God's faith or faithfulness. The Hebrew has "*his* faith," i. e., the righteous one's faith. Paul does not restore "his" because he wants to make the statement entirely general by stressing the function of faith as such. On the context in Hab. 2:4 see Rom. 1:17. The great point is that "the righteous one" has "faith," something that he could not possibly get from any connection with law. Righteousness and faith go together and are never separated.

There is no need to explain, for this has been done already in v. 6 and again in v. 8. So there is also no need to explain the predicate that the righteous "shall live" out of the faith by which he is righteous. We have been told in v. 7 that spiritual sonship with Abraham is due to faith, and in v. 9 that all spiritual bless-

ings come from faith. Both statements include what
the prophet says: spiritual life is due to faith. This
future tense does not refer to some distant time: "shall
live" when he reaches heaven or at the final judgment.
The righteous man is not dead until that time. John
3:15, 16: "Everyone believing *has* (ἔχῃ) life eternal,"
has it as believing and while believing. This is the
so-called logical future: right out of faith, in the instant of its coming into existence, life springs. Yea,
faith is the new birth.

Von Hofmann and Zahn advance the view that we
should combine into one word δηλονότι = *videlicet,
scilicet*: "Now that in connection with law no one is
justified, *namely that* the righteous shall live due to
faith while the law is not of faith, but, etc., therefore
Christ," etc. (v. 11). Glance at this *videlicet* in Liddell and Scott and note that it cannot be used as proposed. See how three parenthetical statements are
thus added one on top of the other — a curious proceeding; nor has Paul the "therefore" that is supplied
in v. 13. It is true that δῆλον is often placed first, but
that does not prevent its being placed last when this
is desired. Regarding the absence of the copula, this is
most common in the Greek.

12) The one who is justified will ever live as a
result of the faith by which he is justified. **But the
law does not belong to faith; on the contrary, He
who has done the things shall live in connection with
them.** That is why no connection with law justifies
with God (v. 11). That is why Habakkuk wrote concerning the justified man that faith alone will give him
life (v. 12). The law is a stranger to faith; it knows
nothing of a faith that justifies a sinner; it only curses
sinners (v. 10); it knows of only one way to get life,
and that is that the man must do, do completely, the
things the law lays down, failure to have done so is
absolutely fatal.

It is important to note that in the term "the law" the article is generic: everything that definitely deserves the name "law." We should not restrict this word to the Mosaic law; this is included, and the Judaizers in Galatia operated with this law, namely with its ceremonial requirements but not with its moral section (the Ten Commandments). Paul includes the latter as well as all that can rightly be called law.

We should also note what constitutes "law" and "the law." This is not the statutory formulation in a code but the *Rechtskraft,* the power of right involved in the law. C.-K. 758 defines: *die mit Rechtskraft ausgeruestete Forderung, die sich immer aufs neue durch die Rechtsfolgen zum Bewusstsein bringt, die daran geknuepft sind* (also p. 753), the demand endowed with the power of right, ever forcing itself into the consciousness by the consequences of the justice thereto attached. Thus an integral part of law in the Biblical sense of the word is the promise and the curse operating in the law. Paul speaks of the former here, of the latter in v. 10.

Here ἐκ πίστεως is construed with ἐστίν in the partitive sense of ἐκ (B.-P. 366, 4 δ) : to belong to something (R. 599 does not list εἶναι ἐκ). Because of its very nature the law has nothing to do with faith. It always *demands* with the power of right and justice; faith always *receives* gratuitously. The two do not match in any way. The fact that they are entirely opposite Paul again establishes by appropriating the well-known Scripture passage, Lev. 18:5: "He who has done the things shall live in connection with them," the connection being that he has done them. The substantivized participle is an aorist and thus denotes complete doing. Our versions lose this important point by translating, "he that doeth." The two are opposites even in this regard: faith has justification and life the instant it begins; doing works of law would get life only when the doing is ended and complete. But the point Paul makes is that faith and doing are opposites. Doing furnishes what is legally and of right *demanded;* faith receives what is gratuitously *bestowed.*

What makes the two quotations so striking is the fact that ζήσεται, "shall live," occurs in both. There *are* two ways to get eternal life: in one instance life is *earned* by complete doing; again life is *given* to us. The trouble with the former is that it is closed to the sinner. Before he can begin any doing, his sin bars the way to life by any use of law. 'Εκ πίστεως, life flows as a pure gift "out of faith"; ἐν αὐτοῖς, life lies as an earned merit "in them," i. e., in all the deeds of law when these are complete.

Now we may note that Paul has built a regular negative syllogism. The conclusion is put first: By the law no one is justified. The major premise is: The righteous one shall live by faith alone; the minor: the law does not belong to faith. Hence, it is true beyond a doubt that by the law no one will live, no one is justified. Thus the line of thought begun with Abraham's justification by faith is duly unfolded.

13) One thought remains to be mentioned, to show how God set aside the law and opened the way of faith. This showing forth is done in typically Pauline fashion. He never lets his explanation run out into a duality, he always brings it to rest in a unit point. This exemplifies the penetration with which his mind works. Here he has two divergent lines of thought, the one a positive thought regarding faith, the other a negative thought regarding law, the one ending in a blessing, the other in a curse. He now ties them together into a knot. He does it in Christ. Christ took the curse upon himself and so made the blessing possible to faith. Thus also — and this is another feature of his masterful mind — Paul brings us back to Christ crucified who was mentioned in v. 1, yea, also to Abraham and

to the Spirit. What a joy to follow a mind such as that!

The absence of a connective in the Greek arrests attention. That is the plain intent regarding the following great statement about Christ. **Christ bought us free from the curse of the law when he became a curse in our stead, because it has been written: Accursed everyone who hangs on wood! in order that for the Gentiles the blessing of Abraham might come in connection with Christ Jesus, in order that we might receive the promise of the Spirit by means of the faith.**

This letter is addressed to the Galatians. When Paul says "us" and in v. 14 that "we" receive he refers to himself, to all the brethren who were with him at the time of this writing (1:2), and to all the Galatian readers, the great majority of whom were former Gentiles. "Us" and "we" are not the Jews. The argument that these pronouns are in contrast with the phrase "for the Gentiles" (v. 14) is untenable. How does Christ's purchase of the Jews bring the blessing of Abraham "for the Gentiles"? This can be done only by his purchase of the Gentiles as well as of the Jews. And how can Paul add that "we" Jews get to receive the Spirit? Do Gentiles not receive the Spirit? Did Paul not say that the Gentile Galatians had received the Spirit (v. 2)?

The argument that the Jews alone were under the law is unconvincing. This view misunderstands the force of "the law" by thinking that it refers to the Mosaic law code, and that the Gentiles were not under this code since it had not been given to them. Paul does not use the phrase "under the law" in this section. When he refers to the law in v. 23; 4:4, 5; 5:18 (Rom. 6:14, 15), the phrase he uses is "under law" (without the article). See v. 12 on "law." Men can be in only one of two conditions, under law or under grace (Rom.

6:14, 15), *tertium non datur*. This refers to Gentiles as well as to Jews. Rom. 2:12-16 is Paul's own exposition regarding Gentiles and law. All who are under law, no matter of what kind, be they Jews or Gentiles, are "under a curse" (v. 10), most of all those who seek to get salvation "out of works of law." The great thing proclaimed in the gospel is the fact that Christ bought them all free from the curse of the law.

When Paul writes: bought *us* free, us believers, he does not have in mind a limited atonement. In II Pet. 2:1 those who bring swift destruction on themselves (damnation) are said to be bought by the Lord. Christ redeemed the world and not only the elect. When we believers are mentioned as those who were ransomed and bought by Christ, this is said because we are the ones who appropriate this redemption. In fact, our ransoming is certain only because Christ ransomed the world. It has been well said that, if Christ had left out one person, I, who know my own unworthiness and sin so fully, must conclude that I am that person.

Furthermore, the law itself declares that only he who keeps its precepts completely shall live (v. 12), all others shall perish. Does this exempt the Gentiles? Rom. 2:12-16 is the answer. Had the Galatians been exempt who had at one time been pagans? Finally, if "he bought us" refers only to the Jews and not equally to the Gentiles, the appended ἵνα clause cannot be properly understood, then the blessing of Abraham was to come for the Gentiles by some other act than this purchase. Such an idea is unthinkable. The Bible knows of no partial redemption, one of Jews only.

᾿Εξαγοράζειν is stronger than ἀγοράζειν, but both are used with reference to the purchasing act of Christ, the former again in 4:5, the latter repeatedly in I Cor. 6:20; 7:23; II Pet. 2:1; Rev. 5:9; 14:3, etc., although it is variously translated in our versions as buy, purchase, redeem. The compound verb with the following ἐκ phrase means, "to buy out of" i. e., "free from." We have a close synonym in the noun ἀπολύτρωσις, "ransoming" by the payment of a λύτρον or ransom. The idea of ransom cannot be eliminated from this noun, so that it means only "deliverance." The two verbs mean literally "to buy," and that means to pay a price for something. That price is the life of Christ laid down in death, cf., v. 1, Christ crucified. His life, blood, death are the price, the λύτρον. This entire imagery goes back to the Old Testament, to its idea of substitutionary blood sacrifice.

Yet, as is the case with regard to a number of concepts and expressions, many modern interpreters search in paganism instead of in the Old Testament for an understanding of the idea of ransom. Thus Deissmann refers to the pagan way of freeing slaves. The slave's earnings were deposited in a temple; finally the master brought his slave to the temple and took the price. Henceforth the slave was under the god's protection and thus free from human masters. C.-K. 63 accepts this and says that Paul deepened the idea while he retained the outward features connected with it. C.-K. disregards Zahn's views on this matter. This pagan transaction is misunderstood. Neither master nor pagan god *buy* anything, the slave *buys himself.* The price is paid in cash; yet I Pet. 1:18 specifically denies that we were ransomed "with corruptible things as silver and gold" and in contrast affirms that our ransom was "the precious blood of Christ, of a lamb without blemish or spot." Neither master nor god died in order to buy the slave's freedom. All the essentials are different; there is not even an outward resemblance.

Meyer states the facts with precision: "Christ bought them free; and he did it by this that he gave

away his life on the cross as the *lutron* (ransom) that
was paid to God, the *dator et vindex legis;* thereby he
obtained for them the forgiveness of sins by his *mors
satisfactoria* which was suffered according to God's
gracious counsel in obedience thereto, so that now the
curse of the law, which should have struck them, had
no more application to them." Here there is no slave
who buys his own release. Here there is the curse of
which v. 10 speaks. From this curse Christ "bought
us free by having become (aorist) a curse in our stead"
(or: "when he became"). The two κατάρα, "curse," are
the same. That means substitution: Christ took the
curse of the law upon himself. "Became" is the completed act. We were not freed from our peculiar curse
by Christ's taking some other kind of curse upon himself but by assuming ours.

The expression is powerful; it is not "became accursed" but "became a curse." Not some part of our
curse affected him through his contact with us, but our
whole curse was on him so that he was all curse. The
expression used in II Cor. 5:21 is still stronger: God
himself made the Sinless One "sin in our stead" (see
this passage). Isa. 53:6; I Pet. 2:24. It is said truly,
"Christ became the embodiment of our curse." He became this voluntarily; he gave himself (1:4; 2:20).

This fixes the meaning of ὑπὲρ ἡμῶν. R. 631: "There
are a few other passages where ὑπέρ has the resultant
notion of 'instead,' and only violence to the context can
get rid of it. One of them is Gal. 3:13. In v. 10 Paul
has said that those under the law were under a curse,
ὑπὸ κατάραν. In v. 13 he carries on the same image.
Christ bought us 'out from under' the curse of the law
by becoming a curse 'over' us, γενόμενος ὑπὲρ ἡμῶν κατάρα.
In a word, we were *under* the curse; Christ took the
curse on himself and thus *over* us (between the suspended curse and us), and thus rescued us *out from*

under the curse. We went free while he was considered accursed. It is not a point here as to whether one agrees with Paul's theology or not, but what is his meaning. In this passage ὑπέρ has the resultant meaning of 'instead.' The matter calls for this much discussion because of the central nature of the teaching involved." The curse would have crushed us forever; it crushed Christ in death, but his death satisfied the law and thus ended the curse, Christ arose from death. On the preposition see also 2:20.

The fact that a curse is involved in Christ's death is substantiated by Deut. 21:23, which Paul quotes in brief but does not follow the LXX with its participle "having been (and thus still being) cursed." He uses the adjective: "because it has been written (3:10): 'Accursed everyone who hangs on wood'." The Hebrew has the noun: "A curse of God the one suspended," curse in the metonymic sense of "an accursed object" (Ed. Koenig, *Woerterbuch*). Paul's translation by means of the adjective is very accurate. The fact that he omits the word "God" causes no change in meaning, for it is God's law and thus God who renders "accursed."

Let us note what is implied. After the execution and as an added disgrace the body of a criminal was suspended on a post and became an accursed object, one whom God's curse had struck down. That is why the LXX could use κεκατηραμένος, the perfect participle which conveys the idea that the object remained accursed. But that is why Paul declined to use this participle: Christ did not remain so. The passage applies to Christ when he hung on the timber of the cross. The Jewish eye regarded that dead body as an accursed object. It saw correctly: that body had suffered God's curse. In Paul's own words: Christ became a curse (a cursed object) in our stead. Paul intends to say that this fact was visible even to the eye.

If Christ had been treated as Stephen was, this would not have been apparent. Stephen's dead body was not hung up as an accursed object. We now see why Jesus said that it was necessary for him to be delivered into the hands of the Gentiles and to be crucified. We see why Paul emphasizes Christ crucified, crucified. God wanted Christ to be seen as what he actually became: a curse. Read Acts 5:30; 10:39; 13:29; I Pet. 2:24 in this light. Note that in the first two passages Christ's being hung on timber is appended to his being slain. It was the cross that said to all Jews that Jesus was accursed. Yet this very cross brought the infinite blessing of Abraham for the Gentiles. The symbol of the curse was the symbol of this blessing for all the world.

14) That is what the two ἵνα clauses state. Christ became *an object* accursed "in order that for the Gentiles *the blessing* of Abraham might come (aorist to express actuality) in connection with Christ Jesus." This was God's purpose, the aorist implying that it was attained. The Galatians are evidence of the attainment. The thought is paradoxical in the highest degree: a curse of God gets to be the greatest blessing of God. And yet it is not at all paradoxical. The curse that struck Christ like a fiery flame was quenched in his blood and death, and so the blessing of that quenched curse flowed out to all the world in life and salvation.

"The blessing of Abraham" is the one promised to him, cf., v. 8. It blessed Abraham as a believer; it blesses all other believers (v. 9) together with Abraham. It is εἰς, "for," all Gentiles, not in connection with law and works of law, but "in connection with Christ Jesus," this man "Jesus" who was anointed as our Redeemer (Purchaser). The connection is faith. The fact that it is intended for the Jews as well as for the Gentiles need not be stated, for Jesus himself was a Jew. The other does need to be stated because the Gentiles do not need to become Jews in order to share this blessing.

The blessing of Abraham is one that is intended for the whole world in Christ Jesus. Its chief content is justification by faith in Christ, our Substitute under the curse. We do not understand the commentators who make the blessing to Abraham and to the Jews one thing, and from this blessing send another thing upon the Gentiles.

The first ἵνα clause is objective although "in connection with Christ Jesus" points to the subjective side, namely faith by which alone the connection is made. The parallel purpose clause brings out the subjective side: "in order that we might receive the promise of the Spirit by means of the faith," aorist, actually receive. A glance shows how this harks back to v. 2, the Galatians had so received the Spirit. As in v. 2, so now again "faith" is combined with the Spirit. Since it is placed last, this phrase has the emphasis.

"The promise of the Spirit" has the appositional genitive just as in Acts 2:33 (R. 498). Jesus calls the Spirit "the promise of my Father," whom he will send (Luke 24:49); in Acts 1:4 the apostles are to wait for this promise. Faith is the means for the Spirit's reception (διά), the means which he himself works. To receive and to have the Spirit is to be declared righteous, to have life, and thus all the other spiritual blessings of Abraham, grace upon grace (John 1:16).

"We" in the verb is identical with ἡμᾶς and ἡμῶν in v. 13. Therefore "us" in v. 13 cannot refer to Jews only, and "we" in v. 14 to both Jews and Gentiles. "We" and "us" are Paul, the brethren with him (1:2), and the Galatians. In the case of these the reception has taken place, and that by means of faith only. Paul has the Galatians themselves say so in v. 2; has them deny that the source was works of law. That is the sense of the phrase here at the end.

Thus everything, everything excludes works of law. Every pertinent Scripture statement on both law and faith. Christ himself is in harmony with these. Faith opens righteousness to all the world. No man is saved except by faith; any man may be saved by faith.

Paul's exposition is like an arrow hitting its mark. From beginning to end there is not a single weak statement. Not one that deviates from the other by a hair. Here there is compactness, every sentence is freighted to the last word. Try and write a paragraph like this! Inspiration guided Paul's pen. Here is convincing light and power for the Galatians. In fact, here is conviction even for Paul's opponents in Galatia, the Judaizers, which should take hold of them mightily in order to draw them away from seeking justification in works of law and to bring them, too, to faith, to the blessing of their ancestor Abraham.

2. *The Galatians must Know the Limitations of the Law, 3:15-4:11*

It certainly cannot upset or alter God's own testament.

15) All Judaistic errors rest on misconceptions regarding law. Too much is then naturally expected of law. Paul has already shown that it leaves all who trust in works of law under the curse, that it cannot possibly justify, that this is done only in connection with Jesus Christ who has borne that curse in our stead. All this will become still clearer when the limitations of law become known. These are indeed great. In the first place, the law on which the Judaizers rely came all of 430 years *after* God put his testamentary promise into force. It ought to be as plain as day that no testament, not even a merely human one, can be

annulled or even altered *after* it is in force.   It is preposterous to think that the Mosaic law altered God's testament.   This is the first great point.

Again Paul cites history.   He has already stated what the testament is and also presented what it conveys by means of its immense promise and the first heir and beneficiary under that testament (v. 8) plus those who are excluded by the testament (v. 10).   Now he takes up the Mosaic law in its relation to this testament as to the point of time.

Brethren, I speak in human fashion.   Though (only) a man's, having (once) been confirmed, no one voids a testament or adds thereto.

The thought as well as the address indicate the beginning of a new section.   "Brethren" is significant for the Galatians, see 1:11.   Here the touch of affection is added which reaches out to win the readers.   "In human fashion" means in a way so simple that anyone can understand.   Paul will in particular use an ordinary illustration, the inviolability of a confirmed human will and testament.   That illustration will help to make the main thought clear.   By drawing attention to the fact that this is a human illustration Paul does not excuse his use of it but rather states in advance just what it is so that his readers may at once catch the point he presents.

Ὅμως, here and in I Cor. 14:7 = "although" and is purely concessive.   True, this is not ὁμῶς, "likewise," (R. 233 on I Cor. 14:7).   When R. 1154 makes it adversative, its position an instance of hyperbaton (423), and has it modifying the participle (1155), we cannot agree.   Our versions are correct; B.-P. 903 and B.-D. 450, 2 leave us uncertain; the classics do not help us.   In both passages the concessive adverb is in the most natural way to be construed with the very next word: "though (only) a man's," though only a mere human covenant; I Cor. 14:7: "though (but) soulless" instru-

ments. This is concession although we may continue
with "yet."

The word διαθήκη is evidently to be understood in the
sense of "testament" and not "covenant" although our
versions leave us in doubt, and some writers prefer the
latter. Regarding the meaning of the word in the
LXX who used it to translate *b^erith*, regarding the reason for this, and then regarding the New Testament
use see the summary given in Matt. 26:18 or I Cor.
11:25. "Testament" is beyond question the meaning
here where it is used with the singular "a man's," a
human testament being referred to. If a human covenant were referred to, we should have the plural. Human covenants are made between at least two persons
or parties and are mutual. A human testament is
always made by an individual, is always one-sided, the
testator alone makes disposition of his property. That
is why this illustration fits the promises of God to
Abraham, which constituted the old covenant. They
and it were absolutely one-sided, from God to Abraham, and not mutual, not between the two. The imagery is here that of a testament with an heir and with
an inheritance.

It is a confirmed, ratified, we should say probated
testament that is the basis of the illustration, the perfect participle stating that it is still in force. This
belongs to the *tertium comparationis*. Paul's illustration should not be regarded as an allegory, and the
making of the testament and the details of ratifying it
should not be introduced, plus the death of the testator,
etc. Then counterparts are sought in God's testament, and none are found. No; this is a testament
that has been probated and has been in force, and the
point of comparison is the inviolability, the fixedness
of such a testament. Nobody can void, annul it, and
put something else in its place. Nobody can "add anything thereto," affix a codicil to it and thus alter the

original testamentary provisions. Of course, the testator can tear it up and write a new will or can add codicils to the one he has written. But this is not a will that is still in the testator's hands but one that is already in operation.

No ancient or no modern legal practice allows a will that is duly in force to be set aside by a substitute that is offered by somebody else, or allows the additions of codicils by any person. Once in force, the will stands exactly as it is. There is no need to inquire to what law Paul refers, to Roman, Jewish, or that of some nation or province. The Galatians were a mixed people. Paul's illustration is one of universal applicability, not for quibbling lawyers, but for common people. In fact, the illustration is true everywhere today.

16) After the chief point of the illustration has been fixed, Paul states the fact he is illustrating. **Now to Abraham were spoken the promises and to his Seed. Not does he say, And to the seeds, as for many, but as for One, And to thy Seed, who is Christ.**

These promises resemble a human testament that is duly in force and in process of administration. Although they were repeated at intervals, they are one confirmed testament that became operative the moment it was spoken. Although they were spoken by God himself and were not at once written, they stand like a man's testament that is administered after his death.

In these testamentary promises two beneficiaries are named: Abraham — his Seed. One is placed first in the sentence, the other last, both are thus strongly emphasized. Since Paul specifies that "his Seed" refers to Christ, comment so often neglects Abraham and expands on this Seed. We should not neglect Abraham. He is here not named as a mere individual, as one of many beneficiaries of the testament. Even

Isaac, Jacob, and the patriarchs could not be named here as Abraham is. Whatever promises God spoke to them were entirely Abraham's. *He* was the heir. All others only share in his inheritance. They inherit only as spiritual "sons of Abraham" (v. 7).

But God named two heirs. These were, indeed, two individual persons, for the second heir is called "his Seed." This very word connects the two. There would be no Abraham, the father of believers, who has multitudes of spiritual sons, without this Seed. The whole blessing of the testamentary promises were Abraham's and made him the father of these sons, but only through this Seed. As the Seed of Abraham he was himself promised to Abraham when no hope of fulfillment seemed possible. That promise Abraham believed (v. 6) and is thus named the heir together with the Seed. Here Paul writes that the promises were spoken to Abraham's Seed; in v. 19 we have the coming of the Seed. When they were spoken to Abraham for him to believe and to become the earthly ancestor of Christ, these promises were at the same time spoken to Christ who was himself both the fulfillment and the one to fulfill the promises. "To Abraham — and to his Seed" thus differ according to the nature and the relation of the two persons. They, indeed, belong together as do no other two, as already stated, but the Seed is supreme.

When Paul writes that God does not say: "And to seeds," as placing the promises upon (ἐπί) many (plural), but as placing it upon One: "And to thy Seed" (singular), and with the demonstrative ὅς adds "he who is Christ," the repetition of καί in the cited words points to Gen. 13:15 and 17:8, where this "and" appears with the dative. Some consider only these two passages and overlook Gen. 22:18 and thus get into difficulties. For is *zera'* as it is used in those two passages not a collective? How can Paul then say: "Who is Christ"? Some think that the way out of the difficulty is to make "Christ" a collective; the reference given in the A. V. is to I Cor. 12:12, i. e., to the mystical Christ, he plus all believers. Then "Christ" would include Abraham, and "thy Seed" becomes unintelligible. Then v. 19, "up to when the Seed comes," is contradicted, for here "the Seed" is decidedly an individual and not a collective group. The mystical Christ is not the solution.

In its place we are told that Paul reverts to the rabbinical type of exegesis which he learned under Gamaliel in the days when he was a rabid Jew. Zahn answers this supposed use of *midrash* in Paul: "Paul knew his Old Testament and his Hebrew rather better than his commentators; it is ridiculous to defend him against the charge that he misreads the collective *zera'* and imagines it to be the individual person Christ." We add that this is the more unwarranted when we read Gen. 13:15 and 17:8, both of which promise the land of Canaan to Abraham's Seed. In various passages of his epistles Paul himself uses "seed" as a collective. The Hebrew plural is used only once in the Old Testament, in I Sam. 8:15.

Paul considers the collective singular in the light of Gen. 22:18 and of the other promises made to Abraham. That is why, to begin with, he says that the promises were spoken to these two. They applied to others only because they applied to these two in a peculiar way, yea, because they applied to Christ in a most particular way as "Abraham's Seed," as we have already shown. This appears so clearly in v. 19 where "the Seed" is individual and not collective. What Paul says is that a plural like "seeds" would not do even in Gen. 13:15 and 17:8; it had to be a singular "as for one," it had to be this collective: "and to thy Seed." The plural would lose, would at least render uncertain, the reference to Christ; the collective singular conserves this vital reference.

Paul is not writing for scholarly but for common readers. These will see that he is not confusing a collective with an individual, and that "Christ" is not a collective. They will see that the collective is the collective it is because it focuses in Christ. In all the spiritual seed of Abraham (collective) there appears "Christ," the individual. Hence he also writes "who," not "which" is Christ. The gender of the relative is attracted to the gender of the predicate "Christ," but here this is done for more than a grammatical reason. Some have called this attraction harsh, but they overlook the inner reason for this. Paul expects his readers to read the prophecies as he reads them, at least to follow him in getting what those prophecies contain. As all of them start with Abraham, no matter how great a collective group they include ("sons of Abraham," v. 7, "thy seed"), so all of them focus and center in "Christ"; for Abraham and Christ, these two, in the way already explained, produce the collective.

A word needs to be said regarding Ishmael, the descendants of Keturah, Esau, etc., since all of them are so often excluded from "thy seed." Please remember how many Jews were also excluded (Rom. 9:6b). "Thy seed" is spiritual. Both Rahab and Ruth (born of pagans) belong to "thy seed." If Ishmael, if any of the children and the descendants of Keturah believed, they, too, belonged to this spiritual collective. It is only an assumption that all of them disbelieved the promises made to Abraham. Note, too, that the assumption is incorrect that Paul here traces the line of descent for Christ: Abraham, Isaac, Jacob, Juda, David. This assumption leads to wrong deductions about Ishmael, the children of Keturah, etc., and overlooks the exclusion of so many Jews from the seed.

17) Now Paul makes the application of the illustration used in v. 15, that even a human testament, after it has been confirmed, cannot be voided or altered. **Now this I mean: a testament that has been confirmed in advance by God, the law that has come four hundred and thirty years later does not unconfirm so as to put the promise out of effect. For if the inheritance** (is derived) **from law, no longer** (is it) **from promise; but to Abraham God has graciously granted it by means of promise.**

Here we have the stunning confutation of all Judaizers and of all those who are Judaistically or legalistically inclined. A confirmed human testament stands. God's testament, duly confirmed, stood for hundreds of years before the Mosaic law was even given, before anybody could even conceive the idea that this law in any way altered the testament or its divine confirmation. These hundreds of years confound all Judaizers.

When Paul places the divine reality beside the human example that he used he advances the argument from the less to the greater.

Paul uses direct discourse in apposition to τοῦτο. He simply states the fact: the law does not unconfirm God's confirmed testament for the simple reason that the law came so much later. The perfect participle (see v. 15) = "still standing confirmed." It is not stated how God made the confirmation but compare Heb. 6:13-18. Do not ask why any testament of God's still needed confirmation. It needed none for its own validity; the confirmation was made wholly for the sake of men in order to give them the strongest possible assurance for faith. This reveals the enormous sinfulness of unbelief which calls the very oath of God perjury.

The participial phrase introduced by μετά is attributive and is thus a compact unit with the noun it modifies. The time, 430 years, is an understatement.

When men are eager to prove something they are inclined to exaggerate their arguments and thereby defeat themselves. The opponents note the exaggeration, discount or reject the argument, and even question the person's veracity. But an understatement acts in the opposite way; the opponents see that the statement spoken against them could be made much stronger. The effect is according. In I Cor. 10:8 Paul writes 23,000 although Num. 25:9 reads 24,000. The latter is a round number, so also is the former; Paul purposely does not make it as large as possible; he lets his readers say: "There were even more slain!"

He does so here. Instead of making his own discount, Paul takes one from Exod. 12:40, etc.; 430 years (Acts 7:6 has the round number 400 which is used also in Gen. 15:13). Paul's readers see that he uses Exod. 12:40, that this covers only the stay in Egypt, that Paul might add the years the patriarchs remained in Canaan before Jacob migrated to Egypt. No one knows how long a period this was; the estimate is about 200 years. Paul excludes all dispute about an estimate regarding this time spent in Canaan, he ignores it. The Scriptures have this 430. Any testament that has been confirmed and has been in force for over four centuries certainly cannot have its confirmation upset or modified by something that comes into existence at so long a time afterward.

We have the same verb in the participle "having been confirmed" and in its opposite ἀκυροῖ, "does not unconfirm," i. e., deprive of confirmation. They are purposely chosen so as to match. "Disannul" in our versions is too narrow, for the verb intends to include both verbs that were used in v. 15: complete annulment (voiding) and also modification (adding codicils which change the original will). Neither in whole nor in part is God's testament deprived of confirmation by the law which was given 430 (to name only this figure) years later.

Paul names the feature of the testament here in question which is no less than its very heart: "so as to put the promise out of effect." "The promise" is properly singular, for it refers to Christ, the Heir, the full inheritance in him. Nothing that came 430 and more years later cancels or puts out of effect this promise by voiding the whole testament or by changing it in part with a codicil. The will would be wrecked in either case, for "the promise" is really the whole will. Εἰς τό denotes result; when it is called contemplated result, this is done only because it is negative and denied (understand R. 1003, 1072, 1090 in this sense).

18) "For" makes still clearer the fact that the law, which came into being hundreds of years later than the testament, does not alter its confirmation, does not put its promise out of effect. Paul states it conditionally: "If the inheritance (is derived) from law, no longer (is it derived) from promise." If, since the days of Moses and Sinai, the source of the inheritance lies in law, then a mighty reversal has certainly taken place, then the source is no longer what it was before, in Abraham's time and in the centuries following, namely promise. Then no one is able to get this inheritance by simply believing the promise as Abraham, the patriarchs, their families and descendants did during those centuries; then one is now able to get it only by doing works of law as the Judaizers claim by meeting all the legal requirements. Then God's own confirmation, the oath he made when sealing the testament promise, is canceled and no longer confirms as it did confirm prior to the coming of the law. With such a confirmation the testament promise, the promised inheritance, falls to the ground; it is put out of effect, abolished.

Paul does not reason about it. He does not ask whether it is thinkable or possible that God's oath-bound confirmation and the promise which it sealed can be thus abolished. The only possible answer is "no." Paul does something that is still stronger. He is a theologian of fact. Facts are invincible. He sets down the cold fact: "but to Abraham God has graciously granted it by means of promise," i. e., by means of promise alone without law or works of law of any kind. He uses the perfect tense "has granted it," so that after it was thus granted it stands. Here is the staggering fact that stands forth as plain as day. Paul lets it confront the Judaizers and the Galatians who are inclined to follow them. Abraham had the inheritance of the confirmed testament by faith in the testamentary promise alone without any law or works of law, and these Judaizers are now telling the Galatians that they can have it only by obeying the Mosaic law that was given hundreds of years later. This is not even modification, it is utter cancellation of God's testament.

The Greek is able to emphasize all the terms by a proper placement in the sentence. "To Abraham" is placed forward; the Judaizers say, *"not* so to the Galatians." The phrase "by means of promise" is placed before the verb and the subject, and verb and the subject are reversed, all three are emphatic, especially "God." This is what *God* has done; this is the *means* he used, the only one; this is his *act,* a gracious granting. We cannot reproduce all this in English but must see it in the Greek in order to get the full meaning of what Paul writes. Note, too, that God's testament is entirely promise without a single legal stipulation; testaments convey an inheritance, the one term connotes the other. Some human testaments may require something on the part of an heir as a condition of receiving the inheritance; God's testament does not, it is pure promise.

19) Paul has completely refuted the idea that the law affected the testament in any way. But this leaves the positive question, in fact, raises it: **Why, then, the law?** Indeclinable τi = "why" (B.-P. 1310: *Wozu in aller Welt das Gesetz?*) ; B.-D. 480, 5: *Was soll also das Gesetz?* If what Paul states are historical facts regarding the testament and the Mosaic regulation, there seems to be no reason for God's giving the law although he did this so much later. Those who have the question read: "*What,* then, is the law?" (R. V.; the A. V. is correct) think that the answer is delayed until v. 24; that Paul had to delay it until he had disposed of other pertinent questions. But the question is "why," and the answer follows at once. It is

The temporary nature of the Mosaic law.

Not only did this law come in 430 years later, it remained in force only for the Jews, only until their historic mission was accomplished, only until Christ came, and then it was abolished even for the Jews.

For the sake of the transgressions it was added until (the time) **when the Seed came, to whom the promise had been made** — (this law) **put into force as an ordinance by means of angels in connection with a mediator's hand.**

The question that is here answered is not one that is raised by some Judaizing objector. The Judaizers had probably never faced the fact that the law, which they made so essential to Christianity, came in centuries after Abraham; had never asked why it came in then. It is Paul who sees all these facts and God's intent in so arranging them. There is, of course, no

question that God gave the law although the fact is
added that it was given in a way that was much inferior to the giving of the testament.

"For the sake of the transgressions" has the word
χάριν which is merely a preposition: *wegen,* B.-D.
160, and may denote the reason or the aim (B.-P. 1398).
Here the latter is the case. When Paul says that the
law "was added," this cannot mean as a codicil to the
testament, an idea that has already been completely
excluded. It was not added to the testament as a part
of it or for testamentary purposes. It did not have to
do with the testament and its provisions but with "the
transgressions." These were its aim and purpose. But
not: "in order to check or to stop the transgressions";
the very contrary, "in order to bring them out fully as
what they were, namely transgressions." The idea is
not that there were a lot of transgressions, and that
these needed a check in order to prevent undue spreading, and that the law was introducced to do the check-
ing. Rom. 4:15 shows that without law there is no
transgression. The very word παράβασις implies a law
or norm which is overstepped. The Greek has the
image of walking "beside" the law or norm and thus
spurning it while our word "transgression" suggests
the picture of a boundary that is illegally crossed into
forbidden territory.

It is astonishing yet altogether true, the purpose
of the law is transgressions. It is for sinners only;
sinless persons need no law. But the moment the law
meets a sinner, he reacts by transgression because of
the sin in him. The law brings it out so that he and
all men may see it. Compare Rom. 5:20 and 7:13. Let
us make it drastic. While it is latent, sin stirs but
slightly. It is like a lion who is asleep or is moving
about quietly. Apply the stick of the law to it, prod
it a little, and its fangs flash, its rages and roars, it
tries to rend and tear, it displays what a wild beast it

really is. That stick does not make the beast a beast;
it cannot kill or change the beast; all it can do is to
make it show what it is. That is true even when the
stick is heavy enough to subdue the beast for the time
being; the very subdual is brought about by overpow-
ering force alone.

Again Paul speaks historically: "up to (the time)
when the Seed came." He refers to the law of Moses
with its many regulations which was given for the
period from Sinai until Christ and Calvary. This is
the law with which the Judaizers were operating on
the thoughtless Galatians. It was abrogated in Christ,
"to whom the promise has been given." The Greek has
the perfect for which the English would use the past
perfect "had been given." The historical mission of
the Mosaic law ended when the promise to Abraham
(v. 18) was fulfilled in Christ who is here called "the
Seed" as explained in v. 16.

Paul carefully keeps the connection. We may say
that the Mosaic law was given when the Jewish nation began to be a nation after leaving the Egyptian
bondage, and that the law ended when this nation lost
its national existence by rejecting Christ. This law, of
course, also segregated the nation, was a strong hedge
about it, kept it from mixing with other nations; but
Paul is not speaking of this function of the law.

We may add still more. The Mosaic law also contained elaborate regulations for removing the guilt of
the transgressions of the Jews. This law established
the priesthood of the Jews, the sacrifices, the cleans-
ings. They were entirely law since they had been ordered by God, and yet in all of them there was gospel,
the adumbration of Christ, whose blood cleanses us
from all sin. This shows that when Christ, the substance, came, the adumbration, having served its purpose, vanished. The letter to the Hebrews has much
to say on this phase of the subject.

This still leaves the larger question about the time from Adam until Moses and Sinai and about the time since Christ and Calvary. Rom. 5:14 refers to the former period and shows how men died because of sin. Rom. 2:12-16 adds that even the Gentiles, who never had the Mosaic law, have God's law, although it is blurred, written in their hearts, their own conscience condemning them. This is the moral law which Moses formulated in full clarity for the Jews. Rom. 7:7-13 shows how this law smote Paul and revealed his sin and his subjection to death. This is the law that still operates in sinners. Romans 2 shows that moralism, the effort to keep this law, is *not* the way in which to escape condemnation, is only the surest way of sinking into greater condemnation. It is this to the present day. The only escape lies in justification by faith, Rom. 3:20, etc. This escape delivers us from all condemnation of law.

This clears up what Paul says to the Galatians regarding the whole Mosaic law, its ceremonial as well as its moral content. The Judaizers laid great stress on the ceremonial phase of the law and demanded that the Galatian Christians keep this in order to be saved. Not only a part of the Mosaic law is abrogated in Christ, but all law with all its condemnation is ended for the believer in Christ; Rom. 8:1: There is no more κατάκριμα, verdict of condemnation from any law, for those who are in Christ Jesus by faith.

Christ is "the Seed" of Abraham, to him the promise has been made, i. e., in God's testament. He is the Heir who has the whole inheritance; and all of us who are joined to him in faith, all of us who are "in Christ Jesus" (Rom. 8:1) are joint heirs with him (Rom. 8:17), who have escaped from all condemnation of law.

The temporary nature of the Mosaic code, as far as it was intended only for the Jewish nation, is evidenced also by the way in which this code was given to the Jews. Paul uses the same word which Stephen employed, but he has the aorist passive participle διαταγείς, "put into force as an ordinance," while Stephen uses the plural noun διαταγάς (see Acts 7:53). The agent in the passive is God; the aorist records the historical fact. God used the angels in his communication of the ordinances to Moses. We must include far more than the two tables of stone, namely also the whole Tabernacle and many other features. Paul and Stephen refer to Deut. 33:2, compare Heb. 2:2.

Just how the angels functioned in the giving of the law to Moses we do not know. Deut. 33:2 speaks of the thunder, lightning, earthquake, trumpet on Sinai. Over against the Gentiles, who had no law that was given in such a glorious way, this mode of giving exalted the law of Moses; the Jews were proud of having such a law. Here, however, the reverse is stressed. The glory remains, it was given "through angels," but Christ, the Seed, who received the promise is vastly greater than all angels. So also the testament promise is far greater than the ordained law.

Ἐν differs from διά; the angels were God's servants, his means, but Moses was not Israel's servant and means but Israel's representative. Exod. 20:19. This shows us the sense of μεσίτης, which does not here mean *Friedenstifter* but *Uebermittler,* not a mediator or an intermediary between two estranged parties who brings them together again but one who merely transmits. In the matter of the law God functioned through angels, yet not with Israel itself but with Israel's representative who bore all the ordinances to the people.

"Hand" = service. Moses is not mentioned by name. The anarthrous nouns say that he belongs to the class of men who represent others; there is a class of them. In the case of "the Seed," Christ, this was far different. He inherited the promise of the testament; he was the Mediator in the highest sense of the

term, himself the God-man who reconciled the world
to God.

20) This helps us to understand the statement
which, despite its simplicity, is said to have received
about 250 different and divergent interpretations.
**Now the mediator does not belong to one person;
but God is one person.** One person acts for himself;
it is a multitude such as Israel that needs a mediator
in the sense of a representative to receive what the
one (God) transmits to all of them. Let us keep to
the context; this is said with reference to the transmission of the law to the whole people of Israel by
Moses. It is also said in contrast to the way in which
the testament and its promise were given. Being one
person, God acted for himself and needed no representative when he was giving the law; being a young
nation, Israel had a representative when it was *receiving* the law from God. God did not give the law to
each Israelite separately; Moses received it for all of
them.

The article in the expression "the mediator" is
generic, it generalizes from what is said about "a mediator's hand" in v. 19. "Is not of one" is the Greek
idiom for "does not belong to one." God is one person
and can act for himself. The διά used in v. 19 shows
that the angels were not regarded as God's representa-
tives even also as there was a number of them. The
observation is correct that, if Paul had intended to
say that a mediator does not belong to one party only
but always to two parties, he would have said "two."
But then "mediator" would signify a go-between who
brings two separated parties together. The giving of
the Mosaic law was not at all a transaction of this kind.

The point is that Paul brushes away the idea that
the law is in some way an addition to or an alteration
of God's will and testament to Abraham which was
already in full force for hundreds of years. It is only

a temporary and a subordinate set of regulations that were intended for the Jewish nation. Hence the great difference in the mode of procedure. When God established his testament with Abraham, God appeared to Abraham (Gen. 17:1-21) in person, and when the testament was executed, God was in Christ (II Cor. 5:19). The testament was given in person to the one Abraham; correspondingly, the inheritance was paid out to the one Heir, Christ. But the law was intended for the whole nation of Jews, their representative Moses brought it to them. The difference is so great that without perversion of the facts nobody can possibly make this law anything that is even remotely like a late codicil to the testament, to say nothing of substituting the law for the testament and thereby making it void.

The great lack in the law: its inability to produce life.

21)   In v. 15-18 Paul stresses the late date of the law and the fact that this excluded any modification of the testament by means of the law. In v. 19, 20 he shows the temporary nature of the law which was evidenced also by the way in which it was given. Now he adds the fact of the inability of the law to give life, which means that it could not possibly produce righteousness.

The further question is raised. If the law is so distinct and different from the testament, is only temporary in its function, etc: **Is the law, then, contrary to the promises of God?** Paul repudiates the idea as being altogether wrong: **Perish the thought!** This expression is explained in 2:17. To have the law alter the testament, to attach it to the testament (gospel) as a vital part, or to substitute it for the testament, is the one extreme; to make the law a contradiction of the testament (gospel) and thus to cast aside the law (antinomism), is the other extreme.

By rejecting the first of these alternatives we are not forced to accept the second; and, of course, vice versa. Both are false, contrary to the facts. We do not have to decide between extremes.

Since the Judaizers would not think of rejecting the law of Moses as being contrary to the testament, since they would point to this extreme alternative only in order to force acceptance of the opposite extreme, Paul does not at once show that the law is not contrary to the gospel but points to the lack and the inability of all law. It is not κατά, "against or contrary to," the testament (gospel) but differs from it in that vital point which the Judaizers fail to see.

For if there had been given a law, one able to make alive, actually the righteousness would have been (derived) **from the law.** "Law" in general (no article), thus also the Mosaic law but equally all other law lacks the ability "to make alive" (aorist, punctiliar), to produce spiritual life. That is why it cannot produce "the righteousness" we need to attain salvation. For one must have life in order to live in righteousness even to the slightest degree. That is why Paul points to this inability to bring forth life.

With regard to the testament of promise matters are different; it produces faith which is life. It grasps God's righteousness in Christ (Rom. 3:21,22), (the imputed righteousness), which means salvation, and it brings forth a life of righteousness (acquired righteousness). See the vast and the essential difference between the testament (gospel) and all law!

Yes, the law "was given," John 1:17. The Mosaic law was, indeed, a great gift of which the Jews were rightfully proud — if they had only used it aright (Rom. 3:20). The implication of the statement is the fact that law is always given, it is never produced by man himself. All evolutionary origin of law is denied. The passive includes the agent: there must

always be the divine Lawgiver. This is true also of
the law written in the hearts of Gentiles which is
greatly blurred by the darkening effect of sin.

We may find a condition of past unreality in the
apodosis as well as in the protasis. For ἦν with ἄν may
be either present or past unreality, the imperfect of
"to be" doing duty for the aorist of this verb (R. 1015).
Only the context decides. Here past unreality is more
in place than present: "would have been" and not
"would be." For Abraham must be included, he who
certainly obtained righteousness without law (v. 6),
he who received the testament of the promises (gospel), v. 16. On "righteousness," the quality due to
God's verdict, see v. 6. "A law, one able," etc., leaves
"law" (without the article) general, while the articulated participle makes a particular application (R.
777).

If a law had ever been given by God that was able
to produce life, then and then alone the righteousness
would have been ἐκ νόμου, have its source in this law.
But the world has never received a law of this kind.
If a law were of this kind, it would not be law; if it
were law, it would not be of this kind. The very idea
of a law producing life is a contradiction. That means
an equal contradiction in the idea of law furnishing
righteousness. When the Judaizers and the Pharisees
in general sought to do "works of law," these were not
righteousness but filthy rags (Isa. 64:6), a pretense,
a spurious imitation; God did not declare these workers of law righteous, they declared themselves righteous (Luke 16:15) as the criminal always likes to
acquit himself.

22) How the matter really stood since there was
no law that was able to make alive and afford the
needed righteousness, is now stated in a striking
way. **But the Scripture locked up everything together under sin in order that the promise might be**

**given as a result of faith in Jesus Christ to those be-
lieving.**

'Αλλά is placed in contrast with the question Paul
has emphatically denied in v. 21. No, the Mosaic law
is not contrary to the promises made to Abraham; no
law can compete with the promises since it is unable,
as the promises are, to produce life and thus righteousness. "But" this was the situation: God locked up
everything together under sin in order to achieve his
great purpose, the gift of the promise to all believers.
It could not come out of law which because of its very
nature cannot produce life and righteousness. The
gift was pure promise, and faith, faith alone was to
receive it as a possession.

Paul does not say that "the law" locked up everything together under sin but that "the Scripture" did
so. He again identifies the Scripture with God (v. 8).
"The Scripture" is God's recorded will. The supposition that this refers to one particular passage such
as Deut. 27:26 (see v. 10) is too narrow. When "the
Scripture" is named, there is a reference to many
passages; we have a sample in the list Paul uses in
Rom. 3:9-18. Many more may be cited. They all express God's judgment on sinners. Rom. 3:9 states that
this includes Jews as well as Gentiles.

"The Scripture locked up everything together under sin." The verb is placed forward for the sake of
emphasis: no less did the Scripture do than lock up
everything together in one mass, allowed no difference
(Rom. 3:22), made no exception. It is striking to note
that Paul does not say "all men" but uses the neuter
"all the things," i. e., "everything." Yet τὰ πάντα is not
the indefinite πάντα; "everything" refers definitely to
all that pertains to men, all of whom were sinners. We
may think of their thoughts, words, and deeds, of their
whole character and life. The view that this neuter
plural means σπέρματα, "all the seed," i. e., all Jews, is

strange. Everything without exception was locked and sealed and thus doomed "under sin" by the recorded judgment of God. "Under sin" = under the curse and the power of sin. Nothing pertaining to men could possibly escape the divine judgment which condemned all of it as sin.

The law extended back only to Moses. While it was recorded later than the giving of the law on Sinai, the Scripture reaches back to Adam by whom sin came into the world (Rom. 5:12). This is the reason that Paul writes "the Scripture" and not "the law." The other reason is this, because the Jews had the Scripture they could thus see what this Scripture did with "everything," namely lock it all up together under sin. What hope was there, then, that those who had all of this Scripture before their eyes might escape this locking up by means of works of law? Absolutely none.

For the purpose which God had in mind in this Scriptural judgment of his was by no means to leave men with "everything" they had, thus locked up and doomed to damnation. The Scripture itself recorded his ultimate purpose which was man's salvation: "in order that the promise might be given as a result of faith to those believing." This was the one way of escape. This promise is the one Abraham received, by which he received righteousness through faith (v. 8, 16), the promise to be fulfilled in Abraham's Seed who is Christ. It was God's purpose to convey this promise to men, to bestow it upon them as a gift with all that it contained. How the gift was to be bestowed is stated most clearly: "as a result of faith in Jesus Christ to all those who believe." Faith is doubly emphasized, both as a source (ἐκ) and as a mark of all who have the gift (the characterizing participle). The Scripture placed Abraham before all the Jews who had the Old Testament by pointing to his faith and by calling attention to the

fact that he believed the promise even long before the
Mosaic law was given.

How, then, can Judaizers say, or the Galatians for
a moment believe, that the substance of the promise
(gospel) is received by means of law and works of
law? A promise is received only by faith. Promise
and faith are correlatives. See this in v. 6-9; also that
works of law leave one under the curse in v. 10. Faith
and believing are the subjective means as the promise
(gospel) is the objective means of righteousness.
"Faith" always has its contents, is never empty; it is
"faith in Jesus Christ" (objective genitive), he in
whom as Abraham's Seed the promise given to Abraham is fulfilled.

It is all so plain in Scripture. But the Jews found
only law and then misused this law for works of law.
And now the Judaizers were trying to draw the Galatians back under law where righteousness could never
be obtained, where they would again be locked up
under sin. "Locked up together" is a characteristic
term of this epistle which proclaims the gospel of
Christian liberty.

The law was only a guardsman and a paidagogos.

23) The Scripture locked up everything under
sin. The Scripture record goes back to Adam, the
first sinner. What, then, had the Mosaic law to do
which came in so late after Abraham's time (v. 17)?
Its function was very secondary and also ended with
Christ (v. 19). **Moreover, before the faith came,
we were being kept under guard by law, being
locked up together for the faith about to be revealed.**

During the period when the Mosaic law was in
force it functioned as a legal guardsman — that is all.

It stood as a guard over those who were locked up together under sin. Call the law a warden for that
period. In v. 17 Paul states when the Mosaic law
arrived; in v. 19 until what time it functioned, "until
the Seed (Christ) came." "Before the faith came"
covers the period thus already marked out: from Moses
to Christ.

"Before the faith came" thus = "until the Seed
(Christ) came." What the coming of the faith means
we see from the phrase "for the faith about to be
revealed." The coming refers to this revelation. It
occurred with the coming of Christ, with his bringing
the great fulfillment of the testamentary promise. This
fulfillment stood forth in complete revelation for Jews
and for Gentiles alike (v. 8, 9). Paul uses a striking
term when he speaks of this as "the faith" arriving
and being revealed. Note the article, it is not "faith"
in general but *"the* faith" in a specific sense. Abraham
certainly had faith (v. 6), so did all the Old Testament
saints, namely subjective faith.

"The faith" is to be taken objectively yet not as
designating a period. It designates the substance of
all justifying and saving faith in the hearts of believers. Before this substance came in Christ it existed
only in promise and was embraced by faith as the sure
promise of God (Abraham is the example). Then
Christ brought the fulfillment, and in him this stood
fully revealed; from then on believers embraced the
fulfilled and revealed promise, i. e., the Christ who had
actually come as promised, "the faith" in this sense.

Δέ is not adversative; it = "moreover" and adds
the new point as to how the Mosaic law functioned
during this period with reference to Christ, "the faith"
in the sense of substance. This law could do nothing
toward bringing the faith. Christ's coming was completely assured by the promise. Only this much is
true, the Mosaic law would have had no object and

would never have been given save for the promise and
its fulfillment in Christ.

What, then, did this law do during this entire period of waiting since it came in on Sinai? It was
posted as a guard or sentry over us, Paul says, who
were locked in together under sin by the Scripture as
stated in v. 22: "By law we were being kept under
guard as being locked up together for the faith
(Christ)," etc. "By law" (no article) means that the
Mosaic law acted as law. The Mosaic law was, of
course, "law" and therefore acted in the capacity of
law. One of its functions was to stand guard. So the
Mosaic law stood guard as law, like a sentry, until it
was relieved of its duty by the arrival of Christ, "the
faith."

When Paul says "we were guarded" he, of course,
means "we Jews." But this is to be understood in the
sense of Rom. 3:19; the law speaks to those who are
under it, to whom it was given, and these were the
Jews and not the Gentiles; but when the Mosaic law
held all the Jews under guard as it did, it thereby
stopped every mouth and declared the whole world
guilty and subject to God's judgment. What this law
did for the Jews had its bearing on the whole world,
also on all the Gentiles who did not have the Mosaic
law. If God dealt so with the descendants of Abraham, how would he deal with those who were nothing
but pagans? In v. 22 the Scriptures locked up "everything" under sin. Paul now adds that the law stood
sentry even over the Jews as those who were locked up.

The imperfect "we were being guarded" reaches
back to Sinai and covers that entire period; it is
matched by the durative present participle "as being
locked up together"; but both tenses imply that this
condition was to be followed by another, for both are
open tenses, their action is not final. The idea of the
verb is not that of being guarded against hostile attack

but that of being in a prison and prevented from any possible escape; yea, there stood this mighty sentry all the time so that all Jews might see that they could not escape.

Yet he stood there because they were to escape. We have this stated already in v. 22. From Adam onward the Scripture confined everything under sin only in order that men might accept the promise by faith in Christ and thus escape from sin. Now Paul adds (δέ) that even then the Mosaic law kept its guard over the Jews, including those who believed, as locked up together for the fulfillment that was to be revealed in Christ. During the period from Sinai until Christ the sentry stood guarding even the believers. All the old Jewish believers had to observe the Mosaic law. The idea is not that they were still held under the damnation of sin like the unbelieving Jews but that they were held by this sentry "for the faith about to be revealed," for the Christ about to come. With their faith in the promise they were not to stray off from the fulfillment of that promise. The fulfillment would come from the Jews and from no other source (John 4:22); the Samaritans, for instance, worshipped they knew not what. It was the Mosaic law which kept the Jews for the fulfillment.

"About to be revealed" is a periphrastic substitute for the future tense and is not often found with the aorist infinitive (R. 857), but is punctiliar in the case of this aorist infinitive (R. 878). The revelation was to occur at a definite future time, namely when Christ came (v. 19). That would be the complete revelation for the Jews and for the whole world. Then the sentry duty of the Mosaic law would no longer be needed, it would end.

That time was now past. The guard had been recalled. What folly for the Judaizers to claim that he

was still on duty and to invent for him an outrageous
duty, one that he had never had, namely to hold believers to works of law by which nothing could be
attained except the curse (v. 10) !

24) **And so** (ὥστε, R. 999) **the law has been
our slave-guardian for Christ in order that as a result of faith we might get to be declared righteous.
But the faith having come, no longer are we under a
slave-guardian.**

With a closely allied figure Paul restates what he
has just said about our being kept under guard by law.
The sentry has been a παιδαγωγός for the Jews until
Christ came. This term is literally, "boy's leader" and
refers to the attendant, generally a slave, whom a
wealthy Greek or Roman father provided for his son
during the years between seven and seventeen, whose
duty it was to attend and to watch over the lad. He
took the boy to school and to gymnastic exercises,
watched and corrected his deportment so that it might
befit his station, and kept him from hurtful associa-
tions and influences, from foolish and hurtful actions.
The lad was thus trained early and long ever to be a
gentleman. The forbidding *vultus paedagogi* came to
be proverbial. This "boy's guide" was not the boy's
teacher except as indicated; nor was he appointed to
administer punishment, for the father attended to the
latter.

"And so," Paul says, "the law has been our boy's
guardian for Christ," γέγονεν, "hath been" (R. V.),
"was" (A. V.), but not "is become" (R. V., American Committee) ; for this function of the Mosaic law as
also this law itself with all its ceremonialism ended
with Christ. This perfect does not reach from the past
to the present (Paul's time, our own time), it stopped
when Christ came; the graph is not. ⸺⸺⸺→ but
⪢⸺⸺⸺→. (R. 895).

Paul's statement is historical and not general or doctrinal. The American Committee seems to have confused the past historical fact which Paul presents to the Galatians, that during the period from Sinai to Christ the Mosaic law functioned as a *paidagogos* for the Jews, with the doctrinal statement which we formulate when we now adopt Paul's language about a *paidagogos* and call the moral law, no matter in what formulation, in that of the Ten Commandments or in any other, a means for directing or driving us to Christ. Paul is speaking of the ceremonial contents of the Mosaic law which were completely abrogated when Christ came, which had fulfilled the purpose for which they had been given when the faith was revealed (v. 23).

Yes, all the ceremonial regulations served just as a slave-guardian did for the boy in his charge. These regulations kept the Jews from mingling with the Gentiles, the bad boys who had no guardian, whose influence and association would bring pagan contamination. All these regulations focused on Christ; they were full of types of Christ. Think of the high priesthood, the sacrifices, the Temple itself (John 2:19-21). All these were "for or towards Christ." None of them had any meaning apart from Christ who was about to be revealed; all of them had served their historic purpose when Christ was revealed.

"For Christ" is elucidated by the purpose clause even as εἰς denotes purpose or aim: "in order that we might get to be declared righteous." This does not mean to get this declaration when Christ came. Millions of Jews died during the period between Sinai and Calvary. But this entire law ever pointed them to Christ, their Messiah, so that these Jews might believe in him as Abraham had believed and had been declared righteous as a result of faith. So the Jews were to believe and to be declared righteous (see v. 6, "righteousness"). The Old Testament believers were justified just as we are by faith in Christ, but they had the Christ who was to come while we have the Christ who has come.

This does not mean that the law worked faith and justification. The law never does that (v. 21b). But this we may say: as regulations all these were law; but all the types and figures in these regulations that referred to Christ were gospel. And this gospel content of the legal regulations helped to work faith, for this content went with the promise made to Abraham.

It is a misunderstanding of Paul's figure of the boy's guardian when the figure is made an allegory. This loses the *tertium comparationis*. Compare R., W. P., who regards Christ as "the Schoolmaster" and says that the guardian is dismissed, and that we are now "in the school of Christ." But the guardian sat in the school (and in the gymnasium), watched the boy there, and then took him home. The guardian went everywhere with the boy. He was not only his teacher. The point of this figure is the immaturity of the boy (4:1-3). He was rid of the guardian only after reaching maturity. As far as school was concerned, the school ended for him even before he was seventeen and was considered mature enough to dispense with a guardian slave.

It is startling in a way that Paul says: ἐκ πίστεως δικαιωθῶμεν, for with ἐκ he makes faith *the source* of God's act of justification. But Paul does this already in v. 12, and twice in Rom. 1:17, and in Rom. 4:16. How can faith be the source of justification? If we conceive the essence of faith to be an activity, *ein Holen Christi*, as it has been called, we must say that Paul is wrong, for in this sense faith could not be the source of God's justifying (and we may add his elective) act. But Paul presented faith as a passivity, *ein sich geben lassen*. In the instant of its creation by the gospel

Christ *is given* to faith. When I lie unconscious, say as I drift into death, and am capable of not the least activity, Christ is mine by this divine gift. Faith, so defined, is, indeed, the source of justification. Thus our fathers speak of election "in view of faith" and most carefully explain this phrase as signifying "in view of *the saving merits of Christ* perseveringly apprehended by faith." The power in the source lies in this content of faith and not in an activity. When faith is correctly defined, like Paul, we need not fear to attribute too much to it.

25) Paul continues: "But the faith having come," the faith in the sense of v. 23 (Christ), "no longer are we under a slave-guardian" (no article). With the arrival of "the faith" all mentorship, whether of the Mosaic law or of any other kind, ended automatically. The aorist participle is again historical. With the arrival of Christ everything changed for all believers whether they were native Jews, foreign proselyte believers, or pagans who were converted by the apostles. "No longer are we" refers to the "we" of the previous verses, namely Jews. Everything resembling a *paidagogos* was abolished, not only for believing Jews, but for all Jews; and if for them, then naturally also for all others. Since Christ came there has never been a *paidagogos* such as the Jews had by God's appointment. The apostles were not sent out into the world by Christ to offer the Gentiles the old Jewish legal system but to offer "the faith" alone.

26) The "we" forms occurring in v. 23-25 speak of Jews, the aorists of the time before Christ. In v. 25 Paul comes down to the arrival of Christ and thus says of the Jews that "we (Jews) are no longer under a guardian." He now turns to the Galatians and tells them what this abrogation of the Mosaic law, this abolition of the *paidagogos* means for them.

"For" = that you may understand what this means for you, note what you are. **For you all are God's sons through this faith in Christ Jesus.** All of you Galatians, whether former Jews or former Gentiles, are now "God's sons," nothing less. The predicate, which is placed before the copula, is emphatic. "Sons" is the significant term, mature, full-grown sons, who are in possession of the inheritance, the fulfillment of the promise (v. 18). The A. V. translates "children of God"; but τέκνα could not be used here. Its connotation is dearness; but the believers of the Old Testament time were as dear to God as those of the New Testament. "Children" may also connote immaturity, and it would do that here. Υἱοί, as the context requires, suggests the idea of standing, independent standing, that is free from any mentor such as children would have (a nurse, a slave-guardian).

The point is that the Galatians are not in a position that resembles that of the Old Testament believers. Theirs is full Christian liberty. More than this. The Judaizers were trying to put the Galatians back under the Mosaic regulations, and that not as the Old Testament believers were once under them but in a monstrous way such as God never thought of during the Old Testament period, namely that the Galatians should seek to be saved by observing these regulations. God had appointed the law as a mentor for his children, the Judaizers wanted this mentor turned into a tyrant slave driver for his sons. Paul tells the Galatians that even the mentor is gone, that they are now free sons.

"God's sons through the faith in connection with Christ Jesus" speaks of "the faith" exactly as was done in v. 23-25 where the article appears three times as it now does a fourth time. "The faith" is again objective. This objective substance of the faith is, of course, retained in the heart by subjective faith, by believing;

but Paul stresses the objective means (διά) of the sonship of the Galatians. When this is noted, the debate
about the phrase "in Christ Jesus" becomes superfluous. The A. V. does not separate by a comma; the
R. V. does and thereby has two separate modifiers of
"you are." The A. V. is correct: "the (objective)
faith" is ever connected with (ἐν) Christ Jesus. All
that we believe centers in Christ, the Messiah who is
Jesus. Paul's thought is not clearly apprehended when
we take the sense to be: by believing (subjectively) in
Christ (as the object). When Paul has this in mind
he writes: "faith (no article) of Jesus Christ (genitive) as in v. 22. C.-K. 1083 is misleading when he
speaks of *Gotteskindschaft* (it should be *Sohnschaft*)
as though a corresponding conduct is implied. The context makes no reference to conduct.

27) With an explanatory "for" Paul adds: **For
as many of you as were baptized in connection with
Christ did put on Christ.** "As many as" takes up the
"all you" of v. 26 and is to be understood in the same
sense: whether formerly Jews or formerly pagans.
Paul points the Galatians to their baptism as the date
when they received "the faith" into their hearts. Baptism is an essential part of "the faith" (substance). By
receiving the one the other is received. Both are objective to be, of course, received subjectively.

Robertson's grammar (592) is most convincing regarding static εἰς in Rom. 6:3, etc.: ὅσοι ἐβαπτίσθημεν εἰς
Χριστὸν εἰς τὸν θάνατον αὐτοῦ ἐβαπτίσθημεν, and declares, "The
notion of sphere is the true one." It is most decidedly.
Rom. 6:3 must thus be translated: "As many of
us as were baptized *in* Christ (not *into*) were baptized
in his death (not *into*)." And in Matt. 28:19 the sense
is, "*in* the name (not *into*)." This the papyri have
taught us. All the former labored explanations of
this εἰς are thus permanently corrected. The New

Testament was written when εἰς was being used with
verbs of condition and even verbs of being which formerly had been using ἐν so that we meet εἶναι εἰς. This
usage continued until in the Greek of the present time
ἐν has disappeared. Here Paul writes just as he did
in Rom. 6:3: "as many as were baptized εἰς Christ," *in*
Christ.

Have no fear in regard to mysticism in the preposition, for the sense of εἰς is ἐν, and the sense of this latter
is connection, location in the same sphere: "in connection with Christ." Baptism is ever in connection with
Christ, in connection with his death (Rom. 6), in connection with the Name of the Father, etc., (Matt.
28:19), in connection with the remission of sins (Acts
2:38), the sphere and connection being indicated by
the noun or the nouns that follow the preposition. Here
the idea is not *auf Christum* (Zahn), which would require the Greek ἐπί, or *in Beziehung auf*. The whole
action of baptism, the command, all the promises included in the sacrament as well as all else are wholly
and completely *connected with* Christ, in one blessed
sphere with him.

Paul says: By being baptized in Christ all you
baptized Galatians "did put on Christ," or, as the middle may be rendered, "did allow yourselves to be
clothed with Christ." On the permissive middle see R.
808, etc.; B.-D. 317. This verb does not mean "to play
a role," the Galatians, like actors, being dressed up as
Christ (Zahn). Nor does the idea of putting on Christ
mean to acquire the same relation to God that Christ
had, the relation of sonship. Nor is baptism "a badge
or uniform of service like that of the soldier," his
sacramentum, oath of fealty, a "symbolic picture" (R.,
W. P.). He who puts on Christ becomes partaker of
his salvation. The imagery is not pagan but that of
the Old Testament.

To put on Christ is to receive justification: "I will greatly rejoice in the Lord, my soul shall be joyful in my God; for he hath clothed me in the garments of salvation, he hath covered me with the robe of righteousness, as a bridegroom decketh himself with ornaments, and as a bride adorneth herself with her jewels," Isa. 61:10. Compare Luke 15:22; Matt. 22:11; Ps. 132:9, 16. The objection that this is not a wedding is unwarranted. Why must allowing oneself to be clothed refer especially to a wedding? Were the grown sons of Greeks and Romans not invested with garments that marked them as sons?

We should not lose ourselves in these details. The stress is on the name "Christ" which repeats "Christ Jesus" of v. 26. The point is the difference between the Old Testament believers who were still under the *paidagogos,* immature, still waiting for the revelation of the faith about to come, and the New Testament believers, God's sons, mature, free, not needing a mentor. This is the position "the faith" and our baptism give us: Christ is here at last, and we are joined to him. Verse 27 explains "in Christ Jesus" as it is used in v. 26. As the latter is a real, saving connection, so v. 27 is not mere symbolism, not an act of ours such as swearing fealty.

28) The new statement is without a connective and simply parallels the previous one. In baptism all the Galatians are alike clothed with the garment of Christ's perfect righteousness. In God's eyes they are all alike. During the time the Mosaic law was in force, this law itself recognized and maintained differences. It had provisions for Jews over against Gentiles — many of them; for free men over against slaves; for men over against women. When the faith and Christ came, these distinctions were abolished. **There is no Jew nor Greek, there is no slave nor free, there is no male and female; for you**

all are as one person in union with Christ Jesus.
Ἕνι = ἔνεστι and is an old idiom (R. 313). Yet ἕνι (the
preposition ἐνί [= ἐν] turned into an adverb) implies,
not ἐστίν the copula, but ἔστιν, denoting existence: *es
gibt,* "there exists."

The old distinction between Jew and Gentile is
placed first; it extends to nations. Next is that between slave and free, and we must remember that this
extended through the whole Roman world at that time.
These two pairs are placed chiastically: for Jew was
greater than pagan Greek, and free, of course, greater
than slave. The last difference is a coordinate pair
(note καί), two neuter terms: "no male and female,"
i. e., no male and no female sex. Paul stops with this;
any other distinction can readily be added. He says:
Since you Galatians are all sons of God by faith, clothed
with Christ's righteousness in baptism, all these and
similar distinctions and differences are wiped out as to
your spiritual standing.

This does not involve a physical mutation. Christians of Jewish or of Greek descent retained their descent, free men and slaves kept their social positions,
men and women kept their sex. The gospel changes
nothing in the domain of this world and this natural
life. In a way the gospel effects changes also in this
domain. It has driven out slavery and has elevated the
status of woman. But Paul is here speaking of the
spiritual domain, of God's household in which all believers are equally sons of God.

Paul states this in a striking way: "For you are
all one person in union with Christ Jesus." There are
still many individuals, πάντες ὑμεῖς, and these remain
"many." But in their union with Christ they are all
εἷς, masculine, not ἕν, neuter, "one person," not just
"one thing or body." The idea to be expressed is not
that of the *Una Sancta,* namely Christ as the head and
all of us one great organism or body of many members,

each with his special gifts as pictured in Eph. 4:11-16. What union with Christ signifies for Jew, Greek, etc., is this that they are all alike in their spiritual standing, everyone has been baptized, declared righteous, etc., none are higher, none lower, none richer, none poorer, none better, none worse, none with more, none with less, in every respect they are exactly as "one person in Christ Jesus." All the Galatians are not a lot of sons of God with many differences in their sonship but a unit person. Whichever you take, the sonship is identical. Paul loves to end with a focal unit idea beyond which thought cannot go.

29) Now he even completes the circle by combining the end with the beginning. **And if you belong to Christ, then you are Abraham's seed, heirs according to promise.** The condition of reality assumes the fact which is indeed the fact, that the Galatians belong to Christ. "To be of Christ" is a Greek idiom: to be his, to belong to him. This defines what "being in Christ Jesus" means. Yet belonging to Christ fits exactly being heirs with him.

Ἄρα introduces the self-evident deduction: "then you are Abraham's seed," his true spiritual descendants (see v. 7). But this is only the intermediate thought; the final one is the apposition. With the word "promise" Paul reaches back to v. 8 where the promise is quoted, to v. 16-18 where the promise is connected with the testament, the inheritance, and the Supreme Heir. With "heirs" Paul recalls what he says of the testament in v. 15, 17, 18. God granted the inheritance to Abraham by promise (v. 17). So, then, as Abraham's seed we are heirs with Abraham, Abraham and we belong to Christ by faith alone. Or recalling that Christ is "the Seed" (v. 16) of Abraham, the Heir of the testament of promise, we who belong to Christ as Abraham's spiritual seed are heirs with Christ according to promise.

A silent contrast runs through all these blessed statements: the Mosaic law does *not* make sons of God, does *not* make us Abraham's seed, does *not* constitute us heirs. It is the promise alone which was fulfilled in Christ; it is faith and baptism and not works of law. Here is the answer to the Judaizers. Could the Galatians fail to feel its convincing power?

CHAPTER IV

2. (Continued): The Galatians Must Know the Limitations of the Law, 3:15-4:11

The law marked the heir as a minor; Christ brought him to majority.

1) When Paul says in 3:29 that by belonging to Christ the Galatians are Abraham's seed and thus heirs according to promise, one may well ask, "Were the Old Testament believers not also Abraham's seed and heirs according to promise?" In their capacity as heirs those Old Testament believers had the law of Moses; should the New Testament believers not also have it? This question is now answered in the most adequate and the most lucid way.

Now I say, for such a time as the heir is a minor he differs in nothing from a slave although he is lord of everything but is under guardians and stewards until the time fixed in advance by the father.

This is an illustration that is similar to the one employed in 3:15 regarding a human testament. This deals with an heir who is still a child, still a minor. Paul takes as his illustration a lad whose wealthy father has died and has left the boy a great estate. In this figure everything has to do with this orphaned lad and not with his dead father, hence the father is introduced only incidentally. We should not turn this illustration into an allegory. "Now I say" intends to emphasize what is said; it lays the finger on the point now stated about minors who fall heir to an estate. "The heir" has the generic article. Paul is not offering a fine legal point; so he writes merely νήπιος, infant, child, and thus a minor.

During the time that the heir is a minor he differs in nothing (adverbial accusative) from a slave although he is lord of everything (concessive participle) and really owns the entire estate. He is fed, nourished, and sheltered in the house, which is true also of a slave in the house. He has no control of the great property, which is likewise true of the slave.

2) Paul himself states what he has in mind. Just as a slave has his superiors who control him and his affairs, so this young heir. Paul thinks of a large inheritance as befits the great spiritual inheritance which he is illustrating. Hence he names two classes of superiors, ἐπίτροποι and οἰκονόμοι, which some regard as identical. But the former are those who are placed in charge of the young heir himself, call them guardians; the latter are those who manage his estates, stewards. The latter were often slaves yet were competent men, one being placed over this, the other over that estate of the owner. In our estimation the "guardians" were those who, among other things, attended to the boy's education.

Since Paul is writing to Galatians who are not merely Roman citizens, it is doubtful whether he refers to Roman law. This provided for a *tutor* (or several) until the age of puberty, the fourteenth year, was reached, after that for a *curator* until majority was attained, which occurred at the age of twenty-five years. The "guardians" of whom Paul speaks do not seem to be the *tutor* and the *curator* but those whose duty it was to provide the necessary teachers for the young heir. The point is that the minor heir is *under* others and that of necessity because he is still a minor.

The other point is the length of time he is under others, which is thus again mentioned, but now more specifically: "until the time set in advance by the father." Supply ἡμέρας with προθεσμίας, the genitive "of the father" is subjective. We need not puzzle about the legal date when majority was attained. Wherever the law specified the age, the will would naturally comply with this specification; wherever law and custom allowed latitude, the father's will would set a date that was agreeable to the father.

Much more important for Paul's illustration is this mention of the father. It is he who made the testament, he who designated the heir, he from whom the inheritance comes. Thus it is he who in one way or in another fixes the time when his heir is to enter upon control of the inheritance. The heir is no more of an heir after this date than he was before it as the participle used in v. 1 indicates; but after this date the heir is, indeed, no longer under anybody as he was before. This is the *tertium*, the essential point: once *under*, then *no longer under* according to the testamentary provision of the heir's own father.

3) **So also we, when we were minors, had been put in slavery under the elementary things of the world; but when the fulness of the time came, God commissioned his Son, come to be from a woman, come to be under the law, that he should buy free those under law, that we should receive the sonship.**

With "so" Paul introduces the great reality he has just illustrated by the standing of a minor heir. By "we were minors" he means "we Jews" just as he does in 3:23-25. Before Christ came, we were nothing but minor heirs. The distinction between believing and unbelieving Jews during the period before Christ is not stressed in this "we"; if we desire to stress it, we shall, of course, have to say that only believing Jews could be included. Yet "we" refers also to Paul himself as well as to all the Jews who came to faith after Christ came. So it is best to take "we" in this broader sense. God intended the inheritance for all Jews, treated all of them as minor heirs before Christ came, intended that all of them should enter upon the freedom from guardians and stewards after Christ came. The fact that so many frustrated all this for themselves by their unbelief is not considered here in order to make the main facts stand out the more.

During that entire period before Christ, while we were minors, "we had been put in slavery under the elementary things of this world." These στοιχεῖα were our "guardians and stewards." Paul has said that the minor heir does not differ from a slave in respect to being under superiors; hence he now says, "we had been put in slavery." The passive verb is causative. God is the agent in the passive. This condition of slavery had been imposed by means of the Mosaic law. The periphrastic past perfect reaches back to Sinai when this enslavement began and extends forward to Christ when it ended. A present perfect would imply that the enslavement is still in force; the past perfect reaches only to the time when God commissioned his Son.

What are these στοιχεῖα? This word has quite a range of meanings, M.-M. 591; C.-K. 1021: etymologically it means anything placed in a row, thus the letters of the alphabet; since Plato's time is was used to refer to the basic elements of which the world is composed, metaphorically it designates the elements or rudiments of knowledge. Of late the effort has been made to refer it to "the great angel powers which were said to preside over natural happenings and to rule over stars, wind, rain, hail, thunder, and lightning," "the spirits of the elements," "astral spirits." The usual discussion is limited to the meanings "elementary instruction" and "actual physical elements": we were under the *abc* instruction, in the primer department; or, we were under physical, material elements, were bound by law to all types of regulations regarding them. The point is not one that is difficult to decide.

Paul himself helps us. The genitive "of the cosmos" points to the physical. In v. 9, 10 he calls these elements "weak and beggarly," observing days, months, times, and years; in Col. 2:20 he adds regarding these elements the ordinances: "Handle not, nor taste, nor touch!" things which perish with the using, which are after the precepts and doctrines of men. These *stoicheia* need not be persons so as to match the guardians and the stewards of the illustration who are persons; for the point of the illustration is the fact that the young heir is really under those who are far beneath him. So the Old Testament believers were placed under material, earthly things that were beggarly, indeed, all of them far beneath these believers. They had to submit to regulations about food and drink, washings and purifications, sacrifices of all kinds, rules about places, times, bodily actions of all kinds.

These *stoicheia* were not the law itself but the earthly things with which the law had to do. In dealing with these perishable elements the law descended to the plane of human precepts and doctrines, Col. 2:20; for in all the pagan religions these likewise dealt extensively with material things. In the case of the Jews they were not self-chosen as they were in the case of the pagans but prescribed by God. Yet they constituted an enslavement, a burdensome one, indeed, and they became worse when the Jews laid all the stress on these beggarly things and lost sight of the purposes of God, of the promise, the spiritual inheritance, and faith in these. This divine purpose was the essential thing. Like a father, God so placed his young heirs under guardians and stewards and regulated all these earthly things only in order to safeguard them during their minority.

We thus do not accept the interpretation *Buchstaben* (Luther), elementary or rudimentary parts of religious knowledge; likewise the idea of "stars" and

of heavenly bodies, and certainly not that of astral
spirits or spirits that govern natural manifestations.
"Under the elementary things of the world" contains
a strong implication: God's sons ought to be *above*
and not *under* these things. Since God placed his heirs
under them, this could be only a temporary arrangement. What folly for the Judaizers to claim that this
subjection to things beneath us is intended to be permanent!

4) This temporary period passed. In the illustration Paul has already said that in the case of the heir
it was to last only until the date fixed by the father.
We should keep to that and not suppose that the heir
grows up and thus attains his majority. Let us stay
with the *tertium* and thus with the reality itself. The
idea that the Jewish Old Testament believers finally
grew up is beside the mark. Think of how few such
there were when Christ came.

"The fulness of the time" is the condition of being
full as regards the time ($\pi\lambda\eta\rho\circ\tilde{v}\nu$ with the accusative),
i. e., the full time. This fulness of the time should
not be explained by means of philosophizing: "Until
generations of mankind had learnt through years of
social training to control some of the animal instincts
of their lower nature, to rebel against its brutal passions, and desire to live in obedience to their higher
nature," etc. (*Expositor's Greek New Testament*).
Some think only of the Jews and find the fulness of
the time in a certain ripeness and maturity that were
finally reached by the Jews. But if Judaism was ever
at a low spiritual ebb, it was so when this fulness of
the time arrived.

All we are able to say is that God knew when the
proper time had arrived. Judaism was bankrupt, and
paganism had always been so. We can enumerate
some of the providences which helped to open the way
for the gospel such as the vast extent of the Roman

Empire, the spread of the Greek language, the facility of travel throughout the empire, the extensive diaspora of the Jews, its many proselytes from Gentilism, etc. All of these aided the spread of the gospel. What God saw and regarded as the fulness of the time in the spiritual condition of men, barbarian as well as Greek, is too difficult for us to predicate because his thoughts and judgments are too unsearchable for us. Paul, too, refrains from stating details.

Then God "commissioned forth his Son." This verb is the more vivid because it is not the usual compound with only ἀπό but has an added ἐκ. This means that the Son went out on his commission not only "from" God but "out from" God. John says that he was "with" (πρός) God (John 1:1) and was God and that he became flesh (v. 14). Not as an angel might be commissioned but as one of the three Persons of the Godhead. It is usually stated that the pre-existence of Jesus is indicated here, but that would apply also to an angel; no less than the deity is expressed here. When we translate "sent forth" we should note that the verb means more. While πέμπω is also used with reference to the Son even as he calls the Father "my Sender" (John's Gospel), ἀποστέλλω and ἐξαποστέλλω mean to be sent or sent out on a commission, to execute a great mission, the one here briefly described.

The action of the two aorist participles is, of course, contemporaneous with the aorist "commissioned," but what is their relation to the verb? The Greek and our two versions leave the answer to the reader. The relation is that of mode, hence participles are used which indicate subsidiary action. The son's commission involved his getting to be (derived) from a woman and thus also getting to be under law. The second participle states what the first involves; both are alike historical: the Son "got to be" ἐκ and ὑπό or "became" the one and the other. Our English has no word that can adequately render these two participles which mean neither the passive "was made" (A. V.) nor the intransitive "was born" (R. V.), the Greek for which latter is γεννηθέντα. Either will do as a translation if the English is not stressed.

In this connection we take note of the effort of some to eliminate the virgin birth from this passage. These can be divided into two groups: those who determine *a priori* the absolute impossibility of such a birth and cancel Matthew's and Luke's accounts; secondly, those who are more or less affected by the argumentation of the former. Over against all of them stands the church of the ages with its faith in the statements of the Word. The one aim of the church is to read what the Word says and then to believe that. "The Son of God" is the second person of the Godhead; he "became out of a woman" in executing his mission. This is the Incarnation, the miraculous conception, the virgin birth. God's Son became man, the God-man.

The phrase that begins with ἐκ denotes more than the separation from the womb, it includes the entire human nature of the Son as this was derived from his human mother. The word γενόμενον is exactly the proper word to express this thought, even the tense is very accurate. The Son's going out from God on his mission is seen in his becoming man. He did not cease to be the Son of God when he became man. He did not drop his deity, which is an impossible thought. He remained what he was and added what he had not had, namely a human nature, derived out of a woman, a human mother. He became the God-man.

Thereby he became, got to be, under law. The one getting to be involves the other, and both had as the object of his mission "that he buy free those under law," etc. The Son could do this and did it by having become man, by having come to be under law. The

God-man is our Redeemer from the curse of the law, "having become a curse in our stead" (3:13). Look at it from either side, from his going forth from God for his mission or from the accomplishment of that mission, and we see what the participial statements declare, namely the Incarnation of the Son and his subjection to law. By means of these two God's Son accomplished our purchase and our liberation. Cancel his deity, consider God's Son a mere human "son," and both are eliminated, his going forth from God and his purchase of condemned mankind.

It is true, the Galatians know that "out of a woman" refers to the Virgin Mary, and that Paul does not need to mention her name or her virginity in this connection. But these specifications are side thoughts. The two thoughts needed here are general: out of a human mother — hence "woman"; and under law — hence not "the law." The facts that this was a specific woman, and that this was a specific law are self-evident. The idea that ἐκ predicates only the birth and not also the conception is untenable. Does birth or does it not involve conception?

"His Son — out of a woman" pointedly omit mention of a human father. Why? Because this is God's Son who is co-eternal with the Father. He became man by way of "a woman" alone. Incomprehensible? Absolutely so! A miracle in the highest degree? Beyond question! Yet, if we were asked to state how God's Son could become man, should we say that it could not be done in this way as God says that it was but would have to be brought about by way of a human father? Would that remove the miracle?

The Christian mind rebels against speculations of this kind. It turns the pages of Holy Writ; it reads Matt. 1, Luke 1 and 2; Gen. 3:15, the woman's seed; Isa. 7:14; Micah 5:3; and all the others in this line, John 1:13, 14; Luke 3:22, 23, Mary's descent; Matt.

1:16 (see the author on the interpretation of these three passages). All of these present the *fact* of which Paul writes tersely, which is back of all his other references (Rom. 1:3 and many another) ; why *speculate* about how the fact might have been other than it was? *"Come to be* out of a woman" is not like Job 14:1: "man *born* of woman," which designates the frailty and the mortality of all men (hear the funeral bells ringing!). The participle is "became" and not "born"; it is predicated of God's Son and not of man in general or in particular. The God-man could die but did not need to die. He laid down his life voluntarily (John 10:18) as the ransom or purchase price for us (Matt. 20:28).

The point to be brought out in "come to be out of a woman" is expressed by the second participle which is appositional and specifying: "come to be under law." He who was greater than all law placed himself under law just as he who was greater than his mother became her child. Only this point is here brought forward, that by coming to be of a woman the Son of God came to be under law. This is due to the fact that Paul is speaking of the latter, of the Jews being under the elements of the world by virtue of the Mosaic law until the time set by God. Paul is speaking of the arrival of this time. It is when the Son of God became man, when he, too, came to be under law once for all to end this domination of law. The figure of heirs, of testamentary provisions concerning minority and majority merge into the reality as the Son's mission is described, which is too great for that figure; only the echoes of it remain, cf., v. 5-7.

We must note the anarthrous "under law" here and in v. 5. When "law" refers to the Mosaic law it often deals with it as belonging to the general category of law. It does so here. This point is important because of v. 5. How many did the incarnate Son buy free?

Only the Jews? No; all men. How many were "under law"? We have the answer in 3:10. In Rom. 3:19 we have more: when the Mosaic law spoke to the Jews who had this specific law, it stopped every mouth and made the whole world guilty before God as Paul shows at length in Rom. 3:10-18 from the Scriptures themselves, as he has shown it from the fact of the universality of sin in Rom. 1:18-32. Not only does such law as the pagans have condemn them in view of the final day of judgment (Rom. 2:12-16), the Mosaic law, as the pure revelation of God's opposition to sin, by condemning the Jews, stopped every mouth and made the whole world guilty before God.

The Son "came to be under law" in general and not only under the pure code of Moses, but by virtue of this code under all that mankind had left of God's law as written in their hearts. That is why Paul connects the Son's Incarnation with his coming to be under law and does not say that by his circumcision he came to be under the Jewish code. But why bring in the Roman law, Christ's dying because of a verdict pronounced by a Roman governor? That verdict was a travesty on Roman law as the Sanhedrin's verdict was a travesty on Jewish law. Paul says "law" and not all manner of civil and criminal codes.

"Under law" implies that the incarnate Son was to fulfill law and thereby purchase our Christian freedom. Paul is nullifying the contention of the Judaizers regarding the permanent validity of the Mosaic ceremonial laws for all Christians. That is why the sacrificial death of the Son, i. e., the passive obedience, is not treated here. It is the active obedience that nullifies all Judaistic ideas. By this, Paul says, the Son bought us free.

This answers the mistaken idea that the Son fulfilled the law *for himself* so that he might remain spotless in order to offer himself as a lamb without blemish to die for our sins. This at best conceives the Son's active obedience only as pertaining indirectly *to us*. But Paul says that the Son bought us by this active obedience. It was thus just as much substitutionary as his passive obedience. In fact, the two cannot be separated. Even in death the Son gave himself (active) and so was slain (passive). The two were indissolubly united during all of his life. We should never stress the one against the other because the passive obedience is more frequently mentioned in Scripture than the active.

This answers Meyer's attack upon the statements: "because of the sole merit, *complete obedience*, bitter suffering, death, and resurrection of our Lord Christ alone, whose obedience is reckoned to us for righteousness," *C. Tr.* 919, 9; "before God's tribunal only the righteousness of the *obedience*, suffering and death of Christ, which is imputed to faith, can stand," etc., 927, 32. We mention Meyer only because others agree with him.

5) God's purpose in his Son's coming to be under law was "that he should buy free those under law." In 3:13 Paul has said: "Christ bought us free from the curse of the law by having become a curse in our stead." Here he uses the same verb ἐξαγοράζειν (see 3:13). The fact that God's purpose was achieved is intimated by the aorist of the subjunctive. This first purpose clause is objective, for those bought free are "those under law"; the second clause is subjective, for those who are to receive its benefits are "we." We have already stated why "those under law" (no article with "law") describes men in general and not merely the Jews under their Mosaic law. But "we" in the second clause is the same as the "we" occurring in v. 3 and does denote Jews. By the purchase of all men who were under law the Jews in particular were to

be set free from the Mosaic law, this sentry (3:23), this *paidagogos* (v. 25), the subjection to guardians and stewards (4:2).

We cannot see that with "those under law" Paul refers only to the Jews and with "we" to the believers (either himself or Jewish Christians or the Jewish and the Gentile Christians combined). In Rom. 3:19 Paul himself states how what was done for Jews affected every mouth, the whole world; here he does not state anything that is similar, namely that what the Son did for the Jews also affected certain Gentiles.

The whole thought is a refutation of the Judaizers. God's Son set free all those who were under law; this purpose, being objective, was achieved. Furthermore, it was achieved in order that we Jews should receive the sonship. This was a subjective purpose that was also achieved, but only in the believing Jews, the unbelieving were hardened and cast away (Rom. 11:7). "The sonship" is modified by the context (v. 1-3) and thus signifies the status of sons who have advanced from their minority to their majority, to the status of full-grown sons who are no longer under guardians and stewards. "Adoption" is not the proper word, for it may apply to a babe, a minor son and heir.

This eliminates the question as to whether regeneration as well as justification is included in this "sonship." In their minority, before Christ came all the heirs were both regenerated and justified although they were still under the guardianship and the stewardship of the Mosaic law (v. 2). When Christ came, when their majority was attained, this involved the end of the guardianship and stewardship of law for them. Ever after that time they were entirely free of it.

6) Jewish believers were formerly minors, now that God's Son has bought free all those under law. Jewish believers have received the standing of sons who are in their majority. This fact pertains to all

Christian believers whether they are former Jews
or former Gentiles and thus to the Galatians, most
of whom were such Gentiles.   It helps us to understand Paul's thought if we remember that during
the period before Christ the many believing Gentile
proselytes to Judaism also did not get beyond the
status of minors. But now Paul is able to say to all
the Galatian believers: **And because you are sons,
God commissioned the Spirit of his Son for our
hearts as crying: Abba Father! Wherefore no
longer art thou a slave but a son. And if a son also
an heir through God.**

Some think that ὅτι = "that," and that the whole
clause is an adverbial accusative: "Regarding this that
you are sons" the evidence is that God, etc. This translation assumes that the sonship of the Galatians is
now to be proved, and that the possession of the Spirit
is the proof. But the sonship is proved in v. 4, 5, and
what is now added is the result of this sonship, the corroboration of it, exactly as is done in Rom. 8:14, 15,
which treats the possession of the Spirit as one of
the great results of justification. A result may, of
course, be used to prove its cause; but here Paul does
not reverse matters in this way, he states the cause
and then its result. In 3:2 he inquires for the source of
the effect and thus does reverse the two.

The moment we note that "sons" means sons who
are no longer in their minority but in their full majority, we see how Paul has, indeed, proved the Galatians
to be such sons: God's Son has abolished all minority,
no minor heirs now exist, all guardians and stewards
over minors are now and forever abolished. It is in
this sense that the Galatian believers are "sons" also
with the evident result of such mature sonship and
freedom from superiors, namely that God commissioned the Spirit of the Son with the cry of sons, "Abba
Father."

Note the close parallel: "God commissioned forth his Son" (v. 4) — "God commissioned forth the Spirit of his Son." These are the two great historic acts. All the promises of Jesus regarding the sending of the Spirit apply, John 14:16, etc.; 15:26; 16:13, etc.; Acts 1:8. The fulfillment came on Pentecost and remained for all believers of all time. The things to be noted are not the outward miraculous signs which occurred at the time of Pentecost, which are like the angels singing at the time of the nativity; but all the statements of Jesus that the Spirit could not come to the disciples until Jesus had gone to the Father. When redemption was entirely complete, the Spirit came, "commissioned forth" as Jesus had been. Then all the guardians and the stewards were dismissed, the Spirit took their place, for the heirs' minority was ended, the Galatian believers were "sons" in this full sense.

We need scarcely say that the Spirit wrought in the Old Testament, that the faith of the Old Testament believers was produced by the Spirit. To think that the Old Testament believers were devoid of the Spirit is to imagine an impossibility. Pentecost ushered in a new era, the era when the Spirit is able to glorify Jesus as one having come, to take all that Jesus has achieved, to declare it unto us, John 16:14; this is his world-wide mission. And this means: no longer minor heirs waiting for this era. "You are sons."

For such "sons" the Spirit of God's *Son* is intended. When Paul says that he is in *"our"* hearts and changes from the second person plural to the first, we must go on to v. 7 where he changes to "thou," the singular, every individual. These different pronouns are not stressed over against each other; they merely turn the thought in every direction. "Our" hearts thus include Paul and the Galatian believers. Paul himself and the great mass of Jewish believers in the Christian

Church had come to faith *after* the Son brought redemption. This includes the 3,000 who came to faith after the Spirit was poured out at Pentecost. Like the Gentile believers, all of them at once became "sons." Do not forget that among the 3,000 there were not a few proselytes (Acts 2:10), former Gentiles. All of them were not minors but sons in their majority. There was no further waiting for the testamentary promises to be fulfilled, no further supervision for minor heirs.

Κράζω may, perhaps, be rendered "exclaim." *Sermo vehemens, cum desiderio, fiducia, jure, constantia,* Bengel. We do not see how this can refer to congregational praying. Nor does "Abba Father" recall the Lord's Prayer which begins, "Our Father who art in heaven"; it brings to mind Christ's prayers in Gethsemane (Mark 14:16) together with Heb. 5:7, "strong crying" (κραυγή which is allied to κράζω). While the crying of the name is predicated of the Spirit, this is evidently to be understood mediately as in Rom. 8:15: "in whom we cry." The Spirit is said to utter this cry when he moves us to utter it. The fact that he is in our hearts is the result of our sonship, and his presence makes this cry possible.

The nominative form ὁ Πατήρ is quite regular after the vocative Ἀββᾶ; it is the repetition of the Aramaic and the Greek terms for Father that is so exceptional. Various Hebrew and Aramaic expressions were taken over by the early Greek Church, but this one is a combination of Aramaic and Greek. Jesus himself certainly spoke Aramaic in Gethsemane and thus would not add the Greek "Father" to the Aramaic "Abba." It seems that Mark, who loved to report original Aramaic expressions and who alone tells us that Jesus cried "Abba," added ὁ Πατήρ to it for the sake of his Greek readers. This had probably been done before when the Gethsemane story was told. Thus, we may assume, "Abba Father" entered the language of the church and became an established liturgical expression which combined the word that was dear to the Jewish ear and tongue with its Greek equivalent. The thought of the apostle is that we sons who are now in full possession of all that we have in the Son and in the Spirit of the Son direct our "Abba Father" to God in our fulness of sonship.

7) Paul makes this most personal and individual by harking back to v. 1 and the thought that the minor heir differs from a slave in no respect. "Wherefore no longer art thou a slave (in the sense of v. 1) but a son" who has attained his majority; and that means "an heir through God," one who possesses and enjoys the spiritual fulness of the inheritance accorded by the testament (3:15, etc.). The inheritance involved is not yet the heavenly glory but the salvation that has been fully wrought out by the Son. He is the Heir Supreme, we are his joint heirs (Rom. 8:17).

There is no reason for raising a question in regard to the υἱοθεσία (v. 5) when this is taken in the sense of "adoption" and asking whether Paul has in mind the Jewish law regarding adoption or the Roman law. In this section Paul does not discuss the question as to how we become "sons" (by adoption) but discusses what the position of minor and of major sons is irrespective of the point as to how they become sons and heirs. Therefore it is better to translate this word "sonship" rather than "adoption." We thus consider irrelevant to the present connection the evidence of adoption adduced from the Old Testament: that of Esther by Mordecai, of Eliezer by Abraham, of the sons of concubines as legal sons, of Joseph's sons by Jacob to share equally with uncles, etc.

The phrase "through God" is, however, vital. Our present standing as heirs in possession and not merely in anticipation is due entirely to God. Διά views God

as the medium by whom this our high standing has
been effected; the explanation appears in v. 4 and 6:
God commissioned his Son and the Spirit of his Son.
Thus we are what we are today and have what we have
as heirs.

*Do the Gentile Christians in Galatia want to go back
into the old bondage?*

8) In contrasting the condition under the law
with that when one is freed from the law Paul used a
comparison (v. 1) which applied directly to the Jewish
Christians and indirectly (v. 3, "the elements of the
world") to the Gentile Christians. He now completes
this by doing the reverse, by speaking directly about
the Gentile and indirectly about the Jewish Christians.

Paul has said of the former that they, too, are
"sons" who are not minors (v. 6), that everyone is
an "heir" in possession of the inheritance and not
a slave (v. 7), i. e., a minor who does not differ from
a slave (v. 1). Just what had the position of the
Gentile Christians been before they became Christians? **Now at the time, not knowing God, you
slaved for those who by nature are not gods.**

Ἀλλά is merely copulative and adds the further fact
(R. 1185, etc.); it is *not* adversative, does not mean
"but." Τότε μέν, "then" or "at that time," is in contrast with νῦν δέ (v. 9), "but now." The condition of
the Gentile Christians before their conversion and during the whole time when the Jews were still in the position of minors is described by the constative participle,
"not knowing God." Οὐκ instead of μή makes the participial negation more clear-cut, R. 1137. It is a simple
fact, the Gentiles did not even know the true God; they
lived in utter pagan darkness and blindness. The Galatians will not question that fact.

In correspondence with that ignorance "you slaved for those who by nature are not gods." In this way these Gentiles were most miserable slaves; they slaved for idols. Note the likeness: under the Mosaic regulations even the Old Testament believers were in a position that was no better than that of a slave (v. 1); the Gentiles, who were ignorant of God, were outright slaves under idols. There was, indeed, a difference: the Mosaic law was divinely given while the false gods were human inventions; Jewish believers had sonship as minors, pagans had nothing. Yet a certain likeness existed regarding the point of slavery. The frightful condition of the slavery of the Gentiles was the fact that "they slaved (constative aorist, expressing the entire action as a unit) for those who by nature are not gods." They were imaginary beings, fictitious gods. The negative with the participle is the common μή, which, however, does not express only Paul's judgment; it negates the fact in the ordinary way.

All of the paganism found in the world today presents the same picture of the vilest and the most pitiful slavery. The pagan gods are not gods in any true sense of the word. The thought that Paul expresses a certain measure of excuse for the Gentiles because they did not know God contradicts Rom. 1:19-32, especially v. 19-21. The context is against the idea of an excuse, for the idea to be expressed is that of a most wretched and base condition.

9) But now, having come to know God, rather having come to be known by God, how are you turning back to the weak and beggarly elements for which you are wanting to slave over again?

The two participles are good examples of the ingressive aorist. We have trouble in conveying by translation what these two participles mean in distinction from the one used in v. 8. C.-K. 388 distinguishes: εἰδέναι = the knowing of an object which enters the per-

ception of a subject; γινώσκειν = the attitude or relation
of self to the object that is known. The latter is not
exact enough. The Lutheran fathers defined the latter
as *nosse cum affectu et effectu.* They also gave the
same meaning to the Hebrew *yada'*, "to know with
affect and effect," a knowing with approval and love,
with full acceptance, John 10:27; II Tim. 2:19. In
Matt. 7:23: "I never knew you," means I never knew
you in love as my own. God, of course, knew them
intellectually or mentally.

Note that both οὐκ εἰδότες and γνόντες have the identical
object, and these are direct objects. This is one of the
evidences for the view that in the case of the latter the
basic idea of knowing remains and is never altered to
signify an act only of the will: to choose or elect, a
synonym of ἐκλέγεσθαι. R., *W. P.*, expresses this prede-
stinarian idea when he comments on the passive participle "known by God": "God's elective grace." Does
Paul say that we *elected* God, and that we *were* elected
by God? The question answers itself.

"Rather having come to be known by God" is not
intended to cancel "having come to know God" nor to
correct the active by means of the passive. The addition is a fuller statement as to how the great change
with regard to the Gentiles came about. They got to
know God as their own in faith and in love but not
by their own ability and effort. God wrought upon
them so that he could know them as his own in love,
and so these Gentiles got to know God of whom they
had been totally ignorant before. The change of
voice in the two expressions is most effective. Luther
states it in a fine way: non *ideo cognoscuntur quia*
cognoscunt, sed contra, *quia cogniti* sunt, *ideo* cognoscunt.

The ingressive aorist participles speak of the start
the Galatians have made and thus leave room for the
question, "What about the present and the future until

the end?" "How are you turning back" = how is it that you are turning back? The first meaning of πάλιν is "back" (place), the second "again" (time); both are used here. Observe the two present tenses "are you turning — you are wanting": the defection was not yet accomplished, it had just recently begun. Are the Galatians turning back "to the weak and beggarly elements"? Here we have the same term that was used in v. 3 (which see), and the relative clause, "for which you are wanting to slave anew," attaches the same thought of slavery. These elements make slaves (passive in v. 3), and men are willing to slave for them (active here in v. 9). The Mosaic law formerly held the Jews to "the elements of the world," regulations about food, drink, and all kinds of material things and outward actions. They were no better than slaves. The Galatians were formerly in a similar state, the Gentiles among them being tied in slavery to their pagan religion with all its material, cheap earthly elements of sacrifices, temples, ceremonies, etc. God's Son bought them all free (v. 4), and the Galatian Christians, Jewish and Gentile, had, by faith in the Son, entered on this freedom, the great and complete sonship. Paul asks how they can possibly now turn back and become slaves again, actually willing slaves in a slavery they had so happily left.

By accepting the works of law of the Judaistic teaching these Gentile Galatians would only exchange their old pagan *stoicheia* for the abrogated Mosaic and and Jewish *stoicheia*. Paul places these *stoicheia* on the same plane and even calls them "weak," unable to bring man into the blessed relation with God, most certainly not when they are used as works of law after the manner of the Judaizers; in addition he calls them "beggarly" (poor in this sense), having no wealth to give such as the Son gives, keeping those who cling to these "elements" in servitude as slaves. Both adjectives have the strongest persuasive force, both state undeniable facts.

As in v. 8, "you slaved for those who are not gods," so here Paul again has the dative "for which you are wanting to slave." We need not identify the *stoicheia* with the pagan god although the idols were material, carved images and thus could be called "elements." It seems better to think of all that was connected with pagan worship, temples, sacrifices, ceremonies employing material objects just as "elements" of this kind were used in the Mosaic regulations. The difference that the elements in the Jewish regulations had been appointed by God while those in paganism were merely of human choice, is disregarded as being immaterial. John 4:21-24 helps us in the interpretation. Worship in spirit and in truth is devoid of all elements of the world in the sense in which Paul uses the term.

10) Paul's intensity of feeling is reflected in the lack of connectives for introducing v. 10 and 11. "The intense pulse beat of the agitated mind expresses itself in the short hammer blows of speech." Zahn. These are declarations and scarcely questions. **Days you are carefully observing and months and seasons and years! I am afraid about you; perhaps I have labored for you in vain!**

Here we see what success the Judaizers had had with the Galatians, which agrees with the present tenses used in v. 9; also in how far they had failed, for the Galatians had not yet accepted circumcision otherwise Paul would have mentioned this and most likely have named it first.

The terms used refer to Mosaic regulations. While all of them refer to time, the terms expressing time are not themselves the *stoicheia* but refer to the elements involved in these terms. Thus all labor with earthly things was forbidden on the Sabbath, the Jewish fasts forbade eating food, etc. Material, earthly things are always involved. "Days" are singled out by being placed before the verb; the compound verb is perfective: "you are carefully observing" (R. 613), and is an indirect middle: "for yourselves," R. 810. These are the days fixed by the Mosaic law, the Sabbaths, the fast and the feast days such as the Passover, the new moons, etc.

"Months" are often referred to new moons, but these are "days." Months signify entire months such as the seventh month Tisri, called Sabbath month since its first day was treated like a Sabbath; also Nisan, the first month which introduced the Jewish church year and was distinguished by the Passover.

The καιροί or "seasons," as distinct from "days" and "months" on the one hand and from "years" on the other, are the seasons of prayer and fasting prescribed by the law. The "years" refer to the sabbatical year and to the interval of years. It would be speculative to conclude that a sabbatical year was in progress at the time when Paul wrote. His meaning is that the Galatians had accepted the Jewish system as far as it was marked by these terms referring to time. The Galatians had been under Judaistic influence for only a brief period yet had begun the observance of time; how many Sabbaths, etc., they had already kept is immaterial. The tense of the verb means that the Galatians were launched upon this Jewish legalism.

11) "I am afraid about you; perhaps I have labored for you in vain!" J. M. Moulton, *Einleitung in die Sprache des Neuen Testaments,* 303, etc., offers the best explanation of μή as it is here used. Φοβοῦμαι has its direct object; the μή clause is paratactic, and μή = "perhaps," to which πῶς or ποτέ is commonly added. This is not a verb of fearing with μή meaning "lest" (our versions and the usual explanation); B.-D. 370, 1; R. 1169. The perfect indicative of the verb

"to labor" is used which fits the actual work done during the extent of time in the past. Note the emphasis on "in vain" which is placed before the verb, also on the phrase "for you" which is placed at the end and pointedly repeats the pronoun, "I am afraid about *you.*" Can it be that *for the Galatians* Paul has done all the hard work he has done entirely in vain? The verb denotes trying labor. Luther comments: *Lacrymas Pauli haec verba spirant.* The simple accusative in the sense of "I fear *for* or *about* you" (not "I fear you") is unusual.

Paul's work would certainly be in vain if all that it eventually accomplished would be to make the Gentile Galatians exchange their old pagan elements and observances for the old abrogated Jewish elements and observances. Neither brought justification and salvation. Worse than never having had salvation with its liberation from these "elements" is to have had it and then to give it up and to turn back to such "elements."

3. *Paul Admonishes the Galatians to Drop Their Legalism, 4:12-5:12*

From this point onward the epistle is admonitory yet with a difference: 4:12-5:12 deals with dropping legalism itself, while 5:13 to the end deals with the evidence that it has been dropped, the Christian life exhibiting this fact.

Personal appeal: the Galatians and Paul once and now

12) The break in thought is marked by the turn to admonition and thus also by the warm address "brethren" (see 1:11). The transition from the previous section is made in a natural manner by v. 8-11. **Be** (ever) **like me; for myself also** (became) **like you, brethren** — (this) **I beg of you!**

This is admonition in the form of direct, most personal petition: "I beg of you!" Note the durative present imperative which we express by adding "ever." The Greek uses γίνεσθαι, not as differing from εἶναι, but as expressing movement. It is generally recognized that in the ὅτι clause we must supply the aorist and not the present which loses the thought; hence not: "for I *am* as you *are*" (our versions), which contradicts the facts, but: "for I, too, *became* like you," i. e., I became as you yourselves once were. The view that we should construe together: "for I myself beg you as (once) you yourselves (begged me)," is peculiar; the Galatians never begged Paul.

The thought is striking, paradoxical, involving a chiasm. The Galatians were formerly Gentiles without the Jewish legal system. Paul was formerly a Jew under this Jewish legal system. Then he became a believer in Christ, dropped this legal system, and thus became like the Gentiles who never had it. But the Galatians, who were originally without the Jewish system (insofar as they were of Gentile descent) and, on becoming Christians, were still without this system, were at this late date beginning to adopt at least large parts of it (v. 10). Paul begs them not to do so but ever to be as he is who had dropped all of it. Once he became as they had been while they were pagan — without the Mosaic law. Now the Galatians are to reciprocate — after having taken up a part of that law under the influence of the Judaizers, they are to drop it entirely just as Paul had done.

But note that there is a plus on Paul's side. It was a revolutionary act for a bigoted Jew such as Paul once was to relinquish the Jewish regulations; it was a far slighter thing for the Gentile believers in Galatia to relinquish these regulations which had been only recently foisted upon them. Paul is begging them to do a thing that is far easier and much smaller than the one he had done.

Paul's appeal involves still more. He was the one who had converted the Galatians, who had brought them full Christian liberty, freedom from all material and earthly *stoicheia,* pagan as well as Jewish. He did that and could do it only as one who was himself wholly free. Think of the blessed fruits of Paul's arduous labors on the Galatians! Are they now to be lost (v. 11)? Will the Galatians now become unlike Paul to whom they owe everything? Do they intend to turn to the abrogated Judaism from which Paul had turned when salvation came to him? This personal relation of the Galatians to Paul is here touched upon in "like me — like you — I beg of you" and in the affectionate "brethren." Paul intends to make it prominent in what follows. He will contrast the love with which the Galatians first received him with the way in which the Judaizers try to gain the Galatians for themselves.

Without a connective Paul adds: **No wrong did you do me.** From his present petition Paul turns to the past, to the time when he first came to the Galatians. Note the aorist which accords with those that follow so that we must regard all of them in the same way. Paul has no complaint to make concerning the treatment he had received during his past relation with the Galatians. The negative statement to the effect that the Galatians had done Paul no wrong is in fact a litotes: they had treated him properly, how very properly he describes in the following. Because of the way in which the Galatians had hitherto treated Paul he feels that they will now heed his request (v. 12); they will surely not wrong him now.

Because of the constative aorist and its connection with what follows it seems unwarranted to interpret: by their defection the Galatians had in a way done Paul wrong, had shown themselves ungrateful (although, unlike the Corinthians, they had not turned against Paul personally), but that he did not want the Galatians to think that personal feeling and resentment moved him to take his readers to task, that he is jealous of his own honor. This would place the force of the aorist into the immediate past. It would also not be true. If Paul had anything approaching this in mind he would have said so and have done so with more than three words.

13) Paul refers to his previous connection with the Galatians in which they had done him no wrong: **but you know that because of illness of the flesh I preached the gospel to you at the first; and the temptation to you in my flesh you did not despise nor loathe; on the contrary, as an angel of God you received me, as Christ Jesus.**

This is the lovely treatment the Galatians accorded Paul when he first came among them. Instead of stating merely the facts Paul adds "you know," a touch of intimacy, friend speaking to friend about an experience shared together.

"Because" Paul was ill he preached to the Galatians on that first visit to them. All of the texts have the phrase with the accusative: "because of my bodily illness"; the proposal to change this to the genitive: "despite my bodily illness" ($\delta\iota\acute{a}$ as in Rom. 2:27; 4:11), is unwarranted. This proposal is due to the supposition that when Paul came from Paphos and landed at Perga and then continued on to Pisidian Antioch in Galatia, he had not intended to stop here but purposed to go on past this country.

But whither did he intend to go? We are told, "To Ephesus." A glance at the map shows that this conjecture is unconvincing; for if that had been his intention, he would have landed at Attalia and taken the road westward or would have sailed on to the harbor of Ephesus. Acts 13:13, 14 says that he landed at Perga and, instead of preaching here, went forthwith to Antioch and to the other Galatian cities. The wrong supposition is that sickness prevented Paul from going beyond Antioch; the right conclusion is that his sickness forced him to leave Perga at once and to hurry to Antioch. He could not remain and work in Perga which lay in the lowlands, he had to seek the higher elevations; Antioch and the Galatian region lay over 3,000 feet above sea level. Here Paul could hope to work even while he was sick, could gradually shake off his illness and then later on evangelize Perga — the very thing he did.

Thus, *because* of illness he preached in Galatia. This fact lends great support to Ramsay's conclusion that Paul's illness was malaria combined with severe headaches. He simply had to hurry to higher altitudes. In Perga he would have been completely prostrated; in the uplands of Galatia he would gradually recover. We have no reason to think of the thorn in the flesh, for this affliction, whatever it was, was permanent; the ailment that drove Paul from Perga to Galatia was not permanent.

Τὸ πρότερον is more definite because it has the article. It is comparative and thus implies at least one additional visit for the purpose of missionary work, and we do know of a second visit made by Paul (Acts 16:1-4). The idea that this epistle is the second evangelization cannot be entertained because it is addressed only to those who are already "brethren," already evangelized.

14) The translation *"my* temptation" (A. V.) follows a very inferior reading. The genitive is objective: "the temptation of (to) *you"* — "of you," the objective genitive. When this sick man appeared in Galatia with the gospel, the Galatians were tempted to

despise him. A sick man is never impressive and assuring. A sick man who claims miraculous powers and heals others while he himself remains sick would certainly raise serious doubts regarding any message he might bring. Yet the Galatians received Paul as if he were an angel of God, yea, as if he were Christ Jesus himself. Luke corroborates this regarding Antioch in Acts 13:43-48, when Paul's ailment must have been at its worst.

Paul uses a concentrated expression when he writes: "The temptation to you in my flesh you did not despise nor loathe." To do this with a temptation is to get rid of it, not by resisting and overcoming it, but by being overcome by it, by yielding to the loathing. The Galatians did the opposite. We thus do not make this accusative adverbial: "with respect to the temptation you did not despise nor loathe me." B.-P. 431 offers a mixture of two ideas: that the Galatians did not despise Paul in his illness, and that they did not yield to the temptation to despise him on account of his illness; but the construction is rather simple.

Does Paul intend that the aorist of ἐκπτύω, "to spit," is to be taken literally? This word occurs only here in the New Testament. Some prefer the literal meaning (B.-P. 380) and say that spitting was a sign of disgust or was a prophylactic to ward off evil spirits. Yet Homer uses the word in the sense of loathing, and Plutarch in the sense of rejecting. Since the metaphorical usage of the word is assured, we are satisfied; the more so when some say that spitting was an evidence that Paul's ailment was epilepsy, for the ancients expectorate at the sight of a person who is in an epileptic fit. On the question of epilepsy see II Cor. 12:7.

The Galatians received Paul "as an angel of God." Because of the genitive "of God" the term certainly means "angel," a supernatural being and not merely "messenger"; but "as" reduces the phrase to a comparison. How little is gained by reducing it to the meaning "messenger" we see from the addition "as Christ Jesus," which plainly recalls Matt. 10:40: "He that receiveth you receiveth me." Paul states it strongly because of the contrast: once the Galatians listened to the gospel that was coming from Paul's lips as if they heard the voice of an angel from heaven or the voice of Christ Jesus himself, but now they had started to drink in the false words of the Judaizers as if these were a divine message. The Galatians have had many followers.

15) **Where, then, is the felicitation of yourselves?** What has become of this counting yourselves blessed for having received the gospel from my lips? The genitive is objective. It was not possible that the Galatians deemed Paul blessed (subjective genitive); nor would such a question be fitting, nor could "me" be omitted.

So great was their feeling of being blessed by the gospel that Paul is able to add: **For I testify to you that, if possible, your very eyes you, having dug them out, would have given to me.**

This is the testimony Paul gives the Galatians when he thinks back of those early days he spent with them. These *carissima membra corporis* (Pelagius) they would have sacrificed for Paul to show their gratitude. The condition is one of past unreality, $\check{\alpha}\nu$ being omitted as is sometimes done in the Koine. "If possible" shows that Paul is speaking hypothetically only. The expression about digging out the eyes and giving them to another is surely proverbial for making a sacrifice of something that is really priceless. So greatly blessed the Galatians counted themselves that nothing that they had could be too great a price to offer in return.

From this statement some conclude that Paul's ailment was ophthalmia, a bad disease of the eyes, which made him look so loathsome that people would spit in disgust or in superstition at sight of him. But how would Paul be able to use the plucked out good eyes of others in place of his own diseased eyes? Are we to carry the idea to this absurd length? A man who had disgustingly diseased eyes would never have obtained permission from the elders of the synagogue to address the meeting, but in Antioch the elders even asked Paul to do so (Acts 13:15, 16).

This supposed eye disease is also connected with 6:11, as though Paul wrote with large script because he could not see well. See 6:11. But in Acts 13:9 Paul's eyes were certainly effectively used on Elymas. All is quite clear if Paul suffered from malarial attacks in Galatia which still left him periods of respite. Ἐξορύσσω is the verb commonly used to express blinding by piercing the eyeballs, thus "digging out."

16) Paul's emotion betrays itself in the ellipsis of his thought. At one time the Galatians counted themselves blessed for having Paul in their midst, but this is passed. Is the opposite now the case? **And so have I become your enemy by telling you the truth?**

Read this as a question; ὥστε means, "and so," R. 999. "An enemy of yours" is active, one who hates you, and not passive, one who is hated by you (C.-K. 459). The perfect tense "have I become" is used in the Greek fashion from the standpoint of the readers and refers to the time when they read this letter in which Paul tells them the truth. Will they then say: "Paul has become hostile to us"? Ah, but it is the best and the truest friend who honestly tells us the truth about ourselves even when he knows we shall not like it. False friends are the ones who hide such truth from us and do so in order to remain in our favor.

Some regard this statement as a declaration: "Wherefore I have become your enemy by telling you the truth." But that is not true (v. 19). If he intends to imply that the Galatians now consider him as being hostile to them, this thought is expressed far better by a question. The declarative idea is made more confusing when the inferior reading in v. 15 is adopted: τίς οὖν ἦν; *"What, then, was your felicitation of your-selves?"* and supplying in thought: "Nothing but superficiality," and then attaching: "Wherefore I have become your enemy." Paul regards the self-felicitation of the Galatians as being genuine; he even states the strongest reason for his so doing: that they were willing to sacrifice their eyes for him.

Again, Paul is not their enemy. Finally, the ὥστε clause cannot be construed across the intervening γάρ statement and attached to the question asked in v. 15. The reason: "I testify," etc., would be contradicted by any declaration that Paul is an enemy of the Galatians. Regard the sentence as a question, and all is readily understood.

17) Paul is the truest friend the Galatians have even as he is telling them the truth. But, in contrast, what about the Judaizers? **They are zealously seeking you in a way not honorable but want to lock you up in order that you may zealously seek them.**

Paul has characterized the Judaizers in a brief and succinct way in 1:7. Here he refers to them only by the plural verb ending, the indefinite "they." The slight is both marked and intentional. They more than deserve this treatment. Here the slight comports with the characterization that their whole action is "not honorable"; it is not done καλῶς, "honorably." The adjective means "good" only in a general way; specifically, especially when it is referred to persons and their actions, it signifies excellent, noble, admirable. To the Greek one is *kalos* who bears the character of a gentleman in our nobler use of that term.

Ζηλόω, when used with the accusative of persons =
sich um eine Person beeifern, to busy oneself about
somebody, "they zealously affect you" (A. V.), one
might say, "they court you." Paul had done the same
thing in a noble way, in a noble and an honorable cause
(the gospel, preached to the Galatians in Christian
love). Not so the Judaizers — their whole courtship
of the Galatians is decidedly "not honorable." To state
it in this negative way is really an understatement
which is the more damning because it is expressed only
in this way. Paul might have used a positive adverb;
if he had done so, any adequate adverb would have
been much harsher. Yet we should not think that Paul
intends to deal mildly with these people who ruin the
church. Quite otherwise. By using a positive adverb
Paul would invite the Galatians to challenge it by any
possible denial that might occur to their minds. This
he prevents by using the negative "not honorably"
which makes the Galatians think of what would be
honorable, of what the Judaizers should at least
have done.

Paul's psychological handling of the Galatians is
most masterly. We often make serious mistakes in
estimating the effect of our words upon the people we
seek to win from error; however excellent our intention may be, by our mistakes we cause them to cling
only the more firmly to their wrong ideas. Paul is a
good master to teach us. One might write a wonderful book on the way in which Paul handled the people
and the situations of his ministry.

With ἀλλά he does mention the positive. This is in
opposition to the entire clause and not merely to the
adverb "not honorably." The entire zealous concern
of the Judaizers is that "they want to lock up the
Galatians in order that the Galatians zealously seek
(only) the Judaizers." The present tenses say no
more than that the action is in progress. The Juda-

izers have not as yet accomplished their will. We have
noted similar tenses in the preceding; all of them are
significant as to this vital point. The object of these
men is dishonorable because of its pronounced selfishness. They want the Galatians completely for
themselves.

Whether we translate "lock up" or "shut out" we
see from the purpose clause, which names persons
("them"), that the infinitive indicates separation
(aorist: complete) from other persons: to lock up and
keep away from Paul and his assistants, thus, of
course, also from their influence and their teaching.
The Galatians had hitherto zealously sought Paul, had
listened only to him (see an example in Acts 13:43);
the Judaizers worked hard to substitute themselves
for Paul and his assistants. Since Paul was far away,
they hoped to succeed quite easily. While ζηλοῦτε
might be subjunctive by contracting οη like οε (R.
325, 342, 984), the Koine allows the indicative after
ἵνα so that the question of mode is here an unessential
problem.

18) The whole subject of zealously cultivating
people is now clarified by being expressed abstractly.
This is always the proper thing to do: brush all personal considerations aside and look at the principle by
itself. Clarity of thought is thus achieved. Otherwise
personal considerations becloud the issue. When he
does this Paul uses the passive since, as he has just
said, the Judaizers wanted to be sought zealously by
the Galatians to the exclusion of all others, of Paul in
particular. This passive not only turns the thought
so as to take in being sought besides seeking (being
sought involves someone who is seeking); it enables
Paul to make an application to the Galatians and to
himself in the simplest and the briefest way. Principle
and immediate application are thus joined in a

few telling words, the quintessence of thought that
penetrates fully.

**Now it is honorable to be zealously sought in an
honorable thing at all times.**

The matter is stated abstractly. We see that it is
true beyond question. But note the implication in the
passive. When somebody seeks us zealously in a dishonorable way, this being so sought is a reflection on us
who permit ourselves to be sought thus. The dishonor-
ableness of the seekers casts dishonor upon those
sought. They must not imagine that they remain
honorable. It is honorable for them only when
they are being zealously sought in an honorable
thing, which will naturally include an honorable way.

The Galatians may apply this to Paul: he had
sought them in an honorable thing, i. e., in the gospel
which is ever supremely honorable. The fact that the
Galatians have been sought thus by Paul and are still
so sought by him is, indeed, blessed and honorable.
Turn it around: The fact that Paul is sought by the
Galatians in the gospel is honorable for him. We
may also think of the delegation the Galatians had
sent to Paul, which caused the writing of this
epistle. But add the reverse, what this means to
the Judaizers and the Galatians. All these applica-
tions become almost automatic once the principle itself
is clearly stated.

It is most unexpected and thus of arresting
force when Paul adds: in an honorable thing — "at
all times." Certainly, "at all times"! At one time
to be sought in an honorable thing, at another time
in one that is not honorable — need we say what this
means? It is as yet stated in general terms but is
food for serious applicatory thought for the Galatians and for us today.

But this matter of being sought applies not only
to the Galatians whom Paul seeks and whom the

Judaizers seek; it applies also to Paul and to the Judaizers. The latter, Paul himself has said, wanted to be zealously sought by the Galatians. Paul makes the application only to himself. He does it in a startling way by suddenly introducing himself and the Galatians into this point of constancy, "always." Yes, always **and not only when I am present with you.**

In a flash Paul makes the Galatians see themselves. He was the one who was once so zealously sought by them when he labored in their midst. He was the one whom they should ever seek because of the honorable thing he honorably brought them. But now that he had left them to pursue his honorable work elsewhere, what had they done? They had begun to listen to men who dishonorably wanted the Galatians to seek them to the exclusion of Paul. Is Paul no longer to be honorably sought by the Galatians? Is his mere absence to end their honorable course?

One must feel what καλός means to the Greek in order to appreciate the turns Paul gives to this word as adverb, adjective, noun. It is typically Pauline. He balances all on the point of moral excellence, nobility, and honor. Will this fade the moment Paul turns his back? Is this so shallow in the Galatians that constancy is so soon at an end? Ἐν with the substantivized infinitive is one of the common ways of expressing "when," and πρός with persons is the face-to-face preposition.

The Judaizers were proselyters; they merely invaded the young churches that had already been founded in order to appropriate them for themselves. Instead of being καλόν, this was meanly, despicably κακόν ("base"). They zealously sought and affected their victims, courted them in every way, clung to them like leeches. The proselyters of today continue this type. Ζηλοῦσθαι is not a middle that is equal to little more than the active; the New Testament affords

no support for such a middle. The form is passive.
The true preachers of the gospel and all true believers
are also filled with a fervent missionary spirit that
earnestly seeks to save the lost. This differs from all
proselyting by its unselfishness, by its purity of motive,
by its spirit which truly reflects the love of Christ. We
see this difference in this epistle and also in Second
Corinthians.

19) Zealously seeking the Galatians is not the
half of it. Paul's concern is like that of a mother, as
if he were giving birth to the Galatians anew, suffering all the pains a second time. Although the Galatians have begun to turn to the Judaizers, Paul's heart
remains constant and true. Yea, their defection
causes him to suffer these pains anew, to suffer them
for the life of the Galatians. This is the acme of love
and constancy. Few more touching passages have been
written.

**My little children of whom I am again in travail
until Christ be formed in you, I would even be present with you now and change my voice because I am
perplexed in regard to you!**

The figure of the mother in travail advances the
thought of zeal for the Galatians; by making this a
second travailing Paul illustrates his unchanged heart:
he would do over again all that he had once done for
the Galatians. Yet the figure does not remain with the
thought that has already been expressed, it extends to
the new thought of pain, for the verb means to undergo birth pains. This also is included, that the Galatians
are making the maternal heart of Paul suffer all the
birth pains a second time, something which no offspring ever does in nature. When a babe is born, it
does not know what pain its birth causes, but these
Galatians have already been born, and they should, indeed, know that unnecessarily, unnaturally they are
causing Paul to suffer all these pains over again in even

a more severe way. But he is ready to suffer so if only Christ be formed in the Galatians by this new ordeal he is undergoing.

The claim is unwarranted that, because Paul ordinarily uses τέκνα, "children," he cannot use the diminutive τεκνία here, where not only the best texts have it, but where also the context so plainly requires this tender "little children." Yet Paul does not use "babes" as though the Galatians were coming to birth for the first time. They have had that birth; what is now happening is something that should not be necessary, a second ordeal of this kind for Paul in connection with the Galatians. But what true mother would not undergo a second ordeal for her "little children" if it were required of her? The relative is masculine and is construed *ad sensum* with the neuter antecedent.

This is one of the rather numerous instances in which a figure is used for something that never happens in nature. Such figures are misinterpreted when they are interpreted as though they were to be understood in the common way. Their very force lies in what may be called their unnaturalness, here the fact that Paul has to suffer birth pains all over again for the Galatians. Why did they compel Paul to do this? Another, moved by thought for himself, might merely abandon them and refuse such second suffering, but not Paul. The Galatians were "my little children" to him. He had brought them forth as a mother in travail. Children can have only one mother. Behold how Paul reaches out to the Galatians in order to draw them to his heart with the most tender love! All the connotations of the figure grip and hold one.

Paul is not dominated by the figure but dominates it and says, not that he is giving birth to the Galatians a second time as though their spiritual life had ceased, and they were to receive it a second time, but that he is in birth pains "until Christ be formed in you." Keep the reality which the figure merely serves to illustrate. This clause is no longer figurative, it is simple reality and is placed beside the figure in order to prevent our turning the figure in a wrong direction. By inculcating trust in ceremonial works of law the Judaistic error was taking Christ out of the hearts of the Galatians, and Paul's strong efforts in this epistle, which wrench his heart like travail pains, sought to put Christ back into the hearts of his little children.

The tense is important, it is an aorist: "be completely formed in you," i. e., so that no Judaistic ceremonialism will ever affect them, that they will ever be immune. The verb itself is expressive, for μορφή is always the form which expresses the essence, the inner reality; it is never a mask or an assumed form which one may lay aside. All that Christ really is Paul is at great labor and pains to have formed in the hearts of the Galatians. The unnamed agent in the passive need not be Paul, for this is really the Spirit, yet he ever uses the gospel for this and thus the true preachers of the gospel; these may thus be considered as means or as agents.

We see what this verb means when we compare pas-pages such as Rom. 8:29: we are finally to be σύμμορφοι with Christ in glory, "to be conformed with him"; even our vile body is to be σύμμορφον, formed like the glorious body of Christ, Phil. 3:21. There is no need to extend the force of this verb. Paul is not speaking of our conduct which is, of course, also to be comfortable to Christ in holy living and abundance of good works. This subject is considered later in the epistle (5:13-6:10). Here Paul deals with faith as embracing Christ, him fully, him alone.

20)   No dash or hiatus is needed, (R.V., American Committee, and others). Omit the relative clause for a moment, and the close connection appears: "My little children, I would be present with you," etc. It is anomalous to suffer birth pangs when children are far away. Paul also labors to have Christ brought to full form in the Galatians and is at a disadvantage by being so far away from them, unable to hurry to them. If he were with them he could change his voice so as to meet their need in the most perfect way; as it is, he labors under a handicap, he must secure his information about the Galatians at secondhand, cannot be perfectly sure of meeting all their inmost thoughts, and must resort to writing, which is never as effective as the voice. What prompts Paul to say this is his intense love which has already been so tenderly expressed.

The imperfect is the tense of politeness (R. 919, a good discussion) like our English "I would" and refers to a strong present desire. Just what the force of δέ is puzzles everybody. It is probably no more than a slight intensification: *ich moechte doch jetzt bei euch sein.* An adversative idea seems too strong although Paul's desire to be with the Galatians is possibly to be placed in contrast with the zealous seeking of Paul on the part of the Galatians only when he was present with them (v. 18). Regarding Paul's changing his voice R. 1199 remarks: "There never was a more nimble mind than that of Paul, as he knew how to adapt himself to every mood of his readers or hearers without any sacrifice of principle. It was no declaimer's tricks, but love for the souls of men that made him become all things to all men (I Cor. 9:22). He could change his tone because he loved the Galatians even when they had been led astray."

Ishmael — Isaac: bondage — freedom

21) It has been well said that, although he is at
a loss because he is so far away from the Galatians, the
fertile mind of Paul, in his attempt to separate them
from all legalism, finds another effective mode of approach. From personal appeal he turns to a clear
case that is recorded in Scripture, which is illustrative
of both bondage and freedom, the account of Hagar
and Ishmael and of Sarah and Isaac. To the subjective and personal Paul thus adds the Scriptural and
objective.

The use of this Scriptural account has been termed
a rabbinical argumentation by which Paul seeks to
turn the arguments of the rabbinical Judaizers against
themselves. But this is not an *argumentum ad homi-
nem,* not a turning of the Judaizers' guns against
themselves. The argument is not merely negative, it
is powerfully positive. Nor does Paul convert the history into an allegory. He uses the history, for only as
historical fact has it the power of conviction that Paul
needs. But this Paul does: he brings out God's own
thoughts that are embedded in this history as they
teach and instruct us Christians for all time. This is
far beyond the old or the new rabbis. It is divine
reality. How the Old Testament histories ought to be
read, not superficially for their mere externals, but for
their real content, Paul shows us in many places,
notably in Rom. 4 (Abraham), Rom. 5:12, etc. (Adam
and the patriarchs before Moses), also Gal. 3:16
(Abraham having the covenant hundreds of years
before Moses and the law came into existence).

The substance as well as the absence of a connective indicate the beginning of a new section. **Tell
me, you who want to be under the law, do you not
hear the Law?**

The question at the head of this exposition is
arresting. The Galatians and certainly those who

were becoming enamored of law as a means of salvation had heard the Law. But that is exactly to what Paul refers: hearing the Law and yet wanting to be under law. "Tell me," Paul says, "how this can possibly be." Whatever one may say about the old Jews (II Cor. 3:14, 15), the Galatians had at least learned to read the Torah without such a darkening, blinding veil. Distinguish between "under law" without an article and "the Law" with the article, here in the sense of the Torah, the Pentateuch, "Moses" (II Cor. 3:15; John 5:46). "Under law" is under law in general, a state which these Galatians were trying to achieve by getting to be under the Mosaic ceremonial system. One gets under law by means of some legal system or other.

The fact that "the Law" refers to the Pentateuch we see from what follows, namely the story of Hagar who lived long before the ceremonial law was given (3:17). Paul is citing one of the histories of the Pentateuch. The Books of Moses were constantly read in the synagogues; they were divided into *paraschas* or regular lections, the other Old Testament books were likewise divided into sections, their lections being called *haphtharas*. The early Christian congregations continued this practice of reading the Old Testament until the New Testament canon was gradually formed when lections were selected from these New Testament writings. We see no reason for excluding reference to these readings in the Christian assemblies, nor for intensifying "do you not hear" as meaning, "do you not understand?"

22) With γάρ Paul introduces the section he has in mind. **For it has been written** (see 3:10), **Abraham got two sons, one from the slave woman, and one from the free.**

Paul sketches briefly what is on record, all of it is well known. The aorist is punctiliar: "got two sons," not "had," which would require the imperfect. In the New Testament a παιδίσκη (John 18:17; Acts 12:13) is always a slave girl or woman; this must have been the position of Hagar (Deissmann, *Light*, etc., 186, and others). She is here contrasted with "the free woman" (the feminine adjective needing no noun). The fact that Hagar was not a wife, and that Sarah was, is not the point; but that one was a slave and the other free is. Thus the one son was a slave, the other free as was always the fact in such a case. The mother and not the father determined the status of the sons.

23) Continuative ἀλλά carries the sketch forward and is not adversative. **Now the one from the slave woman has been born in** (mere) **flesh fashion, but the one from the free by way of promise.**

First the status of the two mothers, then — still more important — the difference between the two births themselves. The one son was born in the ordinary, natural way, the other by a gracious, miraculous intervention of God. Κατά names the norm, the one norm we observe in all human births, ordinary copulation and its resultant conception and birth. Διά denotes means, in this case that special divine means which is God's promise. At the time of this birth both Abraham and Sarah were beyond the age of procreation, he was one hundred years old, she ninety and permanently sterile. Yet God promised them a son despite their age, and so "by way of promise" Isaac was born. Yet, instead of employing a simple aorist which would state the past, historical fact and seem to be sufficient, Paul uses the perfect "has been born," which is neither "was born" (A. V.), nor "is born" (R. V.). B.-D. 342, 5 notes that these two births still have their peculiar significance for us and that this is the reason for the tense; compare the perfect tense occurring in 3:18; Heb. 11:17; 12:3.

24) Matching this perfect is the periphrastic passive perfect: **Things of this character have been spoken as conveying** (also) **another meaning.** Ἅτινα is more than ἅ since it refers to a characteristic of the things mentioned (B.-D. 293,4) and hence does not mean "which things" (our versions) but "things of this nature or character," implying that the ones just mentioned belong to an entire class, that more of them are found in Scripture. This does not refer to the mere words penned by Moses but to the things themselves which are narrated by the words. All such things, thus also the ones here indicated, "have been spoken as conveying (also) something else," something that does not lie on the surface. The perfect tense (here periphrastic) means that all things of this nature permanently carry this additional meaning and convey it even to us when we contemplate properly the things thus spoken. Paul does not say that he gives such things their additional meaning, nor even that God does this. He says that because of their very nature such things have another thing involved in them, and whenever they are told they always have also this other meaning.

The verb contains ἄλλο, "something other," we need not say, "something different." For this "other" agrees, corresponds; it is not diverse, heterogeneous. The historical facts are like a shell that has its natural kernel and is not stuffed with a foreign substance. This "other" has always been, will always be included in the original historical facts. They are not an illustration for this "other," an illustration that Paul's mind has found. There is nothing adventitious about the whole matter. This "other" is also not an abstraction, for it, too, is as historical as the facts with which it agrees. The only difference is that the original events happened first and may thus be viewed by themselves. But when this "other" came to be, one can see that it is of the very same nature.

It does not seem adequate to call this "allegory" and to use the verb "allegorize" although this is quite generally done. Luther translates: *Die Worte bedeuten etwas,* which is nearer the truth. The rabbis were great allegorizers, namely inventors along this line. Rabbi Akiba found a mystical sense in every hook and crook of the Hebrew letters; but these were mere fancies. Philo, the past master of allegory, called what he found the spiritual sense. Wherever it suited him, he made free with the original historical data. One should know that only traces of Messianic ideas are retained by Philo, and among them are neither the person nor the name of the Messiah. The Alexandrines copied his method and carried it still farther. We have it even today.

We thus see at once that when Paul uses this verb he has in mind something that is far different from the method of interpretation devised by those ancient Jews and any of their followers. Their allegories dissipate the original sense of Scripture. The simplest and the plainest things no longer mean what is said about them but something the allegorizer's fancy distils from them. The ordinary reader is completely disconcerted; he finds that he cannot understand a thing in Scripture until the allegorizer offers him his distillation. There is an air of mystery, of profound learning, of deep spirituality about such allegorizing; but the most of it is mere fancy which is often unwholesome. The worst feature about it is the fact that the solid Scripture facts are turned into curling vapor.

An illustration is selected, a parable constructed in order to aid in presenting some fact. Both are legitimate and may be more or less successful. Allegory does the reverse; it takes a fact (a Bible statement or an account) and turns it into a picture of something else which is often no more than a fancy. This is really not legitimate and must be condemned in most cases. A type is different from all of these, for both type and antitype are firmly based on Scripture, the type being a miniature that is furnished in advance, the antitype the great major that follows. They are equally divine.

What Paul presents is akin to type and antitype, but only akin. Hence also he does not speak of a type. All types are prophetic; Paul is not presenting prophecy and fulfillment. Paul does not go a step beyond the Scriptural facts; what he does is to point out *the same nature* in both: mere flesh in Hagar's birth and thus slavery — the same slavery in all those whose birth is no better; divine promise in Sarah's birth and thus liberty — the same liberty in all whose birth is connected with promise. Thus in v. 24-28 Paul identifies: Hagar = Sinai = the mother of all who do works of law; Sarah = Jerusalem from above = the mother of all believing the promise. Yet in v. 29 Paul only likens: "even as then — thus also now." In the case of things of the same nature one may do either, identify them: this is that; or liken them: as this, so that. Paul does both in this paragraph.

The word γάρ begins to explain how the Scriptures have spoken with another, an added meaning in their account about the two sons of Abraham. The two mothers, the one the slave woman who has given birth only in fleshly fashion, the other the free woman who has given birth by way of promise alone, present this *allo* or "something other." **For these are two covenants.** Paul at once characterizes the first and then identifies it with the one mother, the slave woman Hagar: **the one from Mount Sinai, giving birth into slavery, which as such is Hagar.**

The feminine "these" is not due to attraction to the feminine predicate, for the women themselves are referred to, of course, in so far as they have given such diverse births, i. e., the two women as mothers. "These *are*," Paul says, "two διαθῆκαι," expressing the thought intensively because slavery *is* in the nature of the birth of the one, being only a fleshly birth, and liberty *is* in the nature of the birth of the other, being wholly by way of promise. The copula should not be stressed beyond Paul's meaning which he makes plain in what follows.

Paul describes only the one woman and does not follow "the one" by formally adding a coordinate statement regarding "the other"; he lets his readers do this. In v. 26 he at once advances to "the Jerusalem above" without first identifying this with Sarah. This is not a grammatical diversity as though the intervening statements have thrown Paul off the track; this is the advance of the great thought itself.

The translation "covenants" says too much. The Sinaitic legal system was a divine "disposition," something that God placed or appointed for the Jewish nation, and is thus paired with the divine promise; the German *Verfuegung* is a good rendering. Paul describes the one with a phrase, a participial modifier, and a relative clause. "From Mount Sinai" = from this place where Israel received its whole system of law. To name the place is also to indicate the late date (3:17) and the character of this "disposition" as law. This brings to mind all that Paul has already said on the inability, the inferiority, the temporal nature of this law in contrast with promise (3:17, etc.). Here all of this is concentrated in the participial addition: "giving birth into slavery."

The idea of motherhood continues. The law produces children, but ever only slaves "for slavery," and in this sense the law "is Hagar," who, as a slave woman, could do no more. Note that ἥτις is like ἅτινα and adds the note of character: "which (disposition or covenant) as such." Not Mount Sinai in general or even the Sinaitic law as law is Hagar but this system which brings forth only "for slavery." In regard to this point and to this alone the identification is made. As we have said, they are of the same or of an identical nature and produce mere slaves.

25) Textual evidence as well as meaning support the reading τὸ γὰρ Σινὰ ὄρος ἐστὶν ἐν τῇ Ἀραβίᾳ, **For the Sinai mountain is in Arabia.** This is not a trivial geographical remark but a significant statement. Arabia includes the Sinaitic peninsula. Hagar went south to Beersheba, and Ishmael dwelt in Paran, the territory near Sinai. Sinai is thus connected with Hagar's son and his descendants, and Arabia, in which Sinai is located is *not* connected with the promise as all Bible readers know. Not in the promised land but in the Arabian desert, which separated Israel from Canaan when it was at Sinai, was the law given. This law was thus not the fulfillment of the promise given to Abraham. The very place where the law was given, Arabia, Sinai, connected it with the slave woman Hagar and with her son Ishmael, born "to slavery." Paul's statement that Sinai lies in Arabia thus justifies the identification of Hagar with Sinai, with the law and slavery.

Our versions have unfortunately translated the reading τὸ Ἄγαρ, the R. V. even the one that has δέ instead of γάρ. But this means that the *word* Hagar = Mount Sinai. Yet the word Hagar means *se separavit, reliquit,* "flight," and Sinai means "connected with the coast strip *Sin*" and is used to designate the peak *Musa;* see Ed. Koenig, *Woerterbuch* (Hebrew). Thus neither in sense nor only in sound is there a play on the words. All the labor spent on establishing a connection of this kind has netted very little; nor is it clear how Paul could resort to anything that is so superficial. When Paul puts the name "Sinai" before "mountain" he may intend to emphasize the name "Sinai" in contrast with the other name and the other place, namely "Jerusalem."

For he continues: **and is in one row** (or line) **with the present Jerusalem, for she is in slavery together with her children.**

The original military meaning "to be in line with," to be in the same row with, is quite expressive (M.-M. 612) although some prefer the modified meaning "to correspond with" ("answers to," our versions). Sinai is in the same line with the present Jerusalem. The two march together step by step. This is not merely the Jerusalem of Paul's day but the Jerusalem of the legalistic Jews of all ages including the present. The idea of the mother is retained: she and her children, all whom she has brought forth in her legalism. "For" explains: she with all her children are "slaves," do nothing but slaving. We may say that she is a very Hagar in all the births she gives. Hagar — Sinai — the present Jerusalem are all just one on the score of giving birth to nothing but slaves.

But Hagar is not merely a slave like any other slave, she is a slave in Abraham's family. So also Sinai has Moses who wrote all that he wrote concerning Christ (John 5:46, 47) and who himself was a type of Christ (Deut. 18:15, 18). So also the present Jerusalem has this same Moses with his writings about Christ and eventually has come to have the whole Old Testament. In spite of all this connection with the gospel the story is one of slavery, is stamped entirely with Hagar and not with Sarah.

Paul speaks only historically. While no promise, while only flesh was connected with the birth of

Ishmael, it would be hasty, indeed, to conclude that both Hagar and Ishmael disbelieved, spurned the promise of the covenant made with Abraham, and, when they left for Arabia, were lost spiritually. Remember that Ishmael received the covenant sign, circumcision, from Abraham (Gen. 17:23). Not from Ishmael was the Christ to descend; the line of descent went through Isaac, Jacob, Juda, David, etc. But this is only the line of descent. All the other sons of Jacob, for instance, and so also the nations that descended from them were to have the Messianic blessings of that line by faith. Even as Abraham, the head of that line, had it only by faith, so Hagar and Ishmael were not excluded from this faith. The home of Abraham was filled with gospel promise that appealed for faith.

So it was with Sinai and its Moses, so it was with Jerusalem which even had its promise. There were always the Old Testament saints, the true believers. Theirs is the story of faith. The Messianic line ran through a succession of individuals, among them were the former pagan, Rahab, a Canaanite, and Ruth, a Moabitess. This line itself was heavily stained with sin. As the line advances in the individuals who formed it, thousands of believers and by no means only Jews held to the promise by faith. Distinguish this succession of hosts of believers from the Messianic line as such. Down to the time when Christ was born we see these believers. Forget not the Magi who followed the star and worshipped the newborn King of the Jews. And yet for even these there was Sinai with the effect described in v. 1-4; they were only minor heirs, no better, as Paul has said, than slaves.

That is why Sinai, located in Arabia, is here connected with the present Jerusalem. The promise to which all the believers held did not come from Sinai, only the law came from there, the law which made even the believers only minor heirs. Although the present Jerusalem was located in the promised land and should, therefore, with all her children have been marked by faith as minor heirs, this Jerusalem clung only to Sinai, only to the law, only to works of law as though it, too, were located in Arabia, the land that was devoid of promise.

The Ishmaelites eventually lost the promise and the faith, and the present Jerusalem with her children, i. e., all those Jews who bore her distinctive stamp of Sinai and law alone, were no better than the Arabian Ishmaelites: "She is in slavery together with her children." The great facts are plain once they are pointed out. The history is composed of the facts; there is no allegory about them. The *allo* presented is only the real inwardness of the facts. The superficial reader sees only the surface, but there is much more to see, the facts in their full reality.

26) **But the Jerusalem above is free, who as such is mother of us.** "The present Jerusalem" implies another that also deserves the name Jerusalem but in a higher sense; this is "the Jerusalem above." The name of no other city is mentioned as having a higher counterpart. "Jerusalem" = city of peace. The capital city of the Holy Land was to be the center and the source of heavenly grace and peace for the chosen nation, a type and symbol of heaven itself which is thus also called "the new Jerusalem" where all that the earthly Jerusalem was to be reaches its consummation and final realization. But the Jerusalem that is "now," as Paul sees it in its long history up to the very time of his writing, had failed of its spiritual purpose. Hear the cry of Jesus: "O Jerusalem, Jerusalem!" Matt. 23:37, 38. Soon it was to sink into ruin. Paul places it in the same

row with Sinai. It no longer knew the promise, it knew only the law. Its own significant name testifies against it. But that significance abides in "the Jerusalem above." "Now" and "above" do not seem to form a perfect contrast. In order to obtain it we should not introduce the idea of a *future* Jerusalem. An ordinary contrast is not intended. For "now" points to the depth to which the earthly Jerusalem has sunken; the one "above" is ever the same, namely higher, spiritual. "The Jerusalem now" has descended to a Sinai, a Hagar, a slaving mother of slaving children.

Motherhood is the thought connected with both Jerusalems, the one mother slaving and bringing forth slaving children, the other mother being free, all her children being free like herself. This second mother is therefore not the *"new* Jerusalem" (Rev. 21:2) which is heaven with its blessed inhabitants. "Our mother" has her children here on earth and is thus herself on earth where she can be a true mother to them. Her name is "the Jerusalem *above.*" The other mother is identified with an earthly city which is in line with an earthly mountain; not so "our mother." The one is engrossed with the law, which Paul has said deals with "the weak and beggarly (earthly) elements" (see v. 3, 9); the other is "above" anything of this kind, works with promise and the gospel, all her children are spiritual. She is thus bound to no city or place (John 4:21-23). Call her the Christian Church on earth.

On ἥτις, "who is such," see the two relatives occurring in v. 24. In "mother of us" Paul includes himself plus the Galatians, whether they be former Jews or former Gentiles. Do not overlook the appeal that lies in "our mother." Will the Galatians desert their free, noble mother who has born also them as free men and will they adopt this Hagar-mother with her slavery? What folly especially for Gentiles who had been brought to the Christian Church apart from Judaism!

27) Paul corroborates what he has just said about "the Jerusalem above" being "our mother." In Isa. 54:1 the prophet addresses Israel after the Messiah, the great *Ebed Yahweh,* has died and risen again (chapter 53). Paul follows the LXX. **For it has been written (3:10):**

Rejoice, thou sterile that dost not bear!
Break forth and shout, thou that dost not travail!
For many more the children of the desolate than
of her having the husband.

The prophet is speaking of the Christian Church as it appears after Christ's redemption and exaltation. He bids her be happy and shout because of her many children. But he uses imagery that is taken from Sarah and Hagar, the very two who are here used by Paul, and the chief point of this imagery is motherhood. Paul's quotation is not merely apt; the Scriptures themselves are the source which provides him with the identification of Hagar with Sinai and Jerusalem and of Sarah with something higher.

"The deserted" and "she having the husband" are expressions that allude to Sarah and Hagar, but to these two at the time when Sarah gave Hagar to Abraham. We should not, however, translate *die Vermaehlte.* This ἀνήρ, "husband," was not Hagar's. She was not even a concubine. This was Sarah's husband, Hagar "had" him only for the purpose of copulation. Sarah thought she could get an heir by such proxy. Human scheming never fulfills the promise. The whole proceeding was useless. But it is highly interesting to find Jerusalem prefigured by Hagar. It is not some other city, it is the Jerusalem which should have been the holy city, should have been Sarah but

made herself nothing but Hagar. The episode with
regard to Hagar transpired in Abraham's household.
It was Sarah who substituted Hagar for herself and
secured no heir. Yet God's promise was carried out
despite all this.
     We thus see what the "sterile" one means. It is
confusing to say that this does not mean that she had
no children before this time. The idea back of this
view is the thought that there were many saints in
the Old Testament, many long before the Christian
Church came into being. But all these Old Testament
saints — and these include also Gentile believers, think
of Rahab and of Ruth — were spiritual Isaacites, a
part of Sarah's many children of promise *after* Sarah's
sterility was turned into fertility.
     "Thou sterile one" is even re-enforced by the appo-
sitions, the substantivized present participles: "thou
that dost not bear," "thou that dost not travail." Present participles describe conditions that last a long
time. The clause about Sarah's many children who
were at last born to her through Isaac shows that
the sterility ended. We know how it ended in Sarah's
old age by a miracle of grace. Blass observes that
the LXX regularly used οὐ with participles when it
translated the Hebrew *lo*; B.-D. 430, 3 thus lists
this negative as a Hebraism. Moulton notes that in
the Greek individual concepts are negatived by οὐ (*Einleitung* 366; see also 205). R. 1138, etc. We may
translate: "thou non-bearing one," "thou non-travail-
ing one."
     The contrast is only between Sarah and Hagar, the
present Jerusalem and the Jerusalem above. But in
the case of Sarah it includes all her spiritual children
until the end of time, in the case of Hagar only those
who slave with her in the present Jerusalem. We
should keep to what Paul says and not lose ourselves
in self-made expansion regarding Hagar. Thus

Sarah's children are, indeed, "many more." Μᾶλλον ἤ
is used with the positive as a substitute for the comparative (R. 663).

28) **Now we on our part, brethren, are, in accord with Isaac, children of promise.** This is the
complement to the statement that "the Jerusalem above
is our mother." The address "brethren" is significant.
All these children of the sterile Sarah are, indeed,
brethren, all one family, thus also Paul and the Galatians are brethren. Paul reaches the climax of his instruction and thus draws the Galatians to himself in
this great brotherhood of freedom. The silent contrast implied in the emphatic "we" are the Judaizers,
children of the present Jerusalem.

But now Paul advances from Sarah to Isaac and
does this with the κατά phrase. This means more than,
"as Isaac was," more than, "as brothers of Isaac,"
we as he (our versions). Isaac, like Abraham and
Sarah, is not only a product of, he is the channel of the
promise. In accord with him we are "children of
promise," its spiritual product. "In accord with
Isaac" is the opposite of "in accord with Ishmael," i. e.,
"in accord with flesh" (v. 23), mere physical nature. It
is "promise" full of divine grace, that is "above."
"Children of promise" is a practical compound like
"children of light" and similar combinations, the genitive being ethically qualitative. In Paul's time the
promise was already fulfilled in Christ. Children of
promise are those who hold to the promise and its
heavenly contents by faith.

29) Paul completes his account by a reference
to a further portion of Scripture in which the main
point is the command to cast out Hagar and Ishmael
because the latter is not to be a co-heir with Isaac.
**But even as then the one born in accord with flesh
kept persecuting the one** (born) **according to spirit,
so** (it is) **also now.**

Instead of continuing with the identification, Paul uses a simple comparison: "as then — so now." The idea of birth is retained, for both Ishmael and Isaac are indicated by the vital difference obtaining in their birth, "the one born in accord with flesh," "the one according to spirit." The two phrases are such direct opposites that we cannot follow our versions when they capitalize "Spirit." The idea that the Holy Spirit was especially involved in Isaac's birth does not appear in Scripture; all we know is that his birth was miraculous. Flesh and Holy Spirit are not proper contrasts, for in such a contrast flesh would be too highly elevated.

There is a reference to Gen. 21:9. When Isaac was weaned, Ishmael made sport of him, *lachte ihn aus* (Delitzsch), not in mere playfulness but in scorn of Isaac's being the heir. That this attitude was due to Hagar is easy to imagine; we also see why Sarah proceeded to be rid of both Ishmael and Hagar. When Paul calls Ishmael's action "persecuting" and even uses the durative imperfect, some think this is too strong a term for the word used in Gen. 21:9, that Paul must be following the late Jewish tradition which tells of Ishmael's shooting arrows at Isaac in apparent playfulness but with murderous intent. Paul is excused for doing this sort of thing because it is no more than *harmlose Ausspinnungen*.

Now tradition did report some facts that are not otherwise recorded; their use in New Testament Scripture is legitimate. But these late fancies about Ishmael are not true tradition. When Paul writes "kept persecuting" he gives full expression to what was involved in the action of Ishmael. Paul does this because of the parallel that the same thing is continuing now; he that is born in accord with the flesh still keeps persecuting him who is born in accord with spirit.

The debate as to whether Paul refers to the persecution instigated by the hostile Jews against the Christians, or whether he has in mind the Judaizers in Galatia, seems unnecessary. Why restrict the reference to the Judaizers? Why modify the verb "persecute" so as to mean only opposing the gospel? The great instigators of persecution during the apostolic time were undoubtedly the Jews. While we read nothing about outright bodily attacks on the part of the Judaizers, yet, as in Corinth, these certainly attacked Paul and his helpers by slander and vilification.

But any distinction between Jews and Judaizers is beside the mark; the real point is that those who, like Paul and the Galatians ought to be children of Sarah, born of promise, spiritual offspring of Isaac, by their very action showed themselves to be Hagarites, Ishmaelites by repeating in full and complete form the early act of Hagar's slave son. Yet Paul does not mention this in order to comfort the Galatians. This whole section is not written for comfort.

30) Paul writes in order to induce the Galatians to hold to their liberty since they were born spiritually to freedom and to reject the yoke of slavery the Judaizers were trying to impose on the Galatians. That is why he adds: **Yet what says the Scripture?** What does it say to this day, present tense? What does it say in its record that we may today apply to those Ishmaelitic actions from which we are made to suffer? This is more direct than if Paul had said, "has been written," the perfect tense with present implication which is so often used in quotation. **Cast out the slave woman and her son, for the son of the slave woman shall in no way inherit together with the son of the free woman.**

Paul quotes Gen. 21:10 with slight modification, which relates the demand that Sarah made on Abra-

ham when she saw the action of Ishmael that had been
inspired by Hagar. God himself endorsed Sarah's
demand and bade Abraham act upon it. Hagar and
Ishmael were cast out. This verdict stands in the case
of all who have no higher birth than Ishmael's. It
stands in the case of "the present Jerusalem." This
present Ishmael shall not inherit in company with
(μετά) the son of the free woman, the Isaac of promise,
the believers in that promise. Oὐ μή is used with the
subjunctive and with the future indicative. The aorist
is decisive.

Von Hofmann and Zahn interpret this as an order
that the Galatians are to throw out the Judaizers. But
God alone decides who shall inherit. This Scripture
passage means much more to the Galatians and to
us today. If the Galatians and we forsake the
gospel freedom for the slavery of the law and legalism
we make ourselves one with Hagar and Ishmael so
that: "Throw them out — they shall not inherit!"
becomes God's verdict on us. "God forbid!" should
be our answer to that. This is the real object of Paul's
exposition.

31) **Wherefore, brethren, we are not children
of a slave woman but of the free woman.**

Paul draws the conclusion from his entire discussion, the conclusion at which he and the Galatians
ought to arrive: no slave mother for us (no article;
no mother of this kind) but only the one free mother
(the article specifying her). While the same thought
is expressed in v. 26 and 28, we here have the
negative and the positive side by side and in the
simplest form. This befits the final statement. This
is what we (Paul and the Galatians) are; now you
Galatians stand firm as you are. The reading διό is
textually well assured. A few other variants have
about the same meaning except δέ which commends itself neither textually nor in meaning.

5:1) The variants are found also in this verse. The one which starts with a relative, and the one which inserts a relative pronoun lack manuscript attestation and stand discredited already on this score. The latter is translated by the A. V. In regard to inner evidence we might state that any wording that has relative clauses would be far weaker than a wording that has brief independent sentences, especially here where Paul concludes the whole subject. If this verse starts with a relative clause, the clause may belong to the preceding: " . . . but of the free woman by means of the freedom with which Christ did free us." If it is drawn to the following, we get the arrangement found in our A. V.

Associated with this is wavering regarding the point at which Paul closes the paragraph. Some begin the new paragraph with 4:31; some with 5:1; we with 5:2. The distinctive terms freedom and slavery continue through to 5:1 and stop there. A new line of thought begins with 5:2; all the characteristic terms used in 4:21-5:1 are absent in 5:2, etc.: slave, free, mother, birth, children, inheritance. This means that the great paragraph is not intended to be didactic but admonitory. All that is didactic is only to be the basis for the call: "Stand fast, therefore!"

Thus we have the ringing declaration: **For freedom Christ did set us free.** For nothing less. This is not a dative of means that is merely cognate to the verb: "With freedom Christ freed us," i. e., merely emphasizes the verb: "Christ *really* did free us." This is the *dativus commodi*: "for freedom" he freed us (R. V. margin) so that we should have, maintain, exercise, enjoy this freedom. Hence also the article is used. We are children of the free woman (4:31), and for the very freedom involved in this our birth Christ freed us.

Christ is not mentioned until this point. The paragraph could not end without a mention of him. All that has been said about Abraham, Sarah, Isaac, freedom over against slavery, and its application to the Galatians and to us, has its consummation in Christ. As befits the conclusion, the terms are now literal. Christ is not presented as a parent, he is our great spiritual Liberator. The aorist "he freed us" is to indicate the historical fact. But the pronoun "us" (Paul and the Galatians) makes us think not only of Christ's redemption on the cross but of this together with its saving effect in the hearts of the Galatians.

For freedom Christ *freed* us! Shall this blessed act be annulled, this freedom be lost? Never! **Keep standing fast accordingly!** Ever and always as the durative present tense implies. None can set themselves free; this is the work of the Liberator alone. But after we are once set free and endowed with the spiritual power of that freedom, our Liberator moves us to exercise that power. He is now doing that for the Galatians in these words of power through his apostle.

How this positive command is to be understood the accompanying negative states: **and stop enduring again a yoke of slavery.** The verb is middle, "to hold up for oneself," "to endure," and is here construed with the dative (Moulton, *Einleitung* 93; it is often construed with the genitive). R., *W.P.*, translates, "ensnare by trap" and speaks of "trying to lasso," but that is scarcely the meaning of this word. Perhaps it was suggested to Robertson by our versions which translate, "be entangled." A yoke galls, and thus one endures it. The present imperative is conative according to Moulton 203, etc., "do not try to endure"; R. 851, etc., is better, "stop enduring." The present imperative is often used when an action has been begun and is to cease. That is the case here. The Galatians had begun their Judaizing and were to stop enduring such a yoke.

Note the absence of the articles: the Galatians are to tolerate no yoke of any kind of slavery. They are to keep clear of anything of this nature. The genitive is appositional, "yoke" is figurative, but "slavery" is literal. Paul has in mind the Judaistic legal slavery but broadens his expression so as to include this in slavery in general; he also includes the yoke of paganism which the Gentile Galatians once bore.

Paul's admonition and urging are most effective because they are based on the strongest grounds, which reach back even to Abraham and to Isaac, and also operate with the noblest motive, that of the desire for freedom from slavery. All this is enriched by what is said of the promise and the inheritance. The positive is placed beside its negative throughout the paragraph.

CHAPTER V

The sharp warning against accepting circumcision

2) Language as well as substance indicate the beginning of a new paragraph. The Judaistic yoke which Paul wants the Galatians to avoid is assumed by accepting circumcision. This, of course, refers to the former Gentile Galatians. The former Jewish Galatians had been circumcised while they were still Jews; what their circumcision amounted to Paul tells them in v. 6, compare Rom. 2:28. Such Christians were to disregard their circumcision entirely.

See, I myself, Paul, declare to you that, if you let yourselves be circumcised, Christ will profit you nothing! The new subject is circumcision. Ἴδε has become stereotyped since it is used also with plurals (B.-D. 144). It helps to make the statement dramatic. With the words "I myself, Paul," the apostle puts forward all the authority at his command. There are times when this must be done. Apostolic and ministerial authority is to be used at the proper time.

In 4:10 Paul has stated what the Galatians were accepting from the Judaizers. But he did not mention circumcision; so we are forced to the conclusion that the Galatians had not yet advanced that far. Circumcision was the crucial requirement of the entire Judaistic system. It was that already in the case of all proselytes who united with the Jewish synagogues. The reason the proselytes of the gate were considered outsiders was that they had not accepted circumcision. The Judaizers had not yet gained that victory in Galatia. The observing of Jewish holy times (4:10) could never satisfy them. Their goal was to persuade the

Galatians to accept circumcision. A man placed himself under the entire Mosaic system by submitting to circumcision. Circumcision would make the defection and fall of the Galatians complete. The Judaizers knew this although we may be sure that they were very careful in working toward this goal. Paul exposes the whole issue in the most open, direct, and decisive way.

With ἐάν he vividly supposes the future case that the Galatians let themselves be circumcised. This form of condition is used, not because Paul expects this to happen, but in order to confront the Galatians with the actual results in case it does occur. Due to the common ground occupied by the middle and the passive, the latter may be used to express the idea of "subjecting oneself," "allowing oneself or letting oneself," for which use we have a good example here (Moulton, *Einleitung* 225). It is the causative (R. 816) or permissive passive: "cause yourselves or permit yourselves to be circumcised." Paul says: "If you are going to accept that, you will inevitably lose Christ, he will profit you nothing." R. 482, 484 explain "nothing" as a second or cognate accusative. Why not make it adverbial: "in no respect"?

But is Paul's statement true? The Judaizers did not give up Christ and did not ask the Galatians to do so. They merely mixed the gospel with their Mosaic legalism and asked the Galatians to do the same. Yet Christ cannot be halved. Remove a fraction of Christ, and the entire profit or benefit of Christ is lost. One may mean ever so well when doing this, the result is fatal nonetheless.

This does not seem to be obvious to all Christians. Stand on Christ with both feet, and you are safe. Place one foot on something else, that something else gives way, and you fall. Christ is the entire bridge; on him you may cross safely. But if only one foot of that bridge is made something else, the whole bridge collapses. This is a case of either all or none; ninety-nine per cent Christ plus one per cent anything else is just as fatal as no per cent of Christ. *All* the saving power lies in him alone, and no less than all of it saves. "Christ" = all that he is in his person and his work. In 4:11 Paul says that he has perhaps labored in vain among the Galatians. He now advances the thought — Christ would be in vain.

3) Paul adds with full solemnity: **Moreover, I testify once more to every man letting himself be circumcised that he is debtor to do the whole law.** The preceding, "I, Paul, say to you" is now varied to "I testify." A witness is to tell the truth, and this Paul does in the most simple and direct way. With δέ Paul adds another, a clearly corroborating fact. "Once more" or "again" states that Paul has testified to the Galatians at a previous time. We have no difficulty in determining the time when this had been done; it certainly happened during Paul's second tour through Galatia when he brought with him the resolution adopted by the Jerusalem conference which asked the Gentile Christians to abstain from certain things for their own sakes and for the sake of their Jewish fellow Christians (Acts 16:4, 5). All the Gentile Christians received this conference resolution with joy. Paul certainly told the Galatians how the resolution had been passed, how it disavowed the Judaistic demand for circumcision and submission to the Mosaic regulations (Acts 15:1, 5). Then Paul also had the call to testify fully to the Galatians what submission to circumcision involved.

It is Paul's way of writing to change from the plural of v. 2 to the singular and at the same time from the specific "you" to the general "every man." The latter brings out the fact that what Paul testifies to the Galatians is true for every Christian no matter

when or where he may be living. The passive participle is again causative or permissive. Its tense is
properly present, not because the act is extended, but
because of "every man," no matter *when* a man
subjects himself to circumcision in obedience to the
Judaizers.

Every man of this kind "is debtor to the whole
law." It was ever thus: circumcision made one an
out-and-out Jew. Circumcision was not only a part
of the Jewish ceremonial law like observance of the
Jewish holy days and seasons (4:10), it ever involved
the observance of the whole system just as Paul states.
The aorist "to do" involves completeness. Even a
Jew who did not do the whole law was a recreant,
spurious Jew because of the fact that he was circumcised and did not discharge his resultant obligation.
That is why the pivotal point of the Jerusalem conference was the Judaistic demand for circumcision
(Acts 15:1, 5), it involved all else. That is why circumcision was so incompatible with Christ and the
gospel. R. 1062 explains the infinitive as a complement to the noun: "debtor for doing." It is often
so used with substantives (R. 1076). To accept the
Judaistic circumcision meant to abandon the liberty
for which Christ liberated us and to go back under
the yoke of slavery (v. 1), to exchange Isaac for
Ishmael.

4) Paul once more states his warning in a
direct personal way. **You get severed from Christ,
such of you as try to be declared righteous in connection with law; you get to fall from grace.** Paul now
broadens his thought. In v. 3 he states that it is Judaistic circumcision which subjects to the Mosaic legal
system, "the law." But anything that is "law" (no
article) is useless for obtaining justification ("without
works of law," Rom. 3:28), yea, worse than useless,
it is actually fatal. It is difficult to translate κατηργήθητε

ἀπό so as to conserve the force of the verb, the tense, and the preposition. Paul uses the verb in all manner of connections (again in v. 12) which necessitates various translations, all of which are more or less inexact. The basic idea is, "to make idle, inactive" so that nothing results; the preposition adds the idea that this action removes "away from Christ," separates from him.

Both aorists are timeless (Moulton, *Einleitung* 218) but still punctiliar and thus different from timeless presents. Our versions render them quite well. The A. V. translates the sense of the first verb well, the R. V. the sense also of the preposition, and both versions reproduce the timelessness of both aorists by means of the English present. The punctiliar idea is, however, not conserved; we try to convey it: "you get severed — get to fall," such of you as try to be declared righteous in connection with law. The moment one even tries to be justified in connection with anything in the nature of law, this is what happens, then and there the terrible damage is done. It all happens in an instant: completely out with Christ and fallen from grace.

These are clashing opposites: anything in the nature of law — Christ and his grace ("law," 3:12; "grace," 1:3). They are as exclusive as the two aorists indicate. It is impossible to combine them. Although it is worded in the second person, the statement is general, and thus, of course, applies to the Galatians. The sense is: if there are any such among you Galatians. Paul neither asserts nor denies that there are such.

The present tense is conative (R. 880): "try to be declared righteous," try to obtain a favorable verdict from God. The R. V.'s "would be justified" comes much closer to this conative present than the A. V.'s "are justified." The thing is impossible, any attempt

to do it not only fails but causes defection from Christ
and fall from grace. The trying is both hopeless and
itself fatal. 'Ev = "in connection with," and the connection is the fact that we drop Christ and grace by
starting to do works of law (v. 3), whether these be
Jewish or some other kind.

Paul states the straight facts as they always are
and always will be. The result is ever the same. The
Galatians are put face to face with it by an effective
warning.

5) Over against all such who seek justification
in connection with law Paul places the emphatic ἡμεῖς
with an elucidating "for." **For we on our part by
means of the spirit out of faith wait for the hope of
righteousness.** This is what *we* are doing, the direct
opposite of what such as those mentioned in v. 4 are
trying to do. By changing to "we" Paul includes himself and the Galatians as being people like himself.
Nor does he divide the Galatians into two classes,
those who are one with him and those who have fallen
from grace. He gives up none of them. What he says
with "if" and "such as" in v. 2 and 4 is a warning
and not a statement of a sad actuality regarding the
Galatians.

We hesitate to render the simple dative as do our
versions, "through the Spirit," or as do many commentators, "in the Spirit." True, the Greek does not
need the article with "Spirit" when it names this divine
Person. The thought is also attractive: Spirit, the
causa efficiens salutis, the objective means; faith, the
causa apprehendens, the subjective means. One may
then expand the thought and say much about us who
have the Spirit and about all that our having him
means. But note that none of the four nouns has the
article, that the four are consequently to be understood
in their general qualitative sense. Can the one noun
then refer to a person?

Again, this is an unmodified dative without a preposition such as "through" or "in"; it is to be construed
with the verb "await" and denotes means. Now the
analogy of Scripture never makes the Holy Spirit a
means that *we* use just as Christ is not a means
or medium used by *us*. Is this analogy set aside
here?

Then consider the thought itself: "we await with
or by means of the Holy Spirit," which is so incongruous a combination that we decline to make it. This is
simply "spirit." "Law" deals with outward works; all
our waiting is inward, spiritual. It is done "by means
of spirit," by means of that in us which has spirit
quality. Nor do we thus lose the Holy Spirit, for he
alone produces in us what can be truly called "spirit,"
the opposite of flesh.

Our waiting grows "out of faith," which is again
qualitative, again opposed to "law" in v. 4, coordinate
with "spirit" but not to be construed: "with a spirit
(derived) from faith" although we admit that this
construction, too, has its attraction. Faith is the
source of our ardent waiting, which is done entirely by
means of spirit in a truly spiritual way.

What arrests attention most of all is the fact that
Paul speaks of the "hope of righteousness" and of our
awaiting this hope. To wait for a hope is, of course,
to await its fulfillment. Hope and waiting go together
(Rom 8:25). One also sees that "hope of righteousness" contains either the objective or the appositional
genitive: hope for righteousness or hope (objective)
which consists of righteousness, with little to choose
between the two. The genitive also makes the anarthrous "hope" definite. But does faith not *now* possess
righteousness, i. e., the quality produced by the divine
verdict of acquittal? How can we still be waiting for
and hoping for righteousness? The answer is not difficult. Now our righteousness is due to the secret ver-

dict pronounced by God in heaven the moment we believe. Our assurance of that secret verdict is the Word
of Scripture which we must believe. We await the
great hope when, on judgment day, the heavenly Judge
will pronounce that verdict face to face with us before
the whole universe. Then our great hope of righteousness will be consummated.

This is what Paul opposes to "such as try to be
declared righteous in connection with law." Vain is
their trying. Neither now nor on that day can they
possibly attain it. Faith produces the sure hope, the
glad waiting which can never make ashamed. "We are
saved by hope" (Rom. 8:24), a hope that does not make
ashamed (Rom. 5:5) at the last day.

6) Paul returns to circumcision as such with another γάρ. For us Christians circumcision amounts to
nothing; the one thing that is everything for us is
faith. **For in connection with Christ Jesus neither
circumcision amounts to anything nor foreskin, but
faith working by means of love.** Paul does not say,
"for the Christian" but, "in connection with Christ
Jesus." Apart from him, outside of the circle which
he forms, men may value either foreskin or circumcision as they please; but in the saving sphere or the
connection with Christ Jesus (office and person)
neither has strength, i. e., neither is effective in any
way. To imagine that circumcision is effective is to
hug a delusion.

At one time this was a great issue, namely when
the gospel advanced from the Jews to the Gentiles; it
is now dead save as it involves the great principle set
forth by Paul that all legalism is abolished root and
branch by gospel liberty. The church is still troubled
on this score and men like Paul and Luther are needed
to keep it free. The present-day Jews, of course, still
circumcise, but they in no way affect the church.

One thing and one alone is effective. It is already stated in the phrase "in Christ Jesus," which is placed forward for the sake of emphasis, and that is faith. But why does Paul add "working or showing itself operative and effective by means of love"? Because he has in v. 5 referred to the final judgment and our hope for that day. The whole Scriptures testify that in the great judgment the Judge will refer to the works of faith. As such evidence the works will substantiate the public verdict of the Judge, and all the universe will declare that verdict just.

There is a sharp contention with the Roman Catholic Church regarding the voice of this participle. This church insists that it is the passive and stakes its doctrine of the *fides caritate formata* on this voice and calls faith that is not so formed by love a *fides informata*. Love and works thus give form and substance to faith; to the Romanist, faith without these is *informata*, without form and void. The R. V. margin supports this claim with its Romanizing translation: "wrought through love." But this verb is never passive in the New Testament; it appears only in the active and in the middle voice, and when it is used in the middle it never has an object or a personal subject (C.-K. 441; B.-P. 412). This is the linguistic side of the matter. The middle is always = *vim suam exserere.*

Then, too, to the Romanist "faith" is not faith in the Biblical sense of the term. The Romanist doctrine is not understood until one understands what Romanist faith is. Rome hurls its anathema against the teaching that faith consists of knowledge, assent, and *fiducia*, confidence or trust. It cancels the first and the third factors, especially the third. It leaves only assent, namely blanket assent to whatever Rome teaches, whatever that may be. Such assent is indeed *informata* and needs something to make it *formata*, to give it form and substance. Rome declares that this substance is love and good works. When assent has enough of these it is fully formed. Since we seldom know when we have enough we cannot be certain of salvation. Hence also justification is not forensic, not instantaneous and complete but medicinal, gradual, for the most part completed in purgatory; any certainty is doubtful in this life according to Rome's own teaching.

Luther uses strong language when he writes on this subject: "Therefore faith is not such an *otiosa qualitas*, that is, a thing so entirely useless, lazy, dead, that it may lie hidden in the heart of a mortal sinner like light, useless chaff or like a fly in wintertime sticking in a crack so long until the dear sun comes to it and wakes and makes it alive."

There is logic in the Roman Catholic doctrine. *If* faith is, indeed, only assent, then it certainly needs a good deal to fill out its form. Rome says that what it needs are love and works. Many others besides Rome have conceived faith to be only an opinion, something in the intellect, and thus also preach love and works as the real essentials. Many opponents of Rome live on Roman contraband although they deny the source of their goods. In any dispute about what faith does it is essential to lay bare with exactness what "faith" is conceived to be. A Romish, a Pelagian, a Semi-Pelagian, a synergistic, a rationalistic or modernistic "faith" is not the faith of Scripture. It is a waste of effort to dispute about the predications made about such a "faith." Get back to faith itself, define that from the Scriptures; then true agreement is reached, and the predications will fall in line.

Paul here makes "love" (see 2:20, the verb) the means (διά) with which faith works. The means is certainly not the faith, still less its real *forma*, con-

tents, or substance. Faith is ever complete in itself.
No *fiducia* or trust is without the person or the object
which it trusts. It is a cup that is never empty but is
always filled with Christ Jesus. It may be a small or
a large cup, it is never an empty one. The entire value
and the power of faith lie in this its divine content.
And since this is Christ who loved us and died for us,
faith ever brings forth its fruit of love. How can a
heart embrace him who is supreme love without glow-
ing with love and love's energy? Circumcision and
foreskin, any legalistic outward observances? They
fade away automatically.

Paul's final warnings and his confidence in the Galatians

7) The subject of circumcision has been concluded. Paul begins dramatically with a rhetorical
question. In v. 2 it is *he*, Paul himself, who makes
a declaration to the Galatians; now he asks *them* a
searching question. He has had to correct them regarding circumcision and regarding faith. Should
this be necessary for people such as they are? **You
were running well. Who cut in on you for you to
start not to obey the truth?**

The course of Christian faith is often likened to a
race for a prize. The Greeks had their great games,
and, as is the case in our athletic era, everybody knew
all about them. Thus Paul's figure is natural although
the running of races is vastly older than the Greek con-
tests. The imperfect pictures the Galatians as running
well with every prospect of reaching the goal.

Now the question of shocked surprise which is
similar to 3:1. The tenses are important here, an
aorist in the main verb, a present in the infinitive.
Somebody did cut in on the Galatians, but thus far only
to induce them to begin not to obey the truth. The
present infinitive is inchoative. The Judaizers had not

as yet succeeded. The usual translation is, "who did hinder you"; R., *W. P.*, has the more expressive, "who cut in on you." The picture is not one of halting the runners but one of throwing them off their course. One may run with all his might, but if he gets off the course he is automatically disqualified and might as well never have run at all. The course is narrow and never broad so as to allow running over to works of law. The runners do not lay out the course, nor can they change it while they are running.

Thus far Paul has employed a figure; now he turns to the reality. This is constantly done, thereby he makes the figure self-interpretative. This method of Paul's writing is often not appreciated, is perhaps even criticized; yet it is both beautiful and certainly most valuable. We must get clear in regard to the use of μή with the infinitive. Zahn finds it so incompatible, so contrary to Rom. 15:22 which has no negative that he resorts to a very inferior reading and makes a new and a separate sentence with the help of this reading: *Solchem, was Wahrheit is, nicht zu gehorchen, (darin) gehorchet niemandem.* But while this μή is not necessary and thus is at times not used it is frequently found with verbs of hindering and denying; it is pleonastic (R. 1177; B.-D. 429), "a redundant negative repeating the negative notion of the verb just as double negatives carried on the force of the first negative" (R. 1094). Why let this common negative move us to a change of reading? B.-D. 488, 1b also alters the reading without a convincing reason.

Paul purposely states the matter mildly by using this negative. "For you to start not to obey the truth" is really a litotes which is milder because it states only what was being omitted instead of what was being committed. "The truth" is also far better than the reading "truth" without the article, for this is the truth of the gospel, which is decidedly definite as it should be in this closing admonition. This truth marks out the narrow track for the runners; it is run by faith that is active by means of love. Obedience to this truth is the essential, even the elementary requirement.

8) The mild negative form of expression continues. **This persuasion** (is not derived) **from him who calls you.** It has a far different source which is sinister, indeed, if Paul should name it. Our English loses the *paronomasia* in πείθεσθαι and ἡ πεισμονή, "to be persuaded (i. e., and thus to obey) — the persuasion." The agents in the passive infinitive are the Judaizers, and "the persuasion" is their activity which is not "from him who is calling you," not from God. These Judaizers are not God's agents. That ought to be enough for the Galatians. Theirs is an alien voice; read John 10:4, 5 for a fine commentary. The article is plainly demonstrative: "this persuading or persuasion," that indicated by the preceding infinitive.

So rare is this hapaxlegomenon that it affords opportunity for those who, like Zahn and B.-D., alter the reading to dispute its meaning and to make the word passive: *Folgsamkeit* instead of persuasion, i. e., obedience on the part of the Galatians instead of persuading coming from the Judaizers. B.-P. 1025 rightly rejects a passive sense for this word since this supposed passive sense is based on an altered reading.

9) There is a close connection when Paul adds: **A little leaven leavens the entire lump.** The object is placed before the verb in the Greek for the sake of emphasis. Only the beginning of wrong obedience had been made in Galatia. It was like introducing a little yeast into a mass of dough. Let the Galatians not close their eyes to the danger. Give a little yeast time and it will penetrate the entire dough. The expression may be a proverb or common saying. Paul's use of it here and in I Cor. 5:6 has led to its being quoted frequently.

Here the little leaven refers to doctrine and not to persons. In I Cor. 5:6 the application is made to a different matter (see that passage). Those who refer it to persons point to the singular "who" in v. 7 and to ἐγώ and to ὁ ταράσσων in v. 10 which designate persons. But they disregard "not to obey the truth" in v. 7 and "this persuasion" in v. 8, both of which refer to doctrine which is insidious like spreading yeast and seeks to penetrate all that the Galatians had hitherto believed. The whole lump = the Galatians and all of the doctrine they had hitherto believed.

To say that the Judaistic doctrine was not a small bit of yeast but a great mass of doctrine, the whole of which opposed the whole gospel, and that, therefore, doctrine cannot be referred to, overlooks what Paul is saying. He is not placing the one doctrinal system over against the other but is issuing the warning: *Principiis obsta*, resist the beginnings. The Judaizers were not so foolish as to unload their entire doctrine upon the Galatians at one time; they injected it little by little. Paul refers to the little leaven that had already been injected, the fact that the Galatians had begun to observe times (4:10) although they had not as yet yielded to circumcision. If it be not stopped, that little would eventually leaven and alter everything.

To speak of persons is beside the mark, i. e., that a few false teachers are enough to pervert the entire church. We know nothing about the number of the Judaizers in Galatia, in fact, the number is irrelevant. These teachers, whatever their number, could corrupt the entire church only by their doctrine and in no other way. Instead of this reference to persons it would be rather profitable to note the aptness of likening yeast to evil persuasion. Both work silently, insidiously. The figure of yeast is used in a good sense only once (Matt. 13:33), otherwise it is used in an evil sense (Matt. 16:6-12; I Cor. 5:6; here).

It is only too true: the admission of a little false doctrine into the true is highly dangerous. One infected apple infects many others; the many sound ones never make the infected one sound. A little yeast alters the entire dough; and the entire dough never turns the yeast into dough. In our day especially, when so much is known about spores, ferments, and bacteriology, Paul's homely warning should be most effective. This proverb should be death to doctrinal indifference. But many still imagine that a little deviation from the truth of the gospel will do no harm to them and to those who hear them. They even pride themselves on harboring at least some deviation and, while they want their food and their drink pure, cast their flings at the *reine Lehre.*

10)   Not until this point has been reached does Paul contrast the persons, and now he does it plainly. Here, too, is a warning that is plain and direct. **I on my part am confident regarding you in the Lord that you will mind nothing else; but he that disturbs you shall bear his judgment, whoever he is.**

The opposition, "I on my part — he who disturbs you," is marked. The second perfect is used with present force: "I am confident," and this confidence of Paul's regarding the Galatians is not merely light optimism that exists in his own mind but is connected with the Lord who will give power and efficacy to Paul's words.

Paul is confident "that you will mind nothing else." This "nothing else" does not refer to the contents of the entire epistle but to what has just been said in v. 9. The Galatians will see that a little Judaistic leaven will eventually leaven the whole lump, that they must fear the very beginnings they have already made and end them forthwith.

Paul has his confidence in the Lord. But what Paul says about his own sure confidence implies that "he who disturbs you" is also to have *his* confidence, one that is also connected with the Lord, namely, that "he shall bear his judgment," no matter who he may be, of what quality or in what class (R. 727). The idea that Paul has in mind a single individual, the leader among the Judaizers, cannot be upheld. In 1:7 we have the identical designation in the plural; compare 4:17; 5:12; 6:12, etc.

The indefinite relative clause "whosoever he is" is intended for any disturber. Every disturber of the Galatians shall bear his judgment for his nefarious work. Excuses, pleas of good intention, etc., shall not avail. The future tense is prophetic. Paul uses the indeterminate κρῖμα, "judgment," and does not say outright κατάκριμα, "condemnation." He does not mean that this will not be an adverse judgment. Paul leaves this in God's hands. It may come in part already in this life, but will come surely and fully at death.

This is a passage which the disturbers of the church might well take to heart. It is no light thing to scatter the leaven of false doctrine, it never was. Paul, however, writes this to the Galatians in order to warn them. Will they continue to listen to men whose doom is awaiting them? If they do so, will they not come to share that doom?

11) The thought of the judgment awaiting these Judaizers brings to Paul's mind the foul and even fatuous means to which they resort when they are spreading their leaven. Recently, while he was in Lystra, Paul had taken Timothy as his assistant and, in order to enable him to work among Jews, had circumcised Timothy, Acts 16:3. Paul had also very likely not objected when Jewish Christians chose to circumcise their male children and had not made an issue of it as long as no legalistic and Judaistic ideas were connected with such circumcisions. Thus Jewish Christians also continued to eat

kosher as James himself did. This was a matter
of liberty. But, it seems, the Judaizers sought to
make capital of this liberty in support of their legalistic demand for circumcision. Did Paul thus not
preach circumcision by his own acts? These
Judaizers were blind to the common fact that, when
two do the same thing, it may not be the same thing.
Paul blasts them with the most withering irony.
**But I on my part, brethren, if I still preach circum-
cision, why am I still persecuted? Has the deathtrap of the cross been abolished? Would that
they who unsettle you would even have themselves
castrated!**
The condition of unreality deals with an assumed
reality. Paul did *not* preach circumcision. What he
preached on that score, v. 6 restates. The Judaizers
asserted, on the grounds indicated, that Paul *did* still
preach circumcision. This alleged fact Paul picks up
and for a moment speaks of it as being a fact. He
places the pronoun forward for the sake of strong emphasis: "I on my part, if I," etc. The address "brethren" likewise lends weight.

The statement is so silly that Paul is still preaching
circumcision. Paul tears it to pieces with two questions, "Why am I still persecuted?" Why, then, are
the Jews still after me? It is not necessary to assume
that the Judaizers were persecuting Paul. This persecution is also actual persecution and not mere vilification such as these Judaizers launched against the absent Paul whom they had never met. The unthinkable
thing is the fact that the Jews would still persecute a
man who preached the central demand of Jewdom,
namely circumcision. The worst persecution Paul had
suffered so far was experienced at the hands of Jewish
fanatics — because he preached *against* circumcision.

One may make the following statement a deduction
with the reading ἄρα (our versions) or another question

with the reading ἄρα; either is good. We regard it as
a question because a question precedes. Paul is above
thinking of himself alone, of his still undergoing persecution; his thought automatically reverts to Christ.
The second question also rests on the assumption of
fact "if": "Has the deathtrap of the cross been
abolished?"

Σκάνδαλον is the trigger stick of a trap, to which the
bait is affixed, which springs the trap when the bait is
touched. It has nothing to do with "stumbling block"
despite our versions (on the verb see M.-M. 576). The
difference is not one of the figure only but of the sense.
A *skandalon* is a fatal, deadly thing, it kills and is intended to kill; a stumbling block (for which the Greek
has a different word: πρόσκομμα) at most causes a fall
from which one arises and generally designates a lesser
hurt. In Rom. 9:33 the two are found together so that
our versions could not repeat their usual translation.
To be sure, *skandalon* is used metaphorically, but if we
translate it "offense," it must always be mortal, fatal
offense, no less.

If I am still preaching circumcision as the Jews
have always preached it, has this astounding thing then
been done, has the deathtrap of the cross been abolished? Why, then these Judaizers would have all they
want! "The *skandalon* of the cross" = I Cor. 1:23,
"Christ crucified for the Jews a *skandalon*." The cross,
the crucified Messiah, is deadly to the Jew to this day.
Although it is the very power of God to save (I Cor.
1:24) by freeing us from the curse of the law in that
Christ on the cross became a curse in our stead (3:13),
by clinging to their law the Jews are still struck by
this curse, by scorning Christ crucified have him as an
odor of death unto death. At the heart of their fatal
legalism is circumcision. If they could keep their legalism, if they could put into the cross something that is
not atonement but only example, a great model, a so-

called inspiration, the Jews would adopt the cross.
Many modern Jews, as also all deniers of Christ's deity,
do this very thing. But the *skandalon* cannot be abolished. The cross can be perverted, it cannot be
changed. It means atonement, justification by faith,
abolition of law and works of law, complete Christian
liberty. No, brethren, Paul would say, the *skandalon*
of the cross is not abolished by such a silly allegation
as that I still preach circumcision.

12) Paul's hot indignation against these Judaizers
who stoop to anything they think may further their
cause is expressed in the ironic wish that they might
have themselves even castrated. This still rests on the
condition stated in v. 11. But the sense is not that, by
having themselves castrated, they might become even
holier than by being merely circumcised. The idea of
holiness does not lie in the context. With their circumcision these Judaizers want to outdo Paul and take the
Galatians away from him. But if they have no more
to offer than Paul offers, if, as they claim, he, too, still
preaches circumcision, how will they be able to outdo
him? Well, there is a way — would that they might
try it! Let them have themselves castrated! Then
they would, indeed, leave Paul behind who, as they
say, still preaches only circumcision. But this is said
with an eye to the Galatians, a fact which we should
not overlook. These Judaizers, who are unsettling the
Galatians in order to get them away from Paul, who
boast that they have something better than he has, can
outdo him only by going to the full length of their
claim: if they can say that Paul still advocates circumcision they should adopt castration. How the Galatians would then admire and follow these eunuchs!

Ὄφελον is a mere particle for expressing a wish, it is
developed from the imperfect ὤφελον with the infinitive
by dropping the augment. Here alone it is followed by
the future in order to express a wish regarding the

future; elsewhere it is followed by the aorist in order to indicate a wish regarding the past, or by the imperfect in order to designate a wish regarding the present. R. 923. B.-D. 384 calls Paul's wish fulfillable; R. 923 non-fulfillable. It all depends on how the wish is regarded.

The verb itself is the regular term for "to castrate" whether it is used alone or with a term that names the parts cut off. There is no gain in thinking of a figurative modification: cutting the Judaizers off from the congregation, from sin and error, or from the truth and the mercy of God. The form is middle and not passive, R. 809 makes it the causative middle, B.-D. 317, "let themselves be," etc. They would, of course, castrate themselves by having the operation performed by a competent person — no issue regarding that.

The point of castration was highly effective in the case of the Galatians, who had among them the castrated priests of Cybele, a Phrygian goddess, who was by the Greeks identified more or less with Rhea, the mother of their gods. Castration appears in various other pagan cults. So these Judaizers, who had advanced to castration, would be out and out pagans! On the status of eunuchs among the Jews compare Deut. 23:1; Isa. 56:3.

The gospel of Christian liberty has thus been unfolded anew for the Galatians (3:1-5:12). In the last part of this section Paul admonishes the Galatians to drop their legalism (4:12-5:12). This brings us to the third main part of the epistle.

PART III

How the Galatians Should Use their Christian Liberty, 5:13-6:16

After the liberty itself has been unfolded for the Galatians so as to remove them from the slavery the Judaizers were seeking to impose on them, it remains necessary that Paul show how this liberty manifests and exercises itself in the Christian life. To be liberated, to be free is to act with freedom. Action is freedom's very domain. Christian liberty, however, is always controlled; its controlling power is love. It remains liberty only when it is under this control, otherwise it becomes license which runs wild. Thus an anomaly results which Luther has put into a striking paradox (Erlangen ed. 27, 176):

"A Christian man is a free Lord over all things and subject to no one.

"A Christian man is a subservient slave of all things and subject to everyone."

Luther learned this from Paul whose best pupil he is. The key to the paradox is love. Love makes liberty both the safest and the most valuable possession. It fills this liberty with both beauty and happiness.

Liberty exercised by means of love

13) **For you on your part, brethren, were called unto freedom; only** (use) **not this freedom as a starting point for the flesh, but by means of love slave for each other.** "For" at the head of a paragraph = "in order to elucidate still further." The elucidation now offered concerns the use of Christian freedom. Paul places "you" emphatically over against the Judaizers, those making it a business to unsettle you (v. 12).

Whatever Paul may wish for these men, the great fact remains, and the Galatians must ever keep it before them: for their part they were called unto liberty.

The aorist states the past fact, and throughout the epistles the calling is always to be understood in the effective sense, i. e., including acceptance of the call. When the gracious gospel call won the Galatians to faith, it was entirely for freedom. The call itself was a liberation and ushered into the fullest liberty. Ἐπί with the dative is used to indicate an aim or a goal as in I Thess. 4:7 (B.-P. 447). The address, "brethren," is placed after the sentence as in 4:12 and is thus less emphatic although it still marks a new section, acknowledges the Galatians, and expects them to heed.

But this fact, that they were called to freedom, is only the basic statement, the summary of the entire second part of the epistle. On this basis rests the new part regarding the use of this freedom. Paul also states this in a summary fashion, both negatively and positively. In the negative statement the verb is absent. It is not necessary that we supply a verb, yet the negative μή conveys an imperative tone. The thought is complete: for freedom, "only not this freedom as a starting point, an impetus for the flesh," i. e., in favor of the flesh still left in us.

Here lies the danger for all the called. They are ushered into a wonderful land of freedom. Yet freedom is like a great fortune of money, it may be a great blessing if it is used aright, a curse if it is abused. It is like being a great king who must be kingly and not a tyrant. As the freedom mounts, so does the responsibility for its use. Otherwise the freedom itself disappears. The danger lies not on the side of the reborn spirit in the Christian but on the side of his flesh, the power of sin still left in him. In a war an ἀφορμή is a basis of operation, and in the metaphorical use of the word this idea is retained. Our sinful flesh may ap-

propriate this freedom as if it were intended for itself
and may thus start turning it into license. "Only not
this!" Paul writes. The flesh must be checked at the
very beginning.

The positive statement is paradoxical: "but by
means of love slave for each other." Our freedom
means that we must slave. It seems contradictory yet
is perfect harmony. Freedom is the free exercise of
love. This is the love born of faith, the love of real
intelligence and understanding coupled with corresponding aim and purpose. The Greek article is quite
in place although it is not needed in English. Love
itself is free. Love goes out toward its object with
intelligent and purposeful devotion. Here the object
is expressed by "each other," and the devotion by the
strong verb "to slave." Compare I John 4:20, 21. Paul
does not write that we are to be "slaves of each other"
(genitive) ; we are God's and Christ's slaves. The
slave of another is bound to make the other's will his
own. To slave "*for* each other" (dative) is to do our
work for each other according to our Lord's will.

Here we have the whole exercise of our Christian
freedom. Its great medium is the love that fills us,
its great activity, voluntary slaving for each other.
When we exercise ourselves in this work we have freedom indeed. The reading of a few texts which have
the dative: "with the love of the spirit (or Spirit)"
has nothing to commend it either textually or as far as
the thought is concerned. Such a dative still leaves
love as the means, and the combination "the love of the
spirit (Spirit)" would occur only in this variant.

14) Luther writes on this verse: *Theologia brevissima et longissima; brevissima quod ad verba et sen-
tentias attinet, sed usu et re ipsa latior, longior, pro-
fundior et sublimior toto mundo.* What impressed Luther so deeply is the fact that Paul sees that the law itself establishes the gospel freedom since the free love

brought forth by gospel faith freely fulfills the very heart of the law, its demand for the love the law could never achieve. That is what Paul states in words so brief, that involve amplifications so long, wide, profound, sublime as to comprise the whole law and the gospel. **For the whole law stands as having been fulfilled in the one word, namely, Thou shalt love thy neighbor as thyself!**

"For" substantiates, and the marvel is the fact that the very law from which the Christian believer is free should substantiate this very freedom. Yet this becomes simple and clear the moment we stop looking at the many individual requirements of the Mosaic legal system, especially those of a temporary ceremonial nature, and see what really fulfills "the whole law," namely love. The moment the Christian freedom from law is exercised, its one means is love, it does what love prompts down to actual slaving for others. That is the very fulfillment of the whole law as this is voiced in its own one, summary command: "Thou shalt love thy neighbor as thyself!"

Real freedom from law is not license for the flesh but slaving for others by means of love, and the law itself proves that this is freedom from law. The law should certainly be able to demonstrate who is still held as a slave by it and who has been set free from it as at last being a free man. It does this by setting up the commandment of love. A slave of the law he must remain who, despite a thousand labors in complying outwardly with other commands, fails in regard to this one which asks love. He who clings to law ever remains only such a slave, for no law ever produced love no matter how strenuously it may make this demand. But he who accepts the gospel gift which frees from law, by his freedom, if that freedom become not license, without the law achieves the whole law, its very crown, namely love. The whole law says so since its fulfillment lies in love. This has often been put into the simple statement: "What the law demands the gospel gives."

From one viewpoint the law and the gospel are direct opposites; hence the only salvation is freedom from the law. Yet from another viewpoint these two correspond, the one dovetails into the other although they lose their identity; hence the very love produced by the gospel freedom stands as the fulfillment of the law's demand which is love. The law, once a tyrant, becomes the free man's servant. Theologically expressed, this is called the third use of the law.

Observe that this was true also in the time of the Old Testament. Paul cites Lev. 19:18. The Old Testament had the gospel just as we now have it; only the form differed: then it was in the form of promise, now that promise as fulfilled in Christ. That gospel promise which was older than the law of Moses (3:17) ever wrought faith and love just as it now does. Therein the whole law was fulfilled also for those Old Testament saints, therein alone. Yes, they had the ceremonies of Moses which are now abolished since Christ has come. They were the shadows, he the substance (Col. 2:17). But also in the Old Testament love and not in mere outward observances lay the fulfillment. Paul has elucidated this subject at length in 3:23, etc.; 4:1, etc.; also the freedom in Sarah, Isaac, etc., in 4:21, etc.

"The whole law" places this in contrast with single commandments such as those mentioned in 4:10, and especially the Judaistic demand for circumcision. Piecemeal dealings with the law lead to nothing (Matt. 23:23). The whole of it alone suffices. It is entirely "in the one word," ἐν τῷ, "namely," the definite article makes a substantive of the quotation. Paul cites only the love to our neighbor, but this is never without the love to God (I John 4:20, 21). In Mark 10:17 Jesus cites only the Second Table, and in Luke 10:30 he exemplifies the concept of neighbor by pointing to the good Samaritan. As regards "one another" in v. 13 and "thy neighbor" here in the commandment note Paul's own statement in 6:10.

The perfect tense "has been fulfilled" has its present connotation so that we translate: "stands as having been fulfilled." See Rom. 8:13; 13:10. The future indicative: "thou shalt or wilt love," is common in legal precepts (R. 874). It is the love itself in the Christian's heart, born of faith in the gospel, which stands as the whole law's fulfillment despite the fact that this love still lacks so much in its outward manifestation. Yet the law cannot object on this account, for Christ has freed us from all its condemnations (v. 1), and Christ's righteousness covers all our imperfections.

15) The negative side of the Christian's freedom in slaving for others by means of love is stated drastically: **But if you keep biting and devouring each other, take heed lest you be consumed by each other!** Freely to slave for each other is to *conserve* each other; to let the flesh (v. 13) have its way is to be *consumed* by each other. The figure is taken from the jungle and the forest where tooth and claw reign and the denizens are exterminated by each other. The first two verbs are durative: "if you go on biting and devouring"; the last is an aorist derived from ἀναλίσκω and states what the end will be: "you will be consumed."

We note that Paul does not use negative imperatives: "Be not biting, etc.," which, if they were expressed by present imperatives, would mean: "Stop biting," etc. This would imply that the Galatians had, indeed, begun to bite each other. Nor does Paul use ἐάν with a condition of expectancy. This would imply that he has reason to expect such biting, etc. He uses the ordinary condition of reality which may mean that Paul conceives an actual reality and speaks of it as being real; yet it may mean only that he assumes the acts as being real in order to speak of them more drastically although the acts are not real. In other words, no conclusion as to the occurrence of actual biting and devouring in Galatia can be drawn from the conditional clause here used. This is also true with regard to the apodosis, "see to it," which merely matches the protasis and adds nothing beyond it but means only: "then see to it."

In regard to admonitions that involve conduct we must observe that the extreme is mentioned because it includes and intends to include all that is less down to the least. The extreme must, of course, be mentioned, for sins sometimes go that far. So the commandments forbid murder and adultery, but in Matt. 5:21, etc.; 5:27, etc., Jesus expounds and shows how these extremes include all that is less and yet of the same nature. A tiny sprout is as poisonous as the full-grown plant. So Paul mentions the extreme in order to include all that is the opposite of Christian love which serves others even to the extent of slaving for them. It will not always be necessary to slave thus, often only a kind word, a little help will be necessary in the exercise of freedom in love.

The catalog of sins listed in v. 19-21 is objective, and one should not draw from it and say that "enmities, strife, jealousies, wraths, factions, divisions" were prevalent among the Galatians because biting and devouring are mentioned in v. 15. Paul did not include these sins in his catalog in v. 20 because they were prevalent among the Galatians, nor did he list the other sins in v. 19-21 because of their actual prevalence in Galatia. The admonitory form used in v. 15 warns against what lack of love causes. It emphasizes the admonition: "by means of love keep slaving for each other."

We thus decline to accept the conclusion that biting and devouring were actually in progress among the Galatians at this time. Those who think that this was the case admit that this one verse alone reflects the actual bad moral condition prevailing in Galatia and expresses surprise because of that fact. We think that if such conditions were actual in Galatia, Paul would undoubtedly have written more than one line regarding them. With this one line and this condition of reality Paul points out what the reality is bound to become where the freedom of Christian love is lost. At this very time the Jews, from whom the Judaizers sprang, were biting and devouring each other. Read their history during these years and note Acts 21:38 as an incident and Acts 23:12, 13 as another; in a few more years their whole nation was no more, they had consumed each other.

Love conserves, lack of love consumes. The fact that this consuming means destruction of the bond of Christian fellowship needs no further proof.

Following the spirit and not the flesh

16) Paul has mentioned "the flesh" in v. 13 in his preliminary admonition that our freedom must be exercised by means of love. Not to yield to the flesh means ever to follow the spirit. This is what Paul now presents. **Now I say** (my meaning is): **Keep walking with what is spirit, and you will not carry out any craving of what is flesh.** This is what Paul intends to convey to the Galatians as regards their daily life and conversation: that in thought, word, and deed they ever use what regeneration has brought to birth in them; then any stirring of what is still left in them of sinful flesh, their old depraved nature, will not be carried out into action but will be crushed in its incipiency (v. 24). The translation seeks to conserve the anarthrous nouns, all three of which are qualitative.

Throughout the rest of the chapter "spirit" and "flesh" are contrasted, the new and the old nature. We see their antagonism, the freedom of the former, their fruits *in extenso,* finally the flesh crucified, the spirit living on in full activity. Rendall says that throughout this section Paul has in mind "spirit" and not "Spirit"; Lightfoot says it in regard to v. 17. Our versions plus the majority of the commentators prefer "Spirit."

All that we have already said in regard to v. 5 applies to this section. A comparison with Rom. 8:1-11 is decisive. In Romans we have "God's Spirit," "Christ's Spirit," etc., which leave no doubt as to the meaning; although the word is used seven times in Galatians, such a genitive does not appear in a single instance. Four times Paul has no article, and where he has it, the article denotes previous reference. All seven *pneuma* must be translated alike; our versions translate "Spirit" throughout. The commentators who follow them hurdle the difficulties that result and brush aside "spirit."

Here and in v. 25 the simple datives denote means and ought not to be translated "in the Spirit" (A. V.), for which thought Paul would use ἐν. The analogy of Scripture shows that *we* never use the Spirit as a means (see v. 5), but we do so use our own "spirit." So Paul here bids the Galatians to use in their walk and conversation what is spirit in its nature, i. e., the reborn, new man. Then when any craving, lust, evil desire of what is by nature flesh starts in them, they will not let it come to a head in action. "Flesh" and the "Holy Spirit" are not a contrast, but "flesh" and "spirit" are. Ἐπιθυμία is regularly used in an evil sense in the New Testament (C.-K. 501) although the classics use it as a *vox media*.

17) The reason for this admonition is: **For the flesh has cravings against the spirit, and the spirit against the flesh. For these lie opposed to each other so that you are not doing what you may want.**

The articles in "the flesh" and "the spirit" denote previous reference. Here ἐπιθυμεῖ is a *vox media* because it is used also with regard to the spirit; "lusteth" (our versions) is thus not a good translation because this word is too regularly used in only an evil sense. The old nature in us wants things that are contrary to the new, and vice versa. The two natures in us thus lie in constant conflict with each other. They are not opposites that as such live far apart, each following what it craves; they lie ἀντί, face to face, in constant clashing. Paul knows of no exceptions to this fact; he is not a perfectionist.

Lightfoot recognized that ἵνα is here consecutive, and Moulton, *Einleitung* 333, as well as R. 998 support him and free us from the labored interpretations that operate with purpose and even make this God's purpose. Paul says that *the result* of this clashing of flesh and spirit is that we do not go on doing (present, durative) what we may want to do. The indefinite relative clause means, "what we may want to do" in carrying out some craving of our flesh. The spirit in us succeeds in blocking this.

In v. 16 Paul urges the Galatians ever to walk with what is spirit and assures them that they will, indeed, not carry out any craving of what is still flesh in them. It is this context which makes v. 17 different from Rom. 7:15, etc., where the victories of the flesh are recorded. These are not denied here, but here the victories of the spirit are the subject. The fact that the flesh is also active is stated, but what it accomplishes beyond its cravings is not mentioned. This is also true

in regard to v. 24. This makes plain that Paul does
not here mean that what we may want according to
our spirit is always blocked by our flesh (μὴ ποιῆτε, durative) even as this is not the fact. In the believer the
spirit does, indeed, dominate; he has crucified the
flesh (aorist, v. 24).

The verb ἀντίκειται cannot mean that God created the
spirit and the flesh for the *purpose* that we should not
do what we want. This view assumes the activity of
three forces: we and our will, the flesh, and the spirit.
God has then arranged it so that we never get to do
our will but must do either what the flesh or the spirit
(Spirit) dictates. A strange psychology! Regeneration renews, liberates, frees the will. The spirit = the
liberated will. This liberated will is still hampered by
the flesh which ever seeks to obtain control again in
order once more to usurp the throne. The flesh does
not succeed; we need but to keep on walking with
what is spirit.

18) **Now if you are being led by what is spirit
you are not under what is law,** in other words, you
have the gospel freedom to which you have been called.
This links back into the great idea of freedom (v. 13)
by showing what this freedom involves in our daily
experience. To be led by what is spirit (dative of the
agent) is another way of saying that we are walking
with what is spirit (v. 16) save that "spirit" is now
pictured as our guide while in v. 16 it was our means.
Under this blessed leadership you are free men; the
opposite is equally true, without it you are slaves. Rom.
8:14 is a similar statement, but there "God's Spirit"
is the leader, and the result is expressed accordingly,
"sons of God." To be sure, where "spirit" leads,
"God's Spirit" leads, for "spirit" is his creation in us.
Nothing is lost by the qualitative term "spirit."

The freedom which Paul has described to the Galatians at such length is freedom from "law," which is

equally as qualitative as "spirit." In Rom. 6:14: "not under law" = under grace which is spiritual freedom. Both the tyranny and the curse of anything in the nature of law are thus removed. This includes the Mosaic law but also every other law. The anarthrous noun allows no restriction. The Judaizers, of course, wanted slavery under the Mosaic code, especially under its ceremonial requirements. But Paul has passed beyond this Judaistic restriction and has carried the entire subject down to its basic principle, law as such, whatever in its nature is law. This makes slaves one way or another; to be completely free from law, wholly under grace, is alone freedom indeed. John 8:32-36.

19) **Moreover, public are the works of the flesh, of which kind are fornication, uncleanness, unbridled conduct — idolatry, sorcery — enmities, strifes, jealousies, wraths — factions, splits, separate notions, envies — sprees, carousings, and the things like these, concerning which I tell you in advance even as I told you in advance that they who perpetrate such things shall not inherit God's kingdom.**

Δέ adds this catalog of vices. Works betray and advertise their source. Paul lists the actual works after speaking of "flesh craving" in v. 16. The craving produces these wicked works and others like them. Again the full outgrowth is described, but again it includes everything from the first secret craving to these complete works. Where the flesh is in full control works like this result. They show publicly what the flesh is. One does not need to speculate in regard to the flesh; look at what is "public," open to the eyes of all. When a Christian gives way to his flesh he will head for some of these works.

In every one of Paul's catalogs the items are carefully chosen and carefully placed into proper groups, the groups themselves are carefully arranged so that they form a whole. The entire list is always present to Paul's mind in its complete order before he sets down the first item. The most perfect arrangement appears in the list in II Cor. 6:4-10, which deserves the fullest study and appreciation. The world's godlessness and unrighteousness have never been described more adequately than in Rom. 1:18-32. As it was in 4:24, ἅτινα is qualitative, not merely "which" (our versions) but "of a kind which," thus already intimating that the list is not exhaustive.

We indicate the groups by means of dashes. Some make four groups: 3 — 2 — 8 — 2; we find five: 3 — 2 — 4 — 4 — 2. Eight would be unrhetorical, and a glance shows that it contains two fours. Five is the half of ten. Ten indicates greatest completeness (ten commandments, ten virgins, ten slaves in the parables, etc., i. e., in each case all) ; hence the broken ten = incompleteness which allows the reader to supply the remainder.

Some texts begin with "adulteries" and thus have four in the first group; this addition is probably due to Matt. 15:19, and Mark 7:21. This is the *sex* group, the nastiest, the most degrading, on which a special curse seems to rest, *Fleischessuenden* in a specific sense. "Fornication" = all illicit sexual intercourse. "Uncleanness" is broader and includes not only the other sexual aberrations but also all that leads to them — the whole mass of this filth. Ἀσέλγεια = *Zuegellosigkeit*, having restraint removed, plunging onward like a runaway horse; it is here associated with sex. As uncleanness spreads in all directions, so this third rushes on through to the limit and lets no consideration halt its course. These three and the next two are comprehensive singulars and thus again a significant five.

20) Now a closely associated pair that is probably placed next to the sex group because in the pagan

world they are so closely connected with sexual sins, call it the *godless* group. "Idolatry" was a constant danger to Gentile Christians. This was due not only to the fact that superstition drew them toward the old false gods; what often drew them still more were the festivities of the whole Roman world, celebrations and the mass of customs that centered in idol worship in one way or in another. Pagan skeptics scoffed at the gods but participated in the festivities and yielded to the customs.

All sorcery, witchcraft, charms, and the superstitions which furnish the soil and the atmosphere for their existence, are pagan throughout. In our times Christian words, names, and symbols have been introduced into witchcraft in Christian lands, but the basis is always pagan and idolatrous. So also is the notion that the devil operates in sorcery, etc. The writer here summarizes the results of an extensive study of this subject and of occultism in general. The sin is here named according to the drugs and medicaments so widely employed in secret pagan arts. But the word was used so as to include all magic and sorcery and is most properly paired with idolatry. All sorcery is idolatrous and thus pagan. Acts 19:18-20.

After five singulars we have ten plurals, yet not ten combined into one group but into three, hence not a unit ten (grand completeness) but a diverse ten (only hinting at completeness). There are two fours and a broken four: 4 + 4 + 2. Four is the common, brief, rhetorical expression of completeness which is constantly and even intuitively used by writers and is thus distinct from the conscious ten. Paul breaks off in the middle of the third four; instead of completing it he adds: "and the things like these," thus in a double way ending his list as an incomplete catalog. *Addit "et iis similia," quia quis omnem lernam carnalis vitae recenseat?* Luther.

Who cares to review the entire hydra? When one of its many heads is cut off, two grow in its place. We accept the reading that has the nominative plural ἔρεις instead of the singular ἔρις (B.-D. 47, 3; R. 265) ; this plural occurs in a number of texts and could easily be made a singular since the more usual plural is ἔριδες. One singular amid a long list of plurals would be an odd usage in Paul's writings. Some texts also have the singular ζῆλος, but here the plural is textually well assured. Some texts insert φόνοι after φθόνοι as is done in Matt. 15:19; Mark 7:21; Rom. 1:29; I Cor. 6:9 (thus the A. V.). But already Jerome counted only fifteen items. The R. V. is textually correct.

Four types of *personal animosity* are listed. The first denotes personal hatreds or enmities; the second, the strifes and wranglings that result; the third, the motives so often involved, jealousies; the fourth, the outbursts of hot passion in anger; the first and the third point to motives, the second and the fourth to their product. Hateful animosities produce strifes; jealousies produce passionate outbursts of anger.

Four types of *partyism* follow properly. When persons clash, each so often has his following. People take sides. Relatives and friends rally to the support of the one as do those of the opponent to him. Thus the flesh produces "factions," this word indicates mercenary motives. Next there are outright "splits," divisions, sunderings. Third, αἱρέσεις from which our word "heresy" is derived. It denotes a choice of a special opinion for oneself. Thus the Pharisees had theirs and formed a *hairesis,* a sect with peculiar views and doctrines, and aligned itself especially against the Sadducees, another *hairesis;* see Acts 5:17; 15:5; 26:5. This word was applied to the Christians by the Jews, Acts 24:5, 14; 28:22. Its philosophic use came later, according to which it denoted a peculiar school of philosophy.

Here and in I Cor. 11:19 Paul uses the word in the plural with a severer meaning. These "heresies" are results of the flesh and are to be condemned. Paul also lists them after "splits" or divisions, for they are evidently their cause. The context in II Pet. 2:1 is the most damaging of all: false prophets, false teachers, *haireseis* of destruction brought in on the side by such as deny even the Master who bought them, bringing upon themselves swift destruction. It is easy to see the course the word has followed; it soon reached what we call "heresy," any false doctrine down to the very worst.

21) Paul has been criticized for adding "envies" which, we are told, should properly appear after "wraths." This criticism rests on the conception that Paul refers to cases of envy between individuals in common matters of life as when one envies what another has. Then "envies" might, indeed, appear in the group headed by "enmities." Paul places "envies" in the group headed by mercenary "factions" and intends to convey the idea that "envies" are one of the motives which help to create such doctrines and the parties and splits which they cause. Here we may note Matt. 27:18 and also Phil. 1:15.

The last pair: drunkennesses or "sprees" and carousings, *Gelage*, Luther translates: *Saufen, Fressen*, which is very much to the point. From the fact that Paul has four terms to denote hostilities and four to denote divisions the deduction has been made that such conditions prevailed among the Galatians at this time. Any deduction made would have to apply to the whole list, including even "the things like these." And Paul says that concerning all these things he has told the Galatians in advance as he now does again "that they who perpetrate such things shall not inherit the kingdom of God." This catalog evidently does not present a special selection of sins that had but recently devel-

oped among the Galatians. The present participle
characterizes: "those whose mark is the practice of
such things"; πράσσω is often used in the evil sense, "to
perpetrate."

When Paul writes "shall not inherit" he calls to
mind all that he has said regarding the testament
(3:15, etc.), regarding the inheritance (3:18), regarding minor heirs (4:1, etc.), regarding full-grown sons
(4:7), regarding inheriting like Isaac (4:22, etc., note
v. 30). All this shows that Paul does not mean: shall
not enter heaven, "God's kingdom" in that sense. His
kingdom is inherited in this life.

"God's kingdom" is one of the grandest concepts of
Scripture. See Matt. 3:2; Mark 1:15; Luke 1:33;
John 3:3. The kingdom is the rule of God in grace
and in glory. Wherever he so rules there is this blessed
kingdom. Unlike earthly kingdoms, the divine King
alone makes his kingdom. These kingdoms exist apart
from their kings, make and at times unmake their
kings; not so this kingdom. The genitive is possessive:
the kingdom belongs to God; but it is difficult to exclude authorship from this genitive: God makes the
kingdom. It extends from Adam to eternity. On earth
his rule is in grace, in heaven it is in glory. Jesus
expounded this kingdom in his parables, each parable
revealing one side of it. The new birth admits to this
kingdom, John 3:3, 5. This is effected by repentance,
Matt. 3:2.

We "inherit" the kingdom. Since we are sons of
the King, it is ours. We are not subjects as are those
of ordinary earthly kingdoms but royal princes (I Pet.
2:9) who bear themselves as such. Grand vistas open
up here. "The kingdom *ours* remaineth," Luther. We
own it as heirs. We already rule in this kingdom and
shall rule. Since we are heirs of the kingdom, crowns
await us. Only kings are crowned. This crowning
takes place at the consummation of the kingdom. We

shall sit with Christ on his throne. Superearthly is the kingdom, for all earthly kingdoms have only subjects, but this kingdom is composed of nothing but kings. It carries the idea of a kingdom to its *nth* degree. See the author's *Kings and Priests* for a full exposition. The future tense "shall not inherit" = shall never possess this inheritance, because they are doing these works of the flesh they cannot be reborn and become the King's sons.

22) **But the fruit of the spirit is love, joy, peace, longsuffering, benignity, goodness, faithfulness, meekness, self-control. Against such things there is no law.**

We have discussed the fact that Paul has in mind "spirit" in v. 16. He does not say, "the *works* of the spirit" (v. 20, "the *works* of the flesh") but uses the nobler word, "the *fruit* of the spirit." Compare the significant expression, "the unfruitful works of the darkness" (Eph. 5:11). "Fruit" is also singular although it is a collective. The flesh spreads out in many directions with its evil works; all its many activities are bad. The spirit follows one direction, produces unit fruit. The flesh has "works," deeds. In listing them Paul has used many plurals. As fruit of the spirit Paul lists nothing but virtues, the highest moral qualities, and thus also lifts this list above the other. The other list is heterogeneous: 3 — 2 — 4 — 4 — 2; this list is homogeneous: 3 — 3 — 3: each group has three members, and there are three groups. The other list is a jangle, this one a sweet harmony. While it may be only rhetorical and apparent only because we have the lists side by side, this appears intentional to the writer. Paul has the capacity for such perfect rhetoric.

First Corinthians 13 is Paul's own description of "love," the most essential product of faith, the mother of all other Christian virtues, hence the first in this list. Although it is little used in pagan Greek, this

word has a fine history. In the LXX it still has lower
meanings down to erotic love; but in the New Testament it rose to its fullest glory. God is love. It is not
always adequately defined. As distinguished from
φιλία, the love of mere liking and affection, ἀγάπη is the
love of intelligent comprehension united with corresponding blessed purpose. So God loved the world, understood all its depravity and purposed to remove it.
He could not embrace the foul, stinking world in *philia*,
but he did love it with *agape* and sent his Son to cleanse
it. We cannot offer affection to our enemies who would
smite us in the face; Jesus did not love the Pharisees
with *philia* and does not ask us so to love our enemies.
It is *agape* that he asks, the love that understands the
hatefulness of the enemy and purposes to remove it.
This distinction comes to full view in John 21:15-17.
Some of the lower uses still appear in the New Testament as when publican loves publican, but even here
intelligence and purpose are involved. Warfield's idea
that *agape* sees value in the loved object breaks down
when the main passages are studied.

With this love goes "joy." This is a remarkable
combination that was written by the man who composed II Cor. 6:4-10 on the basis of his own experience,
yet note that "always rejoicing" appears even in this
list (v. 10). Yes, joy is one of the cardinal Christian
virtues; it deserves a place next to love. Pessimism is
a grave fault. This is not fatuous joy such as the
world accepts; it is the enduring joy that bubbles up
from all the grace of God in our possession, from the
blessedness that is ours (Matt. 5:3, etc.), that is un-
dimmed by tribulation, that merges into the joy of
heaven. This joy is the sunshine that ever beams for
the believer. On "peace" see 1:3. As a Christian virtue it is subjective, the assured quietness of the soul,
the opposite of dread and terror, the feeling of all who
walk with what is spirit and indeed know that all is

well between themselves and God. These virtues form
the first trio as being the virtues which fill the spirit
itself.

The second trio is composed of virtues which appear
in our contact with men. "Longsuffering" — the mind
holds out long before giving way to action. The Rheims
Version has "longanimity" (Trench). This word is
used also with reference to God. Men may provoke,
the spirit holds out quietly.

Trench has written well regarding the synonyms
χρηστότης and ἀγαθωσύνη. The former is exhibited by
Jesus when he received the penitent sinner, Luke 7:37-
50. It is always sweet, kind, mild, full of graciousness. The best English word for it seems to be "benignity." Close to it lies the other. "Goodness"
seems to be a little pale; perhaps "beneficence" would
be better since the derivation from ἀγαθός points to the
bestowal upon others of what is good and beneficent.
It is goodness, not as mere quiescent moral excellence,
but as goodness doing good to others. Trench finds an
exhibition of it also in the expulsion of the traffickers
from the Temple by Jesus and in his invectives against
the Pharisees in Matthew 23.

The division into verses places "faithfulness" into
v. 22 and makes it a fourth member of this group.
This division would be satisfactory if πίστις meant
"trustworthiness," the fact that men could always
trust us. But the sense is not passive, it is active,
it is the German *Treue* and not *Glaube* (Luther), which
latter the A. V. imitated with its translation "faith."
It is a Christian virtue and not saving faith. We see
that the term belongs to the third trio when we note
that our being true and faithful refers to *God*, to his
Word and his will; our being meek refers to *the world
of men*; and our self-control refers to *our own selves*.
Do not object that we are faithful also toward men,
for this is only an exercise of faithfulness to God. The

essential thing is ever to be faithful and true to God
and to Christ.

23) So we shall also be full of "meekness" among
men. When we are wronged or abused we shall show
no resentment by threatening vengeance. The opposite
is to be arrogant, vehement, bitter, wild, and violent.
The greatest example of meekness is Jesus himself.
Compare the author on Matt. 5:5, including the startling promise given to the meek. The last of this final
trio is "self-control," κράτος, holding all our desires and
passions in check. The "temperance" of our versions
is inadequate, cf., Acts 24:25.

Some regard τῶν τοιούτων as a masculine since no
antecedent is visible; some are undecided; some regard
it as a neuter. We note the correspondence with τὰ
τοιαῦτα in v. 21. When we are told that it is rather
idle for Paul to say that law is not against "such
things" (neuter), and that we therefore have the
masculine, the question arises as to whether it is less
idle to say that law is not against "such men." As
far as grammar is concerned, since all of the antecedents are feminine, the neuter is preferable to the
masculine. Of far more importance is the correspondence of this clause with the relative clause in v. 21.
Still more important is the meaning that "law," of
whatever kind it may be, is not opposed to these Christian virtues. That means freedom, the great gospel
freedom which Paul has set forth. "Not against such
things" means: as against the works of the flesh.
"Such things" implies also that there are still more besides the nine here listed. This makes it unnecessary
to add "things like these" as was done in v. 20.

24) Now Paul speaks of the persons. **And they
who belong to Christ Jesus have crucified the flesh
with the passions and the cravings.** The genitive
denotes possession: "of Christ" = belonging to Christ.
The Greek uses the aorist to express the past fact

whereas we prefer the perfect "have crucified." When we compare passages such as 2:20 and Rom. 6:6, it is well to note the fact that in these passages the expressions are passive and speak of a crucifixion we have undergone while here the active speaks of a crucifixion we have performed. Rom. 8:13 is active: we put to death (A. V. mortify) the deeds of the flesh; but it is durative, a mortification that ever continues, here one past act of crucifying the flesh is referred to. What Paul indicates is the fact that all who really belong to Christ have performed this act on their flesh, a decisive, effective act. It was not performed upon them, *they* themselves did it; it does not continue, it is done and over with. While it is expressed in the third person, v. 25 shows that the reference is pointedly to the Galatians. Once for all, at the time of their conversion, they killed the flesh. In Romans we died to the sin. This reverses the expression but has the same meaning.

The expression "they did crucify the flesh" is even more significant than "put to death" in Rom. 8:13. Yes, we murdered the flesh, it was a violent act to kill this old tyrant and thus to remove him from his throne in our hearts. But the verb "crucified" contains more, for is recalls the cross and the crucifixion of Christ. In conversion we accept the crucified Christ, "the cross" (5:11), in order ever after to glory only in this cross (6:14) as our deliverance. Then and there we nailed the flesh to this divine cross, to let it hang there.

Paul reminds the Galatians of this decisive act, and the third person states that all who are Christ's have done this. The act was radical, for with the flesh all its passions and all its cravings (singular in v. 16) were crucified. The fact that the flesh still troubles us changes nothing on this score. In conversion we did make a radical break, the one here put into strong figurative language.

Παθήματα, originally a *vox media*, is used fourteen times by Paul and always in an evil sense (M.-M. 473) to designate the affects and the stirrings forced upon us by the flesh in order to enslave us. They would literally carry us away (C.-K. 841) ; the ἐπιθυμίαι are the evil desires and cravings kindled in us. They are the flesh in its activity and were thus crucified with the flesh. Let them remain so crucified, let them never attain a resurrection so as again to control us!

25) The asyndeton states this in an effective way: **If we are living with what is spirit** (as we surely are), **let us also keep in line with what is spirit, brethren!** The two datives are abutted in a telling way in the Greek. Having crucified the flesh, let us be done with it! To crucify a man is to get rid of him as a shame and disgrace, as an utter abomination. So now we live "with what is spirit" (see v. 16). Our spiritual life lies in this spiritual means. In v. 16 the verb used is περιπατέω, the ordinary word for "to walk"; here it is στοιχέω, "to keep in line, to march in rank and file." Thus it is a little more precise than the other verb. The dative again indicates means: let us keep marching in rank and file by the aid of what is spirit, all of you, Paul included, he and the Galatians in one line. The picture is both beautiful in itself and full of effective appeal to the Galatians.

CHAPTER VI

Let each man look first to himself!

5:26) The absence of a connective helps to indicate the beginning of a new paragraph. The address ἀδελφοί belongs to 5:26 and not to 6:1; "brethren" is placed at the end as it is in 5:13; 6:18. **Let us not be vainglorious, challenging each other, envying each other, brethren.** How can "brethren" do such a thing! Paul comes to speak about direct personal admonitions in the use of our Christian liberty. This liberty is devoid of all selfishness. The hortative subjunctive is softened by the fact that Paul includes himself; this agrees with 6:4, 5. B.-P. 669: *Wir wollen keine Prahlhaense sein,* let us not be braggarts. The word "vainglorious," κενόδοξος, does not refer to empty (κενός), fictitious glory which the vainglorious person imagines to be real and genuine glory; the word denotes the praise which men seek without a genuine reason.

Persons who are covetous of all possible glorification on the part of men will thus challenge one another as though in combat, each wanting more credit and praise than the other receives. Back of this lies envy. Each will envy the other because of the praise he may obtain, especially if this is greater than his own. Phil. 2:3; Rom. 12:10b; I Pet. 5:5. The two participles are modal; they show how desire for honor among men manifests itself. "Brethren" indicates a new paragraph; more than that, "brethren" who are what the word means cannot and will not act in this manner, such actions are far beneath them.

1) Those who are filled with unholy ambition would be glad to see a brother blemished by some

transgression and do not see that they themselves
are thereby already blemished in the worst manner.
Paul applies the teaching of Jesus who bids one pull
the beam out of his own eye before he attempts to
extract the speck out of his brother's eye. Cleanse
thyself first and then help cleanse also the brother
who may need thy service.

**If also a person gets to be overtaken in some
transgression, you on your part, the spiritual ones,
do you proceed to restore such a one in a spirit of
meekness, watching thyself lest thou also get to be
tempted.**
Paul visualizes such a case as one that may well
happen "also," i. e., besides the serious faults just mentioned. The idea that παράπτωμα means only a slight
"fault" (A. V.), and that the word is chosen because
of this mild meaning, cannot be upheld; this word
is never used in the mild sense in the New Testament.
Literally meaning, "something fallen by the side," i. e.,
as an auto that goes off the road into a ditch, in our
idiom it denotes a "transgression," something that runs
across or against what is right. The idea is something
that is plainly wrong.

The aorist is punctiliar, "gets to be," etc. Luther's
von einem Fehl uebereilet wuerde, which is followed by
our versions, is quite correct and better than the proposed meaning, "gets to be caught or surprised in a
transgression." The sense cannot be: if *you* catch a
brother doing wrong; it could at best be only: if *the
wrong* catches or surprises him into a fall. Paul cannot mean as the opposite: if *you* surprise him "before"
(πρό) he can cover up his wrong.

Paul is excluding wilful, deliberate sin; he deals
with sins into which one may be "tempted" (last verb)
in some way. Include *Uebereilungssuenden* but also
sins that are due to ignorance, weakness, the deceptive
power of sin, the persuasion and the bad example of

others. Deliberate sin is a fall from grace; the transgression here referred to is one that has not as yet reached such a fall. In every case of this kind brotherly love must come to the rescue and put the auto on the road again. Paul says emphatically: "you on your part, the spiritual ones," i. e., who walk, are led, and keep in line with what is spirit (5:16, 18, 25), "do you proceed to restore such a one" (durative present). Only "the spiritual" can naturally do this restoring, but all of us ought to be spiritual. This is not a task for such as are not able to master their flesh. The present imperative is scarcely conative: "try to restore"; it may be iterative to include every case of this kind since "such a one" points to repeated cases that may now and again occur. Each case may also take time and patience.

We have "artisan" from this verb and its adjective, and κατά is perfective. The verb is used to designate framing a mechanism in an expert manner (Heb. 10:5; 11, 3) but more often to denote restoration, setting a broken limb, mending nets (Matt. 4:21), it is always an action that requires expert skill.

The task here mentioned requires spirituality in general and especially that feature of it listed in 5:23, "a spirit of meekness," the opposite of arrogance and harshness. Pour in oil and wine and with gentle fingers bind up the wounds. The addition: "watching thyself lest thou also get to be tempted," is not intended merely as a warning but as the motivation for meekness. We shall be meek in our treatment and show our expertness in this way when we remember that temptation may catch us also as it has caught this or that brother.

The aorist is effective, "be tempted into a fall." Let no one think he cannot be so tempted. Let everyone think what he would need in case he, too, should fall. Such a spirit will quickly mend a brother's case. It is, of course, remarked that Paul drops into the singular, which is not anacoluthic (R. 439) but intentional. Each must watch himself. "Watching yourselves" might be misunderstood as keeping an eye on each other — no, keep it on your own self.

2) This thought of correcting a brother who has fallen into some transgression leads Paul to broaden his admonition. There are many other burdens which we ought to help each other to bear. **The burdens of each other keep bearing and thus fulfill the law of Christ.** Support each other in every way. Weakness, ignorance, inexperience, difficult surroundings, grief, affliction, etc., are some of these burdens. This is the blessedness of Christian fellowship that each is not left to bear his load alone, others will help him to bear it. When many come to the support of one, he will be helped, indeed.

Paul might have said, "Thus you will fulfill the law of Christ." He retains the imperative but now uses the effective aorist: "and thus actually fulfill or fill up the law of Christ." This is the law of love, John 13:34, the law of true Christian liberty. No law is able to produce this love, only the gospel can do it. James 2:8 calls it "the royal law," it is devoid of all slavishness. This second imperative furnishes the motive for the first. Our one desire should ever be to fulfill the law of Christ to whom we belong (5:24), and bearing each other's burdens is the way to do this.

3) With "for" Paul substantiates his admonitions by pointing to the opposite. But not to the opposite action, refusal to bear the burdens of others; he at once goes deeper, namely to the delusion from which such refusal would spring. **For if**

one deems he is something while he is nothing, his mind deludes himself. Self-satisfied, such a man thinks that he is something and needs no help from his brethren in bearing any burdens he may have, he himself being capable enough. Thus also he will have no heart for his burdened brethren. For what makes us tender and helpful, meek and kindly toward others is the realization that we ourselves are nothing and that we, too, need our brethren. Satisfaction with self makes poor helpers for those in need of fraternal support.

The natural negative with the participle is μηδέν, and this belongs to the protasis although some would construe it with the apodosis: "being nothing, his mind deludes himself." But Paul does not claim that everyone is nothing. The fault he scores is that one who is nothing thinks himself something. It is no fault to be something and then to think accordingly in all honesty. Rom. 12:3 is plain regarding this. Grace made a good deal of Paul (I Cor. 15:10), and he says so. "To be something, while being nothing" naturally goes together as it is placed together, and as every ordinary reader would read it. The compound verb contains "mind" and "deceive" and is found in no earlier writing. The whole protasis warrants the conclusion: "his mind deludes himself," even his own mind which ought to know that nothing is never something.

4) Against such empty-headed self-estimation ("vainglory," 5:26) Paul advises: **But his own work let each one keep testing, and then in regard to himself alone he will have his cause for boasting and not in regard to the other person.** Instead of entertaining a vacuous opinion about himself, let him diligently test his own actual work. It is so easy to have a good opinion about oneself, but carefully weigh and test your actual accomplishment, that will tell

the story. The singular "work" with the durative
"keep testing" is the sum of accomplishment and
this submitted to constantly renewed and revised
testing.

By no means does Paul say, "Then you will have
no reason for boasting." The context is: "in regard
to himself alone — and not in regard to the other person," and this context does not permit us to have ἕξει
mean, "he will hold off his boasting" because he will
find that his whole work amounts to nothing. Quite
the contrary. The diligent tester — Paul was one —
will find that he does amount to something, that he
actually has a definite καύχημα, "ground for boasting."
He will, of course, thank God for that. This constant
tester may revise his estimate from time to time as he
learns to make his tests more accurately by means
of the Word. But, proceeding as he does, he will have
his reason for boasting "as pertaining to himself alone
(εἰς) and not as pertaining to the other person" (again
εἰς). This does not mean that he will keep it to himself and will not, when occasion warrants or demands,
tell anybody else. For then Paul disobeyed this rule
in I Cor. 15:10, and still more in II Cor. 11:21-12:6.
What Paul says is that this tester will get no wrong
estimate by pitting himself against the other person
and deciding that he is better than that other person
(definite article). That is what happened to the Pharisee in Luke 18:9-12. *Wer sich an einem andern misst,
vermisst sich.* Besser. He will stand on his own feet,
"for himself alone."

5) **For each one will carry his own cargo** (Acts
27:10 has this noun) without reference to any other
person. "Will carry" matches "will have" in v. 4,
both refer to the final judgment. "Their works do
follow them," Rev. 14:13. The opposite of vainglory
(5:26) is not spurious self-abasement but genuine testing. Vainglory accompanies Judaistic and pharisaic

work-righteousness; love which tests itself, which restores others accompanies gospel freedom. Carry this
and its work as a blessed cargo.

Receiving and imparting spiritual excellence

6) It would be a trivial thought so close to the
end of the epistle to admonish the Galatians to be
generous with their money. Yet this interpretation
has been put upon this paragraph by not a few. The
more the writer seeks to read Paul's words in this
light, the more he feels that he cannot accept this interpretation. Δέ does turn to a different subject, yet to
one that is allied. Verses 4, 5 emphasize, as does the
participial clause in v. 1, that each must look well to
himself even as each must carry his own load. The
allied subject is fellowship, but certainly not merely
in money and in earthly goods. The word "poor" does
not occur in v. 9, 10. In v. 1 the spiritual life of an
erring brother is at stake. In v. 3 we are to bear
each other's burdens, which is already one kind of
fellowship, the one that steps in to share the other's
hardships. Paul now adds the rest of it: both our receiving and our imparting spiritual and moral good.

**Moreover, let him who is being instructed in the
Word be partaker with the one instructing him in all
good things.** The verb κοινωνέω is seemingly not
properly understood. When this is regarded as meaning "communicate," "all good things" become material,
and somehow or other it is thought that Paul says
that pupils should reward or pay their teachers, congregations their pastors. This idea is also put into
κοινωνία, the noun, which is thought to mean "contribution" in Rom. 15:26; II Cor. 8:4; 9:13; Heb. 13:16;
this view has gotten into some of the dictionaries. The
noun always = fellowship, and in the case of alms a
fellowship that is exercised (*Teilnahme*, C.-K. 614)
by means of alms. If the noun means "contribution"

of alms in the four passages referred to, the verb would here practically make the teachers the recipients of alms, men who receive contributions as alms.

The verb means *participem esse* and then *participem facere*, to be or to make participant, the latter, however, in the sense "to share something with somebody, thereby not making him a fellow with oneself but *oneself* a fellow with *him*," C.-K. 612, on our passage. Consider in connection with this C.-K. 4 on "all good things," *im Sinne von heilbringend*, "good" as bringing salvation. The one who instructs has the good things; the one being instructed is to proceed to participate in them, in "all" of them. The riches are with the teacher of the Word, the poverty is with the pupil, and the pupil is to institute "fellowship" with the teacher so that he, the pupil, may be enriched.

Yes, there are not only burdens in which we must fellowship and aid those who bear them, there are also "good things," spiritually and morally beneficial things, in which we should delight to have fellowship with those who possess these good things. Who should have more of them than our teachers? The burdens are painful, the good things are conducive to salvation, delightful. With those who have the burdens and with those who have these good things we should keep fellowship, making *ourselves* fellow with *them*.

This is just about the opposite of the common view. In addition to the context and the meaning of the words themselves one must note that when Paul writes about the one instructing, the Galatians would at once think of their first and greatest instructor together with his assistant who had twice been in their midst. Could Paul tell the Galatians in this letter that they owed material contributions to him and to his helpers? Could he do such a thing with no further word of explanation? Paul never took money for his work. When he speaks of this subject in I Cor. 9 he does so with the fullest and the clearest explanation. See the same thought in II Cor. 11:7-12, which should be read in its connection with I Cor. 9.

We ought also not to forget the Judaizers who also came as teachers, on whose greediness II Cor. 11:20 enlightens us. When such greedy fellows were working in Galatia, Paul could scarcely write the Galatians to share "in all things" (material) with their teachers. Aside from the implication involving himself, such an admonition would reflect on the true teachers in Galatia and suggest that they were also men who were to be paid.

We need not discuss "the one instructing." Paul had not left the Galatian churches in an unorganized state; he had them elect elders and pastors who were qualified to teach. Apart from this office the gift of teaching was exercised as one of the most valuable gifts (Rom. 12:7); we constantly read of teaching in the Acts, note the teachers mentioned in Acts 13:1; I Cor. 12:28, 29. "In all good things" that were possessed by their instructors, Paul and his assistants among them, the Galatians should ever cultivate fellowship for their own enrichment. Then all would, indeed, be well with them. Pay for these teachers? There is no reason for mentioning it in this epistle.

7) The efforts to have what Paul now says support the idea that teachers are to be duly rewarded show that this conception is untenable. Paul and his assistants took no such reward. Sowing for the flesh and sowing for the spirit deal with a subject that is far greater, namely with the desire for all good spiritual things in which the Galatians should seek to share.

Be not deceived, God is not sneered at. The verb means, "to turn up the nose at someone" in disdain.

The implication is that God lets no one do that with impunity. Γάρ at once explains in what respect this warning is to be heeded. **For what a person keeps sowing, that very thing also he shall reap.** In II Cor. 9:6 the point to be stressed is the identity of what is sown and harvested. You cannot sow one thing and reap the opposite or even another thing. You will ever get the same thing, only very much more of it. Let nothing and nobody deceive you on that score. Turn up your nose to God on that if you will; inexorably you will be caught in the law of God.

The absence of the article with "God" seems to make the word qualitative: he who is no less than God. You may turn up your nose at men with impunity, but "God" is far different. The form σπείρῃ may be either present or aorist subjunctive, progressive sowing or just one act. Here it is the former, because ὁ σπείρων follows, the present participle: "he who keeps sowing" not the aorist: "he who finishes one sowing."

8) First the universal law or principle and God back of it. Now the application to the whole spiritual life in the form of the reason that we should never be deceived, and that God is never mocked with impunity. **Because the one sowing for his own flesh, from this flesh will reap corruption; but the one sowing for the spirit, from this spirit will reap life eternal.** The truth that what a person sows he will also reap is an axiom, it needs no proof, no "because." This clause proves what the "for" clause written in v. 7 elucidates, namely that we must not be deceived as to any possibility of God's being mocked.

We cannot understand those who refer "flesh" and "spirit" to two different kinds of *soil* and then say that the soil conditions the two harvests, and in addition to that state that Paul has not altered his figure from the *seed* to the *soil*. But it is not true that the *soil* decides the harvest. In Matt. 13:3, etc., we have four kinds of soil, but three kinds bring *no* harvest at all. These interpreters state that the seed is our material wealth: if we use that wealth by sowing it "into our own flesh," our harvest will be according to this soil, while if we use our wealth by sowing it "into the spirit," our harvest will be better. Supporting our teachers with our wealth is then thought to be sowing it "into the spirit."

This interpretation makes the second soil "the Spirit." But the idea that the Spirit is *soil*, and that this Spirit as soil is paired with flesh, flesh as also being *soil*, is untenable. We have already shown that Paul places "spirit" in opposition to "flesh"; see throughout 5:16-25 and the discussion under v. 16 and v. 25. Some direct attention to the fact that Paul writes "his own flesh" but not "his own spirit" since one cannot say "his own Spirit." But Paul means that the flesh is always our very own while the spirit is the new nature that is born in us by divine operation. To call both our own would be a mistake, for it would say that the spirit is our own in the same sense as the flesh, which would not be true.

The two sowers are contrasted. The one sows "for or unto his own flesh," the other "for or unto the spirit." Εἰς is not "into," one does not sow "into"; it is like the dative (R. 594). The one sows *for* his own flesh, to promote his flesh; the other for the spirit, to promote its interests. The sowing is figurative for what has already been stated literally in 5:16: walking by what is spirit; 5:18: being led by what is spirit; 5:25: living and keeping in line by what is spirit; thus the opposite is walking, being led, living, and keeping step with the flesh. Our life here is a sowing of the one kind or of the other.

The thought is the same as that expressed in Rom. 8:12, 13: debtors not to the flesh to live after the flesh and thus to die, but with the spirit (not Spirit) to kill the deeds of the flesh and thus to live (see this passage). The stress is on the two sowers and what their sowing promotes. Neither seed nor soil is mentioned, for no one sows without them. As to the seed, this is plainly implied. He who sows for his flesh will sow the seed his flesh furnishes and certainly not the seed furnished by the spirit; the same is true with regard to the other sower. We need no special statement on this point.

When Paul says, "from this flesh (of his) he will reap corruption," and, "from this spirit he will reap life eternal," the articles point back to the very flesh and the spirit for which each sower sows, so that we may translate: "from this flesh — from this spirit." The one sower does his sowing in order to promote his flesh, to get more and more of this flesh of his, for one always sows in order to get more of the same product. Paul has already said, "That very thing he will, indeed, get." Yea, in 5:19, etc., he has already listed the works of the flesh, the products which the flesh wants and brings forth. The other sower does his sowing in order to promote the spirit, to get augmentation of this product. He certainly gets it (v. 7), and 5:22, etc., states in detail what the spirit wants and produces. One should not overlook this connection with 5:19-25, for this passage shows the intermediate products of the flesh and of the spirit.

Paul does not go over this ground again, his readers are to remember what he has already said. Here he mentions the two final harvests. What one can grow *for* the flesh (the works of the flesh, 5:19, etc.) one reaps *out of* this flesh, *from* it, this very flesh furnishes the harvest. This is also true with regard to

the spirit. Paul does not expand the thought so as
to include seed and soil; he keeps what he says compact. The final harvest of the flesh-sower is "corruption." This has been explained already in 5:21, yet
only negatively: he shall not inherit the kingdom of
God. Here this is stated positively: "he shall reap
corruption." The final harvest of the spirit-sower is
the opposite: "he shall reap life eternal," i. e., shall inherit the kingdom. Thus each reaps what he sows.

Beyond question "corruption" and "life eternal" are
extreme opposites. Rom. 8:13 is the parallel: "ye shall
die — ye shall live." "Corruption" matches "the
flesh," but not in a physical way. Yet R., *W. P.*, remarks: "Nature writes in one's body the penalty of
sin as every doctor knows." True as this is, here Paul
states far more. "Flesh" is not the body but our own
sin-corrupted nature. Disease invades also the body
of the godly person, his body, too, sees corruption in
the grave (I Cor. 15:53). Paul is not speaking of this.
Here φθορά has its first meaning, *Vernichtung* (C.-K.
1200), *Untergang* (B.-P. 1369 for our passage),
ἀπώλεια, eternal death, the opposite of "life eternal."
John uses the latter fourteen times.

The spirit itself is ζωή. It is the spiritual life principle itself; we get it by regeneration. It manifests itself as is indicated in 5:22, 23. Those who are without it are dead in trespasses and sins. This life may
be lost, but it is to go on and on, is to pass unscathed
through physical death, is to be "eternal," beyond
death. It includes the body which only sleeps in
physical death and is raised at last to have its full
part in this everlasting life in heaven: "he shall reap
life eternal."

All that Paul says goes beyond the proper use of
our earthly wealth, being generous to spiritual instructors, and the like. Sowing for the spirit and
reaping from the spirit include all our spiritual activ-

ity. The idea that Paul teaches the merit of good
works with eternal life as their reward does not appreciate what "the spirit" is and what sowing "for the
spirit" means. The kingdom of God is inherited (5:21)
and not earned by works or human merit.

9) Sowing for the spirit is hard work, long-con-
tinued work, and, although the harvest is eternal
blessedness, we may, while we are waiting for it,
grow discouraged. Hence the admonition: **Moreover, in doing the excellent thing let us not be discouraged, for in proper season we shall reap if we
do not relax.**

The connective δέ adds this as being something different. It certainly is very necessary. "The excellent
or noble thing" = sowing for the spirit and comprises
all that 5:22, 23 contains. The neuter is used in the
Greek fashion as the equivalent of an abstract noun;
it is all one noble unit with which our spiritual activity
is concerned.

Paul employs this verb in II Cor. 4:1, 16 and uses
it in the same sense: "let us not be growing tired, discouraged, faint, or fainthearted." The verb does not
mean, "to give in to evil." It contains κακός in the sense
of "inferior"; the "to be weary" of our versions is quite
correct, as is also the "to faint" in II Cor. 4:1, 16.
Many start well but tire sooner or later, especially
when exertion becomes hard.

What is to keep our energy up to the mark,
strengthen us ever anew, is the shining harvest which
we shall reap in its own season. That season comes
to each one as God arranges. The negative participle
at the end: "we not relaxing, not being exhausted, not
letting down," once more emphasizes the thought that
we should not tire in our blessed task. The implication is a condition: "if we do not relax" (R. 1023).

Participle and subjunctive are present tenses
denoting state or condition. To be doing "the (spiritu-

ally) excellent thing" is itself an inspiration, but in addition to this Paul points to the coming harvest. When the blessed harvest season arrives, we shall wonder why we ever thought of getting tired and of relaxing; to have waited a hundred times as long will then seem to us no reason at all for thinking of tiring.

10) This brings the concluding admonition which is based on the foregoing: **Accordingly then, while we have opportunity, let us work the thing that is good toward all and especially toward the house-members of the faith.**

Verse 9 is negative: let us not grow tired, not be exhausted. So we now have the positive: do with energy. The emphasis is on "while we have opportunity" (the correct reading has the indicative and not the subjunctive as in Westcott and Hort). The idea is, however, not a reference to special opportunities which come now and again, "the good" then being some material help extended by us in charity. No; this is an ever-present *kairos*, "season" or opportunity; ὡς = *jetzt wo* (B.-D. 455, 2), "now while." In place of "the excellent thing" whose spiritual excellence is contained in itself we now have "the good thing," *heilbringend* (C.-K. 4), spiritually beneficial to others who are also named. This articulated neuter singular is classic and equal to an abstract noun; the article is generic (R. 763), all the good is a unit. In v. 6 we have the plural; it is characteristic of Paul to change from the plural to the singular.

It is true, v. 10 looks back to v. 6, but not in the way so commonly supposed, namely that in v. 6 we dispense material gifts to our teachers and now in v. 10 to all men in general and especially to our fellow believers. Quite otherwise: we are first to make ourselves participants with our teachers in all the spiritually good things they have to offer us. This is to be the *source* of our enrichment. Then we are to dispense our spir-

itual wealth to others with all tireless energy so that
they may share it with us. This is to be the *outflow*.
It is to go on "while, as long as, we have opportunity,"
as long as life lasts and without weariness. Jesus is
the example, Paul is another.

We are told by some that moral good (spiritual
would be correct) is our universal duty, in which no
distinction can be made such as doing this good "especially" to our fellow believers; so, it is argued, Paul
must here refer to material good. But dispensing
Christian charity, no matter to whom, is ever as much
a spiritual act as any other and is to be performed only
in the same spiritual way. Dispensing charity especially to our brethren is required no more than doing
other spiritual good especially to our brethren. They
have *first* call upon us and our energy. It would be
strange indeed if this were not true. Does Paul not
call them the οἰκεῖοι of the faith, those who are in the
same house with us, with whom we are in closest contact as "house-members"? All their spiritual needs
are seen and felt by us in the most immediate way.
They and we are of one divine family or household, we
are joined together with them as we are with no others. This is the reason for Paul's "especially"; it
applies to "the good" in every respect.

Paul might have said, "especially toward the brethren"; by saying "house-members" he justifies his special mention of these. In Eph. 2:19 he uses "house-
members of God," those who belong to God's household,
the church. The genitive is possessive, it is like "of
the faith." The latter is thus another instance in
which "the faith" (articulated) is objective faith, *quae
creditur*, not subjective, *qua creditur*. It is interesting to compare ὑμῶν τὸ ἀγαθόν in Rom. 14:16 with τὸ ἀγαθόν used here and to ask ourselves whether the two have
reference to the same thing.

Conclusion

All my glorying is in the Cross of our Lord
Jesus Christ!

11) The final paragraph is no longer admonitory but thetical and summary and ends with a prayerful wish. It is marked as the conclusion by the first sentence. **See with what large letters I have written to you with my own hand!**

This simple sentence has caused much discussion. Paul is not exclaiming because of the size of his epistle. Yet Luther and others translate, "with how many words." The dative means "with how large letters." Others, like R. 846, regard the aorist as epistolary: Paul places himself at the time when his letter is read in Galatia, and his writing is then in the past. These assume that this letter was dictated, that, as in other dictated letters, Paul wrote only the concluding verses with his own hand, and that in this letter he wrote these last words in large, bold script. But Paul never uses the aorist ἔγραψα to designate the writing of only a few concluding words. He uses the aorist "I wrote" when he refers to an earlier letter, or to an entire letter that is reaching its close, or to a discussion he has just finished (I Cor. 9:15). He uses "I write" to indicate a statement just written, something he continues to write, even a letter that is almost finished. From this we conclude that Paul is here referring to this entire epistle and says that all of it came from his own hand, that none of it was dictated, that all of it was written in large script.

This raises two questions: "Why did Paul write with his own hand instead of dictating? Why was the script notably large?" The natural answers are: "Because no amanuensis was at hand; because Paul's hand had been badly hurt in one or the other of the severe beatings he had received when he was flayed by the lictors at Philippi or when he was stoned and left as dead at Lystra." The latter, namely a badly damaged hand, may be the reason that Paul dictated his other letters.

Writing at Corinth shortly after starting his work there, the delegation from Galatia found Paul alone, without a scribe, with nobody to send greetings to the Galatians. Thus Paul wrote this epistle with his own hand. The supposition that he did it in order the more to show his personal interest in the Galatians could be entertained only if Paul had had a scribe at hand and yet did not use him. Even then we think he would have used him.

The large script has been referred to as indicating eye trouble, this together with his practice of dictating, 4:15 is also introduced. Between this supposition and the one that Paul's right hand had been hurt we prefer the latter. The damage to his hand may well have been one of the stigmata to which he refers in v. 17. At least, we deem this the most tenable idea that has been offered on the subject.

12) The issue in Galatia centered on circumcision in a special way (5:2, etc.) ; hence Paul reverts to this in his conclusion. **As many as want to make a fair show in the flesh, these** (are the ones who) **are trying to compel you to have yourselves circumcised in order that they may not be persecuted because of the cross of Christ. For not even those who are circumcised themselves observe what is law, but they want you to have yourselves circumcised in order that they may get to boast for themselves in your very flesh.**

Paul exposes the Judaizers, these circumcisers, as to their base motive. They are not at all concerned about "spirit" but only about "flesh" (v. 8). In this domain they want to make a fair showing. This verb has finally been found in one of the papyri. This is a sample of what may occur in the case of other words that have hitherto been found only in the New Testament. B.-P. 506: "they want to play a role before men," which gives the sense but not the exact equivalent of the word. The German *gleissen* is better. They were good Jesuits.

These, Paul says, men of this type, are the ones who "are trying to compel you (conative present, B.-D. 319; R. 880) to have yourselves circumcised (permissive passive) only in order that they may not be persecuted because of the cross of Christ" (dative of cause, B.-D. 196; R. 532.) They want to make a fine showing with you Galatians by inducing all of you to get circumcised so that the Jews, who are otherwise so hostile to Christianity, may not persecute them, i. e., the Judaizers, although they confess the crucified Christ. The aim of the Judaizers is to win so much merit with the Jews that these will not attack them as they constantly attack Paul, having nearly killed him at Lystra.

Pause and note that, if Paul had yielded on the point of the necessity of circumcision, he, too, could have escaped this persecution, the instigators of which were uniformly Jews. It was his stand on circumcision that fired the dynamite of Jewish hate. See what it did to Paul in Acts 21:18, 19; he was nearly killed in the Temple on the suspicion of having brought an uncircumcised Gentile into the sacred precincts. What a temptation for Paul to advocate circumcision in order to curry favor with the Jews! Was circumcision not a matter that was merely ceremonial? Today many would compromise on a thing like that. The Judaizers also accepted Jesus and the cross; all they did was to soften the offensiveness of the cross to the Jews. Was that not wise? If many of our day had been in their place they would have agreed to this. Do they not today still make the cross palatable by removing its offense?

13) With "for" Paul explains how the Judaizers make only a fair showing in the flesh: although they demanded circumcision they themselves are not observing what is law. Note the absence of the article. We may also regard this present tense as conative: "do not attempt to observe law." Some think that the Judaizers failed to keep the moral parts of the law. But the unmodified word "law" does not allow such a restriction. It includes both the circumcision of the Judaizers and their demand upon the Galatians to be circumcised. For it is certainly not observing law in any true sense of the word to advocate circumcision only in order to escape Jewish persecution. To comply with the outward form of law with such a motive is anything but true compliance. Abraham did not do so when he accepted circumcision as a seal of God's covenant. What the Judaizers did with circumcision they did with law in general. Do the Galatians want to listen to and to follow such men?

The readings vary between the less well-attested perfect participle: "they that have been circumcised," and the present participle which is more adequately attested and which appears to be more difficult since it seems to mean, "those being circumcised" or, "those letting themselves be circumcised," which could then not refer to the Judaizers but only to Gentiles who allowed themselves to be persuaded to circumcision while here the former are undoubtedly referred to. Zahn regards the present as being timeless, as stating the custom which these people advocated, that of being circumcised. Paul wants to say more than that the Judaizers were once circumcised and then, of course, remained so (perfect participle). Paul and all Christian Jews were such men. These Judaizers were men who ever advocate being circumcised, *Beschneidungs-leute* as they have been called, or rather *Leute des Beschnittenwerdens.* The term is intended to be derogatory.

So little are they concerned about actual observance of law that their purpose in having you Galatians subject yourselves to circumcision is only "that they may get to boast in their own interest (middle voice) in *your* flesh." That is why they want you circumcised so as to be able to point to *your* flesh, the amputation of your foreskin as their great accomplishment in order to win vast credit among the Jews. The possessive pronoun is used for the sake of emphasis; a simple genitive ὑμῶν would be without emphasis. "*Your* own" flesh like *their* own and like the *Jews'* own — to achieve that boast (aorist) in their own interest (middle) is their great purpose. This positive ἵνα supplements the negative one used in v. 12. These are the selfish, despicable Judaizers.

14) Throughout v. 12, 13 we have a description of men who are the direct opposite of Paul. This is made evident by the fervent wish: **But for me on my part let it never get to be** (that I) **try to boast save in the cross of our Lord Jesus Christ, by means of which for me the world has been crucified, and I for the world!**

The dative of relation is placed forward for the sake of strong emphasis and is thus set into opposition with all men such as have just been described. Paul uses this aorist optative of wish often, most frequently with only the negative particle: "Let it not be!" which in our versions is rendered, "God forbid!" The aorist is effective and has the infinitive as its subject, which is either a conative present: "that I try to boast," or durative in general: "that I go boasting" save in one thing only, namely in the cross, etc. The Judaizers wanted to escape the persecution that was connected

with the cross by making their boast to the Jews that
they were getting the Gentile Christians to submit to
circumcision. Verse 15 shows that Paul has this in
mind in his prayerful wish that the cross may ever be
his one and only boast. Let what persecution will come,
no other boast shall be his. The Judaizers are sincere
only regarding themselves and not regarding the cross;
Paul is the opposite.

His wish is made regarding himself but in such a
way that every Galatian, every true Christian will
repeat it with Paul. He adds the full, solemn genitive:
in the cross "of our Lord Jesus Christ." The plural
"our" includes all the Galatians and thus says much
more than "my" would imply. He is "our Lord" in the
full soteriological sense of gracious Lord who purchased and won us as his own, to whom we belong,
under whom we live happy to be his and to serve him
alone, whose name is "Jesus" or Savior, whose title is
"Christ," which indicates his mighty office: the Messiah anointed of God.

"The cross of our Lord Jesus Christ" as Paul's one
boast and glory is most comprehensive. We see this
when he makes it exclude Judaistic circumcision and
thus all legalism. When we today adopt Paul's great
wish for ourselves we forget those old Judaizers. They
have long ago faded from the life of the Christian
Church. Oppositions to the cross bearing other names,
using other legalistic tenets, dissolvents of newer kinds,
have replaced the Judaizers. Against all of them we
vow allegiance to the cross with Paul's words. Whatever side of the cross, whatever doctrine involved in
the cross are attacked today, the cross, the whole cross
and nothing but the cross is our one treasure.

Our poets have sung its praises in noblest strains,
our congregations ring with these exalted strains, symbolic crosses decorate our altars, our pulpits, our spires,
and our gravestones. It is the cross of "the blood

theology," the cross on which the Son of God died for
our advantage, the cross of expiation, substitution,
ransom, and atonement, the cross which brought the
resurrection of the crucified body and its exaltation at
God's right hand of majesty and power and the future
resurrection and exaltation of our mortal bodies. God
help us ever to see it in the fulness with which it filled
the eyes and the gospel of Paul!

The relative is to be connected with "the cross," on
which also the genitive depends, even as the Lord cannot be dissociated from the cross which made him "our
Lord." By means of this cross, Paul says, "to me the
world has been crucified, and I to the world." Both
pronouns are emphatic, both are in opposition to the
Judaizers, both are to be uttered by every Galatian as
they are by Paul. "The world" needs no article in the
Greek as is the case with regard to other nouns that
designate objects only one of which exists. "The
world" as here used is all that among men is in opposition to God, to Christ, and to his cross (C.-K. 622),
men who are themselves filled with this opposition or
the opposition which fills them. The perfect tense "has
been crucified" has its present connotation: once crucified and thus remaining so.

There is a causal sense in the double relative clause:
Paul glories in the cross because by means of it a crucifixion has taken place for him and in him. When he
came to faith in the cross, then the world was crucified
and remained so for him, and he himself was crucified
for the world and remains so. Both datives may be
called ethical. The verb is figurative and not mystical.
Crucifixion means death and more than death, a death
of shame and abomination by which the dead one is
cast out as one execrated. Here a double crucifixion,
a double death of execration took place: in the one the
world was nailed to the cross as far as Paul was concerned, in the other Paul was nailed to the cross as far

as the world was concerned. Each was forever done
with the other. This double thing was done entirely
"by means of the cross of our Lord Jesus Christ."

So brief the expression, yet so tremendous. Perfection in wording to attain concentrated penetration
of thought. The effect of the cross for and in the believer cannot be stated in a more adequate way. Even
the two datives and the two nominatives are placed
chiastically, and one verb is enough. Yet the two pronouns are placed first, for the change takes place
entirely in Paul. The world is the same old wicked
world of which Paul was once a part. Then the cross
came into his heart and changed him completely. It
was not he who then crucified the world in execration.
This was done for him in his heart. So, too, it was the
world which was crucified for him; this was done for
him by another, again done in his heart. The passive
leaves unsaid who did both. It was not the cross, for
this was the great means. Was it not "our Lord Jesus
Christ" who entered Paul's heart with his cross?

15) The cross has placed a great gulf between
Paul and the world. It has liberated him from the
wicked world. This liberation is the subject of the
whole epistle. When Paul writes "world" he
broadens to the greatest extent. So with "for" he
now explains how the Judaizers are involved. **For
neither circumcision is anything, nor foreskin, but a
new creation.**

This recalls 5:6, and the substance is the same. The
three abstract terms are often regarded as pure abstracts, yet the observation is correct that here, as is the
case quite often, they are used as marking three concretes: all those who are circumcised — all those who
have foreskin — all those who have been made new
creatures by regeneration and faith in the cross. The
two former are nothing at all, but the latter are something, the latter alone. Yet "neither — nor" is not

parallel but diverse. For those who have been circumcised considered their circumcision as being something, yea, the great decisive advantage. Those with foreskin, of course, never boasted thus about their foreskin. The Judaizers and the Jews considered the uncircumcised as nothing. Thus Paul's meaning is: circumcision is nothing of advantage — foreskin is nothing of disadvantage; the one no gain — the other no loss. But to be a new creation is everthing.

This statement puts the whole matter into succinct and final form. It expounds the main clause of v. 14, Paul's glorying in the cross, and not merely the relative clause regarding what the cross effects. On the new creation compare II Cor. 5:17.

16) **And as many as shall keep in line with this canon, peace on them and mercy, even on the Israel of God!** Verse 15 states the objective canon; "and" in v. 16 adds the subjective use of this canon. "As many as" includes all of them whether living in Galatia or elsewhere. See 5:25 on the verb. From κανών we have our "canon" which eventually came to be applied to the Scriptures. The word refers to a measuring rod by which we take measure of something to verify whether it is of proper size or length. So we measure our doctrine and our life by the Scriptures, for these alone are the exactest measuring rod we possess. Paul speaks of those who will make their faith and their life tally with the blessed principle he has just stated.

On them "peace" shall rest, the peace of God, the condition in which all is well with them. See 1:3. We generally have "grace and peace," peace being named second as the result of having grace. We several times also have "mercy and peace" in the same manner. Paul reverses the order and places the phrase between the words, which leads some to think that he refers to "peace" in this life and "mercy" at the time of the final judgment. While one may mention the cause first

(mercy) and the effect second (peace), it is also proper
to name the effect before its cause. We so understand
the order used here. We shall certainly enjoy mercy
also in this life. To point to II Tim. 1:18 is of no help
since it does not mention peace; neither do Matt. 5:7;
James 2:13; Jude 21.

We need not be puzzled about καί and "the Israel
of God." The future tense "shall keep in line" confines us to the future which is now beginning, and
"as many as" omits none who could be added to this
number. Is it possible to restrict "as many as" to the
Galatians and then to add to them "the Israel of God"
(believing Jews)? What about the other churches
with their believing Gentiles? Gentiles and Jews in all
the churches are together conceived as those who will
keep in line with the canon.

This καί signifies "even" or "namely." "As many
as will keep in line with the rule" constitute "the Israel
of God." The objection that Paul should then say,
"upon the whole Israel of God," is answered by the
preceding future tense. The whole or all the Israel
would include all the Old Testament saints; but Paul
is not speaking of these. Paul has a special, telling
reason for adding this explicative apposition. It is
a last blow at the Judaizers, his final triumph over
them and their contention. As many as shall keep in
line with this rule, they and they alone constitute "the
Israel of God" from henceforth, all Judaizers to the
contrary notwithstanding.

17) Paul has reached the end of his epistle.
**Henceforth let no one go on furnishing me troubles,
for I on my part carry in my body the scarmarks of
Jesus.** Paul is done with this trouble in Galatia. He
considers the issue ended. So little does he expect any
further danger from it that he will have no one extract
further troubles from it for him. Paul was justified
in this view. The Galatians must have taken a simi-

lar attitude, for we hear of no more Judaistic trouble for them or for Paul from them.

With "for" he assigns as the reason for thus calling the troubles from this quarter ended the fact that he is carrying in his body the scars that were inflicted by the Jews who hated him for successfully promulgating the great canon just stated in v. 15. He calls them the stigmata of Jesus, the marks the Jews inflicted on the body of Jesus. These scarmarks show the stand he has ever taken; they show to what extent he has already suffered for this canon. Let the Galatians think of these scars in Paul's body and then they will stand as firmly as he does.

It has been objected that the man who, as it were, was made for troubles and labor could not say he wanted no more of them. But this word is addressed to the Galatians in connection with one specific instance of trouble, and it is beside the mark to generalize. Κόποι enough awaited him, even further scars; but this Galatian matter he considered at an end. Let no one in Galatia prolong it.

This objection has led to a modification of Paul's meaning. The opinion of Marcion is revived that τοῦ λοιποῦ (supply χρόνου) is not adverbial: *fortan* (B.-D. 186, 2 and 160), but a partitive genitive: let no one "of the rest" of the Israel furnish me trouble, i. e., none of the Judaizers. This view is supported by the doubt as to whether Paul ever uses this genitive adverbially as do the classics; in Eph. 6:10 it is eliminated in preference to the other variant. But Marcion himself, as it seems, cancelled the reference to "the Israel of God" from v. 16, which eliminates this idea and any modern modification of it.

A good deal has been said regarding the stigmata and regarding what Paul means by referring to them. That they were the scars remaining from the scourgings, from the one stoning (II Cor. 11:25; Acts 14:19),

and from other blows, is generally admitted. What is
debated is whether Paul borrows the expression from
paganism. Runaway and misbehaved slaves and crim-
inals were branded on the brow or the hand; but this
does not fit Paul although some think that by the mention of these stigmata Paul intends to designate himself a slave. M.-M. 590 adds: "Nor is there any evidence that the practice of soldiers tattooing themselves
with their commanders' names, which others (i. e.,
commentators) prefer, was at all general." Devotees
of a goddess or of a temple sometimes bore a brand;
but this, too, seems out of place when speaking of Paul.
The whole matter of branding and of tattooing as
found in the pagan world is inapplicable to Paul.

The latest evidence is a papyrus found by Deissmann. It is thought to have a bearing on our passage
because the find contains the words βαστάζειν and κόπους
παρέχειν: carrying an amulet of the god Osiris in a godly
act is to ward off getting trouble from any adversary.
Paul's scars are made equivalent to the amulet. Deissmann lets Paul speak to the Galatians as to his "naugh-
ty little children," "smiling, with uplifted finger telling
them: 'do be sensible; you cannot make me any trouble, for I am protected by a charm'" (*bin ja gefeit*),
C.-K. 1021. Then Paul would end his great epistle in a
jocular way! Zahn accepts this and excuses the pagan
language!

Paul writes, "the stigmata of Jesus," the Jesus
who suffered on the cross. There are no pagan implications of any kind; this is only a plain historical reference. Luke 24:39; John 20:25, 27. The scars on
Paul's body belonged to Jesus, were like the wounds he
himself suffered, for Paul's scars were truly suffered
because of Christ. Compare II Cor. 1:5; 4:10; Col.
1:24. A far later age invented "stigmata of Jesus," a
reproduction of the marks of the five wounds in the
hands, the feet, and the side of Jesus. These "stig-

mata" are either violent pains in these parts of the body or marks that turn red and, in some cases, bleed. All of these peculiar phenomena are pathological and have nothing to do with Paul's scars.

18) The most probable reason as to why no greetings are added is noted in v. 11. Paul closes with a benediction. **The grace of our Lord Jesus Christ with your spirit, brethren. Amen.** His grace is to pardon and to bless (see 1:3). Paul writes the full title and name as he did in v. 14. But here he does not write, "with you," but "with your spirit," as he does in Phil. 4:23, and Philemon 25; the spirit is to triumph over the flesh. Note that the spirit has been mentioned repeatedly in 5:16, 18, 22, 25; 6:8. A heartfelt address "brethren" is placed at the end. It is placed at the end of a sentence in 5:13; 5:26; and nearly at the end in 4:12. Paul never uses this word without a due reason, see 1:11. "Amen" seals the closing wish as it does the opening greeting in 1:5. Paul parts from the Galatians as being his brethren. They remained that by the grace of the Lord.

Soli Deo Gloria

St. Paul's Epistle
To the Ephesians

INTRODUCTION

During the late summer of the year 62, while he was a prisoner in Rome awaiting the outcome of his appeal to Caesar (Nero), Paul wrote three letters, possibly on the same day, and dispatched them by the same messenger, namely Tychicus.

Onesimus, a slave, had run away from his master Philemon, a Christian in the church at Colosse with whom Paul was well acquainted, although Paul himself had not been in Colosse. This slave had come into contact with Paul in Rome, had been converted, and had become deeply attached to the apostle. Paul is sending him back to his master under the protection of Tychicus with a letter to Philemon which speaks for itself.

From Epaphras, the founder of the church at Colosse, a man who was devoted to Paul, the apostle had just learned about the peculiar errors that were making themselves felt in the Colossian church. To eradicate these errors and to build up the church in the true faith in Christ, Paul writes the letter to the Colossians.

Ephesus was the port for which Tychicus probably sailed on his way to Colosse. Here, in this greatest Asian city, Paul had founded an influential church. Here he had worked at least two years, a longer period than he had labored in any other locality. By means of his assistants Paul had spread the gospel from Ephesus into practically the entire province of Asia (Acts 19:10, 26; I Cor. 16:19). He had been absent from Ephesus for nearly five years and now embraces the opportunity to communicate with this church through Tychicus.

All the news Paul had received from Ephesus was favorable (1:15). No troubles of any kind had developed. This explains the general character of

Paul's letter. Ephesians is unlike any other of Paul's letters in that it treats a great subject for the purpose of edification only. Even Romans has the special purpose of preparing for Paul's proposed visit and in 14:1-15:13 treats a peculiar situation which had developed in the Roman church. Tychicus duly delivered the three letters and the slave Onesimus.

*   *   *

We turn to the divergent opinions. One of these is the view that these three letters were written by Paul while he was in *Caesarea*. It is adduced as proof that it is far more likely that the slave Onesimus would seek refuge in this city than in Rome which was so much farther removed from his master in Colosse. Yet distance from his former master was exactly what a runaway slave would seek. It was an easy matter for such a fugitive to lose himself in populous Rome which offered much more advantage to a fugitive slave than Caesarea would. The *fugitivarii*, slave catchers, in Rome would not receive the description of a fugitive from Colosse for some time. To say that such a slave would be in more danger in the proximity of a prisoner of state such as Paul was is to state the improbable. What slave would seek the company of a guarded prisoner? And would the danger on this score not be greater in Caesarea where Paul was kept in the governor's own praetorium?

It is argued that, if Tychicus took Onesimus with him from Rome, the two would arrive first at Ephesus and then proceed to Colosse. Accordingly, Paul should have commended Onesimus also to the Ephesians in Eph. 6:21, 22 as he commends him in Col. 4:8, 9. Since Paul does not do this, it is assumed that the two started from Caesarea and reached Colosse first, and that Tychicus alone proceeded to Ephesus.

The answer is obvious. Onesimus needed all the commendation he could get in Colosse where, if his master forgave him, he hoped to be instated as a member of the congregation. On arrival at Ephesus it was best to keep his whole story quiet. It would have been the height of tactlessness on the part of Paul to commend this slave to the church at Ephesus or to any other congregation before this slave's Christian master had acted in his case, and before the congregation directly concerned had also acted.

Again, καὶ ὑμεῖς in Eph. 6:21 is stressed, and it is argued that Paul could not write *"also* you" unless Tychicus had first reported about Paul's affairs elsewhere before he made a report in Ephesus. So we are told that Tychicus came from Caesarea and stopped first at Colosse and then went on to Ephesus. But the chief mission of Tychicus was to Colosse, and only because this took him to Ephesus, Paul sent a letter also to the Ephesians and had Tychicus make a report "also" to them. For Tychicus undoubtedly told the Ephesians that he was on his way to Colosse with most important letters from Paul.

Philemon 22 is cited, where Philemon is requested to prepare lodgings for Paul who trusts that he will be returned to his friend and to his friend's family. This request is thought to place Paul at Caesarea where he expresses the hope that he would soon be released and could then go on to Phrygia and thus to Colosse. But this is improbable. There was no hope for Paul's release through Felix except by paying a bribe (Acts 24:26); besides, already in Acts 23:11 the Lord had told Paul that he must testify in Rome as he had done in Jerusalem, which meant that his next destination was to be Rome, whither Paul had planned to go when he wrote Romans while he was in Corinth before his journey to Jerusalem and before his imprisonment. This note in Philemon 22 places Paul in Rome at a time when his appeal to Caesar is in prospect of receiving action by the imperial court. Paul had little doubt that the action would be favorable. We see this also in Phil. 2:24. It has been well said that in Philemon 22 Paul is not ordering a lodging as we now order a room in a hotel. Philemon heard all about Paul's prospects from Tychicus and from Onesimus.

The supposition that upon his release from custody Paul would travel from Caesarea to Phrygia and then on to Macedonia is untenable. Released in Rome, Paul intends to visit both Colosse and Philippi and, no doubt, other eastern churches. If it be asked, "What about his plans regarding Spain (Rom. 15:24)?" the answer is that he did go to Spain as tradition assures us. We lack an account of Paul's travels after he was set free in Rome. The probability is that he visited the eastern churches and then went to Spain.

Finally, the prayers for which Paul asks in Eph. 6:19 and Col. 4:3, 4 fit his captivity in Rome and not that in Caesarea. In the latter place Paul was kept in the governor's castle, only his friends were admitted to see him; in Rome he lived in his own rented house where already on the third day the leading men of the Jews had a session with him which was followed a few days later by an all-day session with a still greater representation of Jewish leaders (Acts 28:17, 23). Luke informs us that Paul worked for two years in Rome, no man forbidding him. These three letters were written from Rome.

*   *   *

In recent years a few attempts have been made to establish one or more imprisonments of Paul in *Ephesus* which occurred during the two years of his labors in this city, the object being to date the writing of one (Philippians) or of all of the imprisonment letters during these two years; sometimes also one or two other letters are said to have been written during this time. The starting point for these attempts is Paul's phrase used in II Cor. 11:23: "in prisons exceedingly," which was written sometime after Paul's ministry in Ephesus. We should, of course, like to know when and where these imprisonments occurred. One need not be averse to the idea that Paul was locked up once or twice while he was laboring in Ephesus. But this does not support the plausibility of assigning even a single one of the letters to the time of such imprisonments. The transfer of the writing of any of the letters from Rome to Ephesus raises a number of difficulties; the attempts thus far made contradict each other at many points.

It is easy enough to say that Ephesians was written in Ephesus, "where, being temporarily under restraint, Paul sought to reach by his pen those whom he was forbidden to address by word of mouth." But the man who made this assertion needed to write a book in order to establish his argument, and the argument itself presents improbabilities at almost every turn. Let us mention just one: we are told that Luke omitted the mention of the Ephesian imprisonments of Paul from Acts because he intended that Acts should come to the attention of the judges who were to pass on Paul's appeal to Caesar's tribunal. Acts an apology for Paul at his trial in Rome!

*　　　*　　　*

Far more acute is the debate about the readers for whom our epistle was intended by Paul. The preceding paragraphs assume that the ancient tradition is correct: this letter was sent to Ephesus, to *the Ephesians*. In the middle of the second century all copies of this letter bore the title "To the Ephesians" or an equivalent. While it is only a title and not a part of the text, its simple testimony extends far back into history. The entire early church regarded this as a letter that had been sent to the Ephesians by Paul.

The first man to doubt this was the Gnostic Marcion who expressed his view in the middle of the second century. He read Paul's request that the Colossians and the Laodiceans should exchange letters (Col. 4:16), drew the conclusion that the letter "from Laodicea" referred to our epistle, and thus altered the title from "To the Ephesians" into "To the Laodiceans," for which Tertullian, some fifty years later, took him to task. Few have adopted Marcion's alteration. All that we know about the letter "from Laodicea" is stated in Col. 4:16. The general opinion is that this is another of those letters that are now lost to us, it is like the one mentioned in I Cor. 5:9. Paul must have sent it not long before he sent the three letters through Tychicus.

From Eph. 1:15 and 3:2, etc., the opinion has been derived that our epistle was not intended for the Ephesians but for a number of *other churches in the province of Asia* that had been founded during the five years since Paul had left the province, churches about which Paul had only heard. This view is supported by argument and by what is deemed compelling textual evidence and is held by a goodly number of scholars. They call our epistle a circular letter, an encyclical. A few include the church in Ephesus among the churches that were circularized, but very few, because Paul had only "heard" about the churches he addresses (Eph. 1:15). Col. 1:4 is referred to as a sample of churches of which Paul had only "heard," never having been in their midst in person.

Some suppose that, on reaching Ephesus, Tychicus sent Onesimus on to Colosse with the two letters intended for that place, and that Tychicus himself began the round of these "other churches" with the encyclical; some think that Tychicus took Onesimus along with him while he was making this round. One wonders why the third course is not suggested, namely that Tychicus went straight on to Colosse with Onesimus and then proceeded with the circulation of the encyclical.

If we accepted the supposition of an encyclical we should advocate this third course, for Col. 4:7-9 makes the impression that Tychicus and Onesimus will arrive in Colosse together. Onesimus could not travel alone; the nearer home he got, the greater was the danger of being recognized and summarily arrested. The idea of having this runaway slave suddenly reappear in Colosse with two letters, one that was intended for his master and one that was intended for the congregation, is unacceptable. As for taking the slave along during the distribution of a circular letter before delivering that slave and the two letters in Colosse, this is rather improbable.

True, Paul had never been in Colosse (Col. 2:1) and thus had only *heard* about the Colossians (1:4). But from this fact to argue that Eph. 1:15 must mean the same thing, namely that Paul likewise only *heard* of these people and had never been among them, is untenable. May one not *hear* of friends from whom one has been absent for five years? This is our answer to Zahn, *Introduction* I, 483, that, if our epistle is intended for Ephesus, it must have been written *before* Paul worked in Ephesus, and that John and not Paul was the founder of the Ephesian church. I often hear from my relatives from whom I am separated and not only from people whom I have never seen.

The argument on which the greatest reliance is placed for regarding this letter as an encyclical is the general nature of our epistle. A letter to his own beloved Ephesians, we are told, should contain intimate references to Paul's personal labors in their midst, should also contain many personal greetings. Since these features are absent, this epistle could *not* be intended for Ephesus, it was intended for churches with which Paul had never had personal contact.

A deduction that is made from the absence of greetings is unconvincing. Second Corinthians, Galatians, and the two letters to the Thessalonians lack greetings. If it is intended for Ephesus, Ephesians is in the same class with these other letters on this score, all of them were written to congregations that had been founded by Paul. On the other hand, Romans, which was addressed to a congregation that had not been founded by Paul, has more greetings than any other letter; and Galatians, which was addressed to a number of congregations that had been founded by Paul, has none. Therefore, the presence or the absence of greetings determines neither whether a congregation was founded by Paul nor whether a letter written by him is intended for only one or for several congregations, whether these were founded by him or not.

Eagerness to prove a thesis should not lead us to make deductions that do not follow from the available data. Just why greetings appear in some letters and not in others, and why, where they appear, they are what they are, we are able to explain only in part, and some of the explanations that have been offered are open to doubt. To regard our epistle as an encyclical because it lacks greetings is thus unwarranted. Many of those who do not accept the idea of an encyclical justify the absence of greetings and of all personal matters by referring to the exalted subject of the epistle. This may well be a part of the correct explanation. Colossians is not of the same type and was also to be read to the Laodiceans.

A more convincing point can be made against the idea of a circular letter that was addressed to congregations outside of Ephesus: Laodicea possesses a letter that was recently written by Paul, Colosse now receives one, all these other congregations are to receive another, Ephesus alone is then to be passed by! This is improbable. Consider Paul's relation to Ephesus and also its position in this entire province. Tychicus passes right through Ephesus, Paul has been absent for five years, yet not a line from Paul to the Ephesians! We cannot regard this as being credible.

Now the argument based on the subject of the letter. It is the *Una Sancta,* which is presented in a manner that is more exalted than the treatment of any other subject in all of Paul's letters. The first chapter, for instance, is composed of only two sentences the like of which do not appear elsewhere in the entire New Testament, as far as magnificence of either structure or of contents is concerned. Only the ethical sections, from 4:17 onward, drop to a lower level because they include many detailed injunctions; yet even here we have two arresting paragraphs, 5:22, 23, on marriage, and 6:10-20, on the spiritual hoplite.

Can we say that a letter on so lofty a subject, composed in so impressive a style, was *not* addressed to the Ephesians, among whom Paul had worked in person for over two years, whom he had taught the entire counsel of God, etc., Acts 20:17-38; that such a letter befits only congregations that were not founded by Paul but were founded by other men during the last five years, congregations about which Paul had only heard without saying from whom he had heard? The contents of this epistle befit a church such as that at Ephesus, one that had been under the tutelage of the apostle himself.

Paul had a special reason for writing to the Colossians; his letter shows what this was. He did not have such a reason for writing to the Ephesians. The fears he expressed in Acts 20:25, etc., had not yet been justified. All was still well in Ephesus (Eph. 1:15). On the other hand, in a measure Paul's work was completed. He had planted the church in the Gentile world, the gates of hell could not overthrow it (1:19-23; 6:10-17). From his confinement in Rome he surveys the great spiritual structure; his heart swells with joy. To the Ephesians, his largest, most prominent, and most spiritually advanced church, he unfolds the vision of the *Una Sancta* of which they are a part. He would augment their knowledge, their spiritual power, and their life. The epistle is personal throughout, but personal on this plane. A holy propriety pervades it to the very end. *Die Gemeinde Christi hat ihre Wurzel in der Ewigkeit, in Gottes Vaterherzen . . . und treibt ihre Krone wieder in die Ewigkeit an Gottes Thron, und verzweigt ihre Aeste in alle von der Schoepfung Gottes her gegebenen Ordnungen bis ins Einzelnste und Kleinste durch alle Jahrhunderte der Entwicklungsgeschichte, und das alles in Christo.* Braune. The omission of more intimate personal matters, past and present, is most proper in a letter that develops this theme. Paul at least thought so, the more since Tychicus served as a channel to present all minor matters.

*   *   *

One wonders whether the idea of an encyclical originated on the basis of the textual question as to the absence or the presence of the phrase "in Ephesus" in 1:1 or on the basis of the interpretation of 1:15 that the readers were personally unknown to Paul, that he had only "heard" of them. Let us consider the phrase "in Ephesus."

The ancient tradition unanimously attests the fact that this epistle was addressed to the Ephesians. All manuscripts bore the title: "To the Ephesians," to which "Epistle," also Paul's name, and sometimes other words were added. As noted above, Marcion is the one exception. All the texts we possess contain the phrase "in Ephesus" in 1:1 with three exceptions that are noted below. All the versions have this phrase; we meet it in the comments of writers from Chrysostom onward. Since an issue is made of this phrase, it is well to note these facts.

The three texts above referred to are Aleph, which has the phrase added by a later hand; B, which has it in the margin; codex 67, from the twelfth century, which had the words, but they were erased by a later hand, a correction that was apparently made in order to conform to B.

As to Marcion, it is argued that he could not have altered the *caption* or title if the *text* he possessed had the phrase "in Ephesus" in its first verse. So the conclusion is drawn that in the middle of the second century the texts of our epistle were without this phrase. This was corroborated at the end of the second century by Tertullian. Against Marcion's alteration of the caption from "Ephesians" to "Laodiceans" Tertullian appeals, not to the text itself, not to 1:1 with its phrase "in Ephesus," but only to the *veritas ecclesiae*. We are thus told that, if Tertullian had the phrase in his text, he would surely have used that fact against Marcion's alteration of the caption. So once more the conclusion is drawn that as late as the beginning of the third century "in Ephesus" was *not* in the texts, that Paul did not write the phrase, that it is an interpolation, that our epistle is an encyclical.

Let us look at these conclusions. They do not consider all of the facts. We should discuss the assumption that Marcion would not have dared to alter the caption if the texts of his day contained the phrase. This heretic cut and slashed texts to suit his purposes in an astounding manner. Since he altered the caption to suit his idea of Col. 4:16 he was the last

man to be deterred by the phrase in the text, the last
man to stop at also cancelling the phrase from his
text. The idea that no doctrine was involved that
might prompt Marcion's act is met by the observation that not all of his alterations of texts are due
to his heretical doctrinal interests. In fact, the
reason that Aleph and B are without the phrase may
well be due to Marcion's tampering with the text of
his day.

As regards Tertullian, in his battle with the old
heresies he constantly appeals to the "verity of the
church." By this verity he does not have in mind
merely tradition but includes the Scriptures themselves. In his refutation of Marcion he points to Ephesus as being one of the *ecclesiae apostolicae* which
possess the *authenticae litterae*, i. e., the original docu-
ments written by the apostles. Ephesus had this
epistle in its possession because Paul addressed it to
Ephesus. The idea that it was an encyclical that was
intended for other churches, and that it was at last
deposited in the archives of Ephesus, is rather improbable.

Note how Tertullian comes to refer to Marcion's
alteration of the caption. He does so only in passing.
He is about to cite passages from Paul's letters in
refutation of Marcion's doctrinal errors and thus
brings out the thought that, even if Marcion altered
the title of this epistle, this does not alter the power of
proof of any statement of the epistle itself. So Tertullian remarks that he has no special interest in the caption since what Paul writes to some he really writes
to all. Tertullian has at least this much interest in
even the title that he corrects Marcion's falsification
in passing. He even remarks ironically that Marcion
acts as if he were "a most diligent explorer in this
matter." Tertullian needs to say no more. To have him
imply that all the texts of his time lacked the phrase

"in Ephesus" is to attribute to him more than he himself writes.

It is reported of Origen that he applied a peculiar metaphysical exegesis to the τοῖς οὖσιν occurring in 1:1. Since Christ is ὁ ὤν, the One who truly is (Exod. 3:14), Origen regards the saints and believers as ὄντες, "those who truly are." When Jerome calls this rather curious, he takes it to be a reference to those *qui sunt Ephesi*. Yet the deduction is made that Origen, if not also Jerome, found only this participle in their texts and not the phrase "in Ephesus." This deduction does not follow. Quoting Origen when he follows his own ideas is unsatisfactory. Note Lietzmann, *Roemerbrief* 17: "He cannot be cited at all as a witness for a pure Egyptian text but rather furnishes us an instructive picture of the *Durcheinander und Ineinander* of Bible texts prevailing in the third century in learned Alexandria and Caesarea."

Finally, at the end of the fourth century, in attempting to prove the deity of Christ to Eunomius, Basilius revives the peculiar exegesis of Origen. In doing so he states outright that the epistle was sent to the Ephesians. However, when he quotes from 1:1 he uses only the words: τοῖς ἁγίοις τοῖς οὖσι καὶ πιστοῖς ἐν Χριστῷ Ἰησοῦ, and omits the phrase "in Ephesus." Then he adds: "For thus also those before us have delivered, and we have found in the old (writers) of the copies." Even those who reject the idea of an encyclical take this last remark to mean that Basil's texts contained only the words he quotes and not also the phrase "in Ephesus." We do not share this opinion. Not, indeed, only because Basil has just said that the epistle was sent to the Ephesians although this may be one reason; but because he adopts Origen's exegesis, because he thus does not need the phrase because it would be out of line with the point he is making. Like Origen, he is concerned with τοῖς οὖσι, those who truly *are* or exist, and not with *where* some of them may be, whether "in Ephesus" or elsewhere. He appeals to the old copies for the reading that has this participle; he is not discussing the entire reading nor the presence or the absence of the phrase "in Ephesus."

One feels obliged to discuss Origen, Tertullian, Jerome, and Basil because so much is made of them as offering proof for the absence of the phrase in the texts of their day and thus for the idea of an encyclical. As far as texts are concerned, we have two which in a manner lack the phrase, codex B from the fourth and codex Aleph from the fifth century. But because these are *not enough* to eliminate the phrase so much is made of the fathers named above, the object being to establish the fact that *all* the texts from Marcion to Basil (150-400) were minus the phrase, ergo, that Paul never wrote it, ergo, that we have an encyclical. A careful examination of what these fathers say reveals that none of them support this rather startling conclusion of the complete absence of "in Ephesus" in the old texts; they, too, had the phrase. Moreover, if until the year 400 all texts lacked the phrase, it is incumbent on those who make this claim to explain how the phrase came to be interpolated into all the other texts, even into Aleph.

*   *   *

In scores of instances, e. g., use of a special word or expression, use of a construction, etc., analogy is generally accepted as being rather decisive. What Paul does in one or in more places he may do in another place. While this is not in itself entirely conclusive, the argument from analogy often has some weight. It has weight here. In all of Paul's other letters to churches he indicates their location. Can it be that this one letter is an exception? It is not only natural, it is even necessary to indicate the location. Some ade-

quate reason ought to be apparent as to why the letter
omits the location of the church or the churches
addressed.

The answer that this letter is an encyclical, and
that, therefore, no location is indicated, is not an adequate answer. For the omission of the phrase "in
Ephesus" would make this letter, not an encyclical, but
a catholic letter that is addressed to all saints and believers everywhere. This would make inexplicable how
a letter of this kind received the caption "To the Ephesians," or such an interpolation into the text itself as
the phrase "in Ephesus." If Paul intended the letter
for only a number of churches outside of Ephesus in
the province of Asia, excluding Ephesus, it would have
been incumbent upon Paul to designate these particular churches, which he certainly would have known
how to do without the least difficulty.

A recent supposition is that, when Tychicus carried
the epistle from church to church, the top corner of the
first sheet became frayed, and the last three letters of
the first line were lost. In the effort to restore them
four letters were substituted. The original read: "to
the beloved," etc.; the restoration was made to read:
"to the saints," etc. The purpose of this supposition is
not clear. It has nothing to do with the phrase in question. The question centers on this phrase, *which*
"saints" — or, if you will, *which* "beloved ones" —
Paul addresses. Calling them "beloved" instead of
"saints" in no way justifies the absence of this important phrase

*　　*　　*

Since Marcion found the caption "To the Ephesians" and substituted another caption, the question
should be answered as to how this letter received such
a caption if it was not addressed to the Ephesians. We
are told that Ephesus was the great center of all the

Asian churches, that thus this encyclical eventually came to Ephesus and was placed in the Ephesian archives. After it had been copied, the copyists affixed the caption "To the Ephesians."

Did none of the churches for whom the letter was intended retain copies? Did they let Tychicus read the letter to each church and then pass on to the next until after making the round he did not know what to do with the letter and left it at Ephesus? Did none of these churches protest when copies appeared with this false caption? Would any church, to say nothing of Ephesus in particular, permit a scribe to affix a false caption to any letter it might have in its archives?

*   *   *

Did Paul write this epistle? Not a few answer, "No."

For the most part these negations are based on the contents of the epistle. They are either not viewed as Pauline, or they are ascribed to a time that was later than Paul's. Thus the epistle is regarded as resisting Gnostic and even Montanistic tendencies. Again, the type of doctrine, especially that of the church as the *Una Sancta,* is thought to lie beyond the time of Paul. In addition, the language is considered non-Pauline. Comparative word lists and other tables have been compiled with great labor. Those interested may refer to Bishop Brooke Foss Westcott, *Saint Paul's Epistle to the Ephesians,* where these lists appear. Paul Ewald summarizes the findings: "One may roll the lexicon or rather the concordance around as one will, there almost always appear with almost comical precision the identical percentages in the disputed as well as in the acknowledged letters." These comparative percentages are certainly remarkable and disconcerting for those who would assail the Pauline authorship from this angle.

The hypothesis that some brilliant pupil of the apostle impersonated his great teacher and wrote this epistle invents a second St. Paul, one who stooped to falsification and succeeded in deceiving the entire church. Such a view scarcely merits serious consideration. Let us curtail this most uncongenial part of the subject and turn to the delightful task of following the inspired thoughts and words of the apostle himself. Permit the personal remark that every time the writer of these lines has studied this epistle he has experienced the deepest spiritual satisfaction. Drink of this fountain of the Spirit and live in peace, purity, and victory.

CHAPTER I

The First Half of the Epistle
Three Chapters

Paul Recalls to the Mind of the Ephesians:

THE BLESSEDNESS OF THEIR MEMBERSHIP IN THE UNA SANCTA AS IT IS IN CHRIST

The Greeting

1) The form of the greeting is stereotyped: a nominative to indicate the writer, a dative to indicate the intended readers: A to B; then nominatives to express the greeting itself, which are exclamatory (although the grammars supply a verb): Grace to you! Lysias, Acts 23:26, and James use the classical infinitive, Paul and Peter the nouns. **Paul, apostle of Christ Jesus through God's will, to the saints and believers who are in Ephesus in Christ Jesus: grace to you and peace from God our Father and the Lord Jesus Christ!**

In addition to calling him "Saul" his father gave his baby boy the Roman name "Paul" since the child was born a Roman citizen. When he worked among the Gentiles, the apostle naturally used only his second name.

Since he is writing in his official capacity, Paul adds his official title: "apostle of Christ Jesus," one commissioned and sent by his superior, the Lord's ambassador. The word apostle is to be understood in the narrow sense as the added phrase "through God's will" indicates. Paul had received an immediate call; those who are termed apostles in the wider sense had received only a mediate call. The genitive is possessive: this apostle belongs to Christ; but this possession involves origin and agency: Christ appointed and sent him. This was done "by God's will," i. e., by what God willed. Paul did not become an apostle through a set of fortuitous circumstances, nor did he grow into his office. See II Cor. 1:1. Paul is discharging his apostolic obligation by writing this letter. He is conscious of his responsibility and is meeting that responsibility. Apostolic dignity and authority are naturally involved. The Ephesians are receiving an apostolic letter, one that is to be appreciated accordingly.

Ἅγιοι is one of the earliest and the most frequently employed designations for the Christians (Acts 9:13) and thus is regularly used in the plural. A variant term is the perfect participle ἡγιασμένοι, "those who have been sanctified" and are now in that state. Both signify separation unto God by faith in Christ. The idea expressed by ἅγιοι is passive just as is that expressed by ἡγιασμένοι: "saints" as being separated from the world by God for himself.

Here one article combines the two designations: "to the saints and believers." The Ephesians are both. By placing "believers" after "saints," both nouns after the one article, Paul shows that "saints" refers to sanctification in the wider sense. "Saints" includes all that makes us Christians. "Believers" adds what is most essential in this sainthood, namely faith. The thought is: you who are separated unto God, separated thus as true believers. In this epistle, as in Colossians, the readers are to be fully conscious of both their separated state and their faith. The great *Una Sancta* to which they belong is *holy* unto God and is thus composed only of true believers. The combination of terms is highly significant. It is the basis of Luther's teaching that the church consists of only true believers.

Our versions translate πιστοί "faithful." One also meets the explanation that Paul is addressing the saints who are faithful, as if there could also be unfaithful saints. C.-K. 868 shows that the word is to be taken in the specific New Testament active sense: those who trust another, and not in the classic passive sense: those whom another trusts. The word "believers" is here used as a noun exactly as is its companion, "saints." When it is used as an adjective it may mean "faithful" or "trustworthy." Here it means "believers," *Glaeubige* (Luther). See the discussion in C.-K. "Faithful" would lift out only one of the moral qualities of the saints but by doing so would inject an implied contrast, namely that of unfaithfulness, a contrast that is indicated nowhere in the epistle. The opposite of the πιστοί ("believers") are the ἄπιστοι, "unbelievers," who are in no sense "saints," who are altogether without faith.

It is debated whether we should construe: "believers in Christ Jesus," so that the phrase names the object of the faith of these believers. In the first place, note that one Greek article combines "saints and believers" and thus regards the two designations as a unit. This answers the assumption that the phrase modifies only "believers" and not also "saints." The Greek makes this very plain. In the second place, this phrase occurs again and again throughout the epistle and in all manner of connections. It always has the same meaning: "in connection with Christ, with the Lord." To obtain the meaning of the phrase we must collate all the passages in which it occurs.

Deissmann has done this in *Die neutestamentliche Formel in Christo Jesu*. He finds the phrase occurring 164 times in Paul's writings and concludes that it was original with him and means that all Christians are locally united "within the pneumatic Christ" insofar as they form one body. R. 587 calls the phrase mystical;

we have explained mystical language when interpreting Rom. 6:4. Some let "in" denote the element in which Christians move. We are usually referred to John 15:4. "I in you, you in me." So also the phrase is thought to refer only to the glorified and not to the historical Christ, which is misleading. Paul, indeed, wrote after Christ was glorified, but John 15:4 was spoken by Jesus before his glorification. Besides, Christ is one and is just as historical after his glorification as he was before it.

'Εν denotes a vital spiritual connection so that we translate: "in connection with." This connection is established objectively by the means of grace (Word and Sacrament), subjectively by faith. That is why we often read: "in connection with the Name," etc., i. e., with the objective revelation (Matt. 28:19; Acts 2:38; 8:16; 10:48; 19:5; etc.). This ἐν, this connection, applies to every individual believer as such and only thus to all of them as one body. Since each one is connected with Christ, all form one body.

It is mechanical and misleading to stress the idea of sphere or of element when defining the force of ἐν. While all prepositions can be diagrammed, and thus a circle represents ἐν, this device is only helpful and must not be stressed so as to make "in Christ" = as living creatures *in* the air, as fish *in* the water, as plants *in* the earth; man living and breathing *in* the air, and the air also being *in* him (Deissmann, 84, 92). Our connection is the sphere which embraces both Christ and us and does not extend beyond him. We enter nothing that resembles air, water, or earth. We are *in* the connection only by virtue of its being formed by the objective and the subjective means named above. The connection joins us to the crucified, risen, and glorified Christ. This is wholly spiritual and not mystical unless everything that is spiritual is also to be called mystical.

We see practically no difference between "Christ Jesus" and "Jesus Christ." One may indicate the office first as is done in General Washington, President Lincoln. Office and person are often united in the one word "Christ."

The fact that the phrase "in Ephesus" is genuine we have shown in the introduction. The flexibility of the Greek and its ability to make a unit of "saints" and "believers" by means of the one article enables it to place οὖσιν between these two nouns and to have it modify both by simply repeating the article and thus making the participle attributive. The English cannot do this; our versions make an unsatisfactory attempt. Translate: "to the saints and believers in Christ, those who are in Ephesus." Compare II Cor. 1:1: "the saints who are in," etc.; also Rom. 1:7: "all those who are in," etc. Both passages have the word "saints"; see also Phil. 1:1 and Col. 1:2; I Cor. 1:2 has, "having been sanctified" plus "called saints."

Those who cancel "in Ephesus" from the text have difficulty with regard to construing the participle. They should translate: "to the saints who are also (καί) believers in Christ." Zahn says that this "is not quite satisfactory." Yet he offers no alternative. Ewald has another construction; he connects as belonging together: "to the saints and (καί) believers who are in Christ Jesus." He overlooks the rule that adverbial modifiers are placed next to their verbs (or participles) unless there is obvious reason for a separation. If Paul had in mind what Ewald says he should have written: τοῖς ἁγίοις καὶ πιστοῖς τοῖς οὖσιν ἐν Χ. Ἰ. These are the facts of the case. In other words, those who cancel "in Ephesus" are left with a participle which cannot be properly construed. All attempts at construction either offer a new sense (Zahn) or overlook the grammar (Ewald).

2) The greeting itself is exactly like that found in Rom. 1:7; I Cor. 1:3; II Cor. 1:2, which see.

In Colossians Paul mentions Timothy as a fellow writer. Although Ephesians was written at this same time, Paul alone addresses the Ephesians, and does that in the simplest manner. There is nothing in Ephesus that needs correction. The epistle is an apostolic message which comes from Paul himself. The greeting thus fits the epistle closely.

The Great Doxology

3) Other epistles begin with thanksgiving; this one, Second Corinthians, and First Peter begin with a doxology, and the greatest of these doxologies is this one found in Ephesians. The one found in Second Corinthians is due to the intense emotion of comfort, this one to the profound contemplation of the whole work of God for our salvation. Paul glorifies *God, the Fountain of our Salvation.* The doxology is Trinitarian. It reaches from eternity to eternity. Both in contents and in structure it towers above all other doxologies. It is comparable to Ps. 103.

The whole of it in all its details was present to Paul's mind when he began his dictation. This is clear from the structure, especially from the three phrases: "for the praise of the (his) glory," in v. 6, 12, 14. Little attention is usually paid to the structure. R. 433 lists this doxology among Paul's noble periods but detracts from his praise when he adds that Paul would have had many more such but for his impatience with the fetters of a long sentence and his passing over into anacolutha. We have expressed ourselves on the latter in connection with Rom. 5:12; 15:23; II Cor. 5:12; and elsewhere. Much remains hidden and is lost when the doxology is printed in the usual way. Let us conserve as much as we can.

BLESSED

The God and Father of our Lord Jesus Christ,
he who blessed us with every spiritual blessing
in the heavenly places
in Christ,
Even as he elected us *in him before the world's foundation*
to be holy and blemishless before him in love,
having predestinated us to adoption through Jesus Christ for himself
according to the good pleasure of his will
For the Glory-Praise of his Grace
which he graciously granted us
in the Beloved One

* * *

In whom we have
The ransoming through his blood,
The remission of the trespasses,
according to the riches of his grace
which he made abound for us in all wisdom and intelligence,
having made known to us the mystery of his will
which he purposed *in him* for administration
during the fulness of the time-seasons,
to summarize all things *in the Christ,*
those in the heavens and those on the earth;
in him in whom also we were given a lot
as having been predestinated
according to his purpose who works all the things
according to the counsel of his will,
that we may be *for his Glory-Praise*
as those who have hoped in advance *in the Christ*

* * *

In whom also you,
having heard the Word of the Truth,
the gospel of your salvation —
in whom also having believed
you were sealed with *the Holy Spirit* of the promise,
who is pledge of our inheritance
for ransoming the possession
For his Glory-Praise.

The First Member of the Doxology

The phrase "in Christ" ("in him," "in whom")
occurs ten times, the number of greatest rhetorical
completeness. Christ is the golden string on which all
the pearls of this doxology are strung. He is the central diamond around which all the lesser diamonds are
set as rays. "The Beloved One" is the divine designation made prominent. "For the Glory-Praise" marks
the close of each of the three parts, these three indicating the persons of the Trinity. "According to the

good pleasure" occurs three times. A large number of the greatest New Testament concepts is worked into a grand whole with consummate mastery. Proper printing aids the eye; proper reading, especially of the original, aids still more.

When Paul begins with this lofty doxology he shows that his whole heart is filled with the contemplation of God, here in his relation to the *Una Sancta* in Christ. The apostle at once strikes the most exalted note; all else in this epistle rings in harmony with it. The verbal εὐλογητός is common in doxologies. The grammarians feel that a copula should be supplied. So they debate as to whether to supply ἐστί, declarative, or εἴη the optative of wish, or ἔστω, the imperative of command. Supply nothing but read this word as an exclamation. This word means "well-spoken"; we speak well of God when we say what he is and does in his attributes and his works. No task should delight us more. There is too little contemplation of God, too little praise of him. The Scriptures, however, show us no sinking of the mind and the emotions into God as this is cultivated by the mystics, even the best of whom are morbid, the rest, like those of India, pagan. Paul sings the true glory of God as his mind moves amid the gospel glories.

The full liturgical name, "the God and Father of our Lord Jesus Christ," designates God in an effective soteriological way: he in whom our whole salvation in Christ is bound up. This name is really a concentrated confession. All that the Scriptures reveal regarding our Savior God is packed into this blessed Name. The discussion of the commentators as to whether Paul intends to say that God is only the Father of our Lord Jesus or also his God, generally overlook the point just stated.

On this subject see II Cor. 1:3. Let it suffice here to state that in 1:17 Paul himself writes: *"the God* of our Lord Jesus Christ." Note also Matt. 27:46 and John 20:17. For Jesus in his human nature God is his God, and for Jesus in his deity God is his Father, his God since the Incarnation, his Father from all eternity. But note *"our* Lord" which connects us with Christ and through him with God. "Lord" is wholly soteriological: he who purchased and won us, to whom we belong as our Savior King.

Those who do not accept this obvious meaning of God's designation overlook the fact that one article makes a unit of the two terms: "the God and Father" just as we see this in v. 1. They would eliminate everything "metaphysical," in particular the *generatio aeterna* which the church has always found in the name Father of Jesus Christ. For this they substitute the view that "God" refers to the omnipotence and "Father" to the love which are displayed in "our Lord Jesus Christ" in the work of salvation. Yet, unless our Lord is "true God, born of the Father from eternity," and then also "true man, born of the Virgin Mary," no salvation remains for which to glorify God.

"Blessed, he who *blessed* us with every spiritual *blessing"* form a beautiful *paronomasia.* Our blessing rises in answer to God's blessing. His lies in the bestowal of saving gifts, ours in the response of praise. The substantivized participle "he who blessed us" is a constative aorist which sums up all the blessing of God in one grand act. "With every blessing" adds the cognate noun in order to emphasize the idea of the participle. We may translate, "with every, or with all blessing," since in the case of abstract nouns the meanings "every" and "all" flow together. Here "every" is preferable since it individualizes the whole number which makes up the sum.

The nature of these many blessings is "spiritual"; all pertain to our regenerate spiritual nature, to the new man born in us. They thus benefit both soul and body. The adjective does not refer to the constitution of man as being composed of an immaterial and a material part, for all men have these two parts. It is true, all of these blessings come from God's Spirit and might be called "spiritual" because of this origin. This interpretation is often found. Yet the idea is that "spiritual blessings" are intended for spiritual men. They are not intended for fleshly men, fleshly blessings do not exist, such men remain unblessed.

Although Luther translates *in himmlischen Guetern*, and C.-K. 829 adopts this, our versions are correct when they translate, "in heavenly places." One arrives at this translation by noting the same phrase in 1:20; 2:6; 3:10; 6:12. The A. V. margin to our passage offers the translation, "in heavenly things" but does not have this marginal rendering of the other four passages. One must also note the article. Not *bona* but *loca* are referred to. They are the definite heavenly places, supreme over all the earth, where God dwells. God blessed us in the heavens above (ἐπί in the compound). His blessing is according: infinitely superior to anything here on earth below. All that follows accords with these "heavenlies," notably the very next most fundamental blessing, God's eternal election.

He blessed us "in connection with Christ." We have explained this phrase in our comments on v. 1. The phrase is evidently to be construed with the participle. The point is important for the understanding of v. 4 where we propose to construe the same phrase in the same way: "he elected us in connection with him." The sense of the phrase has been given in v. 1. When "through Christ" and "on account of Christ" (*per* and *propter*) are offered as translations for ἐν, or even as interpretations, the thought is changed. It may seem harmless in the present clause, it is not so in v. 4. "In" denotes union, vital connection. The whole action of blessing with every blessing as well as the recipients of these blessings are in the sphere formed by Christ and not an inch beyond that sphere; are in the union and vital connection expressed by this significant preposition.

"Us" = Paul and the Ephesians whom he has just designated as "the saints and believers in connection with Christ Jesus" and stated expressly that *they* are in this connection. When Paul's "us" is regarded as including all Christians, this is done by way of application only. Paul is not writing a catholic letter, he is writing to the Christians in Ephesus. The question is raised as to how he can call all of them "saints and believers" and say that all are "in Christ." May there not have been a few hypocrites among them? The question is answered by the designation itself and by what it implies. "To the saints and believers in union with Christ Jesus" certainly does not include hypocrites, it excludes them. It does so throughout this epistle in the case of all the pronouns which refer to these saints and believers in Ephesus.

4) In perfect correspondence with this constative action of blessing us with every blessing in connection with Christ (καθώς) is the fundamental act of God which antedates the foundation of the world, that "he elected us for himself in connection with him" (Christ). God selected us and appropriated us unto himself (middle voice) by a specific, eternal act. The preposition in the verb points to a mass or a number out of which the choice was made; here the entire fallen race is that mass.

In view of the Hebrew equivalent *bachar,* and of the Old and the New Testament use of ἐκλέγεσθαι, ἐκλεκτοί, and ἐκλογή, the distinctive meaning of a choice out of many should be noted, and the verb should not be regarded as meaning that God merely appointed us to something. The claim that the emphasis does not rest on the verb but on the infinitive clause, "to be holy," etc., is untenable (C.-K. 694). The verb is in the emphatic position and must have the resultant strong emphasis. It was a divine election and no less that took place in eternity. The fact that it also had a great object or purpose in view, which is here duly stated, is what we expect.

The entire multitude of spiritual blessings which have come upon Paul and the Ephesians here in time is in accord with the eternal act by which God elected them, chose them for himself. Perfect agreement exists between that election and this blessing. The latter has its explanation in the former. Here we have another instance in which Paul penetrates to the very bottom and does not stop halfway.

Note also that this election before the world began explains the blessing "in the heavenly places." The two correspond also in this regard. The heavenly and thus eternal nature of these blessings is thereby indicated. The word καθώς is sometimes interpreted as expressing source; Paul stated only a correspondence, which is also ample in every way. He mentions two distinct acts, one that took place in eternity, the other that occurred in time, but both are in heavenly correspondence.

Our older exegetes construed: "us (as being) in Christ," i. e., by faith, this faith being foreseen by God. The assertion that a phrase cannot thus modify a pronoun unless the participle "being" is inserted, is met by the examples in which even the indefinite τίς is so modified. Prominent English and German exegetes still construe as our fathers did. One says pointedly: "In Christ = included in Christ, and this including is conditioned by faith." Matters are only complicated when *in Christo* is regarded as meaning *per Christum*. This alters the text. When Paul wants διά he writes it as he does in v. 5. The reason for this objection to the exegesis of the fathers is dogmatical, namely the idea that, when God entered upon his election, he saw nothing but a *massa perdita* and yet from this vast vile mass, for some mysterious reason that is never revealed in Scripture, chose some to become believers and to be saved, and that he did this "through Christ."

Yet we, too, decline to construe: "us (as being) in him" for the reason that in v. 3 "us" is found unmodified, and "in Christ" modifies, not this pronoun, but the participle. The reason is purely linguistic and not dogmatical. But look at this "us" when it is thus divested of the phrase adjacent to it. It is the same "us" as that found in v. 3; it signifies Paul and the Ephesians, the people he calls "the saints and believers in Christ" (v. 1). *These,* Paul says, God elected for himself in eternity. He elected them "before the foundation of the world," before a single human being existed.

Is it not correct to say that God foresaw "us" when he entered upon this election in eternity? Did not the whole world down to the last day lie open before his omniscience? Did that omniscience halt at a certain point so that it saw only a *massa perdita* and only Christ's redemption of this mass, and did God thus make his selection and see no more? Did that omniscience not also see all that God's grace would accomplish to the last second of the last day? Did it not see every man's whole life until the moment of death (and beyond)? Yes, in eternity he saw "us" as "saints and believers in connection with Christ" (v. 1), and "*us*" he elected.

This whole act of God's took place "in Christ," in connection with him. It could not have been otherwise. Does this refer to "Christ" only as the *causa meritoria* objectively and in general as *acquisita* for the entire *massa perdita?* Does it exclude "Christ" as the *causa meditoria appropriata,* as made *ours* subjectively by faith? I cannot find this separation in

Paul's words here or in any other passage of Scripture. Surely, the verb "he elected" and its object "us" (the saints and believers in Christ) belong together and are connected with Christ. It has been well said: "If the sphere of an action is Christ, the objects of that act must also be within that sphere or else they would be beyond the sphere of the action itself." Any *eternal* act of God's pertaining to "us" in *time* is bound to offer difficulty to our minds and our thinking. Both Calvinism and synergism rationalize in order to remove the difficulty; it remains, we must let it remain.

The phrase: he elected us "in Christ" may be taken to include *all* that is involved in our connection with him, from the elective act onward to the glory in all eternity, salvation from inception to completion. This is called the wider form or the first *tropus* of teaching divine election. Its best presentation is found in the *C. Tr.* 1067, 13-24. When, however, the divine act is considered only in connection with the persons chosen and all else is disregarded, we have the second form or *tropus* of teaching, called narrower, which was employed by the Lutheran fathers after the time of the Formula of Concord. The doctrine is the same, the presentation takes in more or takes in less.

Each form of teaching has its special purpose. The wider excludes synergism. Covering, as it does, the whole of salvation, it lays the greatest stress on the divine activity as the sole power which works that salvation. The narrower fronts against Calvinism, for by pointing to the truth that God chose the believers in Christ the arbitrary and absolute predestination of a mysterious few is overthrown. The Lutheran fathers called the latter: election *intuitu fidei,* "in view of faith," an abbreviation for the fuller statement: "in view of the all-sufficient merits of Christ perseveringly apprehended by divinely wrought faith." The objection that this is or at least sounds synergistic depends

on the conception one has of "faith." When one has
the truly Biblical conception that faith is *in toto* divinely wrought, that all power lies in the Christ, the
one and only content filling the cup of faith, the objection falls. Until better forms of teaching are developed, those of the fathers will stand. Of course, as in
the case of all the teaching of Jesus and of his apostles,
adequate apprehension is necessary.

Is the infinitive clause complementary: "he elected
us to be," etc., or final: "in order to be," "that we
should be" (our versions)? The difference seems to be
a merely formal one. Is the sacrificial meaning of
"blemishless" to be retained as is done in the LXX?
The question concerns also 5:27; Phil. 2:15; Col. 1:22.
In Heb. 9:14 and I Pet. 1:19 the idea of sacrifice is evident; but in II Pet. 2:13 the noun is without this connotation. In Phil. 2:15, "blemishless children of God,"
the thought of sacrifice is untenable. Lightfoot thinks
that in our passage "holy" refers to the consecration of
the victims and "blemishless" to their fitness for this
consecration. This difference of opinion comes to view
in the translation, some translate *immaculatus*, others
inculpatus. We fail to find the least implication of
sacrifice although we retain the translation "blemishless." On "holy" (ἁγίους) see "saints" (ἅγιοι) in v. 1.

Does the clause, "to be holy and blemishless before
him in love," refer to our justification or to our sanctification (holy life)? Both are included as is also our
glorification. We obtain this idea from 5:26, 27 where
we are told that Christ loved the church and gave himself for it to sanctify and cleanse it by baptism and
thus to present it to himself as a *glorious* church without spot or wrinkle but as *"holy and blemishless."*
Again, in Col. 1:22 Christ reconciled us to present us
as *"holy and blemishless* and unreprovable" before him
(κατενώπιον, as in our passage). These three passages
shed light on each other even as all of them contain the

same adjectives, 5:27 adds "glorious." Two contain the phrase "before him," and the other has the same thought in "present to himself."

In eternity God elected us saints and believers to stand before him to all eternity as being holy and blemishless in love; in time Christ reconciled, washed, and cleansed us in baptism and thus actually presented us as being holy and blemishless and also glorious. That is why God elected us "in connection with Christ," and why we are now called "saints and believers in connection with Christ" (v. 1). In 5:27 and Col. 1:22 all that Christ has done for us is stated together with our being holy and blemishless; in our passage, which takes us back to God's elective act in eternity, this work of Christ's is indicated in the phrase "in him" and is then set forth in the following verses (v. 7, etc.).

Those who find only justification in the infinitive clause "to be holy and blemishless" construe the phrase "in love" with v. 4: "having predestinated us in love," etc. *If* justification alone were referred to we should expect the phrase "in faith" and not "in love" to round out the idea. When this phrase is drawn into v. 4, it would, of course, be God's love that predestinated us. A few leave the phrase in v. 3 but construe "he elected us — in (this) love," a construction which, however, no reader would suspect, for verb and phrase are too widely separated. Still others have it modify the whole infinitive clause: "to be holy and blemishless," to be thus justified "in (God's) love," which is again unexpected and rather peculiar. Of course, the thought that God elected, or that he predestinated, or even that he justified us "in (his great) love" (for us), is in itself quite true.

The rhythm of the sentence requires that "in love" be retained in v. 3 as our versions have it. The full emphasis is required on the participle in v. 4 as it is required for the "he elected" in v. 3. Some may regard this as having no importance; the importance of the rhythm is there nevertheless. The claim that adjectives such as the two used here cannot be modified by "in love" is answered by II Pet. 3:14.

But the main issue lies in the thought, in the reference of the phrase to *our* love. Here we submit I Cor. 13:13, love abides forever. Also Matt. 25:35-40: "You have done it *unto me*," namely all this work of love. On judgment day Christ presents us with this evidence of our faith, the works of our love. Of course, "in love" cannot be restricted to our love for the brethren. We must finally point to Rom. 8:28, 29 where love to God is also brought into connection with predestination. The objection that our love is not perfect in this life and does not render us "holy and blemishless" is answered already in v. 1 where, in spite of our imperfection in this life, we are termed "saints," ἅγιοι, just as is the case here. This love always flows from faith; all its present imperfection is covered by the perfect merits of Christ.

Ἀγάπη is the love of comprehension and of corresponding purpose. See John 3:16 where the verb occurs, also I Cor. 13:1, and wherever else the word is found. In the LXX it is at times still used to designate the lower types of love; in the New Testament the word rises to its fullest nobility. The idea that *agape* finds value in the loved object breaks down in the most vital passages. Φιλία is the love of affection and is thus distinct from *agape* even in instances which call for no special emphasis on the distinction.

5) The participle "having predestinated us" is aorist like the main verb, its action is simultaneous with that of the main verb, its force is modal. Whether we translate "foreordained" or "predestinated" makes no difference, for προορίζειν and προορισμός are the Greek

words for "predestinate" and "predestination." The
meaning is to fix and establish in advance, in this case
already in eternity. In God's great elective act, when
he chose us for himself in connection with Christ to be
holy and blemishless in connection with Christ, he
destined us in advance for adoption unto himself
through Christ. The thought is much the same as in
Rom. 8:28: "them he predestined to be conformed to
the image of his Son that he might be the first-born
among many brethren." The idea that the participle
is antecedent in point of time and thus causal: "he
elected us because he predestinated us," will find little
or no acceptance. The persons involved are again
those mentioned in v. 1. The idea that the participle
expresses the main part of the divine act, that this is
not expressed by the main verb, cannot be correct, for
then the verbal forms ought to be reversed.

Christ is the essential Son, we are sons only by
adoption, *Kuehrsoehne,* as Luther puts it. Little or
nothing is gained by delving into the Jewish and the
Roman ways of adoption. To introduce ideas borrowed
from the pagan mystery cults does not advance an understanding of the subject. C.-K. 1103 says: "The
Greek language offered Paul only the word and not the
thought, which did not agree with the Greek conception." The word means, "placing into the position of
a son." This involves a declaration of God concerning us and is not only an operation of God in us which
changes us inwardly. Yet this is true, the word "adoption" includes the state into which this act places us,
i. e., our sonship, in addition to the act and the declaration.

Paul writes: for adoption "through Jesus Christ"
and not again "in Christ." Now we do have *per,* the
preposition that points to Christ as the Mediator, by

means of whose mediatorial work adoption and sonship
are made ours. The final phrase εἰς αὐτόν rounds out the
expression: "adoption for or unto him" (God). The
participial clause thus adds to the main statement and
gives us still more light; in particular, we see that "to
be holy and blemishless before God in love" is to possess "adoption through Christ to him," to be God's sons
through this Mediator.

The entire statement regarding our election and
predestination is modified by the two closing phrases:
"according to the good pleasure of his will" and "for
the glory-praise of his grace," thereby bringing the
first part of the doxology to a close. The view that
εὐδοκία refers only to the free determination of God,
and that this is made certain by the addition of the
genitive, is untenable; see the phrase also in v. 9. To
be sure, God was prompted by nothing outside of himself, least of all by anything in us. But our election is
not declared to be a matter of merely the will of God
considered in an absolute sense, for this would be the
Calvinist's absolute sovereignty of God. Paul does not
write: "according to his will" but states whath norm
this will followed. C.-K. 354 defines: "the free good
will, the contents of which is something good," and
again: *Gottes Gnadenwille, der damit als aus Gottes
freiem Ermessen hervorgehend und so auf das Heil der
Menschen abzielend gekennzeichnet wird.* Nor should
"the good pleasure" and "the will" be identified. Nor
is "the will" a mysterious and secret will, for in v. 9
Paul says explicitly that God "made known unto us
the mystery of his will." This he did in the gospel, in
the entire plan of salvation.

6) The phrase that is introduced with εἰς may
denote either purpose or result; here it is the latter: so
that praise of the glory of his grace is the result. Here
we have one of the concatenations of genitives noticed
in this epistle. They put into brief form a great wealth

of thought. The first two nouns are without articles and are practically a compound: "for glory-praise." The glory and the praise of it center in the great attribute of God's "grace," the *favor Dei* together with all its works and its gifts. It is unnecessary to restrict "grace" to the *Gesinnung*. We behold the grace in its activity and thus praise it.

Grace, too, is one of the operative and not one of the quiescent attributes of God. Still more important is its wonderful quality: it is always wholly undeserved by those who receive this grace or any of its gifts. In fact, grace, as distinct from mercy, connotes guilt in the recipient, mercy connotes misery, the result of guilt. Thus grace is associated with pardon; we are declared righteous by grace, Rom. 3:24; but mercy relieves our distress. The word sweetest to the sinner in the entire Scripture is "grace." Here it is pictured in its fulness as having its source in eternity and in God's eternal acts. Note "the riches of his grace" in v. 7. This entire doxology is Paul's praise of the glory of God's grace.

The genitive case of the relative is attracted from the accusative, the latter is called an accusative of inner content, R. 716; B.-D. 294, 2: "which he graciously granted us in the Beloved One." The fact that grace is graciously granted is self-evident. We may regard the aorist as constative: all of God's granting to the Ephesians expressed as one comprehensive act. But the main point lies in the final phrase: all this granting of grace was "in connection with the Beloved One." The perfect participle reaches into the past and extends into the present and the future. This designation at once recalls Matt. 3:17; Luke 9:35 (compare II Peter 1:13; Col. 1:13). Christ is "the One Beloved" because of his mediatorial obedience to God. The verb from which the name is derived is ἀγαπᾶν; see the noun in v. 4.

Paul does not again write "in Christ" or "in Jesus Christ" when he concludes the first member of his doxology; nor is this exceptional designation a mere variation in style in order to avoid monotony. As to the latter point, this choice new term to designate Christ does mark a division in the doxology; but in doing so it reveals Christ as the One who wrought out our entire salvation, as the One upon whom in consequence rests all the love of God, his love of fullest comprehension, the whole purpose of which takes up all that Christ wrought in order to carry it to its blessed consummation.

All that lies in the preceding phrases "in Christ or Jesus Christ" is thus made to shine forth with fuller radiance. For "in" draws a circle about "the Beloved One," the same circle that was drawn before and once more places the bestowal of God's grace together with us its recipients into this blessed circle but now as those who are filled with the radiance of this heavenly name for Christ so that we break forth in the praise of the glory of the grace that is thus ours.

The Second Member of the Doxology

7) All that lies in the phrase "in the Beloved One" is carried over into the second part of the doxology by the relative "in whom" and must be present to our minds as we read on. The whole doxology is a unit. It ascribes blessedness to God alone, but to him as to the First Person, to whom is joined the Second, our Lord Jesus Christ, the Beloved One, and equally the Third, to whom also a significant name is given, the Holy Spirit of the Promise. It is thus that Paul makes the doxology Trinitarian.

It is the height of injustice to Paul to regard his grand sentence as a rambling of thought and of language. The whole of it is most carefully and symmetrically constructed; it is so elaborate because it is so grand. Even in our far less flexible English we are not compelled to break it up into several sentences. A spacious and lofty palace is naturally larger than a common dwelling. "In whom we have" is in marked contrast to the preceding, both in tense and in subject; instead of the aorists we now have the present tense, and the object of the aorists, "us," now becomes the subject "we," although it is without emphasis. In this simple and effective way the turn to the second part of the doxology is made.

By the grace so graciously granted us in the Beloved One "we have," we actually possess in all its power and efficacy for us, "the ransoming through his blood." This is the liberation wrought by the payment of a ransom or price, and the price is named, it is "the blood of Christ." The very word ἀπολύτρωσις denotes release by paying a λύτρον or ransom. Captives of war and slaves were thus ransomed. Our word "redemption," in its common use, has lost some of this distinctive sense and has dropped to the idea of deliverance in general. Hence "ransoming" is to be preferred (Warfield). Only the payment of a full ransom releases the sinner in God's court. For a fuller discussion, including synonymous terms as well as Deissmann's pagan ransoming, see Rom. 3:24. The mention of "blood" is more precise than the mention of "death" would be; "through his blood" = sacrifice, when Christ was slain as the Lamb in sacrifice. The ideas of ransom, of sacrifice, and of substitution (λύτρον ἀντί, Matt. 20:28; Mark 10:45) are thus combined.

When Paul says: "we have the ransoming," etc., he refers to "the saints and believers," to their having this ransoming by faith. It is not *had* except by faith. Hence Paul adds the apposition: "the remission of the trespasses," which constitutes the essential effect of Christ's ransoming for all believers. The Scriptures nowhere treat the ransoming and the remission as one act; ἡ ἀπολύτρωσις and ἡ ἄφεσις are two acts. The one took place on Calvary when Christ's blood paid the ransom price for all men; the second takes place whenever a sinner repents and God in that instant sends away his sin and his guilt. The remission rests on the ransoming.

The English word "forgiveness" is not as accurate as the Greek word ἄφεσις, which is the noun denoting action derived from the verb ἀφίημι, "to send away." Ps. 103:12 is the perfect commentary: "As far as the east is from the west, so far hath he removed our transgressions from us." Where does the east begin, where does the west end? When our sins are so far removed from us, sent away so far from us by God himself, they are removed from us forever. The psalmist properly names the east and the west and not the north and the south lest someone think of the poles, of the distance of the north pole from the south pole, which is a definite distance. The psalmist indicates a distance that no man can measure: "as far as the east is from the west," this is the great distance that God's ἄφεσις, God's "sending away" removes our transgressions from us the instant we are brought to faith.

Another commentary is Micah 7:19: "Thou wilt cast all their sins into the depths of the sea," whence they shall never be brought up again. Add Isa. 43:25: "I, even I, am he that blotteth out thy transgressions for mine own sake, and will not remember thy sins." Isa. 44:22: "I have blotted out, as a thick cloud, thy transgressions, and, as a cloud, thy sins." These are human expressions, the strongest that human language affords. Add John 20:23: "Whose soever sins ye remit (ἀφῆτε, send away), remitted are they (ἀφίενται, they have been sent away) for them." And thus the opposite: "whose soever (sins) ye retain (κρατῆτε, hold fast, so that they remain upon the sinners), they are retained (κεκράτηνται, they have been held fast, namely by

me Christ)." Se also John 3:36: "the wrath of God
abideth on him" since his sins remain upon him. Also
v. 18: "He that believeth not is condemned already"
(ἤδη κέκριται, has already been judged, the judgment remaining upon him).

All these Old Testament and New Testament passages show clearly what Paul means by our having
"the remission." They show likewise that in the ransoming and in the remission we have two acts: Christ
ransomed all men, the apostles (ministers) remit (John
20:23), i. e., God remits through them. Remission =
personal justification, the act of God by which the moment faith is kindled in a poor sinner's heart he is
pronounced free from guilt and declared righteous in
God's sight for the sake of the merits of Christ, i. e.,
on the basis of Christ's ransoming. Rom. 3:24-26.
Although they are bought by the Lord (ransomed),
those who deny him by unbelief bring swift destruction upon themselves (remission is not theirs), II
Pet. 2:1.

The idea of παράπτωμα is: the result of *falling* to a
side. The idea in our English equivalent "transgression" is that of *crossing* the line of right. The difference is formal; the one language conceives the sinner as having fatally fallen by plunging off the road
of right, the other as having run counter to the line
of right. To divide the sin and the guilt is abstraction, the guilt hugs the sin like its shadow, and it is
impossible to send the one away without sending away
also the other. As Jesus describes the final judgment
in Matt. 25:34, not a single sin is even remotely in
evidence in the case of the believers; but look at the
others.

Our thus having as our personal possession the
ransoming and the remission is "according to the
riches or wealth of his grace." "Grace" is again God's
unmerited favor toward sinners as explained in v. 6,

the energetic attribute of God. "The riches" brings out the greatness, the magnificence of this grace which are exhibited in the ransoming and the remission we possess — which alone is wonderful beyond our comprehension — but extends even beyond that as the relative clause adds.

8) "Which he made abound for us in all wisdom and intelligence" is to be read together and modifies grace. As in v. 4 "in love" is to be construed with what precedes, so here "in all wisdom," etc., is to be construed likewise. The verb is here used transitively, its object accusative being attracted into the genitive of its antecedent (R. 716; B.-P. 1042); there is no need to discuss the intransitive idea with the verb that governs a genitive. Such is the wealth of God's grace in bestowing the ransoming and the remission upon us that he caused his grace to abound for us in the way in which he did this. God's means was, of course, the gospel which is called "the mystery of his will" (v. 9). By using this means he made his rich grace abound for us "in all wisdom and intelligence." We may also say: "in every (kind of) wisdom" (compare v. 3 "all" and "every"), the sense being the same.

The fact that Paul refers to the "wisdom" and "intelligence" that are bestowed on us need not be questioned, especially in view of the parallel, "in all wisdom and spiritual understanding," in Col. 1:9, where σύνεσις replaces φρόνησις. Paul uses the latter only here; it appears but once more, in Luke 1:17, although the verb and the adjective are frequently found. It would, indeed, seem peculiar to predicate φρόνησις of God, likewise to use "all" wisdom and intelligence when speaking of God. And it would be still more peculiar to say of God that he "abounded" (intransitive) in all wisdom and intelligence toward us.

"Wisdom" is here used with reference to us (C.-K. 1009) and in the noble sense of the word even as its

substance is the gospel. It is more than knowledge
with which it is often used. Here and in Col. 1:9 it is
greater than intelligence and understanding, both of
which are sensibleness as applied to our lives and our
actions. Wisdom is the penetrating insight into the
divine realities. Christ is made unto us wisdom,
I Cor. 1:30. So great are the riches of God's grace
in Christ that God must make us abound in "all
wisdom" and must add "all intelligence" so that
we may apply all of it in the varying situations of
our life.

9) The riches of his grace God made abound for
us by filling us with all wisdom and intelligence, "by
having made known to us the mystery of his will."
The participle is modal and modifies "made abound,"
its time is contemporary with that of this verb. The
true wisdom is knowing "the mystery of God's will,"
of his θέλημα, of what he actually willed. This God
must make known to us. He is the only source of this
wisdom, for it is he who originated this will. To
apprehend it is also true intelligence, the ability to
shape life and conduct according to what God has
willed, which is the only sensible thing to do (φρόνιμον).
To make known a mystery is to reveal it. "The
mystery" belongs to "the will," i. e., to what God
willed; the genitive is possessive.

Paul is speaking of the gospel, the will of grace,
the mystery hid from the ages during all these generations but now preached and published in all the world
by Christ's messengers and fully manifest to the saints,
Col. 1:25, 26. Paul is not speaking of some secret
decree of God. Paul's use of the term "mystery" has
nothing to do with the pagan "mysteries" and their
cults. Since "all wisdom and intelligence" precedes,
"the mystery of his will" is not this or that part of
the gospel but the whole gospel. The word is here
comprehensive as in 6:19: "to make known the mys-

tery of the gospel." Once hidden from the world in
general and known by preparatory revelation only
in Israel, it is now thrown open to the whole world.
C.-K. 742 advances the idea that the word implies
the necessity of impartation or revelation, without
which man cannot know the contents of the mystery:
*die Kunde der Heilswahrheiten, sofern diese durch
goettliche Offenbarung kundgemacht werden oder wor-
den sind.*

God made known to us, Paul says, the mystery of
his will "according to his good pleasure which he purposed in him," i. e., in Christ. We leave the order in
its natural sequence, the phrase modifying the participle. In making known the mystery to us as he
did God followed the norm set by his good pleasure.
Here *eudokia* is again not merely God's free determination but this as it is filled with what is good. The
phrase is shorter than the one used in v. 5 and yet
much longer; for instead of a mere genitive the relative clause is here attached: his good pleasure "which
he purposed (literally, set before himself — middle
voice) in him" (in Christ). Πρό in the verb is not temporal but a part of the reflexive voice. God set this
his good and gracious pleasure before himself in order
to carry it into effect. This he had begun by making
known the mystery to Paul and to the Ephesians, but,
of course, it would continue in the same way for others
during all future time.

We consider the debate as to whether ἐν αὐτῷ means
"in him" (Christ) or "in himself" (God) pointless
because the middle voice of the verb is already reflexive and needs no added phrase to express the idea
"in himself." No one purposes anything save in himself. Paul has already used "in Christ" and "in him"
so often that this new reference is perfectly clear.
Certainly, all that God set before himself in regard to his good pleasure was "in connection with

him" (Christ), in connection with whom were all the
other acts of God that have already been mentioned
in this doxology.

10) God set his good pleasure before himself in
connection with Christ "for administration." God's
good pleasure was to be carried out or realized; God
set it before him "in Christ for administration."
Christ was to administer God's good pleasure so
as to carry it into effect. Read together: "In him
(Christ) for administration" (no article). The object
implied in "administration" is "his good pleasure
which," etc., and not the following genitive. For this
is a designation of time exactly like "the fulness of
time" in Gal. 4:4. It is the genitive of time within
which something is to occur: "for administration during the fulness of the time periods." All of the previous time periods reached their fulness when the New
Testament Era began; this fulness continues until the
last day. Within it falls the administration which
Christ exercises.

Christ is now God's great οἰκονόμος, administrator
or manager. To his administration God purposed to
commit the good pleasure of what he had willed.
Christ's administration is to carry the good pleasure
into execution. From his eternal election onward God
has connected everything with Christ, especially during this New Testament Era, during the fulness of
the καιροί or time periods. Christ will eventually lay
everything at God's feet, I Cor. 15:28.

We need not puzzle about the different meanings of
"fulness." C.-K. 785 regards οἰκονομία as a passive:
a disposition or *Hausordnung* arranged by God "relative
to (thus the genitive) the fulness of the time periods."
This confuses the thought. Keep the active sense:
"for administration," i. e., for Christ to administer.
Paul repeatedly uses the word in this active sense to
designate his own apostolic administration. The word

oikonomia with its suggestion of an *oikonomos* is most apt. Great proprietors still have a manager for some great estate, who carries out the good pleasure of the owner. So great is the riches of God's grace, even so bound up with Christ that its administration since the completion of the redemption is placed wholly into his hands.

When the infinitive is made epexegetical, it becomes difficult to see what it would elucidate. Would it be "the mystery of his will" or "his good pleasure which he set for himself" or "administration"? The idea that these expressions are only formal and need something concrete to fill out either one or all of them, is a misunderstanding. In fact, the last two belong together: "his good pleasure which he set before himself in him (in connection with him) for administration." The infinitive states purpose or intended result. This administration during the fulness of the periods, during the New Testament Era following the completion of those previous periods, is "to sum up all the (existing) things in the Christ, those in the heavens and those on the earth." The thought is the same as that expressed in Col. 1:20: "to reconcile all the (existing) things unto him, . . . whether those on the earth or those in the heavens." Compare also Phil. 2:9-11, where the things under the earth are added since Christ's exaltation shall cause even the demons to bow before him. We add Rom. 8:19-21.

Paul uses this verb only once again, in Rom. 13:9, to express a logical summing up of the various commandments into one, to love one's neighbor as oneself. Here, however, the summing up is one of actual objects. What seems to cause so much difficulty in apprehending Paul's meaning is the preposition *ἐν* when this is translated "in." "To sum up *in* the Christ," to sum up "all the (existing) things" *in* him, seems abstruse. So modified meanings are sought for the

infinitive and for "all the things," and a variety of
interpretations results, in fact, the passage is called
a *locus vexatus.* Yet the words are not vexatious.
Christ's administration of God's good pleasure is to
have this result: to cause the summing up (the verb
is causative, R. 809) of all the things that exist, to
do this *in connection with* him as "the Christ." Did
not the risen Savior say that *all authority* was given
to him in heaven and on earth (Matt. 28:18)? Is not
this what Paul says, that he is to administer God's
good pleasure so as to sum up all that exists? Matt.
28:18 contains *"all* authority" and the very phrases
here used, "in heaven" and "on earth." *All* authority
covers "all the (existing) things."

To cause a summing up of all things "in connection with the Christ," with him in his capacity of the
Anointed One (appellative article, also in v. 12), is the
same thing as v. 22: God "gave him as head over all
things to the church." Yet this is not accepted because
of the word "head," because our infinitive does not
mean "to head up," in fact, is not derived from κεφαλή,
"head," but from κεφάλαιον, "sum." True enough,
Christ is head only of the church which is his body,
and not in this sense head of all things as if they were
his body. Yet, if he has absolute authority over all
things in heaven and on earth, if he is "over all
things," he is certainly their head in the sense of their
supreme ruler, to whose "authority" all things must
bow (Phil. 2:10, 11), whose authority all things must
acknowledge. The head of the church is no less a one
than he who in his authority is "over all things." We
feel that Matt. 28:18; Phil. 2:10, 11; and Eph. 1:22
help to expound our passage.

R. 773 lets τὰ πάντα with the article signify "the
sum of things," "the all," the Germans say *das All.*
It is more exact to say πάντα = all things in general
while τὰ πάντα is definite: "all the things" that exist.

One may use either according to the way in which
one desires to conceive of them. In v. 22, 23 we have
both.   Yet, whether this expression occurs with or
without the article, a plurality, a vast multiplicity
is referred to; the German *das All* is misleading because it is a singular and expresses a great unity. What
Paul says is that all the things, multiplied and varied
as they are, are to be summed up in connection with
the Christ; this is to be the result of his administering the good pleasure of God. The connection is that
he has assumed authority over all of them and is thus
over all things whatsoever. Under him they now constitute a sum. This thought underlies Matt. 28:18;
Phil. 2:10,11; Eph. 1:22; in our passage it is expressed. Yet only the summation is expressed that
God brings it about in connection with the Anointed
One, v. 22 adding that he is the head of the church.

Although it is grand beyond comprehension, the
thought is quite clear. These many things are not
left to drift or to operate for themselves; they are
made to constitute one sum. It is our Lord and Savior,
the head of the church, the administrator of God's good
pleasure, of his grace and his gospel, who takes in
charge all the things in heaven and on earth in order
to rule all of them with all authority. It is thus that
he makes "all things" work together for good to them
that love God, i. e., to his church and to every individual in it. In the language of the catechism this is
called the kingdom of power which Christ rules in the
interest of his kingdom of grace.

We are satisfied with the reading ἐν instead of ἐπί:
"those *in* the heavens."   Like the English, the Greek
may say either "heaven" or "heavens." When Paul
writes: "all the things, those in the heavens and those
on the earth," he refers to all of them. It is a misunderstanding to say that he has in mind only the
aggregate and not every individual thing or being.

Only the demons and the wicked are usually dropped from "all the things," this being done either silently or designedly. A few go even farther and drop everything save the good angels and the elect and tell us that for the first time we here meet the *Una Sancta.* But do the angels belong to the *Una Sancta?* All of their service to the elect is pointed to to show that they do. Still more surprising is the claim that this *Una Sancta* is called τὰ πάντα, "all the things, those in the heavens, and those on the earth."

These ideas result from the sense that is put into the infinitive. It is thought to mean that Christ makes a grand unit of "all the things," and the aorist is conceived as being accomplished at the end of time. From this final unity the demons and the wicked are of necessity excluded since the Scriptures do not teach an *apokatastasis.* John 11:52 is referred to: "to gather together in one the children of God that are scattered abroad." Why not also John 10:16: "one fold and one Shepherd"? The good angels are included on the plea that they are called "the sons of God." One wonders why Rev. 21:1-5 is not mentioned, the union of heaven and earth, "all things" made new.

These difficulties disappear when we abide by Paul's words. There is no restriction in "all the things," and the infinitive is not dated at the last day. All the things are summed up in the Christ "for administration" during the fulness of the periods, i. e., during the New Testament Era. His administration deals with all of them. All of them are taken together like a great sum and placed definitely (aorist) "in connection with the Christ," not to form a great harmonious unity, a spiritual entity "in him," some say "centering in him," but "for administration" by him.

As far as heaven is concerned, he there prepares a place for us, John 14:3. As far as "all things" on earth

are concerned, his "administration" makes them work
for good to those who love God. As far as the
demons and the wicked world are concerned, he has
already overcome them (John 16:13), the devil is
already judged. During Christ's administration the
gates of hell shall not prevail against his church; we,
indeed, pass through much tribulation, but the kingdom is already ours. If one makes *oikonomia* passive
and not the active "administration," if one makes "in"
and "to sum up" a spiritual unity, if one disconnects
the administration from what follows, and if one misunderstands *ta panta*, then everything seems to be a
vexatious puzzle.

11)   "In connection with him" is appositional to
the preceding "in connection with the Christ." Paul
shows what our place is in this administration of
Christ, in which all these things are summed up in connection with him. It is surely a most blessed place:
"in connection with him, in connection with whom
also we were given a lot, as having been predestinated
according to his purpose who works all things according to the counsel of his will." The verb simply means,
"we were assigned a lot" in connection with the Christ,
i. e., under his administration. The verb means neither,
"we have obtained an inheritance" (A. V.) nor, "we
were made a heritage." While the Greek words for
"inheritance," "heir," "to inherit" are derived from
κλῆρος or "lot" — a lot or allotment assigned by a testament — the present verb does not stress the idea of
inheritance.

The translations of our versions are so attractive
because they embody such rich Biblical thoughts; for
we certainly have obtained an inheritance, and, like
Israel of old, we are also made God's heritage although
we note that these two thoughts differ materially. Yet
the word here used has reference to neither of them. It
is to be construed with the participle: "we were

assigned a lot as having been predestinated." This represents the thought of v. 4, 5, and yet in a form that fits the present connection, which should not be overlooked, for the thought is now advanced to Christ's administration and to all the things in heaven and on earth. In this vast complex which is in connection with the Christ our lot is one that has the purpose — or is it the result? (εἰς τό may mean either) — that we are to be for his glory-praise.

"We" in the verb = Paul and the Ephesians, and καί notes that also others have received the blessed lot. The passive implies that God gave the lot, that it is received by grace alone. If we regard the verb as indicating an allotment that was bestowed on us in time, the added participle, nevertheless, carries us back into eternity, for it is the same as the one used in v. 5, save that it is now passive and is applied to God. We obtained our lot in connection with Christ, under his administration, "as having been predestinated," etc. Already in eternity God determined the lot he assigned us in time. Paul does not need to repeat that God predetermined our lot as being that of "adoption"; his readers will have kept that in mind from v. 5. One might also say that he would not need to remind them of their predestination; yet his thought has advanced to Christ's administration as it is now exercised and is thus connected with eternity with which the doxology begins.

Thus also the modifiers are different. In v. 5 we have the goodness of what God freely willed; here we have the purpose which God carries into effect under Christ's administration. Κατὰ πρόθεσιν lacks the article and is not the equivalent of the adverb "purposely," which denotes manner; κατά states concord, and the noun is the norm of the concord. God's predestinating act tallies with this governing and normative purpose, and he is the One who ever works (durative present participle) "all the things" that his purpose covers according to the counsel of what he wills. His purpose cannot fail of realization, for there is never a thing that God does not work in concord with the counsel of his will. The lot God has accorded us and which we now enjoy (our adoption, v. 5) must be viewed in this blessed light.

Πρόθεσις = the act of setting something before oneself to carry it into effect, "purpose," *Vorsatz*. God's purpose, like his good pleasure (v. 5), is entirely free, is determined entirely by himself. *Selbstbestimmung* (C.-K. 1173) makes this plain; *Ratschluss* is more like the following βουλή, "counsel." But to stress only the freedom and the determination of the "purpose" is to go astray. Calvin has carried this idea to its extreme. Even in the case of men "purpose" involves certain motives, and these determine the purposing itself and the aims and the objects intended to be realized. So God's purpose emanates from his *agape* and his *charis* and is thus directed to man's salvation. The term is not abstract as it is used by Paul here and in Rom. 8:28; it can never be separated from the motives nor from the aim. This is apparent in the present passage, for here is Christ's administration and our blessed lot. God's "purpose" is his free determination which springs from his love and grace to effect salvation in accord with this love and grace.

Man's purpose often fails, God's never does so. "He works all the things." Here τὰ πάντα does not denote objects as it did in v. 10 but must denote effects and results. They are conceived as definite, hence the article is used. An illustration of the mightiest of these things is presented in v. 20, etc., where also the same verb ἐνεργέω is used; compare Phil. 3:21 and the ἐνέργεια of Christ. But the stress is on the norm and principle governing all this working, namely "the counsel of his will."

"Counsel" and "will" are often synonymous, C.-K. 226: "often completely" so. Yet, since they are here used side by side, their distinction is evident. The Hellenic θέλημα (the suffix μα to indicate result, R. 151) = the will as expressed in a volition although some add the action itself as one use of the word; βουλή implies deliberation: thus a decision based on reasons and considerations. We consider the question as to which of the words implies inclination, which deliberation, as being illy put — "inclination" seems inadequate. C.-K. uses "plan" when he explains "counsel." We take Paul to mean that in all the things God works he follows the plan with all the wise reasons on which it rests as these have been settled by what he has willed. In this no one has been his cousellor (Rom. 11:34); all of it lies on too high a plane. Note θέλημα in v. 1, 5, 9.

12) The clause introduced by εἰς τό states the purpose for which we were given a lot. This is "that we may be for his glory-praise as those who have hoped in advance in the Christ." Our whole condition in this our lot is to be that of praise for God's glory. Here and in v. 14 the genitive "of his grace," which is found in v. 6, is omitted, but this omission merely abbreviates. The glory of God is the sum of his attributes or any one attribute shining forth to men; the attribute whose glory is here most prominent is grace. Once this is said (v. 6), it need not be repeated. We do not make the phrase "for his glory-praise" parenthetical so that the predicate would be the participle: "that we may be for his glory-praise those who have hoped before," etc. The phrase is too prominent in the three places in which it occurs, marking, as it does, the conclusion of each of the three parts of the doxology, so that it might be unemphatic here where it occurs the second time. One also naturally reads it as the predicate.

The substantivized participle forms an apposition to ἡμᾶς (R. 778). We are to be to the praise of God's glory "as those who have hoped in advance in the Christ." Πρό in the perfect participle refers to the future fulfillment of the hope; we now hope "in advance," hope shall finally turn to sight (Rom. 8:24, 25). The note of hope is struck here because of what follows in v. 14; we now have only the pledge of our inheritance, we shall eventually enter upon our entire inheritance. The apposition forms the transition. It is suggested that we read the whole clause as a unit idea: God's intention is that our hoping in advance be for the praise of his glory. This would make the entire statement more compact.

We do not find a restriction in the participle so that it reduces the "we" found here at the end of this second part of the doxology to Paul and the *Jewish* Christians at Ephesus. From v. 3 onward we have "us" and "we" as a reference to *all* the Ephesian Christians plus Paul, and now, without warning or preparation of any kind, this ἡμᾶς cannot refer to "us Jewish Christians," and do so by only an apposition. What kind of Jewish Christians would these be? Very few of those who had been converted to Christianity had ever had a true, spiritual hope in the Christ; almost all of them had had a carnal hope in a political Messiah. Had this been to the praise of God's glory? The true hope had entered the hearts of these Jewish Christians in Ephesus when they were converted. Furthermore, "for praise of his glory" marks the conclusion of the three parts of the doxology *equally*. It cannot in one instance ascribe this praise to all the Christians and then only to Jewish Christians. "In the Christ" (Rom. 15:12; I Cor. 15:19) does not make the Christ the object hoped for but connects our hoping with "the Christ" (the article is used as in v. 10).

The Third Member of the Doxology

13) Like the second, this begins with the phrase "in whom," i. e., "in connection with whom" (the Christ). But now, addressing the Ephesians more directly, Paul writes, "also you," and drops the reference to himself as found in all the preceding "us" and "we." When this "you" is thought to mean "you Gentiles also," the question naturally arises whether it is possible for Paul to restrict the sealing with the Holy Spirit to these Gentiles. "You" is directed to *all* the Ephesians; and καί joins them to all other Christians, it is like the καί occurring in v. 11. We regard "you" as the subject of ἐσφραγίσθητε; hence we suppy neither, "also you were given a lot," nor, "also you have hoped," nor, "also you are (i. e., in him)." Because Paul changed to "you," ὑμεῖς had to be written in order to show that the two following participles refer to the Ephesians.

The very first participle shows the propriety of this change to "you," for the Ephesians — certainly all of them — "had come to hear the Word of the truth, the gospel of your salvation," from Paul himself. The fact that he, too, had come to hear it is taken care of by καί which combines Paul with all the other Christians: he and they are now one group, "also you" are joined to them as another group. Both participles are ingressive aorists: "having come to hear," "having come to believe." At the same time both are effective aorists: the Ephesians really heard and believed. Paul repeats "in whom" before the second participle. This emphasizes the phrase which has already been used so often. But this shows that both "in whom" phrases are not to be construed with the participles but with the main verb. In regard to the first participle this is plain since we cannot say: "in whom having heard"; in regard to the second one might raise the question, for

in a few instances πιστεύω is construed with ἐν. But
here the parallelism of the phrases is too marked. We
all believe "in" Christ, regarding this there is no question. The question is regarding what words Paul
would have us construe together. We take them to
be these: "having come to hear the Word of the truth,
the gospel of your salvation, and having come to
believe." Πιστεύω is used without a modifier, which is
proper here where the Word and gospel are already
mentioned.

Hearing and believing belong together as correlatives; together they lead to the sealing. That is why
"having come to believe" is the ingressive aorist. The
moment we come to faith the sealing occurs. The
thought is not that we must believe a while, and that
some time later in the course of our believing the Spirit
is bestowed. "The Word of the truth" is the *logos*
which conveys to our ears and thus to our hearts the
divine reality (ἀλήθεια) which we are to apprehend by
the faith this reality creates in us. Truth should
always be believed; not to believe it, is to trust a lie,
and that is the greatest guilt because it is so abnormal.
The devil is the liar from the beginning. It is the judgment of those who refuse to believe the truth that they
should believe a lie (II Thess. 2:11). It is well to note
the article: "the truth," for this is the specific reality
which deals with our salvation. It consists of the facts
of God's grace and Christ's work.

What we have come to hear is so important that
Paul adds the apposition: "the gospel of our salvation." "The gospel" defines "the Word," and "our
salvation" describes "the truth." We may regard both
genitives as objective: the Word which deals with the
truth, the gospel which deals with our salvation. The
Word is, indeed, "the glad message" that has reached
our ears through the grace of God. Its very goodness
should kindle faith even as it is full of the power to

do so. Nothing is so good for the sinner as his "salvation," his rescue from all the guilt and the damnation
of sin plus his entrance into an abiding condition of
safety. Both ideas are contained in this word. Also
the fact that we have a "Savior" who is able "to save"
to the uttermost. After these objects of our hearing
have been named, our believing does not call for the
designation of an object.

"In connection with whom (the Christ) you were
sealed with the Spirit of the promise, the Holy One."
The first ἐν ᾧ is repeated in the second ἐν ᾧ; this is
done because of the intervening words and in order to
make certain of the emphasis on "in connection with
whom." The idea that the Christ is the container into
which we were placed, and that this container is then
sealed up, will scarcely find acceptance. We were
sealed "in connection with the Christ." This connection is clearly stated; it was effected objectively by the
Word and gospel heard, and subjectively by our coming to faith. In this connection God sealed us with the
Spirit, for God is the agent in this passive. The dative
might express the agent but it cannot do so here where
the Spirit is at once called "the pledge," etc. Besides,
throughout this doxology it is God who is glorified
in connection with Christ and now also in connection
with the Spirit. The aorist "were sealed" fits one act
of sealing. This act God performed in our baptism
(C.-K. 1031), which only those will deny who conceive
baptism as being merely a symbol. To be thus sealed
with the Spirit is the same as to be anointed with the
Spirit (both expressions are found in II Cor. 1:22),
the same also as being gifted with the Spirit.

The secular uses of sealing are pointed out by M.-
M. 617, etc.: for security, for concealment, for marking, and for authenticating. Here and in II Cor. 1:22
the idea is that of ownership: by means of the seal,
i. e., by the bestowal of the Spirit, God marked us as

his own, II Cor. 1:22 has the middle voice. Sealing,
confirming, and "pledge" (down payment) — though
not anointing — have been listed as legal and juri-
dical terms, as technical or semitechnical court terms.
The modicum of truth in this claim is the fact that
these terms sometimes appear in legal connections, but
only sometimes, they occur far more often in non-legal
connections. The examples cited in M.-M. suffice. The
tomb of Jesus was sealed by Pilate's special seal. The
claim that Paul borrowed the word "to seal" from the
pagan mystery cults is one of many similar claims
which, if taken together, might well lead us to conclude
that Paul himself had been initiated into at least some
of these pagan mystery cults. In I Cor. 2:13 he tells
us that he uses "spiritual words for spiritual things."
He himself calls circumcision a "seal (Rom. 4:11)
although we doubt that Paul had in mind a parallel
between circumcision and the Holy Spirit as being seals.

The Spirit is a living seal, thus a mark that is
proper for the divine life kindled in us. The Greek
is able to lay special emphasis on the adjective "Holy"
by appending it with a second article at the end like
an apposition and a climax (R. 776). The Spirit himself is called "the promise of the Father" in Luke
24:49, and Acts 1:4 (compare Acts 2:33; Gal. 3:14).
This makes it certain that "the promise" here referred
to is to be understood in the same sense: not the Spirit
who *makes* the promise, but who *is* the gift promised
by God in the Old Testament. He is emphatically
Ἅγιος so that those who are sealed with him are ἅγιοι
(v. 1), marked as being separated for God.

14)   If we prefer the reading ὅς, this is only an
attraction of the gender to the predicate ἀρραβών. The
personality of the Spirit is in no way involved by the
reading ὅ or ὅς. To the figure of sealing Paul adds an
allied one by means of the clause, "who is the down

payment of our inheritance." Ἀρραβών is the Hebrew '*irabon*, yet it is found in the Greek already before the LXX and is thus perhaps of Phoenician origin. It denotes the pledge money or down payment and in the papyri involves the guarantee of completing the full payment in due time. It is considered a technical term.

The Spirit is the first down payment of our inheritance and makes certain that in due time the inheritance in full will be turned over to us. As God has fulfilled the vital promise that he would give us his Spirit, so he will fulfill the rest of his promise and eventually give us our heavenly inheritance. The Spirit is more than an affixed seal, he is even the first part of our inheritance and is already now made ours. Doubly blessed is our lot. The idea is that of the greatest assurance. It is personal for each believer although Paul uses the plural. Since the Spirit is received in the soul, the assurance remains individual and constitutes no means for our judging each other. The expressions here used imply no obligation on our part; homiletical deduction is free to bring in our obligation even as we are often told elsewhere in Scripture that we should let the Spirit lead and control us.

We were sealed with the Spirit "for (effecting final) ransoming of the possession, for his glory-praise." The two phrases introduced with εἰς express goal and aim. The first evidently states in what the possession of the Spirit is finally to result as far as *we* are concerned; the second what the result is to be for *God*. We are to obtain our final ransoming; God is to receive the praise of his glory. We already have the ransoming through Christ's blood, that part of the ransoming which consists of the remission of all our sins (v. 7). The same word ἀπολύτρωσις is used to designate the final act when we are ransomed from all evil, when even our dead bodies are ransomed for eternal glory (Rom. 8:23).

It will be difficult to show that the word as it is used in v. 7 implies Christ's ransom (his blood) but that it is now used without this idea and means only deliverance apart from any price. 'Απολύτρωσις signifies not only the payment of the λύτρον but includes the freeing of those for whom the "ransom" is paid. This release consists of two stages: first the remission of the transgressions (v. 7), finally our transfer to heaven. It is thus that the word "ransoming" is used to include both, and the latter is as much due to the ransom as is the former.

This appears also from the context. Our present possession of the Spirit is only the first down payment and not the full inheritance involved in our adoption (v. 5). The transaction as a whole includes much more. Christ's ransom has bought the glory of heaven. The transaction is not complete until this glory is completely ours.

Περιποίησις it at times discussed at length; also the force of the genitive. We take it that the word means "the possession" and that the genitive is objective. The suffix -σις is active, and there is no reason for thinking that the term is intended to be passive. It is what God possesses and not what is possessed. This point is really immaterial, for whatever is possessed (passive) somebody possesses. More important is the thought that God's possession is referred to, that we constitute this possession, and that as such he will complete his ransoming of us. See the word in I Thess. 5:9; II Thes. 2:14; Heb. 10:39; I Pet. 2:9. Isa. 43:21 (LXX) and Acts 20:28 are especially helpful, for both contain the verb with God as the subject.

Westcott points out that in this doxology, which reaches out to "all the things," God's "possession,"

which shall attain final ransoming, includes, besides us
believers, all the creation which shall participate in
the liberty of the children of God (Rom. 8:20, 21). We
thus reject the various interpretations which speak of
our possession: "a complete redemption which will
give possession" to us (a modified objective genitive) ;
"the redemption which is to become our possession"
(an appositional genitive) ; possession as *haereditas
acquisita*; etc. Some have the final αὐτοῦ modify also
"the possession" mentioned in the first phrase. Can it
be made so retroactive? Is this needed in order to
mark "the possession" as God's and not as ours? We
say, "no."

"For his glory-praise" ends the third member of
the doxology. This phrase marked the ending of the
other two members (v. 6, 12), but each time it had an
addition since another member follows; this third
time nothing is added since the doxology is concluded. "We were sealed — for ransoming," for
heaven.

*   *   *

The Great Prayer for Knowledge

15) Like the doxology, the prayer is but one
sentence. After blessing God for his heavenly grace
and gifts to the Ephesians (v. 3-14) Paul tells them
of his intercession for them, prays God to increase
their knowledge of Christ, and mentions also some
of the wondrous features of this knowledge. **Because of this I, too, having heard of your faith in the
Lord Jesus and of your love for all the saints, cease
not in giving thanks for you, making mention** (of
you) **in my prayers, that, etc.**

We cannot make "because of this" refer only to v.
13, 14, the last member of the doxology, for this last
member rests on the other two and cannot be made

independent of them. The fact that v. 13 begins with
"*you* also" as Paul now writes "*your* faith" only shows
that already in v. 13, 14 Paul focuses on the Ephesians as naturally he intends to do in v. 15, etc.   Yet
in v. 14 he writes "our inheritance."   "You also" (v.
13) implies that others, too, were sealed; so now "I
also" means that others besides Paul have heard of the
faith of the Ephesians and thank God for their faith.
Some of these others were with Paul in Rome.

The deduction that, since Paul *heard* of the faith
and the love of his readers, he intends to imply that
he was not acquainted with them, and that they were
not resident in Ephesus but in other places in which
new congregations had been founded since he had
left Ephesus, is unwarranted; see the introduction.
To point to Col. 1:4, where Paul speaks in the same
way, is inconclusive.   He had, indeed, never been in
Colosse, had *only* heard about the faith and the love of
these Christians.   But how about Philemon 4, 5, where
the same language is used?   Yet Paul was personally
acquainted with Philemon, a fact that is unquestioned.
One may hear about persons whom one has never met
(the Colossians) as well as about persons whom one
has met (the Ephesians, Philemon).   Five years had
elapsed since Paul left the Ephesians, and during this
time many new people had united with the congregation.   The fact that this church continued in faith and
in love Paul could know only because he heard about
them.   The idea that this epistle is an encyclical finds
no support in Paul's "having heard" of his readers
during his long imprisonment in Rome.

The thing heard is expressed by the accusative; the
person heard speaking by the genitive.   The usual
order is: "faith — love" (here and in Col. 1:4), for
faith produces love. When the order is reversed (Philemon 5), this relation is not altered; the fruit receives
special stress because some special exercise of love is

referred to. One of the textual conundrums is the fact
that ἀγάπην is absent from a number of important texts.
Of course, explanations for the absence are offered by
those who adopt the texts which have this word, the
best being that the omission is due to an old error in
transcription. Those who adopt the other texts call
the word an importation from Col. 1:4 (compare Philemon 5). One might consent to the omission if a
satisfying meaning could be secured when "love" is
absent. But this seems hopeless. The best that is
offered is the suggestion that, to the Greek ear, πίστις
conveys both the idea of faith (trust) and of faithfulness so that the word would here refer first to Christ
and faith in him and next to the saints and faithfulness toward them. The trouble with this suggestion is
the fact that a dual sense of the main noun must be
accepted. We find ourselves compelled to agree with
the conclusion of the American Committee of the R.
V.: Paul wrote "love."

In this connection it may be remembered that the
best text critics are unable to explain how many of the
variant readings originated. Nor do we blame them,
they have no means of knowing. In such instances
commentators likewise should confess that they, too,
do not know. The present instance seems plain. When
Paul heard of the true and constant faith of his former church he would unavoidably also hear of their
love, and why should he omit a reference to their love
when he so frequently combines these two essential
virtues?

Καθ' ὑμᾶς = ὑμῶν, the possessive or the subjective
genitive, yet with this difference that, like the German
bei euch, the former refers to the faith as it was when
Paul heard of it, the simple genitive ὑμῶν would refer
to their faith in general also as it was when Paul was
in Ephesus. We are satisfied that πίστις ἐν should denote sphere but do not accept the view of C.-K. 889,

who follows Deissmann (see v. 1), that this expression
indicates that faith has its root *in* Christ. Vital, spiritual connection of faith with Christ is the thought and
not the local inherence of a root in the soil. When Paul
writes "the Lord Jesus," this is like "Christ Jesus":
title plus name. "Lord" is soteriological (see 1:1),
and "Jesus" the name the Master bore on earth, implying what this our heavenly Lord wrought while he was
here on earth (C.-K. 891).

Paul does not need to repeat καθ' ὑμᾶς with "the
love," for the readers understand that their present
love is referred to. Chrysostom calls faith and love "a
wonderful pair of twins"; yet love is always the product
of faith, the evidence of faith's genuineness, and thus
not a twin virtue of faith. Bengel says that this love is
the characteristic mark of Christianity, John 13:35;
15:12. This is better. One may note that Paul writes
about love for all the saints (the word is used as it was
in 1:1) since the church in Ephesus had existed for
over seven years, while in I Thess. 1:3 and II Thess.
1:3 this broad area of love is not yet indicated, this
church being quite young when Paul wrote.

Moreover, "for all the saints" is most appropriate
in a letter dealing with the entire *Una Sancta.* Today
some lay practically the entire stress on love and neglect the faith once delivered to the saints (Jude 3) and
"the work of the faith" (I Thess. 1:3), which is the
confession of faith, the first obligation of every believer. One cannot raise fruit without having the tree
on which alone it grows, nor pluck flowers without
growing the plant which alone bears them. "Mighty
works," even when these are done in Jesus' name but
apart from true faith, are not acknowledged by the
Lord, Matt. 7:22, 23. The faith and the love of a
congregation reach far beyond its own neighborhood.
When a church is widely known for its faith and its
love it has a blessed fame.

16) The good reports which Paul heard from Ephesus set his thoughts turning to this former place of his labors: "I cease not in giving thanks for you, making mention of you in my prayers." Paul is grateful to God for all the good blossoming of the gospel in Ephesus, doubly so because he himself had first planted the good seed there. During his imprisonment the triumphs of the gospel in the fields of his former labors made him happy and lightened his captivity. "Cease not" takes the complementary participle, the second participle adding something to the first. With μνείαν ποιούμενος the genitive ὑμῶν is not needed although some texts insert it; it is implied in the phrase "for you" which precedes. Ἐπί is to be understood in its temporal force: *bei meinen Gebeten,* B.-P. 445.

17) Paul's thanksgiving flows over into intercession for the Ephesians. Having such great spiritual blessings, it is most necessary that they know and realize ever more fully what these blessings are, their greatness and their value. We often take God's supreme gifts as a matter of course, which may result in our regarding them lightly, perhaps even losing them. It is thus most proper that Paul's doxology passes over into intercession; the transition is thanksgiving.

Is ἵνα final or non-final, and is its verb form subjunctive or optative? Are we to translate: "in order that God may give to you" (purpose); or: "that he give to you" (optative of wish in indirect discourse)? Robertson champions the latter; others, also Moulton, *Einleitung,* Rademacher, and some dictionaries, decide for the former. The answer to those who think that the optative is impossible — one even calls it "monstrous" — after ἵνα and a primary tense is that the optative is not due to ἵνα; it is a volitive optative of a wish regarding the future, and its use after ἵνα is not unknown in the classics (R. 983). This clears the atmosphere, the supposed Ionic subjunctive included. In fact, ἵνα may be regarded as appositional to μνείαν, Paul is stating that the "mention" he makes is this, "that God may give," etc. If this seems too daring, the fact still stands (although R. 994 seems to hesitate to accept it) that the primary tense of the main verb has no effect upon this optative of wish. Apart from the grammar involved, we desire to say that we rather expect Paul to state *what* mention he makes for the Ephesians in his prayers and not merely *for what purpose* he makes mention.

So we translate: **That the God of our Lord Jesus Christ, the Father of the glory, give to you a spirit of wisdom and revelation in connection with knowledge of himself, the eyes of your heart enlightened, so that you know, what is, etc.**

By calling God "the God of our Lord Jesus Christ" Paul himself settles the dispute raised in regard to v. 3 and elsewhere as to whether both "the God and Father" apply to "our Lord Jesus Christ," which they certainly do (see v. 3). According to Christ's human nature God is his God. For the sake of his readers Paul brings out the truth that the God to whom he and they go in prayer is the God who sent Jesus into the flesh as Christ to work out our redemption and made him our blessed Lord who is exalted forever. As the God of our Lord he is our God, the fount of infinite grace. At the same time he is "the Father of the glory" to whom all "the glory" of deity belongs. This *doxa* distinguishes God as God, his infinite greatness, excellence, perfection, and majesty ever shine forth. It is the sum of all the divine attributes in their manifestation.

Both terms of this double designation pertain to the blessings which Paul requests for the Ephesians. Since God is the God of our Lord Jesus Christ, we may freely ask of him, as Paul does, all that God has provided for us in our Lord Jesus Christ; and since he is the Father of the glory, we may freely ask him to help us to see and to realize this glory of his as it manifests itself in our exalted Lord for our salvation.

The gift which Paul desires for the Ephesians is "a spirit of wisdom and revelation in connection with knowledge of himself." Our versions have "spirit", yet not a few interpreters think this should be "the Spirit." Anarthrous πνεῦμα often means the latter so that the word alone may be indecisive. What is rather decisive is the apposition: "the eyes of your hearts enlightened," etc., an apposition that fits "spirit" but not "the Spirit." The close parallel Col. 1:9 shows that the gifts for which Paul prays are really wisdom and revelation, enlightened eyes, to know, etc.

"A spirit of wisdom and revelation" = a spiritual quality or, let us say, nature that is marked by wisdom and revelation. The claim that then revelation should be placed first and wisdom, its fruit, second overlooks the fact that the cause is often mentioned after its effect. We are perfectly free to say that wisdom results from revelation as we are also to say that revelation works wisdom. Compare the analogous use of "spirit" in I Cor. 4:21; Gal. 6:1; Rom. 1: 4; 8:15; 9:8; II Tim. 1:7; Rev. 11:11; "*the* spirit," I Cor. 2:12; I John 4:6; John 14:17; 15:26; etc.

It is misleading to speak of the active sense of ἀποκάλυψις and to state that here the revealer is indicated by πνεῦμα. "A spirit of revealing" by which *we* make revelations to others would be out of place. Christians are not the source of revelation; if this were Paul's meaning, "the Spirit of revelation" would alone be in place, for *he* makes revelation to us. But revelation is used objectively. Even in Rev. 1:1 God *gave* to Jesus Christ "a revelation" (objective) which he was *to show* to God's servants. The word is here so used by Paul and therefore follows wisdom. Paul wants God to give the Ephesians a spirit that is marked and graced by wisdom and revelation (qualitative genitives), a spirit that is rich in the wisdom derived from God's revelation. See v. 8 regarding "wisdom": "in connection with all wisdom." The revelation here referred to is that embodied in the gospel.

"In connection with (ἐν) knowledge of himself" (αὐτοῦ, referring to the subject, "the God of our Lord Jesus Christ," objective genitive) modifies "revelation." The following verses show that Paul wants the Ephesians really and fully to know God, the full, great revelation he has made of himself by what he has already done for the Ephesians and by what he will yet do according to what he has already done in regard to Christ. Centering all the knowledge on "him" (God) so that the revelation is connected with the knowledge of him, will put the Ephesians into the fullest possession of the entire gospel contents. This harmonizes perfectly with the doxology (v. 3-14) which focuses everything on God.

Ἐπίγνωσις is the proper word: it is not merely *Kenntnis* but *Erkenntnis*, the knowledge which really apprehends God, true realization in the heart and not merely that of the intellect. John 17:3. "Christian knowledge does not consist of certain finished intellectual apprehensions, certain doctrinal statements and formulas impressed upon the memory, but in a living and constantly growing experience of the saving truth, in an ever-fresh apprehension of what the grace of God has given us in Christ Jesus." Besser. The intellect is exercised to its fullest capacity but only as the avenue to the heart and the soul. Unless the latter is reached, the intellect fails to serve its purpose; mere historical or head knowledge is not enough. Some connect the phrase with what follows. But who could surmise that a pause is to be made before the phrase? If it modifies the following participle, why does it precede it and thereby receive a strange emphasis?

18) Those who translate "Spirit" in v. 17 have trouble in construing the accusative "the eyes," some call it an anacoluthon in order to solve the difficulty. Paul has in mind "spirit," and "the eyes of your heart," etc., are an elucidating apposition. The participle is placed forward because of the emphasis it requires as being the important predicate. "Wisdom," etc., means eyes "having been enlightened and thus remaining so (perfect tense)." God has enlightened them (passive).

Leb (Hebrew), καρδία, and the Greek and the Biblical idea of "heart" deserve considerable study; one may start with the data provided by Delitzsch, *Biblische Psychologie*, 248, etc., § 12, and C.-K. 581, etc. "The heart" is in brief the central organ of the personal life and as such the seat not only of the feelings (the common English idea) but also and especially of the intellect and of the will. Here the spiritual life pulsates, here dwell God and the Spirit. Here, in the unregenerate, wickedness and even Satan himself dwell. Thus Paul speaks of "the eyes of your heart having been enlightened" ("spirit of revelation"). The unregenerate heart is stone-blind; it must first receive sight, i. e., be given eyes to see. II Cor. 4:3-6 is most instructive; add John 9:39-41; Eph. 4:18. "The eyes of the heart" are the spiritual powers of sight. But even when we have these inner eyes, they must be more and more filled with the heavenly light of revelation in order to receive all that this light reveals.

Εἰς τό indicates contemplated result: **so that you get to know what is the hope of his calling, what the riches of the glory of his inheritance in the case of the saints, and what the exceeding greatness of his power for us believing ones in accord with the working of the strength of his might, which he wrought in the Christ, etc.**

We may regard the infinitive as an ingressive aorist: "get to know," also as effective: "actually get to know." Here we have εἰδέναι which expresses the relation of the object to the subject (the object comes to our knowledge) ; γνῶναι would express the relation of the subject to the object (we consider in a certain way, as affecting ourselves, the object known), C.-K. 388. Here Paul properly speaks only of the former. What our attitude to the things here mentioned will be need not be stated, for it will be like that of Paul as expressed in his doxology (v. 3-14).

The three indirect questions constitute a unit and form a pyramid. From the hope in our hearts Paul looks up to the object of that hope, the heavenly inheritance, and then looks up still farther to the divine power which guarantees this inheritance to us. All of this is to move fully into the range of our vision and our knowledge.

"What is the hope of his calling" is the hope in our own hearts belonging to (possessive genitive) God's call by which he made us his own. In the epistles noun, verb, and verbal are always used with reference to the successful "call" of God and not as in Matt. 22:14 also with reference to the rejected call. This call offers us a hope regarding the future, and we are to perceive fully just what this hope in our hearts is, what its substance is and its immense certainty, thus its vast superiority over all mere human and self-made hopes. Let us note the mention of faith and of love in v. 15 and that hope is now added.

Now the object or the substance of this our hope: "the riches of the inheritance of him" (αὐτοῦ, genitive of the author). God has promised us this inheritance for which we hope, we already have the down payment of it (v. 14). This inheritance possesses glory, and this glory unspeakable richness. It is promised by "the Father of glory," whose sons we are by "adoption" (v. 5, 17). How could it be otherwise than rich in glory? I Cor. 2:9. Our heavenly state shall shine with wondrous splendor, a reflection of our Father's own glory. "What a full, grandiose heaping up of terms, actually symbolizing the importance of the subject!" Meyer. Yet some complain about Paul's style.

But this inheritance is intended for the whole *Una Sancta*, hence we have the great phrase about "the saints." Ἐν puzzles the commentators. The solution is not that *we* are here called *God's* inheritance; here, in v. 14, and throughout the New Testament the word κληρονομία always means the inheritance intended for us. "Among the saints" will also not do. "In the person of," or "in the case of the saints" (R. 587) seems to be the solution; we offer it as such. Ἐν is quite often used with persons and refers to what is mentioned as pertaining to them: "in their case."

19) Now the power which guarantees the final bestowal of this inheritance in the fulfillment of our hope. This power is beyond question God's omnipotence, but it is viewed by Paul, not abstractly, but concretely in regard to what this omnipotence has already done in the exaltation of Christ. It is well to remember that, as the humiliation pertained to Christ's human nature, so also does his exaltation. He who has so exalted Christ, he guarantees our inheritance, the fulfillment of our hope of glory.

Paul wants the Ephesians to know "the exceeding greatness of his power" as it is effective "for us believing ones." It exceeds all other power that might interfere to nullify our hope, to prevent the bestowal of the riches of the glory of the inheritance God intends for us believing ones. When we know the excessive greatness of this power, nothing will ever disturb our hope. Other men also hope; alas, their hopes are built on air, there is no power to fulfill their hopes, to bestow that for which they hope. God's power is only "for us the believing ones," for us who trust him and in that trust hope. Paul writes "for us the believing ones" because he must include himself and the Ephesians and all others who are believers. The substantivized appositional participle τοὺς πιστεύοντας describes us as the kind of people we are: the ones who continue in believing. The participle is added for the purpose of elucidation.

It seems that Von Hofmann was the interpreter who originated the exegesis which has the κατά phrase modify the participle and states that this phrase, which includes all that follows to the end of the chapter, shows that our believing is due to God's omnipotence. Von Hofmann has his followers today who use his exegesis as their *sedes doctrinae* for establishing their contention that saving faith is wrought by omnipotence. They generally quote Eph. 1:19 as establishing this doctrine. When an exegesis is given, a specious alternative is introduced, an either — or: If you do not believe what we say, you must believe this other, i. e., something that is manifestly wrong. The fact that a third, even a fourth interpretation exists, is ignored. We are confronted with the choice: Paul either speaks of the power of God at the Parousia (which he does not) or of God's present power which is the cause of our believing, omnipotence as a future or as a present reality.

Both views are untenable. God's omnipotence is timeless, but here Paul uses the aorist: "which he *wrought* in the Christ," etc. The Ephesians are to know God's omnipotence by what it has already wrought in the exaltation of the Christ. What they see as having occurred in the *past* is their guarantee regarding the bestowal of their inheritance in the *future*. The greatness of God's power accords (κατά) with what God has *already done*. The immense κατά phrase (v. 19-23) modifies "the exceeding greatness of his power for us the believers"; this "greatness" is exhibited in what God has done and stands as thus exhibited forever. The Ephesians are to know this "greatness" accordingly.

The idea that Paul is here explaining how we come to believe and continue to believe, that our believing is due to omnipotence, is foreign to his thought. The combination πιστεύειν κατά is not used, κατά never modifies this verb. The long elaboration introduced by this preposition could not modify the incidental participle attached to ἡμᾶς. The cause of faith is the power of grace in the gospel; to make *Allmacht, Allgewalt*, omnipotence, the cause is contrary to Scripture teaching. This conception is carried to the extreme claim that "the greatest triumph of the divine almightiness" is to crush "the intensest exercise of their (men's) power" in resisting God. This is the irresistibility of Calvinism. Why, then, does God use this all-crushing omnipotence upon only so few? Is it because of his sovereign, absolute will? To escape this plain Calvinism it is assumed that there are two kinds of *Allgewalt*, one that may, and one that may not be resisted. The Bible knows only the latter; the other does not exist.

Paul heaps up the terms when he says that "the greatness of his power" accords with "the working of the strength of his might": ἐνέργεια is the operating activity in some task; κράτος is the strength exercised in the activity; ἰσχύς is the *vis, virtus*, or strength possessed, whether it is exercised or not. Paul knows how to describe "the exceeding greatness of God's power," δύναμις or dynamic power; the other three nouns unfold this δύναμις.

20) The feminine relative modifies the first (feminine) noun. Paul recites the deeds of God by which he crowned the saving work of the Messiah: his resurrection from the dead, his enthronization in supreme glory and majesty, the two together often being called the exaltation. These deeds are, indeed, works of omnipotence; they make certain

also our exaltation. Our hope rests on what God has thus wrought in Christ, on the working **which he wrought in the person of the Christ by having raised him up from the dead and having seated him at his right in the heavenly place far above all rule and authority and power and lordship and every name named not only in this eon but also in the one to come; etc.** Note the cognate accusative: "the working which he worked," τὴν ἐνέργειαν . . . ἢν ἐνήργησεν. Ἐν = "in the person of," "in the case of" (R. 587). "In *the* Christ," as in v. 10 and 12 = in him who is the Christ, the one anointed for his great office.

Two complementary participles state what God wrought; they are aorists because they were single acts. God raised the Christ from the dead. The Scriptures say both that God raised him and that he himself arose, for the *opera ad extra sunt indivisa aut communa*. The phrase ἐκ νεκρῶν has been thought to mean: "out from among the dead." This is done in the interest of chiliasm. This phrase occurs many times and is always without the article; it is idiomatic in the Greek and signifies "from death." See further Matt. 17:10; Mark 9:9; Luke 9:7; John 2:22; Acts 3:16. Christ's resurrection exceeds that of Lazarus and of others who were raised up as he was, for Christ rose with glory. He is himself the Resurrection and the Life, in whom the blessed resurrection of all believers is assured.

The second participle καθίσας is causative: "having caused him to sit at his right" (feminine adjective, supply "hand"). Sitting expresses permanency. The expression "the right hand" is God's infinite glory, power, and majesty, which the risen and exalted Christ exercises completely. In the state of humiliation he exercised these powers only to the degree that they were necessary for his redemptive work; now he exercises them in an infinite way. Both the raising up and the seating at God's right hand pertain to the human nature of Christ; so also God's putting all things under his feet (v. 22). "In the heavenly places," explained in v. 3, means in the heavenly world to which Christ ascended visibly, from which also he shall come again in like manner, Acts 1:11. The glory of the exaltation is brought out most completely by the added phrase: "far above all rule," etc. How far above is apparent: as far as infinite exaltation exceeds finite exaltation whether it is earthly, "in this eon," or heavenly, "in the eon to come."

21) The terms "rule — authority — power — lordship — name" do not signify five ranks so that "rule" is one rank, "authority" another rank, etc. Moreover, the five are found on earth ("in this eon") as well as in heaven. Nor have we an ascending or a descending scale of rank. There are ranks, lower and higher; the five terms apply to each rank both in this and the next world. What the ranks are, and how many there are, is not stated, but all of them are included. Each one has a certain ἀρχή, "rule" or domain, greater or smaller, an emperor, a king, this and that minister, this and that official, other men in their various stations. With that rule there naturally goes the corresponding "authority"; with that the corresponding "power"; with that the corresponding "lordship" which exercises the power; and with that the corresponding "name" or title. So it is in heaven: one is set over ten cities, another over five.

Only to the last, "the name," does Paul need to attach the modifier: "named not only," etc.; for the name or title one bears involves the other terms. Αἰών is eon or age, *saeculum*, yet as marked by what transpires in it. When it is translated "world," the sense is the world in its course of affairs. Since in its course and current "this eon" is marked by sin, "this world" has an evil connotation and is in contrast to "the eon

about to come" when this eon shall end. The coming
one is perfect. Christ shall usher it in at his Parousia
although it exists now and we may already taste the
powers thereof (Heb. 6:5). It is called "the eon to
come" only because we now wait for it in hope. We
may also note that human language is compelled to use
terms that indicate time when it speaks of eternity
although eternity is timelessness, the opposite of time,
succession, progress, etc. The Scriptures themselves
condescend to our limitation in language in this matter.

22) When Paul continues with a finite verb instead of a third (and a fourth) participle, this is not
anacoluthic nor a change in construction. The two
new statements are no longer subordinate; they are
intended to be independent and coordinate even as
they are written: **and he ranged everything under
his feet and him he gave as head over everything to the church since she is his body, the fulness of him who fills all the things in all ways for
himself.**

Even the change of the object from "him" (Christ)
used after the participles to πάντα justifies the finite
verb. Πάντα means "everything" in general. The idea
of subjecting hostile things is not conveyed but only
that of ranging all things as a footstool under Christ's
feet (it is like Matt. 5:35 and not like Matt. 22:44).
The idea is that of supreme exaltation. The language
is that of Ps. 8:6 (compare, I Cor. 15:27; Heb. 2:8).
The psalm speaks only of man as the ruler of the earth;
the apostle elevates the word about man's dominion by
using it with reference to Christ and includes far more
than the creatures of the earth, namely "everything"
no matter where it is found. Man's earthly dominion
is only a shadow of Christ's universal dominion.

Now the astounding statement: "and *him* he gave
as head over everything to the church," "him" (forward for the sake of emphasis) under whose feet God

had ranged everything, "him" as thus "head over
everything." This was a gift of grace to the church,
a stupendous gift. Christ in his supernal exaltation
"as head over everything" is God's gracious gift to
the church, to the *Una Sancta*, to the Communion of
Saints composed of all true believers. This is all that
Paul says thus far. "Head over everything" only repeats the substance of "everything he ranged under his
feet." What Christ as this gift is to be for the church
is not stated. Some think it is, namely that he is to be
our head also; but "head over everything" is not to be
taken in a double sense; omnipotent ruler over all
creatures and besides this spiritual Lord of the church.

23) The forms of ὅστις often imply the causal idea;
R. 728: "There is no doubt about the causal use of
ὅστις (cf., *qui* and *quippe qui*)." Here: "she being such
as," i. e., "since she is," etc. Paul indicates the reason
for God's gift to the church. This lies in the nature of
the church, namely that "she is his (Christ's) body."
To the church as this body of Christ God gave Christ,
gave him in his entire exaltation over everything. Of
course, not to be a member of this body, but as its spiritual head. Here *this* headship is implied, not in v. 22.
Even here it is introduced only by way of implication,
only by calling the church "his body."

God gave Christ in his exaltation over everything
to the church since she is Christ's body, "the fulness
of him who fills all things in every way for himself."
The sense of this apposition is not noted by those who
overlook the tremendous paradox here expressed and
this paradoxical apposition (also the predicate after
ἥτις ἐστί), the astonishing statement that he who has
everything under his feet and is "head over everything" is yet himself bestowed as a gift to his church.
The fact that she is his body is a part of the solution.
Not because she consisted of mere creatures could she
receive this supremely exalted Christ as her gift, for

as so composed she, too, is under his feet. But she is far more, she is different from the other creatures, she is spiritual, Christ's spiritual body, and as such, and only as such, is able to receive and does receive this supreme Christ as God's gift to her. Not even the angels could so receive Christ, to say nothing of the rest included in "everything." She has this special, unique relation to Christ, that she alone is "his body."

And it is this fact that makes her "the fulness of him who fills all the things in all (possible) ways for himself." The paradox lies not only in the fact that he who fills all that exists, fills all in all possible ways, should yet himself have a fulness filling him; the paradox is even more intense, namey that "all the things" filled by Christ "in all (possible) ways," that this church, itself so filled, should yet be its own Filler's fulness. Yet this is what Paul says.

Here we have the definite τὰ πάντα, all the things that actually exist, thus including the church. Ἐν πᾶσι is adverbial: "in all (possible) ways," B.-P. Christ fills some things in one, some in another way, for all are by no means alike, some being inanimate, some only animate, some rational, some spiritual (the church), some angelic. The fact that the exalted Christ fills the church in a special spiritual way is thus plainly stated. Some misunderstand ἐν πᾶσι. The idea is incorrect that Christ fills each of all the things in all ways. In how many ways he is able to fill a stone, for instance, we cannot say, but certainly it is not in the ways in which he is able to fill a saint or an angel. Christ does not ignore the nature and the capacity of each being. We regard the middle πληρουμένου as a true middle, as saying more than the active. Christ fills all the things for himself, in his own interest, even as he has all of them ranged under him.

This filler of all the things has his own πλήρωμα, which is the church, his own body. We recall Christ's own words, not only that *he* is *in us* (ἐν ὑμῖν), but equally that *we* and each one of us is *in him,* ἐν ἐμοί, John 6:56; 15:4-7; 17:21; I John 3:24. His being in us = he fills us; our being in him = we fill him. The Vine has its "fulness" in the branches; the Christ cannot have his "fulness" in any save the Christians, the church. The very paradox demands that "fulness" be taken in the active sense: we are "that which *fills*" him who *"fills"* all the things. The point is lost when the noun is made passive, for if he fills all the things in all possible ways, it is superfluous to say that we are "that which is filled."

The statement of some of the commentators that πλήρωμα is always only passive is unwarranted. Instead of considering only their examples and their arguments, let us study what is offered by B.-P. 1077; M.-M. 520; Liddell and Scott; and other comprehensive tabulations. The word "fulness" is so common that it cannot be called a technical or a theological term which was later clothed with the glamor of mystery by the Gnostics. Paul uses it in v. 10, here, and in the following without the least polemical intent or even the least linguistic uncertainty.

With the exalted apposition "the fulness of him who fills all the things for himself in all possible ways" Paul reaches his final unit conception which brings the whole period (v. 15-23) to its climax and close. He can add no more to what his prayers for the Ephesians ask of God.

CHAPTER II

The Great Quickening

1) The great doxology, praising God for all that he has done for us (1:3-14), closes with the earnest of our inheritance and the reference to our final ransoming. This is followed by the contents of Paul's prayer for the Ephesians regarding the power guaranteeing their hope for this inheritance, the power so fully exhibited in the supreme exaltation of Christ, and closes with our wondrous relation to Christ. Now there follows what God has done in us in order to establish this relation: we who were dead have been quickened and made spiritually alive (2:1-10). It has been well said that the preceding verses rise to such a climax that what Paul now writes cannot be a continuation. A new section begins. Paul is no longer stating what he is praying that the Ephesians may know but is reminding them of what they once were, and of what God has now made of them.

We again have one grand sentence in v. 1-10. The two γάρ statements (v. 8-10) may be punctuated as separate sentences, but only in English.

The Deadness

And you, being dead due to your trespasses and sins, in which at one time you walked in accord with the eon of this world, in accord with the ruler of the authority of the air, of the spirit now operating in the eons of the disobedience, among whom also we all lived at one time in the lusts of our flesh, doing the volitions of the flesh and of the reasonings, and were children by nature of wrath even as the rest, etc.

New paragraphs often start with "and," which indicates a general connection with the preceding. Paul begins with the object "you" but adds so many descriptive modifiers that, when he comes to the subject "God" and the main verb "quickened," he repeats the object which he has changed into "us" and thereby includes himself. The structure is thus regular. These pronouns show that in this paragraph no distinction is made between former Gentiles and former Jews.

They were all spiritually "dead," completely separated from God and the true life that is in God alone. "Dead" is preparatory to the predication "quickened" or "made alive" mentioned in v. 5. The datives are causal: "due to your trespasses and sins"; the articles are repeated as is done in the German because the genders differ. Two concepts are used, not because there is a distinction between them, but because this repetition states the cause of this condition of deadness more emphatically. The two plurals make plain the continuation of this cause; every trespass (see 1:7) and every sin (missing the mark) exhibited the deadness.

2) The relative is feminine because of the last antecedent but applies to both trespasses and sins. "In which at one time you walked," with its historical aorist, describes the former life as being wholly in the sphere of what was filled with spiritual death. But two important phrases add to the picture. This former walk in trespasses and sins was "in accord with the eon of this world." This combination of terms is unusual. Paul does not say simply, "in accord with this eon," the opposite of "the eon to come"; or, "in accord with this world," the opposite of "the kingdom of heaven," he combines the two. "This world" (ὁ κόσμος οὗτος) is the order or system of this earth as it now exists since sin and death have invaded it; and since this invasion was due to man, "the world" refers

especially to mankind in its depraved state. "Eon" adds the idea of long existence but as marked by the added genitive and as finally to give way to another eon or era that is not so marked.

To walk "in accord with the eon of this world" is to live in a way that harmonizes with the whole age in its present corrupt and debased order which is due to the fallen state of mankind and thus contrary to the kingdom of heaven which shall last forever. To walk so is to follow the transient norm of worldly life as it exists around us everywhere, which is the opposite of the spiritual norm set by Christ in the kingdom of God. Thus, obeying this norm, the Ephesians once walked in nothing but trespasses and sins, in flagrant opposition to God's norm.

The parallel phrase reaches deeper. To walk "in accord with the eon of this world" is to walk "in accord with the ruler of the authority," etc., i. e., in accord with Satan; for that he is this ruler is admitted by all (John 12:31; 14:30; 16:11; II Cor. 4:4). So much is clear; the rest is not. The crux lies in the second genitive: "of the air." Is this to be understood literally as referring to the air surrounding the earth, or is the word to be taken figuratively as referring to the evil atmosphere (the depraved influence or condition) in which the spirit that is operative in the sons of the disobedience moves? The other two genitives are interpreted according to one or the other of these views. The writer is compelled to confess that he is satisfied with neither alternative and that he is unable to suggest a third choice.

If "the air" is taken literally, we are offered the following: the ruler of authority (collective for demons) located in the air about us, this authority (ἐξουσία) being called by apposition the bad spirit (singular, or collective) that is operating in the sons of the disobedience. Or: the ruler of the power domain (ἐξουσία) located in the air and thus the ruler of the bad spirit (parallel genitive, no apposition) operating, etc. B.-P. 432 has "the authority of the air" = *Luftreich.* C.-K. 404 and others conceive "the air" as being located lower than heaven where the good angels dwell (Matt. 24:36) yet above the earth but related to the earth so that Satan operates in wicked men. But how can "the authority" or call it "the power" (ἐξουσία) be a collective for demons? The two passages that are said to assure the other meaning, "power domain," Luke 23:7 and Col. 1:13, do not offer this assurance, for the idea of "domain" is added. Although these proponents of the literal meaning do not claim that Paul adopted the rabbinical and the Pythagorean (sixth century) ideas, they must base the idea that the air is the home of Satan and the demons on nothing more definite in Scripture than the one word ἀήρ, here used by Paul.

When "air" is made figurative as we speak of a certain atmosphere, we are offered: the ruler of the power domain of the atmosphere (figurative) which consists of the spirit (apposition to "the air") that operates in the sons of the disobedience. Here we again have the questionable "power domain" which is now, however, located in the figurative "atmosphere" instead of in the physical air. What kind of a location is this? And how can "the spirit" operating in the disobedient be an apposition to this figurative "atmosphere"? A third suggestion is to regard the genitive "of the spirit" as an apposition to the accusative "the ruler"; but this is a rather gross violation of grammar. Besides, it still leaves us with the real crux which lies in the genitive "of the air."

The idea that the definite authority of which Paul speaks has a definite ruler who wields it (objective) presents no difficulty. So also the thought that a definite spirit or animus (τὸ πνεῦμα) operates in the sons of the disobedience. The fact that these sons and Satan are connected is also obvious; likewise the fact that his authority rules their spirit in all its disobedient operations. But what about this second genitive? We confess that we are unable to answer.

"The sons of the disobedience," like "the children of wrath" (v. 3), is called Hebraistic, but why it should be so called is usually not stated. It is an Old Testament way of using "sons" and "children" in connection with what may be termed an ethical genitive. These "sons" are like their fathers; together they second "the disobedience" of Adam, into which Satan lured him. "Children by nature of wrath" are all who are born subject to divine wrath.

3) "Among whom," namely "the sons of the disobedience," "also we all lived at one time," all you Ephesians as well as I, Paul, myself. "Among whom" means that we were a part of these sons of disobedience. "We all" puts former Jews and former Gentiles on the same plane. The second aorist passive "we lived" indicates the past fact exactly as does "you walked" in v. 2; the passive is to be understood in the sense of the middle. The two verbs are quite synonymous, the one (v. 2) meaning "to walk around" in the daily life, the other (v. 3) "to turn about" and thus to move here and there.

The emphasis is on the subject "we all," next on the phrase "in the lusts of our flesh," and is continued by the participial clause and by the following coordinate clause and ends with the concluding phrase "even as the rest." "The disobedience" revealed itself "in the lusts of our flesh." These ἐπιθυμίαι are the evil desires that arise out of the flesh as its natural products; when they are παθήματα they are stirred up by something outside of us (C.-K. 501). They are many and varied and are evil in various ways. Σάρξ is the Hebrew *basar* in the full ethical sense, our fallen and depraved nature. At one time "our flesh" governed us completely. It is

its nature to produce nothing but sinful desires and
appetites that call for sinful satisfaction. With this
phrase Paul reaches down to the inmost source of sin
in us. In Rom. 7:18 Paul declares that in his flesh
there dwells nothing good. All Pelagianism and all
semi-Pelagianism are here contradicted.

From the phrase Paul advances to the participle, a
durative present: "(ever) doing the volitions (the
things willed) of the flesh and of the reasonings." The
lusts lead to acts. We take θελήματα to mean, not desires, but volitions in the sense of things willed. "Flesh"
is used in the same sense as before. Because "the
flesh" is combined with "the reasonings," we consider
the two as genitives of possession rather than of
agency. The volitions are formed by the will, but in
the natural man the will itself is wholly subject to
the flesh. Hence the volitions are responses to "the
lusts of our flesh."

But since they are actual volitions, the διάνοια, the
reasoning mind, helps to produce them. The will resolves to do this or that according as the mind directs
the choice. This lies back of the plural (which is used
only here in the New Testament) διάνοιαι, which does
not refer to the individual minds but to their products.
Some translate "thoughts" (R. V. margin), others
"purposes" (less good), our versions simply "mind."
It is best to think of the reasonings, reflections, conclu-
ions formed by the thinking mind as these direct our
volitions and the resulting acts. By adding this second
genitive Paul is not speaking of two sources of our
volitions. We question whether he refers to source
at all. The psychological source of all volitions is the
will. Paul is connecting the volitions of the natural
man with his flesh and his fleshly reasonings in order
to designate their character; they are such as belong
to the flesh and its ways of reasoning and concluding.

Now Paul advances to an independent sentence:
"and were children by nature of wrath." Phrase —
participle — finite verb: rhetoric corresponding with
thought. First, lusts — next, deeds — now, what we
actually were. Lusts and deeds as the evidence, now
the final fact: "children by nature of wrath." The
dative is like the double one used in v. 1; thus, "*due*
to nature." By placing it between the other two words,
it does not receive the emphasis which is thus left on
"children of wrath." The genitive is like "the sons
of the disobedience." The article is absent because
this is the predicate, and here subject and predicate
are not identical: "we" were not the only children of
wrath; many others besides us, who are now children
of God, were and still are in this great class.

The fact that Paul refers to God's wrath and not
to our own wrath, needs no proof. His wrath is the
unvarying reaction of his holiness and righteousness
against all that is sinful. It is like fire when it touches
tinder. Holiness and righteousness are always energetic in God. While the term is anthropopathic, it is
adequate to express the dreadful reality. To attribute
to God's wrath the sinful passion of our own anger and
then to deny that there is a wrath of God, in no way
removes this wrath. "Children of wrath" are those
who are subject to God's wrath. There is a contrast
between what we once *were* and what by grace we now
are. "Even as" or "as the rest" refers to mankind in
general, to what all men are by nature, and thus rounds
out the lengthy description of the object "you" ("us")
begun in v. 1.

While φύσις may occasionally be used in contexts
which describe something that is habitual and gradually
developed so that it becomes, as we often say, a person's "second nature," this word is regularly used to
designate what is innate and original. Here we even
have "children by nature of wrath," τέκνα (from τίκτω,

to beget, to give birth to), which indicates their nature already at the time of conception and of birth. The view that Paul refers to a nature that is developed by actual sins disregards this context. Paul does not again use "sons" as he did in v. 2. Since already our conception and our birth connect us with God's wrath, it is unwarranted to argue that because of our very nature we are not subject to God's wrath. In other words, Paul's expression rests on the fact of what is commonly called "original sin," man's inborn, utter sinfulness and depravity, a doctrine which is taught in the entire Scripture. And not in Scripture alone, the reality is before us in all of humanity, notably in the death of babes unborn and born. We are by nature "flesh" (John 3:6). Our one hope lies in the new birth even as Paul here speaks of it.

4) In v. 1-3 we have an example of the richness of Paul's mind. He sees the object in all its relations and implications and unfolds them to us in modifier after modifier. By placing the object forward, ahead of the subject, he makes both object and subject decidedly emphatic, in fact, this includes the predicate as well: *You,* dead, etc., — *God,* rich, etc., — *made alive,* etc.! No less *God* did to *you!* It is marvelous before our eyes. The sentence continues: **God, being rich in mercy, because of his great love, wherewith he loved even us while we were dead due to the trespasses, he quickened together with the Christ — by means of grace have you been saved — and raised us up together and seated us together in the heavenly places in connection with Christ; etc.**

We find no "break" and no "change in the structure of the sentence," *contra* R., *W. P.* This is true even of the English, still more so of the far more flexible Greek. Some attach the whole object (v. 1-3) to the participle used in 1:23 and start a new sentence with v. 4: "But

God," etc. This construction disregards the formulation of the object, which Paul matches with the verb in v. 5; "you *dead* — he *quickened*," and substitutes the incongruity; "he *filling* — also you who are *dead*."

Some, like our versions, think that δέ is adversative because "dead" and quickening are opposites. They only correspond; only those who are dead can be quickened and raised up. Δέ is not adversative, for it is added after the numerous modifications of the object in order to mark the fact that the subject now appears. The English has no equivalent and hence must omit the word in translation. "God, being rich in mercy," describes him according to his motive; the διά phrase modifies the three verbs and describes this motive still further as causing the threefold act. "Rich" in mercy brings out the sufficiency in God.

Paul uses the three terms: ἔλεος — ἀγάπη — χάρις. While they are synonymous, each is distinctive, and the three are not to be confused by ignoring this distinction. "Love" is the broadest: as in 1:4, it is the love of fullest comprehension and corresponding purpose. It sees our deadness and is moved to bring us to life. This divine, infinite love will ever remain the most wondrous and glorious mystery which is too deep for full penetration by our finite minds: "God is love," is so revealed to us in the gospel. Let us fall down before him and adore the glory of his love.

"Grace" is this love as it is extended to us sinners in our *guilt* and unworthiness and pardons the guilt for Christ's sake in spite of our unworthiness. "Mercy" goes out to the *wretched* and miserable. Grace deals with the cause, the guilt; mercy with the consequences, the wretched death in which we lie. All three are active in our restoration. Paul names them in the proper order. Having described us in our pitiful deadness, mercy is applied in order to remove this consequence of guilt; it is the mercy of love with its full knowledge and blessed purpose; and this love also in the form of grace as wiping out our guilt and its penalty of death. Here Paul again presents all the angles; his readers are to see them all.

He dwells on this love because it is the divine motive in its comprehensiveness: "because of his great love wherewith he loved us even while we were (yet) dead due to the trespasses." All of this belongs together. Some punctuate so as to combine: "even when we were dead — he quickened us"; but the fact that only dead persons can be vivified is too obvious to be stated. The fact that God loved us while we were yet spiritually dead, that is indeed astounding. The thought of love is expressed in three terms: "his love — with which (love) — he loved us." A dwelling thus on the term by means of noun, relative, and verb, is a frequent construction in Paul's writings; R. 478 has an example from Plato. The relative forms the cognate object, "he loved" having two objects, one of the inner content, the other of the persons. The aorist indicates the great past fact, call it constative if you wish. The "you" of v. 1 has already been changed into "us" ("we" in v. 3). Our being dead due to the trespasses is significantly repeated from v. 1 since the verbs in regard to our being made alive now follow.

5) Paul uses mystical language: "you" ("us") as dead "he quickened together with the Christ and raised up together and seated together." Mystical means neither mysterious nor mystic. Compare the other notable passage where Paul uses mystical terms, Rom. 6:4, etc. Here we have no figures, symbols, or verbal beauties but concentrated facts. One set of facts applies to the Christ physically, in his human nature; the other set applies to us spiritually. The two sets are drawn together into one. The interval of time

is ignored. All are viewed as one, what God did with the Christ in the three acts and what he later did with us. Yet the difference remains. God vivified Christ in the tomb, raised him up from the dead, seated him at his right hand. God then did three similar spiritual things with us, the spiritual effects of what he did with the human nature of the Christ. The verbs compounded with σύν, "together," combine Christ and us in these acts. Cause and effect do go together; this σύν is a fact. Rom. 6:4, etc., states that this effect, namely making us alive with Christ, was mediated for us by baptism. That makes baptism the divine means of regeneration (John 3:3, 5).

When in 1:20 Paul names the resurrection and the session at God's right hand he includes the vivification in the former as this is commonly done in the Scriptures and in our own way of speaking. Yet here and in I Pet. 3:18 there is reason to distinguish the vivification from the resurrection. God made the dead body of Christ alive, he quickened it. The soul or spirit of Christ was returned from Paradise, from the Father's hands (Luke 23:43, 46), where it had been since the moment he expired on the cross, God returned Christ's spirit to the body in the tomb. In the same instant the body, animated by the spirit, left the closed tomb and then now and again appeared to the disciples during the forty days. God "raised him up" includes both acts; here "God quickened and raised him up" distinguishes between the two. After the tomb was empty, after the living body had left it, the angel descended, touched the stone that closed the door, hurled it away, and thus revealed the fact that the tomb was empty. Only the grave bands were left behind just as they had been wound round and round the body and the limbs, but these wrappings had now collapsed and were flat, the body having been miraculously removed from their winding embrace — mute testimony to the vivification and the resurrection. John 20:5-8.

Us God "quickened together with Christ." This expresses more than likeness: Christ physically dead and then physically quickened — we spiritually dead and then spiritually quickened. This is not allegory like physical leprosy — the leprosy of sin; physical blindness — spiritual blindness. "Together with the Christ" states a vital connection, that of cause and effect. Yet "together with" must not be stressed to mean that in the instant of Christ's physical vivification in the tomb all of us Christians were also spiritually vivified; the preposition in the verb is not that strong. The interval of time remains. The spiritual effect produced in us coincides with our baptism (Rom. 6:4, etc.). The aorist denotes instantaneousness. No evolution, no development is even conceivable between either physical or spiritual deadness and physical and spiritual life. Paul has repeatedly used the appellative "the Christ" (note 1:12), here it differs from the official name "Christ."

Paul reverts to the second person when he inserts the necessary parenthesis: "by means of grace have you been saved." This adds "grace" to "mercy" and "love." The remark is so necessary because Christ was physically vivified by the omnipotence of God (1:20) while our spiritual vivification was not due to omnipotence but to the power of grace. Hence God also used the means of grace in our spiritual vivification (Word and baptism); in vivifying Christ physically he used no means whatever. This has been denied. When we were considering 1:19 we already noticed the claim that omnipotence causes our faith. So here, despite Paul's explicit statement that *grace* has saved us, i. e., by this quickening and kindling of spiritual life, we are told that *omnipotence* did this. The fear of synergism in conversion has produced the assertion: "no kind of God's operation of grace in our hearts" precedes vivification and regeneration. Omnipotence is made to do all of it in one instant.

Two facts are true: 1) the life is kindled in an instant as already noted; 2) nothing that God works in us prior to that instant makes us better in our dead, sinful state so that we ourselves even in the least degree contribute anything to our quickening. Yet the Scriptures are full of instances of prevenient grace. See how this grace operates upon Nicodemus, upon the Samaritan woman *before* life and faith were kindled in them.

Grace operates according to a certain τάξις or order and never effects regeneration all at one blow. The law always first takes hold and works the knowledge of sin and contrition for sin; this is combined with the knowledge and the saving power of the gospel that is drawing us to Christ (John 6:44, 65). The instant faith is thereby produced we are vivified, grace has saved us. God's work is accomplished (John 6:29). It is all pure monergism of grace, absolutely no synergism, which has never been anything but a theological fiction. Take baptism in Rom. 6:4: no adult comes to baptism with saving effect without first learning what baptism is. Baptism is part of the gospel, and it is hearing the Word of God that kindles faith. "By means of grace," working as thus sketched, "you have been saved." Omnipotence does not work in the spiritual domain, grace and grace alone does. The periphrastic perfect denotes the instantaneous act of rescue by vivification plus the resultant and enduring state of safety. Lifted out of our death by grace, we live on spiritually in the new life. God is the sole agent in the passive (monergism).

6) Vivified, the Christ was raised up, left the tomb, and appeared to the disciples in his glorious life (Acts 1:3). This was accomplished by God's omnipotence (1:20). Spiritually vivified by grace, this same

grace raised us up, took us out of and away from the
tomb of our spiritual death, henceforth to live spiritually in newness of life (Rom. 6:4). "Raised us up
together" (with Christ) once more connects the two
acts mystically as cause and effect.

Paul completes the thought by adding the exaltation: "and seated us together (with him) in the heavenly places." Forty days after his resurrection God's
omnipotence seated the Christ in the glory of heaven
(1:20, 21). This, too, has its resultant counterpart in
what God's grace did spiritually for us: "he seated
us together with (him) in the heavenly places." Paul
cannot say as he did in 1:20: "at his right hand in the
heavenly places far above," etc. The counterpart is
not a duplicate. The result matches the cause but is
not the cause repeated.

"In the heavenlies" denotes *loca* and not *bona,* but
the term now appears as a flexible expression. In 1:3,
20 the context indicates that the heaven of glory is
referred to; here the kingdom of God on earth is evidently the meaning; in 6:12 only the supermundane
regions are referred to. The kingdom of the heavens
(Matthew's expression), established here on earth, is
heavenly throughout and not of this world (John
18:36). It is the threshold of the kingdom of glory and
is located wherever God's grace has sway. God seated
us in his own gracious presence in the church, amid
all his children, at the table of his Word and Sacraments, under the shadow of his mercy and love. All
the high and prideful places of the world are dung-
heaps compared with the heavenly places in the kingdom of grace.

The dative after the first verb, "he quickened us
together with the Christ," need not be repeated after
the next two compound verbs; so we translate: "raised
us up together with him and seated us together with
him." This means that the closing phrase: "in con-

nection with Christ Jesus" (here the actual title and personal name) modifies all three verbs. On the phrase itself see 1:1. All three acts were "together with the Christ" because they were done "in union, in vital connection with Christ Jesus." Nor is ἐν equal to διά, which Paul writes when he means "by means of" or "through" (1:5). So also Paul's thought is changed when the three aorists are thought to mean that what God did in Christ's vivification, resurrection, and enthronement he did not do spiritually for us but only "objectively", assuring us of our transformation at the Parousia, so that Paul might have used *future* tenses.

7) The purpose clause takes care of the future: **in order that he might show forth in the eons that are coming the exceeding riches of his grace in goodness upon us in connection with Christ Jesus.** The aorist subjunctive denotes the complete and full showing forth. The verb means that God intends to make such a grand display of his wondrous grace before all the angels and the saints in heaven that all may see, admire, and glorify. "In the eons that are coming" means in those that follow "the eon of this world" (v. 2); the plural denotes their endlessness: when time shall be no more, when all God's saving work shall have reached its glorious goal, when the timeless eons of eternity have come. Because of the limitation of our finite minds the Scriptures use terms that denote time when they speak of eternity, which, in reality, is timelessness.

See "the riches of his grace" in 1:7 and "rich in mercy" in 2:4. Here the same riches are referred to. But the adjective "exceeding" points to their superlative greatness, and the modifying phrase "in goodness upon us" to the quality of the grace as it will be displayed upon us in the world to come. To the great concepts: love, grace, and mercy, Paul thus adds a fourth, the χρηστότης, which Trench defines as benignity and sweetness such as invites to familiar intercourse and sweet converse and bestows all manner of good. Christ's ministry was full of this quality of grace; some of its fairest manifestations we see in the reception of the sinful woman in Simon's house, in his blessing the little children, and in his words of comfort and healing. In the eons to come, when everything sinful has forever been removed from us, the benignity of God will display itself in still higher ways. Who can describe all that God has in store for us?

We construe, "of his grace in benignity upon us"; τῆς does not need to be repeated in order to insure this construction. Even in the eons to come all will be pure grace, undeserved favor; but after having removed every trace of sin from us and having brought us to perfection and glory, grace will still have endless goodness and kindness to lavish upon us. Paul freely interchanges "you" and "us" in this paragraph. To think that "you" refers to the Gentile Ephesians and "us" to Paul and the Jewish Ephesians creates confusion. The final phrase: "in connection or in union with Christ Jesus," modifies the verb and thus the entire statement. Paul rings the changes on this phrase from 1:1 onward: from eternity to eternity everything is connected with Jesus who is the Anointed. By repeating the phrase in the same form in v. 6 and 7 Paul lends it significant emphasis. This the more since in both instances the reference is to Christ Jesus in his exaltation. To all eternity all that is in the kingdom of glory applies to us only in union with him.

8) In English the two "for" statements may be punctuated as continuations of the grand sentence or as two separate additional sentences, the sense remains unchanged. The brief explanatory parenthesis in v. 5: "by grace have you been saved," indicates the thought that underlies this entire para-

graph. That is why Paul uses so many terms to designate the divine motive: mercy, love, grace, goodness. So important is "grace" that he not only repeats the parenthetical statement but now amplifies it as an explanation of (γάρ) all that he says: **for by this grace have you been saved through faith, and this not from yourselves: God's (is) the gift: not from works in order that no one shall (ever) boast; for his workmanship are we, created in connection with Christ Jesus for good works, which God prepared in advance for us to walk in them.**

"For," as just stated in v. 5, "by this grace (by it alone, the article to indicate the very grace just mentioned) have you been saved," etc. This repetition is emphatic: the past act of rescue plus the resultant condition of safety (periphrastic perfect) is entirely due to God (the agent in the passive) and to the grace he used as his means. The emphasis is again on the dative. *Gratiam esse docet proram et puppim.* Bengel. On "grace" see 1:6; 2:4. But now Paul expands the statement by adding: "by means of (or through) faith," living trust in Christ and all his redemptive work. God accomplishes his purpose of delivering the Ephesians when by the power of his grace and the means of this grace (Word and Sacrament) he kindled faith in their hearts. Faith is not something that we on our part produce and furnish toward our salvation but is produced in our hearts by God to accomplish his purpose in us.

Col. 2:12 states this directly: "through the faith of the operation of God." One often meets careless statements such as: "Grace is God's part, faith ours." Now the simple fact is that even in human relations faith and confidence are produced in us by others, by what they are and what they do; we never produce it ourselves. Even deceivers know that they must cunningly make their deceptions of such a nature that they may appear true and grand, and that they may thus produce faith in those whom they wish to deceive. There is no self-produced faith; faith is wrought in us. Saving faith is wrought by the saving grace of God. Salvation is received "by means of faith." The dogmaticians call it the ὄργανον ληπτικόν, die *Nehmehand*, by which God makes the gifts of grace our own. In this matter of being saved by God faith is the trustful reception wrought in us by God, only this reception, which is distinguished from the subsequent activity of gratitude and works of faith. On this account faith is essential, and he who does not believe is lost because he does not by faith receive the salvation he ought to receive.

Grace and faith are thus always correlatives. "As often as mention is made of mercy" — the same is true with regard to grace — "we must keep in mind that faith is there required, which receives the promise of mercy. And again, as often as we speak of faith, we wish an object to be understood, namely the promised mercy." In the German: "As often as we find the word *mercy* in the Scriptures or in the fathers, we are to know that there the *faith* is taught which grasps the promise of such mercy. Again, as often as the Scriptures speak of *faith*, they mean the faith which builds on pure grace." *C. Tr.* 136, etc., § 55.

So important is this matter that Paul adds explanatory specifications: "and this not from yourselves." The neuter τοῦτο does not refer to πίστις or to χάρις, both of which are feminine, but to the divine act of saving us: this that you have been saved. Paul denies categorically that this is in any manner due to the Ephesians themselves. The source and origin (ἐκ) is not in you; it is wholly and only in God. As little as a dead man can do the least toward making himself alive, so little can the spiritually dead contribute the least toward obtaining spiritual life.

Without a connective or even a copula Paul introduces the opposite: "God's the gift!" his and his alone. The emphasis is on the genitive. "The gift" (definite) = the salvation he has given to you. This is a "gift" pure and simple, gratuitously, freely bestowed by abounding grace and mercy. Poor sinners are not even in a condition to go to God and to beg the gift from him; God devised all the means for appropriating the gift. Everything about us is a gift.

9) "Not from works" expounds "not from yourselves." If we were in any degree saved by ourselves, this could be possible only by some work or works we ourselves had done. But among all our works done before our quickening there was not one in which God could find pleasure, not one that could aid toward our salvation; all were wide of the mark, all were so damnable that it took infinite grace to save us. As grace would be excluded if our salvation came from ourselves, so faith and the gift would be excluded if our salvation were due to works. A salvation coming "from ourselves" would, of course, exclude also faith just as a salvation obtained "from works" would exclude grace. Yet it seems best to parallel the two negatived phrases, both of which also have ἐκ; the other contrasts are implied. Works earn something, "the gift" is unearned. "Works" and "faith" are exclusive of each other, even complete opposites.

We may regard the aorist as ingressive: "in order that no one shall (ever) get to boast." The aorist also includes the fact that every boast of any kind is excluded. In our human way we may say that, when we consider what it cost God to save us by his grace through faith, namely the sacrifice of his Son on the cross, it should be plain why he wants all human boasting excluded. But there is more, namely the fact that God alone saved us, that we contributed absolutely nothing, that God is truth and could not possibly allow anyone by boasting to deny even in part that God alone saved him. Now nothing so militates against God's grace and what it does in saving us as the boasting of self-righteousness, the falsehood of Pelagianism and of synergism. To know what grace is, and to have saving faith in that grace, is to glory only in the Lord, I Cor. 1:31.

10) But what about "good works" for which even Christians are inclined to take at least some credit? Instead of there being any in advance of our quickening and having been saved, so that they could have contributed something, or so that God could have in some way used them in saving us, the very reverse is the fact: "for his workmanship are we, created in connection with Christ Jesus for good works," etc. This is what we are and how we must think of ourselves in regard to good works. They are nothing but the product of what God himself has made us to be when he created our spiritual life by his grace. The emphasis is on the αὐτοῦ which is placed forward: *"His* handiwork are we," ποίημα, the result of ποιεῖν, the thing wrought or made. As this is true of our entire being, so it is true also of our being God's children. "Know ye that the Lord he is God; it is he that hath made us, and not we ourselves; we are his people, and the sheep of his pasture," Ps. 100:3.

The participle completes the thought that we are *God's* product, something made by him: "having been created," etc. No less an act is involved. In κτίζειν we have the equivalent of the Hebrew *barah,* to call into existence from nothing. Paul has in mind a close parallel between the first creative act when God brought man into being and this second act, which is likewise creative, when God brought our spiritual life into being. There are, of course, great differences, for the one is the act of omnipotence, the other the act of grace; yet in regard to the essential point both acts are alike. God

alone could perform these acts; both produced something from nothing. Where there was no being and no
part of any being, God called Adam into existence; and
again, where there was no life and nothing but spiritual death God brought into existence the spiritual life
that is now in us.

The difference is brought out by the phrase "in
Christ Jesus," which means more than that we are now
in Christ Jesus as the result of God's work in saving
us; it says in so many words that the creative work
itself, from beginning to end, took place in union with
Christ Jesus. "Wherefore, if any man is in Christ
(in union with him) he is a new creation" (the noun
for the participle: κτίσις), II Cor. 5:17; Gal. 6:15; Eph.
4:24. Paul reiterates emphatically what he says in v.
5, 6 that God quickened, raised up, and seated us together with Christ in the heavenly places. Just as our
redemption is in Christ Jesus, so our new creation and
our personal possession of this redemption are in him.
In fact, he is the specific life element outside of which
the spiritual creative act cannot possibly occur. The
very life that is now in us is the life that Christ brought
to light (II Tim. 1:10) and that God made ours as a
gift by means of the gospel.

But the main emphasis is on the phrase: "for good
works," plus the relative clause: "which God prepared
in advance that we should walk in them." So completely is the idea that our salvation is due to works of ours
excluded that Paul states that all good works on our part
are only the result of God's saving work in us. Harless
says correctly that on the basis of the apostolic declaration Lutheran theology has always taught: *Bona opera
non praecedunt justificandum, sed sequuntur justifi-
catum.* "Good works" are such as God adjudges as good
and not the world in its superficial judgment. They are
all of the thoughts, words, and deeds in which the righteousness and the holiness of the new life manifest them-

selves. They all spring from faith, are all done unto
Christ (Matt. 25:40). Such works are an utter impos-
sibility before our quickening; only the new creation in
Christ Jesus is able to bring them forth.

This, too, is God's purpose (ἵνα) that every one of us
who lives in Christ should produce the fruits of such a
life. "Herein is my Father glorified, that ye bear much
fruit; and so shall ye be my disciples," John 15:8. Not
in order to be saved but because we are already saved
are we to do good works. As the sun was created to
shine, the rose to give forth its delightful fragrance, the
bird to fly, so we are created anew to do good works and
thus to glorify him who created us as what we are in
Christ Jesus. This is the text for all who are slothful
in good works and need to be driven.

Long in advance of doing a single good work God
himself prepared and made ready the good works in
which he wanted us to walk. Even this God did and
not we. All the ways of holiness and righteousness
are God's design and preparation. We need not puzzle
about and search for what may please God, he has long
ago mapped out the entire course. What Paul says is
not that God prepared *us* that we should walk in good
works (so Luther), but that he prepared the good
works. Οἷς is attracted from ἅ and is not = ἐφ᾽ οἷς.
Nor does the verb mean "ordained" (A. V.) or "foreordained," which would require προώρισεν; it means
"prepared in advance" so that, when the time came, we
might walk in them. Stoeckhardt writes: "Christ, in
whom we live and move and have our being, makes us
partakers of his gifts and virtues; is formed in our
life and walk; his holiness, purity, humility, gentleness, goodness, tenderness, kindness, etc., shine forth
in our walk as Christians. And thus all self-praise is
excluded. A true Christian does not boast even of the
truly good works which flow from his regeneration, his
faith. To God alone belongs the honor for what we

are and do as Christians." Thus in Christ the good
works have been prepared in advance.

We need not prepare them at this late date; all we
need to do is to walk in them. Bengel says finely on
this subjunctive: *Ambularemus, non salvaremur aut
viveremus.* All the works are ready, they only await
the living doers and their doing. The road is entirely
made, all that is needed is that we walk thereon. God
and what he has done stand out in the whole paragraph. This continues the emphasis on God in the doxology (1:3-14) and in the substance of Paul's prayer
(1:15-23). It is essential that this be noted, and that
all the points of detail be focused accordingly. The
glory-praise of the doxology runs through the prayer
and through the quickening.

*   *   *

The Great Peace

11) "You" and "we" have been freely used thus
far. Some of the Ephesians were of Jewish, most of
them of Gentile antecedents. Thus far Paul has left
this difference untouched. Efforts to introduce it by
way of the pronouns in 1:13 and in 2:1, etc., are unconvincing. Now, however, this difference is introduced by Paul. Especially in Paul's day the great *Una
Sancta* was composed of these two classes who, outside
of the Christian Church, stood antagonistically apart
with apparently no hope of a union. How did it happen that in Ephesus and elsewhere these two classes
had actually been made one, all equally and peacefully
members together in the church, the *Una Sancta?* When
he was describing the church and what God had done
for it and in it Paul could not pass this question by.
He now states the answer: Christ is our Peace.

This truth is freighted with especial import for
the Gentile portion of the church. Hence Paul ad-

dresses the Gentile Christians in this portion of his letter. He begins a new paragraph. **Wherefore remember that at one time you, the Gentiles in the flesh, those called foreskin by the so-called circumcision, handmade, in the flesh, that you were at that time apart from Christ, having been alienated from the commonwealth of Israel and foreigners to the covenants of the promise, having not hope, and without God in the world.**

Διό naturally refers to the entire preceding paragraph since this is a unit, even one sentence. "Wherefore" = because you Ephesians, once dead, have been made alive and have been created for a new life in good works. The connective is properly consecutive: for this reason the Gentile portion of the Ephesian church should remember and bear in mind how far removed and how totally separated they once were from all the provisions God had made for saving men, and how in the most marvelous way Christ ended this separation which seemed so permanent and so hopeless.

The statement that διό and its consecutive meaning are illogical, and the consequent efforts to adjust the connection by either altering this meaning or by changing the text itself (by following the heretic Marcion) do not correlate what Paul presents in these two paragraphs. These Gentile Christians were not only dead and then quickened by grace like the Jews; they were also, unlike the Jews, so completely and so utterly removed from all the institutions of God's grace that the hope that they might ever be reached by this grace seemed groundless. Yet God's grace reached even them. Here they now are, these Ephesian Gentiles, in the great *Una Sancta,* on a perfect level with the Ephesian Jews, these Gentiles brought from afar, the wall of separation completely removed, believing Gentiles and Jews made one in Christ, he their Peace. "Wherefore," because they as Gentiles were thus quickened from death, they certainly ought to remember from what distance God had reached even them.

The Jews were always near the institutions of grace, Christ himself was a Jew, and the fact that Jews should be in the *Una Sancta* was to be expected; but that this entire multitude of Gentiles should also have been brought in, have been united in perfect union with these Jews, and placed on a perfect par with them, this, indeed, no man could have expected. "Wherefore remember" these things is the connection between the two paragraphs when the thought in them is noted as this connective binds it together.

The Gentile Christians are to remember (present, durative imperative) what they once were in distinction from the Jews, and what in spite of that fact they now are in Christ Jesus. The subject of the object clause is fully described from this angle so that ὅτι is repeated in easy fashion when the predication is introduced. "You, the Gentiles in flesh," together with its apposition, addresses the Gentile Christians in Ephesus. Whenever only a part of a congregation is addressed, Paul leaves no doubt in the readers' minds.

"The Gentiles in the flesh" is explained by a second apposition: "those called 'foreskin' by the so-called 'circumcision' in the flesh, handmade." Jews used these two terms when they distinguished themselves from Gentiles. They would use them with reference to even converted Gentiles and Jews. Both terms are abstract collectives. It is Paul himself who adds ἐν σαρκί (the Greek needing no article in such general phrases) to both "the Gentiles" and "the circumcision" and emphasizes the second phrase by adding even the significant verbal adjective: the circumcision "handmade." The Jews, of course, added no such modifiers.

In both instances "in the flesh" = in what is merely flesh, the physical body. Both foreskin and circumcision were only physical marks and were this only because the latter was made by the human hand by cutting away the natural foreskin of the *membrum virile*. Paul is not speaking slightingly of circumcision, for he well knows that it was given by God to serve as the covenant sign from the days of Abraham onward (Rom. 4:11). This function of circumcision, however, had ceased when the redemption was accomplished by Christ. The Jews still sought to maintain it by their empty formalism and despised the "foreskin" (Gentiles). Paul thus speaks of foreskin and circumcision as being only a physical distinction, "manmade" by the Jews, now artificial and thus valueless. Yet even then the distinction still indicated one thing, namely that the "foreskin," the Gentiles, had never, like the Jews, been in contact with the saving institutions of God.

It is this fact that Paul wants the believing Gentiles in Ephesus to remember because it means so much to them personally when they see what God has now done for them. The Jewish believers in Ephesus will also hear what Paul thus calls to mind for their Gentile fellow believers. They, too, will praise God for the riches of his grace which reached out even to the "foreskin." Paul, however, removes all occasion for pride in their circumcision since it is now only a thing of the flesh and merely handmade.

In addition, these Jewish believers will feel ashamed; for as circumcised Jews *they* had been in contact with God's saving institutions but had not profited thereby, had trusted in the mere sign of the old covenant and not in the covenant itself, had waited so long until at last the covenant fulfillment in Christ had won their hearts. These are the silent implications for the Jewish believers in what Paul writes to their Gentile fellow believers. For so long a time they had been what Paul in Acts 28:26, 27 quotes to the Jews in Rome. Thank God this has changed.

12) The imperfect "you were" should be noted, for it points to the aorist (v. 13) "you have come to be." At one time you went on in the most deplorable condition; then, all at once, this ended, and you got into an entirely different position. The predicate does not begin with χωρὶς Χριστοῦ just as in v. 13 it does not begin with ἐν Χριστῷ. "At that time apart from Christ" is a designation of time and belongs together just as "now in connection with Christ Jesus" is temporal and belongs together. Until these Ephesian Gentiles came into contact with Christ, their state was the one the four predicate terms describe: "having been alienated," etc. There were Jews in Ephesus, a synagogue, and Jewish worship. But even these Jews were mere formalists and did not bring even the few proselytes they made into contact with salvation. So the Gentiles remained "in the condition of alienation from the commonwealth of Israel" (extensive perfect passive participle).

Πολιτεία is either the right of citizenship or the organization of citizens, here it is the latter. "Of Israel" is not the appositional but the possessive genitive: "belonging to Israel." The commonwealth of Israel is, of course, not the Jewish nation but the body of the true Old Testament believers, who were named after "Israel," the last of the three great patriarchs, "Contender with God" (Gen. 32:26-28), the name of honor given to Jacob because of his faith which prevailed. Since the Jews were such people in those days, how could the Gentiles come into real contact with the Old Testament church of God? "Being alienated" evidently implies no previous acquaintance but only the state of being foreign to something. The passive leaves unsaid who produced this state.

The second predicate with its noun (adjective used as a noun) : "and foreigners to the covenants of the promise," is the second part of what the participial predicate states. The state of alienation is that of being "foreigners." The figure is that of a state or a city which gives all sorts of valuable rights to its own citizens and withholds them from foreigners. The ablative genitive denotes separation: foreigners "from (we say: to) the covenants of the promise." This first double predicate names the objective features from which the Gentiles were during the past excluded; the second double predicate adds the subjective blessings from which the Gentiles were in consequence also debarred. Judaism as it was in those days could bring neither of these blessings to the Gentiles. The commonwealth of the spiritual Israel had dwindled down to small proportions. The true church of God was all but submerged by the empty formalism of the Jews. The entire Jewish officialdom was itself foreign and even hostile to the kingdom of God. The rabbis in the synagogues, also those in the Diaspora, taught rank work-righteousness. How could Gentiles attain contact with the spiritual polity through their mediation?

The heart of this polity or commonwealth consisted of "the covenants of the promise." The Jews had falsified this promise (the Old Testament gospel). They had made it a promise of earthly glory for the Jewish nation under an earthly Messiah-King. The covenants in which the true promise was imbedded, those old covenants made with the patriarchs, were equally falsified by the Jews. The Jews, themselves foreigners to these blessed gospel covenants, could not and did not open them to the Gentiles even when they made proselytes of the Gentiles.

The word διαθῆκαι cannot here denote "testaments," nor can this plural be equivalent to the singular "testament," nor does the word refer to the stone tables on which the commandments were inscribed (ideas advanced by C.-K. 1069). The singular does mean "testament," and the Greek word even entered the Hebrew in the form of a transliteration. How this meaning developed from the Hebrew word *berith,* "covenant," by way of the LXX we have sketched in Matt. 26:18 and I Cor. 11:25, which see. "Testament" is the proper word in Gal. 3:15. Here, however, Paul is speaking of the Old Testament promise and thus uses the word in the Old Testament sense of "covenants," and even uses the plural. The plural is in place because God repeated his covenant promise. Each repetition was in a way a new covenant. The word *berith* does not signify a mutual agreement, with mutual promises and obligations, and διαθήκη does not have this force, and therefore it is not necessary to translate *Verfuegungen, Erbrechtverfuegungen,* testamentary dispositions. The whole Old Testament covenant and all of its repetitions were absolutely one-sided, pure promise from God to Abraham and not also from Abraham to God. Never is it called anything but God's covenant, never also Abraham's (or Israel's). That is why the LXX translated as they did, and why this word came to be employed as a designation for "testament" even by the Jews.

By being aliens to the Old Testament church, foreigners to the gospel covenants, the Gentiles were also subjectively in the worst plight: "having (thus) no hope, and without God in the world." "And" connects these two as "and" connects the two objective modifiers. The mistake that μή is subjective is still made; but this word is the standard negation with participles and needs no comment (R. 1136, etc.). The fact that the conditions now named are subjective appears from their meaning alone. "Not having hope" = having no real hope, no objective basis of hope. Whatever the Gentiles subjectively hoped for after death had no reality, rested on air, would never be realized. "Hope" matches "the promise"; for God's promise (gospel) is man's only basis of hope. The hopes of the Jews were equally empty. This is also true with regard to all self-made hopes of men today.

The companion predicate: "and without God in the world," really states the reason for being devoid of hope. What gods the Gentiles had were vain, dead idols, imaginary, non-existent beings; the true God they did not have. Yet he alone can promise and fulfill and thus justify our hope. The Jews themselves had lost the true knowledge of God and of his promise and hence could not aid the Gentiles in attaining either. Ἀσέβεια = the conduct of "godlessness"; ἄθεος in the passive sense = devoid of connection with God and thus without his help, left without God (C.-K. 490).

Paul's picture of the Gentiles during this period apart from Christ is one of sadness: far from the safe haven, from the sure promise (gospel), devoid of real hope and help. They were lost, indeed. Judaism as it then was did nothing for them; it, too, had lost all it had. Rom. 3:22b, 23; 11:32; Gal. 3:22.

13) **But now in connection with Christ Jesus you, those at one time being afar off, have gotten to be near in connection with the blood of Christ.**

The sad story has changed into one of great joy. We regard this as an independent sentence and not as one that is still dependent on "remember" in v. 11. The expression of time, "now in connection with Christ Jesus," is the opposite of, "at that time apart from Christ," used in v. 12. The one period was marked by χωρίς, the present is marked by ἐν; once separation and thus a hopeless condition, now connection, union, and the happiest condition. In the phrase introduced by "apart" "Christ" is proper, for this period extends far back to the time before the Messiah came in the person of Jesus. The Jews had lost the spiritual conception of the Messiah, and thus the Gentiles also remained far from any spiritual contact with him despite the widespread Jewish Diaspora. The phrase introduced by "in" properly has "Christ Jesus" since this happy condition of union dates from the time when the Messiah came in the person of Jesus.

The emphatic "you" is elaborated by the apposition "those at one time being far off," which summarizes the description given in v. 12 and at the same time emphasizes the great point of that description, that the Gentiles were formerly μακράν (sc. ὁδόν), "far off," a long way from the true God, the true church of God, the promised Messiah and his salvation. This sad situation has changed now that Jesus Christ has come. Now the gospel is preached "to those far off"; in fact, the Jews, too, so long sunken in formalism and work-righteousness, are also having this gospel preached to them (v. 17). And thus the Ephesian Gentiles, once as far off as anyone, "have gotten to be near" (ingressive aorist, at the same time also historical); how near the phrase "in connection with the blood of Christ" states. They are actually *in* the polity of the kingdom, believing the promise, possessing the true hope, joined to the true God (v. 12, compare v. 19-22). "Now in Christ Jesus" only connects the present time as such with Christ Jesus, his name and the gospel preached in the whole world forming the connection. The final phrase, the connection with Christ's blood, applies to the Gentile Christians in Ephesus who were actually saved by Christ's blood.

The blood of Christ is the objective means, yet any true connection with that means includes faith. This scarcely needs to be said. Christ shed his blood for the whole world of men, and in the gospel its efficacy was now being proclaimed to all nations. Thus these Ephesian Gentiles had been brought to saving faith. The Koine loved passive forms and even coined a number of them such as the one here used without giving them a passive meaning. The blood is to be considered

together with "his flesh" (v. 15) and with "the cross"
(v. 16). The blood = the sacrificial, expiatory death
which "cleanses us from all sin" (I John 1:7). It
brings us "near," into union with God, by removing
our sins. Like his cross, the blood of Christ is comprehensive, and we consider it a mistake to eliminate
the idea of price or to reduce it to the idea of sprinkling
the mercy seat. Paul thinks of the blood in all its
effectiveness but does not give details.

Much more may be said on "the blood of Christ."
It is always the blood shed in sacrifice, the blood of
the Lamb of God, the blood by which Jesus laid down
his life for us. It is the ransom, the price ($\lambda \acute{v} \tau \rho o \nu$, $\tau \iota \mu \acute{\eta}$),
is substitutionary, effects the $\grave{a} \pi o \lambda \acute{v} \tau \rho \omega \sigma \iota s$ or ransoming
on which rests the $\ddot{a} \phi \epsilon \sigma \iota s$ or remission of sins (1:7).
The entire gospel centers in Christ's blood. Follow the
word "blood" through especially the New Testament
and thus discover the whole "blood theology" against
which modernism, like the older rationalism, stands
arrayed. This word "blood" involves the Incarnation
itself; without becoming incarnate the Savior could not
have shed his blood. Blood is far more specific than
"death" ($\theta \acute{a} \nu a \tau o s$) although both are used. One may die
in various ways without shedding of blood. The cross
($\sigma \tau a v \rho \acute{o} s$) denotes the curse, Gal. 3:13, and is specific in
this sense; hence "Christ crucified" appears so often.
In Revelation he is the Lamb "having been slain"
(Isa. 53).

14) All that v. 14-18 contain explains ($\gamma \acute{a} \rho$)
what precedes. The entire section deals with the
union of Gentiles and Jews in the *Una Sancta.* In
this union they both form one spiritual body. All
separation is removed, not only that which is due to
nationalism and perverted Jewish religionism, but
also that which is due to pagan Gentilism ("afar
off"). This union is formed in Christ: **For he is
the peace** (that is) **ours, he who made both parts**

one part and destroyed the middle wall of the fence
by having abolished in connection with his flesh the
enmity, the law of the commandments in decrees, in
order that he might in connection with himself create
the two into one new man, making peace, and might
reconcile the both of them in one body unto God
by means of the cross, having slain the enmity in
himself, etc.

Αὐτός is emphatic, "he," he himself and no other;
emphatic, however, because it resumes the preceding
phrase "in connection with the blood of Christ." "He"
= this Christ with his blood, *he,* the one crucified who
shed his expiatory blood, *"he* is our peace."

The predicate is ordinarily without the article, but
when it has the article, the predicate is identical and
interchangeable with the subject (R. 768). It is so
here. To name Christ with reference to his blood is
to name the peace that is ours; to name this peace is
to name him. He is the personification or rather the
embodiment of our peace. This identification is the
strongest way of saying that he wrought out our peace,
and that we have this peace by spiritual connection
with him.

The question is raised as to what "peace" means,
and who is included in "our." The answer is furnished
by all that follows: "the peace" that unites Gentiles
with Jews in the *Una Sancta* in God and Christ; "ours"
meaning that of the Gentile Ephesians plus Paul, a
former Jew, and thus the Jewish believers, for the
two are named as such in the next breath and repeatedly. True peace between Gentiles and Jews was impossible save in Christ. It is so to this day.

The apposition defines: our peace, "he who made
both parts (neuter) one part (again neuter) and destroyed the middle wall of the fence," etc. The middle
wall = the wall in the middle between Gentiles and
Jews, separating them. This word = the dividing wall,

Jews being ön one side, Gentiles on the other. The appositional genitive "of the fence," the middle wall that consisted of the fence, adds the idea that this wall was the fence that fenced in, not the Gentiles, but the Jews. The whole Mosaic law and system of legal regulations kept the Jews away from the Gentiles. It was like a tremendous city wall that protected the citizens from invasion by outside enemies, a fence that keeps the flock within safe from outside marauders. This dividing, separating wall Christ broke down with his blood; it had served its appointed purpose. Because of the person who removed it and because of the way in which it was removed the abolition of this wall and fence was not an exposure of the Jews to pagan Gentilism; it was a union: with his blood Christ "made the two parts one part," created the *Una Sancta*, the Communion of Saints, which was drawn from all nations without distinction.

We note that ὁ ποιήσας — — καὶ λύσας are placed chiastically, their objects being placed between the two participles. This chiasm forms a unit in thought and in formulation. And this means that the following accusative is not an apposition that is still dependent on λύσας: "and the middle wall of the fence (he) destroyed, i. e., the enmity (he destroyed) in connection with his flesh." This spoils the chiasm and produces an abstruse apposition. If Paul desired to say this, he would have placed λύσας before "the middle wall of the fence" and not between this object and its apposition.

15) Καί connects the two chiastically arranged participles. A third is added without a connective and thus modifies the two: he who made, etc., and destroyed, etc., "by having abolished," etc. The objects are placed forward and hence are emphatic. Καταργέω is the causative of ἀργέω: to put out of commission, make ineffective, i. e., to abolish or wipe out. When Christ made the enmity between Jews and Gentiles pointless

he broke down the wall and fence, he made the two parts one part. But "the enmity," emphatically forward, advances the idea of the wall and fence to the effect these produced. The Jews utterly despised the *goyim* or Gentiles; they considered them dogs, vile, unclean (Matt. 15:27; Rev. 22:15). One must know the status of dogs in the Orient. This attitude toward Gentiles is reflected in many New Testament passages and flashes forth in shocking language in rabbinical literature. The Gentiles reciprocated in kind and hated the Jews because of their arrogance, their scornful separatism, their peculiar religious laws and ways. The enmity was mutual.

The world of men was actually divided into two classes, Jews and Gentiles; there was a gulf between them so deep and wide that it seemed impossible ever to close it. Of course, renegade Jews adopted Gentile ways to the scandal of the faithful, and Gentiles became proselytes of the synagogue, but such occasional incidents left the gulf unchanged. Uncompromising rabbis spoke derogatorily even of the proselytes. The stone screen (*chēl*) in the Temple court forbade by an inscription that any Gentile pass into the inner courts under penalty of death (Josephus, *Ant.* 15, 11, 5; Acts 21:28). Paul's "middle wall of the fence" may refer to this screen although there is no evidence that it was so named. The fact that this screen still stood when Paul wrote makes no difference since Paul's language is figurative to designate what Christ's blood did on the cross. The old hatred persists even to this day. Jews have been restricted to Ghettos, persecution followed them, in bloody pogroms they were decimated.

Paul inserts the phrase "in his flesh" immediately after "the enmity" before he adds the apposition "the law," etc. This means that we are to think of the abolition of the enmity as being effected in connection with Christ's flesh, and that the apposition, "the law,"

etc., is an added thought. The flesh of Christ is his
human body which was nailed to the cross (v. 16), by
which he shed his sacrificial blood (v. 13). What the
connection (ἐν) with his body was we see from the context. Without giving his flesh or body into death for
us he could not have made this deep, divisive enmity
ineffective so that, like a flame which is robbed of fuel,
it went out.

The apposition to "the enmity": "the law of the
commandments in decrees," is decidedly broad; for
"the enmity" is a subjective feeling that divides men
into hostile camps while "the law" is objective, imposed upon the Jews by God in order to keep them
fenced in and separate. Yet the two may be made
apposite since the second is the cause from which the
first emanates as the effect so that putting out of commission to one does the same for the other. Matt.
5:17-19 speaks of the law in the sense of the Old Testament and cannot be adduced here, where "the law"
is defined by the genitive of *content* "of the commandments" and even their *form* is described, "in decrees."
On δόγμα, "decree," compare Luke 2:1.

Paul has in mind the entire Mosaic legal system
with all its commands that decree: "Thou shalt! Thou
shalt not!" Christ set it all aside when he died on
Calvary. Admission into the *Una Sancta* was ever
accomplished by faith in the gospel alone, by the Christ
to come, and then the one who had come, the end of the
law, he having met all its requirements and satisfied
all its penalties. Even its function as a dividing wall
and fence for the Old Testament saints was abrogated
by the cross.

The purpose clause states the intent of Christ's putting the law of the commandments out of effect. It
repeats and thus emphasizes the unification Christ
wrought and at the same time amplifies and thus explains more fully: "in order that he might in connec-

tion with himself create the two into one new man, thus making peace," etc. The verb "create" is the same as the one used in v. 10, "to bring into existence." No less than a creative act was required and thus intended by Christ when he died. The aorist implies that this purpose was actually carried out. Ἐν αὐτῷ or ἑαυτῷ (the texts vary) is more than an ideal that existed only objectively, ideally in Christ; the two were created one new man in actuality, Jews and Gentiles became a unit by being one in union with Christ, namely with his blood and his cross.

The two neuters in v. 14 are advanced to two masculines: "the two (men) into one new man." This is personification: Jews are one man, Gentiles another, and when they were brought to union by faith in Christ and his blood these two created "one new man," this being the personified *Una Sancta*. We have the predicative use of εἰς (R. 481, etc.) ; καινός is "new" as something different from what is "old." A church without a law fence, composed of believing Gentiles as well as believing Jews, was "new" as differing from the church during the Old Testament period, into which Gentile proselytes could enter only by being admitted within the Jewish fence.

The modal addition, "making peace," resumes v. 14: "He is our peace." Christ as the embodiment of our peace is this embodiment for all believers (Jewish and Gentile) by ever making or producing (iterative present participle) peace. His great peacemaking goes forward constantly as he brings more and more Gentiles and Jews into the *Una Sancta* and welds them into one by faith in his atoning blood. He is our peace in this active, creative sense.

16) Paul expands and explains still further: in order that he might create, etc., "and might reconcile the both of them in one body to God by means of the cross, having slain the enmity in himself." The aorist

is again effective, i. e., might actually reconcile. Ἀπό in the compound verb seems to add the idea of restoration to that of reconciliation: "might reconcile back to God," back to him where both belonged (C.-K. 133). This is, of course, personal reconciliation which occurs when faith is produced in the heart. God and Christ do the reconciling, we are the objects. We need to be made thoroughly other, God and Christ make us so. They need no reconciling; they are never the object of this verb. Its root is ἄλλος, "other," κατά is perfective: "to make thoroughly other."

Here we have a striking case of Paul's use of the singular and the plural and of the neuter and the masculine: two parts — one part (neuter plural and singular) ; the two men — one man (masculine, two individuals and one) ; now the masculine plural: "the both of them," i. e., the two groups consisting of many persons, "in one body," one spiritual organism. Each term explains the other. "One body" = "one new man" = ἕν, "one part." This is enough. We do not extend it into "one body of Christ with him as the head," as some do. The idea is that of oneness combined with peace which is opposed to duality, division, and thus to enmity. How Christ is concerned in this is plain throughout, namely by his great acts and by his great sacrifice and its effects.

Here we have "by means of the cross," the blood in v. 13, his flesh in v. 15, each again defining the other. The cross was the mode of death by which Christ shed his sacrificial blood by having his flesh or body nailed to it. This mode (hanging on the ξύλον or wood) involved the curse which Christ bore in our stead, Gal. 3:13. Thus was the one body formed as the New Testament *Una Sancta.*

Here, too, a participial modifier is added: "having slain the enmity in himself," i. e., in his own person on the cross. Ἐν αὐτῷ is so much like the same phrase used in v. 15 and like the many preceding phrases "in Christ," "in him," that we cannot translate it "thereby" (our versions), i. e., instrumental: "by the cross." The A. V. margin is correct. Paul has said that Christ put the enmity out of commission (v. 15); yes, so thoroughly that he killed it. All that we have said on this enmity might be repeated here. Ἐν αὐτῷ is emphatic, "in (in union with) his own person," the phrase echoes αὐτῷ at the beginning of v. 14.

17) Thus far Paul has stressed the great objective means for producing the New Testament *Una Sancta*: Christ, our peace, his blood, flesh, cross, and what was done through these. Together with these means their result is stressed: oneness, unity: "one part" — "one new man" — "one body." Not in two grand divisions, the one Jewish, the other Gentile was the church to be brought to God, but as one perfect unit, even as God, Christ, his blood, flesh, and cross are one. Now the subjective side is added: **and having come, he brought as good tidings peace to you, those afar off, and peace to those near by that through him we, the both** (of us), **have our access in one spirit to the Father.**

The Greek uses the participle to indicate the subsidiary action of coming and the finite verb to express the main action of conveying good tidings and uses this verb transitively with "peace" twice being its object.

This coming of Christ is often taken to be the coming for his earthly ministry. The hysteron proteron that Paul here records Christ's preaching *after* he records the expiation of the cross is accepted as fact, and it is stated that Paul disregards the sequence of time. Yet some avoid this thought by translating with past perfects: "had come and had announced good tidings." Yet these aorists are exactly like those that precede. All of them are historical and follow in proper sequence. To be sure, Christ's own personal preaching was full of universal statements, full of peace for both Gentiles and Jews; on that point no question need be raised. But we recall that when Christ sent his message to all the nations he told the messengers: "I am with you alway, even to the end of the world," Matt. 28:20. He assured them: "He that heareth you heareth me," Luke 10:16; "Verily, verily, I say unto you, He that receiveth whomsoever I send receiveth me," John 13:20. These statements make Paul's words rather plain: "having come, he brought as good tidings peace to you that are afar off," i. e., Christ did this after his death and his glorification; did it through his gospel messengers. For the fact remains that those afar off, the Gentiles, heard Christ's voice of peace only through Christ's heralds even as we hear it today.

"Having come" is by no means merely picturesque or incidental; Bengel calls it *insigne verbum.* It is that, indeed. Christ came to these people, wretched as they were (v. 12), "far off" as they were, their paganism constituting a gulf of enmity between them and the Jews. They could never have come to Christ, he had to come to them. "Go!" is still his command to us for our mission work. This going is his coming. Thus did he "gospel peace to you (Ephesians), those afar off." Note the keyword "peace" (v. 14 and 16), now combined with the precious verb "to bring as good tidings," an effective aorist to indicate the successful work among the Ephesian Gentiles. "Those afar off" is repeated from v. 13 and is to be taken in the same sense. This peace brought them near as already stated.

"And peace to those near by" repeats "peace" (this reading is textually assured despite its omission from the *textus receptus* and the A. V.). This means that "to those near by" is not a second apposition to "to you," which it also could not be, for no Gentiles were "near by." In v. 13 we have: "got to be near in connection with the blood of Christ." As the added phrase shows, this means the actual nearness of faith in Christ's blood. The unmodified dative "to those near by," paired with the similar dative "to those afar off," signified Jews. They were "near by" as Jews, as descendants of Abraham, as being in possession of the Old Testament, and thus different from the Gentiles. Yet they, too, had to have peace preached to them, the same peace, because their nearness was only external and had to be made internal. Paul is still addressing the Gentile Ephesians and thus speaks to them of the Jewish believers with whom they were one. When the epistle was publicly read in Ephesus, the Jewish believers heard this reference to themselves, heard it with the same gratitude as their Gentile brethren who were personally addressed.

18) Some assert that ὅτι is not explicative. But it is explicative of "peace." Just what did Christ preach as peace to the Gentile as well as to the Jewish Ephesians? Why this, "that through him we, the both (of us), have the access in one spirit to the Father," this that both of us through Christ may approach God as our Father in the same spirit of sonship. Good tidings, indeed! Our versions translate ὅτι "for." But we fail to see that the clause presents either the logical reason (*Erkenntnisgrund*) or the factual reason (*Realgrund*) for Christ's having preached peace to Gentiles as well as to Jews. The real reason that Christ preached peace has already been most adequately stated in v. 14, namely that he *is* our peace. The fact that we now have access to the Father is not the cause of Christ's having preached but the contents of his preaching, the substance of the peace he preaches. Those who believe this preaching "have" what the words say and contain.

"Through or by means of him" is emphatic as its position shows. Those who deny this may compare the same emphasis in John 10:9; 14:6; Rom. 5:2; Eph. 3:12. "We have the access," with its present tense, is general as in doctrinal propositions: the way to the Father is ever open to us by means of Christ who is himself the Way. M.-M. 545 affords no help for understanding προσαγωγή; C.-K. 69, etc., shows that the verb "we have" calls for the intransitive sense "access," that we may come to the Father and not that we are brought or led to the Father (transitive). The additions found in 3:12 point to this same meaning in that passage. The meaning is not *Zufuehrung* but *Zutritt* or *Zugang*. C.-K. finds it "pedantic" to insist on the former when even the classics have examples of the word in both meanings. "Through" Christ, following, as it does, the significant mention of his blood, flesh, and cross, involves these three as constituting Christ the means for our having this blessed access to the Father. And the fact that "we have" it surely includes the truth that it was given to us by this redemptive means. "The access" is definite; none exists but this one through Christ: "No one comes to the Father except through (διά) me," John 14:6. That we might have the access called for both the sacrificial expiation accomplished by Christ as well as the gospeling of peace; "by means of him" includes both.

The Greek is able to add the apposition to the "we" by means of the verb ending after the object "peace," thereby helping to emphasize the apposition: "we — the both (of us)," Gentiles and Jews alike. They come to the Father, not by two roads, but by one. Hence also the phrase "in one spirit." One hesitates to leave the consensus of the commentators who here translate "in one Spirit" as do our versions. This consensus also finds the Trinity in Paul's wording: "through him"

(Christ) — "in one (Holy) Spirit" — "to the Father."
Yet, attractive as this appears, we question its sound-
ness. In v. 16 we have "in one body" to which there is
now added as the complement, "in one spirit." This
correspondence extends much farther when we note
that "one" recurs together with "both" ("two") : v. 14,
"*both* the parts *one* part"; v. 15, "the *two* men *one*
new man"; v. 16, "the *both* of them *one* body"; now,
"the *both* of us in one spirit." In this chain of four
"both — one," one part, one man, one body, the last
link is surely one spirit (not one Spirit). Not the
thought that God or Christ or the Spirit are one fits
into the chain, but one spirit, a unit mind and heart
filled with one life and one faith by Christ, his blood
and his cross, his gospel preaching of peace does. The
decisive word is "one."

"The access to the Father" implies that the Ephesian Gentiles and Jews have an approach to him as
his children and sons, οἰκεῖοι, "household members."
All the rights of children are theirs as also all the
gifts that this divine Father bestows. All come to
him as a unit, come "in one spirit," and are thus in
one and the same blessed relation and position, no
matter if they once were two, some of them Gentiles, others Jews. Πρός is the face-to-face preposition; "there is something almost intimate as well as
personal in some of the examples" (R. 624, etc.), it is
so in fact.

* * *

The Great Sanctuary in the Lord

19) From all that Paul has been sketching regarding the church as being composed of Gentile
and of Jewish members he now draws the grand
conclusion. He loves the combination ἄρα οὖν (the
former word no longer being postpositive in the
New Testament) which expresses correspondence

between sentences or clauses ("fittingly," "accordingly"), the latter indicating result. **Accordingly, therefore, no longer are you foreigners and outsiders; on the contrary, you are fellow citizens of the saints and family members of God.**

This is the deduction from the four "one" terms in which all that precedes is focused. Once the Gentiles were "foreigners" (v. 12), aliens, strangers, were "guests" in the nation or the city to which they had come for a shorter or a longer stay, and were tolerated only as such. Paul adds the synonymous "outsiders," πάροικοι, literally, such as live beside others, tolerated neighbors and no more. M.-M. 496: "a licensed sojourner in a town, whose protection and status were secured by the payment of a small tax," who add an inscription which shows the mixed nature of the population in Graeco-Roman towns. A ξένος might be a mere traveler, a πάροικος was one who dwelt in a city that was not of his own people. Nothing like this is the present status of Gentile Christians in Ephesus.

Quite the contrary. They are "fellow citizens of the saints," members of the holy commonwealth or polity (see v. 12), with all the rights of citizenship. They are "saints" as much as any other saints (1:1), as much as the believers of Jewish descent. Paul is speaking of the present citizenship of the church in which all are on a perfect equality. He is not making a comparison with the Old Testament saints. The *Una Sancta* of Christ is composed of one class alone and not of two, one that is superior, the other inferior, one that has more, the other fewer rights.

From the image of a city or commonwealth Paul advances to that of a household or family even as he has just written "Father" (v. 18): "and family members (Gal. 6:10) of God," he being the Father equally of all of them as his children and sons. The notion that

some are only servants or even only slaves is not to be
entertained.

20) A third step carries the figure still higher.
The Christians dwell in the οἶκος or house as οἰκεῖοι,
members of God's family; but now Paul views them
as themselves constituting the house, they are the
"living stones" (I Pet. 2:5) of which it is built: **having been built up upon the foundation of the apostles
and prophets, Christ Jesus himself being the cornerstone, in connection with whom all the building
framed together grows into a sanctuary holy in the
Lord; in connection with whom also you are being built together into a habitation of God in the
Spirit.**

Paul is speaking of the invisible church, the Communion of Saints, a great temple in process of construction, rising on its foundation and its cornerstone.
The Ephesian Gentile Christians are what they are
since they had been built up upon the foundation of the
apostles and prophets, etc. The participle is causal,
and God is the agent back of the passive. With the
aorist Paul points to the past fact: the Ephesians have,
indeed, been built up on this foundation and have ever
since been what Paul says they now are (v. 19). The
fact that God placed them on the divine foundation as
living stones when he wrought faith in their hearts
and brought them to baptism, does not need to be
added. The great point is that these former pagans
and Gentiles (v. 11, 12) have been made an integral
part of the great spiritual Building of God.

God built them up "upon the foundation of the
apostles and prophets." The one article makes the
apostles and prophets one class (R. 787) although
scarcely with the idea that the apostles are themselves
the prophets here referred to. All is clear in regard
to the apostles. Although Paul is one of them, he
speaks of them in an objective way (so also in 4:11;

I Cor. 12:29). The dispute regarding "prophets" is whether the Old or the New Testament prophets are referred to. It is well to know that prophecy was one of the charismatic gifts (Rom. 12:6; I Cor. 12:10, 28, 29) of a nature to be desired and cultivated by *all* the members of the church (I Cor. 14:1, etc.). Prophecy and prophets of this kind refer to the proper transmission of the saving truths already revealed. Prophets in this sense rank with teachers, evangelists, and pastors. Then we find prophets like Agabus and the daughters of Philip (Acts 21:9, 10) to whom God communicated this and that special revelation about coming events. What we know of them places them far below the great Old Testament prophets as well as below the apostles. Their function was only incidental, their revelations only occasional, they were few in number.

Involved in the question regarding the identity of these prophets is the force of the genitive plus the meaning of "the foundation." One view is that Paul means the foundation which the apostles and prophets lay whenever they promulgate the gospel in any place. So Paul laid the foundation of the Corinthian congregation (I Cor. 3:10) and declined to build on the foundation already laid by some other man (Rom. 15:20), the latter referring to the church at Rome which was founded by no apostle but by Christian believers. Those who think of foundation in this sense regard the genitive as subjective or as causal or as possessive. All amounts to this that the apostles and prophets lay it where they start to work, they being the agents, the cause, the foundation being theirs in this sense. This conception thinks only of the New Testament prophets.

As far as men of the type of Agabus are concerned, these would be ruled out, for we have no record that they ever founded a single congregation. We

should have left only ordinary Christians such as
founded the church at Rome, such as fled from Jerusalem after Saul's persecution and started churches
in the places where they found refuge. We might
include Barnabas (Acts 13:1, "certain prophets and
teachers") who worked with Paul and afterward
worked by himself (Acts 15:39), also other assistants
of Paul and of others of the Twelve like Mark who in
later years was with Peter. If we think of founders
of congregations we shall not get beyond the charisma
of prophecy as it is noted in Rom. 12:6; I Cor. 12:10;
14:1, etc. We do not find this satisfactory. It will
not do to refer to 4:11 and to other passages in
Acts and in the epistles that contain the word
"prophets"; we must see just who is meant in
each case.

In I Cor. 3:11 Jesus Christ is called the foundation,
not laid by Paul, but by God, not laid in founding this
or that congregation, but laid by God once for all, for
the church as such, for all time. In Ephesians "the
foundation" is to be understood in the same sense, the
one laid by God. Then the genitive is appositional:
"the foundation which consists of the apostles and
prophets," not, indeed, of their persons as being the
first believers, or of their faith as being the original
faith, but of their office as "the apostles and prophets,"
the recipients of the entire divine saving revelation for
inspired transmission to all future ages. This revelation on which the faith of the *Una Sancta* rests as
its foundation is "the impregnable Rock of Holy Scripture" as found in the Old and the New Testaments.
Although it was at first spread orally, the apostles and
prophets later committed it to a written form under
the Spirit's inspiration.

Thus also Paul adds: "Christ Jesus himself being
the cornerstone." God laid him as he laid the foundation. In I Cor. 3:11 Christ is viewed as the entire

foundation; the whole church is built on him alone, and a foundation other than this cannot be laid. In a variation and an extension of the figure Paul now views Christ as the cornerstone in the foundation. Christ is the determining factor in the saving revelation of the inspired Word in both Testaments.

It is stated that Paul should then have reversed the words: "the foundation of the (Old Testament) prophets and (New Testament) apostles." It all depends. The apostles added the testimonies of the prophets to the revelation they transmitted. Their constant refrain is: "As it has been written." The apostles brought Christ and then the prophecies; they did not present the prophecies and then offer Christ. This order is perfectly proper when addressing Gentile Christians; if Paul had addressed former Jews in this passage he might have reversed the terms.

But note that the apostles are here placed on the same level with the Old Testament prophets. The idea that they are paired with lesser men (New Testament prophets, Agabus, Barnabas, assistants, men who had only a charisma) does not commend itself. The Twelve and Paul belong in the same class with Moses, Elijah, Isaiah, Jeremiah, etc., because they exceed all others as the inspired transmitters of the Word. All these together constitute the foundation of the church. Our faith rests on the Word that has come to us through them (διά, the great preposition for inspiration). We believe, preach, and confess only what these apostles and prophets wrote; and to this date we use the apostles more than the prophets, and use the latter in the light of the former.

One might refer αὐτοῦ to "the foundation" and translate, "*its* cornerstone Christ Jesus." But it seems far better to join the pronoun to "Christ Jesus": "Christ Jesus *himself* being (the) cornerstone." The predicate noun is marked as such by having no article.

The purpose of a cornerstone does not seem clear to some interpreters. When preachers use our text on the occasion of the laying of cornerstones they often express strange ideas. One such idea is that the cornerstone connects two walls that meet at a corner, and another is that it holds them together. So Christ connects and holds together Jews and Gentiles. This thought is expanded: the cornerstone holds the entire building together, but no stone ever did that. Next the idea of stability is emphasized: this stone is said to give strength and cohesion to the whole building. A little stronger idea: it carries the whole building, but this would make it the whole foundation.

We also meet the idea that it completes the foundation, yet all the stones at all the corners are necessary for completeness. Von Hofmann has the cornerstone "enclose, as it were," the whole building. Ewald regards it as the first stone that is laid and quotes Robinson to the effect that the cornerstones had greater dimensions than all the others. Yet at Baalbek in Syria the writer saw the greatest stones ever quarried, two of them were laid up high in the flat of the immense wall, the greatest one had been moved part of the way out of the quarries; it was evidently also intended for the walls and was not to be the first to be laid at the bottom of the foundation.

'Ακρογωνιαῖος, "at the tip of the angle," is an adjective, and τό makes it a noun that is applied to the stone set at the corner of a wall so that its outer angle becomes important. This importance is ideal, we may say symbolic: the angle of the cornerstone governs all the lines and all the other angles of the building. This one stone is thus laid with special, sometimes with elaborate ceremonies. It supports the building no more than does any other stone. Its entire significance is to be found in its one outer angle. Its size is immaterial and certainly need not be immense. It is thus also placed at the most important corner, in or on the top tier of the foundation, so as to be seen by all. The idea that its place was originally at the bottom of the excavation appears improbable when we note that in the case of large buildings the foundation is broad at the bottom, and that the angels are rough, not always exact. The purpose of a cornerstone is ideal only, i. e., a special meaning is attached to it for the building with its lines and angles. One could build without this idealism, but it has found approval since ancient times. Aside from the LXX (first in Isa. 28:16) and the New Testament the Greek term has not as yet been found save, of course, in later church writers.

Paul uses the idea thus connected with a cornerstone to indicate what Christ Jesus is in reality in regard to the church plus its foundation (the Word). Figuratively speaking, Christ Jesus (title plus personal name) is the cornerstone of the divine building, the *Una Sancta.* There is not a single line or an angle in this building that is not determined by this Stone, *ein Stein der Bewaehrung, ein koestlicher Eckstein wohlgegruendeter Gruendung* (Isa. 28:16, Delitzsch). To speak of Christ as such a stone is no bolder a figure than when Isa. 8:14 calls God a stone and rock; the psalmist also again and again calls him a rock. Paul's figure is beautiful and expressive in every way.

21) Paul is using what Trench calls Biblical allegory, namely figure and reality interwoven, which is thus self-interpretative as it moves on: "having been built up upon the foundation (figure) of the apostles and prophets (reality), the cornerstone (figure) being Christ Jesus (reality), in connection with whom (reality) all the building framed together grows into a holy sanctuary (figure) in the Lord (reality); in connection with whom also you (reality) are being built together into a habitation (figure) of God in the Spirit (reality)." See another beautiful example of

this weaving with double thread, the gold of figure
and the silver of reality, in John 15: "I (reality) am
the Vine (figure), you (reality) are the branches"
(figure), and thus on through.

When commentators declare that "in whom," here
and in v. 22, drops the figure they evidently do not
understand what Paul is doing. He weaves reality and
figure together for self-interpretation and for great
riches. Does Paul "drop" the figure in "the apostles
and prophets" or in "Christ Jesus himself"? Why,
then, say that in the relative pronoun he now "drops"
something? Some regard "in whom" as figurative
language and write about the cornerstone which
umschliesst the building or make the phrase mystical.

Ἐν ᾧ signifies "in connction with whom," the connection with Christ being like that of a building with
its cornerstone, the angle of this stone dominating
every line and every other angle in the building. Call
the figure a simile if you wish, it is all simple and
lovely. The A. V. is perfectly correct: "all the
building," πᾶσα οἰκοδομή, even as R. 772 puts it: "With
the abstract word 'every' and 'all' amount practically
to the same thing." Yet in his *W. P.* R. is uncertain
despite the examples such as Col. 1:15, "all creation";
I Cor. 1:5, "all knowledge," and many others. B.-D.
275, 3 adopts the variant reading with the article. The
R. V. adopts the text that is minus the article and then
becomes pedantic with its translation "each several
building" as if there were several or many buildings
while Paul speaks only of the one great "sanctuary."
The result is that some commentators seek to discover
the several buildings. R., *W. P.*, thinks of the individual Christians, others of the individual congregations, others, leaving the matter indefinite, of the individual parts of the building. Ewald's conclusion is

to the point: not, indeed, *der ganze Bau* but *aller Bau*,
i. e., all that is building and is not foundation, all that
as building is erected on the foundation, for which the
foundation was laid by God.

Paul adds the participle: "by being framed or fitted
together" all that is building grows into a sanctuary. The idea expressed is that of "the Communion
of Saints." An inner harmony, oneness, correspondence, attachment pervade all that forms the building.
What the foundation and its cornerstone demand is
carried out in all that is superstructure even to the
joining of every stone and timber. So it grows (the
verb is intransitive) into a holy Sanctuary in (in union
with) the Lord (Christ). Both participle and verb are
the present. Αὔξω means, "make grow," in later Greek
it is intransitive, "grow," it is like a passive (Liddell
and Scott). In v. 20 the aorist participle states that
the Gentile Ephesians have already been built upon
the foundation. Now Paul speaks objectively of all
building as being still in progress. The fitting together
and the growing continue. The great *Una Sancta*
actually "grows." Some day it will be complete, "a
glorious church," indeed (5:27).

There is no incongruity unless we stress the figure
and forget the reality which the figure is intended to
serve and not to control or to change. This is a spiritual, living Sanctuary. It will not do, then, to think
of the erection of a stone building by human hands,
in which, when a stone is properly put in place, all
is done as far as that stone is concerned. Paul does
not forget the reality which the figure of dead, earthly
stone and material cannot picture. Peter boldly speaks
of "living stones" (λίθοι ζῶντες), I Pet. 2:5. Justification places us on the foundation, but this is not the
whole of God's work of building us into a holy Sanctuary. We need daily forgiveness, progressive sanctifica-

tion, constant blessing. In 1:16, etc., Paul prays for great increase of knowledge for the Ephesians. So we need strengthening, comfort, help of all kinds, and much more besides.

Skillful as he is, Paul covers all this by saying "fitted together" and "grows"; the figure scarcely reaches the reality, the wording of it does, and that is the main thing. One might also urge that a building is not occupied until it has ceased to grow and is complete. But in this entire section God is the prominent subject. He builds this Sanctuary and is ever in it with his operative grace. He is not like one who lets another do the building and then finally moves in. Keep firm hold on the reality, then the figurative language will be much better understood and will serve the purpose which it is intended to serve.

Our versions translate "temple," which word they also use to translate ἱερόν. The latter denotes the entire complex of buildings and courts of the place of worship in Jerusalem while ναός was the "sanctuary," the central structure containing the Holy and the Holy of Holies. The idea that Paul has in mind any sanctuary, including those of pagans, is unwarranted; he thinks of the Sanctuary at Jerusalem, which was a type and a symbol of Christ (see John 2:18-22) and of the church. "Holy in the Lord" belongs together; the holiness of the *Una Sancta* lies in the union with Christ (5:27). The idea to be expressed cannot be that the *Una Sancta* increases in holiness from age to age; the church of the present age is not more holy than that of earlier ages. What Paul means is that the church is a Sanctuary, and that its being this is due to its union with Christ. It always grows, outwardly and inwardly, in this direction only (εἰς), to be a Sanctuary, holy only in this its connection.

22) The tenses are instructive: first, the aorist to denote the simple fact that the Gentile Ephesians had

been built up upon the great foundation; then the present tenses, which throw on the screen the church as such, ever growing into a Sanctuary; now another present tense which applies to the Gentile Ephesians what has just been said (v. 21) of the church as such. "In connection with whom" is parallel to the same phrase in v. 21 and has the same antecedent ("Christ Jesus" — "the Lord"). In this very same union which connects the whole church with Christ (thus including all Jewish believers) "also you (the Gentile Ephesians) are being built together into a habitation of God in the Spirit." They are receiving and are to be no less than other members of the church. They are not like the minor buildings of the *hieron* or Temple at Jerusalem; they belong to the *Naos* or Sanctuary itself.

"Being built together" is a variation for "being fitted together"; in both terms σύν denotes inner, spiritual union ("in one body," v. 16, also "one part," "one spirit"). We make the application that everything that interferes with this σύν, all false doctrines and wrong living, hinders this building process no matter what the apologists of error may say. While there are children of God in the erring churches, they are such only because of the truth that is still found in those churches and never because of the error that is mingled with that truth. The oxygen in the air keeps us alive and not the dust or the noxious gases which may be mingled with the air. If these deleterious elements increase sufficiently, they prevent even the oxygen that is left from energizing our blood through the lungs; when they are present in lesser degree so as not to kill, they seriously damage.

"Into a habitation of God in the Spirit" parallels and also explains "into a Sanctuary holy in the Lord." This Sanctuary = the habitation of God, where he dwells (John 14:21). Both denote what the church calls the *unio mystica*, God's indwelling in us, which is mediated objectively by Word and Sacrament, subjectively by faith. Here ἐν Πνεύματι is parallel to ἐν Κυρίῳ, which shows that here, unlike in v. 18, the Holy Spirit is referred to. Here we do have the Trinity, the Lord — God — the Spirit. In neither phrase does "Lord" or "Spirit" need the article, both terms designate persons. "In the Spirit" explains "in the Lord," for union with the former mediates union with the latter and thus makes us a habitation of God.

CHAPTER III

Paul's own Great Work

1) After telling the Gentile Christians in Ephesus to keep in mind what they once were and what God has now made of them, in particular that they together with all other believers are built together for a habitation of God, Paul continues by bringing to their minds his own great part in this work of God among the Gentiles (v. 1-13), adds the intercession he ever offers for them, and states its contents (v. 14-21). Although he has been absent from Ephesus for about five years, Paul's inward connection with his readers is as close as it ever was when he worked in their midst. While he still addresses the Gentile Christians (2:11), all that he says in both parts of this chapter has its great significance also for the Jewish Christians in Ephesus. In fact, in v. 15 and 18 he also draws them in, for in his mind he ever sees the *Una Sancta* as a whole.

For this cause I, Paul, the prisoner of Christ Jesus in behalf of you the Gentiles, etc. The adverbial accusative χάριν has become a preposition, which is usually postpositive, that governs the genitive. The phrase is practically the same in meaning as διὰ τοῦτο. Yet we are not to supply the copula as if Paul here says that he is Christ's prisoner in behalf of the Gentiles for the reason stated in the preceding. The phrase is to be construed with a verb that has not yet been written. We have it in v. 14. We drop the debate as to whether "for this cause" connects only with 2:22, or with 2:11-22, or even with more, since 2:22 is itself vitally connected with what precedes.

What Paul intends to say about himself is due to what he has said about the blessed condition into which

(461)

God has placed his Gentile readers. That, too, is why he speaks of himself as he does, first emphatically naming himself: "I, Paul," then adding the significant apposition: "the prisoner," etc.; the two must be read as a unit. He, Paul, was the one whom Christ had chosen especially to be his apostle to the Gentiles, and in this very work he had come to be a prisoner, not one who had been arrested for only a few days, but one that had been held bound for several years. Paul was, indeed, "Jesus Christ's prisoner in behalf of you the Gentiles."

He was a prisoner in their cause. His very arrest in Jerusalem indicates that (Acts 21:28, 29). The Asian Jews who brought it about were probably from Ephesus, for they knew that Trophimus, an Ephesian, was a Gentile. In reality the Ephesian Gentile Christians, who were converts of Paul's, were the occasion for Paul's condition as a prisoner. He suffered in the great cause that benefited them because they belonged to "the Gentiles." Ὑπέρ need not be stressed to mean "for your benefit"; "in your behalf" is enough. Paul does not write "*a* prisoner," for while others, too, were imprisoned from time to time, Paul was "*the* prisoner in behalf of the Gentiles," his imprisonment had now lasted for more than three years. While we need not stress the article: "the prisoner *par excellence,*" he was certainly "the prisoner" in a rather definite sense. In I Cor. 1:1 Paul writes: "Sosthenes, the brother" (II Cor. 1:1; also elsewhere); this, indeed, characterizes (so would "a brother") yet with definiteness even as here "the prisoner" does so. Some make "of Christ Jesus" the genitive of cause or agent, but while Paul was a prisoner by the Lord's will (Acts 21:14), there is no reason that the imprisonment "by Christ Jesus" should be stressed here. The possessive is enough: "the prisoner belonging to Christ Jesus." As the prisoner that he was he was and remained Christ's own.

2) Only a few exegetes supply εἰμί in v. 1 in order to avoid the break in construction in v. 2. The break is there. It is intentional. The common explanation is, however, unsatisfactory. This supposes that after dictating v. 1 it occurred to Paul that he really ought to tell his readers, especially the new converts made since his departure from Ephesus, about his office in connection with the work among Gentiles in the church before he proceeds to dictate his intercession for all his readers. Thus, we are told, he swung off into an elaborate digression which became longer than he had intended when he began as he did in v. 1. This digression is then attributed to Paul's nimble, agile mind because all the thoughts in this digression crowded in upon it — grammar and construction being forced aside as being negligible. But this cannot be the correct explanation, for a mind so nimble and agile would see everything from the start, could not help but see it all. Such a mind would choose all its expressions from the first word onward to the last. That is what Paul did in the dictation of this entire chapter, from the start he *wanted* it as he then also dictated it.

The break at v. 2 is *not* due to a sudden flood of new thoughts, it is deliberate, made for a purpose, made so that the purpose for making it lies on the surface. This break itself conveys a most important thought. It is the most adequate means for conveying it to his readers. Paul does not have thoughts come up in his mind and thus veers off into anacolutha and broken constructions. Paul uses the anacoluthon as a regular means for expressing what he plans to express from the start. The grammars do not seem to perceive this intentional and significant use of Paul's anacolutha. They should not be called "irregular" as though they violate grammar, as though they need excuse. Every anacoluthon in Paul's writings is a means for saying what he intends to say.

In the present instance Paul himself simplifies the matter for his readers. In the first place, he begins with τούτου χάριν, a phrase that is exceptional in his style, and then repeats this exceptional phrase in v. 14. This makes it easy for the ear and the eye to catch the connection. In the second place, in v. 1 Paul leaves the subject suspended. As he enters upon v. 2, the reader sees that this subject is to remain suspended, suspended for a reason. That reason is obvious and even striking. In this elaborate paragraph (v. 1-13) Paul presents his apostolic connection with the great work among Gentiles. He intends to do just that in this paragraph. And just because of that he places the suspended subject at the head of it, for that subject contains the climax of his career as the apostle to the Gentiles, namely that he, Paul, is the prisoner of Christ Jesus in behalf of you, the Gentiles. All that follows in the paragraph is illumined by the suspended subject, is to be read in the light of the climax it presents. It is suspended in order to make it stand out like a beacon, to make it shed light over the whole paragraph. If it were embodied in v. 2 it could not have done this with such strong effect. Paul knew how to get the full effect he wanted. Admire his skill and mastery in using language fully to convey his thought.

This is not all. Along with the subject he suspends the exceptional phrase τούτου χάριν, which resumes all that is said on the work among Gentiles in Ephesus in the preceding paragraph. This suspended phrase adds to the light which the subject sheds on what follows. What is already accomplished for Gentiles in Ephesus, together with the climax of Paul's imprisonment for these Gentiles, lights up all that is now added. This phrase does more. Suspended as it is even more than the subject, it implies that the suspension will presently be removed just as this is done in v. 14, etc., where the phrase is reiterated. Because this construction is so exceptional, the reader catches the reiteration without effort. The complete effect is that by means of their striking suspension both phrase and subject dominate the entire chapter. We thus also disregard the efforts to connect v. 1 with v. 8 or with any other intervening point.

Paul continues: **If, indeed, you have heard of the administration of the grace of God, the one given to me for you, that by revelation there was made known to me the mystery even as I have already written in brief, in view of which you are able, on reading it, to perceive my insight into the mystery of Christ, which in other generations was not made known to the sons of men as it has now been revealed to his holy apostles and prophets in connection with the Spirit: that the Gentiles are fellow heirs and fellow body members and fellow partakers of the promise connected with Christ Jesus through the gospel, of which I became a minister according to the gift of the grace of God, that given to me according to the operation of his power.**

All is one great sentence like several others that have preceded in this epistle; we may even write a semicolon or a dash and continue the sentence through to v. 13. The whole of it is a pendant to the suspended phrase and subject in v. 1 as we have attempted to show. Paul is the prisoner of Christ Jesus. Here is all that has brought him to that climax, and v. 13 points back to this climax of v. 1 in a telling way.

It is difficult to imitate the little intensifying γε in English; our "indeed" is a little too strong. The condition of reality with its gentle participle states the matter in a mild and polite form: "if, indeed, you have heard" (the Greek is satisfied with the aorist "heard,"

the simple past fact), meaning: I know that you have.
Here there is another "heard" (see 1:15). Again we
are told that this word implies that none of the readers
had seen Paul, had only heard of him; that therefore
this epistle was not written for Ephesus but for other
congregations that had been founded in Asia since Paul
had left it; that it is an encyclical letter. But after
having been absent from Ephesus for nearly five years,
during which time many more Gentiles had come into
the congregation, Paul could well write as he does.
Even the older members "have heard" what they knew
about Paul from Paul himself when he labored among
them and since that time from others who had been
with Paul. To make this letter an encyclical stronger
proof is required than this verb which is so naturally
explained without such an assumption.

By "the grace given to me for you" Paul refers to
his office as an apostle to the Gentiles (Acts 9:15;
22:21; 26:17, 18; Gal. 2:8). He calls it "the grace
of God" with reference to himself, for his office was
wholly undeserved. "Grace" is a wide term, it is
therefore made specific: "the (grace) given to me
for you," "given" as grace, "for you" (Gentiles), i. e.,
to serve you. Paul makes the designation personal by
referring it to these Ephesians; they were represen-
tatives of all the Gentiles whom he served. This grace
put Paul to work: "you have heard about the administration" of the office bestowed upon me.

It seems uncalled-for either in 1:10 or here to make
οἰκονομία passive: "the dispensation" arranged by God
for me (our versions), *Einrichtung* (C.-K. 785), when
the active meaning is so appropriate: "the administration" of the grace, how Paul from the start conducted
his office especially since God opened the whole Gentile
world to him. "The dispensation (passive) of the
grace of God" gives us a genitive which C.-K. does not
solve, nor do others. The matter is not helped when

"the grace" is not referred to Paul's office but to the divine favor which selected Paul for his office.

Paul says that the Gentile Ephesians have heard of the administration of the office God has given to him. It was naturally "the administration," the actual work Paul did, of which these people heard. To be sure, the Jewish Christians also heard of it; but it had a most personal appeal to the Gentile part of the church since it brought salvation to them. The fact that this was done entirely by God's own gracious arrangement is taken care of in the finest way by the objective genitive "of the grace of God," etc., God granted that grace, the office.

3) Ὅτι specifies by indicating what underlies Paul's office and the administration of it that was heard by these Ephesians: "namely that by (special) revelation there was made known (A. V. 'he made known,' inferior reading) to me the mystery," etc. Yes, these two belonged together, Paul's immediate call to his apostolic office and the revelation to him of what Paul terms "the mystery," which he presently defines in v. 6, namely that the Gentiles were to be received into the church on identical terms with the Jews, to an identical standing in fellowship with the Jews. In what sense this was a mystery and all about its revelation Paul himself describes. The word "mystery" is used in the current sense, it is not something to remain hidden but something that requires revelation to become known.

Paul adds, "even as I have already written (the aorist, R. 842) in brief," namely in 2:11-22, where he told the Gentile Christians to remember what they were and what they have now become, full and complete members of the *Una Sancta* on an equality with the Jewish Christians.

4) Although he has written of it only briefly he adds: "in view of which (πρὸς ὅ) you are able, by

reading it, to perceive my insight into the mystery of Christ." By reading 2:11-22 the Gentile Christians will get to understand (ingressive aorist) Paul's full grasp of this mystery which God's direct revelation had opened up to him. Infinitive and noun are synonyms in meaning: νοέω, "to receive into the mind," mental bringing together, a full grasp, which is construed with ἐν, the field where this takes place. Certainly 2:11-22 shows such a grasp and insight regarding the Gentiles. A few have thought of 1:9,10; others of an earlier epistle written to the Ephesians by Paul (a hypothesis); but 2:11-22 satisfies Paul's reference.

The A. V. makes a parenthesis of v. 3b, 4. The purpose is to attach the relative ὅ occurring in v. 5 to τὸ μυστήριον. This is perfectly correct as far as the relative is concerned although a parenthesis is scarcely necessary, the clause beginning with καθώς already being parenthetical in its meaning. The parenthesis is at times made to include also v. 5; but this alters Paul's meaning. The point of the matter is that the infinitive clause in v. 6 defines τὸ μυστήριον in v. 3. "The mystery" made known to Paul is "that the Gentiles are fellow heirs," etc. The moment this is clear, we see that the relative clause in v. 5 also refers to this mystery, for in the past generations this was not made known to the sons of men as it has now been revealed to the apostles so that they might make it known to men. All this, however, means that τὸ μυστήριον in v. 3 and ἐν τῷ μυστηρίῳ τοῦ Χριστοῦ are not identical. The observation is correct that, if the two were intended to be the same, "the mystery of Christ" should come first since because of its genitive it is the fuller term, and "the mystery" should come second as merely referring to "the mystery of Christ." The reversal of the two expressions differentiates them.

"The mystery" = the one stated in v. 6 regarding the Gentiles; "the mystery of Christ" = the whole gospel which had to be revealed to men. Paul received "the mystery" regarding the Gentiles by revelation alone, and, reading what he accordingly says about the Gentiles in 2:11-22, the Ephesians will perceive his understanding or grasp of "the mystery of Christ" (objective genitive), his insight into the whole gospel mystery dealing with all that Christ is, has done, and still does for all men and for the great *Una Sancta*. The mystery regarding the Gentiles is a part of this entire gospel mystery. We decline to construe as an appositional genitive which makes the mystery = Christ; nor as the possessive genitive: the mystery belonging to Christ. Col. 1:26, 27 is quite the same mystery.

5) This clears up the relative clause: "which in other generations was not made known to the sons of men as it has now been revealed to his holy apostles," etc. The A. V. connects this with "the mystery" in v. 3; but why not leave the connection that seems to be indicated in the text? The whole gospel mystery regarding Christ includes the mystery regarding the Gentiles even as Paul's grasp of it is "according." While the whole of it, including also this significant part, was revealed in the Old Testament, which in so many places speaks of the participation of the Gentiles in the coming Messianic kingdom, it was nevertheless "not made known in other (i. e., past) generations (dative of time) to the sons of men (in the way) it has now been revealed to the holy apostles," etc.

It was indeed *revealed* in those past generations, for all of the prophets tell about it, but it was not *made known* to the sons of men, not carried abroad to men in general, as Christ now revealed it to his apostles when he revealed to them that they should go and proclaim it to all the nations (Matt. 28:19), to every creature (Mark 16:16), starting with Judea and

Samaria and going even to the uttermost part of the earth (Acts 1:8). This was the new revelation that came to the apostles after Christ had completed the redemption. Before that time even the Twelve were ordered not to go into the way of the Gentiles or to enter into a city of the Samaritans (Matt. 10:5). The Old Testament was confined to Israel, only a few Gentiles obtained it. Revelation itself now carried the New Testament gospel to the whole world. Moreover, this gospel does not direct the Gentiles to become proselytes to Judaism in order to be saved; it admits Gentiles to salvation in Christ on the same basis as Jews.

"To the sons of the (generic article) men," an exceptional term in Paul's writings, seems to be the counterpart to "the sons of Israel," but refers to all men generally. It is clear that the one article regards the apostles and the prophets as one class, and that the adverb "now" limits us to New Testament prophets. "Holy apostles and prophets" appears to be the counterpart to "holy prophets" (Old Testament), which is used quite often (Luke 1:70; Acts 3:21; II Pet. 3:2; Rev. 22:6) when their high standing is to be stressed. Like "the holy (Old Testament) prophets," to whom revelation was made, are "the holy prophets and apostles" (New Testament) who likewise receive revelation.

Some find this adjective "holy" un-Pauline and state that it betrays the fact that Paul did not write this epistle, or that with the word "holy" he claims too much for a modest man. But ἅγιοι is a standard term that is applied even to all believers (1:1), "holy prophets" is also frequently found. When the Holy God uses men for receiving and for conveying his holy revelation he thereby makes them his holy instruments. It is also suggested that "holy" is here in place in contrast with "the sons of men," the world. Besides, Paul includes all the apostles; although he is one of them he designates himself as objectively as he does the rest of the apostles.

Is "his apostles and prophets" a hendiadys, a double designation for the Twelve plus Paul? Does "holy" modify both nouns? What about "his"? Finally, does ἐν Πνεύματι modify the verb or both nouns or only "prophets"? These questions are variously answered, with arguments according. We accept as assured the fact that the apostles can certainly be termed prophets because they received direct revelation as did the Old Testament prophets. Here the stress is on "it was revealed," the verb being placed forward for the sake of emphasis. We know of none save the apostles who received by direct revelation either the whole gospel of Christ or that part of it pertaining to the Gentiles, all others, like Barnabas and the apostolic assistants, like Agabus, and like Christians exercising the charisma of prophecy (I Cor. 14:1, etc.) received what they knew of the gospel and about the Gentiles from these apostles.

If these are the facts, it seems very proper for Paul to add to "the apostles" the second term "prophets" in the present connection in which the preceding clause refers to "other generations" when only the word of the Old Testament prophets was available. At one time the Old Testament prophets who had no commission to make the gospel known to all men; now the men who were commissioned for that very purpose, thus "apostles" (their distinctive name because of this commission) yet also "prophets" as much as those of old because, like those of old, they received a direct revelation of the gospel and of all its parts.

Then αὐτοῦ, like "holy," modifies both nouns. Even if "prophets" were other men than "apostles," would they not both be "his" (Christ's)? The fact that "prophets" is used in different meanings should not be disputed; compare the remarks on 2:20. It is the

context that decides in each case. For instance, in
2:20, "the foundation" decides (the Scriptures, New
and Old Testament); here "it has now been revealed"
(the New Testament revelation to apostles who are
therefore also prophets); in 4:11, "the perfecting of
the saints," points to "prophets" as men who have
the charisma of promulgating the revelation like
the assistants of the apostles and others of similar
type.

To construe "in connection with the Spirit" (no
article, "Spirit" being the name of a person) with the
verb or with the object makes little difference. The
apostle-prophets were themselves connected with (ἐν)
the Spirit, and the gospel "was revealed" to them "in
connection with the Spirit." We prefer to construe
with the verb as being the most natural construction.
Those who construe with the object bring in the *unio
mystica,* which is rather unnecessary.

It is necessary to think of Pentecost in connection
with Acts 10:44; 11:15-17: Cornelius and Gentiles;
also Acts 8:15: Samaritans; Acts 15:8-12. Revelation
brought Peter and the apostles to the understanding
that the Gentiles were to enter the church on a par
with Jews. But we dismiss the mechanical idea of
instrumental ἐν as well as the *unio mystica* which is
to be indicated by the preposition. Here the idea to
be expressed goes beyond the thought that the Holy
Spirit was instrumental in making the revelation to
the apostle-prophets; the cardinal part of the revelation here considered is that the Gentiles are included
equally with Jews, and that this was revealed "in
connection with the Spirit" who fell upon the Gentiles
in Caesarea (and upon the Samaritans in Samaria)
just as he descended on the 120 (apostles and disciples) at Pentecost in Jerusalem. Thus came this
significant revelation for the apostles who were also
prophets — a wonderful revelation, indeed.

At the apostolic convention (Acts 15) Peter made his great address on this subject, Paul was present and added his corroboration, and the entire convention adopted the resolution proposed by James which accorded with this great revelation. We note that James had not received any of this revelation, he only accepted it from Peter and from Paul and worded the resolution: "It seemed good to the Holy Spirit and to us," Acts 15:25.

6) The content of "the mystery" (v. 3) which is a part of "the (gospel) mystery regarding Christ" (v. 4) is: "that the Gentiles are fellow heirs and fellow body members and fellow partakers of the promise in connection with Christ Jesus through the gospel." They are no less even as Paul has also written regarding the Ephesian Gentiles in 2:11-22. Three terms are used as good writers often employ them for the sake of rhythm and for the sake of fulness of thought.

"Fellow heirs" (all of the three terms are neuters because of τὰ ἔθνη) = fully on a par with the original heirs, the believing Israelites. "Fellow body members" (a word found only here and later borrowed from this passage) = "together of the body." Many may be fellow heirs like a son and a servant, the latter being remembered in the will with a small portion. Not so the Gentiles in conjunction with the true Israelites. They are a joint body with these Israelites; see 2:14, etc., both "one part," both "in one body," the two being "one new man." It is thus in the fullest sense and on a par with the Israelites that these Gentiles are "fellow heirs." Therefore also as a result they are "fellow partakers of the promise in connection with Christ Jesus." They have an identical share with the Israelites.

The promise is "in Christ Jesus," connected with his office and his person as the substance and the fulfillment of the promise. He is named as the *causa meritoria* of our salvation, which is absolutely equal for Gentiles and for Jews. Hence the addition of the *causa instrumentalis salutis*: "through the gospel," which brings the promise and Christ Jesus equally to Gentiles and to Jews.

7) This brings Paul back (v. 2) to his own special office and to what God wrought for the Ephesian Gentiles through it: "of which I became a minister," etc. Of this gospel, by which Gentiles are made fellow heirs, etc., Paul "became a minister," historical aorist, a Koine passive form that is yet without passive sense. A διάκονος is one who serves in the interest and for the benefit of another, here of the gospel. The connotation of δοῦλος is the fact that the slave's will is wholly subject to that of his master. So also a *diakonos* serves voluntarily, freely, a *doulos* of necessity. Paul became a minister of the gospel of universality in an eminent sense, for he was *the* apostle to the Gentiles (Gal. 2:9).

The language used in v. 2 in regard to the manner in which this ministry came to Paul is now expanded. It came to him "by way of the gift of the grace of God, of that (grace) given to me by way of the energetic working of his power." Paul's office was a special gift (note the article) to him; he obtained it in this way (κατά) alone. This thought is enhanced by the subjective genitive which says that a special grace of God made this gift to him. True, the apostleship was a gift also to the Twelve, came to them by pure grace; Jesus told them that *he* chose *them,* not *they him* (John 15:16); yet in Paul's case this was true in a special sense (v. 8). In v. 2 he calls his office itself "the grace of God," here he calls it "the gift of this grace." In both instances he means that it was wholly undeserved by him who until the hour when the gift

was made was a bloody persecutor of the gospel and
of the church.

That is why he speaks of this grace as being not
merely grace in general but as being one that was
eminent and most specific in his case: "that given
to me according to (by way of) the working of his
power," which recalls the two nouns used in 1:19 regarding the fulfillment of the hope of all believers. We
recall the scene on the Damascus road, the blazing
glory light exceeding the noonday sun. Here was the
vast power of God in its ἐνέργεια or operation but employed by grace so that Paul can call it the special
grace which employed this method (κατά). This does
not imply that omnipotence converted and instated him
into his ministry. Grace did both as Paul states here
and elsewhere. See Acts 9:6. The gospel alone converted Paul, but through the vision of the glorified
Savior God so shaped the outward circumstances as
to outfit Paul for his apostleship, and thus God exercised his power in the interest of his grace.

8) The absence of a connective, the emphatic
ἐμοί resuming μοι from v. 7, plus the repetition of the
thought about grace, show that this sentence is appositional to the preceding. Write a colon or a dash
(not a period) : **to me, the one less than the least of
all saints, was given this grace to proclaim as good
tidings to the Gentiles the untraceable riches of
Christ and to enlighten all (on) what (is) the
administration of the mystery, the one that has been
hidden from the eons on in God, him who created
all the things in order that there may be made
known now to the principalities and the authorities
in the heavenly places through the church the
manifold wisdom of God according to the purpose of the eons which he formed in Christ Jesus,
our Lord, in whom we have the boldness and**

**access in confidence by means of the (= our) faith
in him.**

Heaven and earth, time and eternity, the Creator
of the universe and the work of grace are again woven
together by means of Christ, the gospel, and faith as
centered in the mystery now revealed in the *Una
Sancta* which includes the Gentile believers as well as
those converted from the Jews.

"The gift of the grace of God given to me" (v. 7)
is resumed with the strongest emphasis on the pronoun: "*to me*, the one less than the least of all saints,"
to me as such a one, "was given this grace." "The
gift" — "given" — and now "was given" glorify the
Giver. Paul's office was, indeed, absolutely a gift
given; Paul never tired of saying so. With that goes
"the grace," his office itself, here (as in v. 2) called
"this grace," which was absolutely undeserved, bestowed by the wondrous *favor Dei*. What lies in these
terms comes fully to view in the apposition to the
dative: to me, "the one less than the least of all saints,"
not "the least" but one even less than that. This is
not false humility. To think that a man with a record
like Paul's, a violent persecutor of the church, should
upon his conversion be made one of the chosen
apostles! Incredible but true. We should have re-
legated such a convert to the most obscure corner of
the church, to stay where no one would note his presence; God elevated him to the highest position in the
church, the apostolate. Grace, grace; gift, gift — un-
exampled, glorious.

The comparative formed from the superlative is
quite regular, even the classics furnish a few examples, the Koine has still more. When it is used
as a noun it is followed by the ablative genitive.
Enough examples of πάντες without the added article
occur to show that this, too, is regular.

The fact that "this grace" denotes Paul's office or work, which is called so because God's grace bestowed it, the epexegetical infinitives indicate: "to proclaim as good tidings to the Gentiles the untraceable riches of Christ," etc. The emphasis is on the dative: to do this for the Gentiles, Paul to be their special apostle. Gospelizing is the divine channel for bestowing this wealth also on the benighted (2:12) Gentiles. Once more Paul emphasizes the fact that the gospel is intended also for them.

"The riches of Christ" = all the saving grace and gifts belonging to Christ, which as "riches" abound to the uttermost. Paul was the hand of God to dispense this wealth without money or without price especially to the Gentiles. The blessedness of this office is ever present to his mind. He, an abortion that as a vile thing should have been buried out of sight (I Cor. 15:8), was made a great instrument of God. The aorist infinitive denotes effective evangelization. The most significant word is the adjective "untraceable" which is formed from ἴχνος, track or trace; the same word occurs in Rom. 11:33. In all the universe there was no track or trace by following which men's minds could ever have discovered these riches of Christ. Revelation brought them, revelation alone. "Untraceable" matches "mystery."

9) A second infinitive clause is added in order to bring out more fully what the first states in a more general way: "and to enlighten all (on) what (is) the administration of the mystery, the one that has been hidden from the eons on in God." The aorist is again effective. Πάντας is textually sound. The purpose of Paul's preaching the gospel to the Gentiles was to enlighten all men and to show them what "the mystery" so long hidden in God really was. Preaching the untraceable riches of Christ to the Gentiles was like setting the deep mystery into the fullest light of day so

that all men might see it. To be sure, not all of the
Gentiles as also not all of the Jews would appropriate
the mystery, but the sound and the light of the gospel
would place the blessed wealth of Christ before them
to hear and to see it. Take as an example the great
province of Asia of which Ephesus was the capital
and read the testimony of Demetrius in Acts 19:26,
which is rather eloquent testimony to what Paul is here
saying.

We again meet the question as to whether οἰκονομία
is passive, "the dispensation" or arrangement made by
God, or active, "the administration" Paul carries out
in his office. Here the decision appears to be even
easier than it was in v. 3. "The economy" of the grace
of God given to Paul for the Gentiles (v. 3) is the
administration of his office for the Gentiles; it is "the
economy" of the mystery, the one that has been hidden,
etc., i. e., Paul's administration of this mystery. The
active "administration" contains a complete idea; the
passive "dispensation" (arrangement) would need
something to complete the idea. The Ephesians heard
about the administration of Paul's office (v. 3) which
spoke volumes. Paul operated in a way in which no
rabbi had ever before operated. What these Ephesians
heard (v. 3) enlightened not only them but all men
in regard to the whole administration (whether it
was in Paul's or in any other true gospel preacher's
hands) of this mystery dealing with the Gentiles.
Everybody could hear and even see that this administration was vastly different from what the Jews and
their rabbies were doing. The very word οἰκονομία
suggests the οἰκονόμος, the steward, manager, or administrator operating his trust or stewardship (R. V. margin), and every man could thus hear and see what the
stewardship was.

It was, indeed, "the administration of (nothing
less than) the mystery" so long hidden in God. This

is the same mystery as that mentioned in v. 3 which
pertained to the Gentiles, was a part of "the mystery
of Christ" (v. 4), a part of the entire New Testament
gospel mystery. The fact that the Gentiles were to be
what v. 6 states had been hidden in God during all the
past ages. The Greek starts at the far end and counts
forward to the present, hence "from the eons on"; the
English mind prefers to count backward from the
present time. "In God" means in his mind, counsel,
or plan.

The Old Testament prophets, indeed, revealed this
hidden mystery, but this revelation was confined to
Israel, and, while this much of the revelation stated
that hosts of Gentiles should come in, the fact that
all these should come in, as v. 6 states, on a perfect
equality with Israel's believers, was still left veiled.
Paul's administration of the mystery, when this
mystery was now made known by the New Testament
revelation (v. 3), astonished the Jews and even aroused
their most violent antagonism. What their own
prophets had said should have prepared them for this
fuller New Testament revelation, but they read even
Moses with a thick veil over their eyes (II Cor. 3:14).
They read the whole Old Testament only as law
and never saw the gospel at all, to say nothing of
any part the Gentiles were to have in that gospel.

Many answers are given to the question as to
why Paul adds "him who created all the things" when
he speaks of the mystery having been hidden in God.
Those who stress the sovereignty of God: "making
what arrangements he pleased as to the concealment,"
etc., speak as Calvinists would express themselves.
The idea that his being the Creator intends to remove
the wonder of the mystery is out of the line of thought.
Other thoughts, such as making the mystery great because it lies in the Creator himself, or placing it in
God's eternal plan when he created the world, are

true enough but seem inadequate. Its greatness is self-apparent, and "from the eons on" dates it in eternity. Τὰ πάντα, all the things that exist (definite), leads us to think of the Gentiles as also being God's creatures (see Rom. 3:29) and also of the heavenly world to which the next clause refers. The Creator of all acted and acts with due reference to all his intelligent creatures.

10) The fact that his purpose takes in all men on earth (πάντας, v. 9) is obvious, for it deals with the work of salvation; the thought that it should extend also to the heavenly world comes as a surprise. Yet the expression "the Creator of all the things" prepares us for this thought. Paul's is not the partial, one-sided view which sees only men, and it is not at all the old Jewish narrowness which looks only at Jews and brushes aside others as dogs. In 1:10 he sees the administration of Christ (note "administration") taking in τὰ πάντα (the same as in v. 9), "all the things, those in the heavens as well as those on the earth"; and in 1:21 Paul sees Christ exalted far above all rule and authority (these two terms are now again used) and power and lordship and title, yea, as the head of everything and as such given to the church.

Paul's is an all-embracing view, not because of his own vast mind, but because of what revelation made know to him (v. 3). It is thus that now, when speaking of his Gentile world mission, of his gospel administration of the mystery which pertains to the Gentiles, he once more connects with the angelic world what God, the Creator, does here in the New Testament *Una Sancta.* The mystery now made known, which is full of such wondrous blessedness for the godless Gentile world (3:12), has a bearing also on the angels in heaven.

The fact that this should be so is really not strange. God's creation is a grand unit. Rom. 8:19, etc., shows this as far as the earthly world of nature is concerned; Eph. 1:10 adds the heavenly world. The angels desire to look into the mysteries of our redemption (I Pet. 1:12) ; the general assembly of the church is to come to their innumerable company (Heb. 12:22) ; they are ever employed as our ministering spirits (Heb. 1:14). It is in the light of this connection that Paul says that the divine purpose (ἵνα) of his preaching the gospel to the Gentiles and of his enlightening all men regarding his administration of the mystery now finally revealed is: "that there may be made known (effective aorist) now to the principalities and authorities in the heavenly places through the church the manifold wisdom of God," etc. The clause depends on the two infinitives used in v. 8, 9 and not merely on one of the modifiers occurring in v. 9. The construction is plain when we note that this wisdom is to be imparted "through the church," the product of Paul's evangelizing and enlightening.

"Now" is in contrast with "from the eons on" and with the point of time marked by the aorist in "he created." Yet the emphasis is on the verb which is placed forward, "that there may be made known," of course, "now" that all those eons are past. "May be made known" is in contrast with "having been hidden," and the agent who makes known is God. God's great purpose is to make known the full measure of his wisdom to the very angels in heaven at this time when he made known to Paul by revelation the mystery (v. 4) regarding the Gentiles (v. 6), and when as God's minister by his apostolic administration Paul made plain what this mystery contained.

The angels are called αἱ ἀρχαὶ καὶ αἱ ἐξουσίαι, the abstract plurals for the concrete beings: those who have rule and authority. We cannot use the abstract plural "rules" and hence translate "principalities." Here the question of ranks is again introduced (see 1:21). Dif-

ferences are plainly indicated although we now have
only two terms instead of four with an addition (1:21).
The difference is not this that one angel has rule while
another has authority, but that one has a certain rule
or domain with the corresponding authority, another
a different rule and authority. Of course, each has
power, lordship, and title according (1:21). Paul does
not write οἱ ἄγγελοι ("angels" = messengers) because
this would designate office and work with regard to
men, and here position in the heavenly world is referred to, hence the phrase "in the heavenlies" (*loca*,
not *bona*).

The knowledge of the divine wisdom the angels are
to obtain "through or by means of the church." The
existence and the development of the *Una Sancta* are
to be the medium (διά) for making known this wisdom
in heaven. God's whole plan, hidden so long, now has
the veil withdrawn as Christ's redemption reaches its
consummation in the New Testament *Ecclesia*. In the
church as gathered from over all the world, one great
spiritual household and body (2:16, 19: 3:6), God's
wisdom shines forth most wondrously. What God's
wisdom had in mind from creation onward is made
plain to the angelic world only as the church now finally rises in its spiritual splendor and is actually realized through Christ and his universal gospel.

The verb is placed first, the subject last, both are
thus emphatic. Σοφία is the divine attribute according
to which God arranges his purposes and his plans,
chooses his means, and brings forth the results, all of
which is done in absolute perfection. The most wonderful domain in which this wisdom operates is our
sinful race. The adjective means "many-colored."
M.-M. 527 calls its use here in the sense of *multivaria*
or "manifold," figurative. God's wisdom is one, yet it
can be termed "multifarious" because it weaves a thou-

sand apparently tangled threads into one glorious pattern. So out of the most diverse elements, where the strongest opposites clashed, where men saw only impossibilities, God, coming with means which looked hopelessly inadequate to men, worked out results which no man would have dreamed, and no angel could have foreseen. By thus telling the Ephesians how God makes this wisdom of his appear to the angels in heaven Paul magnifies the church in the highest degree. Let us as members of the church appreciate it. The entire description is exalted and without question deals only with the good angels and not with the evil either alone or in conjunction with the good.

11) This wisdom of his God intends to make known even to the angels "in accord with the purpose of the eons which he formed in connection with Christ Jesus, our Lord." Paul uses the phrase κατὰ πρόθεσιν several times. We have defined it in 1:11 (which see). "In harmony with his free determination, springing from his love and grace to effect salvation in accord with this love and grace." The absence of the article stresses the quality of the word, yet the added genitive, plus the relative clause, make it quite definite. Our versions translate, "according to the eternal purpose," and place "the eons" in eternity, prior to time; but in v. 9 "the eons" refer to those that begin with time and end with Christ. Hence it is best to take this plural in the same sense. The genitive is possessive: the purpose belonging to these eons, marking and distinguishing them. This "purpose" stood during their entire long extent.

"Purpose" is here not equal to "election." Some suggest that instead of "which he *formed* in Christ Jesus" we should translate, "which he *wrought out* in Christ Jesus." In support of this suggestion we are pointed to the historical name "Christ Jesus, our

Lord" (not merely "Christ") ; also to what is called a
tautology: "hidden *from the eons on* — in order now
to be made known — in accord with a purpose *of the
eons* which he formed" — this being avoided by translating, "which he carried out," etc. Πρόθεσιν ποιεῖν is
said to be used like θέλημα or γνώμην ποιεῖν. This seems
attractive at first glance, for this purpose of grace *was*
carried out in Christ Jesus. But the linguistic factor
is not assured except by surmise. Secondly, the name
used is the full liturgical (not merely historical) one
and is used because of the following clause: "in whom
we have," etc. Finally, the tautology is really a correspondence: "the mystery has been hidden from the
eons on," yet God's blessed purpose belonged to these
eons, governed and filled them nonetheless.

We have "our Lord Jesus Christ" already in 1:17
(office, personal name, relation to us believers). The
fact that God's purpose was carried out in him does
not need to be stated, for it was "formed" in him (ἐν,
in union with him), it would certainly not have been
carried out in connection with another. But this
possessive "our" is significant, merging, as it does, into
the next clause with its "we have." Paul has been
addressing "you, the Gentiles," (v. 1), saying what
these Gentiles are (v. 6) how he is administering
God's grace (v. 2) and the mystery regarding them
(v. 9) in his preaching to the Gentiles (v. 8). When
he now writes "our" and "we have" he includes himself, a former Jew, and thus all the Ephesian Jewish
believers. Gentile and Jewish believers alike form the
Una Sancta, the church through which even the angels
in heaven are having God's wisdom made known to
them (v. 10). That is the reason for the full name
"Jesus Christ, our Lord." God's purpose, standing
throughout all past ages, was formed in him. Already
Abraham saw him and was glad, for before Abraham
was he was (John 8:57-59).

12) "In whom we have," etc., attaches to "Christ Jesus, our Lord," with whom the entire saving purpose of the ages was connected, our present possession of all that this purpose contained. How our having this possession is "in him," i. e., connected with him, "through faith in him" (objective genitive) states. Διά names faith as the subjective means, which implies the objective means, gospel preaching (v. 8), even as the object embraced by faith (αὐτοῦ, Christ) is brought to us by the gospel.

Instead of naming any of the intermediate gifts of gospel grace which we of the *Una Sancta* have Paul names the crowning gift: "we have the boldness and access in confidence" through faith in him. He restates 2:18 yet now names the object more fully. When the article used with the second noun would be the same as it was with the first, it is usually omitted. Yet here the two nouns convey one idea even as the phrase "in confidence" modifies them in conjunction: "the boldness and access in confidence" or assurance.

Παρρησία is not used, as M.-M. 497 state, with the meaning "confidence," for this would create a tautology with πεποίθησις; it = the freedom of saying anything and everything, the absence of restraint or fear. We have no exact equivalent and use "boldness" when translating, which then calls for a proper explanation; Luther and the Germans say *Freudigkeit,* "joyfulness." We see at once that this is the lesser or auxiliary term which amplifies "access" (active as in 2:18). We have free, unrestrained, confident access to the Father through faith in Christ. There is nothing to deter us from going to him in Christ's name, nothing to disturb the confidence of our approach. In 2:18 "to the Father" is added: as children we freely go to him in our need with any prayer our faith may inspire and are sure of a paternal reception. This is the climax of our present standing in the *Una Sancta,* the fullest expression of our enjoyment of grace.

We may summarize the great facts:

1) The divine purpose going back to eternity.

2) Formed in Christ Jesus, our Lord.

3) Standing veiled in all past ages yet standing nonetheless.

4) Revealed in gospel preaching to all men including the Gentiles.

5) Establishing the church of the New Testament with its wonderful universality.

6) Unveiling even to the angels in heaven the wonderful wisdom of God contained in the divine purpose from its inception onward.

7) Putting us believers into possession of the enjoyment of the highest earthly communion with our heavenly Father.

In this masterly way and with such a sweep of thought Paul presents the significance of his apostolic work among the Gentiles in the great purpose and plan of God.

13) The entire elaboration regarding Paul's office is now concluded with a request to his readers: **Wherefore I ask** (you) **not to be losing heart in my tribulations in your behalf, which is your glory.**

This request should not be connected only with v. 12, since that itself is in closest connection with the preceding. Moreover, this request itself harks back to v. 1, the tribulations "in your behalf" which refer to Paul's being a prisoner "in behalf of you, the Gentiles." "Wherefore" reaches into the entire paragraph. "I ask" is the common word used to designate asking of men as well as of God. Paul asks the Ephesians not to lose heart on account of his imprisonment. If he were asking God, the word "God" should be expressed. If he were asking that he himself may not lose heart he should not have written "in *my* tribulations." The omission of ὑμᾶς with the infinitive is natural, for "I ask" = "I ask you," so that the infinitive carries this "you" with it. The omission of "you" lends the request a general tone: "I ask that there be no losing heart in regard to my tribulations in your behalf."

Linguists still dispute as to whether the middle of αἰτέω has or has not a business flavor. B.-P. 38 thinks the middle is the same as the active; C.-K. 92 adheres to the reflexive idea in some instances; R. 805 goes still farther, and B.-D. 316, 2 states outright that the middle is used with reference to business transactions and is regularly so used in the New Testament. The old idea that the middle is used when one expects to make a return for what he asks is not apparent. Paul's meaning is not merely, "I ask for myself" (reflexive), his personal interest and gain are not the point; but, "I ask in this my dealing with you," being engaged in an apostolic transaction with you in this epistle. His asking is, of course, that the Ephesians do something, but the gain of it is to be for them.

The infinitive means, "not to grow κακός," good for nothing. A soldier is thus when he is cowardly, a student when he fails to apply himself. So the verb comes to mean, "to grow fainthearted, discouraged, to lose heart" (II Cor. 4:1, 16). We can scarcely say that the Ephesians had already become discouraged because of Paul's long imprisonment, but there was such a danger. At least a few are always pessimists, ready to lower the flag after a long strain. The idea is not that they might give up their own faith, we have no such intimation; it is that they lose heart concerning the great cause of the Gentiles since Paul, the great apostle of the Gentiles, has been a prisoner now for nearly four years, his great work among the Gentiles being apparently stopped. The very statement of what might induce discouragement removes this feature; these tribulations of Paul's are "in your behalf," for the benefit of the Ephesians. In what way they are this the relative clause indicates. After having said "our" and "we" in v. 11, 12, including all of the Ephesians, "your" still includes all of them and is not limited only to the Gentile membership.

The fact that ὅστις is generalizing, qualitative, and often has a causal note, and thus is not merely equal to ὅς, is apparent from many instances. B.-D. 293, 2. Here the sense is: "since this is such as to be your glory." The feminine gender is due to the feminine predicate, the singular is likewise due to attraction. It is a striking statement that the apostle's tribulations are the glory of the Ephesians, not something about which to be discouraged, but something in which to rejoice. But it is true: if Paul is willing to endure everything for his work's sake, that work must be great and valuable indeed; if God permitted Paul to endure so much as the consequence of his work, this showed God's own estimate of his work. Most prominent as the fruit of this work were the Ephesians among whom Paul had spent more than two years of most successful labor.

* * *

Paul's Intercession for the Ephesians

14) With τούτου χάριν Paul repeats the phrase which he used in v. 1 and now concludes what he there began. On the structure and its meaning see the exposition in v. 2. In Paul's intercession for the Ephesians he, the prisoner for the Gentiles, and his whole office in the *Una Sancta* are concerned. This is

an intercession that is apostolic indeed, but apostolic in this manner. Paul's suspended subject together with the suspended exceptional phrase tie v. 14-21 together with v. 2-13 in a most effective manner. **For this cause I bow my knees to the Father from whom all the family in (the) heavens and on earth is named.**

In v. 1 "for this cause" reaches back into 2:11-22: because of the unity in one body (v. 16) wrought by the blood and the cross of Christ (v. 13, 16). This phrase which is now repeated includes the contents of v. 2-13, Paul's work among the Gentiles which has brought also the Gentiles into this blessed unity according to the original purpose of God and afforded boldness and access to God to believing Jews and believing Gentiles alike (v. 12). Christ made all of them one household, all being equally members of it (2:19), all fellow heirs, etc. (3:6), and Paul's office and work have made this evident to all (v. 9) so that even the angels in heaven behold the manifold wisdom of God which wrought out the eternal purpose he formed in Christ Jesus, our Lord (v. 10, 11). From all this originates the great intercession of Paul for the Ephesian believers.

"I bow my knees" refers to actual kneeling in prayer now and again when Paul prays (present tense). The bodily attitude during prayer is important, for it reflects the soul's attitude toward God. Kneeling expresses humiliation and lowly supplication. We kneel when we confess our sins, at a deathbed, or when some calamity presses us down. We stand with bowed head as in the presence of God, the bowed head expressing reverence. We fold our hands in any case, also during any church rite (sponsors, confirmands, communicants, those taking part in a marriage ceremony, etc.). This means that the hands, busy with a thousand things all day long, fold up and put all of them away, the

whole heart and thought being directed to God. One
may pray in any position, even with only a groan or in
silence; but the positions noted have come to mean
much in the church and for the individual. Careless,
thoughtless attitudes of body are not good. Formalism
is no more to be feared than the thoughtlessness of
meaningless attitudes.

R. calls πρός the face-to-face preposition which is
used in intimate personal relations. As a child of God,
Paul prays "to the Father"; compare this phrase in
2:18.

15) The relative clause states in what sense Paul
uses the word "Father": "from whom all the family
in (the) heavens and on earth is named." We are convinced that this clause does not introduce a new definition of "the Father," one that is to be understood by
itself, abstractly, but that it describes "the Father"
according to the entire previous context (2:11-3:13),
in which we note 2:18. Now this entire context mentions "the Creator of all things" only incidentally (v.
9) and in 2:18 uses "the Father" soteriologically, only
in relation to *our* having an approach to him. Already
this rules out any fatherhood and any idea of a family
that is due merely to creatorship. But 2:19 also
speaks of the οἰκεῖοι of God, of those who constitute his
household or family (the word follows "the Father" in
2:18). Paul describes these *oikeioi*, not as being a
duality, but as ἐν, "*one* part" (2:14), "*one* body"
(2:16), "in *one* spirit" (2:18), "the whole building"
(a unit), the Gentile believers being "fellow heirs, fellow body members, fellow partakers" (3:6), a unit
with the Jewish believers.

This rules out any fatherhood of *two* families (Jewish, Gentiles), the very idea of such a duality being
removed in so many words in 2:14-17, etc. It rules
out any multiplication of families such as ranks of
angels, orders, communities, groups, congregations of

men, for instance, "every group of beings united by
a common descent or origin" (Westcott), *jedes Ge-
schlecht im Himmel und auf Erden* (B.-P. 1018), plus
other turns of this nature, "all classes of angels in
heaven and all nations on earth" (Meyer).

The paronomasia in πατήρ and πᾶσα πατριά is unfortunately lost in our English rendering; it is more than
a mere sound, it is really an *annominatio* that involves
also the sense (R. 1201). The real issue is regarding
πασᾶ πατριά (without the article). Must this mean
"every family" as the R. V. has it, and as so many
take for granted? Then we are lost in pluralities,
and it is only a question of the kind and the number
the commentator is pleased to list. Some think that
Paul is alluding to the rabbinical notion of angels and
to certain Gnostic speculations. The A. V. is correct,
"the whole family," or verbally better, "all the family"
(all that is family). It is the same as the πασᾶ οἰκοδομή
(also without the article) in 2:21 (see the discussion).
R. 772 states, " 'all the family' is possible." We say a
little more: this is the meaning here, and it is grammatically perfectly correct with an abstract term in
which the ideas "all" and "every" coalesce. There is
only *one patria*, there are no *patriai* (plural); see "one
— one — one" in 2:14-18.

Whether the addition: the Father "of our Lord
Jesus Christ" (A. V.) is retained in v. 14 or not, the
fatherhood here referred to is soteriological, and the
view that ἐξ οὗ contradicts this is untenable. C.-K. 851:
ὀνομάζεσθαι ἔκ τινος is good Greek for being named after
somebody. The passive does not make God the agent,
for "from whom" forbids this. The name this great
family bears always indicates its Father. This family
is the *Una Sancta*. A part of it is already in heaven,
the other part is still on earth. Some think that the
angels are included since the Old Testament calls them
"the Sons of God." One may debate that, it is imma-

terial; C.-K., although still holding to the plural πατριαί, urges that Paul is throughout speaking of the New Testament revelation, and that we need not bring in the Old Testament term and the angels. That seems satisfactory.

16) Non-final ἵνα with its subjunctive states the substance of Paul's intercession: **that he give to you according to the riches of his glory to be strengthened with power by means of his Spirit in the inner man so that Christ may dwell through the faith in your hearts, in order that, having been rooted and founded in love, you may be strong to grasp with all the saints what (is) the breadth and length and height and depth and to know the love of Christ exceeding this knowledge, in order that you may be filled with respect to all the fulness of God.**

The aorist "that he give" is effective, it is an actual great gift. God's δόξα is the sum of his attributes as these are displayed to the eyes and the hearts of men. The riches or wealth of this glory is all its greatness and its wonderfulness, and this is to be the norm the Father is asked to follow in his gift to the Ephesians. The giving here asked is that which comports with and matches all the attributes of God, his love and grace, his power and wisdom, his majesty and infinitude. As the Giver, so the gift to those in the *Una Sancta*. In connection with v. 12, 13 we have seen that all the Ephesians are now included. Note "the glory of his grace" in 1:7; "the superabounding riches of his grace in goodness" in 2:7; "rich in mercy" in 2:4; "the Father of the glory" in 1:17. All these expressions belong together.

We regard Paul as asking for one gift which he then unfolds in all its richness in order to match the richness of the Father's glory. "To be strengthened with power," etc., is the object infinitive and not epexe-

getical (R. 1086) ; it names the gift. "With power" is
the dative of means. We may note that Paul is here
using three of the terms he employs in 1:19, 20: δύναμις,
dynamic power; κράτος (in the verb), strength as exercised; then ἰσχύς (in the verb in v. 18), *vis* or *virtus* as
possessed whether it is exercised or not. In 1:19, 20
these words are used with reference to God, here they
constitute the gift bestowed on us.

The dative cannot state where the strengthening
is to take place, for this is "in the inner man." This
strengthening is to come to us by the personal medium,
"his Spirit" (διά, the preposition also used in connection with Christ), yet always when God employs the
Spirit or Christ, never when we are the subject (Analogy of Scripture). We must also remember that the
Spirit always operates with Word and Sacrament and
never without these. It is incorrect to say that Paul
is praying for a new Pentecost. Pentecost admits of
no repetition; once poured out, the Spirit remains and
by Word and Sacraments flows out into all the world
and with ever-new power flows into the hearts of
believers.

Εἰς is static (R. 593) : "in the inner man," although
we may also translate: "with respect to the inner
man." "The inner man" is the counterpart to "the
outer man" (II Cor. 4:16). The inner man = the
heart, mind, soul, spirit; the outer = our physical part,
the body. This inner man has been regenerated, quickened (2:5), made spiritually alive and is thus given
power and strength to assert himself in the fullest
manner. Spiritual virility is what we all need. It
comes from the Father through the Spirit in Word and
Sacrament.

17) The infinitive is not coordinate and does not
name a second gift; it is not epexegetical and specifying what "to be strengthened" signifies (R. 1086 and
W. P.) but denotes contemplated result (R. 1090) :

"so that Christ dwells through the faith in your hearts." Like the previous aorist infinitive, this one, too, is effective. It makes no difference whether we regard the verb as intransitive, "dwell," or as transitive, "make dwelling"; we do not see how it could be made causative: the Father "to cause Christ to dwell in your hearts." The fact that Christ is now the subject causes no jar since the subject of the previous infinitive is no longer "the Father" but "you" understood. The Spirit's strengthening us in the inner man produces the result that Christ dwells in our hearts. The very order of these statements answers the objection that this indwelling is already the *sine qua non* of our Christianity; for here Paul speaks, not of the first entrance of Christ into our hearts, but of the further indwelling that is due to the strengthening we receive through the Spirit by Word and Sacrament. The *unio mystica* is progressive; Christ takes possession of us in ever-greater degree. The aorist denotes full possession.

Hence the subjective means (διά) is added: "through faith," which is parallel to the objective means: "through his Spirit." Christ comes by the Spirit and enters and dwells in us by means of the faith which embraces him; hence we also have the definite article. The heart is the center of our being, the seat of intellect, emotion, and will, especially of the latter. Christ will take complete possession of these as one uses the whole house in which one dwells. We are to be "a holy sanctuary in the Lord" (2:21).

The thought of v. 17 is complete; to attach to it the phrase "in love" (whether this be Christ's love to us or our love to him) would confuse its clarity. We likewise do not make the two perfect participles exclamatory: "you, the people who in love have been rooted and founded!" Paul has not written "you." The construction would be broken in a manner that is too strange. The objection to the emphasis that rests on these participles when they are construed with the ἵνα clause is not removed by making them independent and exclamatory; it is rather increased and made disproportionate. We have a number of examples which place some important modifier before ἵνα; to question all of them, as has been done, is unwarranted.

What disturbs some is the fact that the position of the participles stresses "love," hence they seek to reduce this stress. Nevertheless, this remains; in fact, the use of two participles in place of one helps to make "love" prominent. Yet two points should be noted: "in love" has no modifier, and the participles are not finite verbs, are thus only auxiliary modifiers of the subject in the expression "you may be made strong or able." "Love" is to be taken in its broad sense and, unless it is separated from the participles, means our love to the Father, the Spirit, and Christ, for the context has presented only these. Love to the brethren is naturally also involved in this love. On the meaning of ἀγάπη see 1:4.

The perfect participles have their present implication, once rooted and founded and remaining thus. The figures are allied: like a tree that has its roots spreading wide, deep, and strong in the soil of love; like a building that is founded and grounded on a strong foundation. Why the figurative meaning should not be accepted is hard to see. The passive connects this rooting and grounding with the passive in v. 16, "may be strengthened with power." The power the Father bestows on us is to make us like a solidly rooted tree that is growing massive and strong, like a solidly founded building that is rising high and imposing.

Note the progression: the Holy Spirit (Word and Sacrament) — the faith in our hearts — now love in its full development.

18) By connecting love with the subordinate participial modifiers Paul combines it with knowledge and

thus also makes this the knowledge of experience. It comes from the Spirit (Word) by faith when Christ dwells in us and in the love which embraces God. There is a γνῶσις which produces faith and love and is a part of them when they are first wrought (*agape* is always intelligent love); the knowledge here referred to is that which follows faith and love, is mediated by both, and cannot be attained without them; we call it the heart knowledge of full experience with God, the Spirit, Christ, and the Word. Faith and its accompaniment love usher us into a blessed world of knowledge that is absolutely closed to those lacking these prerequisites. We may also note Paul's thesis that knowledge without love is only sounding brass or a tinkling cymbal, I Cor. 13:1.

The thought itself prevents paralleling this ἵνα with the one occurring in v. 16. "That he may give" cannot be followed by "that you may be made strong" (a second object clause). This is a purpose clause: the purpose of Christ's indwelling is this making us strong to grasp, etc. Since Christ's indwelling is itself to be the result of the Father's granting us to be strengthened with power, the purpose regarding knowledge reaches back also to this infinitive in the way indicated. The whole object of Paul's intercession is thus one yet is spread out for us in 1:17, etc., Paul prays for knowledge for his readers. In fact, his entire epistle thus far aims to transmit the wonderful knowledge of "the mystery of Christ" (v. 4), especially as including the plan of God regarding the Gentiles and thus also regarding Paul's office. The strengthening of faith and of love is to fill us with the knowledge of the divine reality on which all our faith and our love rest.

Instead of saying only, "in order that you may grasp," Paul draws in the idea of our being strengthened to grasp: "in order that you may be made strong to grasp." He thus harks back to v. 16 where he uses the two words "to be strengthened with power." The two words match: it takes ἰσχύς, *Staerkebesitz*, to grasp or hold as our own (this is the idea of the middle), to comprehend the great reality Paul has in mind. "With (associative) all the saints" connects the Ephesians with all the other believers (see 1:1), for all of whom alike this comprehensive knowledge is the goal. Paul is not asking anything for the Ephesians apart from the other Christians.

Because of the lack of a genitive after "what (is) the breadth and length and height and depth" there is considerable difference of opinion regarding these dimensions. Some have thought of the Christian Church, the Sanctuary (2:21), on the plea that it alone has four dimensions (Rev. 21:16); others of the work of redemption, the mystery (v. 3, 4, 9), the wisdom (v. 10), etc. The ancients ran riot with their fancies. Estius saw the deity of Christ in the height, his humanity in the depth, his world-wide salvation in the length and the breadth. One article combines the four into a unit concept. Note also the close connective τε, which is a rare construction in Paul's writings (not cumulative καί) and is intended at once to supply the omission of the genitive which is withheld only in order to introduce it the more emphatically as the object in the periphrastic infinitive clause.

19) This clause contains a striking oxymoron: "and to know the love of Christ exceeding this knowledge." Astounding! The breadth, length, height, and depth of the love of Christ exceed all our knowledge (note the article), yet we are to know it in its boundless dimensions, and the aorist infinitive, like that used in v. 18, means effective, actual knowing. We are not to interpret the four different dimensions but only the vastness of this love. Although we know it by actual experience, it ever exceeds all our knowing. We need scarcely say that the genitive is subjective: Christ's

love for us. Note the correspondence: we, rooted and founded in love, i. e., our love to Christ, are to comprehend and know the infinitude of his love to us.

And now the ultimate purpose in this climax which goes from faith to love to knowledge: "that you may be filled with respect to the fulness of God." "The fulness of God" is that which fills him. This is all the riches of his grace in Christ Jesus. The idea in εἰς is not, "filled with all the fulness of God" (A. V.), nor "unto," i. e., up to the limit or measure of God's fulness; but, "with respect or with regard to" all this fulness of God. Again the aorist is effective: we are to be filled to the brim. Our Father is again the agent who produces this fulness. Knowledge is the implied medium, the experimental, spiritual knowledge of faith plus love through the Spirit and Christ by way of Word and Sacrament. John 16:14.

Our fulness "with respect to" (εἰς) all the fulness of God avoids saying that all God's fulness is to fill us, for who of us could contain it all? Paul has also just said that the love of Christ exceeds our knowledge. To be sure, as John 1:16 says, "of his (Christ's) fulness have all we received, and grace for grace" (more and more grace). The fact that we are to be filled from God's fulness is implied; "with respect to" all his fulness means that our being filled is to be done with regard to all this fulness of God until the limit of our capacity is reached.

20) Paul not only states the contents of the intercession he makes for the Ephesians, but also adds as a conclusion to the entire presentation of this first part of his epistle, the doxology: **Now to him who is able beyond everything to do exceeding abundantly beyond what we ask or conceive, according to the power operating in us, to him the glory in the church and in Christ Jesus for all the generations of the eon of the eons! Amen.**

Paul glorifies God for what he is able to do for us and is assured that he will do according to this ability. We find two modifiers: "able beyond everything" — "to do exceeding abundantly beyond what we ask or conceive." Our versions contract the modifiers and attach this contraction to the infinitive alone; we leave the modifiers where Paul places them.

God's ability is "beyond everything." Πάντα is indefinite and hence does not refer merely to all the things that exist but to "all things" in any sense whatever. His power has no limits, is not exhausted by anything he puts forth. It is literally infinite. Thus in his limitless ability he is able "to do (aorist, actuality) beyond what we ask or think" (present, at any time). The compound preposition may be written as one word or may be divided: "exceeding abundantly beyond." Paul uses these vast superlatives more than does any other New Testament writer. The two verbs have the accusative relative ἅ which is changed into the genitive ὧν by being drawn into its antecedent after the preposition which requires the genitive. God can do for us not only more than we ask in our petitions and intercessions but even more than we are able to think and conceive in our mind. This is the strongest kind of an encouragement for us to ask him. On the middle αἰτούμεθα compare v. 13.

Paul does not, however, leave these modifiers regarding the ability and the doing of God in the abstract; he makes them very concrete by adding: "according to the power operating in us," which modifies the entire statement. We have in ourselves the norm (κατά) by which to judge as to what God is able to do; it is the power that now works in us. The view that this δύναμις is his omnipotence should be corrected according to Rom. 1:16. Paul has described the working of this power in us in 2:1, etc., and shown how it quickens the spiritually dead and fills them with spir-

itual life. This is the power of God's love and grace
(2:8) operating in the gospel (Rom. 1:16). Omnipotence does not work in the spiritual domain, which is
a Calvinistic idea; love and grace operate in this domain. These have their own "power," which is as
great in their domain as omnipotence is in its domain.

Confusing the two because "power" is used with
reference to the latter misunderstands the Scripture.
Love, grace, and the gospel and their own power work
their own results. They employ the omnipotence to
work in its own field of providence, to aid the gospel
work, to shield the believer and the church. Yet contrition and faith, regeneration, conversion, justification, the new life and its development, all the Christian virtues plus perseverance to the end are the operations of grace alone. Omnipotent providence opens the
paths for the gospel, curbs the hostile forces, protects
the gospel messengers, prevents the gates of hell from
destroying the church, rules in the midst of the enemies
even when they rage and ravage the church (Ps.
2:1-6). Omnipotence permits martyrdom, grace turns
the blood of the martyrs into the seed of the church.
The Scriptures are very clear regarding the two powers, their separate domains, their operations, their
products. Both work together, yet the two are never
the same.

What the power of love, grace, and the gospel is
doing in us is for us the norm (κατά) regarding what
God will yet do to bring his saving work in us to its
glorious consummation.

21) Emphatic αὐτῷ resumes all that has been said
about God our Father (v. 14) and to him as such
ascribes "the glory," the article signifying the glory
that is due to him from us. We, of course, cannot
augment his glory which is infinite and changeless; but
we can recognize and acknowledge it, and that is what
Paul does here and in every other doxology. The state-

ment is an exclamation: "To him the glory!" We thus prefer to supply nothing; the grammars supply "is" or "be" (optative) and debate as to which is correct.

The text that has the reading καί has the better authority: "in the church *and* in Christ Jesus," etc. The A. V. drops the "and." Those who do this generally combine the two phrases; but the fact that the church is in Christ Jesus needs no solemn statement such as this would be. On "in Christ Jesus" and its interpretations see 1:1. "To him the glory in the church" is a complete thought. The great *Una Sancta* must ever ring with the glory-praise of God (1:6, 12, 14).

Secondly, "to him the glory in Christ Jesus for all the generations of the eon of the eons." While both denote sphere, the two ἐν are yet diverse. "In the church" = in the hearts of all those who constitute the assembly of God here on earth. All the doxologies used in our worship continue the doxology Paul utters here. "In Christ Jesus" cannot mean: also in his heart. The meaning is that all the glory that is due to God the Father is connected solely and alone with Christ Jesus (office and person), and that to all eternity. Ἐν denotes sphere and union in this sense. Thus "in the church" is subjective (in our hearts), but "in Christ Jesus" is objective (connected with him), "and" joins the two.

When "and" is omitted, the interpretation is either that the church is in Christ Jesus forever, or that the glory may be in the church forever in Christ Jesus. In the case of both interpretations the phrase "for all the generations of the eon of the eons" causes difficulty. If Paul means only "to all eternity" he has several ways of saying this: "to the eon," "to the eon of the eons," "to the eons of the eons." Why this statement about "all the generations" (so definite at that)? It is quite

impossible to make "generations" a designation of
time: periods of thirty or more years duration —
especially "*all* the generations" — and then strangely
add "of the eon of the eons." This is what the A. V.
attempts with its odd rendering: "throughout all ages,
world without end" (omitting the article and making
"all the generations" only "all ages"). By introducing "all the generations" with "the eon," etc., Paul's
expression becomes quite exceptional, and it is certainly more than a phrase denoting time.

"The eon of the eons" is not difficult. Like "King
of kings," "Holy of Holies," it means the supreme eon;
the genitive plural produces the superlative idea (R.
660). This is not, however, only the New Testament
eon. The expression is too grand for that; and besides, it is already covered by the phrase "in the
church." Paul means "in eternity," "forever and ever"
(R. V.), which also repeats the word in our English
idiom. Even the Latin *aeternus,* from *aevum,* is a
term denoting time although "eternal" is the opposite
of time: without beginning, progress, or end, without past, present, and future, a *simul tota,* a *fixum,* not
a *fluxum,* which is really inconceivable to the human
mind. We are compelled to use words denoting time
to express what is not time at all, the Hebrew and the
Greek must do likewise. Here the latter raises αἰών, a
vast era or age that is marked by what transpires in it,
to the superlative degree.

By prefixing "all the generations" the concept is
made to refer, not to eternity as following the Parousia, but to eternity as generation after generation
comes to leave this present eon at death and enters
eternity, the superlative eon. God's is all the glory "in
the church" now in time and "in connection with
Christ Jesus" for all the generations as each passes out
of time and comes to be "of the eon of the eons," of
eternity. Thus also Paul does not lose the church in

this addition; all these generations we take to be the generations of the saints, with whom alone the apostle is concerned.

He seals the doxology with "amen," a word that has been taken over into other languages from the Hebrew. This Hebrew adverbial accusative means *wahrlich, gewiss* (Eduard Koenig, *Woerterbuch*); as in the Hebrew, so in the Greek, it was placed at the end of a statement in order to express strong confirmation: "Verity!" or "Verily!" In John's writings it is doubled and placed at the head of great statements. It is senseless to add amen to a set of mere opinions or to anything that is doubtful. Then "Perhaps!" might be in place or just an interrogation point. In the Scriptures this word denotes more than intellectual assent. It always involves an energetic demand for faith since it seals something that pertains to Christ and salvation. *"Christ* covers the word, not *the* word him." C.-K. The divine will is behind it, which carries out what is connected with Christ. This Scriptural significance should be decisive for our present use of amen.

CHAPTER IV

The Second Half of the Epistle

Again Three Chapters

Paul Reminds the Ephesians of:

The Obligations of Their Membership in the Una Sancta as It Is now in Christ

The Admonition to Unity

1) First, *doctrine* which consists of the clear statement of the divine facts on which alone *faith* rests. Next, *admonition* which presents the obligations involved in the faith that relies on the doctrine and thus deals with *life and conduct* in detail. The two stand in a vital connection, which fact also appears where the admonitions are supported by brief doctrinal additions.

After having set forth the great doctrine of the *Una Sancta*, Paul now tells his readers how their lives should be shaped in order to accord with the facts of this doctrine. This is very fitting after having shown that by faith in Christ they are all one in Christ in the *Una Sancta* although they were formerly Jews or Gentiles. Paul's first admonition to the Ephesians is an exhortation that they keep the unity of the Spirit in the bond of peace (v. 1-3). He elucidates and strengthens this first admonition by an explanation of the organism of the church which is so fitted together as to constitute a great unity in its members, their activity and work producing and conserving unity (4-16).

* * *

The Admonition

I accordingly admonish you, I, the prisoner in the Lord, to walk worthily of the calling wherewith you were called with all humility and meekness, with longsuffering, bearing up with each other in love, being diligent to keep the unity of the Spirit in the bond of peace.

The connective οὖν cannot refer to the doxology immediately preceding so as to make our walk according to our blessed calling the outcome of our fervent praise to God. Not only is this connection of thought rather artificial, it also ignores the idea of keeping the unity, the real point in this first admonition, which rests on the substance of the preceding chapters, on the very idea of the *Una Sancta* Paul has described. We, therefore, regard "accordingly" as connecting with all that precedes.

Παρακαλῶ means to call upon someone in order to say something to him, to speak to him in a friendly and helpful way, thus to admonish, to comfort, to encourage, or to cheer. Here "I admonish you" is in place and not "I beseech" as though Paul were pleading. Paul's letters contain much admonition. "You," of course, means all the Ephesians.

Note the juxtaposition of ὑμᾶς and ἐγώ, and the apposition to the latter, "the prisoner in the Lord." This emphasis on "I" is not a call for sympathy on Paul's part nor is his being a prisoner in the Lord the motive that should prompt the Ephesians to heed his admonition. We recall 3:1; but there the addition is "in behalf of you, the Gentiles," which is a reference to Paul's office and work especially among the Gentiles. This is absent here. While Paul's belonging to Christ Jesus in 3:1 is similar to his being in the Lord, even these expressions differ in what they convey regarding Paul, the prisoner. In 3:1, etc., Paul speaks of the mystery that is now revealed regarding the Gentiles, and of the fact that this has brought him into prison as Christ's own apostle to the Gentiles; here he admonishes his readers (Jews and Gentiles alike) and does this as "the prisoner in the Lord," the one whose long imprisonment is evidence of his being *fidele Christi membrum* as it has been well put.

His entire imprisonment was due to his connection with the Lord. In 3:1 the thought is that of special office, here the thought is that of faithfulness to the Lord. As one who is himself faithful he admonishes others. He does not here, as he does at other times, offer himself as an example, this admonition is not of that kind. But from him who has come to be "the prisoner in the Lord" the Ephesians will gladly accept any needful admonition.

The comprehensive sum of this first admonition is at once stated as is done in Rom. 12:1 and is then amplified by means of closer specifications. The sum is "to walk worthily of the calling wherewith you were called." Ἀξίως has the idea of equal weight. Conduct and calling are to balance in weight. The aorist is constative and includes the entire walk of the Ephesians: viewed as a whole, it is to have the mark of worthiness. More is implied than likeness between calling and conduct, namely also corresponding weight and value. God called the Ephesians through the gospel; this call proved effective in bringing them to faith. This was their κλῆσις or calling. In the epistles the noun and the verb and also the verbal κλητοί, "the called," are used in the effective sense: the call that has produced acceptance. Ἧς is attracted from the cognate accusative ἥν. Note that κλῆσις and ἐκλήθητε correspond to ἐκκλησία in 3:21: the calling and having been called makes the Ephesians members of the called assembly (*ecclesia*), whose conduct must be according. To be in the *Una Sancta*, the Communion of Saints, carries with it the obligation of living as saints in Christian sanctification.

2) Considered by itself, walking worthily would include the entire Christian conduct. Paul has in mind that part of the worthiness which conserves true Christian unity. We must read v. 1-3 as a unit admonition. While we consider each item, each must be viewed in its place as bringing out the worthiness here referred to. In the *one Una Sancta* we must walk in true *oneness*. We find four modifiers, two μετά phrases and two participial clauses. The change from phrases to weightier participles should not be overlooked; also the fact that the second participial modifier is the climax of the worthy walking so that the other modifiers support this climax. Humility, meekness, longsuffering as aids to bearing up with each other in love are to attain to the diligence in conserving unity in the bond of peace. To extend the second μετά phrase so as to include the participle: "with longsuffering bearing up with one another," destroys the symmetry of the two participial modifiers. Both are headed by participles in equal, natural fashion; hence "in love" is to be construed with the first participle. The nominative case needs no explanation, for it agrees with the subject of "you were called."

Why does Paul write two phrases instead of placing the three nouns after one preposition? Scarcely because humility and meekness are combined with "all" as applying to our attitude toward God as well as toward men. More probably because these two are broader, and longsuffering is more specific. Humility or lowliness is an attitude of mind, meekness or gentleness likewise, so that the two are combined. The opposite of the former is pride, self-assertion, which make arrogant claims. This virtue fosters Christian unity and, as in Rom. 12:16 and Phil. 2:3, refers to our attitude toward the brethren. The opposite of meekness is violence. "Meek" occurs often in the Scriptures and refers to those who suffer wrong and commit themselves to God (C.-K. 962, etc.). "All" applies to both terms; the article is not needed with abstract nouns (compare 2:21). "All lowliness and meekness" is the opposite of anything that manifests these virtues only in part. Our entire walk is to be accompanied (μετά) by these two; we are to walk arm in arm with them.

Trench defines "longsuffering": "A long holding out of the mind before it gives room to action or passion." It is attributed also to God as his patience toward men while ὑπομονή is patience with respect to things and is thus not attributed to God. The idea of humility and meekness advances to the more specific longsuffering as the outgrowth of the other two.

"Forbearing one another in love" is the preliminary exercise of longsuffering; each is to do this with the faults and the failings of the other: "holding up" under a load of vexations piled upon us. Yet only "in love," the love which understands and has the high purpose of seeking to do what is best for the faulty brother. The idea of standing anything and everything and for any length of time is excluded by ἐν ἀγάπη. Even "longsuffering" has its limits when "love" (in the sense indicated) is no longer able to pursue its purpose by this means and must resort to others.

3) The semicolon in our versions intends to indicate that, while the two participles are alike in form and construction, the second brings the real point of the admonition: by means of lowliness of mind, inner mildness, longsuffering, and loving forbearance when provoked, we are to do all that we can to keep our unity intact. The durative present participle again denotes constant action and matches "all" in the first phrase; τηρεῖν = ever to guard, thus to preserve and to keep that the unity may not be damaged or even lost to anyone who has entered its holy bond.

"The unity (oneness) of the Spirit" (genitive of author) is established by the Holy Spirit when by regeneration, faith, and a new life he joins us all spiritually. Once established, the oneness is not only to remain but is to manifest itself. In v. 13 Paul calls it "the unity of the faith and of the knowledge of the Son of God." Doctrine and life, confession and practice are to be one. There are to be no sects, divisions, schisms; also no strife, dissention, and the like. The *Una Sancta* as such *is* ever one and cannot be rent. In John 17 it is not this oneness for which Jesus prays. Existing as it does, it is the subject neither for prayer nor for admonition. It is the manifestation of this oneness for which Jesus prays and unto which Paul admonishes: that we may all stand as one in the Name (revelation, John 17:6, 11, 12), the Word (John 17:6, 8, 14, 17) and the truth (17, 19), the knowledge (John 17:3, 7, 8), our hearts and lives being ruled by these alone.

Those damage or destroy this oneness who deviate from the Word in any way. Thus they often also separate themselves from the *Una Sancta* herself. We "guard or keep" this oneness by making our faith and our life conform to the Word. In John 17 Jesus stresses the Word; in the following Paul stresses its contents (v. 4-6), the apostolic faith (v. 7-16), the corresponding life (v. 17, etc.), note v. 21. The virtues he has just mentioned in v. 2 are the subjective aids for conserving the oneness in its manifestation.

When dealing with this subject the prayer of Jesus as well as Paul's admonition are often misunderstood so that the inherent oneness of the *Una Sancta* and the manifestation of it in our unified adherence to the Word, and its substance in our confession of lip and life, are confused. Many pray for what needs no prayer and forget to pray and to work for what Jesus did pray for, unto what Paul also admonished. The

fact that we can do the guarding here enjoined only
by the Spirit's help need not be stated.

"Of the Spirit," as in v. 4, must mean the Holy
Spirit; for "the oneness of the spirit" as only the *con-
cordia animorum* or the "community spirit" might be
a wrong concord. Many are today in great concord in
some error, some wrong type of worship, some mode
of life (monks). "In the bond of the peace" rounds out
this particular modifier as "in love" does the one preceding; hence it cannot be drawn to v. 4. The genitive
is not objective: "the bond that binds peace," but appositional: "the bond consisting of peace"; σύν in the
word conveys the idea of "together," the bond joins
most closely. In the Greek as in the German abstracts
may have the article whereas the English does without: *des Friedens,* "of peace." Ἐν denotes the ethical
sphere of the action of guarding and scarcely the instrument employed even as peace is not an instrument.

*   *   *

The Unit Basis

4) This is presented in a triad, each member of
which is itself a triad. Yet sufficient variation avoids
what some might call formalism. There is no connective, no verb; just the nine items which are simply
set down as such for the readers and thus are made the
more striking. These three verses are not an admonition so that "let there be" is implied; they state facts.
Our versions add: "There is," which, however, weakens the effect. Stroke by stroke Paul simply points
to what forms the basis of the unity on which his previous admonition rests. In v. 7, etc., he will say still
more. All of the nine points are objective. They stand
as such. One may leave this great basis, it remains
nonetheless what it is. One may rest on it wholeheartedly or weakly, that, too, does not change it in the least.

Although nine items are listed, Paul has written "one" only seven times. Neither number is accidental: $9 = 3 \times 3$, the Trinity is the basis, the multiplication emphasizes this fact; $7 = 3 + 4$, the three are for us and for all men, we are to be joined with them, for four is the number of the earth. In v. 6 three phrases with the article are joined appositionally to God the Father and thus in a new way express unity. This listing is masterly and expressive in the highest degree. It stands out even in Paul's inspired writing.

One body — and one Spirit — even as also you were called in one hope of your calling. One Lord — one faith — one baptism. One God and Father of all — he over all and through all and in all.

"One body" (see 2:16) = the *corpus mysticum*, the *Una Sancta*, the church. This body is spiritual and hence is invisible: "I believe in the Holy Christian Church, the Communion of Saints." It is "one," without a division, nor can it be divided; nor is there another body besides this one.

"And one Spirit" completes the idea of "one body" since σῶμα and πνεῦμα are correlatives and are always found together in a living body. In this spiritual body God's own Holy Spirit dwells; not a single part of this body, not a single member of it is without the Spirit. Again, he, too, is "one," there is no duality, no division.

The third member of this triad is not stated by the one term: "one hope" but more lucidly and richly: "even as also you were called in one hope of your calling." This is the one item that contains a personal reference to the Ephesians. It reverts to v. 1 in a marked way: "the calling with which you were called." When this item is made personal, all the others also receive a personal touch. The κλῆσις involves the gospel which thus does not need to be named. "One hope" involves eternal salvation. The emphasis is on "*one* hope," another is inconceivable. Since Paul refers to

the Ephesians as being called "in one hope" he includes
their subjective hope, yet as including the one *Hoff-
nungsgut,* for this entire basis of Christian oneness
is objective. What is true of the "one hope" is true of
the one body, Spirit, Lord, etc. The Ephesians are
personally involved, yet this basis of unity stands even
apart from them. "In" one hope = in connection with
it, the ethical union or sphere as in v. 2 and 3.

The first triad centers in the *"one Spirit,"* i. e., as
related to the *Una Sancta.* Hence the call, the treasure
which it brings, namely the hope of salvation, and the
body possessing this treasure. One might say that
already this is basis enough. It is.

5) As Paul proceeds he presents the same basis,
but he does so from the angle of the Second Person.
"One Lord" is meant soteriologically, in the sense of
"our Lord Jesus Christ," he to whom we belong, who
bought us to be his own with a great price (I Cor. 6:20;
7:23), whom we serve in innocence and blessedness,
in whom we have salvation now and forever. He is
"one," there is no division in him, not even a possible
division; thus on his oneness rests ours.

"One faith," followed by "one baptism," connects
us with this "one Lord," makes us his own. These
two are generally conceived as being subjective and
objective, and some question whether "faith" is ever
objective. We have found it so quite a number of
times, it is then generally written with the article, "the
faith." Here "one faith" is like "one hope." The list
presents objective items, our basis of oneness is objective, must be so in order to be such a basis. Yet, as we
have indicated regarding "hope," "Spirit," "body,"
these are ours, for this is *our* basis throughout. Hence
"one faith" includes our personal believing, but the
stress is on the Christian faith as such, on what constitutes its substance. This is one even as it centers
on one Lord, one, whether you and I embrace it or not.

It is all very true that subjective *fiducia* is the same
in every believer whether it be strong or weak, and
that in erring denominations, where the gospel is not
wholly lost, "children of God are still born"; but this
is not the point of Paul's item. It is the fact that the
ground, substance, and truth on which all saving *fiducia* rests, are one and only one. In the *Una Sancta* no
believing saves except that which holds the "one faith"
and trusts that. As hope is *Hoffnungsgrund,* so faith
is *Glaubensgrund.*

"One baptism," one divine door into the *Una
Sancta,* one sacrament of initiation for all who enter
and by which they enter. The relation is obvious: one
Lord to whom we belong; one truth that joins us to
him; one sacrament that seals us as his. "One — one
— one" throughout whether we look at the Spirit, at
the Lord, or at the Father. R., *W. P.,* makes this objective act of God a subjective act of ours by saying:
"There is only one *act* of baptism for all who *confess*
Christ by means of this symbol, not that they are made
disciples by this one act, but *merely so profess* him, put
on Christ publicly by this ordinance." Yet in Matt.
28:19 Jesus himself says: "Make disciples of all nations by baptizing them in the Name," etc. Baptism
is the washing of regeneration and is thus never a
mere symbol. Nor is it an act of ours by which we
merely confess; it is an act upon us by which God
bestows the treasures of salvation upon us.

It has been asked why Paul does not list also the
Lord's Supper for the oneness he presents. Inadequate
answers are offered: that it is in a way included when
he names the one sacrament; that what the Lord's
Supper conveys lies in "one Lord, one faith"; that only
the most basic parts are listed; that faith and baptism
belong especially close together as being subjective and
objective (this regarding faith as being subjective).
The answer is that the *Una Sancta* includes also a host

of babes and children, none of whom are able to receive the Lord's Supper.

The second triad centers in *"one Lord."* The oneness to which Paul admonishes the Ephesians has him who is one as its basis and thus "one faith" and "one baptism" containing him. The omission of "and" lends incisiveness.

6) The third triad, which is entirely different from the other two, consists of the unit: "one God and Father of all" in three relations to the *Una Sancta*: "he over all and through all and in all." These "all" are not only masculine (persons) but are the ones who constitute the "one body" with which Paul begins in v. 4, the *Una Sancta*. This appears from the individualization, "to each one of you," in v. 7. Note that the singular "one body" is now expressed by the plural "all," a thing that is so often done by Paul who truly sees the object as it is. Each "all" takes in the entire sacred, spiritual body, but as composed of the many persons it includes. Paul does not say only "one God" but "one God and Father," thus expressing his soteriological relation to the "all" here referred to. These "all" are his children. In 2:18 we have already had "the Father," and in 3:14, "the Father, from whom the whole family is named." "All" = "the whole family," the οἰκεῖοι of God (2:19), his house or family members.

The apposition: "he over all," etc., is thus also soteriological. The three prepositions radiate from "one God and Father." They cannot be referred to the whole world of nature (as a neuter "all") or to the whole world of men (masculine, indeed, but disregarding the *Una Sancta* as such: "each one of you," v. 7). The three prepositions are quite different and form the third triad, but a triad anchored in the great unit: "one God and Father of all." In a supreme way the unit basis thus stands forth even in the very midst of the multiplicity of "all" these who are "one body."

Look at "all" of us believers. No matter from what angle you look, one God-Father (in Christ) is over, through, and in us all, not two, not more.

The three prepositions ἐπί, διά, and ἐν cover all relations so that Paul is now at an end. He has omitted nothing in the nine items and the seven "ones" and nothing could be added for properly presenting the basis of oneness. The whole presentation is a perfect pattern as to substance and formulation, a spiritual gem in every way. Ἐπί is the German *ob*, "over," which is better than "above" (our versions) and = exaltation and supremacy, but that of the Father: "our Father who art in heaven," with all that this implies for the family of the saints, a part of whom are already in heaven (3:15). Διά = operative power that makes us all his saints, the means through which this Father's hands work. Ἐν = immanence and indwelling, the *unio mystica* of spiritual union. "One" such God and Father "of all" of us and in all relations; a unit basis, indeed. None that is other, different, or greater, can be conceived. On this basis rests the oneness we should ever guard.

Some, especially the more ancient commentators, find a reference to the Trinity in the three prepositions; others voice their objection since all the prepositions are connected with the First Person alone. We do find the Trinity but not as some think and others deny, namely that "he over all" = the Father; "through all" = the Son; "in all" = the Spirit. The one article used with the three phrases makes them a unit, an apposition to "one God and Father." But this one God and Father, who is *through* all, is this by means of our one Lord as the Mediator, mediation (διά) involving a Mediator. Likewise, this one God and Father *in* all is in them by means of the Spirit even as ἐν is the preposition to express immanence that involves the Spirit. So also when we consider how this one God is the

Father of us all in the *Una Sancta,* our answer is: through the Son and the Spirit. While v. 6 completes one Spirit and one Lord by adding one God and Father, it at the same time unites all Three Persons in their soteriological relation to us all. This carries the idea of oneness to its absolutely highest pitch. To know Paul is to know that he would do no less. The reality is exhausted. No man, not even Paul, could add even one more thought when depicting the basis of the oneness of the *Una Sancta.*

*   *   *

The Unifying Work

7) The unit basis has been presented. Now, on this basis, how is the oneness of Paul's admonition to be attained and kept? For there is an endless diversity in the members of the *Una Sancta.* This very diversity is to keep and maintain the oneness of the admonition. Its end and goal is ever one and only one, its entire operation is unifying and constantly excluding all that would divide. This is the burden of v. 7-16.

Now to each single one of us there has been given a grace according to the measure of the gift of Christ.

Transitional δέ introduces the new subject. To call it adversative as placing "each single one" over against the preceding "all" overlooks the fact that it introduces the whole statement including what follows and does not set one term against another. There is an immediate connection with v. 6, and the thought does not leap back to v. 3 or v. 1. The great unit basis involves "all" (four "all" in v. 6), involves all alike no matter how different the individuals constituting this number are. Δέ proceeds to take up the differences found in the individuals: "to each single one of you (now speaking personally of the Ephesians) there was given (the English prefers: has been given) a grace according to the measure of the gift of Christ." Not one of you, Paul says, is without his special grace. The article, which is absent in good texts, is due to the following phrase: "grace according to," etc. Whatever the grace that each one of you has, it accords with the measure applied by the Giver, Christ. The context following shows that "grace" does not refer to forgiveness, life, and salvation, but, as in 3:2, 7, to what is usually called a charisma in the widest sense of this word, some endowment with which to serve the church.

Saving grace is alike for all, but each believer's endowment is different. It is "according to the measure of the gift of Christ." The usual interpretation regards "of Christ" as the subjective genitive: the endowment is measured by the gratuitous gift which in his wisdom and love Christ is pleased to bestow just as this is said of the Spirit in I Cor. 12:11. But this genitive seems to be objective: our endowment is in accord with the measure of the gift bestowed upon Christ. In Matt. 28:19 he says, "All power is given to me in heaven and in earth"; in Phil. 2:9 "the name above every name" is granted to him; compare Matt. 11:27; Luke 1:32; 10:22; John 3:35; 13:3; 17:2. Christ himself received "all things," "all power" as a gift to his human nature, and in accord with the vast measure of this gift to him he dispenses to every single one of us the grace or gift we are to use. It was thus that Paul, for instance, was given the grace of being an apostle to the Gentiles.

8) In Ps. 68:18 the Old Testament speaks about this distribution of charismata to every member in the church according to the measure of the gift made to Christ. **Wherefore the declaration is:**

Having gone up on high, he made captive captivity
And gave gifts to men.

Because Christ makes the gift for us according to the gift made to him, for this reason (διό) Scripture speaks of it. We think it best to regard λέγει as being impersonal, *es heisst,* "the declaration is," and to leave the subject unexpressed instead of trying to supply "the Scripture," "the Spirit," or "God." One may, however, make the subject the same as that of the agent implied in ἐδόθη in v. 7, which would be "one God and Father" in v. 6; yet the simple λέγει points only to the statement as such, and the stress is on "wherefore," the statement is based on the fact expressed in v. 7. So many Old Testament statements read as they do *because.* of what occurred afterward in the person of Christ. The idea that v. 7, 8 imply something like an objection is unwarranted.

This citation is regarded as a *crux* for interpreters as is also the whole psalm which one has denominated the Titan among the psalms, while another confesses that some of its passages are impenetrable. Yet contents and purpose of Paul's quotation are plain. Read both v. 18 and 19 of Ps. 68.: "Thou hast ascended on high, thou hast led captivity captive: thou hast received gifts for men, yea, for the rebellious also, that the LORD God might dwell among them. Blessed be the Lord, who daily loadeth us with benefits, even the God of our salvation. Selah." Jehovah ascends in victory and dispenses gifts to "us," his people. The realization of this statement in the highest degree has occurred in Christ Jesus who ascended into heaven in victory and triumph and gives all kinds of gifts to all the members of the *Una Sancta.* The thought is simple. What Jehovah did the psalmist describes in figurative language because (διό) it was to fit Christ, his ascent to heaven and his dispensing of gifts. The passage is plainly Messianic.

The change of the second person of the psalm into the third is merely formal, so also is the change of the

first finite verb into the corresponding participle. In
the LXX and in Paul this brings out the thought that
the ascending is subsidiary to the making captivity
captive, which it, of course, is. What troubles the
commentators is the fact that the Hebrew and the LXX
have, "thou hast *received* gifts for men" (ἔλαβες), while
Paul has, "he *gave* gifts to men." So Paul is charged
with altering the essential word to suit his purpose,
doing so deliberately, or due to faulty memory, or by
using such liberty as we should not use "in modern
times" (for instance, *Expositor's Greek New Testament*). Those who shrink from such charges labor to
remove the contradiction: Paul had a different Hebrew text; or *laqach* means *to fetch* in order to give;
or Paul offers only an application of the Messianic import of the psalm and not a translation. Some shorten
the quotation to one line and consider the words "he
gave gifts to men" words of Paul's. All this is done
because *received* and *gave* sound like a direct contradiction, the one verb being the opposite of the other.

But the *crux* and the contradiction are not so serious. The reception for men includes the giving to men.
If Christ received gifts for men, i. e., intended for
them, how could he withhold them from men and not
give them to those for whom the gifts were intended?
Even if the Hebrew *ba'adam* is regarded as meaning
an Menschen or *inter homines*, "thou didst receive gifts
consisting of men" (Ps. 2:8: "the heathen for thine
inheritance and the uttermost parts of the earth for
thy possession"), these men would certainly share in
what Christ has.

But much more must be said. In v. 7 the gift made
to each one of us is in accord with the measure of the
gift received by Christ (see this verse) since what
Christ received he was to distribute to us. Many other
passages state this same truth. Therefore, because
all power was given to Christ, he gives to the disciples

their mission and their gifts for this mission on earth
(Matt. 28:19, 20). The words the Father gave to Jesus
the latter gave to the apostles (John 17:8); the mission he had received from the Father he bestows on
the apostles (v. 18); the glory the Father gave him he
gave to them (v. 22); where he is they, too, are to be
(v. 24). So it is throughout: what Christ in his
human nature by which he ascended on high *received*
he was to *give* to us who are his own. These δόματα
or "gifts" include far more than endowment for the
spiritual work in the *Una Sancta;* these are only the
small things that go with the supreme ones.

The Hebrew *hammarom* means "on high" and
never merely the height of Mount Zion. Jehovah ascended to heaven. Some date in the history of Israel
is sought as to when the ascent took place; this effort
considers an ascent to Mt. Zion and results in a variety of surmises which also involve and usually question the authorship of the psalm. In regard to this
let us say that the psalm is too "titanic" to match any
one incident in Israel's history. The more important
question is passed by as to how David could say that
Yahweh could *receive* gifts. This is the word which
clearly points to the Messiah. David saw the God-man
in *Yahweh.* He could receive. Verse 17 of the psalm
with its "thousands of angels" depicts a victorious
ascent into heaven.

When Paul reproduces "received" by "gave" he
translates interpretatively. Delitzsch, *Psalmen,* 4th
ed., 488: "They are gifts which he now divides
among men and which also benefit those that have
strayed away. Thus the apostle understands the words
when he changes ἔλαβες into ἔδωκε. The gifts are the
charismata coming down from the Exalted One upon
his congregation, a grant of blessing connected caus-
ally with his victory; for as Victor he is the possessor
of the blessing, his gifts are like the spoils of his vic-

tory achieved over sin, death, and Satan." R. Kittel, the latest German commentator on the Psalms, does not consider Paul's citation of this psalm.

"He made captive captivity" (verb and noun are used with reference to war captives, II Cor. 2:5) describes Jehovah (Christ) as the supreme Victor. This is not a cognate accusative or an abstract used for a concrete, "captivity" for "captured ones." This is a plain accusative and is highly significant as such. "Captivity" itself was taken captive (Col. 2:15) ; the captivity in which principalities and powers, the hellish kingdom, held and tried to keep men, this was made captive, i. e., abolished (I Cor. 15:57). Thus Christ now divides the spoils.

9) With δέ Paul expounds; the parenthesis of our versions is unnecessary. More must be said about this Ascender, regarding his victory and his ability to give these gifts. **Now this "He ascended," what is it but that he also descended into the lower parts of the earth? The One that descended himself is also the One that ascended far above all the heavens in order to fill all the things.**

With τό Paul introduces the Greek word "He ascended" and uses the finite form in place of the participle used in v. 8. He is not speaking abstractly and saying that every ascent is connected with a descent; nor does he place the descent after the ascent — good texts insert "descended first" (A. V.). Paul is speaking of the One referred to in the psalm, Christ; his ascent was preceded by a descent.

What this descent was depends on the meaning of "into the lower parts of the earth." Is the genitive appositional, the lower parts = the earth? Then the descent of the Son for the purpose of the Incarnation would be referred to, but the expression would then be without parallel and too strange. Is the genitive partitive or ablative (lower than the earth, R. 499) ? Then

hell is referred to and Christ's descent into hell. This
expression is so used in Ps. 63:9, compare Ezek.
32:18, 24. It is asked why Paul does not say "into
hades." The answer is that, when he is expounding
an Old Testament term, he uses an Old Testament expression. The Incarnation will not do because the
psalm describes the supreme Victor, and the Incarnation is not a victory.

We disregard the figment of a *Totenreich,* a realm
of the dead which is situated between heaven and hell,
into which also the soul of Christ passed at death and
from which it emerged at his resurrection. He placed
his spirit into his Father's hands and entered Paradise
(heaven) together with the malefactor's soul. This
fiction of the death realm is often embellished by having Christ execute a ministry there, releasing the Old
Testament saints from the *Limbus patrum,* proclaiming grace to all the dead or to a certain number of
them. Some, indeed, retain the Descent into hell but
have Christ complete his suffering there during the
time that he was dead; or by the Descent they understand only the sinking into death and the tomb and call
the latter "the lower parts of the earth."

This Descent means victory, the capture of captivity itself. Vivified in the tomb, timelessly Christ (body
and soul) descended into hell and proclaimed (κηρύσσω)
his victory to the damned, I Pet. 3:19. This has nothing to do with I Pet. 4:6, for the gospel was not
preached to the dead when they were dead and in hell
but while they were yet alive on earth. This summary
must suffice for the passages found in Peter's letters.
The cross references of the A. V. to John 3:13; 6:33,
62 are misleading as to the descent referred to in our
passage.

Is hell, then, in the lower parts of the earth? and
is this Paul's conception? This question would never
be asked if it is clear that in the other world time and

space as we know them do not exist, also that in all
their thinking our finite minds are now so chained to
time and space that they cannot possibly conceive timelessness ("time no longer," Rev. 10:6) or spaceless-
ness so that, in order to be intelligible to us, even the
Scriptures must condescend to use terms of time when
speaking of eternity and terms of space when referring
to places in the other world. Thus heaven with its
glory is for us ever "up" and Christ ascended; and hell
with its κατάκριμα or condemnation is ever κατά, "down,"
the farthest down we can think, in "the lower parts of
the earth," the comparative being used in the sense of
"lowest" (R. 668). Do not ask, then, how far the
distance and how long the time for traversing it when
in the Ascension a cloud hid the body of Christ. Do
not ask, when considering the *vivificatio* in the tomb,
how far the distance to hell, how long a time it took
for Christ to get there, and how long a time he remained. What his κηρύσσειν (I Pet. 3:19) means Col.
2:15 states, and no man knows more about it than is
said there and in the present passage (v. 8, 9).

10) As v. 9 links up "he ascended" and "he descended" and makes them a whole, so v. 10 points to
the identity of the Ascender and the Descender: he is
the same person, could not have been the Ascender if
he had not been the Descender, and vice versa.

Now, however, Paul explains the εἰς ὕψος used in the
passage cited from the psalm by the new expression:
"away beyond and above all the heavens." The plural
"heavens" often = "heaven" in the Greek as in the
English but it does not equal that here where we have
"all the heavens." In II Cor. 12:2, 4 three heavens
are named, which are commonly thought to be the
atmospheric, the sidereal, and the angelic heavens
(Paradise). This suffices here. The seven heavens of
the rabbis have no Scriptural warrant and cannot be
attributed to Paul. But Christ's ascent "far above"

all the heavens must not be interpreted mechanically as implying a πού (somewhere) beyond all the heavens, beyond the place where God, the angels, and the blessed saints dwell; the sense is that the ascension gave Christ his exaltation and supremacy over all the heavens. We have the commentary in 1:20, 21; Phil. 2:9-11. To be far above the heavens is not to be somewhere that is not heaven — where would that be? Christ ascended "into heaven" (Acts 1:11) but not as Elijah did only to dwell there but to be exalted also in his human nature above, far above this eternal heaven and those beneath it. All heaven bows to him, and hell must.

The ascension and the exaltation of Christ had the purpose "that he might fill all the things," τὰ πάντα, definite, all that exists. As the two participles are aorists and express definite historical past acts, so "might fill" is an aorist subjunctive that is likewise a definite past act which is simultaneous with the exaltation and of permanent effect. The purpose was attained: he did fill all the things, does so now. The A. V. margin "fulfill" is incorrect. Oecumenius: "For, indeed, he long ago filled all things with his bare deity; and having become incarnate, that he might fill all things with his flesh, he descended and ascended." *C. Tr.* 1145. "He has ascended, not merely as any other saint, but, as the apostle testifies, above all heavens, and also truly fills all things, and being everywhere present, not only as God, but also as man, rules from sea to sea, and to the ends of the earth." *C. Tr.* 1025, also 821, 16.

This is the so-called ubiquity of the human nature of Christ, which goes beyond even Matt. 28:20b. It rests on the *communicatio idiomatum,* especially on the majestatic and the apotelesmatic genera. The ubiquity of Christ according to his human nature is best defined in conjunction with the omnipotence that is also bestowed on this nature: *praesentissimum ac*

potentissimum in creaturas dominium; hence it is not
an absolute presence (*nuda essentia*) but one connected with his universal dominion ("all things under
his feet").

To be sure, this is Dogmatics, but it is the dogmatical content of the Scriptural statement. All true Dogmatics merely restates Scripture, otherwise it is false
Dogmatics. Dogmatic exegesis is a different thing,
namely the predetermination of the exegesis itself
according to erroneous dogmatical views. Nestorianism denies the ubiquity of Christ's human nature. So
does Calvinism on the plea *finitum non est capax in-
finiti.* So does the *Einnaturenlehre* of the modern Germans. Against all of them stands this statement of
Paul's and many others of Scripture.

11) Christ, the great Giver, has been described,
also "the measure of the gift" he received in his human nature as "Christ," according to which "he gave
gifts to every single one of us" (v. 7). All this the
Ephesians must keep in mind when they look at any
one of the gifts Christ has bestowed on the church.
Paul now mentions the main ones and shows how they
all operate for the oneness of the *Una Sancta* and make
it grow as one body until it reaches its ultimate goal.
This is the connection with both v. 4-6 and v. 1-3.

**And he, he gave some as apostles, some as
prophets, some as evangelists, some as shepherds**
(pastors) **and teachers, etc.**

These are some of "the gifts he gave" (v. 7). Αὐτός
is demonstrative and emphatic and resumes the αὐτός
of v. 10 and all that has been said about the great
Giver: *He,* it is he who gave. Ἔδωκεν is not ἔθετο; "he
gave" denotes grace in the Giver, "he set or placed"
denotes authority and rule. The objects are τοὺς μέν,
τοὺς δέ, "some — some," and each is followed by a predicative accusative, which is indicated by the punctuation in the A. V. and by the insertion of "to be" in the

R. V. The point is not that some men received the apostleship, others prophecy, etc., but that these men themselves constitute the gift of Christ to the whole *Una Sancta,* yea, "to every single one of us" (v. 7). We now see why in v. 7 Paul uses "the grace" and not "the charisma" (or "charismata") : these men may be termed the grace bestowed on the church by Christ but scarcely the charisma. Paul's word is at times misunderstood, and complaint is made that he does not mention other gifts; but this supposes that the functions here indicated were gifts only to the functionaries whereas these functionaries are gifts to every single one of us. Whatever other gifts you and I have are secondary to this most essential group of gifts.

All these men are named according to their office and their work for the church. Not one of them is what he is just by or for himself. By "apostles" we understand the Twelve plus Paul, Matthias being the substitute for Judas. These were called immediately by Christ in person to serve in the specific way already indicated in 2:20. They constitute Christ's gift to every single one of us to this day. We continue steadfastly in the apostles' doctrine (Acts 2:42) as the foundation of the church and of our faith. While "apostle" is at times used in a wider sense so as to include Barnabas and other assistants of Paul, in a grouping like the present one the wider sense would only produce an indefinite term.

But who are the "prophets"? When we discussed 2:20 and 3:5 we already expressed our conviction that only the context of each passage is able to supply the correct answer, and that we cannot take "prophets" in the same sense in every passage, whether we think of the great Old Testament prophets, or of prophets like Agabus who received only incidental revelations about future events, or of prophets who had the charisma which all Christians are urged to acquire (I Cor. 14:1, etc.).

Between the first two types of prophets our choice would be the former because Agabus and those like him never stood out in the early church despite the fact that their revelations were received immediately. Only Agabus and the daughters of Philip are actually named in the New Testament as belonging to this class. Many, however, think that this class is here referred to. The possibility that Ephesus ever heard a prophet of this kind is not recorded. Now the statement that "Christ gave some as prophets" places us into the New Testament at a time after his ascension (v. 10) and thus eliminates the Old Testament prophets. The further statement that "Christ gave to every single one of us" (Ephesians) in v. 7 fits prophets in the third meaning of the word, those who spoke the revelations received by the apostles and thus benefited "every single one" who heard them.

The view that fixed offices are here listed, and that these prophets held no such office, is not unanswerable. Prophets like Agabus held no fixed office, they were called prophets only because they now and then received some minor revelation. Thus theirs, too, was not an "office" in the ecclesiastical sense of the word but only a certain standing in the church. Prophets in the wide sense of the word supplied evangelists and pastors and teachers. Thus they are here listed before these others. The functions indicated by the names are surely not exclusive, save the first, the specific work of the apostles. An evangelist would transmit the gospel revelation he had received from the apostles, so would pastors and teachers. Even an apostle would teach, and why not also some of these prophets? Church organization had not yet progressed much beyond the calling of regular elders (pastors).

"Evangelists" spread the gospel in new places. We have the very early example of Philip who first worked in Samaria (Acts 8:6-14) and who also worked along the coast up to Caesarea (Acts 8:40). These men resemble our missionaries. We may also think of Epaphras who founded the congregation at Colosse. They, too, were given "to every single one of us," for they did for the ordinary members what these could seldom do, planted the gospel in other localities. It was their gift and their ability that prompted them and not a fixed appointment unless we think of the regular assistants of Paul. The apostles certainly approved such work although the workers supported themselves.

The third τοὺς δέ makes one class of "shepherds and teachers," i. e., pastors of local congregations who were commonly called "elders" (the Ephesian elders, Acts 20:17) and termed ἐπίσκοποι, "overseers" (our "bishops"), by Paul himself in Acts 20:28 when he tells them "to shepherd the church of God." In John 21:15, etc., Jesus uses both "pasture" and "shepherd" my sheep. The latter is wider and includes the former, but the former is important enough to be mentioned separately. It is the feeding by means of teaching, hence "teachers" is the second term added by Paul. In I Tim. 5:17 note the elders "presiding well — especially laboring in word and teaching." So much of the Good Shepherd's work was teaching that one of his titles is "Teacher"; his command to the church in Matt. 28:20 is: "Teaching them to observe," etc.

When he uses these predicate nouns Paul's object evidently is to indicate what these men are as a gift to every one of us, i. e., what good we have from them. As "apostles," etc., they are our great benefactions from the exalted Christ. He had to be thus exalted before he could bestow this gift in accord with the measure of the gift to him himself, i. e., the glorification and exaltation of his human nature.

The challenging question is at times thrown out: "Where did Christ establish the Christian ministry?" Here we have one answer: *"He,* he gave some as apostles, etc." The Holy Ghost sent by Christ made the Ephesian elders overseers of the church of God. The establishment of the apostleship in Matt. 10:5, etc., is the institution of the ministry. In and on this office all else that we call offices rests. But our view becomes warped when the thought in our minds is that of institutionalism. Christ's instituting, as we often term it, is not institutionalism whether hierarchical or otherwise. Christ gave, he gave *men* to the church, men who are named according to their blessed *work.* He still so gives. Call it his institution, but only as Paul describes it, the δωρεά and δόματα, "gift and gifts" ("things given") of Christ.

12) **Christ gave these various workers in view of the complete outfitting of the saints for ministration work for upbuilding of the body of Christ, etc.** This expresses the purpose of the gift that consisted of the workers named. All are servants of the Word by which "the body of Christ," the *Una Sancta,* is to be built up; yet not these workers alone are to do this work, but all the saints are to be equipped and engaged in it like a growing body.

Paul's meaning is obscured by the punctuation of our versions and by that of editors of the Greek text. This happens when the text is regarded as consisting of three coordinate phrases, or when the two εἰς are coordinated, or the last εἰς is coordinated with πρός. We are pointed to inversions: Paul places the Christian ministry second, which he should have placed first; he is said to change his prepositions "without any obvious difference in sense." Three coordinate phrases assume that the second refers to the Christian ministry, but this would be in the wrong place. The coordinating of

the first and the third leaves the second hanging in the
air with nothing being said about it. The coordinating
of the last two in the way in which this is often done
has the ministry alone build the church, which is a
serious fault also in the other two coordinations.

The second phrase depends on the first, the third
on the second, the whole is a unit. Paul cannot say
that the leaders alone build up the church after having
so emphatically said that "to each single one of us"
Christ's grace has been given. Πρός = "with a view
to" and includes the whole of v. 12 as the purpose.
Καταρτισμός = "complete outfitting," it is like κατάρτισις
in II Cor. 13:9; "mending" and "repair" in R., W. P. is
inadequate. The Germans say *zur Fertigstellung der
Heiligen.* "For the perfecting of the saints" in our
versions may be wrongly understood by perfectionists
who point to it in order to substantiate their views of
perfect sanctification. The idea of perfectness lies
only in the preposition κατά in the noun. The saints
are to be perfectly, completely fitted out by all those
in the church who are able to transmit the Word. These
saints include also all the workers in the Word from
apostles down to teachers. They are to preach also
to each other and to themselves as well as to prospective converts and to the other church members and
thereby to fit themselves and all others out more and
more.

The thought is still incomplete. For what purpose
are these saints to get this outfitting? Paul adds: "for
ministration work." All the saints are to be engaged
in a work of ministration. Note the absence of articles. This is not the Christian ministry as some have
thought. It is a task of ministering to each other, for
"ministry" signifies a service rendered to benefit
others. All the saints have this blessed work to do
and are to get their complete outfit for it from the
apostles, etc., given to the church, i. e., from the Word.

But the thought is still incomplete. What is this
work of ministering to achieve? The answer is given
in the final phrase. This work is "for upbuilding the
body of Christ" (of the "one body," 3:16; 4:4), i. e.,
of the church itself. Construe: "ministry for upbuilding." The thought is this: to every one of us as the
saints who form the *Una Sancta* Christ gave some as
apostles, some as prophets, etc., for the purpose of
providing the necessary equipment for all to engage in
the blessed task of ministering to each other so as to
upbuild his body, the church itself. Οἰκοδομή is spiritual edification which consists of everything that develops our spiritual life. Paul is offering a wealth of
the equipment that is useful for this work in this
very epistle.

"Upbuilding" and "body" are not a mixing of figures, one referring to the construction of a building,
the other to the growth of a living body. To this day
we speak of body building; the development of a body
from childhood to manhood is very properly likened
to the building of a house or a temple. So in the following we have "no more children" — "unto a full-
grown man" — "grow up" — "the body fitly framed
together." This rich imagery is carried through.
Some think that "upbuilding" refers to the numerical
increase of the church and even have this consist of
bringing in the elect who were at first not believing
but were finally brought to faith because for some unknown reason *they* were elected in eternity. Paul himself tells us what "upbuilding" he had in mind; numbers are not in his mind nor any un-Biblical conception of the "elect."

It is worth while to note the exactness and the
precision with which every word of this verse is placed.
The composition is flawless; the reconstruction of
editors and of commentators is, therefore, the more
regrettable.

13)   Even the three phrases used in v. 12 have not
fully expressed Paul's thought.   Outfitting — for a
task — for building Christ's body still leave unan-
swered the question of completion, as to when this ἔργον
and this οἰκοδομή in which we are engaged will have
achieved their results.   To build the body of Christ
indicates only the work being done on that body.   When
may we now say that it *is* built?   What work must
be done?   When is the goal reached?   Paul would be
the last person not to answer this question.   He does
it with μέχρι which is used in the papyri with or without οὗ, with or without ἄν.

The clause modifies the phrase introduced by πρός
(all of v. 12) : **until we, the whole number, arrive at
the oneness of the faith and of the knowledge of the
Son of God, at a man full-grown, at an age measure
of** (i. e., marked by) **the fulness of Christ; etc.**

Fully equipped by the teachers of the Word for
our task of building up the *Una Sancta,* we are to work
on until we all attain full Christian manhood, which
means full maturity.   Paul significantly adds the apposition οἱ πάντες, which definitely means "the whole
number" of us.   In their work of ministration (v. 12)
the saints are to neglect none of their number, for all
are to arrive at the goal of spiritual maturity through
our mutual ministration, actually arrive (aorist subjunctive).   In a manner this task never ends because
new generations of children and new converts ever
require our ministration; from another viewpoint it
does end, namely as one and the other does arrive at
the maturity indicated.   The view that this arrival
occurs at the hour of death or at the end of the world
at the time of the Parousia overlooks what follows.
The maturity here referred to is full-grown manhood
in faith and in knowledge in contrast with immature
and inexperienced childhood.   Paul was such a man.
The idea that such manhood is not reached before

death, that the saints are always only children in this life, is contradicted by Paul's own words.

The three εἰς phrases are construed with the verb "arrive at," the second phrase being appositional to the first, the third appositional to the second: "arrive *at* the oneness, *at* a full-grown man, *at* an age measure," etc. The goal is thus stated in a complete way. "At the oneness," etc., reverts to the oneness mentioned in v. 3, which is based on the oneness detailed in v. 4-6. We are to strive diligently for this subjective oneness (v. 3) on the one objective basis (v. 4-6).

The unity of Paul's thought is striking. The oneness we are to attain by mutual ministration is that "of the faith and of the knowledge of the Son of God." In the Greek the last genitive is objective and modifies both "the faith" and "the knowledge." The Greek says regularly, "faith of Christ," he being the object of faith, whereas we say, "faith in Christ." So "the knowledge," too, has this object. The idea that the oneness referred to is that *between* our faith and our knowledge is unsatisfactory. Paul is not discussing the relation of these two to each other. By placing the genitives side by side Paul does not mean that our knowledge is to harmonize with our faith, that, although we have faith, our knowledge is at first imperfect and must be raised to the level of our faith.

The oneness is the one that unites us all. It is the oneness belonging to (possessive genitive) the faith and to the knowledge. At this oneness we are to arrive both regarding our faith and regarding our knowledge. At first, especially in the case of all beginners but often also later in the case of many a saint, faith and certainly also knowledge have much about them that is imperfect, immature, faulty. If these imperfections are allowed to remain, this will damage the inner oneness of the saints; those who have the faults are not welded together with the rest as they should be.

They may even become detached, drift away, or be drawn away. Faults weaken those who have them, but here the weakness referred to is lack of strong oneness with the other saints.

Paul places "the faith" first, "the knowledge" second, and for the latter uses ἐπίγνωσις, which is more than γνῶσις. Not mere intellectual knowledge is referred to, such as *gnosis* might express, but true heart knowledge. True knowledge is a part of faith when the latter begins ("how shall they believe in him of whom they have not heard?" Rom. 10:14); but much real knowledge is the outcome of faith, it is even impossible without faith. When faith reads the Scriptures it finds treasure after treasure of knowledge which unbelief never finds; when faith is exercised by confession and life it discovers by its own experience more and more knowledge of the saving truth which unbelief cannot know.

Paul has written the article with both nouns and views each separately, yet both have the same object, "the Son of God." We see his meaning, a fault in the faith will effect the knowledge, a fault in the knowledge the faith. Although they are distinct, they yet interact and are thus articulated by Paul and placed in this order. Faultless faith and faultless knowledge, whether these be of small or of great degree, form the oneness which is the goal of our mutual ministration task. By setting this as the *goal* Paul by no means excuses the faults of faith and of knowledge which mark so many believers and prevent them from being fully one with the one body of Christ. Note again v. 3. He is also not indifferent to weakness in either our faith or our knowledge. Real oneness = strong adherence.

By not naming the object "Christ" but "the Son of God" Paul makes manifest the divine greatness and glory of him whom he has just described as the

Ascender and Descender who fills all things (v. 10).
Our oneness centers in him. The claim of some that
Paul never called Christ "the Son of God" is here once
more met. We see, too, how serious any fault in our
faith and in our knowledge is, for every such fault in
our oneness involves the Son of God. How diligent
should we then be to guard this oneness (v. 3), to
minister to each other in such diligence, to remove
every rent and rift in oneness, and to overcome all
indifference and carelessness. Be sure you yourself
are fully in this oneness. Many a one who is only
partly in this oneness, perhaps not in it at all, the fanatic especially, is amazingly diligent in undermining
"the oneness of the faith and of the knowledge of the
Son of God," and wrecking many a soul.

A second time, by means of an apposition, Paul
states at what we are to arrive: "at a man full-grown."
He uses a concrete expression to express what is really
an abstract thought: "at full-grown manhood," or at
full spiritual maturity. He uses the right word ἀνήρ,
male man, connoting full maturity of strength, and not
ἄνθρωπος, a human being, which has no such connotation
since a newborn babe is also a human being. Τέλειος =
having attained the goal. It is here in contrast with
"children" and is to be understood in the sense of
"mature," "full-grown." We have no etymological
English equivalent; "perfect" (A. V.) may pass, but it
must not be understood in the sense of perfectionism.
Full-grown manhood or maturity is the goal for all
beginners, also for all others who have lagged behind.
There is a strong argument in the figurative term.

The oneness in the first phrase = the full-grown
man = also the age measure in the next phrase; hence
all are singular. This bars out the idea of individualization in the singular "man" as though it intends to
divide οἱ πάντες. Since "we all" form the church, it
would be incongruous to make "a full-grown man" =

the church and to say that "we all (the church) are to *arrive* at a full-grown man" (the church). This also does not permit making "a full-grown man" = "the body of Christ" (v. 12).

The second appositional phrase completes the statement of the goal at which we are to arrive: "at an age measure (no articles) of the fulness of Christ." The debate as to whether ἡλικία, a person's "age," may also mean "stature" (our versions) need not disturb us since "age" fits the thought quite well. Pointing to "grow up" in v. 15 and "growth" in v. 16 does not establish the meaning "stature," for "measure of age" intends to define τέλειον just as "the fulness of Christ" defines the preceding term, "the Son of God." The indefinite "a measure of age" or "age measure" needs something to complete the concept; this is "the fulness of Christ." Following Luther's *des vollkommenen Alters Christi,* and Calvin's *plena aetas,* some regard "age of fulness" as an adjectival genitive = "the full age of Christ," B.-P. 975, *Vollreife des Christus.* But this cannot be done because the two unarticulated nouns belong together: "age-measure." Secondly, what could be meant by "the full age of Christ"? Is it thirty years when he reached manhood? Can you think of anything else?

Some refer to 1:23 where the church is called "the fulness of him who fills all the things in all ways." But if "the fulness of Christ" = the church, we again have the incongruity that we who constitute the church are to arrive at a certain age of the church. At what age, pray? "Fulness" is also not "perfection" so that we could say, "At the measure of the height of the perfection of Christ." In 3:19 "the fulness of God" is that which fills him, his love, grace, etc., all of which we are to know; so here "the fulness of Christ" is all that fills him. The genitive characterizes: "an age-measure marked by the fulness of Christ." We are to arrive at this age-measure, it is the goal for all of us. Some attain it quickly by maturing spiritually by leaps and bounds. Alas, many lag, love to stay in the infant age. They have only a little of the fulness of Christ but could and should have all its wealth.

Paul rightly uses "the fulness." Yet not in the sense of Christ's perfections so that the sense would be the arrival of every believer at an age of moral perfection, of perfectly Christlike character. "The fulness" makes clear what lies in "the Son of God," he who is the Ascender and Descender and therefore has so many "gifts" for men, among them the apostles, etc., who are to equip us with the Word for attaining our goal. Christ's fulness includes all the divine, saving realities which exist in him. C.-K. 927 has *Inhalt seines Wesens* and so refers to 1:23, Christ filling all things in every way.

By faith and real knowledge we are to appropriate all the realities that are in Christ, thus achieving the goal of oneness in the Word, of full-grown spiritual maturity. The saving realities are presented by teaching and preaching, hence apostles, etc., down to pastors and teachers are mentioned. Any proper and adequate presentation of any one of these realities is a doctrine which faith and knowledge are to receive fully. We are to have their entire fulness, are to attain an age of such fulness. To know only something about Christ, God's Son, is not enough, it is not the full oneness with our fellow saints, not full-grown manhood. We must apprehend all that our faith and our knowledge are able to understand.

As for moral perfections, Christian character, Christlikeness in life, these spring like a living plant and tree from true faith and true knowledge and from no other soil. Take away the fulness of the verities in Christ, and all that is able to grow in our lives are works of our own righteousness, imitations. Remember the Pharisees, study the "gospel" of the modernists who turn the Son into a son and abolish the Ascender and Descender.

14) Paul is not yet through. He first adds the negative result of arrival at the goal, and then in v. 15, etc., the positive result. The negative is striking: **so that no longer we are infants, tossed to and fro by waves and carried about by every wind of teaching in the gambling of men in craftiness after the expert method of the deception; etc.** There is difficulty when ἵνα is regarded as expressing purpose, for no writer would say that we reach manhood and full maturity *in order* to grow up (v. 15). This would be a strange hysteron proteron, for we grow up in order to arrive at manhood. In order to avoid this inversion v. 14 is made parallel to v. 13 and is regarded as a kind of restatement. But this view overlooks the fact that v. 13 is a temporal clause: *"until* we arrive at," the parallel of which cannot be a purpose clause: *"in order that* we may be." Not a few refer the purpose clause back to v. 11: "he gave . . . in order that we may no longer be infants." In order to maintain the idea of purpose the statement is at times made that Paul always uses ἵνα with a final sense and never with a subfinal or a non-final meaning. But read R. 997, etc., regarding consecutive ἵνα. When we are doing so, it is well to know that the old reluctance in regard to thinking that this connective can express anything but purpose, which view dates from the time before the Koine was fully known, is still manifest. We see it in B.-D. 391, 5: "hardly to express actual result," and in the comments on many passages, in which the commentator hesitates to say that ἵνα introduces a result clause.

We have actual result: "until we all actually arrive (aorist) at a full-grown man . . . so that we are (as a result) no longer infants, etc., . . . but have actually grown up, etc." (again aorist), v. 15. Even the view that ἵνα indicates contemplated result weakens the thought. "Infants" is the opposite of "a full-grown man." It is a plural as Paul so often places the plural beside the singular, but here the word is properly the plural because the thought now concerns the individuals. Infants are helpless against assaults; they must be protected, carried in the arms of others, and in the case of these infants such protecting arms are not always present. There is the same argumentative appeal in "infants" as there was in the previous "full-grown man." It is pitiful never to get beyond the infantile stage. Yet some Christians seem to be afraid of growing up; or, remaining infants, imagine they are strong men, which is pitiful in another way.

Every one of the modifiers is important. Paul's mastery in combining so many terms in such a terse manner, each being in its exact place, with supreme effect deserves due recognition. How many secular writers have anything that is equal or comparable? Paul always dominates his figurative terms and does not let them dominate him; he makes them carry his thought, and does not let them sway or swing his thought into a mere accommodation to themselves. "Infants" might dominate us so as to stay with its imagery and to use only what this term affords. Its *tertium* is helplessness; Paul takes that and does not insert another idea.

"Tossed to and fro by waves and carried about by every wind of the teaching in, etc.," advances to a graphic description of the helplessness already indicated. The idea is not that of physical infants in a boat who are helpless to manage it in waves and wind; physical men, who know nothing about managing boats, are infants amid wind and waves. Such is the helplessness Paul describes, which is due to not being fitted out properly with the Word in faith and in

knowledge. The imagery is not that of a violent storm
foundering a vessel but of drifting at the whim of
waves and wind.

Διδασκαλία = "teaching" in the passive sense (C.-K.
294) : what men teach, "doctrine." "Every wind of
doctrine" is most expressive. Winds veer and shift,
blow now in this, now in that direction. "Waves of
doctrine" is not necessary because the winds cause the
waves. The true doctrine is ever one, solid like Gibraltar, because the verities it expresses are the changeless fact. But every doctrine of men is mere wind,
unstable, transient, causing a drift now hither, now
thither.

The waves should not be allegorized. Paul is not
saying that all the saints are afloat on the sea (sea
of life, sea of this world), the babes among them drifting around helplessly, the men among them steering
a safe course to the heavenly haven. Only the babes
are described, we are shown only how their helplessness amid the false doctrines of men looks. The literal word "doctrine" interprets the figurative terms
just as in John 15: "I (literal) am the Vine (figure) ;
you (literal) are the branches" (figure). Greek abstract nouns may have the article when the concept
denotes something definite.

"In the gambling of men in craftiness" belongs together as the absence of the article with the second
phrase shows. The whole phrase does not modify
"infants" or "infants" plus the participles but the
participles alone. From κυβεία we have our word cube.
The idea of chance suggested by waves and wind is
advanced by the allied figure of throwing dice, a game
of chance, one form of "gambling." But Paul advances
still more when he calls it the gambling of men "in
craftiness," πανουργία, the ability to do anything, which
is used in an evil sense: resort to dishonest means,

"knavery." The picture is one of helplessness, exposed to chance, crafty chance at that.

"Of men" is in contrast to God although it is without emphasis. "Whereby they lie in wait to deceive" (A. V.) is not translation but paraphrase. Μεθοδεία (found only here and in the late papyri) = *kunstgemaesses Verfahren;* and πλάνη is "deceit" or "deception" and is accepted also by M.-M. 516 in the sense of "error" in the New Testament passages where it occurs; hence the R. V.: "after the wiles of error." Πρός, "toward," has the force of fostering the tricky expertness or skillfulness which belongs to error when men, like crafty gamblers, take advantage of the unwary in dealing it out to them.

Paul's effective characterization of error and of errorists is surely drawn from his own experience. He had been in vessels that were drifting helplessly in waves and wind; he had seen soldiers and sailors use loaded dice to fleece some innocent greenhorn. They had their expert system which was all fair and honest to the inexperienced eye but deadly in its cunning and trickiness. Paul thus draws his composite picture and combines the significant terms compactly. Error always operates with a tricky expertness. It uses Bible passages (apparently according to their real meaning) and reasonings (apparently sound) and thus easily fools the "infants" in Christian faith and knowledge, who have not yet grown up to Christian manhood and the age-measure of the fulness of Christ.

We cannot say that Paul has any special error in mind such as the beginnings of Gnosticism; he speaks in general terms. Paul's expressions contain no shadow of excuse for error or for errorists; he tears off their mask. Those who deviate from the truth cannot do so with moral integrity. Error perverts its adherents in subtle moral ways. This is often denied

but never by Paul who knew the effects of error fully.
He who is not honest with the true doctrines of the
Word simply cannot be honest with the way in which
he handles that truth, he mishandles it when he filches
it from others.

15) Δέ turns to the positive side. Ἵνα still governs and now states a further result: "until we all
actually arrive (aorist) at a full-grown man . . . so
that we are (as a result) no longer infants . . . **but,**
(as a result) **speaking truth in love, get grown up
with respect to him in regard to everything, who is
the Head, Christ; he from whom all the body, as being framed together and knit together by means of
the supply of every joint, (i. e.,) according to the
working in** (its) **measure of each single part, produces the growth of the body for upbuilding of its
own self in love.**

Paul inserts "speaking truth in love" as the brief
opposite of "the gambling of men in craftiness after
the expert method of the deception" or error they hold.
As in Gal. 4:16, the participle = "speaking truth."
"Speaking truthfully" is practically the same, for lies
cannot be spoken truthfully. "In love" is added because the knavery of error lacks both truth (truthfulness) and love, and because speaking the truth properly goes together with the love of intelligence and
purpose (see 1:4). Those who actually arrive at the
goal indicated by the three phrases in v. 13 always
use only the divine truth of the apostles, etc., (v. 11),
i. e., the Word, in their work of ministering (v. 12);
and even as theirs is a ministry for the spiritual benefit
of others, a true διακονία, they combine this truth with
their love, which understands what others need and
purposes only to meet that need.

We have seen how error and deceit go together,
how falseness to the Word always goes together with
moral falseness in the heart. The opposite is also true.

Faithfulness to the truth and the Word goes together
with purity and nobleness of motive, with true love,
in fact, creates this high motive. Paul knows that
some preach Christ because of envy, strife, and contention, with wrong motives, and speaks of this in Phil.
1:15-18. This is abnormal and a giving way to the
flesh. It is the nature of truth ever to cleanse the
heart, especially when this is handling the truth.
"Speaking the truth" includes all teaching, all confession; the formula of the confessions is: "We believe, teach, and confess." Paul's "we" includes himself as an apostle, all his own preaching and teaching,
admonition, rebuke, comfort. The love with which he
did this never yielded an iota of the truth, it would
not have been love if it had done so.

The view is untenable that if we construe "speaking the truth in love," this would be a love toward
those who cunningly defend error, with whom Paul
wants us to have nothing to do. No matter with whom
we deal we are to speak the truth in love. Since this
participle belongs to what follows, it is plain that Paul
is here thinking of our contact with our brethren and
not of polemics with errorists. To construe "in love
get to grow up" sounds as though Paul has in mind a
growth only in love. The emphasis the phrase would
thus receive would be strange and misleading. Moreover, the main verb has its adverbial modifier, τὰ πάντα,
"in regard to everything," which takes in more than
love. Because "for upbuilding of its own self in love"
in v. 16 is to be construed as one phrase is not proof
that "in love get grown up" is likewise one phrase.
The very rhythm of the expressions used shows where
each phrase belongs.

The present subjunctive ὦμεν is durative; the aorist
subjunctive αὐξήσωμεν is punctiliar, namely ingressive:
"get grown up" (intransitive). The idea of growing
up continues the figure of "infants" and of "a man

full-grown." We cannot agree with translations and interpretations like the ones found in our versions: grow up *"into* him who is the Head, Christ." To be told that growing up *into* the head is not an incongruous idea does not remove the incongruity. Do we, by growing *into* the head, become part of that Head, Christ? Some translate *"unto* the Head" as though he is the aim or goal, which is equally unthinkable. "Unto" also does not mean, *"up to* Christ's stature" (R., *W. P.*), nor "into" the "center of our life *in* him." Paul clearly distinguishes "the Head, Christ," and "all the body" and never confuses them.

He even adds the adverbial accusative τὰ πάντα, "regarding everything," which is definite at that: "all the things that pertain to our relation to this Head." This makes it plain that εἰς αὐτόν means, "in relation to him." This signifies neither "in communion with him" nor "in likeness to him." We "get grown up" in every respect as our relation to him requires of us, and that relation is at once stated, he is the Head, and we the body of this Head. The relation indicated is that the body of any head should correspond to its head. The body cannot remain an "infant" indefinitely. Its growth cannot remain stunted, not even in one or the other respect. Especially this body with its relation to this Head who is Christ. We must all actually arrive at the proper oneness of the faith and of the knowledge of the Son of God, at a man full-grown, at an age measure such as belongs to the fulness of Christ (v. 13). The emphasis is on the adverbial "in every respect."

How natural, proper, even necessary such growth is the relative clause points out: "who is the Head, Christ." The term "Head" puts Christ into connection with the entire body as a unit, which includes "all of us." (v. 13). The body must correspond to the Head with which it is in vital relation. Paul writes "with respect to him" and places the antecedent of the pronoun, "Christ," at the end of the relative clause and thus makes it strongly emphatic as it ought to be.

16) The full relation of this divine Head, Christ, to the body and to all its members is brought out in a second relative clause. This clause is emphatic and has the force of an independent statement: *"he,* from whom the whole body," etc. See other relative clauses of this kind in Rom. 2:29; 3:8; 3:30; etc. The importance of the statement added in this fashion is apparent from the wealth of the modifications which make the thought so weighty.

Here we have another instance in which Paul makes his figurative expressions subservient to the reality he is presenting and does not let the figure dominate the reality. Ordinary bodies and heads grow in their relation to each other. This is not true of the Head, Christ; it is true only of the *Una Sancta,* his body in its relation to Christ. Paul brings that thought out with full clarity; he confines the figurative terms to the body, he remains their master. It is something worth learning from Paul.

We do not translate, "from *which."* Since "Christ" precedes, the only correct rendering is *"from whom."* Christ is the source (ἐκ) of the spiritual growth here described. Yes, Christ is the Head of this body; the emphatic insertion of his name indicates that as the Head he is vastly more than any other bodily head would be. He is himself the life, all the life of his body is drawn from him alone. We have nothing in nature that is comparable to this. The heavenly relations ever dwarf those of mere earth and nature. Our Head does not grow, only we, his body, grow, and our entire growth comes from him.

In this last clause Paul reaches back and combines all the main points he has developed from v. 1 onward. Once more we see the mastery of his mind. Here there

is again the great oneness, the body framed and knit
together, this body being in connection with its Head.
Here there is now still more clearly the place of "each
single one of us" (v. 7) and "the all" (οἱ πάντες, v. 13)
of us framed and knit together in oneness under Christ,
the one Head and Lord (v. 5). Here there is again
every one of us with the grace (v. 7) and the gifts (v.
8) given to him, making his contribution of supply in
the ministry work for upbuilding the whole. Here
there is again the oneness we are to keep (v. 3) with
all its growth that is due to Christ. The description
of the unifying process is thus adequately completed.

"All the body" includes every one of its members,
not one being omitted, compare οἱ πάντες in v. 13 and
"we" in the preceding verbs. The word contains the
thought of spiritual life; hence the predicate speaks
about making growth. Yet *this* body draws all its life
from Christ.

We regard the two present participles as descriptive: "as being framed together and knit together by
means of the supply of every joint." Both are passive.
In regard to the first note 2:21. Body building and
growth are not mixed figures as we have shown in
v. 12. The first participle contains our word "harmony" and is amplified by the second, "knit together,"
which is used with reference to men who are making
a treaty or a contract. We may perhaps say that
"framed together" is the more figurative and "knit
together" more in line with the reality. We prefer to
regard both as passive and not as middle; the agent
involved is omitted because it is not stressed, yet this
agent would be Christ.

But the means used are named: "by means of the
supply of every joint." Our versions offer the meaning by means of a paraphrase. The fact that ἀφή =
"joint" (not "contact, sensation, feeling," or something else) is plain from the close parallel found in Col.

2:19: "through the joints and bands." A note in Galen (Kuehn's edition, XIX, 87) shows that Hippocrates, the father of medicine, used this word in that sense; see Ewald. We, therefore, do not accept the rendering of the R. V. margin which suggests that the Greek means, "Through every joint of the supply," as though the first genitive is the object of the preposition and not the second.

Paul is not speaking of the first formation of the church but of its subsequent growth, not in numbers, but in faith, knowledge, and life. The means for holding the body together as a living unit are like those that are found in any physical body: the *Handreichung*, supply, furnished by "every joint," i. e., by every bone, muscle, and ligament supplying its vital forces. Whether ἐπιχορηγία (not used in the classics) is passive: "supply," or abstract and active: "supplying," makes little difference either here or in Phil. 1:19. Every supplying would surely produce a supply. The *simplex* of the word was used to denote the defraying of the great cost of the solemn public choruses by some wealthy patron. The connotation is generous abundance freely supplied.

The phrase introduced by κατά does not modify "supply," nor does it modify the verb ποιεῖται. The latter would lend the phrase a disorganizing emphasis, and even then the verb and not the object should follow immediately. In regard to the former, "the supply" needs no description, least of all one that is so disproportionate as the one contained in this phrase would be. The phrase introduced by κατά is appositional to the phrase introduced by διά and is thus explicative: framed and knit together "by means of every joint's supply," namely, "according to the working in its measure of each single part." In this manner the means operate. "Every joint" and "each single part" are practically the same, yet "joint" stresses the living juncture with other joints, "part" only the general relation to the body as a whole. But note how "each single part" resumes "each single one of us" in v. 7.

'Εν μέτρῳ, like εἰς μέτρον in v. 13, needs no article since a genitive follows which indicates what measure is referred to. The English is, "in its measure," not, "in due measure" (R. V.). The "working" or energy of each individual part of the body has already been described in v. 11 as "ministry work." As parts of a living spiritual body each one is alive, and in its measure each part, according to the gifts bestowed upon it, especially according to the faith and the knowledge (v. 13), works to aid others in a true *diakonia*.

Thus with each single part energetically contributing its measure of supply, all the body "produces the growth of the body for upbuilding of its own self in love." The source of all the spiritual growth is Christ alone. "Increase" (our versions) is inexact, for αὔξησιν repeats αὐξήσωμεν, "get grown." The object is placed forward for the sake of emphasis. It is blessed "growth" which all the body makes. Drawing from Christ, this whole body is able to make its own growth. The spiritual life in the church develops as life.

Instead of twice using the reflexive pronoun: "all the body makes the growth *of itself* for upbuilding *of itself*," Paul uses the noun in place of the first "itself" and thereby also removes any ambiguity as to the antecedent: "all the body makes growth (not merely of each single part but) of the body." The verb is properly the reflexive middle: the body makes this growth for itself.

A final modifier rounds out the whole thought: this growth is being made "for (the) upbuilding of its own self in love," v. 12, so that the great object, "upbuilding the body of Christ" in all its parts or members, is attained; v. 13, so that "we all arrive at the oneness of

the faith and of the knowledge of the Son of God"
with none being neglected or left behind. This making
growth is ever in progress, hence we have the present
tense. Some who are in the church have reached full
manhood in faith and in knowledge, have actually become full-grown (τέλειος in v. 13) ; they are no longer
"infants" (v. 14). As such they will contribute the more
"abundant and generous supply" in all their "energetic working." But there are ever new beginners, all
the children and the youth, all the new converts; all
these necessarily start as "infants," all these need
abundant "supply" to become full-grown as soon as
possible. Paul's is a perfect picture of the church as
a living, unit body. Compare the picture Jesus draws
in John 15:1, etc. He brings in also the dead branches
that are cut away from the Vine; Paul omits them
from his imagery.

"For upbuilding of its own self in love" names the
sphere in which this upbuilding occurs. The interac-
tion of the members of the church is entirely "in connection with love," the love of intelligence filled with
corresponding purpose. The love here referred to is
not Christ's love for us or our love for him but, as in
v. 15, our love for each other. Paul twice writes, "in
love." Furnishing abundant and generous spiritual
supply to each other is the supreme work of love. The
motive of God and of Christ in all that they do for us
is the motive that prompts us to do all that we do toward spiritually upbuilding the church. Note that the
object of the upbuilding is the body itself and not love.
Love is the motivating sphere. Paul is not saying that
we are to build up love in the body but that we are to
build up the body and to do this with loving hearts.

Paul has presented his admonition to unity (v. 1-3)
and has supported this by pointing to the unit basis
(v. 4-6) and by describing the unifying work (v. 7-
16). He now proceeds with further admonitions, all of

which rest on the fundamental one so fully elaborated thus far.

*   *   *

Four Admonitions for All the Members of the Una Sancta.

17) This group of four admonitions is plainly general and extends from 4:17 to 5:21. A further group which deals with specific classes of members follows in 5:22-6:9. Then comes the concluding admonition in 6:10, etc.

It is worth noting that in the first group of four admonitions each is connected with the preceding one (v. 17; v. 25; 5:1; 5:15). In marked contrast to this connected chain note the second group of four in which each is placed beside the other without connectives (5:22; 5:25; 6:1; 6:5). In 6:4 only "and" joins the fathers to the children and in 6:9 the masters to the slaves. Those four of the first group are properly connected, for the one admonition entails the other, and they also apply to all the members of the *Una Sancta.* Not so the next four, each of which is intended for only a limited class: wives — husbands — children and fathers — slaves and masters. The progression in this group is the natural one of the status of the classes named.

It is certainly worth noting these points of structure. The last admonition is plainly marked as such by "finally" in 6:10. This would give us ten admonitions: one + four + four + one. Ten is the number of greater rhetorical completeness, four the number of minor completeness, both are frequently used by Paul. One might make the first group consist of five admonitions by dividing 5:1-14 at v. 7, where another connective appears, but this would make 5:1-6 entirely negative. It would also make the total number of admonitions eleven with the first group consisting of five, which is quite unusual in Paul's style.

*   *   *

The Admonition to Put off the Old and to Put on the New Man

In v. 1 the statement: "Accordingly I admonish you, I, the prisoner in the Lord," places emphasis on the one admonishing. Now the verb is doubled and thus receives the emphasis. So also "this" is placed first and emphasizes the admonition plus the admonishing and no longer the admonisher. **This, therefore, I declare and testify in the Lord** appears only here, and nothing similar to it is found in connection with the other admonitions. We thus conclude that this preamble is intended to introduce all the admonitions that follow. At the same time this preamble separates these admonitions from the first one (v. 1-16), and properly so since the first one regarding spiritual unity in faith and in knowledge, i. e., in the Word, dominates all the rest. We thus also consider it ill-advised to make οὖν connect only with v. 16, or to refer it back only to v. 1. All that is stated in v. 1-16 is a unit, and the connection is according.

"This I declare and testify in the Lord" is important. Indeed, putting off the old and putting on the new man includes all that Paul has to offer in the way of admonitions. "I declare" makes "this" stand out in an objective way, and "I testify" stands out as personal testimony from Paul himself. "In the Lord" connects Paul's declaration and testimony with "the Lord" to whom all the Ephesians and Paul himself belong. See v. 1 for the same phrase. "In the Lord" touches the motive which prompts Paul to declare and testify and appeal to the motive which ought to make his readers comply by spiritual obedience.

This, **that you no longer walk as also the Gentiles walk in** (the) **vanity of their mind, as having been darkened in their understanding, as having been alienated from the life of God because of the ignorance that is in them, because of the petrifaction of their heart; etc.**

The infinitive is appositional and epexegetical and is really indirect discourse and not a substitution for an indicative but for an imperative: "Do not walk any longer." This verb is commonly used to denote our entire conduct as this is governed by our hearts. "No longer" implies that at one time the Ephesians did so walk as they are now no longer to walk. But the present tense also implies that they had already made the change and are now to continue thus. Paul describes this wrong walk concretely by a reference to the Gentiles in the midst of whom the Ephesians lived, whose wicked mode of life they constantly beheld. This was the kind of a life they had once led, a life that should now be forever impossible for them.

"You = all the Ephesians. The fact that some of them were former Jews we have seen in 2:11 where Paul addresses the Gentile believers separately, and the following discussion shows how the Gentile believers are on an equality with their Jewish fellow believers. This present reference to the Gentiles does not imply that all of Paul's readers were former Gentiles, that this epistle was not intended for Ephesus where some of the members were former Jews but was an encyclical that was addressed to other Asian churches that were composed entirely of Gentile believers. For one thing, it would be strange, indeed, and impossible of proof that even such other, recently formed churches were wholly Gentile. "As also the Gentiles walk" presents these pagans as the glaring example which all the Ephesians should avoid.

These Gentiles were the extreme and thus included all that was less. The Scriptures constantly use extremes in this way. In Matt. 5:21, etc., and 27, etc., Jesus shows that murder and adultery include all that is accounted less by men. So it is here. Their religion might keep the Jews from certain actions of the pagans; even pagans did not always go to the extreme of paganism. But all spiritual vanity, ignorance, hardness of heart, with the resultant conduct, are alike. Thus the extreme of paganism includes it all.

"As also the Gentiles walk in (the) vanity of their mind" includes the entire wrong walk. This is the summary of the negative side; all that follows is elaboration. The summary is stated in the phrase "in (the) vanity of their mind"; all that follows expounds this "vanity," which does not need an article because it is made definite by the genitive. Derived from μάταιος, the noun means that which does not lead to the goal. The companion noun which is derived from κενός = that which is without real content, hollow. The two are often confused. C.-K. 723 and others have ματαιότης mean *Gehaltlosigkeit*, but the Greek word for that idea is κενότης (which is not found in the New Testament).

Paul does not say that the Gentiles are addlepated, that their mind has nothing in it; it is only too full. He says that all that their mind contains leads them to nothing. It puts them on a course that ends far from the goal. Their mind directs them on a wild-goose chase. Κενός would put nothing at the start, in the mind itself; μάταιος puts nothing at the end of the whole career that is directed by the mind.

Νοῦς is the proper word, "mind" as that which produces thought yet not only in the sense of intellect; for "vanity" implies a goal and an aim for the mind. The directing will is included; the thoughts aim to bring the person to the right goal. In this case the goal is vacuity, emptiness, delusion. See Delitzsch, *Biblische Psychologie*, 178, etc. What a picture! Men with thinking, willing minds, rational creatures, walking and walking on and on throughout life, following the dictates of a mind that leads them at every step and at the end to nothing, to monumental, tragic failure!

18) The two masculine participles are construed *ad sensum* with the neuter "Gentiles." The ὄντες modifies both and makes both periphrastic perfects, the tense indicates a past act with its present and enduring result, the periphrastic form stresses the continuing condition: once darkened and alienated, these Gentiles go on in this terrible condition. The agent of these passives is left unnamed, it is Satan. Regarding the second periphrastic participle compare Col. 1:21. Paul mentions the alienated condition in 3:12, but now "from the life of God" takes us farther. It is well to remember that the Scriptures speak of "the darkness" as being a definite evil power or monster, and that the word includes what this power produces. This conception is reflected in the verbs σκοτίζω and σκοτόω, "to darken."

"In the understanding" is the dative of relation: "as regards," etc. Διάνοια, "understanding," is not the same as νοῦς, "mind." The plural = "reasonings," 2:3. The singular = the activity and the product of the mind. The Gentiles live not only as men who have utter darkness all around them but as men whose entire understanding and thought are darkness. They have not merely been plunged into darkness so that, if they could get out of it, they could see; the darkness has filled them themselves in their very understanding where there should be light. One should get the full force of the fact Paul is stating.

The best commentary is Rom. 1:19, etc., to which add John 9:40, 41. Even the light of nature, which is so bright all around these men, they do not see. They consider themselves wise and are become fools. The Pharisees claimed to be οἱ βλέποντες, those who see, and because of their inner blindness, combined with arrogance, saw nothing. Many a present-day "scientist" claims to know but knows nothing as he ought to know it. The same is true with regard to the light of Bible facts. It shines and shines, but the darkened "understanding" of the skeptic and the modernist shuts out the light. How could minds like this arrive at the right destination?

The second participle is added without a connective and states the result of the first. The condition of having been darkened involves the condition of having been alienated from the life of God, the life that belongs to him (possessive genitive). The word ζωή (*vita qua vivimus*), the vital principle itself, is never used in the sense of βίος (*vita quam vivimus*), the course of our physical life. The genitive is often made one of origin, but it is like "the grace, the mercy, the love of God," so that Jesus can say: "I am the Life." In secular Greek ζωή refers to physical life, consider "zoology" as compared with "biography." The New Testament has elevated the word very considerably. It thus carries a soteriological meaning. We see it most clearly in Gal. 2:20: no longer does Paul live, but Christ lives in him. This = that the life of God is in him; and this is "life eternal." It is begotten in us, bestowed by the quickening mentioned in 2:5. Alienation from this life is death in transgressions and sins (2:1), ἀπώλεια, destruction or perdition. The "vanity" of v. 17 consists in this that the life of God is never reached.

The first διά modifies both participles, and the second διά expounds the first. To make the two phrases parallel and to let them modify only the second participle, is unwarranted; nor can the first phrase be construed with the first participle, the second phrase with the second. The underlying reason or cause for having been darkened and alienated is "the ignorance, the one that is in them," and the reason or cause for this ignorance is "the petrifaction of their heart." This looks like reversing things, that Paul should say, "Darkening and alienation cause the ignorance, and the ignorance causes the hardening." But Paul is right, the facts support him, and he is ever true to the facts.

Note that he does not write, "Because of *their* ignorance" (a mere αὐτῶν), but, "Because of the ignorance, the one that is in them." It is not an acquired ignorance that is due to absence of light and information; it is an original ignorance that is in them from the start, the ignorance of inborn sin. Rom. 1:19, etc., states that men had the full light of nature and knew God and then in their wise folly changed his glory into human and beastly forms. This is the inborn ignorance Paul means, and it is this that caused the terrible darkening and alienation that progressed ever farther downward, to ever lower forms of paganism. Jesus says the same in John 3:19: men loved darkness more than light, took darkness in preference to light. The idea of religious evolution is not true to the facts. The fact is not that men eagerly took the light they had and by it rose to more and more light until they came to monotheism, yea, to Christianity. The fact is the reverse just as Paul says: they hated the light they had. Thus their ignorance caused the darkness and alienation in which they now are.

But this ignorance is the proximate cause, under it lies the ultimate one: "the petrifaction of their heart," of the personal center of their being, the seat of intellect, emotions, and especially also will. Ὁ πῶρος = tufa, a mass turned to stone. This term is used with reference to marble and to softer stone, to stalactites, stalagmites, etc. See πώρωσις in Rom. 11:25; on the verb compare Rom. 11:7. An inner petrifaction of the very heart itself was the cause of this inborn ignorance which caused the darkening in spite of all the light in nature and all the light inherited from Adam and from Noah, and with this darkening went the alienation. The very heart was stone-hard, unresponsive to moral and spiritual impression.

This is what is wrong with the natural man; yes, he is blind and ignorant, but worse, his heart is stone (compare Ezek. 11:19). M.-M. 561 refer to the idea of Armitage Robinson that "obtuseness or intellectual blindness is the meaning of the context." But Paul has more than this in mind. The ancients translated *pōrōsis* with "blindness" as if πήρωσις were the word used in the text, and Luther followed them, our A. V. followed him. R., *W. P.*, notes the medical use of this word in Hippocrates to denote callous hardening. But this does not make the word itself medical any more than does our "hardening" of the arteries.

Paul heaps up the terms in his compact way: darkening — alienation — ignorance — petrifaction; but each is in its proper place. This is the condition of the Gentiles. This passage is a *locus classicus* for the state of the natural man and is used by the church against all Pelagianism, semi-Pelagianism, synergism, and moralism. God's miracle of grace is described in Ezek. 11:19.

19) The relative clause is parallel to the two perfect participles used in v. 18. It adds pagan action to pagan condition. Both v. 18 and 19 thus show how the Gentiles walk "in vanity" and get nowhere throughout their lives. Like the participles used in v. 18, the relative οἵτινες has both causal and qualitative force: **they such as, having lost compunction, gave themselves over to excess for practicing all uncleanness with greediness.** Darkened 'and alienated, this is how the Gentiles walk in the vanity. Such they are,

and because they are such, vanity is their entire sphere of life.

The current interpretation finds two sins mentioned here which are joined: sexual excess and greed for money. We are told that they are special marks of paganism and are thus named here. This thought has also been suggested, that sexual excesses require money so that covetousness is here added by Paul. It is rather strange that sexual vices should be mentioned here when in 5:3, etc., Paul centers an entire admonition on these vices. The same is true with regard to covetousness since v. 28 follows. Why speak of only two kinds of sin here, where the entire walk of the Gentiles is described? Two types of sin are not introduced here as notable examples of all kinds. Paul says οἵτινες which pictures the entire Gentile world in all its depravity.

The perfect participle is exactly like the two used in v. 18 and describes the condition that no longer feels pain, here twinges of conscience: "past feeling" (our versions) or "past compunction." In this degraded moral condition the Gentiles "gave themselves over to excess for working all uncleanness with greediness." They literally abandoned themselves to this excess (παρέδωκαν, aorist, R. 1214; B.-D. 95, 1). Ἀσέλγεια = *Zuegellosigkeit, Ausgelassenheit,* "excess." Compare Rom. 1:24, 26, 28, and see how in his judgment God "gave them over" to their vices. In passages where this word is used as one item in a list, it gets to mean sexual excess (Mark 7:22; Rom. 13:13; II Cor. 12:21; Gal. 5:19); not so where, as here, in II Pet. 2:2, 7, 18; Jude 4, it is used as a modifier or in its general sense; then it retains its unmodified meaning "excess," plural "excesses." The R. V. tries to carry the modified meaning throughout by translating "lasciviousness."

Nor should "all uncleanness" be restricted to sexual sins and ἐργασία regarded as meaning *Gewerbe,* regular trade (R. V., margin). Only prostitution can be made a regular business and not *all* sexual uncleanness. The word means: *Beschaeftigung mit allen moeglichen suendlichen Dingen* (B.-P. 478). "Uncleanness" is to be understood in its broadest sense: the Gentiles were such as gave themselves over in excess (without restraint or moderation) "for practicing all manner of moral taint" (*Unlauterkeit, Lasterhaftigkeit*) or vice, and did that "with greediness." No restraint held them back, nor could their greediness get enough of tainted doings. The last phrase does not add the one vice of covetousness to another vice, namely sexual excess.

Paul is describing the whole pagan life and not only two of its vicious features. The whole of it was "practice of uncleanness," was this in all its forms. "Uncleanness" marked their religion and their worship, their pleasures and diversions, their business and their social relations, their politics, their public shows, and what not. "Uncleanness" is the main word. "Practice of all uncleanness" points to all the doings of paganism; and the modifying terms, "having no compunction — excess — in greediness," emphasize the extreme length to which the working out of all uncleanness was carried.

Such was paganism; it is such to this day, an outrageous vile mess. Read the four Gospels and the Acts and see that much similar uncleanness was found among the Jews. In Rom. 1:18-32 Paul combines the ungodliness and the unrighteousness of Jews as well as of Gentiles (see the writer on this portion of Romans).

20) Paul declares and testifies (v. 17) that his readers were done with this kind of life. Emphatically he writes: **But you, you have not thus learned Christ!** We prefer the perfect whereas the Greek merely states the past fact with an aorist. The Ephe-

sians did learn Christ, and not "thus," so as to allow
anything of such practice of uncleanness to continue.
"Not thus" repudiates all of it. The negation is a
litotes; "not thus" = in a manner that is utterly opposite. To learn Christ means far more than to learn
about him, to get acquainted with him, or even to learn
to know his doctrine. To learn Christ is the counterpart of to preach Christ (I Cor. 1:23; II Cor. 1:19)
and means to believe that preaching, to embrace Christ
in all that makes him Christ. We decline to divide this
little sentence: "But you not thus! You did learn
Christ," etc. We also decline to make it a question:
"But you, did you not learn Christ thus?"

21)   Paul appends a parenthetical conditional
clause: **if, indeed, you have heard him and were
taught in connection with him even as there is truth
in Jesus, etc.** This condition of reality does not intend to raise a doubt; it does, however, intend to remind Paul's readers of the unquestionable fact that
they *heard* and were *taught* so that if any one of them
did not *learn*, the fault does not lie with their teachers
or with what these taught. The verbs and also their
tenses correspond: one learns by hearing and being
taught. Even the change of voice is expressive: "you
heard" — because "you were taught." *What* one hears
the Greek puts into the accusative: "him," Christ, who
is the object also of "you learned," but now "him" is
put forward for the sake of emphasis: "if, indeed, *him*
you heard." This is also done in the phrase: "in connection with *him* you were taught." "In him" merely
repeats the object of the teaching with the passive
verb. There is no deep mystical idea in this phrase.
We rather note the emphasis: *"In him"* you were instructed, *in him* as your branch of religious and spiritual knowledge. Paul himself had done this instructing for over two years, and it had been continued by
the elders mentioned in Acts 20:17.

Καθώς is correlative to οὐχ οὕτως: *"not so* did you learn Christ (as has been stated) — if, indeed, *him* you did hear and in *him* were instructed *as* there is truth in Jesus." The last clause makes plain what the two emphatic pronouns "him" (Christ) convey. Jesus himself says: *"I* am the Truth," John 14:6. So Paul says: "There is, indeed, truth in Jesus." He now uses the personal name "Jesus" because the Ephesians are not to think only of "Christ" or the Messiah in a general way but of "Jesus" who lived, labored, died, and rose again here on earth, of this Jesus as the Christ. Ἔστιν should be accented, for it is here not the copula but the verb to denote existence. Paul might have said, "The truth exists in Jesus," and made the subject specific; by omitting the article and writing "truth" Paul says that whatever is truth (i. e., spiritual reality) in any sense exists in Jesus, in him whom they learned if, indeed, they heard him when they were instructed in him.

This clause has had various interpretations: "if him you heard . . . as it is a fact" that you did. Some then draw "in Jesus" to the following: "that in Jesus you put away," etc., Westcott and Hort, Greek margin. "Truth" is at times translated "holiness": "even as there is a pattern of holiness in Jesus." The whole clause is also drawn to v. 22: "even as it is true teaching in Jesus that you should put off," etc. Or "as he (Christ) is truth in Jesus," or: "as he (Christ) is in Jesus in truth," as though there were two kinds of instruction, one dealing with the Christ idea apart from the person of Jesus, the other connecting the Christ idea with this person Jesus. Each of these varying efforts has only a few adherents.

The point of "truth," which means reality and verity, is so pertinent in this connection because the darkened and alienated Gentiles had never even heard it and were thus in ignorance and in hardness of heart walking in the vanity of their mind and giving themselves up to all uncleanness. All this delusion was swept away for the Ephesians who had learned Christ — if, indeed, they had actually heard *him* and been actually instructed in *him* even as real truth exists only in this person Jesus.

22) Paul continues: **that you put away from yourselves once for all, as concerning your former mode of life, the old man which is in process of corruption in accord with the lusts of the deceit, and that you continue to be renewed in regard to the spirit of your mind; and that you put on once for all the new man which, in accord with God, is created in the truth's righteousness and holiness.**

The three infinitives depend on "ye were taught" and state *what* the Ephesians were taught in connection with Christ. Because the minor clause intervenes, it was necessary to add ὑμᾶς; if the infinitives had followed immediately after "you were taught," this pronoun would have been omitted, for the subject of an infinitive is normally that of the main verb. It is written only when, as here, there is a reason, or when the subject of the infinitive differs from that of the main verb. R. 1089, 1038.

The remark of B.-D. 406, 2, that the construction is *wenig durchsichtig* is unjustified and is probably due to the attempts of commentators to make the infinitives appositional to "truth." That construction would require at least "*the* truth," the infinitives then stating its contents. Paul keeps to the main line of his thought, conversion away from the whole Gentile life and walk, and is not defining the general idea of "truth" or reality in Jesus. In fact, these infinitives are not such a definition; they denote actions and thus, as far as "truth" is concerned, only the products of "truth."

It is not necessary to regard these infinitives as indirect discourse for original imperatives. Although the whole paragraph implies admonition, Paul nowhere uses "I admonish," as he did in v. 1. We should not think that he is calling on the Ephesians to do what these infinitives state. They had learned Christ, they had heard and had been taught (three historical aorists), and Paul now states what they had been taught. "Did learn Christ," like the "if" clause, puts beyond question the fact that the Ephesians had followed this teaching. Paul recalls its contents to their minds. The "if" clause implies only this much, that if any member had not truly accepted the teaching — which Paul can scarcely believe — that person certainly should do so now.

The first and the third infinitive are aorists: to put off the old man and to put on the new are punctiliar actions, done once, done once for all; the second infinitive is present and durative: the renewing is continuous and progressive. These tenses express neither past nor present time, they express *Aktionsart*, aorists are punctiliar, momentary (here not constative); the present is durative, continuous. To overlook the force of these tenses of the infinitives is to understand Paul's thought but partially.

In v. 22 we have the negative side, in v. 24 the positive, but there is no interval of time: the old man is put off when the new is put on; either is impossible without the other. "That you put off or away from yourselves (middle) once for all the old man" refers to a definite and permanent break. Paul's aorist views it as being nothing less. The fact that one may fall from grace and be re-converted is passed by. It is quite true that the old man still clings to us after the decisive break and thus must be put away again and again. That is why Paul adds the iterative present

infinitive: "but that you continue to be renewed," etc.
Paul's view is: one definite, decisive break and then a
continuous renewal. We should read the first two
infinitives together: 1) that you put away and (δέ, on
the other hand) be renewed — 2) that you put on.

The κατά phrase, "as concerning your former mode
of life," resumes what has been said about this "conversation" (A. V.) in v. 18, 19 and thus weaves the
thought together. In their former mode of life they
were ruled by what Paul calls "the old man," the old,
sinful ego derived from Adam by our natural birth
plus the entire old, sinful *habitus*, i. e., thoughts, motives, emotions, volitions, in their evil moral quality.
Not merely this or that is wrong with us so that mending will correct the faults (Pelagianism), the entire
nature is wrong. Putting off this old man is not a
painless operation, it is violent, painful; Rom. 6:6 calls
it a crucifixion.

It is self-evident that no person can himself put
off the old man. We put him off by the efficacious
power of grace (2:5). Nor does this power only help
us; we contribute not one iota. *We*, indeed, put him
off just as *we* repent, *we* believe, etc.; but in the very
nature of the case *we* do these things when grace works
this putting off, repentance, faith in us with its divine
power. The old man is put off, crucified; he is not
converted — he cannot be; he is not renewed — he cannot be; he is replaced by the new man by a creative act
of God (v. 24; 2:5, 10).

"Former" and "old" look back; the present participle, "which is in process of corruption in accord
with the lusts of deceit," looks at the entire condition
of the old man. One may regard the participle as a
middle or as a passive: "corrupting himself" or "being
corrupted" by an unnamed agent; the former seems
preferable. The tense is graphic. It presents the old
man as working steadily at his own ruin and destruc-

tion. The word does not refer to a progress of moral
decline, for the old man is wholly depraved and corrupt from the start. The reference is to v. 19 as also
"according to the lusts of the deceit" indicates. In
harmony with (κατά) the lusts in which the old man
indulges he plunges himself down progressively into
everlasting ruin or destruction. To be sure, we and
the old man are to be differentiated, for after having
rid ourselves of him we remain. Paul does not need
to say that by corrupting himself the old man also cor-
rupts (ruins or destroys) us. When a virulent disease runs its course, it wrecks itself, of course, by
wrecking the patient.

᾽Επιθυμίαι, originally a *vox media* for "desires,"
receives its connotation from the context and in the
New Testament is steadily used in the evil sense of
"lusts." The A. V. regards the genitive as adjectival:
"deceitful lusts"; it is subjective: "the lusts which the
deceit uses" to bring on the ruin. Distinguish ἀπάτη
from the πλάνη of v. 14. This is "the deceit" (specific)
that is native to the old man, the lying, deceptive power
that rules him. All lusts have this deceit back of them.
Deceit offers the cup that tastes sweet but has death in
it. The lusts are many, but the deceit is always the
same. Men who have been darkened (v. 18) give
themselves over to lusts with greediness (v. 19) and
even want the deceit. The only salvation is to get rid
of the old man with his deceit, lusts, and ruination.

23) With the slightly adversative δέ Paul adds to
the decisive putting off of the old man the constant
renewing begun in the putting off. This continuation
always follows the definite break. The tense is marked,
it is a present between two aorists.

Putting off the old man is negative, being constantly renewed is positive. Paul might have continued the negative, for the Christian life and walk is
a constant war against the attempted usurpations of

the old man with his lusts and deceit who tries to get back his former control. Paul prefers the positive, for we keep this usurpation in check by a steady and a progressive spiritual renewal. The infinitive is not middle as Luther has regarded it: *erneuert euch,* but passive: "ever being renewed." The middle is always transitive and has an object; none is named here. The agent in the passive is God or the Spirit. While the renewal may be predicated of us since, after the putting away of the old man, we have new spiritual powers and cooperate with God in using them, here the passive attributes this blessed work to God.

Ἀνανεοῦσθαι = ἀνακαινοῦσθαι, which we translate in the same way since we lack two words for "new." The Greek distinguishes νέος, "new" in the sense of not having existed before, from καινός, "new" as different from something old. In the infinitive the former newness is referred to, yet it is followed in v. 24 by the other, in "the new man," καινός. The prefix ἀνά is our "*re*newed." In Col. 3:10 "the new man" is called νέος, and the word for the renewing act is derived from καινός, which again states the newness in both ways but reverses them in the adjective and the activity.

We regard the dative as a dative of respect: "in regard to the spirit of your mind." Some regard this as a reference to the Holy Spirit, the dative being used as the agent with the passive; others regard it as an instrumental dative. But this construction does not agree with the appended genitive. Nowhere else is the Spirit called "the Spirit of our mind." The passive infinitive itself implies the divine agency in the renewing process. This process is, however, an inward one. Our versions make the dative locative: "in the spirit," etc., which is also good. Not only our outward conduct is wholly new; this newness starts from our very spirit. Our immaterial part, which is ordinarily called "the soul" in English, is in the Scriptures viewed in its relation to the body as animating and giving it life; it is then called ψυχή, *Lebenshauch*, life. But when this immaterial part is viewed as receiving impressions from God and his Πνεῦμα it is termed πνεῦμα, "spirit." That is the case here. It is well, however, to remember that in English "soul" is used much like "spirit." We see this when we note that the Greek forms the adjective ψυχικός, "carnal," from ψυχή, which is the direct opposite of πνευματικός, "spiritual." We are unable to form such an adjective from "soul."

Paul does not write merely, "As regards *your* spirit"; he puts it in a richer way, "As regards the spirit of your mind," which recalls "the vanity of their mind" in v. 17. On "mind" see v. 17. Yet this is not to be reduced to "the animus of your mind" as we speak of the spirit a person manifests in some act. This is the limiting genitive. Paul means our "spirit" or soul insofar as the thinking, directing "mind" is concerned, the mind that governs our actions and determines our aim and goal. "Vanity of their mind," as we have seen, is the mind reaching out for an empty goal, engaging in actions that end at no proper goal. Our spirit, freed from the domination of the old man, will use our mind for nothing that supports the old man, will with all our thinking and willing seek only what is new, full of blessedness and salvation.

It has been well observed that, as far as the Holy Spirit is concerned, the analogy of Scripture does not use even the possessive "our Spirit" as it does "our Lord" and "our God"; much less then "the Spirit of our mind" or anything similar. This ought to exclude all the hazy interpretations of a union of God's Spirit with our spirit as far as this expression of Paul's is concerned. Our own spirit in its activity of mind, in its moral and spiritual thought and decisions, is to continue in a new course. A perennial rejuvenation is to bring forth newness of life so that we walk in

newness of life (Rom. 6:4), serve in newness of spirit
(Rom. 7:6), as a new creature (Gal. 6:15).

24) "And that you put on once for all the new
man" is the positive aorist which completes the negative, "that you put away from yourselves the old man,"
and is thus properly added with καί. Both are instantaneous acts (aorists in this sense). Both are really
one: to do the one is to do the other. The joining of
negative and positive is done for the sake of clearness
and completeness of statement. If it be asked why,
after having already added the constant renewal to the
riddance of the old man, Paul now brings in the first
putting on of the new man, we may answer that this
would in a way be unnecessary if all he said were only
that we put on the new man. But he says much more.
As he characterized the old man, so he characterizes
the new man, and the latter is so important as to become necessary. We must not only be reminded of
what the new man is, we must also remember how he
comes into existence ("created") so as constantly to
be renewed.

This aorist, like the first one in v. 22, does not then
state the culmination of the renewing process. The
new man is not put on at the end of this process. The
new man is not the glorified man. Nor does the aorist
indicate successive individual instances: "now and
again, in each individual instance, obeying the good, saving thoughts and impulses of the new man," which, to
say the least, would require an iterative present tense.
Such a tense would then be in place also in v. 22. The
new man is put on as the old is put off, by one decisive
act. Nor could iterations be understood without this
decisive act. The iteration is already provided for in
the durative infinitive used in v. 23.

"The new man" is the opposite of "the old man,"
hence we have καινός in the sense already explained. At
one time our nature, as it centered in the ego, was

"old," like Adam since the fall, "flesh"; by grace this old man is replaced in us by the new man, in the very center of our being or ego. Not this or that part of us has become new but our inward being which was once old. This is more than a new *habitus*, it is the life principle itself which produces the *habitus*.

The attributive, "the one created in accord with God," is like an apposition and thus a climax (R. 776). Both the noun and the attribute have an emphasis. The passive "created" implies God as the Creator of the new man, and κτίζω is used in its proper meaning, "to call into existence." The new man had to be "created" (compare 2:5, 10; II Cor. 5:17; Gal. 6:15). The monergism of grace cannot be more adequately stated so as to rule out even the faintest synergism. Yet "created" does not signify "by omnipotence" as it does in the domain of nature. Spiritual creation is due to the δύναμις of grace, "the power" of the gospel (Rom. 1:16), which works its wonders in the *ordo salutis*. Grace is Calvinized when it is confused with omnipotence, and there is not a twofold omnipotence, one that may, and one that may not be resisted.

"According to God" signifies likeness. God is the model, the new man a copy, and the latter accords with the former. The point of likeness is expressed by the phrase: "in the truth's righteousness and holiness," these two being combined as in Luke 1:75. The genitive makes the two nouns definite. Paul has already mentioned "truth" in v. 11; its opposite is "deceit" in v. 22, "error" in v. 14. "The truth" is the entire saving reality conveyed by the gospel. Why limit it to "moral truth"? Why philosophize: "being as it ought to be," confusing the concept "being" with the concept "the truth," i. e., the saving realities that exist in Christ Jesus (v. 22), with our own regenerated existence?

Righteousness and holiness are God's attributes ("in accord with God") ; the new man has what corresponds to these attributes, has it, however, only as being derived from God, created by him. These attributes are closely allied. Righteousness is God's unchanging love of right, and holiness his unchanging aversion to sin. Both attributes are ever active and never quiescent. The natural man shuts his eyes to both and makes a god for his own use who is an indulgent grandfather; for a righteous and holy God is a terror to impenitent sinners. We may note that by declaring us righteous for Christ's sake God exercises his righteousness (Rom. 3:26) as much as when he damns the impenitent unbeliever.

The new man resembles God in righteousness and in holiness. Both qualities are his because God declares him to be righteous in the judgment of justification, and because the new man then lives in righteousness and holiness. The latter never takes place without the former. Righteousness and holiness are the chief perfections of Adam in his original state, in the *imago Dei*. The restoration of the divine image in us most certainly includes our justification for Christ's sake, the product of which is a righteous and holy life. The creation of the new man in us does not at once stop all our sinning (note v. 23), but it does place the new man in control of our life and our conduct; our imputed righteousness and holiness produce acquired righteousness and holiness, and this product increases until the last and perfect purgation takes place in the hour of death.

Δικαιοσύνη occurs often in the New Testament, but ὁσιότης only twice. The adjective ὅσιος = *chasid* (Hebrew) = *sanctus* as opposed to *pollutus*. We are interested especially in the synonym ἅγιος, *sacer, qodesch*, "set apart," holy in this sense. See the excellent discussion of the four synonyms by Trench. The current

New Testament word is "saints," ἅγιοι (1:1), not ὅσιοι, the latter adjective is, in fact, rarely employed. The mystery cults certainly had nothing to do with that; for those who practiced these cults did not use the latter word to describe themselves.

It is the connotation and the flavor of the words themselves that decide their use in any context. If the word used here were ἁγιωσύνη, which is in form, too, a mate to δικαιοσύνη, we should have "holiness" = the state set apart for God, separated unto him; ἁγιότης (resembling ὁσιότης) would be the abstract quality of such consecratedness and separateness. Ὁσιότης, the word used by Paul, is "holiness" as opposed to all pollution, as being in accord with the everlasting sanctities, and as accepting their obligation. Perhaps the combination of righteousness and holiness is due somewhat to classic writers, but both terms have their distinctive Scriptural meaning and are not used in a pagan sense. It is valuable also to note the remark of Trench that these two Greek words are never interchanged in the Scriptures.

We decline to accept the adjectival genitive of the A. V.: "true holiness," just as we declined to accept "the deceitful lusts" in v. 22. "Righteousness and holiness" are two sides of the same quality and thus convey one thought which becomes the stronger because it is expressed by two words. Trench is right in discarding pagan distinctions such as that righteousness refers to our relation to men, and holiness to our relation to God: "The Scripture gives no room for such an antithesis as this," although some commentators accept it. Both refer to God and only thus to men. Nor does righteousness refer to conduct, holiness to the heart; both refer to heart and conduct. Nor is the former generic, the latter specific. Nor does the second refer more directly to God, for δικαιοσύνη involves the divine δίκη or norm of right. Both equally and jointly belong to "the truth," the blessed gospel realities.

We add the illuminating note given by Trench. When Joseph was tempted by Potiphar's wife he remained ὅσιος by reverencing the everlasting sanctities of the marriage bond ordained of God: "How can I do this great wickedness and sin against God?" ἅγιος in that he separated himself from the temptress since he belonged to God, and ἁγνός in that he kept himself pure and undefiled.

The middle, "put on yourselves," uses the figure of a garment which covers the body and gives it a new appearance. But this garment is intended for the soul so that the idea of hiding anything under it is excluded. The old coat of the lusts of the deceit is forever cast aside for the new robe of righteousness and holiness which belong to Christ's saving truth. In this garment we stand before the all-seeing eyes of God as his new creation and also before men as we are created in Christ Jesus unto good works (2:10), to be the light of the world and the salt of the earth.

In this admonition the important point is the old man and the new. Hence no specific sins or virtues are mentioned. Sin is mentioned only as "uncleanness" (v. 19) and "lusts" (v. 22), godliness only as being contained in "righteousness and holiness" (v. 24). This leaves room for further admonition.

* * *

The Admonitions not to Wrong our Neighbor

25) Those who think that Paul adds one admonition loosely to another are mistaken, for this is never Paul's way of writing. As v. 1-16 is carefully built up, so each new paragraph is added in logical order, and each is likewise carefully constructed. We now come to specific sins and to the virtues that must take their

place. Like v. 17-24, this paragraph is strongly negative. In the next paragraph positive and negative
features are more nearly balanced, and in the one following the positive predominates. All this, too, is
carefully intended.

Διό uses Paul's previous declaration and testimony
(v. 17) regarding the truth they have learned about
putting off the old man and putting on the new as
the basis for the specific admonitions that now follow.
**Wherefore, having put away the falsehood, do you
ever speak truth, each one with his neighbor, because we are members one of another!**

The participle is causal and not modal; moreover, it
is an aorist, and hence does not mean, "putting away
falsehood" each time we speak to our neighbor and
uttering truth instead, but, "since we have once put
away the lie or falsehood," let us not use any of it when
we speak to our neighbor. This is the same putting
away that was mentioned in v. 22, even the tense is the
same. Nor is τὸ ψεῦδος *das Luegen,* "lying," or *das
luegenhafte Wesen,* a course of conduct; but "the lie,"
"the falsehood," the opposite of "the truth" of the
gospel (v. 24), "truth in Jesus" (v. 21). "The lie" =
"the deceit" (v. 22) and "the deception or error" (v.
14). The sense is: because in our conversion we have
once for all cast away the lie that dominated us.

This is the great lie that rules all who have not put
off the old man, the lie by which they are darkened and
blinded, alienated, because of the ignorance and hardness of heart, the lie that impels to all uncleanness in
life (v. 18, 19). This lie lies about God and about
man, about sin and about punishment, about godliness
and about morality. Rom. 1:18, etc., describes how it
operates; it strangles the truth in unrighteousness, it
renders man inexcusable.

This lie is the natural man's religion. It appears
in multitudinous forms but is here viewed as a unit.

Truth is reality, every lie is a fiction, a pretended reality, that asserts that something is so when it is really not so at all, or that something is not so when it really is so. To trust any lie is to head for a great wreck, especially to trust "the lie" which substitutes fictions for the saving realities of God and the gospel; the wreck that ensues is irreparable. The participle is *not* an imperative; it states a past fact, it forms the basis for the imperative verb.

Once for all having put away the lie, which means having once for all embraced the saving truth, how can we after that do otherwise than evermore "speak truth," i. e., what is truth (no article), with our neighbor? This injunction naturally comes first, following, as it does, "the truth" mentioned in v. 24. Those who have the new man, created in accord with God in the (gospel) truth's righteousness and holiness, cannot in any matter lie to a neighbor, whether this be a fellow believer or not. The imperative is durative: "ever be speaking truth." The plural "do not speak" is individualized by adding "each one." This injunction is identical with that stated in Zech. 8:16 and may be intended as a quotation without the use of a formula of quotation.

"Because we are members one of another" does not intend to restrict "neighbor" to a fellow believer. The thought that we may lie to those who are not Christians is itself a lie. The term "members" recalls all that Paul has said about "the body of Christ" in v. 12, 16 and also in v. 4, "one body." All of us are members of this body. But instead of stating the relation of each one to the body as a whole, Paul states the relation of each one to every other one in this body. By lying to any man we should injure the body by injuring one or the other member, perhaps many in this body. A Christian who lies injures not only the person to whom

he lies, whether this be a brother or not, he injures
most of all a circle of his fellow members by grieving
them, giving them a bad example, destroying their
confidence in him, etc. As a liar he is a pest among
them. Here and in the following Paul does not dwell
on God and his penalties. He keeps to his great subject, the *Una Sancta.* As members of this divine body
we must build it up (v. 16) and not injure or tear it
down, whether by lying or by any other sin.

The ethical question is constantly raised as to
whether a lie is ever justified. The casuists offer cases
that are so tight as to lead them to conclude that a deliberate lie is frequently entirely right and justifiable.
The doctor who knows that a patient must die tells him
he will get well because to tell him the truth may
hasten his end. But this is making the end justify the
means, a principle which would then justify any number of sins. Every pastor meets this problem. So also
does the lawyer in court, the soldier in war, the bus-
inessman, the laborer, the members of a family, man
with man. A man confronts me with a gun. He wants
to kill my brother. I know where my brother is hiding.
A lie seems the way out. So Peter lied to save his
own skin.

Panic, loss of presence of mind, cowardice make a
Christian lie. There is always a way out, perhaps there
are several. Confront a direct question asked you with
a question of your own. This turns the tables on the
questioner and often changes the whole situation at
once.

Take the patient. The blunt truth may needlessly
precipitate his death. Telling him the truth in a wise
manner helps him in every way, makes him grateful,
enables him to prepare for death, etc. It is the greatest crime to lie and to send a dying man into eternity
unprepared.

The full injunction is not merely to speak the truth but to speak the truth *in love* (v. 15). It is self-deception to think that we can lie *in love*. Truth spoken without ἀγάπη, the love of Christian intelligence and corresponding purpose, is as bad as a lie spoken with supposed love.

One can at times decline to speak at all. One can at times also take the consequences. Jesus did that when he took an oath that he was the Son of God. The consequences that seem so certain and so terrible often do not follow, are often not so terrible, are often even good. Any profession or business that cannot be practiced without lying or dishonesty the Christian will not enter, no matter what the profit to him might be.

Much more should be said on this subject of Christian ethics. We cannot expand here. Even a worldly man with a conscience who uses his wits with courage need not lie in a tight place, and men will respect him.

26) Next to harm resulting from lying is harm caused by anger. No commentator restricts the thought to anger only against a fellow member of the church. **Be angry and do not sin! Let not the sun go down upon your exasperation, nor give room to the devil!** Only the harm we do to ourselves is mentioned; that done to our fellow members apparently needed no mention after the last clause of v. 25.

The ethics which forbids all anger and demands unruffled calmness in every situation is Stoic and not Christian. If all anger is wrong, as some think on the basis of v. 31, Paul should have written, "Be not angry!" and stopped with that. But he writes, "Be angry!" and then adds, "And sin not!" Jesus, our great example, was himself angry (Mark 3:5); and if εἰκῆ should be the genuine reading in Matt. 5:22, he would speak much as Paul does, namely exempt the anger for a just cause. We thus discard any interpretation that prohibits all anger. When God, Christ, the holy things of God are reviled, shall no anger stir in us? When hypocrites come with their masks of holiness, when injustice parades as right, when tyrants trample helpless victims, anger is justified. These are plain cases. A problem arises only in cases that are not plain, which we need not discuss here.

Yet this still leaves Paul's καί connecting two imperatives (iterative presents). All would be simple if Paul had written, "Be angry *but* sin not!" Ps. 4:4, if Paul has this in mind, affords no help, for the LXX wording is exactly like Paul's. Moreover, the LXX rendering is correct, *ragatz* = to tremble with wrath (Delitzsch on this psalm; Ed. Koenig, *Woerterbuch*). Accept καί as it stands, as adding one command to the other. Instead of separating the two, combine them. We are urged to be angry, *and* in the same breath are urged not to sin in such anger. For, as is rightly observed, the next injunction is directed against overindulgence in even justifiable anger.

We, therefore, do not need the refinements of the grammarians: Buttmann, it is impossible to take the first command as a direct command; Winer (6th ed.), the first imperative is permissive, the second jussive, or the first is equal to a participle; B.-D. 387, 1: "You may be angry as far as I am concerned (if you cannot help it), but do not sin therein!" yet Paul has no "but"; R. 1023, the two imperatives are like a protasis and an apodosis, the first is concessive (949), the second points to an imminent danger (854). Examples such as, "Do this and live," or: *divide et impera*, do not fit because Paul's second imperative is negative.

"Let not the sun go down upon your exasperation!" is a separate command, and hence there is no connective. Παροργισμός, found only here in the New Testament and a few times in the LXX and not at all elsewhere (M.-M. 496), appears to be passive: "exasperation" or provocation, and names the cause for justifiable wrath. All unjustifiable anger is wrong *eo ipso*. But the provocation one suffers in even justifiable wrath must not be entertained too long. Dismiss it before the day is over. This is not what Plutarch says about the Pythagorean custom of giving each other the right hand and embracing each other. Christian forgiveness is mentioned in v. 32 and is another matter.

The sun's going down (descriptive present, permissive passive) is a popular, concrete expression for "before the day is over." To be sure, this is limitation, yet why forbid the reference to the Christian's prayer before he goes to sleep? Since he cannot stop the sun's going down he will lay the ungodliness that has rightly called forth his wrath before God, he will commit it to God (I Pet. 2:23). The lengthening shadows will bring Paul's admonition to his mind. Regarding any unjustifiable anger Paul's only injunction would be prompt repentance irrespective of nightfall.

27) The δέ in μηδέ adds, but adds something different. As in the case of δέ in v. 23, the other side is stated. The amount of importance attached to the particle governs the exegesis as to whether "the devil" is referred to or only "the (human) slanderer" (the article then being generic). The statement that a reference to "the devil" would insert a broad, disconnected injunction, makes too much of δέ. The plea that we must translate "slanderer" disregards the fact that when διάβολος is used as a noun in the New Testament it regularly refers to "the devil." Just as the καί used in the previous clause does not make "and sin not" general and thus a disconnected injunction, so this δέ does not do so. Our versions translate correctly.

The connection between sinning and the devil is rather plain. By manifesting our exasperation too long and not laying it before God in prayer at least by sundown and thus sinning we should not give room to

God to exercise his righteous activity but to the devil
to use his activity in our sinning. Is he not the one
back of the ungodly exasperation which provokes us to
righteous wrath? Is he not the one who tempts us to
carry our exasperation too far and thus to sin? Despite Luther's *Laesterer* we hold to the close connection
indicated and abide by our versions. We may regard
the present imperative as ingressive: "begin to give
room."

28) **Let the stealer no longer be stealing but
rather be laboring, working that which is good with
his own hands in order that he may have to share
with him who has need.**

By far the best discussion of ὁ κλέπτων is that found
in Moulton, *Einleitung* 205, etc. The difference between this form and ὁ κλέπτης is that the former connects more closely with the verb κλέπτω. The substantivized present participle is timeless, descriptive, characterizing. *When* the act or action occurs is not indicated. The tense indicates iteration (R. 1116). "Him
that stole" in our versions (B.-D. 275, 6, *wer bisher
stahl*) translates interpretatively, according to the
present context. Robertson's (892) "the rogue" is incorrect. "The stealer" might still be stealing as far
as this participle indicates, but Paul evidently has in
mind a person who stole before his conversion and is
in danger of falling back into this grave sin, whom he
thus warns. "No longer let him be stealing" no matter
what the temptation may be at any time. Stealing is
here intended to include all forms of getting something
wrongfully, theft, cheating, overreaching, etc. Having put on the new man, the Christian is honest in
every act.

But is such an injunction still necessary for Christians? Many Christians were slaves, and pagan slaves
did not regard it as wrong to pilfer from their masters.

Speak to foreign missionaries about present-day pagan servants. Nor need we disregard servants of our own country. The vice of getting something for nothing is world-wide and is found among all ranks of men. Graft, bribery, so-called "gifts," and any number of other forms of dishonesty tempt the Christian again and again.

Why does Paul say nothing about restitution? Because he is in brief strokes sketching how the Christian's life looks: no stealing or wrongful appropriation of what belongs to others. Paul is not elaborating the ethics of the Seventh Commandment. Paul is also reaching much farther than mere restitution. "But rather" is not a mere opposite (this would be ἀλλά, "on the contrary") but a wider, freer contrast, something that is far better than the former conduct.

Both the imperative and the participle are durative to express steady labor and work as a rule of life, and "let him labor" denotes exertion that tires one. The thief wants to get things easily, with little effort; the Christian gladly undergoes honest toil. To get rich quickly, to do it by shady schemes and means, is not on the program of the new man. Little is gained by making "that which is good" the object of "let him labor" and leaving the participle without an object. Nor is there a reason for drawing "that which is good" into the purpose clause.

Τὸ ἀγαθόν is the opposite of τὸ κακόν and conveys the idea of moral good quality over against any base quality. "The good" is good in the sense of its quality, which extends also to others; hence it is more than "earthly good," *sein redlich Teil*. It is *acquired* in a good way, by honest labor, without doing harm to anyone, also not to the laborer; it is to be *expended* in a good way, to a good purpose: "that he may share with him who has need." The present tense = may continue to have, and the present infinitive = share with at any time when a needy one appears. This is more than restitution, it is conduct for the entire life. The question of the exact reading the text critics may decide; "with his own hands" seems correct, "hands" continue the idea of labor.

29) From the Seventh Commandment Paul proceeds to the Eighth Commandment, from damage done to our neighbor by theft to damage done him by speech. **Let no worthless statement go forth out of your mouth; on the contrary, if there is some** (statement) **good for upbuilding where necessary, so that it may give grace to those hearing.**

The derivation of σαπρός (from σήπω, "to putrify") does not imply that the meaning must always be "putrid," rotten, "corrupt" (our versions). A putrid thing is worthless and is thus thrown away. So in its New Testament use *sapros* = "worthless" and not "corrupt or rotten." B.-P. 1191 rightly asks: "Do rotten (*faule*) fish enter a net? do rotten trees bear fruit at all?" Matt. 7:17. So here the sense is "no worthless statement" (λόγος). As far as "foul" language is concerned, this is fully named in the next paragraph (5:4) which deals with the Sixth Commandment. Here the injunction is broad and covers every statement that ought to be thrown out as being worthless; compare Matt. 12:36. All empty, shallow, thoughtless talk is referred to. Paul is not speaking of talk that is worse, namely vicious, lying, slanderous, foul, etc. Even every worthless word should be beneath us. The Greek construes the negative with the verb, we negate the subject.

Hence also the positive is not "pure" but "some (statement, λογος) good (i. e., beneficial) for necessary upbuilding" (spiritual edification). Προς = toward, tending in this direction, to accomplish this object. The genitive has puzzled many so that a few texts and early versions and several writers altered it: "for edification of the faith." This would be an objective genitive. The A. V.'s "to the use of edifying" is peculiar, as is also its margin, "to edify profitably"; χρεία, however, means neither "use" nor "profit" but "need." One may hesitate between the objective genitive: "for building up the need," which is an awkward thought that is hence modified in the R. V.: "as the need may be"; B.-P. 1410: *da, wo es nottut,* "where necessary"; and the adjectival genitive: "for the needed upbuilding."

Is this an instance of the imperative ἵνα like the one found in 5:33: "the wife, let her fear (or see that she fears) the husband"? R. 994 lists it as such: "On the contrary, if there is some statement good for needed edification, let it give grace to the hearers." But the hearer will, without effort, supply the verb from the preceding clause: "if there is some statement good, etc., let it proceed out of your mouth in order that (or so that) it may give grace to the hearers." The ἵνα clause denotes purpose or purported result.

It is debated whether χάρις is human or divine favor. Some refer to διδόναι χάριν (Sophocles and Plato) for the meaning "to do a kindness"; but Paul himself uses this expression (generally the passive) so often that we need not look elsewhere, note for instance 3:2, 7, 8 (three times in succession). Paul does not say that *we* are to give grace, nor even that *our* word is to do so, but "if there is any word good for edification," *it* is to give grace, edifying grace, and thus certainly divine grace. Our mouth is merely to be the channel. Yes, our mouth, too, is to serve the *Una Sancta.* For the negative compare the famous passage, James 3:3-12.

30) Καί connects the new statement with the preceding admonition. Paul is not speaking of grieving the Holy Spirit in general but of doing this by worthless speech. We may, of course, grieve him

also in other ways. Paul's readers will think of that; but this fact does not alter the close connection here indicated. **And do not be grieving the Holy Spirit of God, in connection with whom you were sealed for redemption's day!**

"To grieve the Spirit" is a highly anthropopathic expression and is the more effective for that reason. Do we wish to make the Spirit sorrowful, who has done so much for us and our fellow members, who wants to do equally much for other men and to use us in his work? The imperative is the present tense. Grief lasts. Moreover, this tense is iterative and matches "every worthless statement" in v. 29. He who starts with one such word will likely let more go out of his mouth. The present imperative at times means to stop an action already begun (R. 851, etc.) ; but here we cannot translate, "Stop grieving!" for this would imply that the Ephesians had already begun such grieving, which Paul in no way implies. He is warning against a sin that has not yet been committed, which is ample in this connection.

By adding the adjective with a separate article this is given special weight: "the Spirit, the Holy One" (see R. 776). The Father and the Son are equally holy. When this adjective is applied to the Spirit, the point is not that he is holy in a special sense but that he is the One whose special work it is to make us holy. He is grieved as the Holy One when his work of making us and others holy is hindered by the speech of those who should be his instruments in this work. Paul brings out the gravity of such a sin when he writes "the *Holy* Spirit *of God*." The entire divine majesty is thrown into the scales in order to deter us from grieving the Holy Spirit with even a single worthless statement.

The motivation thus introduced by the very designation of this divine person is intensified by the relative clause: "in connection with whom you were sealed for redemption's day." Although it is only a relative clause in form, it is emphatic: "*him,* in connection with whom," etc.; yet as a relative it connects more closely than an independent sentence would. This sealing has been explained in 1:13. The agent in the passive is again God. Having occurred in baptism, it is to stand to the last great day. This sealing thus constitutes the central blessing connected with God's Holy Spirit, the guarantee of our final ransoming. The dative "with the Holy Spirit of the promise" found in 1:13 (which see) is here changed into a personal phrase: "in connection with whom" (as the great Sanctifier) you were sealed.

Some regard this as the instrumental "in" and think that this expounds the preposition. But this "in" phrase is like all the "in" phrases used in 1:1-13 and throughout the epistle: "in Christ Jesus — in him — in whom," none of which is instrumental, none of which = διά, *per,* "through." In all these phrases "in" conserves the personality and goes beyond instrumentality. "In union or connection with" the divine person named the divine act was done. The effort to make this "in" mystical is misdirected, especially when the idea of being like a bird "in" air (Deissmann) is added and ideas that are borrowed from pagan mystery cults are introduced.

By baptism every believer has been sealed as God's own in connection with God's Spirit. Then and there by baptism the Spirit was given to us as the seal; that is the connection expressed by "in." How can we then think of grieving this Holy Spirit of God? Will this not force him to leave us? Shall we who once bore him as the seal blot out this seal from our hearts, deny God's ownership of our souls? Paul stops with the grieving and does not advance to our losing the Spirit.

The stronger statements are reserved for later treatment.

Not for a day or for a brief time were we thus sealed but "for redemption's day." No articles are needed; the two nouns are almost like a compound. The genitive makes the "day" definite. Only one such day exists; for this reason, too, no articles are necessary. "Unto the day of redemption" in our versions should not be understood as meaning until that day. Εἰς = "for" that day when our final ransoming is to take place. It is the last great day.

On ἀπολύτρωσις see 1:13; also Rom. 8:23; Luke 21:28. This word means more than "deliverance." The idea of the payment of a ransom is implied. Warfield, *Christian Doctrine*, is right: the idea of ransom is never dropped from this word. He is also right: our word "redemption" has become pale, we should stick to "ransoming" just because it contains "ransom." At the last great day our ransoming, which was effected through Christ's blood, reaches its final consummation for body as well as for soul. This word denotes an act. The ransom price was paid on Calvary; it bought our release, the release from sin and death by pardon in baptism and conversion so that we now have this ransoming (1:7); we shall have all that this ransom bought for us in our final glorification at the last day. "Deliverance," yes, but even that final deliverance as having been bought for us by the blood ransom of Christ.

31) What follows reads like a summary that concludes the admonition against wronging our neighbor. We have first the negative and then the positive side. **Let all bitterness and exasperation and anger and yelling and blasphemy be** (definitely) **put away from you together with all baseness! On the other hand** (δέ), **be** (ever) **benignant toward each**

other, tenderhearted, forgiving each other even as also God in Christ has forgiven you!

Paul uses five terms, the half of ten, which latter is the number of greatest completeness. He stops, as it were, in the middle much as Jesus does in Matt. 5:22, by not adding threatening, striking, knocking down, wounding, killing. The worst is often mentioned as including the less bad (in Matt. 5:21, 27, murder and adultery); here the reverse is done: if what is less bad is completely put away (aorist imperative passive from αἴρω), the worse and the worst will not occur.

The five terms form a climax. First, "bitterness," embitterment, is felt in the heart. The next step is "exasperation," which is still in the heart although hard to be restrained. The third step is "anger" which blazes forth. The fourth, "yelling," is a violent outburst of words. The fifth is a cursing in words of "blasphemy" against the opponent. Trench is right when he says that, while θυμός and ὀργή are often used in the same sense, the second at times only to strengthen the first (C.-K. 805), instances remain where the two are clearly to be "desynonymized." One of these instances we have here, where "and" adds term upon term, and each is distinct.

Trench reviews the efforts to define the difference. We accept the idea that the former word = the boiling agitation of the feelings; so we render it "exasperation." But we decline to make the distinction that this is like a fire of straw that quickly blazes up and as quickly subsides while ὀργή settles down to a habit of mind. The difference does not lie in the duration of these emotions. Both may blaze up and subside, both may also endure, as far as that is concerned. The difference is that the exasperation is still confined inwardly while the anger breaks out. Rising like a tide, the exasperation, if it is not controlled, overflows in anger, and this shows itself in κραυγή or a loud outburst of words, and this, if it is allowed to go farther, becomes blasphemy or cursing; "wrath and anger" in our versions have no tangible distinction.

"Together with all baseness." Κακία is *Schlechtigkeit*; "baseness" is our best equivalent. Our versions add a sixth item to the preceding five and thus translate this word "malice" (so also elsewhere). Trench agrees. But κακός does not mean malicious, it means "base," bad, morally inferior (in moral contexts). So this is not a sixth item but a comprehensive summary. Paul mentions five stages of baseness and instead of going on calls the five "baseness" and throws into the same pot with them (associative σύν) all other types and stages of meanness to our neighbor.

32) Δέ, "on the other hand," places the sacred three over against the secular five, and these three, too, rise higher and higher. The present imperative is in contrast with the aorist used in v. 31: "definitely, once for all, put away" the sins — "ever continue to be" beneficent, etc. First, "toward one another benignant," kind in the sense of helpful; this applies to all contacts and all situations. In contrast with the five no cumulative καί is used, for these three are not climactic, one overflowing to bring on the next; these three simply stand side by side. The second applies to fewer persons, the third to still fewer.

"Tenderhearted" or compassionate applies to those who are suffering any kind of distress. Remember the compassion of Jesus. Paul does not add the action that will follow this feeling; this is understood. Thirdly, "forgiving each other," just letting the wrong done to us go without a claim for punishment or reparation. Here Paul shows what Christian forgiveness is: it insists on nothing when we are wronged, freely lets the wrong pass, and thus for its part ends it at once.

"Even as also" draws a parallel as to manner. But Paul does not write, "As God forgave (our idiom: has fórgiven) you"; he adds and must add the adverbial phrase "in Christ." The phrase does not modify "God": "God in Christ." God cannot dismiss our sins in a summary fashion. That is the rationalistic view: if we can forgive without atonement, God can surely do likewise. Our sins against God are a different thing in regard to him from what our sins toward each other are in regard to us. In the latter case one sinful creature wrongs another sinful creature; the matter occurs among equals on a low level, these equals being alike faulty and sinful. In the former case the sinful creature outrages and challenges his heavenly Creator, God in his holiness and righteousness, who never sins against us   Here, there is, indeed, also free forgiveness, but only "in Christ" whose blood atones for our sins.

Let us put this plainly since even pastors misunderstand it. The moment a man wrongs me I must forgive him. Then *my* soul is free. If I hold the wrong against him I sin against God and against him and jeopardize my forgiveness with God. Whether the man repents, makes amends, asks my pardon or not, makes no difference. I have instantly forgiven him. He must face God with the wrong he has done; but that is his affair and God's and not mine save that in the case he is a brother I should help him according to Matt. 18·15, etc. But whether this succeeds or not and before this even begins I must forgive him.

The Christian way of settling quarrels is the easiest thing in the world. The pastor is not to bring the two quarreling persons together in order to decide who is wronging, who is wronged — when there is perhaps guilt on both sides, what the degree of guilt is, and how it is to be apportioned   Can the pastor act the part of God and see into the hearts? No, let him go to each separately and see to it that each from the heart forgives as God has forgiven him in Christ. Let him make each face God until any grudge in his heart has disappeared. Then, and not until then, let the pastor bring them together in God's name. Then, after each has in his heart forgiven the other, hands and hearts will go out, lips will confess any wrong which either or both have done, and the quarrel will be ended to stay ended.

As God "in Christ" forgave you refers to the justifying act described in Rom. 3:28, that act by which God remits all sins to the sinner the instant he repents and believes in Christ. This is the personal justification and remission of which the Scriptures constantly speak. Ps. 32:1-5. The Ephesians had been forgiven thus (ὑμῖν). This is not the so-called universal justification which is the reconciliation of the whole world as this was accepted and declared by God for all men even before most of them lived here on earth. On this subject see the interpretation of Rom. 1:17. The fact that God forgave your sins and mine "in connection with Christ" is the compelling motive for our forgiving every man who in any way sins against us. Matt. 18:23, etc.

CHAPTER V

The Admonition against Filthiness

1) We cannot combine v. 1, 2 with the previous admonition as though it rounded it out by making us who walk in love like that of Christ's forgive as imitators of God. We have already shown that each admonition begins with οὖν (4:1, 17, 25, διό; 5:4, 15). Each rests on the preceding one and thus connects with it also in thought and even in expression. In 4:24 ἀποθέμενοι reverts to ἀποθέσθαι in 4:22, and "truth" to "truth in Jesus" in 4:21. So in 5:15 the thought contained in "light" in v. 13 is continued in "wise." Paul's οὖν is not merely formal; it connects the thought. So here the new admonition begins with walking in love, love like that expressed in 4:32, and has a καθώς clause like the one found in 4:32. Yet 5:1 begins a new admonition. If 5:1, 2 form the conclusion of 4:32, the new piece would begin with δέ which would be odd and at variance with the other three admonitions. More might be said, let this suffice.

The new subject is *filthiness*. It is treated at length in fourteen verses; Paul does far more than to name and to forbid the sins against the Sixth Commandment. He puts them into a setting of thought that should make them impossible for the Christian. In the following admonition to husbands in 5:25-33 he likewise brings in the grand relation of Christ to his church. The sins against which he warns are seen in their true light when they are viewed as Paul here views them, against the whole background of our holy life in God and in Christ. We have already noted that in 4:19, 29 he is not trenching on the subject which is reserved for the long admonition which now begins.

Be, therefore, imitators of God as beloved children; and be walking in love even as also Christ did love you and gave himself for us as an offering and a slaughter sacrifice to God for an odor of sweet smell.

Γίνεσθε repeats this imperative from 4:32 but now broadens the admonition by means of the predicate "imitators of God," who not only, like God, forgive (4:32) but copy God and Christ in love generally. The durative imperative = "ever be"; it is not necessary to translate it "become" because in so many instances γίνεσθαι rather than εἶναι is used. We can be only "imitators," but we are to be that always. Μιμηταί refers to likeness and similarity and not to complete duplication. It means dependence on God in all our actions and not indepedent sameness.

The closest relation underlies our imitating, and this relation to God is both the reason for our imitating him and the motive that prompts us; be God's imitators "as children beloved." Τέκνα are children born of God who is their Father. The word itself conveys the idea of dearness to God. "Sons" connotes the idea of standing and rights. "Children" is exactly proper here, for in their childhood children are naturally imitators of their parents. To be sure, our Father loves us; but "beloved" makes evident our normal relation. Some ordinary children are unnatural; they act in such a manner that one would scarcely believe that they belong to their parents. Not so "children beloved." This word "beloved" strikes the note of this paragraph: our love is to imitate God's love.

2) Hence the addition: "and be walking in love even as," etc. With love in your hearts, let your lives and all your actions show forth that love. Or walk, with every thought, word, and deed move in the circle

drawn by your love and never step outside of it. "Beloved" = God's love to us, certainly the same love as that mentioned in John 3:16 and yet with this difference that, since we no longer belong to the world but have been taken out of it by God's love and made his "children," his love is able to bestow upon us vastly more than it bestows upon those who are still of the world.

"Walk in love" = in love to God. Here it becomes evident that these two verses cannot be combined with the preceding admonition. "Walk in love" would then mean: in love toward our neighbor so as not to harm him. But here "in love" means that, as God loves us, his children, we in imitation as his children are to love him in turn. Not our relation to each other but our relation to God is stressed, for our relation to God is to bar us from all filthiness.

Three times we have the word for love: the verbal, the noun, the verb. It is essential to know what ἀγάπη means. See the condensed remarks on 1:4: the love of understanding and comprehension coupled with corresponding purpose, which is far higher than φιλία, the love of mere affection (see John 21:15-17). We are to *know* all the love of God and Christ, and our one *purpose* is to respond to this love. That is our *agape*.

Now the special model of love we are to copy: "even as also Christ loved you," etc. The similarity, of course, is found in the love as love and not in the act by which Christ manifested his love. We cannot die in his stead as he died in ours and ransomed us. The thought is like that expressed in I John 4:19: "We love him because he first loved us." The aorist: "Christ did love you," is historical to designate the one supreme act of love on Christ's part; it is like the next aorist: "and did give himself in your stead." God's love to us is identical with Christ's love to us and with Christ's sacrifice on the cross.

"And" is explicative: "he gave himself" expounds "he loved." We should construe: "he gave himself for us as an offering and a slaughter sacrifice," and "to God" modifies this unit and not merely the verb or the predicative accusatives. Jesus delivered himself into the hands of his enemies at the gate of Gethsemane and thereby gave himself to God as the sacrifice to be slain according to God's determinate counsel and foreknowledge (Acts 2:23). Here there is the voluntariness of Christ's sacrifice, and it was this that made it such a sweet odor. Here there is the supreme evidence of Christ's love for us; greater love is impossible.

The better reading is "for us" and not "for you." The phrase makes the whole statement more than a model for our love, it at the same time states the motive for our love and calls forth love from us as nothing else could. Do not pound Christians with the law in order to make them love; the law kindles no love. Set them afire in love by the love of Christ who died for them. Translate as you please: "for us," "in our behalf," "for our sake or benefit," "in our stead," neither here nor in other passages like Rom. 5:6, 8, 8:32, II Cor 5:14 is substitution eliminated; here expiation lies even in the context.

One should read R. 573 and 630, etc., on ἀντί and ὑπέρ, and especially Robertson, *The Minister and his Greek New Testament,* the entire chapter 35, etc., in order to see the evidence for the meaning "instead of." The classics lend their authority, the papyri and the ostraca furnish a whole volume. Scribes write "for," ὑπέρ, others who cannot write, i e., "in their stead," and constantly sign "for" whom they write In Gal 3.13 the curse, like the sword of Damocles, hangs over our heads, Christ interposed, the sword pierced him "instead of" us John 11 50 Jesus is to die "instead of" the people Winer stated that in any number of cases one cannot act "for" another unless he acts "in his stead." The incontestable fact is that ὑπέρ was used as *the* preposition to indicate substitution in preference even to ἀντί. Christ's sacrifice was vicarious, in substitution.

Two predicative accusatives state the capacity in which Christ gave himself: "as an offering and a slaughter sacrifice." Two words are used to re-enforce the idea. The first is derived from φέρω, "to bring," and thus points out the truth that when Christ gave himself *he* brought the offering; the second is derived from θύω, "to make go up in smoke," and indicates the fact that the offering referred to was one that involved the victim's death. Both terms are at times used in a general way, the latter also to designate unbloody sacrifices. Here the reference is historical: Christ died on the cross ("blood," 1:7; 2:13; "cross," 2:16) and so gave himself as an offering and a sacrifice.

The dative does not modify the εἰς phrase, especially since it precedes the phrase. "For an odor of sweet odor" may be an instance of the adjectival genitive: "a sweet-odored odor" ("a sweet-smelling savor," A. V.). Both words are derived from ὄζω, to emit an odor; in fact, our word "odor" is a derivative. Paul has this combination also in Phil. 4:18. The Hebrew *reach nichoach* = odor of soothing, the second noun being *ein Ersatz von "versoehnend," "angenehm"* (Ed., Koenig, *Woerterbuch* 276). It is used thus in Gen. 8:21 and repeatedly in Leviticus. Paul means an odor that pleases to the extent of reconciling us to God. Incense was burned, so were the burnt sacrifices, both emitted an odor, the true sweetness of which consisted in the spiritual condition of the person bringing the sacrifice. Cf., Lev. 26:31; Amos 5:21, 22; Ps. 51:16, 17. In the sacrifice of Christ his supreme love, his absolutely perfect obedience, and its all-sufficiency in every respect made it in the supreme sense "an odor of sweet odor" — the odor of odors for sweetness.

The expiatory character of Christ's sacrifice is often denied. Christ's death is said to be nothing but a sweet odor in the sense of a noble suffering and a martyrdom and thus pleasing God and thus being our noblest example. This is Socinianism. Von Hofmann still maintains that Christ was our representative with God but finds the significance of his death only in the fact that he might appear before God as an acceptable and well-pleasing representative. Other "theories" are offered. They are excluded by ὑπὲρ ἡμῶν combined with "offering and slaughter sacrifice." This was the odor of odors for sweetness, not merely for its moral quality in general, but for its expiatory sufficiency. Its sufficiency is attested by its acceptance on God's part.

It is not accidental that Paul writes about the supreme sweetness of the odor of Christ's sacrifice when he purposes to warn against filthiness on our part. The love of God brought forth such a pure, sweet sacrifice for us on his part. Can we, who were made God's beloved children by this sacrifice on our part return a life that is reeking and stinking with vile odor? It is thus that the idea of *agape* or love is colored and individualized by the additional concepts into the midst of which it is set for the apostle's present purpose.

3) It is Paul's way (copy it!) to lay a great, deep, massive foundation on which to erect some specific appeal and admonition. **Now fornication and all uncleanness or covetousness, let it not even be named among you as befits saints; also indecency and silly talk or wittiness, things not proper; on the contrary, rather giving of thanks!**

Δέ is not adversative but specifies the type of sins to be mentioned in this warning. First is "fornication," prostitution in all its forms. Next we have a pair: "all uncleanness or covetousness," both are unclean, foul, and are often joined together, "or" indicat-

ing the two as being different types of the same class.
The difference in meaning from the broader "uncleanness" used in 4:19 is that here fornication precedes
and thus makes us think of sexual uncleanness. Every
form of lasciviousness is meant. The ancient and the
modern world are disgusting in this respect, the details
are unfit to be mentioned. "Covetousness" is ranked
in the same class with sexual uncleanness; it is the
German *Geiz* and is here to be taken in its specific
sense; the Greek word is not to be understood so in
4:19. We, too, say "*filthy* lucre."

Instead of using a simple prohibition Paul has the
stronger form: "Let it not even be named among you
as befits saints." The thought is, of course, not that
these vices are not even to be mentioned among Christians, for Paul himself does that right here, and we
must warn against them as he does. The view that
Christians are not to discuss them with pleasure and
avidity in conversation does not lie in the text. Paul
means that such vices are to be so far removed from us
that even an intimation or a suspicion of their presence among us should not occur. "As befits saints"
recalls "saints" in the address in 1:1, those separated
unto God as his "children beloved" (5:1), for whom
Christ's sacrifice has been made.

4) In a descending scale three more vices are
added, the second and the third again being joined with
"or" as being two of the same type. The three terms
are *hapax legomena* in the New Testament, rather rare
words. The first is "indecency," "nastiness," *Scheuss-
lichkeit*, which B.-P. 37 limits to speech: *Zoten*, filthy
stories. Next, "silly or vapid talk," combined with
"wittiness," (εὖ plus τρέπω, to turn easily), quick rep-
artee, *elegante Witzelei*, salacious quirks. The three
may refer to speech, the last two certainly do so. And
because of the context these are given a sexual color-

ing. How worldlings so generally love nasty stories, throw out silly, vile remarks, crack supposed jokes of a spicy kind!

If we regard the next expression as the neuter plural participle, οὐ negates the participle: "things non-proper" (R. 1138), that do not come up (ἀνά plus ἥκω) to the mark set for Christians, that are far beneath us. Although the nouns that precede are feminine, this apposition is neuter. If we regard it as the imperfect, it is the Greek idiom in a statement of propriety or obligation that is not lived up to (R. 886): "which are not proper." The Greeks and the Latins start from the past with which the present does not agree: the propriety is not met. The English and the Germans have difficulty with this imperfect which refers to a present duty that is left unfulfilled. Either reading is like a verdict pronounced on "the things" indicated. Its very mildness is damning.

"On the contrary" states the positive opposite, "rather" setting the virtue against the vices as being vastly to be preferred. The striking thing is that Paul considers one virtue enough, and that he does not name as this virtue purity of heart, word, and deed, but "thanksgiving." This deserves more attention. We do not accept the view that εὐχαριστία = grace or graciousness of speech; even if such a meaning could be established, it would not aid us in securing a formal opposite. Nor can "thanksgiving" to men be referred to, for only a few men deserve our thanks; to thank everybody would be silly. This is thanksgiving to God, of whom and of whose love we, his children beloved (v. 1), constantly think. That lifts us above the vileness of worldlings. Amid our Father's blessings, with hearts and lips full of thanksgiving, these filthy vices will not even be named among us. On the great virtue of thanksgiving compare v. 19, 20.

5) **For this you know, realizing that no forni-cator, or unclean person, or coveter, which means idolater, has inheritance in the kingdom of Christ and God.**

Whether we are to regard the Greek verb as an indicative or an imperative depends on the thought alone; hence opinions vary. We agree with our versions and prefer the former. The appeal to knowledge already present is more to the point than the effort to impart such knowledge by a command. Moreover, the fact that sinners such as Paul names do not belong to the kingdom belongs to the ABC of Christianity; every beginner knows that. Γάρ is argumentative and agrees with the indicative better than it would with an imperative. The plea that ἴστε would be a literary Attic indicative involves Heb. 12:17 where the word is plainly an indicative, and James 1:19, where it seems to be indicative. Even B.-D. 99, 2, who prefers the imperative, hesitates regarding Heb. 12:17.

What has caused more discussion is the combination ἴστε γινώσκοντες which is found in a LXX variant of Jer. 42:22, and in somewhat similar expressions in other LXX renderings. Is this a Hebraism, the Greek participle used for the Hebrew infinitive absolute when the verbal idea is to be intensified? But the Hebrew uses the infinitive of the same finite verb, and here the participle is that of a different verb; besides, it is a participle. The Greek would use a cognate noun in the dative. In addition to this Paul is here not translating Hebrew, is not quoting or alluding to a Hebrew passage.

The canon of Ewald should be reversed. Instead of saying that, when we can read Paul's Greek in Hebrew fashion, we ought to do so, all the newer insight into the Koine leads us to say that, when we are able to read Paul's Greek without a Hebraism, we ought to do so. A host of supposed Hebraisms has already been corrected. Although he prefers the imperative, even Moulton, *Einleitung* 119, says that it is at least probable that we must separate verb and participle: "you must be assured of this (ἴστε), as realizing for yourselves that, etc. (γινώσκοντες)." This is acceptable. We prefer the indicative: "this you know, as realizing yourselves that," etc. We add the point that Paul wants both the force of οἶδα, simple knowing (relation of the object to the subject), and the force of γινώσκειν, personal realization (the relation of the subject to the object) ; see C.-K. 388 regarding these two verbs.

So we do not regard this as the periphrastic present (R. 330), which may be the idea of the A. V., but prefer the literary Attic (R. 319). We also do not accept the Hebraism offered in the R. V.: "ye know of a surety." We likewise do not call πᾶς . . . οὐκ ἔχει translation Greek (Moulton 127), a sort of sacred way of speaking. We have nothing but a common Greek idiom which places the negative with the verb: "every fornicator does not have," whereas we place it with the subject: "no fornicator has."

The Ephesians know the fact intellectually, the more so because they realize it personally, "that no fornicator, etc., has inheritance in the kingdom." "Fornicator" repeats "fornication" used in v. 3, and "coveter" repeats "covetousness." These two suffice here, for the other vices mentioned in v. 3, 4 are ethically of the same character. Yes, it is necessary for us to be reminded of what we know and even realize about vice. There is constant temptation. Ephesus presented it on all sides. Apologists defend, excuse, even advocate these sins. This is especially true regarding sex and regarding business.

Western and Syrian texts read: ὅς: "who is an idolater"; but ὅ, the neuter, is textually correct. Yet this does not imply that "the general sense of the thing" is meant (R. 713), for then the abstract should follow: "which is idolatry." "Which" = which word "coveter," this word means "idolater." Because v. 3 contains only the unmodified "covetousness," Paul elucidates briefly what a covetous sinner is. Like a pagan idolater he worships gold instead of God. Some such an exposition of the enormity of this sin is necessary. A Catholic priest states that during his long years of service all kinds of sins and even crimes were confessed to him in the confessional, but no member of his church ever confessed himself as being covetous.

The negative is absolute: not a single one of these sinners, whether he is still regarded as outwardly belonging to the congregation or not, is in the *Una Sancta*. He may so hide his sin that the congregation does not expel him, he expels himself from the kingdom. Paul's language is full of meaning.

On the great concept of the kingdom see either Matt. 3:2; Mark 1:15; Luke 1:33; John 3:3. It is the rule of God's (Christ's) grace here on earth and of glory in heaven. It extends from creation into all eternity. The kingdom does not make the King as earthly kingdoms do; the King makes the kingdom. Where he is with his grace, there is his kingdom here on earth. We are not admitted into this kingdom as subjects, it has no subjects. We are admitted as heirs; we "have inheritance in the kingdom." That does not mean merely a place in it, but that the kingdom itself, i. e., the King's riches of grace, are our own as heirs. Joined to the supreme Heir, we are co-heirs with him, Rom. 8:17. As "children beloved" we have this inheritance. We "have" it now; we shall presently enter upon this inheritance, i. e., upon its full enjoyment. We are now like princes in the King's house. We shall presently sit with the King in his throne (Rev. 3:21).

We thus see what it means "not to have inheritance in the kingdom." "Inheritance" is the vast, eternal possession, but the covetous man, like the fornicator, grasps at the transient and the perishable. What is the wealth of all the kingdoms of this world compared with the inheritance of the kingdom? What the foul pleasures of the world to the kingdom's unspeakable heavenly bliss?

Matthew regularly says, "the kingdom of the heavens," and only occasionally, "the kingdom of God." On inheriting the kingdom note Gal. 5:21; James 2:5. Jesus said "my kingdom" to Pilate; the malefactor said "thy kingdom" to Jesus. Paul says, "the kingdom of Christ and God." The question as to whether Paul refers to one person when he writes "Christ and God" cannot be determined from the English which needs no article but only from the Greek which here uses one article with both nouns. This question is more acute in regard to Titus 2:13, regarding which read Moulton, *Einleitung* 134, which is quoted also by R. 786. Robertson states: "Outside of special cases like these [where a second article appears when *one* person is referred to] only one article is found where several epithets are applied to the same person." Again: a second article lays greater stress on the second epithet. We thus have the fullest justification for regarding "Christ and God" as *one* person. Even if two persons were referred to (Christ and the Father), they would be equal in grace and in glory, i. e., in deity, as owners of the kingdom. The kingdom is that "of the Son of his love," Col. 1:13, in whom the fulness of the Godhead dwells bodily, Col. 2:9.

The plea that "Christ," when this term is used as an official name, may more easily have the article: *des Messias,* is unsubstantiated, for a mere appellative is out of place here where the King in his person is to be named. The same is true as to Θεός and the plea that it does not need the article when it is used regarding

the Father. Of course it does not; but that says nothing about the present case where two nouns are preceded by one article, the regular way of designating
one person by the use of two terms. The reason for doing so is also plain. For the kingdom Paul mentions the
King. He calls him "Christ" because of his great work
and adds "God" because of his deity. The deity and
the Christhood of the King make plain to the Ephesian
Christians what the rule or kingdom is from which
every idolatrous sinner shuts himself out.

Christ is called God so often in Scripture, his deity
is so constantly revealed that one more or one less predication to that effect is of little importance as regards
the fact. The sole interest for us is to see what Paul
says and means. Grammatically and in every other
respect that is as plain as can be. If the deity of Christ
is not a fact, those who reject it eliminate it here as they
do in all the other passages of Scripture that mention it.
Here this is patently impossible. That is enough.

6) **Let no one deceive you with empty words,
for because of these things comes the wrath of God
upon the sons of the disobedience.**

These sins and vices have their apologists, "the
sons of the disobedience," as the context suggests. Even
the greatest men of the Gentile world practiced sexual
vices as something that was quite natural and blameless. Paul warns against their specious arguments
such as that nature requires these vices, that they are
innocent pleasures, at worst pardonable weaknesses,
etc. "Let no one," no matter who he may be, "deceive
you" at any time (present imperative) "with empty
words," devoid of truth or reality, "empty," because
they state what is not so. On κενός compare the remarks made in connection with 4:17. To believe and
to act on such words is to build on a shadow.

Paul's word states the fact; "for" states the reason for not listening to deceivers. Just because of

these things there comes the wrath of God, etc. The
emphasis is on the verb which is placed before the
subject. The wrath "comes" when it blazes forth in
divine judgments and blasts individuals and even rotten nations. To think only of the last day does not
agree with the tense (iterative present) and the sense;
we observe many of these judgments. "The wrath of
God" is the reaction of God's holiness and righteousness against sin. See Rom. 1:18. Considerations of
grace and mercy restrain God's wrath from blazing
forth; this is the patience and longsuffering of God.
But when sinners persist, disregard patient grace,
intensify their disobedience, and literally challenge
God, his wrath finally strikes the sinner down.

On "the sons of the disobedience" see 2:2. This is
the old, original disobedience and hence is definite.
These are "the sons" of it, brought forth by it, and as
"sons" make it their practice. Unbelief is also disobedience, but why make a restriction here? The Gentiles
stifled even the voice of conscience, the law written in
their hearts, the *lex naturalis* (Rom. 1:32). Read Paul's
own commentary in Rom. 1:18-32 and note how the
wrath comes: "God gave them up" (v. 24, 26, 28).
Do God's "children beloved" (5:1) want to listen to
these sons of the disobedience? R., *W. P.,* refers to
Gnostics. Gnosticism appeared later, and these vices
were not peculiarly Gnostic.

7) **Therefore be not their partners!** Συμμέτοχοι =
σύν, supporting and abetting them; μετά, in association
with them; ἔχω, adhering to them, holding and having
what is theirs in sin and in coming wrath. The present imperative, like the preceding, is iterative: at any
time. The negative involves the positive, "Stay entirely aloof." Here οὖν appears to be incidental, it does
not introduce a new line of admonition; see 4:17. This
appears from αὐτῶν, the antecedent of which is "the
sons," etc., in v. 6.

8) **For you were at one time darkness, now,
however, (you are) light in the Lord. As children
of light (ever) walk, for the fruit of this light (is)
in all goodness and righteousness and truth, testing
out what is well-pleasing to the Lord.**

"For" in v. 6 offers the reason lying in the vices
themselves, always and everywhere they are subject
to the coming of the wrath of God. "For" now offers
the second reason lying in the new condition of the
Ephesians, it states what they no longer are. The first
word in each clause has the emphasis: *"You were* at
one time darkness; *now,* however, light in the Lord."
"You were" is emphatic because of its tense; "now" is
therefore the opposite, and the copula "are" is not
needed. How can the Ephesians ever think of going
back, of making that "were" a "now"?

The abstracts "darkness" and "light in the Lord,"
used directly with reference to persons, are highly
effective, compare Matt. 5:14. While both terms are
predicates and may be called spiritual conditions, the
following non-predicative "the light" shows that the
remarks made in connection with 4:18, that "the darkness" (and "the light") are really powers, are correct.
They exist independently of us, and we are either darkness or light only as we are identified with the one or
the other. "You were darkness" = "having been darkened" (4:18). "Now light" is not enough; "light in
the Lord," in union with him who is the Light of the
world, by faith in him, is the proper predicate.

The negative: "Be not their partners" (v. 7), is
now followed by the positive: "As children of light
(ever) walk," etc. In this sense, then, we are light:
"children of light," children born of light when the
Light, our Lord, entered our souls. II Cor. 4:6. In
I Thess. 5:5 Paul has the expression "sons of light."
The difference is that obtaining between "children"

and "sons," between birth and standing; but the expression "children and sons of darkness" is never used, the strongest statement in this direction being perhaps "to be of darkness, of night" (I Thess. 5:5).

"The sons of the disobedience" refers to all of them (v. 6; 2:2); "as children of light" is predicative and needs no article, there are other such children. The genitive is commonly called adjectival (R. 651) and it does characterize, yet it is not like an adjective; it names a power, call it an ethical or a possessive genitive. The simple predicate "be walking" anticipates the following participle (v. 10): "testing out," etc.

9) This leads our versions to place v. 9 in parentheses. Paul builds the admonition against vileness on the broad basis of our being "children of light." It is his way of doing throughout: every individual virtue, every single avoidance of sin he pictures as growing out of the full tide of the new life that fills us in Christ. Not content with the general reference "children of light," he adds what this light produces, for this is a very definite light, is most effective, produces great results, and is known by them. So γάρ explains this feature of "the light" and makes clear what walking as "children of light" means. After this is clear, Paul adds the participle that describes our walk as such children.

We see that "this light" (article of previous reference) is a power. It is productive. Paul has the same view of it that John has (1:4). Light and life go together. Being children of light and walking as such means what Jesus says in Matt. 5:14-16, letting our light shine in good works for the glory of God. We are created (spiritually) for good works (2:10). "The fruit of this light (is) in all goodness," etc. Ἐν indicates the great sphere, and "all" the whole of this sphere. "The fruit" is a collective and summarizes all that "walking" means. Our deeds are marked by three cardinal qualities: "all goodness and righteousness and truth." They fill our hearts, they are the rays of the light which make us children of light, they shine forth in our walk or deeds. The three are, of course, not exclusive. Viewed from one angle, we see nothing but goodness, viewed from another, we see righteousness, from a third, truth. These three complete the view.

"Goodness" has been translated "benignity," *Guete*, Luther, *Guetigkeit*. It means more, it is "all genuine moral excellence." It is more than goodness, kindness, beneficence to men, for the reference to God is not omitted. That is why "righteousness" follows, agreement with the divine norm of right (δίκη) as this is applied by the heavenly Judge. The righteous walk in all righteousness. The approval of this Judge rests upon them. The morality of our modern moralists is the reverse: what is good for the herd, the herd has in its evolution come to approve as "right"; what damages the herd, the herd has come to condemn and to punish.

Paul's circle is closed by "truth," verity, reality, namely spiritual and moral reality as opposed to all lying perversion, sham, deception, pretense. These three are ever the same. Like the sun in the heavens, "the light" never changes. Truth, righteousness, goodness are not one thing in one age and another thing in another age. The only progress possible is to enter more deeply into these three. It is one of the lies of our time that we have progressed beyond them.

10) We should remember that the Greek participle has number, case, and gender and thus great precision. So here the nominative plural participle connects automatically with the subject "you" in the imperative "walk" in v. 8: "as children of light walk . . . testing out what is well-pleasing to the Lord," what accords with his gracious and holy will. We are "light in the Lord" (v. 8) and hence concerned to know and

to do only what pleases the Lord. We are "children
of light," our very birth and nature lead us toward the
Lord. As a plant seeks and turns to the light, so do we.
Paul uses the gospel appeal and not the compulsion of
law. As children of light we know the qualities which
the light produces, we are able to make the test in our
walk and life.

"Walk . . . testing" means examining ourselves.
Δοκιμάζω is exactly the proper word. It is used with
regard to testing metals as to whether they are genuine, of coins as to whether they are the real metal and
of full weight. The word matches v. 6: "Let no one
deceive you." Satan deceived Eve. Endless deception
offers what is morally rotten as though it were perfectly sound. Test every thought, word, and act. That
is why we are children of light and have the standard
for testing (v. 9). I John 4:1.

11) This testing refers to our own walk as children of light. But how about others! **On the one
hand, have no fellowship with the unfruitful works
of the darkness; on the other hand, rather also reprove them, for the things being done in secret by
them it is shameful even to state.**

As far as others are concerned, two things are mentioned: no fellowship with their evil works, reproof
that exposes their shamefulness. "Have no fellowship" repeats v. 7, but the statement now refers to
works, the verb is different, and the thought is amplified. Whereas in the preceding we had the idea of
support and association with persons (v. 7), we now
have the idea of fellowship or communion with their
works. In a masterly way Paul keeps the idea of both
"the light" and "the fruit." For he calls them "the
works, the unfruitful ones of the darkness," and adds
the adjective with a second article like an apposition or
climax with emphasis (R. 776). "What fellowship is
there for light with darkness?" II Cor. 6:14. "Be

having no fellowship" has the dative as the object of the verb, the dative because of σύν.

"The darkness" is the direct opposite of "the light," both are definite, both are powers. Each excludes the other, a union of the two is impossible. The one has fruit, the other is unfruitful; what it produces in the way of works is not fruit. "Unfruitful" recalls "empty words" in v. 6. The discourse is closely woven together by the very terms used. We should note the impact of argument in "unfruitful" and "of the darkness," it is like a volley from a masked battery. Who wants to spend his life in working a field which produces no fruit at all? That is what "the sons of the disobedience" (v. 6) do. Do we want a part of this fruitlessness? Who wants to be in the grasp of "the darkness," a power as black as hell? Call the genitive subjective or possessive. See John 3:19, 20: some love the darkness, hate the light.

But withdrawal is not enough. This is the ideal of monks and of nuns. The light is not to be placed under a bushel, the salt is to bite into the world's corruption. Καί — δέ = "on the one hand — on the other"; δέ is not adversative ("but"), it adds the other thing which is different from the first. Μᾶλλον καί = "rather also" (it is not the ascensive "even"). "Also" means that this, too, must be done; and "rather" means that the obligation of administering reproof is not to be reluctantly added to that of avoiding fellowship but to be added with zest. That is what the light is for: not just to shine for itself but "rather" also to blaze out into the darkness and to expose what that darkness covers up. We are to "reprove" these works as being "unfruitful," as being "of the darkness." There is no need to intensify and to translate "convict"; one reproves works, he scarcely convicts them.

12) "For" does not state the reason for reproving but explains how this reproof gets to be so effec-

tive. Many are puzzled about this verse and the next;
but the meaning is rather obvious. Just to state the
things done by them (by those who do the works of
darkness, *constructio ad sensum*), to state them in our
reproof, is shameful, not for us who make the statement, but for those who engage in these works. It is
"a shameful thing" (neuter) for them. Paul exposed
this shamefulness at length in Rom. 1:18-32. Was he
thereby guilty of doing a shameful thing? Since when
is it a shameful thing for a Christian to reprove dirty
works? The idea that Paul here says that it makes *us*
blush to mention these things, that we hate to do it, is
not indicated.

The emphasis is on the adverb "secretly." Why do
men hide such things? They thereby admit that such
works are a disgrace to themselves. Our reproof is
like the flash of light on these hidden works of darkness which exposes all their shame. Alas, men are not
ashamed before God who sees in secret (Matt. 6:4);
but they are ashamed before men when their deeds are
exposed to the sight of men.

"In secret" matches "the darkness," but the two are
not identical. Many a deed is done openly and is, nevertheless, a deed "of the darkness." "In secret" limits
"the things done by them" to the vile and filthy sins
with which Paul here deals. Sexual vices are not practiced in public; covetousness also hides itself from the
public eye. Γινόμενα = occurrences, and the Greek is
able in the regular way to add the agents involved with
ὑπό. This present participle denotes continuousness,
things that are done again and again.

13) **Now all the things reproved by the light
are made public, for everything made public is light.**

This verse has been found difficult, especially the
last half of it. Δέ introduces a parenthetical remark
regarding the effect of applying "the light," the thing

Paul wants the Ephesians to do. The thought is carried a step farther; it is not adversative ("but," our
versions). It is a simple fact that all the things reproved by the light are thereby made public so that
men see them as they are. Thus Paul let the light shine
on the heathen ungodliness and unrighteousness in
Rom. 1:18-32 and by his epistle exposed them before
all the world for what they really are. That public exposure still stands and is most effective.

The point to be observed is that the things must be
"reproved by the light," the sun of God's Word. Participle and phrase belong together (contra our versions). The fact that they are made public also by this
light, by it alone, is self-evident. The verb is passive
and not middle. The dictionaries translate this passive (which they acknowledge as such) "become visible" (middle); it should undoubtedly be: "is made
visible, plain, manifest." Here even the light is implied as the agent. There is no need to make the participle temporal: "when reproved" (R. V.), or a statement of means: "by being reproved." It is attributive
(A. V.).

"For" explains that everything that is thus made
public is light. This is not "light in the Lord" (v. 8).
The subject is "everything that is made public," and
the context refers to the hidden, secret works of darkness. "The light" (the revealing agent) and this predicate "light" are not the same. "The light," Christ, his
Word and his truth shine on the secret vices of men
when we reprove them, and thus every one of them is
light, is seen as what it is, an unfruitful work of the
darkness. It is not changed, transformed. Darkness
does not become light. Paul is not speaking of the saving effect of "the light" and of our reproof of secret
sins. Up to this point he insists only on our steady
reproof. What the effect will be, whether it will result
in contrition and conversion or not, makes no differ-

ence; as children of light we *must* reprove sin and vice,
our very nature requires no less. What saving effects
may result from our efforts lies with God. See Ezek.
33:8, 9.

14) **Wherefore the statement is:**
Up, thou sleeper, and arise from the dead,
And there shall shine forth upon thee Christ!

"Wherefore" = because of the reproving just enjoined upon the Ephesians. Δέγει (see 4:8) indicates
a quotation without naming the source. The quotation
does not offer a sample of the reproof of the sins and
vices as such but a reproving call to the sinner to rise
up from his condition of spiritual death and a great
promise. These two lines are a sample of the *way* in
which the reproof is to be uttered, of the spirit of the
reproof. The aim is always the sinner's conversion.

Amid the discussion about the source of this quotation the quotation itself seems not to have been sufficiently noted, especially the second line about Christ.
For this line, too, is part of the quotation. It is not
taken from the Old Testament, from the Apocrypha, or
from a pagan Iranian source (B.-P. 473). As for the
Apocrypha, the New Testament never quotes them.
While in 4:8 and elsewhere λέγει introduces citations
from the Old Testament, that is not conclusive proof
that it must do so here. For this is a Christian call, it
even names Christ. This is evidently a couplet taken
from a Christian hymn that was used in Ephesus in
Paul's time. The propriety of quoting such a hymn is
obvious. The Ephesians are to reprove sinners; lines
from one of their hymns are in place.

The first line is a reproof, this sleeper is lying dead
when he ought to "up and arise." The present imperative ἔγειρε (some texts have the middle), like ἄγε,
whether it is added with καί or without, is only our exclamatory: "Up!" and intensifies the aorist imperative: "Up and arise!" Ἀνάστα is the second aorist im-

perative with the suffix dropped (R. 328). Arising is a momentary act. This sleeper is in the sleep of spiritual death (2:1). Telling him to arise implies no synergism in conversion; nor does it imply God's omnipotence as when Christ raised the physically dead. This is the gospel call of grace, of the *gratia sufficiens,* which is ever filled with quickening power (2:5) to raise up those whom it bids to arise. The figure of sleep and of death fits the idea of "the darkness" (v. 11).

Beside the negative there appears the positive: "and there shall shine forth upon thee Christ." The beautiful word ἐπιφαύσκω, *erglaenzen, ueberstrahlen,* "send effulgence upon," matches "the light" (v. 9, 13). But the future tense is not hypotactic, and a condition is not implied as R. 948 assumes: if thou dost arise, Christ will shine forth, etc. This is a peremptory imperative that is effective because of the tremendous promise with which it is combined (καί). The command would be in vain without the life-giving promise; the promise would be in vain without the command. Here there is the same gracious and efficacious call as in Matt. 11:28-30. Subject and verb are transposed, both are thus made emphatic. A wealth of meaning is concentrated in this brief promise. This must have been a missionary hymn, and its other lines unfolded what these two contain.

We have had "the light — the light." Here we see that this light is Christ. As in John 1:4, life and light are combined in Christ. Because these two lines fit the previous thought and expressions so exactly Paul uses them and thus rounds out and brings to a close this great admonition. No loose thread of thought is left dangling; all is perfectly woven together and comes to rest in this gospel call to the sinner.

* * *

The Admonition to Exercise Christian Wisdom

15) We have noted how the preceding three admonitory sections are introduced. Each has its connective (see 4:17) which links each into the preceding and makes the whole one chain. We thus understand the force of οὖν; it adds the last of the four specific admonitions which constitute a group. The summary of this admonition is the exercise of Christian wisdom. It is a natural admonition in this place; for those who are to rebuke others must be wise and not foolish in both heart and conduct.

Therefore see how accurately you are walking, not as unwise but as wise, buying up the opportunity because the days are wicked.

The readings vary so that it is difficult to establish the proper text, whether it is: "see accurately" ("carefully," R. V.), or: "how accurately you are walking" ("that you walk circumspectly," A. V.). It will not do to reject the latter on the plea that "to walk accurately" is an improper combination of ideas, for the answer to that objection is the fact that some of the very best texts place the adverb so as to modify "to walk" and find this combination perfectly proper. Nothing more convincing can be said regarding the position of the adverb so that it modifies "to see." Both constructions make equally good sense. We prefer the former only because βλέπετε usually has no adverbial modifier, it being understood that "see to it" means "see to it carefully."

"How you are walking" might have been written; yet this would only raise the question and leave undecided whether the Ephesians are walking properly or not. Paul does not want to leave the matter open. He wants to say that the Ephesians *are* walking accurately and raises only the question as to "*how* accurately" they are walking. He wants them to examine the degree of their carefulness in life. To walk with some care is not enough in days that are so wicked; we must use the greatest care, must walk accurately indeed. In Luke 1:3 the same adverb is used.

"Not as unwise but as wise" defines the indirect question, "how accurately you are walking," accurately as regards Christian wisdom. One might understand "accurately" as a reference to mere precision in observing the law. Paul is moving on the gospel level. The Christian must walk in the full gospel light (note "the light" in v. 9, 13), and that means the gospel wisdom. "Not as unwise" (negative) "but as wise" (positive) emphasize the point: not lack or deficiency but abundance of wisdom. To be wise is more than to know; it means to use, apply, and thus to get the most out of knowledge in our walking or in the management of our life. Μή is not a subjective negative (Winer), nor is it due to the adjective (R. 1172); it is due to the implied participle: "not as being unwise."

16) Even this amplification is not enough. When are Christians really wise? When they "keep buying up the opportunity," ἐκ in the participle intensifying; "buying it out completely." The classics use a different verb but have the same figure. A καιρός is the special time that is adapted for a certain thing, the season for something, hence the opportunity. Christian wisdom makes the most of its opportunities. These seasons are brief, they soon slip by; one must recognize them and must buy while the buying is good. We say "use" the opportunity; Paul says "buy it out," purchase all that it offers. That means: pay the necessary price in effort and exertion. It is lack of wisdom to hold back and to wait for a still better opportunity, which then often fails to arrive. It is certainly still greater lack of wisdom not to see the opportunity at all and thus to let it slip by. Our lives are brief and present only so much opportunity; he is truly wise who invests 100 per cent at every opportunity and then is

able to report: "Lord, thy pound hath gained ten pounds" (10 = maximum completeness), Luke 19:16; Ps. 126:6, "bringing their sheaves."

Paul uses the same expression in Col. 4:5 but places it after the following injunction: "in wisdom keep walking as regards those outside." Hence some refer also our passage to opportunity for influencing "those outside" of the church. But such a limitation is not expressed in this passage. Opportunity is not lacking for aiding also our brethren, for doing much for our families, for personally building up ourselves. Why narrow the word when Paul leaves it broad and general?

Opportunity itself is always a positive invitation and incentive. But a negative reason for the exercise of the fullest wisdom and the purchase of all that any opportunity offers is: "because the days are wicked." The adjective means viciously, actively wicked. The days are such as to spread wickedness of all kinds among men, to draw men into damnation.

This characterization is true also regarding our days. Paul says far more than that the times are bad, full of trouble and distress. Paul's meaning is not that the more wickedness there is, the more opportunity we have to buy up. Wickedness is not opportunity; it reduces the opportunities. This is the reason for using every one of them that is still offered, using it with all wisdom so as to buy it out completely. What a pity to lose a single one or only partly to buy it out! Luther's *schicket euch in die Zeit* comes nearer to the meaning than many suppose although he makes no distinction between "the opportunity" and "the days." We do accommodate ourselves to the times when we see and use what opportunity they offer.

17) **For this reason,** because the days are wicked, **be not foolish but understand what the will of the Lord is.** The verb does not necessarily mean

"become" since it is regularly used in the sense of "to be" (for instance in v. 1, 7). "Unwise" (v. 15) and "foolish" are practically the same. "Foolish" means not to have good judgment or not to exercise it when the time comes. Here it is, of course, spiritual sense and judgment in things which pertain to the Christian life and secure spiritual advancement and blessing (v. 9) for ourselves and for others. Wicked days are full of temptation that would make us foolish and cause us to yield to the inclinations of our flesh or at least not to make the most of our opportunities.

Over against this negative Paul sets the positive: "but understand," etc. Christians are foolish when they fail to understand what the will of the Lord is, i. e., what it is that he has willed us to be and to do; when they yield to their own will or to the will of men. Συνίημι = to bring the mind into conjunction with some object and thus really to grasp and understand it. In our case the one object to be understood is the answer to the question: "What is the will of the Lord?" We know where to find the answer: in the Word, in the Word alone (v. 6a). This answer is to be decisive.

Others may direct their minds to other questions such as: "What will bring me earthly gain, honor, pleasure, ease, etc.? What do others say, advise, do?" This is not only wrong, it is folly, senselessness. He is a fool who asks thus and determines his judgment and his life accordingly. Yet how few are the Christians who in the various situations of life make Paul's question the decisive one and follow out the answer at every cost! They often even persuade themselves or let others persuade them that the Lord's will is not what the Lord himself plainly says in his Word. Paul usually writes "the will of God"; but in Acts 21:14 we have "the will of the Lord." The latter is perhaps used here because Christ has left us an example that we should follow his footsteps (I Pet. 2:21).

18) **And be not drunk with wine, wherein is dissoluteness, but be filled in spirit, making utterance for yourselves by means of psalms and hymns and spiritual odes, singing and playing with your heart to the Lord, giving thanks always for all things in our Lord Jesus Christ's name to the God and Father, subjecting yourselves to each other in fear of Christ.**

This is the way in which Paul wants us to go about doing the will of the Lord: with joyful, enthusiastic, grateful hearts. This is good sense, the right tone for wise Christians who are living in wicked days. Did not also Luther say that music drives the devil away? He was, of course, not speaking of jazz.

The perplexity of some commentators regarding the occurrence of an admonition against drunkenness in the middle of this paragraph can thus easily be cleared up. The intoxication of drink is not introduced as a mere foil to spiritual exhilaration. It is a concrete example of worldly folly in wicked days and a sample of how fools make themselves utterly incapable of wisdom, sound judgment, and real understanding. They dull and drug even their physical brain and wickedly add to the wickedness of the days in which they live. Paul writes concretely in both the negative and the positive part of this admonition so as to be the more easily understood. The word about drunkenness is not an anomaly in this connection; it fits well into its place. Καί is explicative; Paul particularizes in a concrete manner.

The verbs Paul uses are aoristic presents and simply state what to do or what to shun. "With wine" is the dative of means, and "wine" is named because it was the commonly used intoxicant in the Orient at

Paul's time; it still serves in this capacity. Since he exemplifies, the abuse of any other intoxicant is included in his admonition. The abuse, not the legitimate use, is forbidden. Those who have traveled in southern Europe and in Oriental lands will know that wine is quite necessary because so much of the water is unsafe, and the necessity of boiling it for the sake of safety is so little understood. On the face of it excess of wine is gross folly which produces a physical and a moral condition in which anything resembling wisdom is impossible.

'Ασωτία (see its derivation) has come to mean "dissoluteness," *Liederlichkeit,* an abandoned, debauched life. It describes the condition when mind and body are dragged down so as to be incapable of spiritual functions. "In which" refers to the condition of being drunk with wine or to "wine" as here used, a means for becoming drunk. 'Αλλά presents the opposite course of conduct, yet there is a certain analogy between the two; the one is physical, the other a matter of the spirit — the one is debasing, the other ennobling — the one is open folly and a mark of it, the other is wisdom and one of its signs and aids — the physical stimulus of excessive wine gives base pleasure with bitter dregs, the spirit, when stimulated, is elevated to the highest pleasure with lasting results of the richest benefit. The contrast centers on the verbs, both of which are placed forward for that reason; the modifier of each verb simply goes with it and thus shares a bit of the emphasis. That is why "wine" is a dative and "in spirit" a phrase; being diverse, they are not pitted against each other as are the verbs.

Some regard ἐν as instrumental or think that, besides being construed with the genitive, the dative, or the accusative of that with which the filling is done, this verb may also use "in" with reference to the filler, and thus our versions translate, "Be filled with the

Spirit." But St. Paul would not combine "wine" that is used for the purpose of drunkenness with the Holy Spirit, the third person of the Godhead. In this connection review the writer's exposition of Gal. 5:16-25 and 6:8, where Paul uses "spirit" and not Spirit nine times.

'Εν does *not* state "with" what we are to be filled. Paul is not stating with what we are to be filled, he has no opposite for "wine." He lets us gather what this filler is to be from the context: it is spiritual joy, happiness, enthusiasm, thankfulness that overflow in the utterance of psalms, hymns, and odes even as the mouth speaks from the abundance of the heart. This statement does not deal with the *unio mystica* but with the richness and the abundance of the spiritual life "in" our own "spirit." Our spirit is ever to be filled so that it overflows with spiritual expressions.

The fact that these expressions are due to the Holy Spirit is self-evident, for this spirit is the new life in us, which is to be full of spiritual emotions that press for utterance. Yes, here there is a contrast between base physical stimulation and noble spiritual stimulation. The worldling descends to his body, the Christian ascends to his spirit.

19) The present participles partake of the imperative character of the main verb, "be filled." But they modify the subject of the imperative and thus describe the condition of those who are filled in spirit. They are so happy that ever and again they will be "giving utterance for themselves by means of psalms," etc. The reflexive "for yourselves" is not ἀλλήλοις (v. 21), "one to another" (R. V.), for the benefit of each other, but ἑαυτοῖς, for your own sakes. They simply cannot keep still (λαλεῖν is the opposite of to keep still), they must express themselves, their spirit is so full.

"Psalms, hymns, and spiritual odes" are datives of means and include the different forms of Christian poetic expression. Plain prose will not do, only the more exalted verse will. When we are differentiating the three forms of poetic utterance, not only the etymology but also the use of the terms must be noted. "Psalms" thus seem to refer to the Old Testament psalms, their use being carried over into the Christian Church. They have ever served to voice our feelings.

The word "hymns" originally had a strong pagan flavor, for it was used to designate the songs of praise that were addressed to heathen divinities or to deified men. Paul uses this word twice, the verb appears in Matt. 26:30 and in Acts 16:25. A hymn in the Christian sense of the term is thus an uninspired poetical composition in praise of God or Christ that is intended to be sung. Our present use extends the force of the word beyond the idea of praise.

The Greek word "ode" is wider in meaning and refers to any song or poem, religious or secular; hence it is placed last and needs the adjective, "spiritual odes or songs," to distinguish them from secular songs.

"Giving utterance" is general; the next two participles specify: "singing and playing with your heart to the Lord." Singing is done by means of the voice; playing by means of an instrument. Ψάλλω means to let a string twang and thus to play a lyre or a harp, and then to play any instrument as an accompaniment to the voice. Thus the two are here combined: "singing and playing." "Making melody" (our versions) will do if it is applied to instruments. But the view of some commentators that the dative indicates place: "*in* your heart," and that this is *silent* singing in the heart, is untenable. "Giving utterance" does not refer to audible music, over against which the non-audible "in your heart" is placed. There is no καί before the second participle. The second and the third participle define the first: *all* acts are audible.

"Giving utterance" means: by singing with the voice and by playing on instruments. But this is never to be only mechanical; it is to be done "with your heart to the Lord" and not merely with lips and fingers for men. The dative "for the Lord" is like the reflexive "for yourselves." We ourselves and the Lord go together; all this music is between him and us. He wants no lip service from us. We must sing and play to him "with our heart," and he ever looks to the heart.

Now look at Isa. 5:11, 12 and at Amos 6:5, 6 and see how Paul comes to write as he does about wine and drunkenness on the one hand and about Christian music on the other hand. Paul knows the Old Testament. And this Old Testament seems to be very modern, think of the cabarets! Drinkers yowl their songs. Now add Isa. 14:11 and Amos 5:23 and preach a bit to our church choirs, organists, and other players on instruments in our services. Unless all their music is for themselves and the Lord, sung and played "with the heart," the Lord will have none of it. Worldlings are rank and ribald where they carouse. God knows that they make the days wicked (v. 16). But they at least make no pretense of singing and playing "with the heart to the Lord." They know, and all men know that they are wicked. But the worst sin is pretense and hypocrisy in religious worship; Jesus denounced no other men as he did the Pharisees and the scribes: "Hypocrites!" Matt. 23:13, etc.

20) Another participle, again without "and," defines this utterance in singing and in playing in another direction: gratitude must run through it all, "giving thanks always for all things," etc. This is the main substance that dare not be absent. "Always" might mean simply that the Christian will always find *some* cause for thanksgiving; the addition "for all things" shows that *all* of them actually furnish such a cause.

Rom. 8:28 explains. Under the divine control even
painful experiences, calamities, etc., must bring us
spiritual benefits such as driving us closer to God to
seek his protection, making us search his Word more
earnestly for comfort, etc.

The addition "in our Lord Jesus Christ's name"
should not be read superficially as though we are
merely to add this phrase to our thanksgiving. This
phrase occurs often. The ὄνομα always signifies revelation, the Name which reveals our Lord to us, the
means by which we apprehend him; and ἐν = in union
or connection with (sphere). Hence we are told not
merely to believe in his Name. Our trust is to be connected with his revelation. No man knows God save
by means of his Name. We are baptized "in (not into)
the Name of the Father," etc. The act is connected *in
toto* with the revelation of the Father, etc.

The same is true with regard to our thanksgiving.
The Name includes the person, for it reveals him, that
is its function. His Name is then the sphere that sur-
rounds all our gratitude and its expression. Hence the
full designation "our Lord Jesus Christ," the concentrated formula that expresses all his Lordship, his
Christhood, his person, Jesus (see 1:2, 17) as these are
revealed in all Scripture.

Here there is another example of one article used
with two terms to denote one person exactly as in v. 5.
In connection with the blessed revelation of our Lord
Jesus Christ we have free access to him who is our God
and Father. As God Almighty and our heavenly
Father with infinite love he makes all things redound
to our good, and as his "children beloved" all our
thanksgiving is offered to him "in the name of our
Lord." It is a fine thing that Paul thus adds the word
"Father." We fail to understand the comment that
Paul does not mean "our Father." The nouns go to-
gether. Is he not our God and Father, is he only our

God and Christ's Father? The designation of both persons is plainly soteriological.

21) Does the participle continue the thought and close the paragraph (R. V.), or does it begin the new paragraph? The thought does not continue our utterance in singing and playing with thanksgiving to God. Paul counts on the intelligence of his readers to see that. He writes a durative participle that is just like the three that precede so that we shall connect this last participle with the present paragraph and not with the next. If he had intended to make a break at v. 21, it would have been the simplest thing in the world to write an imperative. Moreover, in what follows (v. 22-6:9) we, indeed, have subjection but no reciprocal, no mutual subjection. Wives are to be subject to husbands, children to parents, slaves to masters, but not the reverse, and husbands and masters are not to be subject to other persons in the family. The whole of v. 22 to 6:9 deals with the *family*, is thus distinct, mentions the classes concerned, and thus cannot be introduced by v. 21.

Those who think that the contrary is the case labor to construe the participle. To call it a nominative absolute is to state that it cannot be construed. To let it mean: "while subjecting yourselves to each other, the wives to their own husbands," is unwarranted because the wives are to subject themselves to their husbands and not as we are to subject ourselves to the rest of us.

It is the wisdom of this world to dominate others, to stoop below others only when one is compelled to stoop. This paragraph is written regarding wisdom, regarding understanding the Lord's will, and thus in spirit singing our happy gratitude to God our Father. This we are to do in happy harmony. No rivalry, no self-exaltation, no devisive pride is to interfere. Rich and poor, learned and simple, high and low are to be one, and that is accomplished by "subjecting themselves to each other in Christ's fear," not in false humility, in sycophancy, or the like. None is to subject another, each is to subject himself, voluntarily, freely. This is to be mutual, reciprocal all around (Rom. 12:10; Phil. 2:3; I Pet. 5:5). What a wise thing, and how fine when none lords it over another, when each serves the other! Matt. 20:27, 28. The songs that arise to God from such hearts will be sweet.

The thought to be expressed is not a contrast between our attitude toward "the God and Father" and that toward "each other," for the latter, too, is to be "in Christ's fear" (objective genitive). This is not the dread of Christ, our Judge, but the loving and devoted reverence of Christ, our Savior, which is ever seeking to do "what is well-pleasing to the Lord" (v. 10), "what the will of the Lord is" (v. 17). R. 690 is probably mistaken when he makes the ἑαυτοῖς found in v. 19 reflexive in the reciprocal sense; here we have the reciprocal ἀλλήλοις, and the two could not be exchanged.

By thus rounding out this paragraph, the last of the general admonitions directed to *all* the members of the *Una Sancta*, Paul has prepared an easy transition to the next group of admonitions, each of which deals with only a certain class of members.

* * *

Four Admonitions, Each for a Special Class of the Members of the Una Sancta

22) See the analysis in 4:17: we have no connectives but only a natural progression of the classes concerned; four groups of them: wives — husbands — children and fathers — slaves and masters. Note the "and" in 6:4, 9. This has been called Paul's *Haustafel*.

For Wives

**The wives to their own husbands as to the Lord!
Because a husband is head of his wife as also Christ
Head of his church — he, indeed, as Savior of his
Body. Nevertheless, as the church subjects herself
to Christ, so also the wives to their husbands in
everything.**

The wives are the first to be admonished, the children the next, then the slaves for whom a special type
of self-subjection is made incumbent. For this reason
wives are followed by husbands, children by fathers,
slaves by masters. No verb is needed, an imperative,
"let them subject themselves," being automatically
supplied by the reader.

Paul counts on the intelligence of his readers. The
very mention of "the wives" (not vocative) and "their
own husbands" shows that a special relation and a
special self-subjection are now referred to, something
that is entirely different from the fact mentioned in
v. 21. For in v. 21 any Christian, whether this be a
wife or not, is to subject himself to every other Christian, whether this be a man or not. The difference is
so clear as to be self-evident. We are now in the Christian family, in the marital relation; "the wives" at
once place us there. Gal. 3:28 lies on the plane of v. 21
and not on that of v. 22.

Paul is not subjecting all women to all men but all
wives to their own husbands. This is not a text on
the inferiority of women to men; it is a text on the
Christian marriage relation. This is also voluntary
self-subjection and not subjugation. Moreover, it is
Christian: "as to the Lord," i. e., as rendering this
self-subjection to the Lord in obedience to his blessed
will. The idea is that the will of God who arranged
the marriage relation at creation is likewise the will
of the Lord Christ for Christian wives. Every Christian wife will then follow "what is well-pleasing to the

Lord" (v. 10), "what the will of the Lord is" (v. 17).
She subjects herself, we may say, for the Lord's sake:
his will is hers. A Christian bride will then rebel
against the idea of altering the marriage ceremony so
that "obey him" is left out; she will do so on account
of her Lord, no matter what worldly brides may do.

23) Back of this reference "as to the Lord" lies a
great reason for all Christian wives who own reverence to this Lord: "Because a husband (no article) is
head (predicate, hence again no article) of his wife
(possessive article) as also Christ is Head (predicate)
of his church (possessive)." There is no need to say
that this is a reference to Christian marriage as Christ
intends it to be. Every Christian bride and every
Christian wife will want her marriage to be like that
of Christ and his church.

Already at this place Paul brings forward his great
comparison which lifts Christian marriage to a plane
which is so high that we are astounded. It is like the
marriage of the Lamb (Rev. 19:7), his Bride, the
church, the Lamb's wife (Rev. 21:9; 22:17). Remember the bridal and the marriage imagery found in both
Testaments. Paul is lifting Christian marriage into
the full light of grace which is to sanctify it throughout
(I Cor. 7:14). Can any Christian wife make her marriage more blessed than that? We see how Paul comes
to do this: the great theme of his epistle is the *Una
Sancta,* her Head being Christ, the Lord. Christian
marriage is a miniature of this. All its loveliness is
brought to view by holding it beside the great original.

Paul has often been accused of having a low view
of marriage, i. e., that non-marriage is better than
marriage. But where in all the Scriptures is there a
more exalted and truly spiritual conception of marriage than that presented here by this apostle?

One point is made to stand out, one that the entire
epistle also presents: unity. One Body, which thus

has one Head (1:22; 4:15). So the married couple
is a unity. It can have but one head even as the Bride,
the church, can have but the one Head, Christ. Two
heads for either would not only cause a duality, it
would produce a monstrosity. Many marriages have
been made into something like that by the "unwise"
(v. 15) who mistake their folly for wisdom (Rom.
1:22). Behold the wrecks everywhere, the freaks, too,
alongside of the wrecks! Two heads, then a division.
Or the wrong head, the thing turned upside down.

Paul is not devising a human allegory, is not losing
himself in a figurative tangle. In one tremendous
respect our divine Lord goes utterly beyond what any
wife has or can have in her husband as her marital
head. Of Christ alone is it true: "he, indeed (emphatic αὐτός), as Savior of his Body," i. e., the church,
repeatedly called so, viz. 4:12. No other head in the
universe is like that. We have seen the same relation
in v. 5, the King to his kingdom who is not made by his
kingdom as are earthly kingdoms but makes his kingdom so that wherever he is he also has his kingdom.

24) Ἀλλά = "nevertheless," it is adversative: in
spite of this fact, which is exceptional with regard to
Christ, that he and he alone is the Savior of his Body,
the headship of the Christian husband is like the headship of Christ regarding the church. Paul now reverses the statement: "as the church subjects herself
to Christ, so also the wives to their husbands in everything." This is a repetition of v. 22, but now the verb
is expressed, "in everything" is added. The repetition is emphatic. This is what the husband's headship
of his wife means. It is typical of Paul to turn the
thought in this way, to state the two sides of it and
thus to round it out.

The verb is the middle voice: the church subjects
herself voluntarily, joyfully. This is her normal and
natural relation to Christ, which could not be other-

wise. Just so is the relation of the wives to their husbands (a fine example of the generic article). The verb to be supplied is either an indicative or an imperative: "subject themselves," or, "let them subject themselves." The passive is out of place: "is subjected" — "are subjected," for this sounds too much like compulsion. The idea is not that of a divine command which forces the church, forces the wives, but of blessedness. Christ has highly honored the marriage relation in that he has made his own relation to the church like that of a bridegroom to his bride, of a husband to his wife, as far as his headship and the church's self-subjection are concerned.

This self-subjection is not partial but complete: "in everything." Yet in the nature of the case, the phrase is limited to the things involved in the marriage or home relation. Luther drew the Scriptural line well when he called Christian marriage *ein weltlicher Handel*. He did not mean "a worldly affair" but an affair pertaining to the natural and not to the spiritual or church life. In all religious matters Gal. 3:28 applies: neither male nor female, for you are all one man in Christ Jesus. But in all earthly matters the husband functions as the head. In this connection read Col. 3:18; I Tim. 2:12; Tit. 2:5; I Pet. 3:1, which are to the same effect.

In the state of innocence the husband was the head, and the wife subjected herself to him as the head. God made marriage so ideal, lovely, blessed, perfect. Sin entered and disturbed this relation. Eve fell, Adam followed, God's order was subverted. In the state of sin the divine and blessed order is disturbed in two directions: wives seek to rule their husbands and refuse loving self-subjection; husbands tyrannize their wives often to the point of enslaving them. Endless woe results. Christianity restores the divine order with all its happiness. Yet when Christianity came and elevated woman and wifehood from their pagan degradation and made male and female one in the church of Christ Jesus, the danger of antinomistic views regarding wifehood appeared. Wives might be inclined to refuse self-subjection because of a false view of emanicipation and independence. For this reason Paul ever speaks so clearly and shows both the original divine intention of the marital relation of husbands and of wives and the sanctification of this relation and its glorious elevation because Christ made it the image of his own relation to the church even as Jehovah had done this in the case of Israel in the old covenant.

In our times not a few Christian wives and husbands also have tried to modify Paul's words, especially concerning what they say regarding the self-subjection of Christian wives, because it is claimed that this view is no longer up-to-date and befitting our advanced age. The more need is there that we understand just what Paul and the Scriptures say on the subject, that we apprehend the inwardness of it all and the impossibility of our ever advancing beyond the true directions here laid down.

*　　*　　*

For Husbands

25) What Paul says regarding the wives must be read in conjunction with what he says regarding the husbands; only thus shall we catch his full meaning. **Husbands, love your wives even also as Christ did love the church and gave himself for her in order that he might sanctify her by cleansing her with the the bath of the water in connection with spoken word, in order that he himself might present to himself the church as glorious, not having a stain or**

wrinkle or any such thing, but in order that she may be holy and blemishless.

We may regard the articulated "husbands" as a vocative; then we shall also have vocatives in 6:1, 4, 5, 9. This construction may be questioned in v. 22, where no verb is used. Perhaps Paul just announces the classes: The wives — The husbands — The children, etc. Thus here: "The husbands — do you keep loving your (possessive article) wives!" This point is merely formal. The word for love is the verb used in the New Testament to designate the higher form of love; it is not φιλεῖν which denotes mere affection, romantic attachment or passion, which is practically all that worldly people know about ideal conjugal love. See the noun in 1:4. Paul has in mind the love which comprehends what God intends marriage to be, which is therefore filled with the desire to carry out God's intention. Let us say that the love now described is of such a kind that makes it a delight for the wife to subject herself to such a loving husband.

Do you ask why Paul does not say also: "The wives — do you keep loving your husbands"? Is this love not to be mutual? You have answered your question. No wife can cultivate the self-subjection intended by the Lord without this intelligent and purposeful love. When Paul asks for her self-subjection he asks for it as the outstanding evidence of her love. Without the presence of this conclusive evidence no wife "loves" her husband with true Christian intelligence and purposefulness.

"Even as" denotes likeness of manner. The supreme illustration for the way in which Christian husbands should love their wives is no less than the love of Christ himself for his church. The manner of his love is described at length; we are told how he gave himself and with what high purpose he did this. The feature that no one can possibly imitate has been elim-

inated in v. 23: his being himself the Savior of his
Body. So the parallel given the husbands in v. 28 is
that they love their wives "as their own bodies," i. e.,
as being no less than their own bodies. In that manner
the husbands are to love their wives; in that manner
Christ loved the church, his own Body (4:12). Where
this love is present in the Christian husband, the manner of it will be the constant evidence, he will treat his
wife as his very own body. So the head intelligently,
purposefully (*agape*) treats its body and shows itself
to be the head indeed. Only too gladly the body sub-
mits itself to such a head in order to receive this manner of treatment. That is the body's love for its head.
Nor can the thing ever be reversed regarding the head
and its body, for in any living organism the one can
never be the other.

"As Christ loved the church" (aorist) is followed
by explicative καί: "and gave himself for her" (aorist).
Both tenses refer to the supreme act of Christ's love,
his death for us on the cross. The fact that ὑπέρ =
substitution we have seen in connection with 5:2.
Here this act exhibits the manner of Christ's intelligent and purposeful love. "For her" does not imply a
limited atonement, does not cancel from the Scripture
all the statements regarding the universality of the
atonement. He bought also those who bring swift
destruction on themselves, II Pet. 2:1. The Scriptures
often speak of the atonement for those who receive its
full effects.

26) First the proximate and then (v. 27) the ultimate purpose which Christ had in mind with this love
and vicarious self-sacrifice. "That he might sanctify
(her) by cleansing her with the bath," etc. Both the
verb and the participle are aorists. When such a participle follows hard upon such a verb, the two are generally simultaneous as to time unless the nature of the
second verb makes its action antecedent in point of

time. In this case the act of sanctifying and the act of cleansing are synonymous, the one is positive: to separate unto God, the other is negative: to remove sin and guilt. Both take place in baptism, the only bath of which we know in which water and the spoken word are combined. Dogmatically stated, i. e., doctrinally, this is the sanctification which makes us ἅγιοι (1:1) and by means of the *justitia imputata* cleanses us from all sin and guilt in justification. The sanctification which presents us in the perfection of holiness, when every stain and wrinkle of the flesh are finally removed from us, follows in v. 27 as Christ's ultimate purpose.

R. 521 regards the dative as a locative. In his *W. P.* he states that λουτρόν may mean "bathing place"; but why the place should be mentioned here (locative) is not clear. Is it the place (here definite because of the article) that effects the cleansing? It is surely the bath, a most definite one, baptism. This is the common dative of means. Christ cleanses us and thereby removes our sin and guilt through his atoning death, thereby sanctifies us by means of baptism. This is the efficacy of baptism. Paul knows only a baptism that actually cleanses (aorist) and thereby actually sanctifies (aorist), which is the aim and purpose effected by Christ's love and his giving himself in our stead (also aorists). Moreover, it should be noted that the subject is Christ. *He* applies this means to us, *he* cleanses, etc. Baptism is *his* act and not *ours*. It is not a mere symbol, not a mere act of obedience on our part to an ordinance and a command.

We have little interest in the debate as to whether λουτρόν means "washing" or not. It seems that this point is raised in the interest of immersion. The word means "bath," and many a bath is taken without a total immersion. Our versions translate "washing," which is to be understood in the sense of "bath." "Bath (washing) of water" is the *genitivus materiae*. Its addition excludes the figurative sense of "bath" as though this might be understood with reference to something that is only spiritual. No; this is the bath that employs actual water. "Water" — no other liquid. The sand baptisms of some dogmaticians as substitutes when water cannot be had in a desert are speculations. "Water" is named as the earthly element of the sacrament besides the spoken word. We reject the R. V. margin to the effect that the Greek word means "laver," the first meaning of which is a basin for washing (the laver in the Jewish Temple), the second "that which laves or bathes," the water itself. This margin and Vincent are unclear. They apparently accept the former; if the latter is meant, "of water" would be a superfluous appositional genitive. As to *loutron* in the sense of place, all that Homer has is a reference to "hot baths" and also to "cold baths," always plural; the singular is rare in other writers. We find "baths of Hercules," "baths of the ocean," "water baths." But this does not yet prove that *loutron* designates a place either in our passage or in Titus 3:5. Until the linguists furnish more convincing examples, the present writer will doubt that the singular λουτρόν was ever used to designate a place.

The ἐν ῥήματι has no article because "the water in connection with spoken word" is one concept. That, too, is why "the water" has the article, and why Luther's compound *Wasserbad* is inexact as a translation for this Greek phrase. This is a most definite water; it is made so by the phrase. The phrase belongs where Paul placed it. Ῥῆμα is also the proper term, "utterance," because the water of baptism is always ἐν, "in connection with," a spoken word; λόγος would refer to a statement that conveys a thought, whether it be spoken or written. What this "spoken word" (ῥῆμα) is should be beyond question, for the very institution of the sacrament orders the administrant to say: "In the Name of the Father," etc. Unless this is uttered, we have no baptism, no matter what we utter or how much water we use. Luther states it simply: "Without the Word of God the water is simply water and no baptism. But with the Word of God it is a baptism, that is a gracious water of life and a washing of regeneration in the Holy Spirit," Tit. 3:5.

This phrase cannot be referred back across the dative and modify the participle or the subjunctive. The phrase should then adjoin the verb or the participle. Nor can it be said that if the phrase is to be joined to the genitive, τοῦ should be repeated. There is also confusion about ῥῆμα itself: whether this is the *gospel* in general or the *preached* gospel. Salmond says, "Set apart, etc., in accordance with the *divine promise*," or, "on the ground of the *preached word* of the gospel," that "word," like "law," "grace," etc., needs no genitive such as "word of God or word of Christ." Salmond offers this as proof that "the bath of the water" has nothing to do with the cleansing, but that the cleansing is wholly "on the ground of the preached Word." Why did Paul then insert "the bath of the water"? And ἐν does not = "in accordance with" or "on the ground of." This appeals to those who regard baptism as a mere symbol without cleansing power. Such interpretations misunderstand the Greek, and R., *W. P.*, says: "Neither there (I Cor. 6:11) nor here does Paul mean that the cleansing or sanctification took place in the bath save in a symbolic fashion."

Such strange ideas are advanced as that Paul here refers to the bath the bride took before her marriage. But the bridegroom does not bathe the bride. It is *Christ* who cleanses the church; and yet some advance the view that the bath does not cleanse, that the Word does that wholly apart from the bath. Von Hofmann

philosophizes and has *rhema* refer to the utterance of
Christ's effective will.

We here have Paul's definition of baptism: it is the
bath of that water which is connected with an utterance, the bath which is Christ's means for sanctifying
by cleansing, "a bath of regeneration and renewing
by the Holy Spirit" (Tit. 3:5).

27) A second ἵνα states Christ's ultimate purpose:
"in order that he himself might present to himself the
church as glorious, not having," etc. Note the points
of emphasis: one is on the verb which is placed forward; another on "he himself to himself"; a third uses
"the church" instead of the mere pronoun "her" and
thereby makes this clause stand out more independently. Paul is speaking of the church as a whole and
not of it as it is now being gathered, with many now
unborn yet to enter. Paul sees a grand vision: the
church at the last day, Christ himself presenting her
to himself, making her stand forth by his side (παρά)
enfolded in glory, beautiful in sanctity, the spotless
Bride of the Lamb. The aorist points to one great act
of Christ. After all that Paul has said on the oneness
and unity "the church" now appears as one glorious
person.

Paul expounds "glorious": "not having a stain or
wrinkle or any of such things." In her present state,
as she passes through this sinful world and still battles
with the flesh, the church has many "a stain" of sin
splashed upon her from without, many "a wrinkle"
due to faults in her own body, also other things of this
kind. Some make no difference between "stain" and
"wrinkle"; Paul does by adding "such things." The
world about the church causes the stains, the flesh still
in her causes the wrinkles.

But note: the terms denote what is only on the
surface, what may thus be removed, and not what is in
the inner being. Nevertheless, these are blemishes,

and they cannot remain. Paul's picture is that of a bride, and he makes us think of one that is beautiful, indeed; but at first we see her with her bridal robe spotted here and there with ugly stains and with her lovely face marred by ugly wrinkles. What bride can appear like that on her wedding day? Why, every eye would at once fasten on such blemishes of robe and face! Feel the argumentative force in these terms so perfectly chosen. How the church must long to be all-glorious — and *we* are this church!

But we ourselves can never attain perfection. Christ himself must bring us this perfection even as he first set us apart for himself by cleansing us with the divine bath of baptism. Paul is thus describing our great hope in Christ. Once more recall v. 23 where it is stated that he himself is the Savior of his Body, that his love for the church and what he has done for her (v. 25) and will yet do for her exceeds all that a Christian husband can do for his wife. Christ is the example for the husband, Christian marriage is a miniature of his relation to the church, but oh, the greatness of Christ and of his love! Must a Christian husband, then, despair before this example? No; he is part of the church that is so loved by Christ, and Christ's love is his constant inspiration and help. "As to the Lord," written for the wives (v. 22), has its parallel for the husbands in "even also as Christ" in v. 25.

The negative terms "spot" and "wrinkle" are figurative; the corresponding positive terms are literal: "holy and blemishless." Instead of continuing with the participial construction, Paul writes: "But in order that she may be holy and blemishless." This is not due to the vivacity of the Greek way of thinking and speaking; it continues the idea of the two previous purpose clauses and at the same time makes the positive clause tower above the negative participle clause.

We have "holy and blemishless" in 1:4; now the words indicate the final perfection of holiness at the last day. First Peter 1:19 has, "a lamb spotless and blemishless," which leads some to conclude that Paul has in mind the idea of a sacrifice also in our passage. But in the passage in Peter's letter it is the word "lamb" that suggests the idea of sacrifice, nor does Peter say "a lamb *holy* and blemishless." The church is never called a lamb. The thought that the church is a sacrifice that is presented by Christ to himself, is un-Biblical and untrue. It is impossible here where *Christ* delivers himself as a sacrifice for the church (v. 25); how can the purpose of this be to present the *church* as a sacrifice to himself? The imagery is that of a bride. This Bride must be like her Bridegroom, a fit spouse for him and therefore "holy and blemishless," dedicated and separated from all that is profane, common, and sinful, with not one sinful blemish or fault remaining. Christ himself, her Savior (v. 22), will at last so present her to himself.

28) Paul brings out more fully what lies in the comparison he has made. **So ought also the husbands love their own wives as their own bodies.** Paul's thought is misunderstood when "so" is regarded as a correlative of "as." The view that this is grammatically possible is untenable because here Paul has only *one* statement, and a correlation of "so — as" requires *two*: so do this as that is done. Here οὕτως is a correlative of καθώς in v. 25: as Christ — *so* the husbands; and ὡς explains "wives" by calling them the own bodies of their husbands. The Christian husbands who follow the example of Christ (in the relation indicated) do so only by loving their own wives as being their own bodies.

Instead of the previously used imperatives we now have "ought to love," which signifies moral obligation.

Here we again have the great word ἀγαπᾶν for "love."
Not *like* their own bodies but literally *as* their own
bodies. The husband is the head, the wife is his body.
The head is to love its body. So the Head, Christ,
loves his Body, the church. Indeed, husband and wife
are *one* flesh, no less. The fact that the relation of
Christ to the church lies on a far higher plane alters
nothing in the earthly relation of the husband to his
wife; only when we compare the superior relation to
the inferior, the latter is lifted and ennobled.

Paul restates his meaning in order to put it beyond doubt and to make it emphatic. **The one loving his own wife loves himself.** As his body she is
to that extent his own self. So closely are husband and
wife connected. The singular follows the plural of
the previous statement. Paul knows how to use number. This is not mere variation in expression; this
singular brings the point home to every individual husband. The statement is terse, axiomatic. In order to
appreciate it and all that Paul says remember how
the Jews regarded marriage: any husband could dismiss his wife for the most trivial cause or for no cause
at all, and she had no recourse. The pagan world was
no better, it was worse. The church was composed
of converts from both Judaism and the world. Paul
knows what he is doing when he especially expounds
the obligation of the husbands as he here does. God
knows that his exposition is still needed.

29) "For" shows how self-evident the statement just made is, how impossible it is rationally and
and normally to entertain the opposite view. **For no
one ever hated his own flesh but nourishes and
warms it.** The fact is universal, unquestioned. We
again first have the negative and then the positive, and
"to hate" is the opposite of "to love." A person may
commit suicide, but living men the world over feed and
warm their bodies. Now the proper word is "his own

flesh," for now the head and the body are referred to
and not the body in distinction from the head. So also
the preceding clause has "himself," and v. 31 has "one
flesh." We see no reason for making θάλπει metaphorical, "cherish," instead of literal. Our physical being
needs two things that are essential for existence, food
and warmth, the one to nourish, the other to make rea-
sonably comfortable.

Paul does not again introduce the application to
the wife, for "himself" and "his own flesh" have
already gone beyond the wife. With **even as also
Christ the church because members are we of his
Body,** Paul reverts to the basis of his whole admonition. He rings the refrain for the husband: "as Christ
the church." There is no need of verbs; the mind gets
the thought, which is enough. The fact that "Christ
the church" lies on the spiritual plane while a man and
his flesh are on the physical level, is not only self-evident but has already been made sufficiently plain so
that the implied verb or verbs will, of course, be
spiritual.

30) "Because members are we," etc., is the reason
for what Christ does in loving provision for the church.
The form now advances to the applicatory "we" and
thus to the individualizing plural "members of his
Body." Thus far we have had only "the church" and
the "Body" (4:4, 12, 16; 5:23), the entire unit; now
the component parts of the church at the time of Paul's
writing are indicated: "members." Every individual
Christian, Paul being one, is a member of this blessed
Body, the Church of Christ, and "because" of this
receives the care of the great Head.

The addition: "of his flesh and of his bones" (A.
V.) lacks both textual authority and internal evidence.
Genesis 2:23 reads: "This is now bone of my bones
and flesh of my flesh." It would seem that someone
amplified Paul's text by adding Adam's word regard-

ing Eve and yet found it advisable to reverse bones and flesh. The trouble is that "members" precedes, that nobody is able to conceive how we as members are derived ἐκ Christ's flesh and ἐκ Christ's bones, whether these are understood physically with regard to Christ or spiritually.

The idea of a mystical derivation from the glorified flesh and bones of Christ is un-Biblical. Mystical union is not mystical derivation. Nor is this a reference to the Lord's Supper as though in that sacrament we receive Christ's flesh and *bones* and are thus derived from him. When one, for instance, reads Harless and others who defend the insertion, he is struck by the way in which they avoid speaking about the last phrase: "out of his bones." They generalize so that "his bones" is not considered.

31) Now Paul does quote with a slight deviation from the LXX, without a formula of quotation, because all his readers are acquainted with the words of Gen. 2:24. In fact, Paul uses Adam's words only in order to express his own thought and makes this more effective because it is taken from Holy Writ. **For this cause shall a man leave his father and his mother and shall be glued to his wife, and the two shall be one flesh.**

Paul is offering no new doctrine and no new ethics regarding marriage; here, as in all his other references, Paul does as Jesus himself did (Matt. 19:8; 22:29): he goes back to the beginning, to the Scriptures, to the institution of marriage itself. The doctrine and the ethics there established for marriage stand for all time, they were approved by Jesus and by his apostles as being valid also for the New Testament time.

Paul retains the phrase "for this cause" (the LXX has ἕνεκεν) although it connects with nothing in Paul's preceding statements. Some seek to discover such a connection, but none is clear and actual. Those who retain the spurious words found in v. 30 refer to a connection with them, for are those words not taken from Gen. 2:23, and is v. 31 not quoted from Gen. 2:24? But this view is untenable, for "out of his (Christ's) flesh and out of his (Christ's) bones" must be allegorized if they are retained, must somehow refer to Christ, and this compels one also to allegorize a man's leaving his father and his mother so that this, too, must refer to Christ. Then if God is the Father left by Christ, who is the mother? We are told "Jerusalem" or "heaven," which makes the allegory rather farfetched.

Nor need we go into the other crass things that result when Christ and the church are made "one flesh." Some say this came about at the time of the Incarnation when Christ's leaving the Father took place; others say that it shall occur at the Parousia when the consummation of being one flesh is to be reached; but at that time Christ is again back with his Father (to say nothing about a mother). These interpretations are to be spiritual; but they rather exhibit morbidity.

"For this cause" means exactly what it means in Gen. 2:24, the cause mentioned in Gen. 2:23, this connection being known to Paul's readers just as the quoted words themselves are so well known. Those early Christians could be counted on for a far more precise knowledge of their Old Testament than our Christians today have. Incidentally, this may serve to explain why the apostles quote so often and in such ways as they freely do. Paul is here speaking of the married state, how it is entered by leaving father and mother, and in what it results. Adam himself uttered this description in Eden. It was prophetic. He had no father and no mother. The prophecy is true. A young man leaves his parents, cleaves (really "shall be glued") to his wife, and so a new home starts. To be sure, in the patriarchal age and often in the Orient the son brought his wife to his parents' home, but Adam was not prophesying regarding all the variations in marriage customs. Ἄνθρωπος is the proper word since ἀνήρ has been used repeatedly in the sense of "husband."

But the main point is this being glued together with his wife, glued so closely that they, "the two, shall be one flesh" (predicative εἰς, R. 481). Here there is still more reason for using Adam's words, they serve to express the very climax of what Paul has been building up. In v. 25 he speaks only of the husbands loving "the wives"; in v. 28 he calls them the husbands' "own bodies," singular the husband's "own self"; in v. 29 "his own flesh." Now comes the peak and this in actual words of Scripture: "the two one flesh." That is the Scriptural conception, that is the Christian conception. This is sexual union. For this purpose God created the two sexes. It was for the sake of marriage not for harlotry and fornication (I Cor. 6:16), the great crime against marriage. With his mind still unclouded by sin, Adam saw this and expressed it, and Paul, with his mind enlightened, found no more adequate expression.

32) Nevertheless, Paul has more than Adam had. The latter could not know that marriage was to be a miniature and a reflection of Christ's relation to the church. Sin had not yet entered the world, the promise of "the Savior of his Body" (v. 23) had not yet been given. Paul has seen the fulfillment of this promise; he is thus able to add these two together, the miniature and its wonderful original. He has done so throughout with "even as" and "thus" (v. 25 and 28) and again with "even as" in v. 29. He now brings this to its final expression. **This mystery is great. Now I on my part am speaking in regard to Christ and in regard to the church.**

"This is a great mystery" (A. V.) is an incorrect translation.

Some make a mystery of the place where "this mystery" lies hidden. Some say that it is found in the passage in Genesis and then offer what they think its mysterious, hidden meaning to be. The allegorizers think that "this mystery" is the allegorical sense of Adam's words. "Mystery" is not something mystical (Alford), nor the "secret meaning" of what Paul is about to say (von Soden) ; nor "symbol"; nor "secret." The early church understood the Vulgate's *sacramentum* as a translation of μυστήριον and of *mis^ethar* as any solemn religious act or custom or anything sacred: "a holy and divine matter or sign" (*C. Tr.* 737) ; its restriction to baptism and the Lord's Supper started with Tertullian. Yet this translation, which was proper enough in its time, led Romanists to make marriage a sacrament. A "mystery" is something that is to be revealed. "Great" does not mean deep and profound, still less forever impenetrable, never to be made known to us; it is "great" because it is so wonderful.

Adam was not revealing a mystery when he said, "The two shall be one flesh." What is so mysterious about the natural sex relation of husband and wife? But when the order of nature is compared with the order of grace as regards Christ and the *Una Sancta,* a mystery great and wonderful stands revealed. Except for proper enlightenment such as Paul furnishes this correspondence of the marriage relation (the husband being the head, the wife the body) with the saving relation (Christ being the Head, the church the Body) would not be noticed. Even now Christians alone see it when they are enlightened by revelation. The mystery is so wonderful in that what lies on the earthly plane of sex should correspond with what lies on the exalted plane of soteriology.

Δέ refers to the brief parenthetical pointer. The emphatic ἐγώ places Paul over against Adam whose statement Paul has just quoted, and who could say nothing "in regard to Christ and in regard to the church." Paul can and does. No more than this pointer is needed. The preposition is repeated because the relation of the church to Christ and also his to her are referred to. The two relations existing in marriage are also mentioned in v. 33. On "mytsery" as regards the *Una Sancta* apart from marriage ("this mystery") see 1:9; 3:4, 9.

33) Πλήν closes the discussion and emphasizes the main point (B.-D. 449). It is not resumptive after a digression, for Paul has not digressed. **Well then, you, too, one by one, let each continue to love his own wife thus as himself; on the other hand, the wife, that she respect her husband!**

Paul's admonition centers on this one point. The distributive καθ' ἕνα, "one by one," is joined attributively to ὑμεῖς by οἱ, and "each" is added to show that no one is omitted. The plural of v. 25, "do you keep loving" is now repeated in the singular, "let each keep loving," it is personal, individual. "As himself" is to be understood in the sense of v. 28: "as their own bodies" — "himself." The two are one.

Yet this admonition to the husbands to love their wives thus may make the wives feel that their husbands are after all placed very much in their service, and may thus materially alter their self-subjection (v. 22 and 24). Such a deduction is excluded. "On the other hand (δέ), the wife (now also singular), that she respect her husband." The verb is to be understood in this sense as Ewald shows from Plato: Φοβεῖσθαι τὸ σῶμα, "to respect one's own body," i. e., by doing what is proper for it. After all the love that is urged upon the husband anything like servile fear on the part of the wife is excluded from her Christian self-subjection.   The older grammars and commentators had no solution for this ἵνα which is itself a substitute construction for the imperative and matches the preceding imperative regarding each husband (B.-D. 387, 3). Robertson calls this ἵνα an expletive which merely introduces a voluntative subjunctive. The tone seems to lend it commanding force.

Thus Paul points out to husband and to wife their proper relation and their attitude and their conduct toward each other. Nothing truer and nobler has ever been written or said on this subject. To tamper with the relation here marked out is only to cause damage, often the most terrible damage. Let the world tell its sad, sad story. Here are two great texts that are not expounded to our people often enough or thoroughly enough,

CHAPTER VI

For Children and Fathers

1)   Paul takes it for granted that the Christian home contains children. Nowhere has he cause to treat the modern crimes of abortion and so-called birth control which defeat the divine purpose of marriage as instituted by God (Gen. 1:27, 28) and its chief blessing (Ps. 127:3-5). **Children, keep obeying your parents in the Lord, for this is righteous.**

Paul assumes the presence of the children in the assembly of the congregation where his letter will be read. Their unnatural absence from the service is thereby tacitly condemned. They, too, are members of the *Una Sancta,* baptized "with the bath of the water in connection with the spoken word" (5:26). In his great epistle on the *Una Sancta* he has a word for all these Christian children, which is an example for the sermons of all Christian pastors. Vocatives may have the article, but see 5:25.

It is the natural law that children obey their parents. This law the gospel sanctifies; hence Paul's addition "in (in connection with) the Lord," in union and communion with him. From their earliest days onward the children are to know their blessed Lord and to connect their young lives with him. This phrase means more than following the Lord's example when he was a child; it means more than submitting to his will. Childhood obedience is to be the fruit of the child's entire relation to the Lord. This evidently implies that those who are thus to obey "in the Lord" have been placed in communion with him as his very own; and this means baptism.

(646)

"For this is righteous" names the simple motive in a simple way so that every child may understand. In Col. 3:20 Paul says, "For this is well-pleasing to the Lord," "righteous" in that sense. There he has also written obedience "in all things," i. e., in no thing disobedience. Whether we translate "right" (our versions) or "righteous," δίκαιον remains forensic and implies the Lord as the Judge who pronounced his verdict on every child's conduct in accord with his divine norm of right (δίκη). Paul's admonition is brief, hence he does not enter upon the pitiful cases when Christian parents demand obedience in something that is unrighteous; this he forbids the fathers in v. 4.

2) Without a connective and now in the singular and thus the more impressively he quotes the Fourth Commandment (Exod. 20:12; Deut. 5:16): **Honor thy father and thy mother, such is a commandment foremost in connection with promise: in order that it may be well with thee, and thou mayest be a long time on the earth.**

Those who divide the First Commandment into two make the fourth the fifth. Honor is the form love assumes toward those who are placed above us by God. God rightly put the word "honor" into this commandment and not merely "love," for it is "love" plus respect, reverence, and corresponding obedience. God places father and mother on the same plane as far as the child is concerned, and Christian ethics is right in extending this commandment so as to include all persons who rightfully assume any part of the parental relation to a child, all the different kinds of parents, teachers, and pastors, even governors and rulers ("fathers" of their people).

It is not necessary to put the expository relative clause into parentheses (R. V.). But we note ἥτις which is not the simple relative but qualitative with a causal touch: it states what kind of a commandment this is, and thus why it should be the more readily obeyed. We should also note that the adjective and the phrase go together: "prime in connection with promise." Such is this commandment. It is usually remarked that "first" will not do as a translation for πρώτη. The First Commandment has a promise atta ˙ ed to it (Exod. 20:6). The fact that this promise is general alters nothing, it is surely "promise." More than that, this promise which is actually first, being what it is, is to be attached to every one of the Ten Commandments so that in his Catechism Luther transposed this promise which is added to the First Commandment to the end and placed it after the tenth as a conclusion to the entire Decalog, a most intelligent thing to do. Paul could thus have said regarding the fourth that it really has a double promise, the one that all the others have and one that is more specific, that none of the rest have.

Again, "first" will not do because no second commandment follows to which a specific promise is attached. Πρώτη is used as it occurs in Acts 28:17: "the first men of the Jews" (even plural), their "foremost" men, rabbis and leaders. The Fourth Commandment is indeed "foremost," an outstanding one; for not only does the promise attached to all ten extend also to the fourth, it extends to the fourth with the definite and notable specifications: "that it may be well with thee, and thou mayest be a long time on the earth."

This shows that God is concerned about the honor which children should show their parents. Humanly speaking, he offers them a special inducement, he makes it more easy for them to obey. The family is the basis of all society. Hence there must be the right relation between husband and wife, the founders of the home and the family (5:22-32), next the right relation between children and parents (6:1-4). If either is destroyed or even disturbed, the results are dire. The world furnishes the heart-rending commentary. Listen to the stories related in the divorce courts and in the juvenile courts of today. The ramifications are endless; our reformatories, prisons, asylums show only the worst of the tragedies. Millions of evil cases begin by dishonoring parents. The worst evil that can strike a nation is the disintegration of its homes.

3) Paul adapts the Old Testament promise which was made to the Jews to children in the new covenant and omits the references to Canaan in Exod. 20:12 and Deut. 5:16. This teaches us to distinguish the substance of the moral law from its Old Testament form. Ἵνα is followed by both the subjunctive and the future indicative, this is perfectly in order in the Koine. The papyri often have the indicative so that the R. V.'s margin, which makes a new sentence: "And thou shalt," is out of place. The aorist denotes permanent well-being in the full Christian sense, to be under God's constant blessing. The future indicative is linear as befits the adjective that is used to indicate the long time. Genuine well-being, and that during a long life, constitutes the promise which God's mercy offers to thousands of generations of godly children (Deut. 5:10). The fact that this promise involves the opposite for children who do not honor their parents need scarcely be stated.

But do some of the best Christian children not die in childhood, in youth, in early maturity? Are some not in great affliction, crippled, very poor, etc.? Do not the wicked prosper (Ps. 73:3, 12)? Divine providence is full of problems for our finite minds. We can never hope to comprehend all the ways of God, especially those observed in individual cases. As to any question of guilt read Luke 13:2-5, and John 9:1-3. God's promise stands; these problems, to which we have only such partial answers in this life, leave it unchanged. Let no one think that he may for any reason mock that promise. The sons of Eli did.

4) First the wives, then the husbands; first the children, then the fathers, the dependent, then those upon whom they depend. What Paul tells the fathers is told them for their own sakes and, of course, also for the sake of the children under their control. The father who mismanages his child makes it next to impossible for his child to be what it should be and thus robs his child of the blessing of the Fourth Commandment and brings God's curse upon his child as well as upon himself.

And fathers, provoke not your children to anger but nourish them in discipline and admonition of the Lord.

"And" connects; it is absent in 5:25. The commandment itself places the mother beside the father, and Paul himself has presented the close relation existing between them. What is said to the fathers thus applies also to the mothers. The present imperative refers to iterative action: do not again and again provoke to anger. Unjust, improper parental treatment angers the child so that it cannot honor the parent. A long list of parental faults may be drawn up under Paul's summary which would include arbitrary, inconsistent, foolish, harsh, and cruel treatment. Parental authority is easily abused. The prevailing sin is Eli's softness, careless indifference, the children rule and dishonor the parents, the parents obey. Turn the home upside down and the results must be according.

The positive imperative is to indicate a steady course of nourishing (this verb is found also in 5:29). It is the phrase that here adds to the verb the ethical sense of nourishing whereas in 5:29 the meaning physical nourishing is sufficient. The best discussion of the synonyms "discipline and admonition" is still that of Trench, *Synonyms*. In the classics and in the papyri παιδεία means "education" in general, but in the New Testament it has a wider force. In Heb. 12:5 one may translate it "chastening," for the next verses refer to painful correction. Some (Thayer) would retain the meaning "education" in our passage so that the difference between the two terms would be small. Trench contrasts the definitions of Plato and of Basil the Great, the pagan and the Christian view. The context of our passage bears out Trench. "Discipline" = measures according to the laws and regulations of the Christian home, the transgression of which brings chastisement, yes, spankings when necessary. This is the proper opposite to provoking to anger.

Combined with "discipline," holding children to proper conduct is νουθεσία, "admonition," i. e., "the training by word, by the word of encouragement when no more than this is needed, but also by the word of remonstrance, of reproof, of blame where these may be required," Trench. Thus training by measures and acts and by words is combined. As children grow more and more mature, "admonition" alone will be necessary. Note I Sam. 3:13: Eli οὐκ ἐνουθέτει αὐτούς, he did not even "admonish" them.

"Of the Lord" has been termed an objective, a subjective, a characterizing, a source, and a relation genitive, and each commentator explains accordingly. Now this cannot be so many kinds of a genitive. We note that the modified nouns are without articles and are thus made definite by the added genitive. That would be a qualifying or a possessive genitive. The comment: "Such discipline and admonition as the Lord would exercise, who does not incite to wrath" (subjective), is unsatisfactory. *Zum Herrn* (objective, Luther) would call for εἰς or πρός; origin would be better but only because it approaches the qualifying idea. Not mere human or humanistic or moralistic discipline, etc., will do but only that which is joined to the Lord.

*   *   *

For Slaves and Masters

5) Slaves, keep obeying your bodily masters with fear and trembling in singleness of the heart as Christ; not in the way of eyeservice as men-pleasers but as slaves of Christ doing the will of God from the soul, with ready mind slaving as for the Lord and not for men, having come to know that whatever good each shall do, this he will receive back from the Lord, whether slave or free.

The Roman world was full of slaves. In Rom. 16:10, 11, "those from them of Aristobulus," and, "those from them of Narcissus," who are named after their deceased masters, were slaves in the imperial household at the time of Paul's writing. While some were servants of a lower type, others were educated, capable, in charge of great and responsible positions. From the way in which this group is introduced in Paul's admonitions we see how many slaves there must have been also among the Christians, and how at that time also Christians were slave owners (v. 9). We know that Philemon was a slaveholder, one of his slaves being named Onesimus. Christ and the apostles did not denounce slavery and call for its immediate abolition. Christianity followed a deeper, more thorough method, it undermined slavery with the spirit of Christianity by destroying it from within.

When Paul calls the owners "the bodily masters," this implies that the slaves were also only slaves κατὰ σάρκα, "by way of flesh," meaning body; since we are without a convenient corresponding phrase in English and are unable to place one attributively we use the adjective "bodily." The relation was one of only this

transient, earthly type and was not a matter of the
spirit. We may regard the following as adding three
modifiers: keep obeying 1) "with fear and trembling,"
a negative motive, lest they be found derelict; 2) "in
singleness of your heart," a positive motive, bent on
one thing alone, without duplicity or ulterior purpose;
3) "as Christ," as though the service were rendered to
Christ himself. It seems best, however, to parallel
only the first two prepositional phrases and to let the
dative with ὡς modify Christ, and with singleness of
heart as obeying Christ; for the two object datives
belong together: "obey the masters as Christ."

6) "As Christ" means: "not in the way of eyeservice as men-pleasers," not as that kind of slaves
who perform service only for the eye, to make a show,
to catch human praise, which is one great vice of slaves
and servants in general; "but as slaves doing the will
of God from the soul (no article is needed in such
Greek phrases), with ready mind (εὐνοία) slaving as for
the Lord and not (just) for men," as that kind of
slaves, which describes the true virtue of Christian
slaves and servants in general. "As Christ" (your
Master) is matched by "as slaves of Christ," the two
nominative participles defining 1) what such slaves
will do, 2) how they will do this. They will be busy
doing no less than "the will of God from the soul," *ex
animo*, the only way in which it can be done.

7) They will keep slaving (doing their work for
their masters) "with ready mind, as to the Lord and
not to men," to gain his approval before all else.

> "Men heed thee, love thee, praise thee not;
>   The Master praises — what are men?"

The participles match: "doing" — "slaving," the one
referring to God's will, the other to the human service.
Likewise, "from the soul" is to be construed with doing

God's will, and "with ready mind" (or "good will")
with the slaving. To draw both phrases together:
"from the soul with good will slaving," does not commend itself: the soul refers to God's will, the good
mind or good will to the daily tasks. Here is the secret
for all of us who work for other men. Whether we are
observed, praised, rewarded by them or not, our supreme satisfaction is that all our labor is done for the
Lord, our praise and our reward cannot be taken
from us.

8) Hence the final participle, now an ingressive
aorist: "having come to know (to perceive as a fact)
that whatever good each shall do, this he will receive
back from the Lord," his real Master. II Cor. 5:10.
Service rendered unto the Lord he will repay whether
men do or not. "Anything good" is to be understood
in the ethical sense. Whether we prefer the reading
κομεῖται or κομίσεται we have the future: "will receive
back." The readings vary in several points and cause
some difficulty for the text critics; fortunately, all
readings leave the sense unaltered. It makes no difference, for instance, where the subject is placed:
"that each, whatever good he may do" (expectancy),
etc.; or: "that whatever good each may do," etc. How
and when each will get back his reward is in the
Lord's hands; it will often be in part already in this
life.

Paul has no fear about fostering work-righteousness by using a frank appeal to rewards for Christian
slaves and workers. We may freely follow him if we
remember that the Lord's rewards are always pure
heavenly grace. "Whether slave or free," it makes no
difference. This is comfort for every poor slave in
his position of inferiority among men. When the Lord
dispenses his rewards, this lowly position never matters. In those days a great many slaves were set free
and even formed a class that was called "freedmen."

By following a regular procedure they were often allowed to buy their freedom. Exceptional acts of service were sometimes so rewarded. Some masters freed their slaves in their will and testament. But this is not at all the chief thing for the Christian. Slave or free, he moves on a far higher plane.

9) **And masters, keep doing the same things to them, refraining from threat, having come to know that both of them and of you the Master is in the heaven, and that there is no respect of person with him.**

"And" joins masters to slaves, it is like the "and" used in v. 4 in force. We need not seek the verbal antecedent of τὰ αὐτά; the expression is used *ad sensum*, "the same things," those that correspond to the difference in position. Beside this positive Paul places one subordinate negative: "refraining from this thing of threatening," that is the force of the article. Since slaves had no recourse, their pagan or their Jewish masters were inclined to threaten them on the least provocation and, as a usual thing, that meant the execution of the threat. By forbidding the threat its execution was, of course, equally excluded.

Note the force of the durative and of the punctiliar participles: "always refraining from — having come to know the fact that," etc.; the construction is like the three duratives plus the one punctiliar participle used regarding the slaves. Each class has come to know a mighty fact, the slaves a fact that stimulates them in heart and in work and lifts them above their physical slavery; the masters a fact that restrains them from misusing their physical superiority. The two genitives have a decided emphasis. We should use datives: "both for them and for you the Master is in heaven." As far as this heavenly Master is concerned you are both in the same position: "respect of person does not exist for *him*," the last phrase being emphatic. It may exist for men but not for him. He is not a judge who "takes the face," sees who a man is and decides his case with partiality, in favor of the one who is a lord and master, rich and powerful, in disfavor of one who is only a poor slave and powerless. This heavenly Master is an absolutely impartial Judge in all his judgments present and to come. Even the emperor's purple will not shield him before this Judge. This admonition is brief but to the point and altogether sufficient because of the importance of what it conveys.

* * *

The Closing Admonition for All to Stand against the Great Enemies of the Una Sancta.

10) The texts and the text critics differ as to whether the reading is τοῦ λοιποῦ or τὸ λοιπόν. Either would be adverbial. Robertson calls the former an incipient adverb, the latter is an adverbial accusative. There is only a shade of difference between them: *des weiteren — was das Uebrige betrifft.* There is no need to have the genitive refer to the future: "from henceforth"; it is logical: "with respect to the rest" (R., W. P.). Beyond question Paul now offers his final admonition which is to cover all that he has yet to say.

Finally, be powerful in the Lord and in the strength of his might!

The dispute as to whether the imperative is passive or middle cannot be decided on the basis of the word itself (R. 816). There is no difference in force whether we make ourselves powerful or let God make us powerful. No agent is indicated here; therefore the phrase, "in the Lord," is probably the middle, which phrase, as always, means, "in union with him," and is even explained: "and in union with the strength of his might." The durative present tense is important: we must constantly appropriate power in this our union with the Lord, since we need it all the time, lest at any time we be caught by the enemy. Note 3:16. As was the case in 1:19, ἰσχύς is the might possessed whether it is exercised or not; κράτος is the strength in its exercise.

This opening command strikes a virile, martial note: power — strength — might! Christians dare never be weaklings. They are joined to a Lord who is their inexhaustible source of power, who is himself filled with strength and might, the Stronger One who conquered the strong one (Luke 11:21, 22). By virtue of his new life the Christian has a certain amount of power, but this needs constant augmentation. We secure this increase through our union with the Lord, our union with the operative strength of his possession of might.

11) Like a general issuing commands and instructions to an army, Paul gives the next order and does so without using a connective. **Put on the whole armor of God for you to be able to stand against the expert methods of the devil!**

Now the aorist imperative rings out, for one decisive act of assuming the armor is referred to. The emphasis is on the verb: "Put it on, put it on!" Thus, equipped with this armor, the Ephesians will be powerful (v. 10). The imagery is that of a Roman hoplite, "man of arms," the heavy-armed legionary, not the light-armed fighter of the auxiliary contingent who was armed only with the bow.

This is a picture of a soldier of the line. These were the dependence of Rome and formed her invincible legions by which she had conquered the world and held it. Isa. 59:17 blends with the picture. We, too, use the word "panoply" in the meaning "the whole armor" as Paul does. Yet we should not think of a false contrast as though a Roman hoplite might have only a part of his armor. This is not an admonition to be sure to put it all on, to forget nothing. Certainly, automatically the hoplite took his panoply. How would he dare to do less? "Of God" is the *genitive auctoris*, God supplies the panoply, this is *his* army. Πρός with the articulated infinitive denotes subjective purpose, R. 1075. We have twelve instances of it in the New Testament; all express purpose and not result. The infinitive is present to denote constant ability and matches the imperative used in v. 10: "for you to be able, to be powerful." But the second, complementary infinitive is an effective aorist: "to stand" successfully, invincibly. The implied opposite is not flight but rather defeat: "to stand as victor, unvanquished." Paul does not say merely "to stand against the devil"; he says more: "against the expert methods of the devil," the same word that was used in 4:14. The idea of expert skill should not be overlooked. "The devil" leads the opposing army, and he is no mean commander, he knows his game.

> *Gross' Macht und viel' List*
> *Sein' grausam' Ruestung ist.* Luther.

12) **Because there is for us not the wrestling against blood and flesh but against the principalities, against the authorities, against the world tyrants of this darkness, against the spiritual (forces) of the wickedness in the heavenly places.** This is reason enough for putting on the panoply of God and never trusting to "our own unaided strength" or "might of ours." Paul lets the whole army of the devil parade before our eyes. This is the tremendous power we face, against this we must stand victorious. Equipped with God's armor, we can.

Paul is not mixing his figures and inserting the idea of the wrestler into the description of the hoplite. "The wrestling" is the proper word and is used here

for that reason. When one contends with "blood and
flesh" he comes to grips, he wrestles with such an antagonist. This is a human antagonist. Wrestling is
also only a game, a human game. In this game the
wrestler only throws his opponent, he does not kill him
as he does in war. Paul says that we have (Greek:
"there is not for us") no mere wrestling match with
an unarmed, human opponent, who at the worst is
able only to lay our back to the floor, we face a tremendous army, all the evil forces of the supernatural
world.

Some overlook the fact that Paul says "blood and
flesh" (also Heb. 2:14, the correct reading) and does
not follow the usual order "flesh and blood"; others regard the two expressions as being without a difference.
In John 1:13 blood is named first, flesh second; in Acts
17:26 blood alone is mentioned. As C.-K. 82 indicates,
"blood and flesh" seems to point only to the basis of
our physical, natural existence and avoids what lies in
"flesh and blood," namely moral quality, a contrast
with God. We add that here the point appears to be
the avoidance of the connotation of the evil in our
nature which is in alliance with the devil, which thus
also requires the divine panoply in order to be defeated.
Anything consisting merely of "blood and flesh," our
physical constituents, could at the worst only stage a
wrestling match with us. This is the best explanation
we are able to offer.

After the negative we now have the positive, and
πρός is repeated four times, thus intensifying the appositional designations. The supposition that after ἀλλά
we must supply the predication "there is for us the
wrestling" is untenable. The idea of wrestling so evidently confines itself to "blood and flesh" that no Greek
would have any difficulty in understanding Paul's
thought. He sees the contrast Paul indicates, gets
Paul's meaning without the verb, and notes that this

is something vastly worse than a wrestling match. The omission of a predication fixes the Greek's mind upon the array of appositional phrases that unroll the power of the devil's army. That, too, is why Paul sets these four πρός over against the one lone πρός.

As was the case in 1:21 and in 3:10, Paul is not enumerating different classes of demon warriors. These phrases are appositions: each one parades the entire demon army before our eyes. Paul gives us four views of it, four for the sake of completeness. We cannot use the abstract plural "rules"; as in 3:10, our best word is "principalities." Every demon has his "rule" or domain in which he exercises his "authority." Paul then gives them their ὄνομα (1:21), they are "the world tyrants of this darkness," and then still more significantly he terms them "the spiritual (forces) of the wickedness in the heavenly places," i. e., of the supermundane wickedness. The two abstract designations are thus defined by concrete personal names or titles.

"World tyrants" is better than "world rulers," for κράτος in the compound noun contains the idea of exerting strength and utter hardness and thus acting like the worst tyrant. Not in a corner but in the whole world these have their vast domain. "Of this darkness" (not merely "of darkness") points to the present spiritual world darkness to which these world tyrants belong. The contrast is "the outer darkness" where there is only wailing and gnashing of teeth (Matt. 8:12) in everlasting doom. Here again "the darkness" is not the mere absence of light; it is the absolute antagonism to light and thus denotes the fearful power that is hostile to God who is "the light" and whose are "the children of light" (5:8). This designation is as horrible as the next. From "this darkness" and the dominion of these "world tyrants" Christ has delivered us; hence their war is waged in order again to subjugate us under their tyranny.

The neuter plural τὰ πνευματικά does not denote "things" (R., W. P.) since this phrase, too, is appositional and the masculine plural "world tyrants" precedes. Instead of writing πνεύματα Paul substantivizes the adjective, not as denoting "the spiritual principles" of the Satanic powers (C.-K. 956), but as denoting "the spiritual beings" as such: "the spiritual hosts" (Westcott: "forces") of the R. V. The neuter is scarcely due to the preceding "blood and flesh" which also may be regarded as a neuter expression, but is like the neuter πνεύματα, "spirits," of which it makes one think. But this is true that, like all the other terms, "the spiritual forces," since they are spiritual, bring into relief their difference from "blood and flesh," which are only physical (men). That is why here, too, the genitive must be added (as in the preceding designation): "of the wickedness in the heavenly places," i. e., belonging not to wickedness in general but to this particular wickedness. This wickedness is a power like "this darkness." It has produced all the wickedness on earth. We war also against the latter, but here Paul describes the worst, that which produced the latter, that which is thus more terrible than the other.

Paul uses ἐν τοῖς ἐπουρανίοις four times, each time to designate *loca* and not *bona*. In 1:3, 20; and in 3:10 we have no difficulty, heaven is referred to. But in 2:6, "the heavenly places in Christ Jesus" in which God has seated the Ephesians, cannot be heaven, for Paul is writing to them while they are here on earth. This shows that the meaning of the phrase is determined by its context, and here the context is not God and the good angels (as in 1:3, 20; 3:10), not Christians (2:6), but demons. So heaven as the abode of

God and his angels is excluded and also "the heavenlies in Christ Jesus," the kingdom of Christ here among men. The phrase must here designate "the wickedness" as being located in the supermundane world and thus being distinguished from the wickedness found in men here below on the earth. Paul is describing the demons as they now are; hence we hesitate to accept the idea that he describes this wickedness as it first originated in heaven when Satan and his adherents fell and were cast out. Some identify the *loca* of this phrase with the ἀήρ of 2:2 and take this to be the physical air; but see the writer's confession in 2:2 regarding "the air." The A. V.'s "spiritual wickedness in high places," margin, "wicked spirits," are incorrect; the plural accusative which is substantivized does not modify the articulated genitive singular, nor is this genitive adjectival. The phrase modifies the genitive.

13) Because of this take up the whole armor of God in order that you may be able to withstand in the wicked day and, having accomplished everything, to stand!

"To stand (v. 11) — to withstand — to stand" (all aorists), so rings the refrain of these infinitives plus the imperative: "Stand then!" in v. 14. The victorious stand — that is their business.

"This" refers to the fact just stated in v. 12. The admonition given in v. 11 is repeated. It is made to ring out doubly, on both sides of the great terms of power which describe our enemy host. Such repetition lends it great emphasis. Yet Paul's repetitions always add new points and variation. For "put on" he now writes "take up," both are peremptory aorists. He keeps unchanged the expressive object "the panoply of God," all other armament is as so much straw against these foes. In the purpose clause only the significant infinitive "to stand" is the same, the rest is an advance. In v. 11 there is stated what we are to stand

against, "the expert methods of the devil." Now we
are told when and how to stand victorious. "To withstand (aorist: successfully) in the day, the wicked
one (the adjective after a second article which makes
it emphatic, R. 776), and, having accomplished everything, to stand" (aorist: as victors when this day of
battle is over).

This day is called "wicked" because the spiritual
forces of the wickedness of the other world will hurl
themselves against us. Recall the words of Jesus
spoken to his enemies: "This is your hour and the
power of the darkness," Luke 22:53. It is not the day
of the last battle at the end of the world, Rev. 20:7-9.
Only the Christians who are then living will see that
battle with Gog and Magog, and not the panoply of
God will win the victory in that battle but "fire came
down from God out of heaven and devoured them,"
the enemy. "The day of death" cannot be referred to,
for this is a blessed and not a wicked day for the Christian, the day of the crowning (II Tim. 4:8). This
wicked day is also not the entire time of our life, for
we are to arm ourselves for this day, to be ready when
it breaks. Paul has in mind the critical and decisive
day which comes for each one of us, sometimes but
once, again repeatedly, in which Satan pounces upon
us with all his forces. Then we must "be able or powerful (the same verb that was used in v. 10, 11) to
withstand" without yielding to a single assault.

Thus we understand the participial clause: "and
having accomplished everything" by using the panoply
of God, "everything" for which it is intended. That
will be the day when this whole armor will be fully
tried out by our expert foe. But, using it to the full,
we shall, indeed, be powerful "to stand" as victors
(aorist) with effective finality. Note the five aorist
forms in this verse. Robertson is right, there are sermons in tenses. Here they have the ring of victory.

Be that day ever so wicked with the wickedness of
hell itself,

> "*All watching to devour us, —*
> *We tremble not, we fear no ill,*
> *They cannot overpower us.*" (Luther).

The preposition in the participle is perfective:
"having thoroughly done everything." In the New
Testament it never means "to overthrow"; nor can the
neuter ἅπαντα refer to τὰ πνευματικά: "having overthrown
them all." Then Paul would have used the masculine,
for then persons would be referred to. The participle
also never means, "having gotten everything ready."

14) Paul now expressly names all the parts of the
panoply of God but so as to retain the admonition with
which he began. **Stand, then, having girded your
loins in truth, and having put on the breastplate
of the righteousness, and having shod your feet in
the preparation of the gospel of the peace, in addition to everything having taken up the long-shield
of the faith, in connection with which you will be
able to extinguish all the arrows of the wicked one,
those that have been set on fire.**

The preceding aorists (v. 13) are picturesque; we
see the hoplite rush to arms — then fight and withstand valiantly — then stand with the enemy defeated
and the victory won. The progress lies, not in the
tenses, but in the verbs themselves. When Paul now
begins the description of the armor with another aorist
imperative, this is not ingressive: "begin to stand, or
take your stand" (R., *W. P.*), this is constative:
"Stand once for all." That is why the relative clause
in v. 16 has the future tense: "you will be able," etc.

Paul might have added a few other points to this
description. So the mind of most men operates: they
let the image and figure dominate their thought and
thus would seek out literal counterparts for all that

the picture of a Roman hoplite presents to their mind. Not so Paul. He makes the imagery subservient and hence uses only as much as really aids the literal facts. Now these literal items are seven (a number we expect Paul to use): truth — righteousness — gospel of peace — the faith — salvation — the Word of God — prayer. The figure of the hoplite is fitted to these. The fact that it cannot be applied to point seven does not disturb Paul even as no one expects a figure for prayer. Paul regards prayer as a part of our equipment, for he carefully uses two nouns after διά which points to means: "by means of all prayer and petition," etc.

The arrangement in expression is interesting. Paul does not, of course, merely enumerate seven in a loose succession but in the natural order and grouping, each item occurring only where it should be found in this list. Thus items 2 and 3 are joined with καί, but 4 with ἐπὶ πᾶσιν. That makes four, but as composed of 3 + 1. This is repeated in the case of the next three (v. 17, 18) where 1 and 2 are combined by καί after the imperative, while 3 (prayer) is added by a phrase which modifies a participle. All this is rhetorical, but it uses rhetoric and flexibility of form to make the thought shine out more lucidly.

The first three participles are indirect middles: the Christian is to belt himself, clothe himself, shoe himself; all are aorists, definite acts, which are to precede the action of the aorist "stand!" The Greek uses the singular, our idiom the plural for "loins." This belting does not refer to the Oriental long, loose outer robe of the civilian, which was belted up for rapid walking and other action. The hoplite wore a short tunic. Any mantle that was worn over his armor was put away when he stood in line and was ready to fight. To his belt the scabbard of the sword and his thorax were attached. The order is the natural one: the belt is buckled on first, then the breastplate, then the sandals. We should carry this order on through; next the helmet and the sword, then the shield. Paul does not do so but keeps to the reality and subjects the figure.

"In truth" (better than the instrumental "with") is not subjective, *sittliche Lauterkeit*, the moral quality of truthfulness. We are surprised that Luther understands "righteousness" in the same way as the moral righteousness of the Christian. To be sure, both must be the Christian's possession, but this is expressed by the participles: belt yourselves, put on yourselves. The "truth" which Paul has in mind is the divine, saving truth or reality. The absence of the article stresses the quality of the term. Therefore "truth" is placed first.

Let us note that the efforts to divide "truth" — "the gospel of the peace" — "the utterance of God" as to their substance are misdirected. They are one in substance. The differentiation lies in the use to which the three expressions are to be put. At one time "truth," the divine, saving reality as such (no article) and all that constitutes it, firmly encircles and holds the Christian warrior in the battle. Paul sees more in this truth than we ordinarily should; hence he uses two more terms to indicate two other effects of the truth in this war.

As truth is to be the belt, so "the breastplate" or *Brustpanzer* is to be "the righteousness." This is the righteousness of Christ put on by faith, the *justitia imputata*. No righteousness of our own, *justitia acquisita*, could be proof against Satan; since it is always still imperfect, it would be promptly pierced. Our righteousness of good works ever needs Christ's merits and righteousness to cover up its imperfection. After describing the horrible power of our demon foes, as Paul does in v. 12, it would be folly to send us against them with works that our own hands have done.

Here the article is in place, and the genitive is appositional: "the breastplate" = "the righteousness." The figure is elucidated by the reality it describes; the language is self-interpretative. This is, indeed, the breastplate that covers the vital organs, especially also the heart. A wound in the arm or the leg would not prove fatal. Only the head is comparable, and we see that the helmet covers that. "The righteousness" is forensic as it is in all other connections (verb and adjective, etc., likewise): that quality bestowed by God's verdict which acquits us of all sin and guilt and declares us righteous for Christ's sake. It is the central part of all saving truth. The heart of the Word makes our heart invulnerable against Satan.

15) The third participial clause is more complex. It means literally: "And having shod yourselves as to the feet in readiness of the gospel of the peace." This literal translation clears up some of the misunderstanding that is due to translations which seek smoothness. The general sense is: ready, eager courage that is due to the gospel which fills us with the peace of God. The context does not support the idea of invading the territory of the enemy, taking the gospel among men in order to snatch them away from the devil. The feet are sandaled for the wicked day, for the battle with the demon host. The idea is not that of solid footing or ground, because sandals furnish no footing, they protect the feet when going over rough ground such as this spirit army might choose for the battle.

The word is "preparedness" and thus "readiness," here the preparedness which makes us fully ready to plunge into the fight. No article is needed, for the genitive of source defines: "a readiness inspired by the gospel." It is the gospel "of the peace," definite, of that peace (objective) which Christ gives us (John 14:27), which then also fills us with the feeling of peace (subjective). The wrath has subsided, God is with us, we are thus ready, eager for the battle unto victory. We are above defeat. We know that if we resist the devil he will flee from us. As the swarms of the Persian armies were scattered like chaff before the onslaught of the Greek hoplite phalanxes of Cyrus as these were singing their battle paean or closing in with ominous silence, so will these countless πνευματικά flee like chaff before the charge of the ready courage instilled by the gospel of the peace.

The peace is in the heart but shows itself in the readiness of the feet. Hence, "having your feet shod." "Of the peace" is the genitive of the substance. *Euanggelion* is the proper word, for to bring peace is to carry good news. To be sure, this gospel with its contents of peace is "reality" or "truth." But see how the words fit! If some "sham" instead of "truth" bound us, we should be lost to begin with. But "truth" must be this peace, made ours by this precious gospel, so that the courage in our *hearts* makes our *feet* march with victorious steadiness and courage into the hostile hosts in order to scatter them in defeat.

The introduction of "the peace" into this picture of battle is highly paradoxical. *Our peace with God* makes us avid for *the battle with Satan!* It is true, indeed. Without this gospel and its peace our feet would not for one moment stand or go forward against Satan. Who save *we men of peace* dares *to fight him?* Occasionally, when these "world tyrants of this darkness" (v. 12) perpetrate exceptional outrages (gangster rule, crimes that cry to high heaven), a protest is voiced by worldly men; but these tyrants are not thereby scattered, the protests soon subside.

We should not overlook the fact that "the righteousness" and "the peace" are correlated as are "truth" and "the gospel." The terms are beautifully interlocked. They also show a progression. The figure only serves; the literal actualities unfold. Rom. 5:1

thus joins our having been declared righteous with the resultant peace with God. Paul's writing is incomparable. Sit at the feet of this spiritual master and learn.

16) The readings vary between ἐν and ἐπί, the former having a little better textual support. But this is reduced when we note that the old Latin versions translate the participle as though it were present and not aorist. This is the very point: "in all things taking up the shield" (present, iterative: "on all occasions"). But not: "in all things having taken up" (aorist like the preceding participle). To let "in all" mean in all the previous acts, makes belt, breastplate, sandals, and shield a confused mass. Nor can v. 16 serve as the preamble to v. 17, for the latter is marked off by καί, and "in all" then hangs in the air. No; the four aorist participles (v. 14-16) belong together. The second and the third are added cumulatively by "and." Instead of using another "and" (cumulative coordination) Paul now lifts the fourth member to a greater height with ἐπὶ πᾶσιν: "in addition to all things" having taken up the shield of the faith.

The genitive is again appositional: "the shield" = "the faith" just as "the breastplate" = "the righteousness." A large number of writers regard "the faith" as subjective: *fides qua creditur*, the faith *with* which we believe, especially those who regard "truth" and "the righteousness" as subjective moral qualities. Nothing is generally said about the article: "*the* faith." The Greek may or may not have the article with abstract nouns; the English often omits it where the Greek needs it. The Greek use of the article *does*, however, make a difference. Look at "truth" and at "the righteousness." We cannot agree with C.-K. when he states that "faith" is never used in the sense of *quae creditur*, that which is believed (objective). We have found "the faith" used in this sense a goodly number of times; it would be strange, indeed, if the English used the word in this objective sense and *not* also the Greek. Some of the interpreters note that "faith" is a correlative term: our believing always involves the object which faith embraces. These come nearer to Paul's meaning. And "the (objective) faith" likewise always involves subjective faith. "The faith" is something that is actually believed by believers; if it were not embraced by believers it could not be called "the faith."

What is meant by "all the blazing missiles of the wicked one," which we shall be able to quench with this shield, "the faith"? "Temptations," we are told. Very well. But what are they, and why are they called "missiles," βέλη, arrows or darts, *malleoli,* arrows tipped with burning cotton and pitch (not poisoned arrows, as some think), not *falaricae,* the great spears hurled from a catapult during the siege of a fortress.

Paul is describing an open battle. The devil tempted Eve by hurling at her the doubt regarding God's word: "Did God really say?" How could and should she have quenched that blazing arrow? As Jesus did when Satan shot the same kind of arrows at him during the temptation in the desert. Each time the arrow was quenched in the shield, not of, "I believe," but of, "It is written." Eve's answer should have been: "Most certainly God *did* say!"

Here is the answer as to what "the faith" means when it is used as the shield against the blazing arrows. Luther: "One little *word* overthrows him." Hold up to the devil, not merely your believing or subjective faith, but the Word, the doctrine, the pertinent Scripture passage, the objective content of faith, of course, also with your whole heart believing, relying on its truth and power. You may believe with all your might, but that will not be a quenching shield; Satan will easily pierce that, and you will be set on fire. Everything depends on *what* you believe. Hold up "the faith" (objective) ; this extinguishes every tempting lie of the wicked one. The participle contains the subjective factor. You do not take up this shield unless you believe that it will do what it did for Jesus, what Paul says it will ever do.

The θυρεός is the long-shield, *scutum,* about four feet high, extending from the top of the greaves at the knee to the level of the eyes. Hoplites in line literally held an extended wall before their bodies. The ἀσπίς, *clypeus,* was round, 2½ feet in diameter, and was carried by the cavalryman. "The wicked one" = "the devil" of v. 11, but the new term recalls "the wickedness" and "the wicked day" of v. 12, 13. This word always means actively, viciously wicked in hostility to God. The singular does not restrict the arrows to Satan as though he alone shot them; they are all his no matter who shoots them An attributive after an intervening genitive has the article. The perfect participle "having been set on fire" has its present implication: thus blazing now. This word is significant. The mind is to be set on fire with lies. On entering, the fire sets up a conflagration which turns everything to ruin and ashes. What a graphic picture of the devil's temptation! What a fire was started by Eve's temptation! It still burns on and on, a world-wide conflagration, and see the ashes it has left!

It is not necessary to make the effort to save Paul from incongruity. Since common shields do not extinguish fiery arrows, some let the infinitive mean only "to make burning ineffective." But where does the verb have that meaning (M.-M. 570)? Then Paul strains the figure beyond the reality. It is a fact. Jesus, too, does the same thing because earthly figures are too weak always to picture the great realities in an adequate way. And these are arrows tipped with unearthly fire, and a divine shield does quench that fire most promptly. Let the reality exceed the image, both will then be better understood.

In the panoply of God note the four objective items: truth — the righteousness — the gospel of the peace — the faith. Again, the subjective, personal appropriation for the purpose of the battle, the participles: girded — put on — shod — having taken up. When "faith" is made subjective, there is an inclination to take it as corresponding to "righteousness"; but Paul has the proper order: truth — the righteousness — the gospel — and in addition to these the faith, which is as objective as the rest.

17) When Paul continues with the finite verb, this is scarcely due to the intervening relative clause, because he could have followed this with participles just as he uses participles after the relative clause in v. 17. The imperative marks the division; first a group of four (v. 14-16), next a group of three, "and" connects the two. **And the helmet of the salvation do you take and the sword of the Spirit, which means God's utterance; by means of all prayer and petition** (ever) **praying on every occasion in spirit and thereunto** (ever) **being vigilant in all steadfastness and petition for all the saints, etc.**

The object is now placed before the verb which makes the object emphatic; then, since the verb is placed between the two objects, the second object also becomes distinct. The genitive is again appositional: "the helmet" = "the salvation." Perhaps the neuter τὸ σωτήριον instead of the commonly used abstract ἡ σωτηρία is a reminiscence of Isa. 59:17 where Jehovah arms himself with the helmet of salvation. But this salvation is neither an ideal possession that is yet to be realized, which would be a poor protection for the soldier's head, nor the hope of future salvation (Thayer and others) despite I Thess. 5:8: "as a helmet, hope of salvation"; for "hope" is lacking in this passage.

This is our present salvation. That which saves and keeps safe (τὸ σωτήριον) protects the head from a fatal or a disabling blow.

Next "the sword of the Spirit," the one offensive weapon in this entire armament. Hear the genitive denotes a person and cannot therefore be appositional. This plainly differentiates "the helmet of salvation" from "the sword of the Spirit" even as the two are as widely separated as possible by having the verb placed between them. Yet these two have been combined by some interpreters: "make your own *the Word* of God as the helmet on your head, pointing to and assuring salvation, and as a sword insuring victory." "Sword" and "helmet" are two distinct parts of the armor. The genitive is the genitive of source: the Spirit's sword is invincible.

The relative clause defines this μάχαιρα, the short sword, the regular weapon of the Roman hoplite. "Of the Spirit" is not explicative, for it is the relative clause that is the explication of the expression "the sword of the Spirit." Ὅ ἐστιν is an idiom which is used without much regard to the gender (or even number) of the antecedent or of the following predicate (R. 411): "which means," etc. The supposition that ὅ has derived its gender from Πνεῦμα or from ῥῆμα is untenable.

"God's utterance" (no article) is purely qualitative. Paul does not use *logos*, which points to substance; but, as in 5:26 and notably in the temptation account in Matt. 4:4, ῥῆμα = "utterance." It is this because it leaves God's mouth. So one need no think of the *writing* in Scripture although this records the utterance by inerrant inspiration; nor of "the *preached* Word", for although it is the same utterance, when it is preached it passes through *our* mouth; nor of the idea of *meaning* (logos), for no utterance of God is devoid of meaning. "God's utterance" as an *"utterance,"* as "going forth out of God's mouth" (Matt. 4:4), makes it "the sword of the Spirit" that is so deadly in striking down the foe of God and of man. When we use it in our battle we are to use it only as "God's utterance." We must also use it unaltered, just as God uttered it. Any alteration takes the power and the edge off this sword.

To be sure, this is "God's utterance" and thus "the sword of the Spirit." In that utterance lies God's power; Rom. 1:16 uses "God's power" to define the gospel. That utterance, we may say, is the expression of God's will. In Rom. 10:17 we have "Christ's utterance" (which is the same) in its beneficent power producing faith and salvation. In Heb. 6:5, "God's good utterance" which one tastes. That "utterance" should be the sword before which the demon host flees is one of the surprising facts of Scripture revelation. Since they are intangible because they are "spirit forces," the opposite of "blood and flesh" (v. 12), we must have a weapon that is able to crush these hosts, and this is it.

This does not imply that the Word can be used by Paul only in one way in this picture of the panoply of God, namely as a sword. That is only its offensive power. As truth the Word belts us; as the gospel of the peace it puts the readiness of courage into our hearts; as the faith, the doctrines which we believe, teach, and confess, it shields us against any and all of the wicked one's lies. In addition to all this (ἐπὶ πᾶσιν) the Word and utterance smites and defeats our foe himself. What a true description this is of the Word of God! What a call, then, to every one of us to arm himself with it!

18) Now there follow two present participles. Being participles, they present the subordinate part of our equipment. Although there are two participles, we see that they are bound together and describe one thing. Being durative present tenses, they differ decidedly from the aorist participles used in v. 14-16, which denote but a single act. These participles do not

modify a verb, neither στῆτε (v. 14), as some suppose,
nor δέξασθε (v. 17), as others prefer; they are nominative plurals and modify the subject "you" that runs
through v. 13-17 and still further describe the armament of the Christians. In one word, this is prayer,
but prayer in the Biblical sense, answered prayer which
brings to our aid the mighty help of God himself.
Since prayer is always an activity, the terms used are
of that kind. We wield the power of prayer. This
does not place prayer on a level with the Word, its
righteousness and its salvation; the very wording with
durative participles excludes such ideas. Prayer must
be listed here because it brings our divine ally to our
side in the battle on the wicked day (v. 13). Thus the
figure of the panoply is no longer needed.

Διά states the means: "by means of all prayer and
petition (ever) praying on every occasion in spirit,"
etc. The word used for "prayer" and "praying" is
the religious term that is used to designate the act
of worship that is directed to God and is never used
when men are addressed. The word for "petition"
(our versions, "supplication") is also employed when
we ask favors of men. "Prayer" includes all forms,
"petition" notes the cries for help when in need. So
also Paul says: "by means of *all* prayer and petition,"
not a single kind being neglected or omitted.

The participle is durative (iterative), yet Paul
adds: "on every occasion," ἐν παντὶ καιρῷ. It has been
denied that this refers to specific occasions, crises in
the conflict, and it is claimed that Paul means "habit-
ually," on all kinds of occasions, "without ceasing"
(I Thess. 5:17). But we should not forget "the wicked
day" (v. 13) and the context of battle. We, indeed,
pray daily, we ever keep the prayerful attitude of
spirit; but every one of us has experienced those special occasions when in dire need we cry to God for
help and strength with intensity.

The phrase ἐν πνεύματι is generally understood to mean: "in union with the Spirit," especially since he is the Spirit of prayer. Then, however, we find the absence of the article strange, the more so since "the Spirit" has just been mentioned, and the article of previous reference would be in place. To be sure, as in the case of "God" and other words that denote that there is only the one of its kind in existence, the article is frequently absent when the Spirit is referred to. The matter is not so simple. The article is omitted in scores of adverbial phrases; look at ἐκ ψυχῆς in v. 6. What is still more decisive is the use of "spirit" (not "Spirit," our versions) in Gal. 5:16-25 and 6:8 (see the author's exegesis of the nine words), and also elsewhere. We are to pray "in spirit." To say that this would be self-evident is to overlook our experience. This is the very point to be stressed because the spirit, the new man in us (4:23, 24), is often languid even in critical days and needs stimulation. Nor does "in spirit" ignore the Holy Spirit; for none of us prays in spirit save by the Spirit's help.

Because "in spirit" is Paul's meaning he adds: "and thereunto (ever) being vigilant in all steadfastness," etc. It is our spirit that must keep vigilant unto prayer, yea, vigilant "in all steadfastness." We have already said that the two participles describe one and not two acts. Satan loves to lull the new man to sleep, at least not to be wide awake, so that he may catch us unawares. Ἀγρυπνεῖν = to remain without sleep, awake, and thus vigilant. Synonymous are γρηγορεῖν, to watch with effort, and νήφειν, to be weary. The verb Paul uses here conveys the idea of never being off guard with respect to these enemies who would like to find us heedless and secure. "In all steadfastness" (which is better than "perseverance," our versions, compare the participle in Acts 2:42, 46) means more than constancy in prayer. It is the steadfastness of the spirit of these warriors in their entire battle, the same idea that is expressed by the command: "Stand, then!" in v. 14.

Keep the phrase where Paul has it, viz., with "being vigilant"; for he himself has tied the two participles together, once by "thereunto," and again by repeating: in all . . . "petition." The latter is especially obvious, for "thereunto" already resumes the idea of praying by means of all prayer and petition. Some find fault with Paul for having a superfluous second mention of "petition," it is really a third mention. But Paul always knows what he is writing. And here the matter is obvious. "Steadfastness" and "petition" are diverse, the one is a virtue and quality of the "spirit," the other a begging prayer. The latter so plainly repeats this word as to weld into one idea the two participial clauses. Prayer is the power we wield, vigilance is not a second power; it is only the alertness in using the prayer power.

Yet the repetition is not a mere reiteration. It would scarcely be that in Paul's writings save for a plain reason. "Petition" ushers in all that follows: "petition regarding all the saints and in behalf of me, that to me," etc. The two phrases are highly significant. The first includes the entire *Una Sancta* and all that Paul has written about it in his entire epistle. "All the saints" = the *Una Sancta*. They include all the Ephesians, and here Paul does not differentiate and say: "petition for yourselves and for all the saints." This is *one* army standing against *one* other army. All the saints stand as a unit, none stands alone. See the full force of that. The thought, so often met today, is far from Paul's mind: If only I myself stand, or only my congregation, I am satisfied. The *Una Sancta* is one. Petition for self is to be intercession for all.

19) But does that not also include Paul? Most assuredly it does. That is why Paul changes the pre-

position (not as a mere matter of style) ; and that is why Paul adds what the Ephesians are to ask of God for him. Ἵνα is not final (contra R., *W. P.*) but non-final; it states the contents of the petition to be offered for Paul. This is something that differs from what the Ephesians are to ask for the whole *Una Sancta,* of which they and Paul are equally members: **and in behalf of me, that to me be given the floor by opening my mouth in boldness to make known the mystery of the gospel in behalf of which I am an ambassador in a chain, that in it I speak boldly as it is necessary that I speak.**

This petition is distinct and could be offered only in behalf of Paul. To make known the mystery of the gospel recalls all that Paul has said in 3:3 about having had this mystery made known to him by revelation, and in 3:9 about the administration of this mystery once hidden in God but now made known even in the angelic world. In 3:11-22 Paul unfolded the whole mystery as it pertained to the Gentile believers in Ephesus, they with the Jewish believers being one body of Christ. Thus as "all the saints" includes all that this epistle contains about the *Una Sancta,* "me" includes all that the epistle contains about the special office of the gospel, that the *Una Sancta* embraces equally Jewish and Gentile believers, all being the one body of Christ.

There is a difference of opinion in regard to the meaning of λόγος. Thayer defines it as "faculty of speech," B.-P., *Reden,* C.-K. passes by our passage; our versions come close to the thought with their translation "utterance." We submit that the expression is parliamentary, forensic, and a court term. The president, judge, or king says like Agrippa in Acts 26:1: "Thou art permitted to speak!" In an assembly one "is given the floor." The German says: *"Ich bitte ums*

Wort!" and receives the permission: *"Sie haben das Wort!"* Here the expression agrees with "I am an ambassador," which points to a court. The emperor or the king receives the ambassador, nods, and thus permits him to deliver his message.

Paul is thinking of the day he was so anxiously awaiting when he would stand before the imperial court or before the emperor to whom he had appealed his case. But see the vividness of Paul's mind. He sees himself in the most paradoxical light: a prisoner before a judge, and yet this role fades out into an ambassador sent by Christ, the King of kings, standing in the throne room of Nero, delivering the message of his King to the pagan imperial court. Wonderful double picture, indeed! To be given *logos* is to be given the floor, the right to speak. The ambassadorial figure adds the note of great dignity to that of order and also the idea of vast import to the message thus to be transmitted.

The A. V. punctuates more correctly than the R. V., for we should construe: "by opening of my mouth in boldness to make known the mystery of the gospel." The point is this bold making known. Some combine λόγος with at least the first phrase: "utterance in opening of my mouth." Opening the mouth is a common expression for making a public address or a long explanation. But the emphasis is on the παρρησία, which is, therefore, also repeated in the verb used in v. 20: liberty to say anything with nothing compelling restraint such as fear. The aorist infinitive is effective: actually to make known; call it an infinitive of purpose. "The mystery of the gospel" has been elucidated by Paul himself as we have shown.

The commonly held view is that Paul is thinking of his preaching in general, that the Ephesians are to pray that he may have adequate boldness for that. But

Paul is thinking of far more, namely of the climax that
would be reached when his case would finally come
before the imperial court, where perhaps the emperor
himself or at least his representative would preside.
Then Paul would be told to give an account of his
teaching and doctrine. Then the hour would come
when he was to lay before the highest tribunal in the
world the gospel of the King who had sent him to bear
his name before kings (Acts 9:15). Then he must
speak not as an intimidated prisoner but as a true ambassador. Paul had the promise of Christ for that
high moment (Matt. 10:19, 20; Mark 13:11; Luke
12:11, 12; 21:12-15). Paul was not worried; but he
knows that the fulfillment is obtained by prayer. He is
not thinking of his own safety but of rising to the
great occasion, of doing full justice to the gospel as a
true ambassador should. That is why he asks for the
intercession of the Ephesians.

20) Hence the relative clause: "in behalf of which
I am an ambassador in a chain," plus the purpose
clause which is parallel to the infinitive, "in order that
I may speak boldly as it is necessary that I speak."
Πρεσβεύω = to be an ambassador (II Cor. 5:20); it is
derived from πρεσβύτερος, because an older person was
usually sent as an ambassador. But to speak of "Paul
the aged" because he uses this verb has no more warrant than to conclude that in II Cor. 5:20 "we are
ambassadors" means that all these ministers were aged
men.

Regarding the question of being chained see the
author's comments on Acts 26:29; 28:20. Since he
was a Roman citizen, Paul wore no fetters; Acts 22:29
shows how frightened Lysias was on discovering that
he had fettered the Roman citizen Paul. During the
entire imprisonment in Caesarea Paul wore no chain
or chains; neither did he do so during the time of the
journey to Rome. Not until Burrhus put Paul into the

lightest military custody in Rome by letting him live in his own house was one light chain employed. This was done merely in order to save placing more than one soldier over Paul as a guard. To the one soldier Paul was fastened by a chain at the wrists. In Acts 26:29 the neuter plural = bondage and not "chains." II Tim. 1:16 refers to Paul's second imprisonment when he was closely confined and soon to be condemned and executed. Even in II Tim. 1:16 only one chain is mentioned.

Yet this light chain and the idea of an ambassador clash as a paradox. To put a chain upon an ambassador is to insult the government he represents. The fact that the imperial court and Burrhus, the head of the imperial guard who had the custody of Paul, acted ignorantly still leaves the strange reality: an ambassador in a chain. The Roman authority that was soon to pass on Paul's case saw him only as a prisoner who had appealed his case to the emperor; Paul sees more. When his case is at last called, it will be his great obligation to act as Christ's ambassador to even that supreme court, even if Nero himself presides as the judge. Men might see the half, Paul saw the whole. He puts it into only two words, but they are striking.

The freedom of speech, usually translated "boldness," is defined by Paul himself: "as it is necessary that I utter." It is the freedom befitting an ambassador of Christ, that he be unhampered in stating his message (gospel) which he is to deliver also to kings (Acts 9:15). No fear about his own person is to act as a restraint. Δεῖ is used to express all kinds of necessity or obligation according to the context; λαλῆσαι is the proper word in the proper tense. The substance has already been stated: "the mystery of the gospel"; this must be adequately "uttered."

*   *   *

The Conclusion

21) Tychicus was to carry the three letters (Ephesians, Colossians, Philemon) to their respective destinations. He was also to deliver the slave Onesimus to Philemon, his master, in Colosse. So Paul closes: **Now in order that you, too, may know the things concerning me, how I am faring, everything Tychicus shall make known to you, the beloved brother and faithful minister in the Lord; whom I have sent to you for this very thing in order that you may get to know the things concerning us, and he may comfort your hearts.**

Colossians 4:7-9 has these same words. The Ephesians were deeply interested in Paul who had founded their congregation (read Acts 20:17-38) and had labored among them for so long a time. They would want to know everything about Paul. Tychicus is commissioned to satisfy this desire. He could tell far more than Paul could write unless Paul wanted to mar the balance he has kept in his letter.

Colossians 4:9 shows that Tychicus was not a Colossian, yet Acts 20:4 calls him an "Asian," a native of Asia Minor. He is mentioned in II Tim. 4:12. We lack further details save that he was one of Paul's assistants, a commissioner that was to help to take the great collection to Jerusalem (Acts 20:4), a man of high character, beloved by Paul personally. "A faithful minister in the Lord" (one concept) means one who rendered voluntary service as a "fellow slave" of Paul's in the work of the church by aiding Paul in this work. "In the Lord" modifies only "minister," the term "brother" needing no further modification. In this capacity of ministering Tychicus was now serving.

The aorist is probably ingressive: "get to know." "Also you" means "like the Colossians." The chief mission of Tychicus was to take Onesimus to Colosse and to carry Paul's letter that was correcting certain errors to the Colossians. Tychicus would tell the Ephesians about his chief mission. We have discussed the untenable conclusion that is based on this "also" (καί) in our introduction, which see. "The things concerning me" is explained by "how I am faring." The latter does not mean, "What I am doing"; it is a classic idiom. The sick Gorgas, for instance, is asked: τί πράττοι; So Tychicus will tell the Ephesians "everything."

22) In fact, Paul sent him to do this very thing, this was one of the purposes for which he is sent. The aorist is epistolary, the writer thinking of the moment when the sentence is read in Ephesus. "I sent (our idiom: have sent) to you" means that Tychicus is sent to the Ephesians and not merely to Colosse for a specific purpose.

Now Paul uses the ingressive γνῶτε and adds this to εἰδῆτε. The latter means to know the facts; it expresses the relation of the object to the subject. The other adds the relation of the subject to the object; it conveys the idea of the personal interest and concern of the Ephesians regarding the facts. But when he touches this Paul makes the object "the things concerning *us.*" To say that "us" = "me" is unwarranted. No writer uses "I" and the majestic or the editorial "we" in one and the same sentence. There were others with Paul (Col. 4:10-15), and he includes them. Paul would never think only of himself. But this generous spirit extends farther. As regards himself Paul uses the verb which simply denotes knowing the facts; but when he combines those others with himself he writes the verb that indicates knowing with personal concern. That, indeed, reveals the apostle's spirit.

Because the verb has this meaning, Paul adds the personal interest he has in mind: "and he may comfort your hearts" (the R. V.'s "ye" is correct). Because they were anxious and uncertain about Paul's situation, the definite news brought by Tychicus in person will assure and comfort the Ephesians. They will get complete answers to all their questions. Paul does not indicate that he expects soon to be set free as he does in Philippians. All that we are able to say is that at this time Paul was faring well enough, much as he had been since coming to Rome. According to the context the verb here used may mean admonish (4:1), encourage, urge, and also comfort, which latter is its meaning here.

Tychicus sailed to the harbor of Ephesus, visited the Ephesians, and then went on to Colosse with the slave Onesimus. See our introduction on this point. The assumption that, after landing, Tychicus sent Onesimus on to Colosse is untenable: no runaway slave could safely travel alone; the nearer he approached home, the greater was the danger of being recognized and summarily arrested. The two were together in Ephesus and then went on from there. "With Onesimus" in Col. 4:9 makes this quite certain. In our introduction we have already stated why Paul could not have recommended the slave to the Ephesians as a brother and otherwise. It would have been the height of tactlessness to commend this slave to any church before his master had dealt with him, before also the Colossian church had accepted him as a brother.

Why does Paul not add greetings from those who are with him? Some assume that this omission is proof positive that Ephesians was an encyclical, was a letter that was not intended for Ephesus. We have answered this question in our introduction. No less than *five* of Paul's letters to congregations lack greetings, only *four* have them, in Philippians there is no mention of an individual. Why this difference? This is the real question and not the one regarding Ephe-

sians alone. A blanket answer regarding the five cannot be given. Each letter stands by itself whether it is
with or without greetings from or to individuals or
from churches. That means that we can give only
very tentative and partial answers to the questions as
to why five letters are minus greetings, why four have
greetings, and why these greetings are what they are,
in one letter (Romans) a long list, in one only a summary (Philippians), both of these letters being different from the other two as far as greetings are concerned. As regards Ephesians, personal greetings
are not missed by those who see the exalted subject and
tone of the epistle. Colossians belongs in a different
class.

23) Now the closing benediction. **Peace to the
brethren and love in company with faith from God
as Father and the Lord Jesus Christ! The grace
with all who love our Lord Jesus Christ in connection
with incorruption!**

This is a double benediction, the second is wider
than the first, both are the more impressive because
they are phrased in the third and not in the second
person. The grace and the peace of the greeting (1:2)
are now reversed, the effect is placed before the source.
This is proper after the full effect has been set forth.
On the meaning of the two words see 1:2.

Paul does not write: "Peace and love and faith."
He inserts the dative between the first two and adds
the third with a preposition. So we take "peace" to
be objective like "the grace." As peace is the fruit of
grace, so love is the fruit of faith, in both instances the
fruit is named first. This is our love to God and to the
brethren, ἀγάπη, the love of intelligence and corresponding purpose (see 1:4). Μετά = "in company
with faith" as the fruit accompanies the tree. Faith
must ever bear fruit because of the peace which God

sheds abroad in our hearts. Behold the great *Una
Sancta* under the sun of God's peace, its faith fruiting
in love!

All this "from God Father and Lord Jesus Christ."
We have the unmodified nouns, and the statement is
striking on this account. In v. 24 we have the usual
form for the Second Person of the Godhead. Both
persons are here again placed on an equality as being
the source of saving gifts. That is the point to be
observed. The fact that the Father is the *causa prin-
cipalis* and *fons primarius* while Christ is the *causa
medians* and *fons secundarius* is not expressed. In ἀπό
the picture is that of blessing coming "from" God and
Christ to us.

24) "The brethren" = the Ephesians who are
Paul's brethren as Tychicus is a beloved brother (v.
21), Paul being one of this blessed number. But this
epistle has dealt with the entire *Una Sancta* of all
places and all ages. So Paul reaches out to all of the
members of the church. He fittingly goes back to "the
grace," which is articulated because no "from" follows.
This source and fountain of all spiritual blessings,
which is itself the supreme blessing for all sinners,
Paul would have accompany (again μετά) "all those
loving our Lord Jesus Christ (on this designation see
1:17). It is worth noting that when blessings are
mentioned the recipients are so often named according
to their love to God and to Christ, compare Rom. 9:28.
The participle characterizes: "all the lovers" of Christ.
The thought of merit in their love for him is cut off by
"the grace" which means unmerited favor and by their
very love which only God's grace has produced.
Whereas in v. 23 "love" means especially love to the
brethren, the love to Christ is now added. What "the
grace" will be for all these lovers is thus apparent:
daily forgiveness and all the gifts of him who first
loved them.

There is some difficulty regarding the final phrase, both as to its construction and as to its meaning. Luther translates with an adverb, *unverrueckt;* English translators have followed him: "in pureness," "sincerely," "unfeignedly," R., *W. P.,* "never diminishing." All of these construe the phrase with the participle. But this meaning cannot be substantiated linguistically and would be a strange way of expressing undying love. Moreover, the phrase should then be closer to the participle and thus make "Jesus Christ" the final word of the entire epistle, a matter Paul would scarcely have overlooked if he had wanted to say what these translators find. A few connect adverbially with "the grace": "grace in eternity"; "grace that all may have eternal life." But the distance between this modifier and "grace" is too great. "Our Lord Jesus Christ in incorruption" also fails to satisfy. If the risen and glorified Lord were referred to, this phrase would not express such a thought.

It is certain that ἀφθαρσία means "incorruption" (I Cor. 15:42, 50, 53, 54; II Tim. 1:10). It is equally certain that Paul does not close this epistle with a minor but with a major concept. Then it is plain that ἐν = "in connection with" and to "the grace" for all Christ's lovers adds "incorruption," a blessed condition that corruption shall never be able to destroy. Such an ἐν may stand at the end of this epistle as this ἐν does. Paul could not write καί and a nominative, for "the grace" and "incorruption" are not coordinate; Paul does not write "and" between love and faith in v. 23 but there, too, uses a preposition. He could not use μετά which he has already used with the lovers because this would make "incorruption" the major and "the grace" the minor even as "faith" is major to "love," its fruit. "In" is the proper preposition, but not as denoting the sphere of "the grace"; "in" may express any kind of a connection or union with something else according to the nature of the concepts involved. So here: "the (divine) grace in connection with incorruption." Yet 4:19 is not comparable (see above). Also, ἀφθορία and ἀδιαφθορία, *Unverdorbenheit,* purity, are not "incorruption."

The surprise felt by so many regarding this closing phrase turns to admiration when Paul's meaning is understood. The *Una Sancta* described in this epistle was founded in the mind of God in eternity and shall endure to all eternity. Since it is composed of all the lovers of Christ, this benediction rests upon them: "the (divine) grace — in connection with incorruption."

Soli Deo Gloria

St. Paul's Epistle
To the Philippians

INTRODUCTION

Gaudeo — Gaudete!

Thus Bengel sums up the Epistle to the Philippians. JOY is, however, not the theme of this letter as justification is the theme of Romans and the church of Ephesians. Joy is the music that runs through this epistle, the sunshine that spreads over all of it. The whole epistle radiates joy and happiness.

In addition to studying Paul's logic and his rhetoric one of the student's delights should be the study of his emotions. Ephesians is filled with lofty serenity as it contemplates the *Una Sancta* through a prisoner's eyes. Romans is filled with apostolic dignity as it unfolds the blessedness of justification by faith alone and rises to exalted admiration in the presence of the wisdom and the unsearchable judgments of God (Rom. 11:33-36). Galatians throbs with intensity in its battle for Christian liberty. It ranges from restrained calmness (1:11-2:21) to indignation, from cold and crushing logic to unquestioned victory. Second Corinthians is also an interesting study in emotions: depression of spirit so deep, triumphant joy so high, a fool compelled to use what he deems folly, a victor who scorns his despicable enemies. And now Philippians, which shows us a prisoner whose appeal to the emperor is finally in process of being heard, and this prisoner ringing all the joy bells in the cathedral! So we might go on.

These emotions are not manifested by an emotionalist. Paul is not an emotional reed that is swayed by the wind. Sound, sane, balanced, solid to the core, Paul is nevertheless alive with a human heart capacity beyond most men. Add to this the spiritual world in which this heart lives, moves, and has its being. No

(691)

unspiritual man is capable of emotions that exhibit the quality, the purity, and the range of these manifested in Paul. Add then the experiences this exceptional apostolic life underwent! Look at the catalog given in II Cor. 6:4-10 or at the sketch drawn in 11:23, etc. These experiences called out all these emotions and often intensified them to so great a degree. Few lives have undergone the like. Yet no emotion ever runs away with Paul. His feelings are ever controlled by the spirit, their expression in word and in act is ever made to serve his spiritual needs. Seventeen times this short epistle mentions the words joy and rejoice, which express in part the joy of Paul and in part the joy he would kindle in his readers. Both kinds of joy are spiritual throughout.

*   *   *

Ten miles inland from its harbor city Neapolis was Philippi. It was the old town Krenides, "Place of Fountains," which was finally made a real city by Philip of Macedon and then also named after him, the father of Alexander the Great. A mile to the east flowed the small river Gangites which emptied into the Strymon thirty miles away. The region contained valuable gold mines. In this valley the battle of Philippi was fought in 42 B. C. between the Second Triumvirate (Octavius, Antonius, Lepidus) and the republicans of Rome under Brutus and Cassius, which resulted in the defeat and the death of these latter. In recognition of the victory Octavius made Philippi a colony. After the battle of Actium in 31 B. C. Augustus transported a large number of Roman veterans to the colony and raised the status of Philippi by granting it the so-called *jus Italicum* which placed it on a par with the Roman colonies of Italy.

Philippi regarded itself as being an entirely Roman city. Its citizens were Roman citizens who enjoyed all the rights of such: freedom from scourging, from arrest except in extreme cases, and the right to appeal to the emperor. The official language was Latin. The city was governed by two officials who were answerable to Rome, the *praetores duoviri* who appeared officially with attendant lictors who bore the official bundles of rods or *fasces* with a mace protruding from the center, symbols of Roman power and authority.

Luke tells the story of the founding of the church in Philippi (Acts 16:13, etc.). The first convert, Lydia, seems from the very beginning to have made this church liberal and generous in appreciation of Paul's work. After her baptism she insisted on lodging Paul and his assistants in her home. Prompted by the same spirit, this church soon sent gifts to Paul who was then in Thessalonica (Phil. 4:15, 16); the present epistle returns thanks for a gift sent by the Philippian church by the hand of Epaphroditus while Paul was in Rome. Now that Paul's appeal to the emperor is in process of being heard, this gift helped to increase his joy. The church had grown and prospered. We learn of no disturbance that was due to either persecution or aberration in doctrine and in life.

When Paul left Philippi in the year 52, Timothy and Luke remained to build up the infant congregation; but Timothy soon followed Paul, and when he was sent back to Macedonia from Athens he most likely again came to Philippi. Luke, it seems, worked steadily on in Philippi. His first "we" section (Acts 16:11-40) stops with Paul's departure from Philippi; the second does not begin until Paul again reached Philippi (Acts 20:5, 6). This occurred at Easter, 58 when Paul and the delegates of the churches (Acts 20:4) took the great collection to Jerusalem. Paul had been in Philippi during the previous summer when on his way from Ephesus to Corinth he spent some time in Macedonia (II Cor. 2:13). Thus Paul was in Philippi three times, the second visit probably being the longest. It seems likely that Second Corinthians, which was written in Macedonia, was written in Philippi.

Timothy is joined with Paul in this epistle (1:1). He was with Paul when the church was founded. When he was sent back to Thessalonica from Athens, Timothy probably went back also to Philippi (I Thess. 3:1, 2, 6). Timothy was also in Philippi when Paul sent him by land on an extended commission from Ephesus to Corinth prior to Paul's own slower journey over the same land route. This occurred in 57. Finally, Timothy was in the party that took the collection from Corinth to Jerusalem via Philippi (Acts 20:4). These connections of Timothy with Philippi cast light on Phil. 2:19-23. Once more this beloved assistant of Paul's is being sent to this beloved congregation.

*   *   *

The occasion for the writing of this epistle can be gathered only from its contents. None of the hortations found in it suggest a necessity for immediate transmission. The matter between the two women mentioned in 4:2 is quite minor and cannot have called for a letter on the part of Paul. Even the gift which the Philippians had sent Paul did not prompt him to write this letter. That gift had arrived some time before he wrote. Epaphroditus had delivered it and in the meanwhile had become sick unto death but had by this time recovered sufficiently to be able to travel back to Philippi. The Philippians had heard of this sickness, and Paul knew that they had heard about it. Surely, as was the custom especially when funds were sent, the Philippians had not sent Epaphroditus alone but had sent others to Rome with him. These had to return alone when Epaphroditus became sick. Paul most certainly sent his thanks for the gift with these messengers and thus knew that the Philippians were informed in regard to Epaphroditus even as the latter knew that they were anxious about him (2:26). Now he is strong enough to be sent back to Philippi, and Paul sends this letter with him.

More than this. Those companions of Epaphroditus' also took back to Philippi a report on the latest developments in Paul's case, namely that the imperial court had begun to dispose of Paul's appeal to Caesar. The Philippians were anxious to obtain further news. Paul also writes them the latest news on this subject. They will want still later news, so Paul promises to send Timothy to them in the near future. Paul's case is progressing so well that he has high hope of being set free. So he promises that he himself will pay the Philippians a visit if he should be freed.

These two developments prompt Paul to write. Both are of a joyful nature and furnish the note of joy. We see how Timothy comes to be made a joint writer with Paul. All the rest of the epistle: Paul's prayers for the Philippians, his instructions and his admonitions to them, finally his renewed fervent thanks for their gift, are introduced most naturally as additions to the two main objects of the writing. So we, too, write letters. Some one or two matters make the writing necessary, to which we add information that is more or less of a nature that does not necessitate our writing.

Attempts have been made to read more than this between the lines. Instead of having news reach Philippi by the return of the companions of Epaphroditus, news is thought to travel in some other way that was unknown to Paul and to Epaphroditus, so that these two found out about it when news from Philippi again came to Rome. This is also amplified. The Philippians are said to have sent a letter to Paul, which he is now answering. A part of the contents of that letter are found in Paul's reply, namely that the Philippians feared that Paul was not satisfied in regard to the gift

sent him: because there had been no gift from Philippi
for a long time, and because the gift that was finally
sent appeared rather small. But none of this can be
found in what Paul writes.

It has also been thought that the Philippians sent
regular remittances to Paul, and that Paul expected
this, so that the delay and the size of the remittance
displeased him. Only twice had Paul received gifts
from Philippi (4:15, 16), and these had been sent
years before he wrote this letter. It was a joyful surprise to him when another gift arrived from this beloved congregation. Paul never accepted support; I
Cor. 9:15 puts this beyond question, as does II Cor.
11:7-12. The two gifts received from Philippi were
another matter. Paul could not refuse them after they
had been sent without offending the kind hearts of the
Philippians. The same was true with regard to this
third gift received while Paul was in Rome. Three
gifts from the same congregation in the course of years
did not annul Paul's principle of ever preaching the
gospel without charge (I Cor. 9:18).

It is true, Philippians is most letter-like. That
means that Paul is not developing a theme as he does
in Romans, in Ephesians, and in Galatians. That
means also that he is not correcting grave errors as
he does in First Corinthians, in Galatians, in Colossians, etc. But the supposition that this letter-like
form of Philippians is due to the fact that a letter had
been received from Philippi, to which Paul is making
reply, is untenable. The form of Paul's epistle accords
with what the epistle itself contains. We have seen
what called for a letter from him. As for the remainder of the letter, its hortatory parts, this has back of it
only what Paul learned from the Philippian congregation from Epaphroditus and from his companions,
which includes 4:2, 3. Efforts to reconstruct situations
should not be allowed to become too ingenious, one's

gift of combining hints and following out clues should not carry one beyond the verifiable facts.

*   *   *

A late supposition is that Paul wrote this epistle during an imprisonment in Ephesus. No more needs to be added to what we have said in the introduction to Ephesians.

The more serious attempts to place the composition of this epistle together with those to the Ephesians, Colossians, and Philemon, in Caesarea meet the contradiction of the entire ancient tradition. In order to defend their composition in Caesarea Acts 23:11 must be ignored or struck out as being spurious. The situation depicted in the epistle argues against Caesarea being the place of composition. Regarding "Caesar's household" (4:22) see the exposition itself; do the same with regard to "the whole praetorium" in 1:13. The composition at Caesarea has few advocates; their argumentation has so often been answered that we may pass on.

Philippians was written after Ephesians, Colossians, and Philemon, shortly before the imperial court set Paul free, which occurred in the year 63. Philemon 22 does not indicate that Paul's appeal to Caesar was already at that time being considered by the court; Philippians states that this stage has finally been reached. That fact settles the order of these epistles. The interval between their writing does not seem to have been a long one.

When Paul first appealed to Caesar (Acts 25:10, 11) he did so because he expected justice from the imperial court; Acts 23:11 should also not be forgotten. The long wait in Rome never lessened Paul's expectation that his innocence would be vindicated in the end. Thus he wrote Philemon 22. Philippians shows that

Paul had had his first hearing, and that this had gone well. Unless, after all, things should go wrong, he would soon be a free man. Thus he writes with great joy also regarding this matter. The Philippians will be equally happy. Epaphroditus will carry the letter. We do not know the route he followed. If he was able he would spread the news in other congregations. Still later, perhaps, the final news would be carried by Timothy.

Yet Paul keeps his balance amid his joy. The final verdict is yet to come. The possibility remains that, after all, the verdict might be adverse and send him to some remote exile, or to the mines, or to the executioner's sword. That, too, is in the Lord's hands. Paul writes accordingly. We know that it does not dim his joy.

Was Paul transferred from his rented house, where only one soldier guarded him, to the barracks of the soldiers in order to be promptly available at the call of the court? This has been asserted. It is a minor point, is possible, but lacks evidence in the epistle itself.

*   *   *

The external evidence for the authenticity of Philippians begins as early as Polycarp and extends onward to Eusebius. The internal evidence is so overwhelming that only the most radical criticism has attempted to set it aside. This letter is so fresh, distinct, inimitable in every way that forgery is impossible. Any effort to divide this letter into two parts with a redactor welding the parts together, or to make this letter a forgery for an ulterior purpose, is obsolete the moment it is published. This judgment accords with that of many other writers, all of whom make short shrift of the few radical critics.

CHAPTER I

Paul Sends to the Philippians Joyful Information about Himself and about Epaphroditus, Combined with Prayer and Admonition

Greeting

1) **Paul and Timothy, slaves of Christ Jesus, to all the saints in Christ Jesus, those who are in Philippi, together with overseers and deacons: grace to you and peace from God our Father and the Lord Jesus Christ!**

The form is stereotyped: nominatives — datives — nominatives (see Eph. 1:1, 2). Regarding the Roman name "Paul" note the discussion in Acts 13:9; and regarding Timothy see Acts 16:1, etc. Timothy joins Paul in this letter, not as though he helped to compose it, but as seconding it. He helped to found the congregation and was to be sent to it again (2:19, etc.).

In I Cor. 1:1; II Cor. 1:1, and Col. 1:1 the distinction between "apostle" and "brother" is retained because of the authoritative contents of these letters. They are apostolic as far as they come from Paul, fraternal as being seconded by the co-writer. In the case of the contents of Philippians this is not necessary. This is the only caption in which one and the same apposition modifies both the writers. Both are termed "slaves of Christ Jesus." What they have to say is to be received from them as being such. Paul is not dropping his apostolic authority for the time being, he is now only not making it felt. The genitive is possessive, and whether the order is "Jesus Christ" (Rom. 1:1) or "Christ Jesus" makes no appreciable difference. These "slaves" belong to Christ Jesus, whose office and whose personal name mean so much to them and to their readers.

"Slaves" does not refer to office although Paul at times applies this word only to himself. Paul and Timothy are Christ's because he has both bought them and taken them into his service. No special form of service is indicated by the word. It, of course, denotes work, and many who today love to be called "church workers" should learn what Paul means by "slaves," namely men who in all their work have no will of their own but only their Owner's will and Word. That is why the Philippians will gladly read what these two men say.

In view of Rom. 1:7 and II Cor. 1:1 no special stress can be laid on "*all* the saints" although this "all" appears a number of times in the beginning of the epistle but not always with reference to persons. The idea that Paul and Timothy intend to be strictly impartial to *all* despite certain pretensions of superiority on the part of some, is refuted when it is noted that this "all" is lacking in the admonitory paragraphs. The use of "saints" to designate Christians is regular in the New Testament beginning with Acts 9:13 and is probably to be traced to Christ's prayer, John 17:16-20, where also separation from the world and the cleansing power of the truth of the Word are indicated. By faith to know, to believe, and to keep God's Word takes one out of the world and makes him a saint (John 17:3-6), and the more this Word of God enters him, the more he is sanctified and deserves the name "saint." Perfectionism is not suggested by the term.

The Philippians are "saints in connection with (ἐν) Christ Jesus." We need not repeat the discussion of this phrase; see Eph. 1:1; also Rom. 6:11. The context always determines the nature of the connection or union with Christ. It contains nothing mystical; anything of a mystical nature is expressed only by the context. Although "Christ Jesus" is repeated, no point is to be made of this as though Paul and Timothy are *"slaves* of Christ Jesus" while the Philippians are *"saints* of Christ Jesus." The latter points to the spiritual blessings received, the former to the work assigned, yet only in a silent way. After an intervening genitive the article is repeated; in English "who are in Philippi" is enough. The name of the city is a masculine plural.

The organization of the apostolic congregations has been much discussed. As far as the πρεσβύτεροι, "elders," and the ἐπίσκοποι, "overseers," are concerned, only the designation and not the function differs. The former is first used in Acts 11:30; Paul himself uses the latter in Acts 20:28, *"overseers* to shepherd the flock," when addressing "the *elders* of the church" (Acts 20:17). This is plain enough.

One might think that an apostle would choose to call himself an "overseer" in preference to an "elder," but the reverse is done (I Pet. 5:1; II John 1; III John 1). "Elder" expressed the dignity of the office, "overseer," the work. In the LXX ἐπίσκοποι was used to designate the overseers of the repairs to the Temple, less frequently to designate army officers. Not until a time that is much later than the New Testament does *episcopoi* appear in the sense of our present "bishops," men who are placed over several congregations and their pastors. This was, however, only a human arrangement. In the apostolic churches a group of elders or overseers attended to the congregation's work, the best men in each congregation being chosen for this purpose.

The difference between these and the "deacons" is most clearly seen in I Tim. 3:1-10. The latter were like the deaconess Phoebe of Cenchreae (Rom. 16:1); they attended to the common needs of the poor and of the sick and to minor chores. The deacons seem to have been duly appointed, the name suggesting voluntary service. No form of church government was prescribed by Christ beyond that of the pastoral office (the ministry), see Eph. 4:11. The arrangement of having several elders or overseers in a congregation was an adoption of the system that was followed in the Jewish synagogues. Yet the Christian office was a divine institution, and its ideal became "to labor in the Word and doctrine" (I Tim. 5:17). What we call church government, the organization of many congregations under one overseer or bishop, developed at a later time, not *jure divino*, but *jure humano*, and was a product of Christian liberty, and the offices were by human appointment only. More need not be said in the present connection.

This is the only letter in which Paul mentions the pastors and the deacons in the address. We naturally ask why. Σύν is associative: "together with," "in association with," and in a beautiful way expresses the relation of "all the saints in union with Christ Jesus" to their overseers and deacons. The absence of the articles makes the two nouns qualitative, lends them the force of "such as are overseers and deacons," and thereby avoids the idea of a particular class. The best answer to our question is that these servants of the congregation were instrumental in gathering the gift that was sent to Paul, that Paul knew this, and in an unobtrusive way indicates his appreciation.

2) "Grace to you and peace," etc., is exactly like Rom. 1:7; I Cor. 1:3; II Cor. 1:2, which see.

Paul Tells the Philippians about his Joyful Prayers for Them

3) In his *Introduction* I, 534, etc., Zahn follows von Hofmann and prefers the reading: Ἐγὼ μὲν εὐχαριστῶ τῷ Κυρίῳ ἡμῶν. The textual support for this reading

is so weak that Souter, for instance, disregards this variant reading. In order to justify its preference Zahn states that those who reject it must explain how it came into existence if Paul did not himself write it. Hundreds of variants exist which neither Zahn nor any other interpreter attempt to explain, which no man can explain, which also are therefore rejected by most text critics. We are not obliged to accept this inferior reading because we may not be able to explain how it came into existence and in a few texts altered the preferred reading.

In the present instance we are able to explain its origin. This inferior reading is that of Codex D, the author of which loves to edit. In the Acts he does this to such an extent that Zahn thinks that Luke wrote two editions of the Acts, the second of which contains many corrections. This editing copyist thought that in Philippians Paul ought to write an ἐγώ, for Paul has just written "Paul and Timothy" in v. 1 and now writes only about himself as thanking God, εὐχαριστῶ, and continues with "my God," "my petition." This insertion of ἐγώ is not an editorial improvement, for the insertion of this emphatic pronoun "I for my part" injects a contrast between Paul and Timothy that is foreign to Paul's mind. We note many similar instances in the alterations made by Codex D. The alterations it offers often spoil the correct meaning of the original.

Zahn's reason for following von Hofmann in adopting this inferior reading is more serious. We see what Zahn has in mind when he offers this translation: "I for my part thank our Lord for all your substantial remembrance (of me and indeed) always in each of my prayers, offering up my prayer for you all with joy on the ground of your participation for the purpose of the gospel (i. e., your cooperation in the missionary

work) from the first day until now," etc. Several
ideas are expressed: 1) that Paul thanks the Lord for
the many gifts the Philippians have been sending him;
2) that by means of these many gifts the Philippians
have been participating in Paul's missionary work until
now; 3) that Paul is answering a letter just received
from the Philippians, in which they express the fear that
their last gift, which was sent by Epaphroditus some
time before this, has been delayed too long to the dis-
satisfaction of Paul and to the regret of the Philippians themselves. So Paul is thought to write: *"I for
my part"* (ἐγώ) do not feel as *you* do about this your
last gift; you have always been helping my missionary
work. What is wrong about this? A good deal aside
from the inferior reading.

Years ago Paul has received two gifts from Philippi
(4:16) and not until recently, after an interval of
years, had he received a third by the hand of Epaphroditus (4:10). The word μνεία does not mean "substantial remembrance," and μνεία ὑμῶν does not mean:
"your remembrance (of me) in sending me regular
support for my missionary work"; but "(my) remembrance of you" (objective genitive).

In v. 3-8 Paul states *what induces him to pray for
the Philippians.* He does not say anything about
money. **I thank my God upon all the remembrance
of you, always in every petition of mine for you all
making the petition with joy on the basis of your fellowship as regards the gospel from the first day until
the present, etc.**

Paul begins in the same natural way as he does in
some of his other letters. There is no reason for
contrasting himself with anyone else by the use of an
ἐγώ. Every time he remembers the Philippians he is
grateful to God. Ἐπί states occasion and time (R. 604):
"upon all the remembrance of you" (objective genitive). Here the article: πάσῃ τῇ μνείᾳ, is pertinent,

R. 772. First Corinthians 4:1 is different, ἐπί states the ground for Paul's thanksgiving, namely "the grace of God given to the Corinthians in Christ Jesus." The difference is due to the objects: "the grace of God" is objective, a divine gift to the Corinthians, while "remembrance of you" is subjective, something in Paul's mind.

"All the remembrance of you" needs no "my," for Paul is certainly speaking of his own remembrance and not of that of someone for him. Moreover, "my God" precedes, and "my" would thus also not be repeated. Here the word means "remembrance"; only when it is used with ποιεῖν does it mean "to make mention." "All" is added, not only because Paul's recollection of the Philippians takes in all that he remembers of them, but because all of it induces him to thank God. All of it comes to his mind whenever he thinks of them, and then his heart is grateful to God. He remembers his first work in Philippi, even the beating and the imprisonment he and Silas suffered, and God's wonderful deliverance. He remembers his other visits in Philippi and all the reports he had received from time to time.

"Of you" makes the Christians in Philippi the objects of Paul's remembrance, their faith and faithfulness, their loyal adherence to the gospel, etc. The fact that 4:16 need not be excluded is self-evident; for 4:16 itself is written in remembrance. To restrict the remembrance to this item and then to enlarge it into a constant flow of gifts, disregards the context that follows, to say nothing of 4:10-19 where Paul dwells at length on the matter of this gift.

4) We construe as a unit: "always in every petition of mine for you all making this petition with joy on the basis of your fellowship as regards the gospel from the first day until the present," not even placing a comma between v. 4 and 5. We cannot construe:

"I thank my God . . . for your fellowship," because too much lies between these expressions. This in answer to our versions. Because in I Thess. 1:2; II Thess. 1:3; I Cor. 1:4; Col. 1:3; Philemon 4 we have "I thank always," some would find the same statement here by joining "always," or "always in every petition," or this plus "for you all," to v. 3. But in the other passages "always" is placed next to "I thank (my) God"; not so here nor in Rom. 1:10 where "always" is to be construed with what follows.

"Always in every petition of mine in behalf of you all" belongs together. Every time Paul makes such a petition, "he makes this petition (article of previous reference) with joy," etc. By expressing this with a participial clause Paul makes it subordinate to "I thank my God." When Paul thanks his God he does so for past blessing to the Philippians which he appreciates; when he then always adds his *petition* for all the Philippians in his whole remembrance of them he *asks* something for all of them for their present and their future needs. The participial clause is thus not modal; it adds a subsidiary thought even as thanks and petition go together. Note: "upon all the remembrance" (article) and: "in every petition" (no article). With abstract nouns the difference is erased, the idea of "all" and "every" flowing together. Here, however, the two nouns appear as concretes so that the difference remains.

Δέησις is *Bittgebet*, petition for some gift, and is much narrower than προσευχή, "prayer," which is general. One may ask why Paul does not use the more general word here. We have already indicated that thanks accompanies remembrance of the past, petition the future. While Paul has so much for which to thank God in all his remembrance of the Philippians he petitions God for all of them that God may ever bless them so that all Paul's added remembrance may also be coupled with thanks.

The two statements make it plain that, as in the past so in the future, all the blessings of the Philippians flow only from God. Him Paul thanks, to him he sends his every petition. "Always in every petition of mine" denotes continuous, ever-repeated petition. Who would become weary when, "Ask, and ye shall receive!" is the command and the promise? "In behalf of you all" is intercession. In v. 3, 4 we have four "all," and more follow. Paul's heart is truly large and wide. "For you all" includes every child, every backward and faulty member. We do not share the view that Paul prays for all although some have been remiss toward him. When the "remembrance" is thought to be remembering Paul with gifts, this derogatory implication in "you all" lies near. This thought can be extended farther; it might seem that, because the Philippians had sent Paul money, he keeps petitioning God for them as a kind of return favor.

The emphasis is undoubtedly on the phrase "with joy." In English we are forced to place it at the end. The more Paul remembers about the Philippians for which to thank his God, the greater is his joy in making his petitions for them. Some place the emphasis elsewhere, yet "with joy" is the distinctive point, the first of the many expressions of joy in this epistle. See the introduction on the emotions of Paul.

5) With joy Paul makes this petition "on the basis of your fellowship as regards the gospel from the first day until now." The close connection with v. 4 should not be interrupted by even a comma (our versions). This "fellowship" is active, devoted to the interest of the gospel as the εἰς phrase shows. When Paul points back to "the first day," he has in mind Acts 16:15, the day he baptized Lydia, the day she

insisted that he and his assistants lodge at her house. That was the start of this fellowship as regards the gospel. "Until now" takes us to the present when this fellowship manifested itself anew in the sending of a gift to Paul while he was at Rome.

Yet neither here nor in II Cor. 8:4 and 9:13 does κοινωνία mean contribution of money. In the latter passage this word is translated "distribution" in the A. V. and "contribution" in the R. V. Commentators adopt it, and some dictionaries follow the commentators. See the writer's exposition of the passages and of Rom. 15:26. Zahn defines the word: "Your cooperation in missionary work" (*Introduction* I, 535). Repeated contributions of money for Paul's work are then supplied, each of which was followed by a receipt on the part of Paul. But "your fellowship as regards the gospel" is as broad as Acts 2:42, the fellowship of faith in the gospel, of confession of the gospel, of worship and of Christian life in the grace of the gospel. The Philippians, of course, had the gospel preached and taught in their midst "from the first day until now" and kept winning new converts. They, of course, continued a lively interest in Paul's work for the gospel. Their fellowship regarding the gospel was active in all manner of ways.

"Your fellowship," with its pronoun, does not mean merely "your fellowship with each other," nor only "your fellowship with me." "Your" means that the Philippians were in the great fellowship that concerned itself with the gospel. Paul's joyful petition for the Philippian church rests on the *whole* fellowship this church had maintained from its birth to the present day. This includes *all* the manifestations of this fellowship and thus not alone their love for Paul and the three gifts they had sent him. Thus, too, we may define Paul's petition for them: he prayed to God that they might ever continue in this fellowship.

6) Paul adds: **being confident of this very thing that he who began in you a good work will finish it up to Jesus Christ's day.**

This clause modifies all that precedes, the main verb in v. 3 plus its participial addition in v. 4. Paul states the inner conviction from which his thanks to God and his petition for the Philippians flow. "He who began in you a good work" takes up the phrase "from the first day until now," all the blessed past for which Paul thanks God. "Will finish it until the day of Jesus Christ" covers all that Paul has asked for in his petition for the future of the Philippians. So also the perfect participle "being confident" has the full meaning of a perfect: this confidence began long ago and still continues, i. e., from the first day until now (B.-D. 290, 4). Many men are confident enough, but when we look at the contents of what they hold to we see that it will never come to pass. The thing of which Paul is confident is of a different sort.

Πείθω does not govern the accusative. Hence arise the difficulties regarding αὐτὸ τοῦτο, Zahn making it mean: "for this very reason," others, *eben deswegen*, referring it back to v. 5, Paul's reason for being confident being the fellowship of the Philippians. When, in addition, "your fellowship" is regarded as referring to contributions of money, this idea becomes untenable. R. 478 and *W. P.* call this an accusative of inner content. Winer 33, 5 is correct: αὐτὸ τοῦτο ὅτι belong to-gether; similarly in v. 25. This verb πείθω is construed with ὅτι, and "this very thing" merely introduces "that he who began," etc. God began a good work in the hearts of the Philippians, certainly not in order to let it end in nothing, but to bring it to its full completion (ἐπί in the verb), which will take him "up to the day of Jesus Christ." This future tense is not merely futuristic (R. 889), it is voluntative: it is God's will to do this. It is to be noted that Paul does not say "the good work" and refer to this fellowship of which he speaks in v. 5. "He who began in you a good work" is perfectly clear; all that God had begun in them was "a good work" because God had begun it, because it was *his* work. Note that Paul attributes all of it to God alone, not only its beginning but equally its consummation.

No article is needed with "Jesus Christ's day" since there is only one day of this kind, the genitive defining it: "Jesus Christ's day," the last great day of the world. The moment we ask ourselves how at that terminus God will complete the good work he had begun in the Philippians, all the doubtful ideas found in Paul's statement disappear. The completion will consist in raising the dead believers' bodies, these bodies being glorified and joined again to their souls. As to the question regarding those believers who may still be living, I Thess. 4:15-17 supplies the answer.

Paul implies nothing as to the time when this day will come; he does not know the time, never pretends that he does but ever keeps to Christ's word that the day may come at any time and that we must ever be ready. Thus we reject the views that "in you" means the congregation as a congregation in distinction from individuals, that Paul thus expected this congregation to continue in Philippi until the end of the world, and that he believed that this end was coming soon. But some of those living in Philippi had died, as some had at a much earlier time died in Thessalonica. (I Thess. 4:13). The completion of God's good work pertains to individuals.

7) Paul now speaks of the relation of the Philippians to himself, which has been only implied thus far: **even as it is right for me to mind this in behalf of you all because of having you in my heart both in my bonds and in the defense and confirmation of**

**the gospel, you all as being my joint-fellowshipers
of the grace.**

"Meet for me" (A. V.) is incorrect; "right for me"
(R. V.) is correct, it would be wrong, ἄδικον, if Paul
were minded otherwise. "To think this of you all"
(A. V.) is likewise incorrect. Paul has not been telling
what he thinks about the Philippians but has spoken
of the confidence that accompanied his continuous
petition "on behalf of them all." In fact, this very
phrase is now repeated from v. 4. It must have the
same meaning in both verses, a fact which R. 632
overlooks when he translates "concerning you all" as
being the meaning in v. 7.

Verses 3-6 = τοῦτο, "this" that Paul is minding "on
behalf of, for the benefit of, you all." To thank God
as he does, to make petition as he states, to do both of
these in the confidence he describes, are so "right,"
that if he did not mind and attend to these things, his
own heart would condemn him. While this verb is
used also in the sense of thinking, it here has its
original sense: the action of the φρήν, being affected
in the *phrēn*, being moved to mind something and to
attend to it (Ewald 51, etc.).

It is right for Paul to be minding this "because
I have you in my heart both in my bonds," etc. All
that follows διά should be read as one clause and not as
two (our versions). Ὄντας is not an accusative absolute (R. 1131), nor does it mean "inasmuch as you
are" (our versions). It merely expands the appositional object: "I have you . . . you all as being
joint-fellowshipers of my grace." As such he has
them, and that means all of them, in his heart. The
R. V. margin: "Ye have me in your heart," reverses
subject and object, both of which are accusatives in
the Greek. But there is no doubt about which is which:
not only is ἔχειν με together, "I have," but in the pre-

ceding φρονεῖν the subject doing the minding is Paul.
The R. V. margin should be stricken.

"I have you in my heart" means more in the Greek
than it does in the English; for in the Greek the heart
is not the seat of the affections, these are located in
the viscera (v. 8). The heart is the seat of the personality with its mind, feeling, and will, notably the
latter. Paul is not merely holding the Philippians
dear, he is holding them, we may say, as part of himself, his mind and his will ever being concerned about
them, and that not in general only, i. e., as being believers, but "as being joint-fellowshipers of my grace"
in connection with both his imprisonment and now
his trial before the imperial court. Permit the coin-
ing of "joint-fellowshipers" in order to conserve the
similarity in wording between κοινωνία in v. 5 and
συγκοινωνοί. In v. 5 Paul rests his petition on their
fellowship as regards the gospel; here this idea is now
advanced, they are all in joint fellowship with Paul's
grace in his bonds and in his stand for the gospel at
his trial.

Instead of τε — καί, "both — and," the former has
been made equivalent to "and" so as to produce two
clauses: "have you in my heart and have you as being
fellow partakers," etc. But Paul has written only one
"have you." The bonds and the defense are also plainly
correlated and call for "both — and." By the δεσμά
Paul refers to his entire imprisonment (all that confines; the masculine plural is sometimes used in the
same sense, v. 13). The word itself does not mean
chains but, like imprisonment, may include also fetters
of some kind among the things that confine. Paul had
been in confinement for nearly four years, a δέσμιος
(Eph. 3:1; 4:1), prisoner. Now his trial had come.

Some would regard "my defense and confirmation
of the gospel" in a broad sense and refer it to Paul's
gospel advocacy in general during his long imprison-

ment; but why, when "both — and" pairs the imprisonment and the defense plus the confirmation? Ἀπολογία is the regular term for what the defendant pleads in a court trial or before a judge (the verb is used in Acts 26:2). Since it is here combined under one article with βεβαίωσις, another term with a reference to a court in this combination, we are sure that Paul is referring to his trial. The imperial court wanted not only Paul's plea in his defense (the *apologia*) but together with it the "confirmation" (βεβαίωσις), the factual proofs that would be convincing to the judge or the judges. Both are regular legal terms.

Yet note the difference: "my bonds" but not "my defense." It is the defense and confirmation of a far greater defendant, namely "of the gospel." The fate of his person was of the least concern to Paul, the fate of the gospel was everything. That it should not suffer when he pleaded his case and proved his facts before the emperor's court was his one concern. Now during both his whole imprisonment and his trial involving the gospel he has all the Philippians in his heart as people who fellowship his grace.

The enclitic μου modifies the noun that precedes it just as it does in v. 3; the following articulated noun: "of the grace," which is dependent on "my fellowshipers," like the articulated "remembrance" in v. 3, thus becomes Paul's also. This grace is the grace of God which was using Paul as a prisoner for so long, was now at last using him at the imperial trial in the defense and the confirmation of the gospel before the supreme court, "to bear Christ's Name before the Gentiles and kings" (Acts 9:15). What fellowship the Philippians had in this grace is evident: they believed and held to this same gospel, their cause was before this court, they would all be affected by the outcome. The fact that they all sympathized with Paul, prayed for him, etc., is natural yet secondary and should not be permitted to overshadow the chief part of the fellowship.

So also, while their recent gift to Paul is not excluded as a manifestation of this fellowship, it is only in the background. If the Philippians had not sent a gift at this time they would, nevertheless, have been in the full fellowship of this grace. Thus also nothing of a pointed nature should be read into πάντας ὑμᾶς, which repeats the "all" of the two ὑπέρ phrases (v. 4, 7a), namely any fear on the part of the Philippians that Paul was perhaps not satisfied with some of them, that a recent letter voiced this fear, and that Paul was now allaying it in his reply. This "all" is to be construed with "all remembrance," "always," "every petition," all the time from the first day until now. A long time has elapsed since Paul had been with the Philippians, and many new members had come into the congregation. *All* of them, whether they had had personal contact with Paul or not, are in this fellowship with him, "the fellowship regarding the gospel," as he has already stated it (v. 5). So now again he puts the gospel forward: "defense and confirmation of the gospel," for this gospel is the bond of this fellowship.

8) With "for" Paul adds the final personal note and completes the picture of his relation to the Philippians. **For God is my witness how I long for you all in the viscera of Christ Jesus.**

This is usually regarded as an explanation as to how Paul has the Philippians in his heart; but his having them thus is a part of what precedes, namely of his thanking God every time he remembers them and thus making petition on their behalf. All of this will be more fully appreciated by the Philippians when they know how Paul longs again to be in their midst.

"My witness God" is not an oath as some seem to think. Note the same expression in Rom 1:9; also in v. 11, the longing to see the Romans. The longing is hidden in the heart, hence God alone is a direct witness of its presence. Paul names him as such, "witness of mine" thus being placed forward. This is Christian assurance and nothing more. Since he had been absent from Philippi for so long a time he longed the more to get back. He had not forgotten ("remembrance" in v. 3) ; he had not grown cold; his love had not lessened. He longed to see the old faces again but he says "all you," for he yearned to see all the new members also.

If Paul had said "in my viscera," all would have been simple. For the Greek made the nobler viscera, lungs, heart, and liver, the seat of the feelings as we now speak of the heart (see M.-M. 584) ; "bowels" (A. V.) is incorrect, for this usually refers to the intestines. "Tender mercies" (R. V.) is interpretative and thus satisfactory.

Many curious interpretations are on file, which are deserving no notice unless one is making a collection of oddities. One of the best interpretations is that of Bengel, which is adopted also by others: *In Paulo non Paulus vivit sed Jesus Christus; quare Paulus non in Pauli sed Jesu Christi movetur visceribus.* Bengel thinks that Paul is using mystical language and confuses mystical language with the *unio mystica.* We have mystical language in Rom. 6:4, etc.: buried, dead, raised with Christ, what happened to Christ physically in these saving acts happens in us spiritually in saving effects, the interval of time being disregarded, the means of grace being the medium. See Rom. 6. We at once see that when Paul longs "in the viscera of Christ Jesus" he is not using mystical language. Nor does ἐν indicate the *unio mystica,* for this denotes that Christ dwells in us and we in him by means of Word and Sacrament; nor can we leave out one of these two, either his "in us" or our "in him." Yet this is what

Bengel does in his exposition. Finally, it is impossible
to think of the physical viscera of Christ, and still more
impossible to think of a union of these with ours in
anything like the *unio mystica.*
Paul omits the article. "Christ Jesus' viscera,"
as in 2:1, is not to be understood in the physical but
in the metaphorical sense: the tender feelings and
yearnings of Christ Jesus (not necessarily "mercies,"
R. V.). The identification goes no farther than the
feelings of Christ and of Paul. We are not taken
beyond 2:5: "Let this mind (here also feeling) be
in you which was also in Christ Jesus." We may say
that this unity of minding the identical thing (2:5)
and thus also having the same feelings (viscera, metaphorical) is the *result* of being mystically, spiritually
joined to Christ. Surely, this is ample in every way.
With Paul's longing for the Philippians we connect 2:24.

**Paul States the Contents of His Joyful Prayer
for the Philippians**

9) We learn what that petition is which Paul
ever makes "in behalf of you all." **And this I keep
praying, that your love may yet more and more
abound in full knowledge and in all perception so
that you may keep testing the things that differ in
order that you may be unalloyed and uninjured in
regard to Christ's day, filled with fruit of righteousness, this** (fruit) **through Jesus Christ, for God's
glory and praise.**
This is the whole prayer in brief form. "And"
joins it in a natural way to what Paul has been saying about his petition for the Philippians, his confidence in God, and his feelings for them. The idea
that "and" connects with v. 8 is untenable because
Paul is not saying that God is his witness that he is
praying for these things and not for other things. His
use of "I keep praying" (durative present tense) is

not an objection to connecting it with "all my petition" in v. 4 as if this construction would require "I keep petitioning." For this prayer *is* a petition, a great and comprehensive one. All petitioning is praying. Perhaps Paul used "I keep praying" because he wants to indicate that this petition was not the whole of his prayer but only the petition part of it, to which he adds the thanksgiving of v. 3.

Ἴνα is non-final in apposition with τοῦτο, an object clause stating the contents of the praying. "That your love may yet more and more abound in full knowledge and in all perception" implies that it is already to a degree abounding in both — surely thus justifying v. 3. This subjoining of knowledge to love is truly Pauline. In Romans 14 love must use the knowledge of the strong Christian so as not to hurt the weak. *Gnōsis* puffs up, love builds up (I Cor. 8:1). To have all *gnōsis* but not love is to be nothing (I Cor. 13:2). Ἀγάπη is the love of true knowledge and understanding coupled with corresponding purpose (see Eph. 1:4). But this understanding and purpose are fully emphasized here as belonging to love. The less of these, the less of love; also vice versa. Paul is only partially understood unless one enters fully into this entire conception of love (*agape*) and its relation to knowledge, wisdom, understanding, etc. In Eph. 1:15 and 17 Paul prays for wisdom, knowledge, and understanding after having heard of the faith and love.

It is unwarranted to discover behind this prayer special failings on the part of the Philippians either in their relation to Paul or otherwise. Since they are already abounding, Paul's desire is that no decline may ever set in but steady, healthy increase, for in every congregation, even also in the case of the best members in it, this is the mark of virile spiritual life. Ἐπίγνωσις, *Erkenntnis*, as distinguished from γνῶσις, *Kenntnis*, is full, true, genuine knowledge, here, of course, spiritual knowledge. Paul often uses the word in the sense of knowledge of the heart and not mere knowledge of the head. He adds "all perception." While this word is used regarding the senses, it applies equally to the mind and the heart. Perceptions are due to experiences, hence Paul uses "all" with this noun. "Perception" is more precise than "judgment" (A. V., and margin: "sense") or "discernment."

Paul's prayer is, then, that love may abound in its natural, native connection with true knowledge of the heart and with all the perception brought by experiences in life. This means stronger, wiser, abler love. Love is an active attribute, it reaches *out* and bestows; knowledge and perception bring *into* love what its nature requires for its work. The fact that this love is the fruit only of true faith, which likewise contains the knowledge of that in which it trusts, is ever understood in the Scriptures.

10) Εἰς τό κτλ., indicates the result contemplated by Paul. Love that has this knowledge and this perception is to keep testing the things that differ. Δοκιμάζειν is a favorite word of Paul's. Metals and coins were subjected to tests; in those days some coins were under weight, and any metal might be spurious or mixed with too much base alloy. The idea of testing the things that differ is thus not quite complete, hence the purpose clause is added in order to indicate the idea underlying the test.

The arresting thing in this clause is the fact that it does not deal with outside objects that are to be tested, some being appropriated because they are genuine, others being discarded because they are spurious or do not measure up to the test, but with the Philippians themselves: "in order that you may be unalloyed and uninjured in regard to Christ's day," when he makes the final test in the last judgment. This is masterly thinking. It drops the intermediate step and at once leaps to the ultimate. We test this or that, find it so or so; but even in the case of coins and metals, to say nothing about divine truth and base religious lies, moral excellence and moral deceits, we who do the testing or fail to do it, we who test with real knowledge and perception or with half-knowledge, not perceiving as we should, really ourselves undergo the test, are ourselves shown to be up to par or to be inferior.

Εἰλικρινής = of unmixed substance and in this sense *sincerus,* pure, i. e., "unalloyed." Some accept the etymology which refers to the sun: the brightest sunlight showing no blemish (C.-K. 636); but this is uncertain, see especially Trench, *Synonyms.* The other etymology refers to rolling in a sieve in order to remove all worthless substances. The difference between this sort of cleanness and that expressed by καθαρός (both words are often found together) is that admixture makes unclean and again stain or filth clings to something. Of course, both "to test" and "unalloyed" are here to be understood in the ethical sense. But the terms correspond. Our versions, which translate "sincere," are inadequate, for one with no real equipment or ability for testing may go at it sincerely enough, but his test amounts to nothing, and he himself is thus tested and found to be below par.

The debate regarding ἀπρόσκοπος is whether this is active or passive, offering damage or undamaged, "uninjured" ourselves. Both meanings are found, here the context favors the latter. Doubly so, for this second adjective completes the idea of the first. For Christ's great day we are to be people who are genuine through and through (without unspiritual alloy or admixture), and at the same time we are to be whole and complete, without injury. Keep the idea of a blow that damages. A genuine article may be damaged and worthless for this reason. The idea of "offense" as a meaning of the blow is only a metaphorical turn. This second adjective rounds out: the ignorant tester first proves himself below par because of his alloy of ignorance, and thus by his ignorant testing gets a blow, gets damage to himself. We are to keep Christ's day before us so that his test may not show any alloy or any damage in us which would necessitate our rejection.

11) The perfect participle, which is added without a connective, is predicative to the adjective: "unalloyed and uninjured" by "having been and thus continuing to be filled (this is the force of the perfect) with fruit of righteousness, (the fruit that is produced) through Jesus Christ." "Filled as to fruit" (the accusative with the passive) and remaining filled means leaving no room for anything that is not such fruit. We have a practical compound: *Gerechtigkeitsfrucht*. The phrase "through Jesus Christ" might modify the participle, but the article unites it with "fruit." The emphasis is thus on the character of the fruit with which we are ever to be filled; no fruit of another character is to be mixed in at any time. It is the "righteousness-fruit" (qualitative genitive) described in Gal. 5:22, etc., and regarded as righteous by the Judge and by the norm of this Judge. This "fruit" consists of good works (Eph. 2:10); filled = Ps. 126:6b. At "Christ's day" the Judge will pronounce a righteous judgment on all men's works (Matt. 25: 31-46). Paul wants all the Philippians to appear then as being filled with nothing but fruit of a righteous quality.

None of it can they produce by their own powers, hence this second and attributive (τόν) qualification "through Jesus Christ." God fills the Philippians, but this fruit that passes the test at Christ's day is such as develops and ripens only through the mediation (διά) of Jesus Christ, he enables its production. His grace, Spirit, Word, and gifts must be productive in us who are to be good trees (Matt. 7:17-19), good soil

(Matt. 13:23). The figures used in v. 10 and 11 match.
Fruit, too, is tested, critically examined, either accepted
on examination or rejected. Let our baskets contain
no admixture of fruit of the flesh or of unrighteousness, none that is σαπρός, "worthless" (Matt. 7:17).
"For God's glory and praise" is like Eph. 1:6,
12, 14, and modifies the entire object for which Paul
prays. See John 15:8. God's glory is to be reflected
in all that our hearts and our lives contain, and thus
his praise is to fill all who have these contents. The
genitive is objective: God is to be glorified and praised.
This final phrase rounds out Paul's prayer and completes its thought.

Survey this most comprehensive and beautiful
prayer as a whole: love abounding (durative present)
— in knowledge and all perception — ever making true
tests (present iterative) — the purpose being that we
ourselves may be unalloyed and uninjured for Christ's
judgment day — our hearts and lives filled with fruit,
all righteous, all mediated by Christ — and all this to
the glory and praise of God. What a sermon *in parvo!*

**Paul Informs the Philippians with Joy about the
Good Effects of the First Stage of his Trial**

12) Transitional δέ introduces the great and joyful news Paul has to impart. We see the fine spirit
which thinks first of the spiritual interests of the
Philippians (v. 3-11) and then turns to Paul's own
situation. Paul has great news to tell. The long-
expected trial has begun, the first hearing has been
most favorable. Since the Philippians are so anxious
about Paul, he makes no delay in the letter, he tells
about it right here. But while all centers on his own
person, on his fate, acquittal or condemnation, Paul
merges all in the gospel, in the effects his trial and its
outcome are bound to have on the advancement or the
retardation of the gospel work in Rome and in the

Roman world generally. Paul is only a pawn, the king
in the game is the supreme issue. This fact is supreme,
and nothing blurs or dims it in Paul's eyes. That is
why this section contains so little detailed information
about Paul himself, the things so many of us would
like to know and yet cannot extract from this man who
writes chiefly about the gospel. Should we, too, not
rise to his height, be less eager about these details, more
satisfied with the great story of the gospel work?

**Now I want to inform you, brethren, that the
things pertaining to me have gone rather for the
gospel's advancement so that my bonds got to be
published as in connection with Christ in the entire
praetorium and (among) all the rest, and that more
of the brethren in the Lord, being confident due to
my bonds, the more dare fearlessly to utter the Word
of God.**

This is the great news about the gospel in Rome.
Paul tells it with great joy. "I want to inform you"
("you to know") is little more than a common epistolary formula for introducing special information.
It is only a bit choice, not so much by using βούλομαι
instead of the commoner θέλω, but by using the present
infinitive γινώσκειν instead of the common perfect εἰδέναι,
which also explains why this infinitive is placed forward. Here is a piece of news that the Philippians
are not to get to know only once, this being enough
(perfect εἰδέναι), but one which will affect them personally for a long time (durative γινώσκειν). The former
expresses only the relation of the subject to the object
(C.-K. 388); hence the tense is as significant as the
choice of the verb. "Brethren" is in line with this
thought, the address also marks the new subject that
is of such interest to Paul's brethren.

"The things concerning me" (Eph. 6:21; Col. 4:7;
Rom. 1:15) means more than "my affairs," for the
phrase is stronger than a mere genitive "my." Paul

has in mind the recent developments in his case. We should like to know the full details, but Paul offers no hint. The messenger who carried Paul's letter supplied the details as Tychicus did in Ephesus (Eph. 6:21). We gather only this, that Paul's appeal to Caesar has recently come before the imperial court for decision, he has had his first hearing or hearings. Claudius was accustomed to attend to these in person, Nero is known to have referred them to his representative, and most likely did so in Paul's case. Paul's case had not yet been decided; it might, of course, still go wrong, but the start had been auspicious, and Paul's hopes are strong. Thus he writes "that the things pertaining to me have gone rather for the gospel's advancement." The perfect tense, literally, "have gone," means that they now continue in this condition.

He adds "rather" and thus touches upon all the fears and misgivings that were rife prior to his first hearing; things have, indeed, gone "rather" better than they might have gone.

The word used for "advancement" (it is not found in the classics, other examples are given in M.-M.) means to administer a blow and impel forward; "furthermore" (A. V.) is good. General advancement is meant, hence there is no article. It is concerned with "the gospel," Paul merges all personal thoughts about his prospective freedom in this supreme concern. What an example for all present-day preachers! How many could write as Paul does?

13) Ὥστε with its two infinitives states the actual double result and thus shows what a great advancement the gospel received in Rome. But note the difference in the tenses: ingressive aorist infinitive, "did get to be" — durative present, "dare the more." The fact result (aorist) is followed by the continuous effect result (present). The fact was published far and wide that Paul's imprisonment was connected with no crime

or criminal charge but with "Christ," and the effect
of this was the greater daring with which so many
brethren told everybody the Word of God.
On "bonds" see v. 7; masculine and neuter plural
have the same meaning: "imprisonment" or "confinement." The assumption that the neuter always =
fetters and chains is incorrect. The datives in v. 7
and 14 seem also to be masculine. We should get the
idea in φανεροὺς γενέσθαι: "got to be public or published."
Read the notes on the grand publication made in II Cor.
3:3. Here there is another. Paul's case had all at once
become a *cause célèbre*. If there had been dailies in
Rome, Paul would have been on the front page. No;
he was not averse to that, he was filled with joy. But
not because of any glory this shed on him but only
because of the publicity it gave the gospel which is
itself news.

Rome's prison had held many prisoners, also many
Romans who made appeal to Caesar and who were
proved innocent. The fact that Paul was another of
the latter class was not news; it would have been such
only if he had been a high Roman official or otherwise
renowned in the empire; but he was not a great figure
of this kind. The great thing on which the public eye
was all at once focused is suggested by the phrase "in
connection with Christ."

Leave it where Paul placed it. It is not a modifier
of "my imprisonment" but is placed between φανεροὺς
— γενέσθαι and modifies this expression. To be sure,
the emphasis on "among" whom this strange fact got
to be public is evident; but this emphasis would be
pointless without its own climactic point that in this
publication in these great circles Paul's confinement
was connected *with Christ*. Christ was the cynosure
of this public news. Paul's innocence of any crime
really interested no one. His release as an innocent
man would scarcely have called out a remark. The

brevity of the phrase "in Christ" should not surprise us. Paul's words: "in my bonds and in the defense and confirmation of the gospel" (v. 7) are our cue. During the hearing of the appeal of this prisoner to Caesar his great legal defense and its legal confirmation of fact presented the *gospel* and all that it contained about *Christ.*

Never had such a case come before the imperial court. Never had such an ἀπολογία and such a βεβαίωσις been heard by its judge. The divine gospel itself and its Messiah Christ were before the supreme court of the world. May we not assume that Christ fulfilled his promise (Luke 12:11; 21:12-15; Mark 13:11; Matt. 10:19) to Paul so that the gospel and Christ lost nothing when Paul stood before this court? It was Christ's own promise that had brought Paul there (Acts 9:15; 23:11). Christ had arranged everything from start to finish in order to produce the very effect here briefly described. Thus came about this great publicity "in the entire praetorium and (among) all the rest."

The A. V. is incorrect in both text and margin. The emperor's "palace" was never called τὸ πραιτώριον, nor was "Caesar's court" so named. This was the name for the barracks of the emperor's guard, the *castra praetoria* outside the Porta Viminalis, or the name of this imperial guard itself which was also called *cohortes praetoriae.* From the time of Tiberius to that of Vespasian this guard consisted of nine cohorts, 1,000 men in each (Tacitus). It was a picked body, all of its members were of Italian birth. They received double pay and enjoyed special privileges, every soldier ranked with the centurions of the regular legions. The entire guard was not always stationed at Rome, certain divisions were at times posted in adjacent towns. Because of its numbers and its position the praetorian guard wielded a powerful influence in the state; the

emperor often courted its favor and on his ascension
bestowed liberal donations upon it. The praetorium
cannot designate a place because "all the rest" cannot
mean "all other places." Both terms signify persons.
We may regard both datives after ἐν in the sense of
"among" although some regard the second as an indirect object: "in the whole praetorium and to all the
rest" of the people.

Was Paul removed from his own rented house
when his trial began? We can only guess. The court
did not sit in the barracks, hence to place him there
would not have made him promptly available at call.
The *praefectus praetorio* had his office in the emperor's
palace, and Paul may have been placed there, say in the
guardroom of the praetorian cohort on duty there.
Wherever he was, his friends had full access to him,
and he is able to dictate and to send this letter.

The way in which Paul writes "in the entire
praetorium" and then refers to "the rest" evidently
has back of it a special connection of Paul's case with
the praetorium. For two years, day after day, soldier
after soldier had guarded Paul in his rented house.
In this way Paul gained entrance into the praetorian
cohorts. His daily guards heard all he said and did,
talked about it in their barracks, became interested in
the case, and, when it was now up for hearing, when
it was established that the imprisonment had to do
with this Christ of Paul's teaching, the whole influential body of the imperial guard became thoroughly
conversant with and interested in the case.

"All the rest" cannot mean only the *praefectus* who
presided at Paul's hearing; he commanded the prae-
torians and thus belonged to what Paul calls "the whole
praetorium." He and his officials heard Paul's defense
and confirmation as a matter of course. "Getting
public" is a different thing from being brought to the
judge's ears in a courtroom; it is getting to the atten-

tion and into the talk of others, and here Paul even
writes *"all* the rest." This cannot mean less than
Rome in general. The people of the capital of the
world and its dominating military force, in the remarkable providence of God, through this lowly prisoner
Paul, heard the whole gospel story of Christ. Since
the imperial court had thus far acted favorably, all
this publicity was likewise favorable. No wonder
Paul was joyful.

14) This had a marked effect upon "the brethren
in the Lord" in Rome. It is thought that Paul coined
this designation, but see Col. 1:2 and remember in how
many ways he uses "in the Lord" and "in Christ." "The
brethren in the Lord" is such a natural expression that
it may well have been current for a long while, and
nobody knew who first used it. Paul refers to the
members of the congregation in Rome. In Rom. 16:3-16
Paul names all those who were prominent in the congregation about four years before he wrote this epistle
(see the author's exposition of these salutations). Two
large groups in the emperor's very own household,
slaves of the deceased Aristobulus and Narcissus (Rom.
16:10, 11), belonged to these brethren in the Lord.
Paul mentions them as "those of Caesar's house" in
Phil. 4:22.

But we must add many more. On Paul's arrival
in Rome he began a great missionary work among the
Jews in Rome. All the rabbis and other Jewish leaders
came to Paul's house; half of them came to faith that
first day (Acts 28:24), and Paul continued this work
among the Jews as Luke describes it in Acts (see the
author's exposition of this section of Acts). Now
Rome had no less than seven great synagogues. After
the conversion of about half of all the Jewish leaders
we can see how many Jewish "brethren in the Lord"
there must have been in Rome at the end of the two
years. The host of Jewish converts did not unite

with the original congregation of Rom. 16:3-16. Several of the synagogues became Christian congregations in the great city, these were composed exclusively of converted Jews.

Now all this favorable publicity about the connection of Paul's imprisonment with Christ inspired more of these many brethren with confidence "the more (περισσοτέρως) to dare fearlessly to utter the Word of God." Our versions are correct, the dative cannot mean: "trusting or relying *on* my bonds (imprisonment)," but means: "confident by or through my imprisonment," i. e., "due to it" (dative of means or of cause), now that all Rome knew the connection of this imprisonment with Christ and Paul's vindication soon to be declared by the court. The clouds that had so long been hanging over the head of the great exponent of Christianity in Rome, no less a man than the apostle, were disappearing. Instead of being silent, more brethren than ever, with more courage than ever, were fearlessly speaking aloud (λαλεῖν) the Word of God. Openly and boldly they confessed their faith by letting all men hear the Word of God, the gospel of Christ.

Brave hearts had done this before when nobody as yet had any intimation as to how Paul's case would fare before the imperial court. Even these now showed greater daring (τολμᾶν). Their number was increased. It was still daring, it still required fearlessness to speak out. Paul's case had not been concluded. An evil turn might yet make it go wrong. If the imperial court condemned Paul to exile, to the mines, or to death, to have talked Christianity so openly in the capital itself might entail serious consequences. But the prospect was now markedly favorable. Paul is praising all these many brethren. He is not blaming either those who had been or those who still were timid. Courage must develop even as faith must have time to grow. But to see so many now so courageous made Paul's heart joyful indeed.

15) **Some, indeed, are preaching Christ because of envy and strife, some, indeed, because of good will — from love, having come to know that I am placed for the gospel's defense; those are proclaiming the Christ from self-seeking, not with pure motive, thinking to be raising up affliction for my bonds.**

All this gold of speaking the Word fearlessly in Rome was not without alloy. Here is the place to recall v. 10, Paul's prayer that the Philippians may be "unalloyed and uninjured." When some read this letter, they think that Paul's words may reflect the conditions found only in Philippi. May they not reflect Paul's own experiences right here in Rome? Well, here were Roman brethren who were not "unalloyed and uninjured."

Τινὲς μέν — τινὲς δέ is exactly like the following οἱ μέν — οἱ δέ: "some — some." The two καί help to emphasize the phrases and have somewhat the force of "indeed." It is plain that Paul is dividing the brethren mentioned in v. 14 into two groups, one that has grave faults, the other of noble nature and motive. The view that he cannot call the former "brethren in the Lord" who have gained confidence due to Paul's bonds clashes with the way in which Paul writes "some — some," which every normal reader will refer to v. 14. These faulty brethren, Paul himself says, preach the Christ; they are not Judaizers, heretics. Paul calls the faulty Galatians, Corinthians, and others, "brethren" despite their very grave faults. Calvin writes: "Paul says nothing here which I myself have not experienced."

"Because of envy and strife" = because these men are envious of Paul and thus intend to raise up strife and dispute with him. The meanness thus manifested is the greater because their own boldness in preaching was due to the way in which Paul's case was going. They had the benefit of that, and this was the manner in which they repaid it! Many of this type have appeared in the church, who are envious because God has given greater gifts and more influential positions to other men. They feel thrust into the background, their authority and their following have been reduced, hence they carp, find fault, raise strife. The fact that Rome had some of these causes little wonder. Not only had Paul been prominent and successful from the start (Acts 28:24), all Rome was now talking about him. All this irked them: people always quoting Paul, praising Paul. Were there not also other men in Rome, meaning themselves? Well, they would show Paul and everybody else; they would preach the Christ with such vim as to draw all eyes on themselves and away from Paul.

Contrast this conduct with the noble and magnanimous spirit with which Paul writes about them. He shows not the least resentment. It takes two to have strife, and Paul is not going to be the other person. He rejoices and will rejoice in the main thing which ever remains that Christ be proclaimed as widely as possible. This does not imply that he is indifferent to the faults of these men. Is he not pointing out the faults which these men display so publicly?

Others, indeed, do their testifying "because of good will," "good pleasure" (used regarding God in Eph. 1:5, 9), the free determination to do the good thing, here, it seems, in their relation to Paul, loving, honoring, aiding him as the great apostle of the church. The word κηρύσσειν is used only in the sense of the preceding λαλεῖν so that we do not restrict it to "preachers" in the narrow sense, "elders" of the Roman congregations.

16) The A. V. transposes v. 16 and 17 contrary to the better texts and spoils the chiasm, the very thing Paul intends for both effect and beauty of form. Since

"some — some" precedes, we regard οἱ μέν — οἱ δέ as subjects: "these — those"; and not as the American Committee proposes which substantivizes the phrases: "they that are moved by love — they that are factious." As is done in v. 15, the verb is omitted in the first clause, and that of the second answers for both in neat and effective fashion.

Ἐκ = the source of the action and states the inner motive: "these, from love" (see v. 9), the love of real understanding and purpose. As in v. 9 Paul wants this love to be full of real, true knowledge, so he here adds: "having come to know (aorist) that I am placed for the gospel's defense." Theirs is enlightened, intelligent love in regard to the very point here involved. They act on it accordingly. "Love is blind," but never ἀγάπη. Nor is it informed only in a general way (which satisfies so many) ; in any of its actions it has to have a knowledge of the special fact or facts involved in those actions otherwise it will after all not be "unalloyed" (v. 10). These brethren did not merely "like" Paul; they saw what his office and his imprisonment meant in the plans of God and acted accordingly.

Κεῖμαι = "to lie"; the present tense is used as a present perfect, a substitute for the unused passive of τίθημι (R. 906) : "I am placed or set," i. e., "I stand for the gospel's defense." This is, however, the same "defense" as that mentioned in v. 7. The law and court term denotes Paul's pleading before the imperial court where in Paul's view not he himself but the gospel is on trial, he being only its mouthpiece, a prisoner in God's plan for that very reason. Knowing this inner fact, these brethren acted accordingly in what they did for the gospel "from love."

17) The others, indeed, also "announce" or "proclaim the Christ" ("speak the Word of God," v. 14) ; and this is the same as "preach the Christ," which is said of those who do it in good will (v. 15). But the

others do it "from self-seeking," ἐριθεία; this word is
explained in Rom. 2:8, which see. Their motive is
mercenary in the sense of being selfish; "of contention"
(A. V.), "of faction" (R. V.) are incorrect renderings.
"Not purely" defines the thought that their motive is
not unmixed; it has this self-seeking as a base alloy.
Their love is not pure gold throughout. "Thinking to
be raising up affliction for my bonds (imprisonment)"
— or is this a dative of place: "in my bonds" (R. V.)?
They thought they were vexing Paul. Imagining him
to be actuated by motives and thoughts like their own,
they supposed that any special success on their part
would make him envious of them, would make him
chafe in his confinement which prevented him from
competing as fully with them as he otherwise might.

18) Little did they understand the man whom
they intended to afflict. **What then? Only that in
every way, whether with pretense, whether with
truth, Christ continues to be proclaimed! And in
this I rejoice, yea, also will continue to rejoice.**

Τί γάρ; is an idiom: "Well now!" "What about it?"
Some would construe it with the following: "What,
then, except that," etc. The writer halts as if to
consider for a moment and then with πλήν singles out
the main thing in the whole affair, which is that in
every possible way Christ be continually proclaimed:
"only," "at any rate" (B.-D. 449; though see R. 646).

"Whether with pretense" is made clear by the
opposite, "whether with truth." The latter is from a
true, unalloyed motive; hence the former is with a
pretense of such a true motive. In the early church
this passage was used to shield heretics so that Chrysostom and others had to protest. R., *W. P.*, says:
"Some Christ is better than no Christ," as though
Christ can be divided! A bridge that reaches within
a foot of the opposite bank is not a bridge. Those who

think that these envious promulgators of Christ were
Judaizers find it difficult to explain Paul's joy. No
false doctrine ever found as much as tolerance on the
part of Christ or on the part of the apostles. The
tolerance of unionism was a later practice of errorists.
The error (lack of ἐπίγνωσις, v. 9) in the early misap-
plication of this passage is evident: motive is confused
with substance.

"Christ" and "the Christ" are used identically with
regard to both kinds of preachers: the substance was
identical. The motives differed; in one group they
pretended to be the true ones but were not; Paul states
what they really were. That is why Paul could bear
them in Christian longsuffering. He did not condone
them; he condemns these motives just as he did when
he was writing to the Christians in Rome.

But he keeps his balance. His own person and its
luster fade into the background; even whether he
lives or dies is unessential (v. 20). This selfish ambition that tried to outshine him and hurt his feelings
did not disturb his equanimity even for a moment. "In
this" that Christ is being preached in every way although from wrong motives by some, he says, "I
rejoice!" Paul was no light-minded optimist who
laughed when he should weep. The faults in Christian
hearts are not held so close to his eyes that he no longer
sees Christ preached over all of Rome. Here is his
note of joy again, doubled at that.

**Paul Tells the Philippians of His One Desire
to Magnify Christ during the Rest of his Trial**

19) From what has transpired at the start of
his trial Paul turns to what the outcome of it may be.
Whether this be life for him as he hopes, or death,
his one desire is that Christ be magnified. The words
in which he concentrates his thought (v. 21) find an

echo in all true Christian hearts; poets have clothed
them in metrical forms:

> "For me to live is Jesus,
> For me to die is gain;
> To Christ I gladly yield me,
> And pass where he has lain."

The last words of v. 18: "Yea, also I will continue
to rejoice!" have been drawn to what follows by some
because Paul now deals with the future. These punctuate accordingly. Since "I will rejoice" is decidedly
emphatic, following, as it does, "I do rejoice," these
commentators seek to find a still greater cause for joy,
one that rises above the preaching of Christ in all
Rome. They find it in the words: "I know that this
for me shall turn out for salvation" by assuming this
to be Paul's own personal final salvation. Yet Paul
never places a personal benefit above the spread of the
gospel. He has no climax of this kind. Paul does
this: with "I rejoice" he lifts himself above all the
despite he suffers from those who proclaim Christ in
order to cause him affliction in his imprisonment; and
with "I will rejoice" he lifts himself above any other
despite that these or any others may in the future try
to offer him. Verse 18 belongs to the preceding.

Paul now turns to the possible outcome of his trial,
and not merely as this may affect only himself, but as
it may affect also the Philippians. The prospect is
bright indeed: he expects to be set free. But he considers also the other possibility. He views both in
their bearing on the Philippians but sees as his supreme desire only this, that Christ may be magnified
among men, whether this be by his own life or by his
death. The thing that is supreme for Paul in v. 12-18
is the same as that which is supreme in v. 19-26: Christ.

For I know that this for me shall turn out for
salvation through your petition and supply from the
Spirit of Jesus Christ according to my earnest expec-

**tation and hope that in not a single thing shall I be
made ashamed, but in all boldness, as always, also
now Christ shall be magnified in my body, whether
by means of life, whether by means of death.**
All this explains (γάρ) how Paul can say, not only
that he is rejoicing, but also that he will continue to
do so. He knows one great fact which rejoices him
now and will do so in the future, however his trial
may turn out: "this for me shall turn out for salvation
through the petition that comes from you (genitive
of source) and the supply (in consequence of that
petition) that comes from the Spirit of Jesus Christ."
Paul "knows" this fact, and it assures his joy in all
that he has yet to face in his trial.

He alludes to Job 13:16: "He also my salvation,"
yeshu'ah, and uses the very words of the LXX but in
the sense of the original. Delitzsch translates:

*"Schon das waere mir zum Heile,
Dass nicht darf vor ihm ein Ruchloser erscheinen."*

"Already this would be for my preservation that no
hypocrite dare appear before him." Job is on trial
as Paul is. He may go down physically but not morally.
Already this is his great moral advantage that no false
person dare stand before God as Job is doing, whose
heart is filled with integrity. The word "salvation"
is not to be taken in its deeper sense; *es bedeutet hier
Heil als Sieg im Rechtstreit,* Delitzsch: being saved
in a judicial trial. The comments which think of
heavenly salvation are beside the mark. Neither Job
nor Paul have that in mind. We must take the whole
of what Paul says just as we must keep to the context
in Job. Neither has in mind a "salvation" that implies
that he is to live on. Job says: "though he slay me";
Paul: "whether through death." Both may, or also
may not, be slain. That is in the hands of God, and
they leave it there. They are saved from what would

be far worse for them. In the case of Job this is the thought that God would find him to be a *Ruchloser* or hypocrite in this trial induced by the accusation of his false comforters. In the case of Paul it is the idea that during the rest of his trial before the imperial court he disgrace Christ and the gospel. Nor are these two men diverse. If in his defense at court Paul should think only of himself he would be inwardly false, the type of a man that Job says dare not stand before God.

Paul says that he knows he will be saved from anything like this. By τοῦτο he refers to his trial: this will turn out safely for him so that he will not disgrace the gospel through cowardice, fear, lack of free utterance, or any inadequacy. He states the thing that will help him in his "defense and confirmation of the gospel" (v. 7), the only thing about which he is concerned. The means (διά) on which he relies is "the petition from you and supply from the Spirit of Jesus Christ"; one article unites the two, both are genitives of source.

Paul makes "petition" for the Philippians (v. 4), they make "petition" for him. We see what the latter is: that he may have an abundance of "the supply" which, according to Christ's own promise (Matt. 10:19, 20; Luk. 12:12; 21:14, 15), the Holy Spirit will furnish the apostle and the Christians when they are haled before earthly judges. Jesus said that they are not even to study in advance what and how they shall make answer, at the critical moment the Holy Spirit will put the correct answer into their mouth. We see why Paul writes "the Spirit of Jesus Christ"; he knows all about that promise. On "supply" see Eph. 4:16. The genitive is not appositional: supply = the Spirit; it is subjective: supply which the Spirit furnishes.

20) Paul unfolds his thought still further. He knows that this trial shall turn out safely for him

as far as his doing full justice to the gospel is concerned since so many besides himself are praying that the Spirit may supply him all that he needs. The thought that this affair of his will turn out safely is modified by the phrase, "according to my earnest expectation and hope that in not a single thing I shall be made ashamed." The thing that he knows accords with this expectation and hope (one article joins these two). Without this knowledge this expectation and hope in his heart would have no basis. Paul has used ἀποκαραδοκία (papyri) also in Rom. 8:19: watching for something with head stretched forward to see its very first appearance, "hope" completes the idea.

The verb is passive and implies an agent; hence the thought is not that Paul will in no thing become ashamed by what he may say or do at his trial but that the Spirit of Jesus Christ will make Paul ashamed in not one thing by failing to give him due supply of what and how to speak at his trial. Paul's hope and expectation is that not even in a single thing (the phrase is placed forward) will the Spirit on whom he counts fail him and thus put him to shame in his hope. Rom. 5:5.

The opposite is: "but (that) in all freedom of utterance, as always, also now Christ shall be magnified," etc. Paul does not say, that *I* shall magnify Christ; the verb is again a future passive, again the Spirit is the implied agent, he will use Paul as the instrument to magnify Christ. This is Paul's earnest expectation and hope. "In all boldness, as always, also now," means free speech that is restricted and cowed by no fear or no consideration of Paul's own person. So he had "always" spoken the gospel when he was a free man, so the Spirit will help him to speak "also now" in the rest of his trial before his Roman judge.

Give this a little thought. Suppose you were to appear as a preacher before the U. S. Supreme Court, and suppose this Court to be thoroughly pagan. Would it be so easy to speak with perfect freedom "as always," as in your own pulpit, your own town? And this free utterance, remember, is not just a free tongue but utterance that in not a single word, expression, or implication hurts the cause of Christ or falls short in doing it perfect justice. That is what Paul means. After a critical occasion we think often too late of just the way in which we should have said something. In the case of Paul such a danger will be excluded. He himself will marvel at what the Spirit led him to say.

In John 7:4 and Col. 2:15 ἐν παρρησίᾳ means "in public." B.-P. 1007, some commentators, and the author formerly (*Eisenach Epistle Selections*) so interpret here. Yet here the phrase has the addition "all." While "in public" would fit "as always," it does not fit "also now" because this refers to the courtroom of Caesar where appeals were heard, which was not open to the public. The idea that the phrase cannot refer to Paul personally because the statement is objective does not note "in my body" which is subjective enough. "In my body" is used instead of "in me" since "whether by means of life, whether by means of death" follows. The reference is to the outcome of the trial "now" in progress. The Spirit will magnify Christ in all the frank and free utterance he will enable Paul to make, no matter what means the Spirit will use for the outcome. He may use life for Paul's body, again he may use death. That is for the Spirit to determine. As far as the Spirit's supply is concerned which enables Paul to speak in all boldness before his judge, Paul's life or his death at the termination of the trial in no way affects that. Note that διά is to express means, and that the agent in the passive (the

Spirit of Jesus Christ) is the one who employs the means.

21) There is no reason to think that γάρ elucidates "I shall continue to rejoice," and to go back as far as v. 18, or "I shall not be ashamed" in v. 20. The connection, the emphasis, the meaning itself are clear. **For for me to live is Christ, and to die is gain.**

Every reader can see that this explains "Christ shall be magnified in my body, whether by means of life, whether by means of death." Here there are the very infinitives "to live," "to die," that take up the nouns "life," "death" that precede. Here, too, is the same word "Christ." He will be magnified as well by means of Paul's death as by means of his life, "for" for Paul to live is Christ, and to die is to have all the gain Christ promises us.

The same is true with regard to the emphasis on the ἐμοί which is placed forward. Here, too, there is a difference of opinion. The majority say: to *me*, whatever the case may be with regard to *others*. But v. 20 has indicated no others. Some refer back to v. 15-18, to those who proclaim Christ from envy, from intent to place Paul into the shade. But the last persons to be mentioned are found in v. 19, the Philippians who are making petition for Paul, with whom he is not in contrast.

This "for me" is in contrast with the divine agent implied in the preceding verb, who will magnify Christ in Paul's body whether by Paul's life, whether by Paul's death. This magnifying is what *he*, this agent (God or the Spirit of Jesus Christ), will do by means of either Paul's life or his death; and now Paul explains ("for") what this living or dying, which this divine agent will use, is to *him*. The one is an objective statement about Paul's body living or dead that tells us what the Spirit will do with it; the other is subjective and tells us what this living or dying is for Paul personally. The Spirit could not magnify Christ in Paul's body by means of life if for Paul to live were not Christ; nor in Paul's body by means of death if for Paul to die were not gain. But both are "for me," Paul says, these very things. In either way, then, by the Spirit Christ will be magnified in my body.

Τὸ ζῆν is properly a present durative infinitive, for living is continuous; but τὸ ἀποθανεῖν must be a punctiliar aorist, for "to die" is a momentary act. Who would think that immediately after saying: "in my body, whether by life, whether by death," the next words: "to be living — to die" are to be understood in a different sense and introduce a new contrast: "to be living spiritually — to die bodily"? Yet after von Hofmann introduced this exegesis others followed him. Despite the exactly parallel wording: τὸ ζῆν Χριστός — τὸ ἀποθανεῖν κέρδος we are told that this is a chiasm, that both infinitives are not subjects, nor both unarticulated nouns are predicates, but that Paul says: "For me Christ (subject) means that I live spiritually (predicate), and that I die (subject) means gain (predicate)." We are told that any reader would at once see this chiasm, that he must see it since in v. 20 Paul writes "body" in connection with "life" and with "death," and in v. 22, "to live in the flesh"; but here in v. 21, "to live" without a modifier such as "body" or "flesh," therefore this unmodified "to live" must be taken in a different sense: "to live spiritually," and is also in a different construction, it is not a subject but a predicate.

But millions of readers, in fact, the church as such have never seen this. Paul's γάρ connects v. 21 with v. 20. The English may have two sentences, but they belong most closely together, no matter how we punctuate. Since Paul starts with bodily life and closely follows with "to live" when he elucidates, this means "to live bodily" even as the new sentence (v. 22) goes on speaking about another thing (δέ) in this bodily living. A contrast that is as great as living in the body and flesh and living spiritually, the spiritual being placed between the other two, would call for an indication by at least a word: "to live spiritually" or "to live in spirit." Even then, in order to have a chiasm Paul would have had to place the terms chiastically: "for me Christ means to live spiritually; to die means gain." Chiasms are written chiastically so the eye may see them: subject — predicate; — predicate — subject. Here: noun — infinitive; infinitive — noun. Yet Paul did not write in this way.

Ζωή and ζῆν may, indeed, be used to designate both bodily and spiritual life and living. That is why Paul adds "in my body" (v. 20) and "in the flesh" (v. 22) in order to indicate that here, where he speaks of "life" and "death" or "living" and "dying," these terms refer to the body. Having referred both to the body in v. 20, they remain so in v. 21. When he further speaks about "fruit," and this is spiritual, one might think that now (v. 22), since Paul has said his life is Christ, he may intend "to live" in the spiritual sense. But no; Paul says that he is still speaking of the bodily life: "to live in the flesh." Also this (in v. 23) is still the subject as in v. 21 where, if Χριστός were the subject, the word would have the article. What impresses some who read von Hofmann's interpretation of living spiritually is this spiritual feature, it sounds more profound. But what profundity is there in saying that to a man like Paul, Christ means to be living spiritually? Even the deeper sense that is sought is, when tested, disappointing.

What Paul says *is* arresting, namely that for him to be living this bodily life "is Christ." He does not identify the two, for that thought would require the article with the predicate "Christ" (R. 768). It would also not be true, for then to die bodily would be to lose

Christ. This statement introduced with γάρ elucidates "Christ shall be magnified in my body by means of life." The great thing said in elucidation is that all Paul's bodily living (durative infinitive), all his bodily life activity, "is Christ." This is a new and a concentrated way of saying that he is a δοῦλος or "slave of Christ" who has no will of his own, that Christ alone moves his body and all its members according to his will. That is why he turns from the noun "life" used in v. 20 to the infinitive "to be living," and to this in the present tense. Recall all that Paul says in different places about the Christian's body and its members, for instance in Rom. 12:1; 6:12, 13; 6:19, where "fruit" follows in 6:22 as it does here in v. 23. Note the connection with the magnifying of Christ mentioned in v. 20. Look at Paul's life and living day by day, it is all "Christ." And it is thus that "Christ will ever be magnified in his body."

"And" is not "but"; nor is there an adversative thought or a contrast in the thought that Paul's getting to die (aorist) is gain. These two go together as though they were one: bodily living — Christ; bodily undergoing death — gain. Here not the noun "death" used in v. 20 is in place but the infinitive "to die." There is not an "antithesis" between "to live" and "to die." If this were the case, the predicates ought to indicate wherein the two are antithetical; but the predicates do not do so: "Christ" and "gain" (profit of any kind) are not in antithesis. Paul does not write δέ. And has Paul not already removed all antithesis by the wording: "in my body, whether by means of life, whether by means of death"? Life and death are not antitheses, they are alternatives.

The aorist infinitive is simply the close of the durative infinitive: "to live" at last reaches the point marked by "to die." The long line eventually comes to this end. Paul views it thus. In their conjunction

both statements elucidate the magnifying of Christ in
Paul's body as v. 20 shows with conjunctive "whether
— whether." Neither statement could stand by itself.
Only the living that is Christ reaches the getting to
die that is gain; no dying is gain unless it closes the
living that is Christ. Christ will not be magnified by
means of a death that does not close a life that has
already magnified him. So Paul might have said what
he does say in a slightly different form in Rom. 14:8:
"For me to live is Christ, and for me to die is also
Christ." It would be true. He practically does say
that in v. 20. By saying "gain" in the second clause
he says more. He tells us what more he means when
he speaks of it in v. 23 as being "by far better" and
calls it "to be with Christ." Yes, he is with Christ
now, both while he lives and when he dies, but only
spiritually, by faith; when he is dead he will be "with
Christ" in the way in which he has long desired to be
with him, namely visibly, gloriously. This is the
"gain."

"Gain" thus goes beyond "Christ" used in the first
clause, but only in the way indicated. "Gain" takes
us only one step farther. "Christ" is not left behind,
"gain" only has him to magnify him in a new, in a
glorious association. Yes, it is "gain" when our living
is Christ. But the word fits better at the end of life,
for it means the profit one obtains from a previous
investment. It is what one cashes in at the end. Thus
"gain" adds the subjective part to the objective, what
Paul gets at the end when he comes to die: that he is
then with Christ in glory after a life of living Christ,
of spiritually making Christ the sum and substance
of his living.

One line on the page, scarcely that; yet so blessed,
so glorious the substance expressed!

22) **Now if** (it is) **to go on living in the flesh,
this for me** (means) **fruit of work. And what shall**

I choose? I do not know. Moreover, I am held from the two (sides), having the desire for getting to depart and to be with Christ, for it is very far better; yet to go on remaining in this flesh is more necessary on account of you.

The margin of the R. V. shows how translators vary regarding v. 22. We need not discuss the matter except to say that "this is the fruit of my labor" is incorrect; Paul writes: "This (to go on living, durative present as in v. 21) for me (is, i. e., means — supply the same copula in the same sense as in v. 21) fruit of work." In an objective way he views the possibility that his trial before the imperial court may permit him to go on living; hence there is no copula in the protasis, and we must supply an indicative: "If it is (or shall be) that I am to go on living." This, he says, means for me "fruit of work," i. e., that I shall do more work as an apostle because of my prolonged life and secure more fruit ("fruit," in Rom. 1:13). To get such further fruit makes Paul want to go on living. All his past apostolic life had been just this: "fruit of labor" (genitive of origin). We have already explained why "in the flesh" is added.

We do not regard this sentence as an anacoluthon (contra R. 1023). When Paul does use an anacoluthon he has a reason for doing so. There is no such reason here. While the question with the indicative future might be indirect and deliberative (R. 875) as in the classics, we agree with B.-D. 368 that this can scarcely be the case here. Robertson admits that it would be the only instance in the New Testament. Nothing prevents us from regarding it as a direct question: "And what shall I choose for myself (middle)?" Paul confesses: Οὐ γνωρίζω, "I do not know." Our versions have the archaic: "I wot not." Here, too, there is a debate, for in the New Testament this verb is used in the causative sense "to make known." Hence some

prefer that sense here: "I do not make known." One
does not, of course, make known a thing that he himself does not know.

The papyri, however, show that this verb continued
to be used also in its original classic meaning "to know"
(B.-P. 256). We agree with C.-K. 257 that it is so used
here: *Ich erkenne es nicht.* The causative sense really
lurks in the word as it is here used, for which reason
neither οἶδα nor γινώσκω is in place. By using γνωρίζω
Paul intends to say: "I am without cause of knowing,"
i. e., God does not let me know. The thought is: nothing has enabled Paul to know just what to prefer for
himself. We should note that he is not speaking of
what will come to pass, whether life or death, but only
of what he should prefer if he alone had the choice.
Any hint from God in either direction would at once
be decisive for Paul, but God had given him no hint
as to the choice to make.

23) That is why he adds something (δέ) regarding
this matter of making a choice: "Moreover, I am held
(restrained) from the two" alternatives or sides, "I
am in a strait between the two" (our versions). Yet
ἐκ points to the source from which the double impetus
comes. "The two" is definite, for Paul has named
them: life or death. When he again names them he
makes a fine distinction in two ways. To indicate the
possibility of dying he uses a participle as if this were
a minor thing; to express the possibility of living for
the benefit of his readers he uses a finite expression.
This is not accidental. Again, the thought of death is
expressed subjectively: "having the desire to depart";
the thought of living is put objectively: "to remain is
more necessary." Both differences show how exactly
Paul weighed the two alternatives. The one was combined with his personal *desire*, which he regards as
minor because it is only his own desire; the other is
combined with a *necessity* regarding his readers, **which**

Paul thus regards as *major*. But note well that he speaks only of the pressing in upon him of these considerations. The real alternatives remain: life — death; this desire and this necessity are only attached to these in exerting pressure upon Paul.

One often simply yields to his own personal desire over against something that is really more necessary. Paul's wording shows that he clearly distinguished between the two and does not yield to the former. He adds no undue weight to his personal desire; he subtracts no weight from the special necessity. In other words, if death is to be his lot, he will be happy in having his desire fulfilled, but if life is to be his lot, he will be happy in serving others with the fruit of his further work (v. 22). What a fine example, and what a perfect way of stating the alternatives! The meaning of ἐπιθυμία is determined by the context which often gives the word the meaning "lust," plural "lusts"; here the connotation is good: "desire for getting to depart," the εἰς phrase = a dative (R. 1076). The infinitive means "to break camp," thus to leave or depart, it is properly an aorist.

Departure from this life means for Paul "to be with Christ," σύν to indicate the heavenly association with him. "The opinion constantly bobbing up, a view of the apostle ever fluctuating and getting into contradiction with itself regarding the nearness of the Parousia and the relation of death to this event, and regarding the proximate circumstances of the end, belong to the most ill-considered and fanciful notions which the newer criticism has cultivated." Wohlenberg's severe verdict is only too true. These critics have Paul say: he is certain he *will* see the Parousia, he is certain he *will not* see it; the believing dead will sleep in unconsciousness, will be in the dim, dark *sheol*, realm of the dead, will come back during the millennium, etc. That a man who so often faced immediate death should reckon with the thought of dying soon is too plain to need comment. That an apostle should pretend to know more than Jesus about the time of the Parousia is incredible. It might come at any time or might be long delayed. Paul speaks accordingly. The body alone sleeps in death, after death the soul is with Christ, glorious, in bliss (Acts 7:59, 60). The millennium is a fiction. Let this suffice. "To be with Christ" is the assured hope of every dying Christian, which all the fancies of "the newer criticism" (Wohlenberg) will never disturb.

24) Paul adds regarding thus being with Christ, literally: "for (this) is rather by much better," in English: "for it is much better." The same thought is expressed in II Cor. 5:8. The two comparatives match: "better" — "more necessary." Each balances between two alternatives; each puts a plus against a minus, but at one time the plus is on the one, at another time on the other side. It is this that puts Paul into his undecided state. Who can blame him? Whichever the Lord will allot to him as the outcome of his trial, Paul is bound to be happy, for he is bound to get either the one plus or the other.

Yet the two plus are diverse. The one is "better" by a good deal for Paul personally, the other is "more necessary on account of you," Paul's readers, namely for Paul "to remain on in this flesh." In v. 22 ἐν σαρκί needs no article, here the article of previous reference is in place. "Flesh" = "my body" (v. 20), and this does not meat "sinful flesh," for sinfulness is foreign to the discussion. The article leads us to think that ἐν is genuine; even without it the dative would = place.

25) Paul does not know which alternative to choose as far as choosing on his part is concerned. So he does not choose. Another will attend to this for him. The point he now treats is: can he determine in any way which the Lord will choose for him? To

a degree he can, and this even on the basis of the analysis he has just made. When it comes to what is better for Paul alone and what is more necessary for many others, the great probability is that the Lord will choose the latter unless, indeed, still other factors enter such as the Lord alone knows and weighs.

And in regard to this having become confident, I know that I shall remain, even remain by the side of all of you for the advancement of you and joy about the faith in order that your reason for boasting may increase in Christ Jesus in connection with myself through my own presence back with you.

This knowing is qualified, is different from that mentioned in v. 19, qualified by the thing of which Paul has become confident, namely that "to remain on in the flesh is more necessary for you." In v. 6, "having become confident of this very thing that" refers forward as the word order itself shows. Now the word order is reversed, τοῦτο refers back, and ὅτι alone belongs after "I know." Paul's knowing rests on only this confidence of his; he does not know absolutely, in an unqualified way. Some refer to their interpretation of v. 19 and thus find a contradiction, but none exists; see v. 19.

Moulton (*Einleitung* 187, etc.) draws attention to the Greek idiom of using a simplex after a compound verb, the simplex to be understood in the same sense as the compound: "to remain on in the flesh — I shall remain," both mean to remain alive. R. 828 points out that in the second compound the stress is on the preposition: "I shall remain (alive in general) — I shall remain *by the side* of all of you (with you all)." Hence καί is ascensive: "even." The latter is more than the former.

But Paul now adds the qualifier: remain with you all "for the advancement of you and joy about the faith, in order that," etc. This alone is the thing

for which the Lord, Paul is confident, will want him
to remain. This, then, is what he thinks he can say
that he knows. If it were not for this necessity regarding Paul's readers the Lord would most likely fulfill
Paul's desire to depart and to be with his Lord.

Paul is not flattering himself as though his readers
still need him. He says only that he is confident they
do, and he describes in what respect he thinks they do.
He was in a position to know, and we know that he
judged correctly, that the Lord did let him remain on.
He was released from his imprisonment and lived on
for a few years. Then came his second and fatal imprisonment, during which he wrote in an entirely different way (II Tim. 4:6-8).

One article connects the two nouns "advancement
and joy" exactly as in the διά phrase in v. 19. Each
noun also has a genitive attached and placed chiastically as in v. 19. Whereas there the genitives are both
subjective: petition which the Philippians make, supply which the Spirit furnishes, here they are both objective: advancement *of* the Philippians, joy *about* the
faith. In regard to the former there is no question,
hence there should be none in regard to the second
since the governing nouns are used with one article.
That means that "the faith" is objective: joy over what
the Philippians believe and not merely over their act
of believing. Yet this does not appeal to some; they
confuse the genitives by making one objective, the
other subjective or possessive, and usually "the faith"
is subjective faith (*qua creditur*), hence *Glaubens-
freude*. We are told that πίστις is never objective although it is so in a score of instances when it is used
with the article.

We should note Vitelli's idea in M.-M. 487, etc., that
παραμένω is a euphemism for "to serve," and Schmid's
finding that in late Greek the word means "to remain
alive" Yet Schmid produces no examples to substan-

tiate his idea of παραμένω, and here Paul's simplex: "I know that I shall remain," plainly means "that I shall remain alive." The examples offered for the meaning "to serve" lack the idea of serving; they mention only length of time: "remain with" so or so long a time just as Paul uses the words here. Εἰς states the object for which Paul knows that he will remain for the Philippians. This object consists of what *he* will furnish them.

26) With ἵνα he adds the purpose, the intention regarding what *they* may have when Paul's object is attained: "that your reason for boasting (καύχημα, not καύχησις, the action) may continue to increase (present, durative) in Christ Jesus in me through my own presence back with you." The "advancement and joy" are evidently referred to as "the reason for boasting" and being elated. They will, of course, abound "in connection with Christ Jesus," for all advancement and joy ever remain in the sphere that is bounded by Christ. The emphasis is on the phrases "in me through my own presence back with you." That is why "in me" is amplified. "In me" == "in connection with my person" (see R. 587), namely Paul's own personal presence back with the Philippians. Yes, when Paul is again in their midst, his very presence and the stimulation (προκοπή) and the joy it will produce will increase their reason for boasting of what Christ has done for them.

Παρουσία is the word used with reference to the presence of Christ when he returns at the last day; it has become technical for that but here has its common meaning. Ἐμῆς, the possessive adjective "my own," is emphatic; the enclitic μου would not be. The first meaning of πάλιν is "back" (place), the second "again" (time). Here the former fits well, for the idea of πρός is "face-to-face." It is often used to indicate intimate personal contact and is very expressive in the present connection.

The note of "joy" is sounded again (v. 25). What a happy time that will be when the apostle is back again face to face with his beloved Philippians, is again able in his own person to preach to them, to advance them, to give them joy in their faith and greater elation in Christ Jesus! All this will be the greater because of the dark days of Paul's long imprisonment, because of the uncertainty about the outcome of his appeal to Caesar. But now the sun is breaking through, Paul is able to write that he will most likely soon be back in Philippi. He writes only about them, and we do not think that *"all* you" in v. 25 refers to all his congregations everywhere. That Paul will visit also other congregations, that these will have similar joy goes without saying. As far as that is concerned, the Philippians will rejoice only the more.

Paul Adds the Admonition
That the Philippians ever Stand Fast,
United and Unafraid,
Against the Adversaries

27) The admonition is added in the most natural way and even refers to Paul's presence or absence. It is naturally general and not directed at any specific evils that were found in Philippi. **Only continue conduct in a way worthy of the gospel of Christ in order that, whether getting to come and getting to see you, whether being away, I may get to hear regarding the things concerning you that you are standing firm in one spirit, with one soul contending together for the faith of the gospel, and scared in nothing by the adversaries; which is for them an indication of perdition but of your salvation, and this from God, seeing that to you there has been graciously granted this in behalf of Christ, not only to believe in him, but also to suffer in behalf of him,**

**having the same conflict such as you have seen in me
and now hear about in me.**

"Only" (μόνον) stresses the main thought. It is
debated as to how much of the idea of citizenship is left
in πολιτεύομαι, and some will naturally think that more
(R. V. margin), some that less is still found in the
verb. Both here and in Acts 23:1 very little of this
idea seems to be left. The examples cited in M.-M. are
political and thus cannot well apply to Paul's two uses
of the word; the two non-political examples given use
the word in the sense of περιπατέω but are not taken from
the papyri. All that can safely be said is that these two
verbs are synonymous and indicate conduct, the former
the conduct that is touched with the connotation of living together as a community or unit body. It is asked
why Paul uses this word instead of the commoner "to
walk," and the answer is given that he prefers πολιτεύομαι. But here, at any rate, the reason for the preference is evident: this πολίτευμα has "adversaries," and
his readers must thus keep together as a unit in order
to stand against them.

We thus do not accept the connotation of living
under gospel rules and regulations; also the other, that
Paul has in mind his own Roman citizenship and, since
Philippi was a Roman colony, the similar standing of
his readers, which seems rather farfetched.

The adverb "worthily (in a way worthy) of the
gospel" contains the idea of weight: the conduct of
weight to the gospel of Christ (genitive of origin).
Yet this gospel is not thought of as laying down laws
and regulations but as offering salvation and blessedness. The conduct of this united band of believers in
the gospel is to match the blessed saving gifts they
have received. The conduct is to reflect what the gospel and its riches have made of the Philippian congregation (I Pet. 2:9).

Paul adds a personal note because of the close bond existing between him and the Philippians: "in order that, whether getting to come and getting to see you (ingressive aorists), whether being away (durative present), I may get to hear (again ingressive aorist) regarding the things concerning you (most likely only an adverbial accusative) that you are standing firm (στήκετε) in one spirit (this animating you all), with one soul contending together (or jointly) for the faith of the gospel," etc. That he expects to be able to come and to see them Paul has already said. This will, of course, be only a visit, aside from that he will be absent from them. Hence we do not understand the participles as balancing between two possibilities, that of getting to see them or of not getting to see them at all (life — death, in v. 20). The texts vary between the aorist ἀκούσω and the present ἀκούω, "get to hear" — "continue to hear," either of which is good. Either is the subjunctive after ἵνα. "Whether — whether" balances only the participles.

"That you continue firm — contending" matches the idea of πολιτεύεσθε as already explained. The present tense to indicate continuousness is important, implying, as it does, that the Philippians are now standing thus. We deem the discussions about the constitutional difference between *pneuma* and *psyche* out of place in the present passage since both are ethical and not constitutional to man's immaterial part. When it is used with reference to many persons, "one spirit" means one animus, here the true Christian animus. It, of course, dwells in the spirit of each person and is placed there by the Holy Spirit; yet "in one spirit" intends to designate neither of these two although some think that it signifies one or the other.

The dative of means "with one soul" is so like "one heart and soul" in Acts 4:32 that the ethical meaning is plain. The variation from "one spirit" to "one soul" is ethically slight; let us say, the one *animus* that dwells in each Christian's spirit, the one *life activity* that comes from each Christian's soul. Hence we *stand* in one spirit but *contend* by means of one soul. The dictionaries are disappointing; C.-K. 1141 has only a meaningless reference regarding "soul"; B.-P. 1422 only *einmuetig* for the same; Thayer 520, 2 is no better: "one soul = "one heart." All seem to avoid even a remark on "one spirit."

The σύν in the participle means to contend (as in an athletic contest) jointly; Jude 3 has the compound with ἐπί, "contend earnestly." Paul is not saying, "Contend together with me," and certainly not, "Contend with each other." "For the faith" is the *dativus commodi*: to get victory "for the faith of the gospel." Here "the faith" is objective (as in v. 25) and not subjective. The genitive "of the gospel" is either appositional: the faith = the gospel; or possessive: "the faith" is the contents which belongs to the gospel. "*The* faith" is as clearly objective as it is in Jude 3. It is to be maintained against "the adversaries" who deny this faith, this gospel contents. The idea that the Philippians are to contend only for their believing is too tenuous to maintain even when this believing is said to be objectivized, the act being made objective by speaking of it, a sort of "technical term" as it has been called, with the genitive naming what is believed.

In the first place, the implied contrast is not that these adversaries might make the Philippians stop believing, that the latter are to fight only for themselves. Their adversaries deny the truth of the contents of the gospel, want to down the gospel contents with their lies, want their lies to be victorious so that the gospel shall not spread. That is the real contest or battle.

In the second place, "faith" is always a correlative term: the act of believing always involves the thing I believe; vice versa, the thing calls for the act. I always trust something, and this something intends that I trust it. Subjective faith is nothing without the objective faith; "the faith," objective, could not have this name without "faith," subjective. Applied here, this means that as being believers themselves the Philippians defend what they believe. Unless they are able to do that they cannot defend their own action of believing. To this day the battle is always about the *what*; only so is our act attacked even as we stop believing and cease this act only when this *what* is made uncertain for us.

28) The two participles belong together: that you stand firm, "contending and scared in nothing by the adversaries" (generic: whoever they may be). The verb is used regarding horses' taking fright. While it is expressed negatively, the thought is really positive: unscared means joyfully courageous. So Paul had been when at the time of the founding of the church he and Silas had sung hymns of praise in their dungeon cell.

It is asked who the adversaries are, and some think of hostile Jews. The trouble with this view is that there were only a few Jews in Philippi, that Paul's clash, too, had not been with Jews, and that he even refers to this clash of his as a sample. No, these opponents must be pagan and, judging from v. 30, such opposition as could move the city authorities. Both "contending and not scared" speak of the fight. Paul wants hearty, fearless fighters. Hence we should not take his thought to mean fear lest the Philippians give up their faith and sink back into paganism. Paul's thought is only that the Philippians may not fight joyfully, assuredly enough, that some at least may fight, indeed, but all the while be exceedingly frightened.

That is why he adds: "Which is for them an indication of perdition (objective genitive) but (an indication) of your salvation, and this from God." Why,

then, should they not stand firm, contend, be unafraid?
Ἥτις is feminine because of the predicate ἔνδειξις and is
qualitative with a causal touch: since this is a thing of
this kind, an indication, etc. The question as to the
antecedent, whether this is "not scared," "contending,"
or "stand firm," is easily answered; for each of the
three, or any two of them, is incomplete in thought
when taken independently. The thought to which the
relative refers is that of all three: this your standing
firm in contending and being unscared, "this is a thing
of such a kind as to constitute for them an indication
of perdition," etc.

Paul does not call it "a sign" but only a pointer in
that direction, ἔνδειξις. It seems that some copyists did
not understand Paul when he wrote: *"For them* an
indication of perdition but *of your* salvation," and so
changed the genitive into another dative: "but *for you*
of salvation," some even making it: *"for us."* But Paul
wrote a dative and then a genitive and placed both
in the emphatic forward position. This thing is an
indication "for them" although *they* do not see that
it is a thing of this kind, but Paul sees it, and the
Philippians are to see it as such a thing. But it is an
indication "of your (ὑμῶν) salvation," the salvation you
already possess and enjoy. Perdition is not yet upon
them, it still awaits them; but salvation is already
yours. They may still escape perdition if they should
get to see this indication of it in the right light, see that
their opposition means perdition for them, see that it
means your salvation.

Ἀπώλεια (intransitive) and σωτηρια are opposites.
The former = "the condition after death, the exclusion from salvation as a final fact, when, instead of
having become what one could have become, he is
ruined, has perished" (C.-K. 789), "the destruction
which consists in the loss of eternal life, in eternal misery, perdition" (Thayer). Both Judas (John 17:12)

and the Antichrist (II Thess. 2: 3) are called "the son
of the perdition." It is said that Paul does not describe
this perdition, but all that he as well as Jesus say about
hell and damnation is all that anybody can ask in the
way of a description. The word never means annihilation as has, in view of the translation "destruction,"
been claimed by those who attempt to abolish hell. In
his *Offenbarung* Zahn agrees with these people: to be
thrown into the lake of fire he states is annihilation.
"Salvation" includes both an act of rescue and the resultant state of safety. This is already ours but attains
its consummation in the future. The fact that "salvation," "to save," and "Savior," are mentioned more
often than "perdition," "to perish," should not surprise
us, for the Scriptures are full of "salvation."

Paul adds: "and this thing (is) from God," τοῦτο,
neuter, this whole thing which is of such a kind as has
just been stated. "This" is neither an accusative nor
idiomatic (R., W. P.) It is a natural and proper nominative. The antecedent of "this thing," τοῦτο, is the
whole clause, yes, this clause as defining what kind of
a thing (ἥτις) the valiant action of the Philippians is;
hence τοῦτο is neuter. The antecedent is not the feminine ἔνδειξις, nor what is said only about "your salvation." Ἀπό points out to the Philippians that everything: their standing firm in contending and being
unafraid comes to them "from God" even as Paul adds
"graciously granted to you," ἐχαρίσθη (v. 29).

29) Here, we submit, is an instance of what R.
1001 calls the consecutive ὅτι, which is best rendered by
"seeing that." Only a few seem to know about it so
that we commonly have the translation "because" or
"for" (A. V.). The point is that Paul does not give us
the reason or cause why "this thing is from God." Does
that need proof? Nor is what Paul says proof. This
ὅτι states what underlies the whole admonition from
v. 27 onward; the whole of it applies, "seeing that" or

in view of the fact that, etc. Consecutive ὅτι does not state what follows from a thing but the thing from which what has been mentioned follows. It does so here: "seeing that to you (emphatic) there was granted (by God's gracious act when you were converted) this 'in behalf of Christ,' (namely) not only this thing of believing in him but also this thing of suffering 'in his behalf.' " Consecutive to what is thus said should be what Paul bids the Philippians do.

So highly God has favored *you.* Graciously he granted (historical aorist) as the most precious gift to you, τὸ ὑπὲρ Χριστοῦ, "this thing that we all know as 'in behalf of Christ,' " the article making a noun of the phrase. All Christians wear this precious jewel as God's dearest gift to them, which is engraved: IN BEHALF OF CHRIST. It is terser and more beautiful in the Greek, ὙΠΕΡ ΧΡΙΣΤΟΥ. The brevity requires the appositional explanation: "this thing (called) *In Behalf of Christ,*" it is "not only 'this thing of believing in him,' but also (as going with the believing) 'this thing of suffering *in his behalf,*' " the significant "in behalf" being repeated. The three τό neatly substantivize, one τό the phrase, two τό the infinitives. The second two τό do not divide the first one, together they state the defining apposition.

This *Hyper Christou* necessarily includes the thing called "believing in him" (durative, εἰς directing all our confidence, *ueberzeugungsvolle und zuversichtliche Anerkennung,* toward him) ; but in addition to this it includes what naturally goes with this believing (καί), the thing called "suffering in his behalf," with suffering (durative, iterative present) belongs ὑπὲρ αὐτοῦ, with believing only εἰς αὐτόν. The former could not be possible without the latter although Paul's contrast in the two phrases is the idea that believing as believing only reaches and embraces Christ for itself, does not yet step in for him, endure and suffer "in his behalf." This "in behalf of him" is implied in God's grant, which, as it were, doubles his gift and crowns the believing *in* him with the suffering *for* him.

30) The nominative participle "having" is not irregular as though it depends on the dative "to you" (v. 29). Calling it "anacoluthic" or "pendent," etc., overlooks the fact that in the Greek the participle has both number and case and is thus used with perfect clearness whereas the English is hampered by lacking both. Being a participle, it expresses a subsidiary thought that goes with the main thought, which here reaches back to v. 27, to the joint contending, and now resumes this with "conflict": "having the same conflict of the kind you saw in me (in my case, R. 587, cf., v. 26) and are now hearing in me" (in my case). The aorist refers to what the Philippians "saw" when Paul was beaten and thrown into prison, cf., Acts 16:19, etc. The present refers to what they "are now hearing" about Paul's imprisonment and trial in Rome.

But Paul qualifies: it is "the same" conflict or contest that requires strength and endurance, yet only the same as being of the same general kind, namely as being due to hostility against the gospel. The treatment Paul received in Philippi was worse than the treatment he was receiving in Rome. So the Philippians will suffer more or less, in one way or in another, now and again after a while. This is even God's gracious grant to them. From the way in which Paul writes we may conclude that the Philippians were not suffering persecution at this time. The fact that they had "adversaries" who were opposed to the gospel is only what they had from the start. Paul's admonition is that they ever continue their firm stand, be ready for any eventualities, and face them unitedly (as a πολιτεία — πολιτεύεσθε in v. 27) and perfectly unafraid.

CHAPTER II

Paul's Second Admonition:
With a Mind like Christ's Humbly to Relinquish
What is Ours by Right
In the Interest of the Brethren

1) First, how the Philippians are to stand firm against their *opponents;* next, how "accordingly" (οὖν) they are to be minded toward their *brethren.*

Two considerations make the translation of our versions unacceptable: first the reading, secondly the thought. The reading is τὶς σπλάγχνα and not τινά, which underlies the translation of our versions. To assume that we have a solecism, a masculine singular construed with a neuter plural, is untenable. That τίς should be indeclinable (R. 744) is equally untenable, for Paul declines τίς and τί in the preceding clauses. To assume that this reading is due to an early error in copying is equally untenable, for the error would produce the solecism. The very few copyists who altered the text evidently sought to correct what they thought was a mistake. The many Greek texts that have τίς are proof positive that this correct reading was correctly understood by those who allowed it to stand. So much for the text.

The thought is disjointed when the correct reading is changed and when we translate as do our versions by making the εἰ clauses protases to v. 2: "If — if, then fulfill my joy that you be of the same mind," etc. The protases do not match the apodosis. Some regard the protases as adjurations and think that Paul adjures the Philippians by the admonition, solace, fellowship, tender mercies and compassions they have toward each other, but how can the *same* mind rest on adjurations of this kind? Others make them conditional affirmations that the Philippians do have admonition, etc.; the apodosis is still incongruous, its thought is not a *conclusion* but *an addition* to the thoughts contained in the "if" clauses.

Von Hofmann has taken the right view, which Ewald sought to improve. Verses 1 and 2 are separate sentences, v. 2 is *not* the apodosis. Each "if" clause has its own apodosis in v. 1, which may be either declarative or imperative, preferably the latter, because v. 2 is imperative.

If, accordingly, (there is) **any admonition,** (let it be) **in connection with Christ; if any solace,** (let it be) **of love; if any fellowship,** (let it be) **of spirit; if any** (such fellowship), (let it be) **tender mercies and compassions!**

All the conditions assume a reality, otherwise they would have to be of a different Greek form. Paul takes it for granted that there is such admonition, etc. The fact that the apodoses are so terse makes them the more striking and effective. Here we have one of the many instances where one should note that Greek is *not* English. The Greek does not need to have everything written out in full as the English does. The Greek mind catches the thought at once without having the copula written out. People who are accustomed to think in other languages are thus often left behind, the Greek is too nimble for them. We shall have to learn this nimbleness and think in Greek.

This "admonition," etc., as also the following shows (v. 2-4), is not directed from the Philippians to Paul but from them to themselves. Παράκλησις, "calling one to one's side," is always modified by the context so that the word may mean having someone come to our side with admonition or with exhortation (R. V., American Committee) or with urging or with encouragement or with comfort (our versions) or even with request. Here "comfort" would trench on the next term, "solace." Since οὖν connects with what is said about standing firm against adversaries (1:28), all the terms used in v. 1 get their coloring from that connection. The Philippians who have to suffer from such adversaries will need from their brethren: admonition or encouragement — solace or comfort — true spiritual fellowship — and all that tender mercies and compassions can bestow. That is why all of these are mentioned. They are, of course, needed also at other times but especially at times such as the previous context suggests.

All such admonition, let it be "in connection with Christ." So Paul offered all his admonitions; take Eph. 4:1 as a sample. "In Christ" is not mystical; it means "in connection with Christ." The admonition will remind them that Christ suffered and died for us, that we are his, under his love, protection, etc. That kind of admonition goes home to the Christian who receives it and cheers, strengthens, helps him. Any other would fall flat.

So with "any solace," let it be "of love," let its source be Christian love that is intelligent and purposeful (see 1:9). Sentimentality, mere humanitarian feeling will not do, and officious intrusion would be the worst of all. Παραμύθιον (παρά, beside, μῦθος, speech) is used "much in the sense of our 'solace'" (M.-M. 488), *Erleichterung* (B.-P.), making things easier by speaking to one in trouble Regarding these first two compare I Thess. 2:11: "You know how we dealt with each one of you as a father with his own children, exhorting you (παρακαλοῦντες) and encouraging you (παραμυθούμενοι)."

"If any fellowship, (let it be that) of spirit." This expression, like "of love," points to source. The majority of interpreters translates "of Spirit"; but this cannot be the sense because this thought is mentioned third, "of love" intervening between "in Christ" and "of the Spirit" (if this means Spirit). Paul says that outward fellowship is not enough, spirit must fellowship spirit. Note, too, that because it is third, "of spirit" is already linked with "in Christ" and with "of love." These four exhortations belong together, one links into the other, the four form a whole. To offer admonition in connection with Christ means also to offer solace from love to a brother, and both mean true spiritual fellowship. Experience has taught the writer the full force of what Paul here writes. When I was in deep distress, the visit of brethren with whom I felt that I was in true, full spiritual fellowship meant everything to me; but my soul turned from those who tried to act as if theirs, too, was such inner fellowship when I was convinced that it was not.

"If any" (elliptical) means "any such fellowship of spirit." In this further reference to what any fellowship must be the subject includes what has just been said of it, that it must be "of spirit" and thus now states that it should consist of "tender mercies and compassions." On the former see 1:8; the latter = pities, manifestations of pity. "Of spirit" characterizes this fellowship according to its source, the nominatives characterize it in its manifestation as coming from that source. This final predication is double, consisting of two closely synonymous terms. That is rhetorically good for the last of a series of statements even as it is good to say two things of the "fellowship" after having said one of each of the preceding terms.

But note the progress from "admonition" to "solace" and then to "fellowship," each predication matches. There are thus seven terms in all, and each is in its proper place, and the seven form a whole. One predicate is a phrase, and this is comprehensive, weighty: "in Christ"; then come two genitives of source which are included in this phrase; then a double nominative to indicate the outflow of feelings. In the

face of so many opponents Christians need all manner
of admonition from each other so as to remain firm,
and this must always be connected with Christ. They
will often suffer hurt and need consolation from each
other, and this must come from intelligent and purposeful love, the love which Christ produces in the true
believers. Thus the fellowship of clinging close together in the face of the hatred of opponents is necessary, but this must have its source in spirit and be truly
spiritual fellowship; and as such it will itself consist of
tender mercies and pities to bind up every wound. The
picture is thus complete.

2) What Paul now asks, not only as giving him
joy, but as filling the cup of it completely, is something
additional to v. 1, we may say the highest (or deepest)
part of the fellowship. It is expressed in a separate,
long sentence as the main part of his admonition in this
paragraph; hence the asyndeton; v. 5 is also introduced
without a connective. It is the *humility* which regards
others so highly as to serve their interests as fully as
one's own. The admonition crowns those stated in v. 1.

Fulfill my joy (aorist: make it completely full)
that (apposition to "joy") **you keep minding the
same thing as having the same love, joined in soul
minding this one thing, not one in accord with self-
seeking or with vainglory but with the lowly-mindedness considering one another as being above themselves, these each one watching out not for their own
things** (alone) **but also for the things of others, these
each one.**

It should be noted that minding "the *same* thing"
is an incomplete idea, this would have to be the *right*
thing. It should be noted, too, that minding τὸ ἕν (some
texts again have "the same thing"), "this one thing,"
still leaves unsaid what it is. What it is v. 3, 4 state,
first negatively: "not one in accord with self-seeking,"
etc., but the very contrary: "with lowly mind," etc.

The idea expressed is not only "thinking" the same thing, having the same thoughts or feelings and thoughts, but "minding" the same thing, attending to the same thing with the same feelings and thoughts. We see this when we note that the following belongs together and forms one idea: "minding the same thing as having the same love." Some think that the participle presents an advanced idea, but it forms an integral part of the one idea. That is why "same — same" is used. This is active minding, the minding of love, ἀγάπη, which is always bent on an intelligent purpose (see 1:9, and on the verb Matt. 6:44).

Again, "joined in soul (cf., 1:27: with one soul) minding this one thing," belongs together and should not be divided as it is in our versions. This is simply a restatement of the minding that is due to the same love. It thus emphasizes the matter yet also amplifies as Paul regularly does in his restatements, for "joint in soul" (σύμψυχοι, "joint-souled") is placed forward and carries the impact. It adds to "love" in this minding the same thing the fellowship of soul that binds together. "This one thing," however, still holds us in suspense, we wonder what it really is.

3) Now we are told what Paul means by the same, one, and identical thing which we are all to keep minding as having the same love, minding as "joint in soul." First, negatively: "not one (or: none) in accord with self-seeking (see 1:17) or in accord with vainglory." Paul does not want the Philippians to act like the self-seekers did who preached Christ in Rome as he has described. Paul uses the preposition (κατά) twice, for "self-seeking" refers to what the selfish are after and "vainglory" to what they get when they succeed, a lot of glory that is entirely κενός, "empty," hollow. Yes, this "self-seeking" is minding a certain thing, and the thing is "empty glory" when it is achieved. Thus to unmask it for Christians is to make them turn from

it; μηδέν, "nothing" of that for them, nothing that
accords with it (κατά), shall we say that smells of it?

"On the contrary (ἀλλά), with the lowly-mindedness
considering one another as being above themselves,
these each one (ἕκαστοι) watching out not for their own
things (alone) but also for the things of others —
these each one" (ἕκαστοι, emphatically repeated). The
thing to be noted is that by means of the use of the two
ἕκαστοι Paul states everything in the third person and
thus finely gives it an objective turn; but he still uses
participles as if he were continuing the participles of
v. 2 which refer to the second person in φρονῆτε. This is
another fine turn. The force and the skillfulness of
this twofold procedure have not been generally noted,
hence we find the emendation of the text, now by one
scribe, now by another, which we need not consider.
Ἕκαστοι was changed into the singular since we here
have the only two instances in the New Testament
where the plural of this word is used.

The article with ταπεινοφροσύνη = "with due lowly-
mindedness," it is the dative of means. Note that it
continues the idea of φρονεῖν and is placed in the emphatic position. This lowly-mindedness is active (like
"minding" in v. 2) : first, it considers the other as being
superior; secondly, it thus looks out for his interests
as much as it does for its own. When the Philippians
keep to "this thing," all of them to "this same thing,"
Paul's cup of joy will certainly be full to the brim.

M.-M. do not list this noun because it does not appear even in the Old Testament nor in secular Greek,
and in Josephus and in Epictetus is used only in the old
base sense of the adjective ταπεινός: "pussilanimity,"
which is a fault and not a virtue. The pagan and the
secular idea of manhood is self-assertiveness, imposing
one's will on others; when anyone stooped to others he
did so only under compulsion, hence his action was
ignominious. The Christian ethical idea of humility

could not be reached by the secular mind; it lacked the spiritual soil. But the New Testament has this noble word, and especially Paul states what humility or "lowly-mindedness" achieves. Read Trench, *Synonyms,* who also deals with πραότης, "meekness" (the two are combined in Eph. 4:2). Where the conviction of sin is absent, which bows us into the dust before God, spiritual lowly-mindedness in our attitude toward the brethren is impossible; but where this conviction exists the humility naturally becomes the result.

It is active, the means (here dative) for making us consider others above ourselves, ὑπερέχοντες, and thus the means for making us look out for the things of others as we look out for our own (σκοπεῖν τά τινος = to secure someone's advantage). Note the reciprocal pronoun ἀλλήλους: "one another." Each one is to consider each other one ὑπέρ, deserving first consideration. Note how astonishingly that works: as I consider you above, you likewise consider me above, and so all around. A marvelous community in which no one is looked down upon but everyone looked up to! The very need of the needy lifts them up to receive the greater consideration.

Paul is not asking the impossible or the untrue, namely that I am to think that every other Christian, just because he is a Christian, has more brains, more ability, more everything than I have. Nor does Paul ask that we merely "consider" one another above although we know that the facts are quite to the contrary, that a large number are far beneath us. "As being above themselves" (genitive after the comparative, R. calls it ablative) means as deserving first attention from us. Rom. 12:10 "In honor preferring one another." Each is to put every other brother first on the list to be considered, himself at the bottom of the list; each one is to have the list arranged in this order. The worldling reverses this: *he* comes first, everyone else comes last, perhaps does not come at all.

4) It is not necessary to punctuate with a semicolon or to supply a finite verb (untenable reading), a comma is sufficient, for this participle expounds the preceding by telling *how* we are to consider one another above our own selves, namely "by not looking out for the things of our own alone but also for the things of these others," the two ἕκαστοι emphasize that each one of us is to do this. In the world each one looks out for the things that are his, the things of others do not concern him. If he does look out for them, it is only because, if he does not, he himself will also lose. His motive is not above ἐριθεία (v. 3), "self-seeking" or selfishness. The Christian reverses this: he looks out for the things of others (Paul puts that first and thus justifies his ὑπέρ used in v. 3) and then looks out *"also"* for his own things (Paul puts this "also" second). Only "lowly-mindedness" can do such a thing, do it truly and sincerely.

Yet the thought is not that the Christian is after all to look out for himself alone, that if all his fellow Christians look out for *his things,* he will fare better than if he alone looked out for his own things. To be sure, everyone will fare better when, instead of disregarding each other's interests, all mutually help each other. But this result cannot possibly be attained if the motive that prompts those concerned is after all secretly insincere, selfishness that is only deeply hidden. That would blight the prosperity down to the very roots, it would simply not result.

Nothing is achieved in the kingdom except by genuine sincerity and unselfishness. That stands once for all. This whole matter is only the old principle of Jesus over again: he who loses his life shall gain it, and he who is out only to gain it, thereby has already lost it. So paradoxical, to the world so incredible, it is nonetheless the fact. Moreover, from v. 1 onward Paul is speaking of spiritual interests; "the

things of our own" and "the things of others" are
spiritual things, note v. 1. Paul means: "Look to the
spiritual interests of others, then also to your own.
Do this, all of you, each one." Now, if 1,000 thus look
out for me, it will be easy for me also to look out for
myself. This will also be true in the case of every
other one. No secret, insincere selfishness can possibly
play into this spiritual reciprocity. But look at Matt.
6:33 and see that when Paul is speaking of the spiritual interests, the material are by no means disregarded or left out. Paul does not dream of saying, "In
material things let each one look out for himself first!"
The Christian's "own things" cannot be thus divided
into two. Spiritual interests reach into the way in
which we deal with the material as Jesus shows in
Matt. 6:24-34. The material are cared for by truly
caring for the spiritual through the mutuality Paul
describes. The moment we see the spiritual interests
and how they control, the impossibility of even the least
lurking selfishness appears

All this is essential for understanding what follows,
namely the model Christ in his self-humiliation. An
inadequacy in understanding v. 1-4 is liable to react on
the understanding of v. 5-11.

*The Example of Christ: his Self-humiliation Fol-
lowed by his Exaltation*

5) This paragraph is a classic, a great *sedes doctrinae*. Meyer says that from v. 6 onward it is like an
epic in its calmly exalted objectivity, even the epic
circumstantiality not being omitted. The dignity and
the rhythm in the parallel clauses are impressive. The
style matches the grandness of the matter. This is
doctrine. Although it is used in support of hortation
(v. 5), Paul presents pure doctrine, which means a
statement of the facts, the realities, which the hearts
of his readers are to receive. The exegete's supreme
task is to note all that Paul thus states. If he is called

dogmatical when he does so, this is praise, not blame.
All that Paul says of Christ is true as it stands apart
from Paul's hortatory interest. Note it well!

This keep minding in your case, (the thing)
which (appears) **also in Christ Jesus' case — he
who, existing in God's form, did not consider his
being equal with God a thing of snatching but emptied himself in that he took slave's form when he
got to be in men's likeness and, in fashion found as
man, lowered himself in that he got to be obedient
as far as death, yea, death of a cross.**

The reading "keep minding" (plural active) is
overwhelmingly attested over against the passive singular: "Let this be minded among you," which then
makes it necessary that another passive be supplied
in the relative clause: "which (was minded, aorist or
imperfect passive) in Christ." Textually so inferior,
this reading is unacceptable also as far as its thought
is concerned; for no one has ever been able to answer
who minded this thing in Christ if not he himself. The
idea is incongruous. This reading also compels us to
make the two ἐν phrases diverse when they are alike.
Yet some prefer this inferior text although they do not
solve the difficulties created by this reading. The plea
is that, unless this is the original reading, it cannot
be explained how it came into existence. Yet many
variants are summarily rejected without our being able
to guess as to how they came to be inserted into the
text.

"This thing be minding" means "the one thing"
Paul tells us to mind in v. 2 and then describes in v.
3, 4, the key word of which is "lowly-mindedness."
Paul now shows us this thing "also in Christ Jesus"
and thus presents it as it was in Christ who is our
model or example. Many find it difficult to render the
two ἐν phrases in the same way although they perceive
that they are intended to be rendered in the same way.

Apply R. 587, ἐν in the sense of "in the person of" or "in the case of": "be minding *in your case*" the thing which appears also *"in Christ Jesus' case."* Note that the balance and the emphasis are not on the verb, for then Paul would at least have a verb in the relative clause. The emphasis is on "this thing — which" and on "in your case — in Christ Jesus' case." What we supply in the relative clause in order to obtain a smooth English translation, whether "is," "was," "appears," makes little difference, for we can in no way stress what is absent in the Greek.

6) Instead of continuing with the neuter: "This thing . . . which . . . (namely) that," etc., with an appositional ὅτι clause that states *what* this thing in Christ Jesus was, Paul continues with a personal relative pronoun: ὅς, "who," etc. We should catch the dramatic, demonstrative effect, for this is not a mere common relative "who," it is like the relatives found in Rom. 2:29b; 3:8, 30, and others that Paul has used: *"He,* he the One who," something great and weighty then following about this person "who." Here it is Christ Jesus, *he* is the One who is supreme in the thing Paul is urging upon his readers. Paul fixes our eyes upon *this person as a person.*

Who is this person to whom Paul refers: is it the Logos ἔνσαρκος or the Logos ἄσαρκος? That question sounds strange, for Paul does not write "logos" but the regular name "Christ Jesus, he who." This is like so many names we use when indicating the office by the first term: King David — General Washington — Doctor Luther, etc. The question raised seems innocent until we see at what it aims. This ὅς is the subject of the three verbs following: "he who did not consider but did empty himself and did lower himself." Some predicate these acts of the logos *before* his incarnation and state that he emptied *his* deity of some or of all of his *attributes of deity* or even of his *deity ego itself.*

The aim is to get a Jesus whose incarnation or whose humiliation consists in this that he gave up *some* of his attributes of deity or *all* of them or even his deity ego itself. The aim is to get a Jesus who is only *partly* divine or only *merely human,* i. e., who has only *one* nature (*Einnaturenlehre,* the one nature doctrine of the Germans). Those who thus drop some of the attributes of deity are the semi-Kenoticists; those who drop all or who drop the deity ego itself are the pan-Kenoticists.

The question regarding ὅς, as to whether this is the logos *ensarkos* or the logos *asarkos,* is by no means innocent. The issue it raises is really the old Arian one in a new form: What think ye of Christ? Is he really God's Son or only partly God's Son or only a man and not even partly God's Son? Against these Kenoticists stand the entire Scripture and the true church of all ages. This is not a squabble among theologians, this is an issue involving the life or the death of every Christian's faith in his Savior. Centered on the humiliation of Christ, it automatically involves the whole saving work of Jesus wrought out here on earth and equally his exaltation. To state it in brief, the whole Christian faith is the real issue.

All grades of Kenoticism are answered by the fact of the *immutability* of God, of the one essence which is identical in the Father, in the Son, and in the Holy Spirit. All Kenoticism which subtracts attributes from God reduces deity to the nature of creatures. From a creature an attribute may be withdrawn and still leave the creature. To withdraw even one attribute from God is to destroy God. The God who, for instance, is no longer omnipotent, is no longer God. The revelation of Scripture regarding God is the truth that his every attribute is his essence or being itself which reveals one side of that being. All that we call attributes of God is not a plurality, is not divisible in its reality, but is the one unity — God. But since our minds are finite and cannot possibly grasp this infinity, our thinking is divided, looks at God now from one side, then from another, and again from still another and so adds all sides together but does not really have all of them at that. So we list God's "attributes," and in their revelation of God the Scriptures condescend to this poor, finite inability of ours and at one time reveal his omnipotence, at another his omniscience, again his righteousness, then his grace, etc., but never so that a single one of these could even in thought be lacking in God. Moreover, what we thus in our helplessness term an "attribute of God" is in every case again incomprehensible to our finite minds. No human mind has ever adequately visualized say God's omnipotence or his omniscience. We see only darkly as in a mirror, glimpse only a little of the infinite reality in God.

This is not a dogmatical excursus as some may think. For to think with the mildest Kenoticist that the logos, whether before, in, or after his incarnation, emptied himself of even one of his attributes of deity, means that by his own act the immutable logos ceased to be. The difference between the various types of Kenoticists is in reality unimportant. To empty out *one* attribute destroys the logos as completely as to empty out *all* his attributes, destroys him as completely as to empty out the logos *ego* himself. A Jesus who is devoid of one attribute of deity is no more the Son of God than a Jesus who had only one nature while he lived on earth, was not at all the logos, was only Joseph's natural son.

Yet, although so much is involved, the fact remains that the Scriptures freely name the person, at one time only as a person, at another according to his office, at another according to one, again according to the other and even according to both natures and, no matter how it is named, predicate of this person something that is native to the one or to the other or also to both of his natures. Knowing this, we might pass on without further concern when Paul writes "Christ Jesus" (office, person), for this name certainly befits all that is predicated of him. The issue is raised by the Kenoticists and by those related to them. They empty out more or less of the logos, of his divine nature, plus also every divine gift bestowed on Christ's human nature. Their first statement is that here "Christ Jesus" = the logos *before* he became flesh. The confessional church emphatically rejects this demand because this demand would contradict all that Paul here says of "Jesus Christ."

The subject of *all* that follows in v. 6-11 is "Jesus Christ." This whole section is one connected sentence. This is Paul's great passage on the humiliation and the exaltation of Christ, on these two states. Both deal with Christ's *human* nature, here and everywhere in Scripture where either the humiliation or the exaltation or both are mentioned. The *divine* nature can undergo neither humiliation nor exaltation, it is immutable.

The participial phrase is to be construed with the relative: "*he* who existing in God's form." It simply describes "Jesus Christ." Luther made the phrase concessive: *obwohl*, "although" existing in God's form; but this relation is not indicated. The temporal idea: "while existing," etc., is untenable because Jesus Christ never existed in any other form even as God cannot exist in any other.

It is often said that ὑπάρχειν, "to exist," and εἶναι, "to be," are quite the same; they are, compare Luke 16:23 with the former and II Cor. 8:9 (a parallel to our passage) with the latter. Yet here, where Paul uses the two side by side, a distinction is implied, the one indicated by the predicative term: existing "in

God's form" — to be "equal to God." In the one instance we have *existence* as such, in the other we have
being in a condition which comports with that existence. Even in the English where "to be" and "to exist"
are as much alike as they are in the Greek we should
here use them distinctively quite as Paul does.

The matter not to be overlooked is the fact that
Paul makes a double predication: "form" is as much
a predication of "God" as the whole phrase is a predication of "Christ Jesus." "God" has a form, and "Jesus
Christ" exists in this form of God. The word "form"
thus cannot mean anything visible (*Lichtleib*), for
God is a spirit. Μορφή = the form native to the essence
(compare Trench). In Mark 16:12 the idea of vis-
ibility is suggested only by the verb ἐφανερώθη. Luther's
Gestalt comes no closer than our "form." It is misleading to say that Paul chooses μορφὴ Θεοῦ because of
the following μορφὴ δούλου, misleading because it would
have us define the former according to the latter, the
"form" predicated of the Creator according to that
predicated of the creature. "Form" applies to both,
but to each according to what each is, the one is "God,"
the other is "a slave."

The German *Art* comes closest to rendering the
idea. Luther uses this in his Christmas hymn: *Der
Sohn des Vaters, Gott von Art.* The point is the
quality and thus the type of existence, one being predicated of God, the other of a slave: *die spezifische
Eigenart* of God — of a slave. However, since God is
immutable, *his* specific form of existing, his *Art* or
Eigenart of existence, is equally immutable whereas
a slave may lose his quality or form of slave-being and
exchange it for another form, and this other may also
be exchanged for a third.

The idea of Zahn and of C.-K. 737 that Jesus Christ
"exchanged" the form of God for the form of a slave
is thus untenable. Paul does not suggest an exchange.

As God cannot lose or alter the form of his existence, so Christ Jesus cannot. More than this. When Paul says "Christ Jesus" he refers to both natures of Christ; "existing in God's form" includes both. For to say that only the logos exists in God's form is saying no more than that God exists in the form that is essential to his essence or being. This would be pointless here, where there is no discussion about a possible difference between the logos, the Son of God, and God, either God as such or God the Father. But the fact that the God-man Christ Jesus exists in God's form, as "Jesus" born of the Virgin, as "Christ" anointed to be our Redeemer, that is, indeed, the basis of all that follows, without which all the rest becomes unintelligible.

The matter is perfectly plain: in the incarnation the human nature which Christ Jesus assumed was made partaker of all that belonged to the divine nature of Christ. The dogmaticians term this the *genus majestaticum* of the *communicatio idiomatum* as taught throughout Scripture. By this communication and by a participation in virtue of the *unio personalis* of the two natures the human nature existed and exists "in God's form." Only those who cancel this personal union of Christ's natures can say that only the logos in Christ has existence "in God's form" and not the human nature he assumed. The logos has this existence "in God's form" as God, and because he is very God was this from all eternity; his human nature has it by gift and communication since its assumption. Thus Paul writes of "Christ Jesus": "existing in God's form."

Existing in God's form as indicated, Christ Jesus "did not consider his being equal with God a thing of snatching" as he might have done if he had considered only himself. The predicate accusative is placed forward for the sake of emphasis: "a thing of snatching"; thus also, by being placed last, the direct object receives an emphasis: this thing "to be equal with God," ἴσα the neuter plural in the adverbial sense (R. 407). How Christ considered it his great act of emptying and lowering himself shows. "To be equal with God" adds the thought of condition to that of existence; for, he who exists in God's form exists and thus is (εἶναι) in equality with God, i. e., equal in power, authority, majesty, etc.

Paul's expression is terse when he says that Christ Jesus did not consider being in equality with God a ἁρπαγμός. The few examples of the earlier use of this word show that it has the active sense as also the suffix -μος seems to require. So some state that Paul here uses it in the active sense: "did not consider it a *robbing* (A. V.: robbery) this thing of being equal with God." But one cannot consider a *condition* an *action,* and those who do so substitute the *result* of the action when they offer their explanations: "did not consider it something robbed." The fact also is that quite a few nouns in -μος are used to denote a result just like the nouns in -μα.

The passive-result idea is generally accepted but with a difference, some preferring *res rapienda,* "a thing to be robbed" (R. V. margin: "a thing to be grasped"), others *res rapta,* "a thing robbed," "a prize" (R. V.). The former meaning is questionable even linguistically. If Paul meant that equality with God was not considered as a thing to be robbed or snatched at, then we expect him to say that Christ wanted to get this equality in some other way, something Paul does not say. Then, too, if the meaning is *res rapienda,* equality with God is conceived as something that Christ had yet to attain, the idea being that he won it by his humble obedience to God and obtained it in his final exaltation, which is about the opposite of what Paul says and all Scripture attests.

We prefer *res rapta, Gegenstand des Raubens,*
viewed concretely: something involving an ἁρπάζειν,
something that is characterized thereby (C.-K. 170).
But in what way did Christ Jesus refuse to consider his
being equal with God "a thing of snatching or robbing"? The view that his being equal to God was *ein
Fremdes,* something foreign, something that really did
not belong to him, that he had to snatch at, is excluded
by the fact of his existing in the form of God. One
who exists in this form or *Eigenart* is *eo ipso* equal
with God, already has the condition involved in this
form of existence. Here again we should stress the
fact that this condition of equality with God, like the
existence in the form of God, belonged to *both natures*
of Christ Jesus, both the existence and the condition
being communicated to the human nature by the divine
which had them from eternity.

Now it becomes plain what ἁρπαγμός means: a thing
for self-glorification. Christ did not consider that the
condition resulting from his form of existence which
involved also his human nature allowed to him only an
ἁρπάζειν, *ein Ausbeuteverfahren,* i. e., *ein Prunken,* a
dazzling display of his equality with God in both of
his natures, regarding this equality as "a prize" (R.
V.), a booty ever to be exhibited. If such had been
the consideration on which Christ Jesus acted when he
assumed his human nature, it would have been useless
for him to assume it, he could never have carried out
the work of redemption for which he assumed his
human nature. His great mission and office and the
consideration of his equality with God as a prize for
display could not be combined. The consideration on
which Christ did act his further acts themselves show
most clearly.

7) "He did not consider, etc., on the contrary
(ἀλλά), himself he emptied in that he took slave's form

when he got to be in men's likeness." This should be read together as a unit thought. It is typically Pauline not to follow "he did not consider" with "but he did consider" but rather at once to state the great acts which reveal best of all what Christ did actually consider. He considered the mission and the work for which he assumed human nature, he considered not "himself" but us: "himself he emptied" in order to fill us that we might be rich (II Cor. 8:9), that we might be made the righteousness of God in him (II Cor. 5:21). This explains the emphasis (the forward position) and thus the implied contrast in ἑαυτόν (the reflexive not being thus placed forward in v. 8).

Κενός = empty, devoid of contents; the verb, "to empty" so that the contents are gone. The self was not, of course, emptied out of the self so that no self was left. "He emptied himself" is an incomplete thought which leaves us with a question. Paul completes the thought, yet not by a statement regarding anything that Christ emptied out of himself but by a participle that defines the act of emptying himself: "in that he took slave's form," and at once adds when all these acts took place: "when he got to be in men's likeness," when he became incarnate. All the aorists in v. 6, 7 are punctiliar, historical, expressing simultaneous action; all are predicated of the God-man "Christ Jesus."

Paul does not say that Christ emptied himself of "the form of God," either as to his divine nature or as to his human nature which at the time of his incarnation was made partaker of this form. He does not say that Christ "exchanged" the form of God for the form of a slave as Zahn and C.-K. 737 state. Because "God's form" and "slave's form" are such vast opposites the statement is so tremendous that one who exists in the former "took" the latter. Paul simply states the fact;

he does not philosophize about its possibility. Facts are facts whether Paul or we are able to understand their possibility or not.

Again, Paul does not say that Christ emptied himself of his equality with God, either as to his divine nature or as to his human nature, which at the time of his incarnation was made partaker of this equality. He does not say that Christ "exchanged" his equality with God for equality with a slave. Here again no exchange is predicated. "God's form" and existence in God's form and the consequent condition of equality with God are immutable also regarding Christ's human nature when they are communicated and bestowed upon this nature. No mutable slave's form, existence, or condition could take their place.

"When he got to be in men's likeness" = when he became incarnate, became man. This recalls the ὁμοίωμα used in Rom. 8:3: "in likeness of sinful flesh" (cf., Rom. 1:23; James 3:9, "according to God's likeness"). "Likeness" is added because, when the incarnation took place, Christ did not cease to be God. Docetism stresses the meaning of the word so that only a sham human nature is left to Christ. So the Kenoticists stress the sense of ἐκένωσε until little or nothing of deity is left. Their very name is derived from this word. F. Pieper, *Dogmatik* II, 321, somehow thinks that Paul says nothing at all about the incarnation, which is surely an oversight.

The clause is temporal. Paul clearly distinguishes "got to be in men's likeness" (the incarnation) from "took slave's form" (the humiliation). Both are simultaneous, but the two are not identical. Christ is still incarnate but no longer in the form of a slave which he took for his redemptive work. The slave's form he dropped but not his human nature to which God gave a glorified form. "He got to be in men's likeness" does not define "he took slave's form," nor does the former state purpose: "he took slave's form in order to appear in human likeness." These ideas of Ewald are reversed. "Slave" does not define "men," nor must a man become a "slave" to prove himself a "man."

When Christ Jesus became man he took slave's form. The exinanition or humiliation pertained to his human nature alone and not to the divine. As man and not as God Christ humbled himself. He took slave's form in order to fulfill his office on earth. His full deity remained (existence, form, condition of equality with God) ; all that his deity bestowed upon his human nature likewise remained a possession of this nature (κτῆσις, as it has been called).

What, then, is this "slave's form," and why is it called a "slave's"? We have already received the answer in ἁρπαγμός in v. 6. Christ laid aside, emptied himself of the constant and plenary *use* (χρῆσις) of all that had been bestowed upon his human nature. If he had not done this he could not have wrought out our salvation. If he had come to earth only as his three disciples saw him on the Mount of Transfiguration, his redemptive obedience in his life, suffering, death, and resurrection, as the Gospels record it, would have been impossible.

Luther aptly calls this "slave's form" *die dienstliche Gestalt Christi.* Pieper (II, 324) writes well: "To be sure, this is a *remarkable* outfitting and form. The earthly warrior, who determines to gain the victory, girds his sword to his side and strives to be high. Christ's equipment for the victory to be gained develops in the opposite direction. Christ ἑαυτὸν ἐκένωσεν, divested, emptied himself to naught, became lowly, altogether lowly. But this strange equipment accords with the nature of the work to be done. It was not to conquer cities. It was also not by a divine word of power to hurl him into hell who by God's permission (*Verhaengnis*) held men captive. It was, in the execution of the *divine* redemption method, by substitution, through being obedient, suffering, and dying, to pay the sin guilt of men. That, to be sure, could not be effected by *laying aside his deity* partly or completely. He could not do without his deity in his state of humiliation. He had to attach the full weight of his deity to his being obedient and to his suffering and dying. Even in the midst of his death he had to be the mighty God in order by his death to conquer death, to raise up again the temple of his body (John 2:19, 21), to take up his life again (John 10:18)." Again (325): "This conquering 'second Adam' is not only man but the Lord from heaven (I Cor. 15:47). He *is* God and therefore also according to his human nature in God's form."

8) "And, in fashion found as man, lowered himself," etc., continues the construction after the relative: ὅς . . . ἐκένωσε . . . καὶ ἐταπείνωσεν. We would not disturb the rhythm and the balance of the clauses as well as the smooth progress of the thought by placing a period after λαβών in v. 7 or after ἄνθρωπος. After saying that Christ Jesus took slave's form when he got to be in men's likeness, explicative καί sets forth what this means. For the statement about taking slave's form at the time of the incarnation is general, we need the particulars about this slave's form. Paul states them, not abstractly, but in the clearest, most concrete way; he states the facts. First, the subsidiary fact which is marked as subordinate by the participle: "in fashion found as man," as real, true man, "found" so by all other men who came into contact with him. This advances the idea of the "likeness of men" by means of the dative of relation which is placed emphatically forward: "as regards fashion (σχῆμα, *habitus*)" Christ Jesus, who was truly man, was so found by men. We have the full record of this in the Gospels. Born of a human mother, he developed from a babe to manhood,

ate, drank, slept, labored, etc., was a true human being. Christ even assumed the weaknesses of man although only those that were serviceable for his office (not disease, deformity, mental deficiency, etc.), yet he remained without sin (John 8:46; Heb. 7:26; 4:15).

All this is only preliminary to the "slave's form," is not yet itself completely this form. The astounding thing, however, is already the fact that he who exists in God's form and thus in the condition of equality with God also as to his human nature to which these are communicated, that he should take this form, this likeness, this fashion. Human reason would declare it impossible, in fact, has done so; but the fact remains.

Men have attempted to make this fact at least somewhat reasonable, but all their attempts leave them with the same seeming impossibility. Kenoticism cannot reconcile itself to the idea of the development of the child Jesus. How could he develop bodily, mentally, with normal human consciousness if his person was the logos? Therefore the Kenoticists cancel the logos in Christ, or cancel some of the divine attributes, and Calvinism, like Nestorianism, cancels any communication of such attributes to the human nature of Christ. Only the outright denial of the incarnation (Modernism) makes Jesus reasonable: it leaves him a mere man. All who do not reason away as much as this are still left with the insoluble mystery that God became man; their reasoning tries the impossible, namely to empty (κενόω) something out of God (the logos). Paul sees and presents the fact as it is; and we — we want and accept no less.

He who was found as man "lowered (humbled, humiliated) himself in that he got to be obedient up to death, yea, death of a cross." Again read this together as a unit thought. Here we have the full explication of "himself he emptied in that he took slave's form." This is the picture of *Christ, the slave,* drawn completely in a few strokes. The old secular idea of ταπεινόω, "to abase," is still present: Christ "abased himself." The New Testament ennobling of the word lies entirely in the moral use to which this word is put: the God-man's self-abasement *for our salvation.*

Paul does not use the reflexive middle but the active with the reflexive pronoun, which is stronger. But now, by placing the pronoun ἑαυτόν after the verb, it thus being without special emphasis, no contrast attaches to "himself," only this is said that Christ lowered his own person. He did this himself to himself. Thus all was voluntary, prompted by his own infinite love.

This lowering was "in that he got to be obedient" down to a point so extreme that it goes even far beyond the miracle of his assuming our human nature. Here we see the connotation of the word δοῦλος, "slave"; it is in the adjective "obedient." Yet the idea of a forced obedience is removed already by "he lowered himself," this is voluntary obedience. Isaiah pictures the Messiah as the great *'Ebed Yahweh,* pictures also his death as that of a slaughtered sheep; but the LXX carefully rendered this Hebrew word, not with *doulos,* but with παῖς, "servant," which the apostles retain when quoting the prophet. May we say that *God* did not make Christ a slave but that Christ *himself* did that? A slave's mark is obedience to the extent of not following his own will. This strong word is here used in paradoxical fashion: by his own will Christ gave up his will by the acme of voluntariness in descending to the cross.

"Slave" matches "cross," for when slaves were executed they were crucified. For this reason "slave" is here used and not "servant." Dramatically Paul introduces the cross. He does not write simply "as far as the cross" but "as far as death, yea, death of a cross," δέ emphasizing the latter. Paul makes us linger at this

death, and with the characterizing genitive "of a cross"
this one final word flashes upon us the full significance
of this death. Yes, it was "death — death," no less
than that: the God-man *died*. Incomprehensible that
he who was God died! Yet not incomprehensible that
he who possessed also human nature and all the fashion
of it should use it for dying. It is his being the God-
man that, nevertheless, leaves us astounded because of
his dying.

But this is only the least of it. The climax is in the
word "cross," *Kreuzestod,* death of one *accursed* of God
(Deut. 21:23; Gal. 3:13; also II Cor. 5:21). To speak
only of the lowest point of the humiliation, to speak
only of the shame of the cross, which is entirely true, is
to remain on the surface. This is "the offense" of the
cross, its *skandalon* (deathtrap), Gal. 5:11, especially
to the Jews, I Cor. 1:23. It is not the suffering and
dying Messiah that made him a deathtrap to unbelief
but his dying as one *accursed of God.* How can one
who ended as one accursed be the Savior of the sinners
who are accursed? How can *he* be God's Son? The
Scriptural answer to this apparently extreme impossibility is equally tremendous, absolutely complete:
Christ was *our substitute,* he bore *our* curse and its
penalty (Isa. 53:4, etc.).

Here we have the climax of it all which leaves un-
sanctified reasoning behind. He who was the Son of
God, equal with God, he who communicated his divine
attributes to his human nature so that all the Godhead
dwelt in him bodily (Col. 2:9), he died, died hanging
on a post of wood (σταυρός), died as one accursed, hanging on wood, ξύλον, the mark of being accursed. Of his
own volition. Hence this is the most noble act the
world has ever seen; hence it is full of infinite merit,
all this is to be bestowed upon us. This is the mystery
of the gospel, into which even the angels of God delight
to look. This is the historic gospel fact which the

gospel attests and publishes in all the world. This is
the fact that saves to the uttermost all those who embrace it in confidence and rest their very soul upon it.

Those who have only the human Christ on the cross
destroy the efficacy of the cross. To say that this is
more "thinkable" is erroneous; to divide the person in
this or in any other way is unthinkable; to leave the
person undivided is the only thing that is thinkable
because it is the only thing possible and the one thing
the Scriptures testify to as being the fact. Luther has
well said: "If I permit myself to be persuaded that
only the human nature has suffered for me, then Christ
is to me a poor Savior, then he himself, indeed, needs a
Savior." C. *Tr.* 1029, 40.

Throughout his life Christ revealed that his human
nature was in possession of the divine attributes communicated to it. John (1:14) testifies about him who
became flesh and dwelt among his apostles: "We beheld his glory, glory as of the Only-begotten, (as) from
the Father." Although all this glory dwelt in his human nature, he used it only to the degree that was
needed for his office. It was covered (κρυπτός), yet at
Cana "he manifested forth his glory," and his disciples
believed on him. This was also true at the time of the
Transfiguration, yet he commanded the three witnesses
to remain silent regarding the glory they had seen. It
was finally also manifested in the *passio magna* when
at the garden gate he delivered himself into the death
of the curse, when one word strikes down the more
than 200 captors, and twelve legions of angels are at
his command. The efficacy of his vicarious death in
becoming a curse to remove our curse lies in his Godhead, not as constituting the logos, but as dwelling in
his human nature bodily (Col. 2:9).

In further exposition study C. *Tr.* 1015, etc., and
the excellent presentation by F. Pieper, *Dogmatik* II,

311, etc, with its masterly refutation of all forms of deviation from Scripture.

9) The mighty basis on which Paul's admonition (v. 1-5) rests includes both Christ's humiliation and his exaltation even as these two naturally go together. The Greek continues the sentence no matter how we may print the English: **wherefore also God highly exalted him and granted to him the Name above every name, that in the Name of Jesus every knee should bow of** (such as are) **in heaven and** (such as are) **on earth and** (such as are) **under the earth, and that every tongue should confess that Lord** (is) **Jesus Christ for glory to God Father.**

Only the human nature could experience the exaltation as it alone could undergo the humiliation. The logos was not withdrawn and then restored. No attributes were emptied out from either the divine or the human nature and were then replaced. The plenary use of the divine attributes communicated to the human nature at the time of the incarnation constituted the exaltation. The "slave's form," in which the human nature employed the divine attributes only for a restricted and mostly a veiled use, ceased when this restriction was lifted. The exaltation thus corresponds to the humiliation. Because it deals with the human nature, we now read that, whereas Christ lowered *himself*, not he but *God* exalted him.

Διό, "wherefore," introduces the consequence. Christ's own word spoken in Matt. 23:12 was gloriously fulfilled in himself. The idea in ὑπερύψωσε is not comparative but superlative: "God supremely exalted him." How this was done is at once explained by the addition: "and granted to him the Name, the one above every name." The two actions "supremely exalted him — granted to him" constitute one act, the two sides of which are given equal importance by the two finite

verbs. In v. 7 the second is a participle: "in that he
took"; in v. 8 likewise: "in that he got to be obedient,"
hence it is subordinate. Observe the difference. Paul
used two finite verbs to designate Christ's action: "he
emptied himself — he lowered himself"; so he now
also uses two of the same importance to describe what
God did in consequence.

Augustine and others find merit indicated in the
connective: Christ's self-humiliation merited his exaltation. Some find the merit especially in the voluntariness of the humiliation and the obedience. We do
speak of Christ's "merits" and that he bestows them
on us although the word itself is not found in the Scriptures. Here Paul moves on a higher plane than that of
acknowledged merit. Even on a higher plane than that
indicated in John 17:5 where Jesus prays to be glorified
in his human nature with the glory he had in his divine
nature before the world was. To be sure, he received
this glory in his human nature in the resurrection, the
ascension, and the *sessio* at God's right hand. The
"slave's form" fell from him, the purpose for which he
had assumed it having been accomplished. But the
thought is not that now his human nature received
"God's form" and the condition of equality with God as
some think. We have seen that Christ's human nature,
by virtue of the *unio personalis,* partook of these already in the incarnation when the *unitio* of his two natures occurred. The only change the exaltation made
on this score was the fact that now, after the slave's
form had been dropped, the human nature ceased the
limited use of its communicated divine attributes
which was required for the work of redeeming us and
entered upon the plenary, unlimited use of these attributes consequent upon redemption in the full royal
work of Jesus. It is of this that John 17:5 speaks, see
the author's exposition which treats the errors of Kenoticism regarding Christ's exaltation.

Paul goes farther than merit and plenary use of the communicated attributes when he says, "Granted to him the Name, the one above every name." We have Paul's own exposition in Eph. 1:9, 10 and especially 1:20-24, see the author's interpretation. This humiliation and this exaltation were entirely God's own plan. God sent Christ on his redemptive mission even as in John's Gospel Christ keeps calling him "my Sender," ὁ πέμψας με. Thus, when this mission of redemption was completed down to the curse of the cross, God crowned it by exalting Christ for the fullest fruition of his redemptive mission. Emptying and lowering himself as man, in his human nature, were not something "granted" to him but something voluntarily done by Christ himself; but crowning all this for its full fruition according to the eternal plan of God was something God could and did do: he granted to Christ the Name, etc. The second article by which the phrase is added: "the one above every name," makes this an appositional climax (R. 776).

There is considerable confusion regarding this "Name," especially since the phrase "in the Name of Jesus" follows. Some think of this Name as being higher than "God's form" and equality with God as though God could grant something that is above himself. This ʼONOMA is soteriological. As such it transcends every name "named in this eon or in the one to come" (Eph. 1:21).

We repeat what we have said in so many other places: "name" = revelation, that by which God and Christ alone can be known, make themselves known, that by which we apprehend them, enter into communion with them.

The very idea of "Name" is soteriological. One may think of "title" but only in the sense thus indicated. In Eph. 1:21 and here the multitude of other names is placed beneath this Name. In Eph. 1:21 the

exaltation at God's right hand lifts him far above every
name no matter in which eon it occurs. All these titles
reveal their bearers as what they are, each is a revelation as we have said. Christ's is supreme because he
is supreme.

Those are not wrong who say that this Name above
every name = "Jesus" or "Lord" (v. 11) or "Jesus
Christ as Lord." The statement that "Jesus" was the
name given to him in infancy, and that "Lord" was
accorded to him by his disciples on earth gives evidence
that "the Name" is not adequately understood. Those
who define it as "Jesus," etc., generally fail to make
their definition include enough, especially the main
point. These individual terms "Jesus," etc., are only
the peaks of the revelation which shines forth. When
the sun falls on a mountain peak that towers to heaven,
we know that the whole mountain carries that peak
even as the sun presently illumines it all. So by his
granting God let the glorious light reveal him who once
lowered himself to the cross and its accursedness. The
term "Jesus" is here no longer a name like Peter, Caia-
phas, Pontius Pilate; it now embodies the whole blessed, glorious revelation of the Savior. The name "Lord"
— and any other individual designation — does identically the same thing.

We said this Name is soteriological. But not in the
narrow sense but in the completest possible sense as
stated in Eph. 1:10; 1:22. This Name and revelation
saves sinners for the glory of God, saves them through
the redemption accomplished by the Bearer by means
of his human nature and its humiliation; but it does
this saving because it forever crushes all opposing,
hostile forces. See Mark 16:16 as far as men are concerned and Col. 2:15 as far as the devils are concerned.
These two activities involve each other, the saving
could not be accomplished without this crushing. Both
shine forth in the Name, in it as the one Name above

every other.   All other names reveal that their owners
either look up with adoration to the Bearer of this
Name with its revelation of who and what he is or
that they are compelled to look up to his revealing
Name in consternation, having fought this revelation
and him whom it reveals.

10)   This is the purpose for which God gave this
Name to Christ when he crowned his redemptive work:
"in order that in the Name of Jesus every knee should
bow of (such as are) in heaven and (such as are) on
earth," etc.   Both the bowing of the knee and the con-
fessing of the tongue are concrete expressions.   It is
pointless to argue that only beings that have bodily
knees and tongues can be referred to.   The anarthrous
genitives are qualitative: "heavenly ones, earthly ones,
subterranean ones," not neuters: "things" (our versions), but masculines: persons.   The first are all the
blessed angels and the saints in heaven; the second are
all the men on earth; the third are all the demons and
the damned in hell.   The three groups include all created personal beings.   All shall bow in submission and
make this acknowledgment or confession with either
joy and bliss or dismay.

This interpretation is challenged.   Angels and demons are excluded.   Who cares about the demons?   The
trouble is that the "heavenly ones" cannot be restricted
to the saints in glory.   The angels who minister to
those who are heirs of salvation (Heb. 1:14), who have
been associated in this ministry with the Redeemer (in
connection with the annunciation to Mary, at the time
of Christ's birth, in Gethsemane, in the tomb, to mention only this much), surely glory in the Name and
revelation of its Bearer.   We think that Paul includes
them.   Then the third term includes the demons.

It is argued that wicked men and thus still more
demons cannot be referred to because to bend the knee
and to confess with the tongue are actions which beings

like this refuse to perform. On this supposition "earthly ones" are thought to be believers who are still on
earth, and "underearthly ones" those who are in Purgatory in the process of being purged for entrance into
heaven, or souls in the *Totenreich,* namely in its upper
compartment.

Purgatory and this *Totenreich* ("realm of the
dead") are fictions. While the Catholics place many
souls into their Purgatory, they at least leave many
others in heaven. But what about this modern Protes-
tant imitation of Purgatory, this intermediate place
which is neither heaven nor hell, which is referred to
by *sheol* in the Old Testament and by "hades" in the
New? If all souls go there at death, the wicked, like
Dives, into the lower part amid flames, the godly, like
Abraham and Lazarus, into the upper part, we still
have godly and wicked in this curious place just as we
have the two classes of the "earthly ones." About the
only ones that would be left for heaven would be Elijah and Enoch. When we are told that at the time of
his resurrection Christ took the godly from this *Totenreich* to heaven, that, indeed, fills heaven with the Old
Testament saints. But does this imply that, after releasing these Old Testament saintly souls from the
Totenreich, he again filled it with New Testament souls
of believers? If *all* godly souls are still in the *Totenreich,* heaven is empty of souls; if only *some* godly
souls are in the *Totenreich* and the rest in heaven, why
this difference? See further Luke 16:22, 23.

11) "Every knee and "every tongue" plainly refer
to all created persons. The two verbs apply to all of
them and are chosen to fit all of them. The thought is
not that the good shall voluntarily bend the knee and
confess, and that the bad shall do so against their will.
The latter will act voluntarily enough. Remember that
"the Name" means the revelation. When that name
and revelation shines forth in all its infinite glory, not

even a demon in hell will be able to deny the Lordship
of the God-man Jesus Christ. It is unwarranted to say
that in Eph. 6:12 Paul does not place the demons in
hell among the "underearthly ones" but in a supermundane sphere. See the exposition of this passage.
Hell was prepared for the devil and his angels (Matt.
25:41). Is hell ever empty of all demons? Even if one
should venture to say "yes," all of them will be there soon
enough; it is hard to separate the hellish ones from hell.

The aorist subjunctive "should bow" has a future
sense as all subjunctives have. The texts vary between
the aorist subjunctive "should confess" or acknowledge
and the future indicative "shall confess." This variation in the second verb after ἵνα is frequently found, even
the future indicative occurs. It makes no difference
which reading we adopt, both verbs have the same construction, the second does not begin a new sentence.

The question is asked as to *when* every knee shall
bow, every tongue confess. At the Parousia, at the
final Judgment. Heaven now rings with the Name, Ps.
24:7-10; Heb. 1:6; I Pet. 3:22. Earth does so faintly
in the confession of the saints. On that day the universe of angelic beings and men shall stand before the
throne of Christ. All his majesty and his power, all his
grace, his righteousness, and his justice ("the Name")
will be revealed with absolute finality. Then *no* knee
will remain unbowed, *no* tongue without acknowledgment.

While we think especially of the Parousia we do not
exclude other effects of the Name. Among these we
may include that of Christ's descent into hell, namely
its effect on the demons and on the damned, Col. 2:15,
the former; I Pet. 3:18-20, the latter. With great exactness Paul writes "in the Name of *Jesus*" and again
that the confession will be that "Jesus Christ" is Lord.
This is he who hung on the cross as one accursed, he
whom they mocked and spit upon, in a word, he who in

his human nature had slave's form and in that nature
descended to this depth. In that nature, by God's own
grant, this "Jesus" now has this Name, this "Jesus
Christ" is Lord; all the universe will not only see it
but see it so that the confession and the acknowledgment of it cannot, will not be withheld.

Κύριος is the predicate and is thus unarticulated.
The Hebrew *Yahweh* is translated Κύριος, but here this
latter term does not refer to *Yahweh.* Some think that
"the Name" is the Hebrew *Hasēm*, a substitute for
Yahweh, which the Jews considered too sacred to pronounce. So God now changed the ineffable tetragram-
maton which was too sacred to pass human lips into a
name that it was possible for men to utter, "desirable
by all the world," the name Κύριος.

Others find either touches of Gnosticism or a refutation of Docetic Gnostic beginnings in some of the
terms used in v. 6-11. But even if all the Philippians
had been Jewish, this play on "Name," etc., would have
been lost on them. The Jews had their substitute for
Yahweh, needed no Greek term, had had the Greek
translation Κύριος for over two centuries in their LXX.
On the whole subject and also on this phase of it see
C.-K. 644, etc., and note 651, etc.

The confession of the universe that Jesus Christ is
"Lord" means divine Lord, all that we have said regarding "God's form" and "to be equal with God" in
v. 6, not only as being inherent in Jesus' divine nature,
but also as being shared by the human nature through
the *communicatio idiomatum,* "Lord," however, as now
evidenced by what the God-man did in his humiliation
and by what God did in his exaltation, thus the Mes-
siah-Lord, the Savior-Lord, the blessed reliance of all
his saints (so many of whom are still on earth), the
joy of all the heavenly angels, the Judge of the demons
and the damned, in the whole universe "for glory to
God as Father" (objective genitive), Eph. 1:6, 12, 14.

Father is added to mark the first person in relation to Jesus Christ as "Lord." Since v. 6-11 contain no reference to the readers, "Father," which is added to "God," has only the objective reference to them which lies in the Name of him whom we glorify. Because he is confused regarding the part which the human nature has in the humiliation and the exaltation, Kennedy (*Expositor's Greek New Testament*) remain a subordinationist: "undoubtedly the New Testament teaches a certain subordination of the Son," like others ruining the heart of his exegesis.

After all this that is so effective when it is properly seen "in the case of Christ Jesus" (v. 5) has been placed before them by Paul, the Philippians will be moved ever to mind "this one thing" which he asks them to mind (v. 2), namely to cultivate in heart and in life "lowly-mindedness" (v. 3).

Paul's Third Admonition:
That the Philippians May Be and May Act as Light Bearers

12) Both the address "my beloved" and ὥστε, which means simply "and so" (ὡς plus τε, R. 999), indicate the beginning of a new paragraph even as "for the glory of God Father" closes the one preceding. It is unrewarding effort to search for an immediate connection to justify ὥστε; this connective does not call for such a connection. It marks this paragraph as being the last in this admonitory group (1:27-2:18). It thus harks back to 1:27 with its reference to Paul's presence and his absence. It advances the appeal to stand firm as one body by a conduct worthy of the gospel, unafraid of any opponents, to the appeal to stand as luminaries in a perverse world. This "and so" is the connective for the whole paragraph and not just for the first sentence, and τε in the connective indicates something that is closely allied.

And so, my beloved, even as you always obeyed, not as in my presence only, but now much more in my absence, with fear and trembling keep on working out the salvation of yourselves; for God is the One working in you both the willing and the working in behalf of his good pleasure.

"My beloved" = you whom I love dearly with the ἀγάπη of intelligence and corresponding purpose. Paul puts the appeal of his personal love into his admonition. It is great praise for Paul to be able to say that the Philippians have always obeyed, not as in his presence only, but now much more in his absence. Paul loves to praise where there is reason for praise, yet he never flatters. Some think that he means: "you obeyed me," my apostolic authority; but "me" is absent, nor is it suggested by the reference to his former presence and his present absence. Paul refers to their obedience to the gospel, which is mentioned at the beginning of this admonitory section (1:27), and the context following indicates that the obedience of faith as well as of life is meant, the aorist stating the summary fact.

The view that "as" (ὡς) is faulty is untenable. Rhythm and sense demand: "even as you always obeyed, not as in my presence only, but now much more in my absence," "always" being defined by "in my presence — in my absence." It would be unsatisfactory to combine: "not as in my presence only, but now much more in my absence with fear and trembling keep on working out the salvation of yourselves." If Paul intended to load the imperative with such a mass of adverbial modifiers that are placed *in front* of it, "as" would require a following "so," and μή would have to be deleted. Paul writes clearly and correctly. "As" modifies both phrases: the Philippians have always obeyed, "not as" in Paul's presence only, "but as now" (not merely "also," nay even) "much more" in his absence. There is always a tendency to relax obedience when the spiritual leader is absent. How great praise was it when the Philippians increased theirs when Paul was gone! And he was gone not only for a short time. Paul had been absent from them for a long while: *"now,"* at this very moment, after so long an absence, they still obeyed "much more" than when Paul was present in their midst.

Verb and object are reversed so that both are emphatic. "With fear and trembling" is placed at the beginning and thus has the primary emphasis: "with no less than with fear and trembling and no less than the salvation of yourselves keep on working out, never relaxing or doing less." This is the same fear and trembling as that mentioned in Eph. 6:5. Joseph exhibited it when Potiphar's wife tempted him and he exclaimed: "How can I do this great wickedness, and sin against *God?*" This holy fear trembles at the thought of doing or omitting anything that will offend God, compel him to turn away, and thus endanger our salvation. It is not a dread that we may after all be damned; it is shrinking from all carelessness in faith and in life. The Christian does not dread God who gives him the life-giving gospel (v. 16, "life's Word"), but he does dread the poison of sin that robs him of strength to work out the salvation of himself. So far from killing the Christian's joy in the Lord, this fear increases this joy by increasing his assurance that the Lord is with him for his salvation.

"The salvation of yourselves" has the objective genitive and not the possessive. "Salvation" includes the act of saving and rescuing and the resultant state of safety. Here the activity is referred to, which matches the durative verb, hence also we have the objective genitive "of yourselves"; yet the activity is never without its product. We understand Paul's idea when we note that Christians are called οἱ σωζόμενοι, "those in process of being saved" (Luke 13:23; Acts

2:47; II Cor. 2:15), in contrast with "those in process of perishing" (I Cor. 1:18). The saving effected by God at the time of our conversion does not place us into the salvation of heaven at one stroke; it makes us σεσωμένοι, "those who have been saved" (Eph. 2:5). But until we attain the safety of heaven we must be kept safe in this dangerous world; the great salvation that is now ours must be kept ours, our heart's hold upon it must be made ever stronger. Paul speaks of that here.

Saved by grace alone by baptism and conversion, the new life is born in us and is nourished by God to develop ever greater spiritual strength, and this divinely imparted strength is to exercise itself constantly in "working out the salvation of ourselves." Theologians call this the synergism of the new man. Here there is, indeed, a synergism. Saved by the monergism of God's grace, the danger for the saved is ever that they grow otiose, secure, and thus through their own fault lose the salvation bestowed on them by God. Hence all these admonitions in Scripture to stir up the new man. Κατά in the verb lends it a perfective sense, and the tense is durative: "keep on working thoroughly" so as actually to get the results.

The position of the reflexive does *not* make it emphatic as some state; that would require the reading τὴν σωτηρίαν τὴν ἑαυτῶν and would then be incorrect. We are certainly not to work only for our own salvation. Verse 4 settles that, to mention only this passage. The more we work for ourselves, the more will we aid also others by our example and by the concern for them that naturally goes with the concern for ourselves.

We do not work out the salvation of ourselves by any kind of work-righteousness. Paul refers to the constant, faithful use of Word and Sacrament ("life's Word," v. 16). These means of grace renew and increase our hold on salvation, for the gospel is the power of God for salvation (Rom. 1:16). This use of the means is the vital part of the working. A live man must eat to remain alive and strong; Word and Sacrament are our spiritual food and strength. Only as the effect of this use we have what are called "good works," the fight against sin, temptation, error, the efforts to do all that we do, even down to our eating and drinking to the glory of God (I Cor. 10:31), shrinking only from remissness in using and in obeying the Word.

13) It sounds paradoxical when Paul substantiates this admonition by the fact that *"God* is the One working in you both the willing and the working in behalf of his good pleasure." A superficial person may conclude: "If *God* does it, why do *we* need to exert ourselves?" R., *W. P.*, expresses such a view when he says that Paul exhorts "as if he were an Arminian" (one who adds his part to God's) but prays "as if he were a Calvinist" (one who leaves everything to God's sovereign will), and that Paul "feels no inconsistency in the two attitudes." Thank God, Paul is neither an Arminian Calvinist nor a Calvinistic Arminian. The Arminians and the Calvinists do better than that; each holds only *one* error instead of combining *two*. Paul held *neither* error. His exhortations and his prayers have the *identical* contents.

The apparent paradox is non-existent. If *God* is the One who works in us both the willing and the working, then we Christians must ever go to God whose continuous grace will move us to will and also to translate the willing into deeds, i. e., into work. How else shall we be able to heed Paul's admonition that we ever keep on working out the salvation of ourselves? Paul's word is an assurance, the one assurance we Christians need for retaining the salvation we have obtained by a gift of God (Eph. 2:8).

Paul does not imply: "You Philippians are responsible, not to me, the apostle, but to no less a one than God." He is not frightening the Philippians with the

gravity of their *responsibility* as an Arminian might
do and as Calvinism often at least tries to do. Paul is
not using law but gospel. He is assuring his Christian
readers that, in their complete dependence on God for
their salvation, this God will never, never disappoint
them but by working in them by means of Word and
Sacrament will ever bring them to keep on in their willing and to keep on in their working, both object infinitives being present and durative. There is no uncertainty, no fear and trembling before God but only gospel assurance that he is the very One to supply all that
we need to keep willing as well as working. This is not
to present God as the *Judge* who holds us to our *ac-
countability*, but this invites us to God as the unfailing
source of all the power and the *supply* we need.

Paul wisely writes "both to will and to work." We
often start to will, even to will strongly, the flower
opens beautifully but it blasts and fails to set fruit. In
Rom. 7:19 Paul mourns because he still finds this in
himself to a degree. Here he assures us that such a
thing will not blast his readers altogether, by God's
grace and help there will also be the fruition of working.

The last phrase introduced with ὑπέρ is not "*of* his
good pleasure" (A. V.; Luther *nach*, "in accord with")
but: to be willing and working "*in behalf of* or *for* his
good pleasure" (R. V.). The discussion about the article and about the absence of αὐτοῦ and thus about
whether this is God's good pleasure or that of the will
of Paul's readers, then also whether "good will" — or
"good pleasure" — or "free determination" is meant,
wearies one. In hundreds of instances the article has
the force of "his" (the translation of our versions are
correct). This is the same *eudokia* as that mentioned
in Eph. 1:5, 9 (see these passages): "God's free good
will, the contents of which is something good" (C.-K.
354), namely grace and salvation How do we keep

willing and working in behalf of God's good pleasure?
By seeking it in Word and Sacrament, yielding will and
effort to its blessed contents and purpose.

When it is applied to conversion, this passage is a
dictum probans for the utter inability of man's will to
contribute the least toward saving himself (*C. Tr.* 884,
890, 894). If God must still work in the converted both
to will and to work, how much more must he work to
turn that will in the first place, not indeed mechanically as a log is turned over, but as our will is always
moved and altered: by inner conviction. There is no
need of fine-spun philosophical discussion regarding
the primary cause and the secondary cause, between
necessity and contingency. Where is the Christian
who will not testify with joy, as Paul does, to the
blessed fact that God works in him both to will and to
work in behalf of his good pleasure, and that this willing and this working work out the salvation of himself?

14) So Paul continues: **Everything keep on
doing without grumblings and reasonings in order
that you may get to be blameless and unmixed, children of God unblemished amid a generation crooked
and distorted, among whom you shine as luminaries
in the world, as holding life's Word, — for a cause
of boasting for me for Christ's day that not for something empty did I run, nor for something empty did
labor.** Paul refers to "everything" that is required
for working out the salvation of ourselves.

Those misunderstand the thought who think that
"grumblings and reasonings" (our versions have "dis-
putings") refer to complaints against each other, lack
of harmony among the members, and then cite 4:2.
No; in this crooked and twisted generation Paul's
readers have much to endure. They are to go on doing
everything that is required for their salvation without
murmuring and complaint about what such faithful

doing nets them from the world and without wrong
reasonings about why this ill from the world comes
upon them and how, by doing less, they might possibly
escape this ill. One preposition combines "grumblings
and reasonings." The nouns are in their proper order,
for one at first grumbles at the disagreeable and then
starts figuring out its cause and its possible cure.
Διαλογισμοί are always to be understood in the evil sense,
rationalizing thoughts and calculations (cf., Rom.
1:21; I Cor. 1:20).

15) The purpose is that the Philippians "may get
to be" or "may definitely and permanently be (aorist)
blameless and unmixed" when God, they themselves,
and others examine them. The two adjectives go together: nothing for which to blame them in their conduct — nothing in their hearts and their motives that
ought not to be there. On the latter see Trench and
our note on Rom. 16:19 (Matt. 10:16) It is not
"harmless" (our versions) ; nor "sincere" (A. V. margin) but "sound," without even a wrong thought,
desire, or motive mixed in, immune to anything of this
kind.

The appositional predicate continues: "children of
God (genuine ones) unblemished amid a generation
crooked and distorted." "Unblemished" includes
"blameless and unmixed" by stating these in a new way
(Eph. 5:27: "not having spot or wrinkle — holy and
unblemished"), namely "undamaged" by the generation, contact with which you cannot avoid. If they
become blameworthy, if they do not keep their thoughts
and their motives free of admixture, this means that
the worldly generation has blemished them who by
their very birth are spiritually "children of God" and
should resemble their Father in all things.

It makes no difference whether we call μέσον a preposition (R. 775) or an adverb (R. 644; C.-K. 215, 3).
"Amid a generation crooked and distorted" has two

significant qualifiers in plain allusion to Deut. 32:5: "a perverse (distorted) and crooked generation — not his children." Crooked is the generation that has left the straight paths of the Lord. Crooked in mind and in heart and thus in acts means lying thought. Truth alone is straight, lies are crooked and bend in all directions but the straight one. The perfect passive participle means "distorted, twisted," being in this condition now, and emphasizes and intensifies "crooked." What a drastic picture of the religious and the moral condition of that generation! "Generation" does not, however, mean those of a single physical succession from father to son but the continuous wicked moral succession as seen in Acts 7:52: "as your fathers, so ye."

"Among whom," plural, is in order because "generation" is a collective. We regard the verb as the middle indicative: "among whom you are shining as regards yourselves (A. V. simply: shine) as luminaries in the world" and not as the passive: "are seen" and not as the imperative: "shine!" Φωστῆρες is used regarding stars, hence it means "luminaries," "lights" (our versions), which should not be changed into "light-bringers" in order to get a missionary thought which is not in the context. The context is that of contrast to the dark world, dark in its moral crookedness and perversity. We do not expect an admonition to do shining in a relative clause. Even imperfect Christians shine; when Jesus spoke to his then very imperfect disciples he did not use the future tense: "You *shall be* the light of the world," but the present: "*you are*" (Matt. 5:14). This very fact is to move Paul's readers to be true luminaries, to achieve the purpose stated by ἵνα. "In the world" needs no article in the Greek, the less since the qualitative sense is thus felt the more: "as luminaries in what is world."

16)   We should not let our imagination carry us
too far, as those do who speak of the Philippians as
being sun, moon, and stars for the world.   This is said
because our versions have the next clause read: "holding forth" life's Word, i. e., offering it to the world in a
missionary way.   Commentators support this as being
the old meaning of ἐπέχω, but it was only one of rather
numerous turns of meaning (Liddell and Scott); it
would be the only instance of this meaning in the New
Testament; B.-P. 443 and C.-K. 1166 do not list it at all,
the latter has it in the sense of *festhalten;* others, like
Thayer, advance the meaning "hold forth" only in support of our versions and of a few commentators.   The
fact is that in later times the compound was used in the
sense of the simplex as was the case with other verbs
because a preference for compounds had developed.

Paul does not insert the simple assertion that the
Philippians are luminaries in the world; he at once
explains how he is able to say this when he has just
admonished the Philippians to get to be blameless, unmixed, unblemished.   It is not so much the conduct of
the Philippians that justifies the assertion that they
shine as luminaries, it is their "having life's Word."
This Word makes them luminaries irrespective of what
the world judges about it and about those who have it.
The world does not have this Word; this is the very
reason that it is "a generation crooked and twisted,"
the Philippians are a different generation.

Ever and ever we must have it impressed upon us
that we are *different* from the world, must be told what
is the matter with the world, and what we have that
makes us so different.   Then we shall not grumble
because of ill-treatment, nor reason about escaping
mistreatment by accommodating ourselves to the
world.   We have and hold "life's Word."   This designation is found only here and certainly is a striking
one, being a practical compound: *Lebenswort,* the gen-

itive being either appositional: "Word that is life," or
qualitative: "Word with the quality of life"; but not
objective: "Word about life." First John 1:1 has "the
Word of life"; I Pet. 1:23: "the Word of God, which
liveth and abideth forever." Jesus: "The words that I
speak to you, they are spirit, and they are life," John
6:63. The soul and center of this Word is Christ, "the
life" (John 14:6). This Word quickens, i. e., makes
alive; it keeps alive, increases the spiritual life. Apart
from this Word all is spiritually dead.

"Word" (λόγος) is not to be taken in the sense of
"preaching" as those understand it who give it the
meaning: "you hold forth (offer) to the world the
preaching of life." "Word" is the divine medium by
which we have life eternal. The spoken Word (ῥῆμα)
makes the water of baptism (Eph. 5:26) a washing of
rebirth (Tit. 3:5) by the Holy Spirit. We have this
"Word of life" by faith. Wrought by this Word, faith
holds this imperishable life (the very life principle
itself: ζωή the life by which we live). The word opens
up all the Scriptural vistas of the spiritual life; follow
them in detail. And do not overlook τέκνα Θεοῦ in v. 15,
"children born" of life's Word and thus "children of
God."

As Paul began with "my beloved" (v. 12), so he
now gives all that he says the strongest personal turn.
Is this, perhaps, a predicative εἰς (R. 481), all this being "a cause of boasting for me (or: for a cause of
boasting) for Christ's day," all that the Philippians
are and that Paul is trying to make them be and do?
The Philippians were a congregation that was not only
founded by Paul but that was also watched over by him
as his present letter shows. See I Thess. 2:19, 20:
"the crown of boasting" for us (Paul and his helpers),
"you our glory and our joy." Paul thinks of the
sheaves he will bring with rejoicing as the fruit of his
apostolic labors (Ps. 126:6). "For Christ's day" =

1:10. Paul is not speaking of already boasting but of the cause of boasting he hopes to have on the final day. This is again taken to mean that the missionary activity of the Philippians is to constitute Paul's cause of boasting. Then Paul should say, "A cause of boasting *for you,*" for you as missionaries as I am one. He certainly would not credit the missionary labors of others to himself.

Paul does not leave undefined what he means by this καύχημα for Christ's day just as he does not leave undefined what he means by shining as luminaries in the world. The ὅτι clause is epexegetical: "that I did run not for an empty thing nor did labor for an empty thing," the phrases being placed forward in the Greek. The aorists are dated from the viewpoint of Christ's day. When Paul then stands before Christ he wants the Philippians as the evidence that he, as an apostle, did not run and labor for nothing.

"Did run" is the figure of a race, "did labor" is the literal interpretation, both imply strenuous exertion. "In vain" has the Greek word κενόν, "empty," and not μάταιον, "useless" as not leading to the goal. To run and to labor εἰς κενόν means at the end to find only something entirely empty, with nothing in it, to run, etc., "for nothing." The great thing for which Paul wants to have run and labored when Christ's day comes is the shining faith and faithfulness of the Philippians as having ever held life's Word that was brought to them by Paul, brought to them even now in this epistle. As to the date of that "day" Paul attempts to say nothing.

17) This personal reference to himself — certainly a stimulus to the love of the Philippians for Paul — he now carries to a climax in the reference to his possible martyrdom. But this would not be Paul if he ended with himself; *he* has to end by joining the Philippians with himself, not in sorrow, but in the highest joy, if, indeed, all his labors are to be crowned with martyrdom. **Yea, if also I pour myself out as a libation along with the sacrifice and public service for your faith, I rejoice and rejoice jointly with you all; moreover, in the same way do you, too, rejoice and rejoice jointly with me.**

'Ἀλλά is not adversative to the previous negatives, not even in the sense of *sondern;* it adds another thing; it is not contradictory but climacteric (R. 1185, etc., clears up this use). Our versions are correct: "Yea," etc. Εἰ καί = "if also," as is likely; while καὶ εἰ = "even if," as seems quite unlikely (R. 1026). Σπένδω = to make a drink offering; the middle to make oneself such an offering. The Jews poured out this wine offering beside the altar, pagans poured it upon the sacrifice on the altar; either usage fits here.

The present tense naturally refers to the future; if I pour out myself at any time, the indicative considering the fact. It should be noted that this verb fits the martyr's death which, as a Roman citizen, Paul would likely suffer, namely decapitation, the sudden gushing out of his blood, not the slow trickling of crucifixion. Again, the noble nature of the action deserves full appreciation: the act is sacred in the highest degree, a drink offering poured out to God or Christ. The tense does not imply a contradiction with Paul's expectation of release from his present imprisonment (1:25). He is thinking of the future; his words are almost prophetic, for he was beheaded a few years later. He feels already at this time that this would be his end.

The voice of σπένδομαι should be noted. Our versions and many others regard the verb as a passive: "if also I am poured out as a libation," but we then ask who the implied agent could be in this passive, the priest performing this priestly function. It cannot be God, for the libation is poured out *for* him and not *by* him. It cannot be the pagan executioner or the pagan judge or court, for how can a pagan function as a priest in a

libation to the true God? The pagans would execute
Paul in the interest of their idols, in bloody hostility to
God. Can we say that the agent is left unnamed because he is immaterial in this passive? This is a middle and not a passive. We have the example of Jesus
himself although "libation" is not used regarding the
shedding of his blood. He is the Priest, the High
Priest, the Lamb, who shed his own blood. Pagans and
Jews executed him, but they were not the priests func-
tioning in his holy sacrifice; nor was God the priest
as we need not prove.

Next, equally decisive: whose is the libation? His
whose is the sacrifice which accompanies the libation.
Does one person come to the priest with only the sacrifice, and a second person with only the wine for the
libation? To ask is to answer. The three words σπένδομαι — θυσία — λειτουργία refer to acts of Paul, and not
the first to an act of Paul, and the other two to an act or
to acts of the Philippians. That is so self-evident that
Paul did no need to add a pronoun: "*my* sacrifice and
public service."

Yet von Hofmann offers the view that *Paul* brings
the libation, and the *Philippians* the sacrifice proper,
and some agree with him. On what plea? The claim
that the genitive τῆς πίστεως ὑμῶν cannot be objective,
that λειτουργεῖν never governs the accusative *rei*, that the
noun also cannot have the objective genitive in place of
such an accusative (C.-K. 667, etc.). The conclusion
is then drawn that this is a subjective genitive: the
faith of the Philippians brings the sacrifice and renders
the public service. The sentence is divided: "But if
also I am poured out as a libation," (then an ellipsis:
all right, I am poured out!). Next, a new sentence:
"At the sacrifice, etc., of your faith (subjective: which
your faith brings) I rejoice," etc. But ἐπί does not
state the cause of Paul's rejoicing, what really produces
the joy is left in the air.

We break off, there is no need to state the further
details. Any grammar (take two: B.-D. 163; R. 499,
etc.) shows the wide range of the objective genitive.
It is not compelled to name only the corresponding
accusative *rei* or direct accusative object which the
active verb would have. "Of your faith" is an objective genitive. To object on the score of θυσία is equally
untenable. But even when the Philippians are not
made the priests, when Paul is the priest, "your faith"
is not the genitive which names the direct object (as
some assert) : "at the sacrifice and priest's service of
your faith," i. e., "while I bring your faith as the sacrifice and (thus) treat it with priest's service." How
can I bring another person's faith as a sacrifice to God,
to say nothing of the word indicating action, λειτουργία,
"public service"? The use of these two nouns: "sacrifice" (a thing), "public service" (an action), both
after one article, is plain evidence that "your faith" is
not a direct object, that the attributive genitive is objective in a different sense, in one that fits both nouns.

Some sacrifices needed no libation. Paul considers
that his may be intended to have one. That thought
rejoices him. To be sure, his would thus be a richer
sacrifice. He who rejoices in bringing the sacrifice
cannot but rejoice in making it richer by adding a libation. Ἐπί = "upon," "in addition to," "along with."
The addition would be a grant of God, compare 1:29, 30
where we see that Paul wants the Philippians to consider any suffering of theirs as an additional grant of
God to them.

"Along with my sacrifice" would be an incomplete
thought even if "and my public service" were added,
both with "my"; hence the complete thought with the
article in the sense of "my"; "along with the (my)
sacrifice and public service for your faith," all this is
a unit. Paul's whole apostleship he views as a sacrifice.
Yet that thought is incomplete; the second noun helps

to define it as a public service. "For your faith"
rounds out both nouns. This is a use of the objective
genitive that is so common as to need no reference to
grammar.

It may well be possible that Paul does not use θυσία
(θύω, "to slaughter") in the general sense of προσφορά,
"offering" (we often make no distinction between "sacrifice" and "offering"), but in the sense of slain blood.
Be that as it may, λειτουργία = official public service.
Paul is an apostle and acts in that public office. Since
priests function thus, some think that this word always
has the priestly meaning. We have discussed this in
II Cor. 9:12. Here the context might lend the priestly
color. But the explanatory force is only that of public
official service; the priestliness is already expressed by
more than this noun could add. All three are Paul's:
libation — sacrifice — official service. In all three *he*
offers and offers his very own. That is his joy, his
joint joy "with all you" Philippians.

They are of Paul's mind. They see the glory of it
all as Paul sees it; σύν is associative. But we are told
that the Philippians would be plunged into grief if Paul
were executed, that the opposite is incredible. Why,
of course, all these Philippians would shed tears to hear
that Paul was condemned to the sword. They did that
when he finally did go to the block. But his glorious
martyrdom, his public apostolic service and sacrifice
for their faith as for the faith of so many others, filled
them with the most sacred and blessed joy. Paul writes
to Christians who have caught the vision he has of his
work, office, life, and death, who are sharers of his own
joy in all of it, ready in their lesser stations with joy
to have granted to them whatever of the same kind
God allots to them.

18) Δέ adds the other side. Τὸ αὐτό is undoubtedly
adverbial: "as to (this) very thing" of which I am

speaking, i. e., in the very same way; and not the object of the verbs. But is this not tautology, telling the Philippians to rejoice and to rejoice with Paul when he has already said that he rejoices with all of them? The matter is not improved by letting the second verb mean "and congratulate me" (Lightfoot, so also in v. 17, "and I congratulate you all"). For in both verses the first and also the second verb would still be alike, tautological.

The question in Paul's mind is: "Do the Philippians rejoice as he rejoices and wants to rejoice with them? Do they rise to the proper level?" These imperatives intend to raise them to a higher level as the emphasis on "you, too," shows. There is no need to divide the cause of this joy as though it is not to include the prospect of the libation of Paul's martyrdom but only Paul's labor for them. Such a separation is meaningless. There is no tautology. We can say: "I am already rejoicing with all of you; do *you*, too, now rejoice in the same way with me!"

Paul Tells the Philippians about Timothy's Coming

19) With the common transitional δέ Paul sends a further piece of information. The first piece was given in 1:12, etc., which is amplified by the three admonitions and extends to 2:18. Now comes the rest of the information, to convey which the letter is written, namely Timothy's mission and the experience of Epaphroditus.

Now I hope in the Lord Jesus soon to send Timothy for you in order that I myself also may be of good cheer when I get to know the things concerning you.

The emphasis is on "Timothy," which name is for this reason placed before the infinitive; secondly, on "soon," which is also placed forward. Hence in the following Paul explains why he sends Timothy and how soon he hopes to do this. He "hopes in the Lord Jesus" to send him "soon." This is said in view of 1:25, 26, namely Paul's confidence that he will be acquitted and released at his trial. This is stated also in 2:24, where Paul again expresses this confidence and advances it to the assurance that also he himself will soon come to the Philippians. So Paul "hopes" and connects this hope with "the Lord Jesus" who is guiding everything about this trial before the imperial court. The phrase is here not general but specifically important.

Here Paul writes the simple dative ὑμῖν after "to send," but in v. 25, after the same infinitive, when he is speaking about Epaphroditus, he writes πρὸς ὑμᾶς. This difference means that Epaphroditus is being sent home "*to* you" whereas Timothy will soon be sent for a purpose "*for* you," a dative of advantage. Verse 23 states what this purpose is, namely at once to report to the Philippians the acquittal and the release of Paul, which he is confident will ensue. All this is quite clear. Also, as we have shown in the introduction, that Paul's letter intends to inform the Philippians without delay how well matters have gone in Paul's case at the start of his trial, and how well matters stand with regard to the gospel in Rome in consequence (1:12, etc.).

All this is presented in the epistle itself. It is so adequate to account for Paul's writing that we see no need for advancing the hypothesis that the Philippians had just sent a letter to Paul, to which he is now writing a reply. How can Paul write that he will send Timothy when he gets to know the outcome of his trial, which will be soon, "in order that I myself also may be of good cheer when I get to know the things concerning you," if a letter had just arrived from Philippi? Not only such a letter but also its bearers would give Paul full information on "the things concerning you" (on "your state," our versions, your affairs). As Paul writes he has only his memory of the Philippians on which to draw (1:3), which includes what Epaphroditus had told him some time ago.

Paul has a double purpose in sending Timothy, which is quite like Paul. His thoughts are ever of a mutual nature. *He* hopes to send great news by Timothy (v. 23), and *the Philippians* are to send back refreshing news to him. Are they not "my beloved" (v. 12)? It is even like Paul to place the latter ahead of the former.

Εὐψυχέω is found often on the ancient epitaphs as εἰφύχει, the Latin *have = ave*, like: *Have pia anima!* "Farewell" (Liddell and Scott). "That I may be refreshed" and thus of good cheer (present tense, durative) "on getting to know your affairs" (aorist, the verb γινώσκω to designate knowing with personal interest). Timothy is, then, not to remain in Philippi but is to return to Paul with a report about the Philippians.

20) **For I have no one** (at my disposal at present) **equal in soul** (to him), **such as will genuinely care for the things concerning you, for they all are seeking their own things, not the things of Jesus Christ.**

Compounds with ἰσο do not mean "like" but "equal to," as good as, here *von gleichen Trieben beseelt* (C.-K.), equally animated as is Timothy (not as is Paul himself). If Paul had Timothy's equal he would plan to send that one and would plan to keep Timothy with himself. The qualitative relative (B.-D. 379 "qualitative — consecutive": *derart dass*) specifies what equality is meant: "such as will genuinely care for the things concerning you" when Paul hopes to do the sending. It is rather fanciful to have γνησίως = "by an instinct derived from his spiritual parentage."

21) "For" explains what is wrong with all the rest: "they all seek their own personal interests, not those of Jesus Christ." This sounds worse in the Eng-

lish than in the Greek, for the latter does not mean:
only their own interest, *not at all* those of Christ, for
then they would not be Christians at all. "They all"
(definite) still let their own interests interfere with
Christ's, do not pursue Christ's interests exclusively.
They are somewhat of the type of those of whom Paul
complains in 1:15, 16, but less so, for those wanted to
grieve Paul, these do not respond wholeheartedly.

Just who these were we have no way of knowing
although every interpreter is certain that Luke is not
among them. The view that Paul writes as he does
because he is out of sorts contradicts all the joy that is
found in this epistle. This joy rises above 1:15, 16 and
more easily above 2:20, 21. Paul, however, hides nothing, he is not that kind of man. Moreover, when the
Philippians read about these others they will appreciate Timothy the more.

But we must heed the Eighth Commandment and
put the best and not the worst construction on everything (Luther's explanation). The fault of these men
seems to have been that, when Paul broached the matter of sending news to Philippi as soon as his trial
should end, he met no ready response. To each of these
men the hard, long journey to Philippi did not seem to
be greatly in the interest of Jesus Christ or greatly in
the interest of the Philippians. Paul saw that very
little would be gained by sending any of these men and
thus gives up Timothy for the journey to Philippi. As
regards Luke and other loyal assistants of Paul, one of
whom Paul might have sent instead of Timothy, we are
compelled to conclude that they were absent from
Rome, away on other missions, for at the end of this
epistle Paul is not able to send salutations to the Philippians from them. This is the situation.

We may say a little more. Paul is thinking of what
he will do when before so very long his trial will be
concluded, when he is set free and is able to leave Rome.

We know what he did do then, what he was already very likely planning. He went from Rome to Ephesus and to Colosse to visit Philemon. He would like to take Timothy along as his companion instead of dispatching him from Rome to Philippi. He intended to place Timothy in charge of the entire work in the province of Asia while he himself would then go on from Ephesus to Philippi and elsewhere. He plans to give up Timothy, to send him to Philippi, then to have him come from Philippi to Ephesus to meet him there and to leave him in the great Asian field as his apostolic representative. This Paul did eventually. It is safe to conclude that he is making this plan now. It certainly accords with the later facts. Timothy's former intimate connection with Philippi makes him especially eligible for this mission, for which reason Paul also has him join in the writing of the present letter.

22) Moreover, the testing out of him you know, that as a child for his father he slaved with me in regard to the gospel.

Δέ adds this as another point for characterizing the ψυχή of Timothy. He has been tested out, αὐτοῦ is the objective genitive, ὅτι is epexegetical. This is the word that is used to designate the testing of metals and of coins, it is like the verb that is so often found in Paul's writings. The Philippians not only know about it, they know it in a personal way (γινώσκω) ; three times Timothy had been with them (Acts 16:13; 19:22; 20:3, etc.). Some think that Paul changed his thought in the middle of the sentence, at least marred the parallel by first writing the dative πατρί and then the prepositional phrase σὺν ἐμοί (R. 441, 1199), the R. V. smoothes out this break by repeating the verb. There is neither break nor parallel (see A. V.). A child may slave *with* his father when he is doing this *for* him. Why does that thought require two parallel sentences? Timothy was Paul's regular associate, which thought σύν expresses. The thought is not that he never left Paul's side; that idea would require μετά, "in company with." The main point is that Timothy showed himself to be a child who closely resembles his father; those mentioned in v. 21 were not showing themselves in such a way. Paul slaved in regard to the gospel (εἰς as in 1:5) ; Timothy slaved *with* Paul, *for* Paul as a true child does for its father; those others could not go to this length of slaving for Paul as regards the gospel. Slaving means not having one's own will but doing only the will of one's superior. Those others had not learned this "lowly-mindedness" (v. 3) which also looks out so completely for the things of others (v. 5) ; had not yet come to mind this thing that was so plain in Christ's case when *he* took "slave's form" (v. 6, 7). Paul had indeed learned completely to be "Jesus Christ's slave" (Rom. 1:1). Note how τὰ ἑαυτῶν is repeated from v. 5, and how the wording recalls the admonition that was based on Christ's "slave's form."

23) **This one, therefore, I hope to send forthwith, whenever I get to see in due course the things concerning me; and I am confident in the Lord that also I myself shall come soon.**

Τοῦτον, our emphatic *"him,"* summarizes everything said about Timothy, and οὖν resumes Paul's hoping to send Timothy mentioned in v. 19 and now adds the statement that he will send him "forthwith" (placed emphatically at the end) and specifies the time: "whenever (ὡς ἄν) I get to see," etc. The aorist subjunctive is punctiliar: "get to see." Both ἀπίδω and ἀφίδω are used, the latter probably because the disused ἀφοράω had the rough consonant φ. But we should not render the ἀπό in this verb: "to turn the eyes away from and fix them on something," and thus make it analogous to ἀποβλέπω. We beg to submit that there is an analogy with ἀποδίδωμι, "duly to give or pay," ἀπέχω, "to have in full what is due," to be paid off in full (Matt. 6:2 and often), and other verbs compounded with ἀπό. Paul's trial would run its due course, he would thus "duly, or in due course, get to see" the eventual state of his affairs. Paul could not hurry this, the Philippians had to wait until Paul was due to see the outcome of his trial. When B.-P. 200 renders: *sobald ich meine Lage ueberblicke,* we note his uncertainty regarding the force of the preposition. Paul was now doing that (1:12, etc.), could do it at any time. Here he speaks of in due course getting to see the final outcome of his trial. Note that Paul here construes περί with the accusative (R. 620) instead of with the genitive (v. 19, 20).

The mission of Timothy was to carry this final news and, of course, also to bring back news to Paul (v. 19). Timothy did bring such news when he again joined Paul in Ephesus. Paul probably used some means to get the great news as promptly as possible also to other places.

24) We cannot reproduce the neat balance in μέν and δέ, the hope, on the one hand, to send Timothy, the confidence, on the other hand, that Paul himself will come to Philippi. He has already promised the latter in 1:25. Here he adds that his confidence is connected with the Lord and states in so many words that he expects to go to Philippi and that "soon." The decision of his trial is not far off.

Paul Reports to the Philippians about the Return of Epaphroditus

25) Δέ is used as it was in v. 19. **Now I considered it necessary to send to you Epaphroditus, my brother and fellow worker and fellow soldier and your commissioner and public servant for my need, since he kept longing for you all and kept being distressed because you heard that he had gotten sick. And, indeed, he got sick very near to death. But**

God showed him mercy, and not him only but also me in order that I might not get to have grief upon grief.

What is the picture here drawn of Epaphroditus? This aorist and the one used in v. 28 ("I sent") are plainly epistolary aorists, written from the standpoint of the readers when they hear this letter read, when Paul's considering and sending will lie in the past. They are a common Greek idiom in letters; the English would use "I consider — I send," which are written from the standpoint of the writer at the moment of writing. Those who regard these as aorists that indicate recent acts assume that Paul had sent Epaphroditus back some time before. They thus create the difficulty that he most probably arrived in Philippi before Paul's present letter, and that v. 29 does not agree with its request: "receive him," etc. So the hypothesis is advanced that Epaphroditus traveled rather slowly since he was a convalescent, and that Paul's letter traveled faster and was delivered before the latter's arrival. Yet Paul could get no one to go to Philippi to carry the expected news of his release in the near future. How did Paul then send his present letter? by some stranger? Epaphroditus is to be the bearer. Whether he is also Paul's scribe as the ancient note at the end asserts (see A. V.) we cannot say; v. 19-23 show that Paul has no other man to take his present letter to Philippi.

The five appositions: "my brother and fellow worker and fellow soldier and your messenger and public servant for my need," plus the adverb in v. 28: "I sent him the more speedily," justify the conclusion that Epaphroditus not only brought the gift of the Philippians to Paul but intended to stay with Paul for some time in order to aid the apostle by whatever work he was able to do in Rome. The impression we get is that, when the Philippians sent Epaphroditus, they did not

know that Paul's case had already been taken up by
the court or was on the verge of being taken up. Paul
had been waiting for two years, might still have to wait
a long time. The Philippians knew that he needed
helpers and sent Epaphroditus to be one of them. Then
the latter fell sick, almost died, but recovered. Paul's
case was actually in court, would soon be settled by the
court. At the moment Paul had far less need of helpers. So Paul now sends Epaphroditus back "more
speedily" than he would otherwise have done. He
makes the whole situation plain to the Philippians.

We see, then, the reason for all these appositions.
Epaphroditus was sent to Paul so that he might have
another "brother" at his side, another "fellow worker"
and "fellow soldier," the terms are arranged in an ascending scale. Although his serious sickness incapaci-
tated him, and although, upon recovering, he was able
to do but little, Paul regards him as more than a brother, as being also a fellow worker and soldier, for Epaphroditus came to enlist as such. The supposition
that all these epithets refer to the past, to a time years
ago when Epaphroditus helped in the work, is untenable, for neither "my brother," the very first designation, nor "your commissioner and official servant," the
last two epithets, can be referred to the past.

Thus, too, we understand "your commissioner and
official servant for my need" (objective genitive).
This "need" is not Paul's poverty as is assumed. The
δέ does not separate, is not adversative ("but," A. V.).
Paul purposely abuts μου and ὑμῶν δέ, a construction that
it is hard to imitate in English. Paul's "need" was
men, not money. Paul is not referring to the money
the Philippians sent him. This designation of Epaphroditus would be extravagant, unlikely even in the
case of a man that was less balanced than Paul, if
Epaphroditus had done no more than to bring the
Philippians' gift to Paul. *"Your* (emphatic) com-

missioner (representative) and official public servant for my need" means: for my need of a brother, fellow worker, and a fellow soldier. The Philippians had sent Epaphroditus as their gift to Paul.

The word used is not ἄγγελος, "messenger" who brings news or a gift, but ἀπόστολος, "one sent on a commission," to carry out a commission. In order to leave no doubt about it Paul adds λειτουργός, "one who acts as an official, public servant" for others, see the remarks on λειτουργία in v. 17 where Paul calls his apostolic work "an official public service for your faith" (with the same objective genitive). Where is a man bringing a gift from others called a *leitourgos*? But a man commissioned by a whole church to assist Christ's apostolic commissioner is, indeed, both a "commissioner" and "an official public servant." So we have the force of the abutted genitives: a brother and fellow worker and fellow soldier of *mine*, (as such, moreover,) *your* "commissioner," etc., i. e., not an assistant of Paul only of his own accord but duly commissioned and officially appointed by the Philippian church.

As such Paul acknowledges Epaphroditus. When he arrived in this capacity and then fell sick, this naturally makes no difference as to the capacity itself. Those who think that the titles refer to the bringing of the gift of money even assume that *leitourgos* refers to a priestly function. The word itself means "a public official," for instance, of the state. Since also priests act as public officials they are at times called *leitourgoi*. But countless public officials were not priests in any sense. Who would call that person who, on behalf of a congregation, brings and presents a gift to a pastor or religious leader *a priest?*

26) Paul states why he considers it necessary to send Epaphroditus back to Philippi: "since he kept longing for you all and kept being distressed because

you heard that he had gotten sick." Instead of being
able to carry out this commission and to act as the
official representative of the Philippians by assisting
Paul in the gospel work and warfare poor Epaphroditus fell sick and became a burden on Paul's hands
although Paul does not state the latter. Whether he
arrived as a sick man or became sick a short time
after his arrival, who can say? It also makes no dif-
fence in order to understand what Paul writes. Epaphroditus, who, on behalf of the Philippians, was to do
so much for Paul, almost died on Paul's hands. No
wonder he "kept longing for you all," wishing he were
back with you who could easily care for him instead
of being in Rome where he felt himself a terrible
burden to Paul and to the brethren who had to take
care of him, all save Timothy being strangers to him.
The imperfect (perhaps the periphrastic, R. 888, 1120)
describes the state in its continuance. The supposition
that Epaphroditus had a bad case of homesickness
merits little consideration. He longed the more to be
back home because Paul would not at all need him
when his trial was over, had only slight need of him
now while the trial was in progress.

Καί adds the other point, the distress of Epaphroditus "because you heard that he got sick." How did
the Philippians hear of it, and how did Epaphroditus
and Paul know that they had heard about it? The
simple answer is that Epaphroditus had not been sent
alone but had been accompanied by a few companions.
These companions returned after a rest in Rome.
Epaphroditus took sick before they left. So the Philippians "heard," and Epaphroditus and Paul knew that
they had heard.

'Αδημονεῖν (derivation in dispute) is used in Matt.
26:37; Mark 14:13 with reference to Jesus: "to be
distressed." What worried the sick man was the fact
that the people who had sent him, probably at consider-

able expense to themselves, to do so much for Paul, heard that all their good plans and intentions had failed, had only put a further burden on Paul instead of relieving his other burdens. All this seems rather obvious. Yet some think that news got to Philippi in other ways and then back to Rome, say by a letter to Paul from the Philippians, all of which, together with the unmanly homesickness, we regard as improbable.

27) "And indeed (or: indeed yes) he got sick near to death," which explains why Epaphroditus longed so to be with the Philippians and worried so because they heard of his illness and would themselves worry about its outcome. Yet, the way in which Paul adds this sounds as though the full gravity of the sickness had not appeared when the companions left Rome, but that these feared that the sickness might turn out to be very grave. Paul reports that it actually almost had fatal results: for a time Epaphroditus hung between life and death. On καὶ γάρ see B.-D. 452, 3.

Paul is sending him back, the Philippians will see him, so he says only: "But God mercied him" (literal, the verb with a direct object in the Greek). Epaphroditus had recovered. Paul at once adds: "and not him only but also me in order that I might not get to have grief upon grief," grief over the illness of the brother who, in the intention of the Philippians, was to be his assistant, and still more grief over his death. The aorist σχῶ, like those occurring in v. 26, is ingressive: "get to have." How this reference to "grief," as some think, conflicts with the joy with which the epistle abounds is hard to see. Had Epaphroditus not recovered by God's mercy? That, surely, caused great joy. Besides, the true Christian freely sheds tears at the death of one that is dear to him without these tears darkening his joy in the Lord.

28) **More quickly, accordingly, I sent** (epistolary aorist: am sending, see v. 25) **him in order that,**

on getting to see him back, you may get to rejoice, and I on my part may be more relieved.

Not "more carefully" (A. V.) or "more diligently" (R. V.) but "more hastily," i. e., sooner than might otherwise have been the case. If Epaphroditus had remained hale and hearty, there would have been no reason to send him back as yet, he could have remained until Paul's court trial ended. But as things were, since Epaphroditus had almost died, since the Philippians knew that he had fallen ill and that he had not been able to function as they desired, and since Paul's own release was pending, Paul felt that the thing to do was to send Epaphroditus back without further delay (v. 25). Oὖν is resumptive, goes back to v. 25 and even takes in v. 24 together with the explanations that follow; it is unnecessary to seek only a single point in v. 26, 27 to which to refer "accordingly."

For one thing, the Philippians will "get to rejoice" (ingressive, second aorist passive) on getting to see Epaphroditus back (πάλιν in its first meaning), now knowing the whole situation and also the nearness of Paul's release. For another thing, Paul himself will be "the more relieved" (B.-P. 63: *sorgenfreier* = *ganz sorgenfrei*), elative comparative: quite relieved or very much relieved; yet with comparative force: more than he would otherwise be (R. 665).

There is no need to stress "more griefless" and to say that this still leaves some grief to Paul. This sounds literal but does not adequately understand Paul's thought. Paul is still a bit sorry for the Philippians who know only that their representative got sick on Paul's hands. This will entirely disappear when Paul knows the joy which the actual return of Epaphroditus will create. Paul could have written that Epaphroditus is well again, but to send him back is better, especially since Paul expects release so that he, too, (Paul) can get back to Philippi.

29) **Accordingly, receive him in the Lord with all joy and hold such in honor because on account of Christ's work he came near to death, having ventured his life in order to fill your absence in the public service toward me.**

The Philippians are to receive Epaphroditus in the manner in which Paul is sending him. He wants this to be done with unalloyed joy. In fact, they ought to hold all who are of this kind in honor. Paul generalizes when he writes τοὺς τοιούτους, but when he describes this kind of men he returns to the singular and states the thing that Epaphroditus, one of this deserving class, has done.

30) **First, that because of Christ's work** (διά, for the sake of it) he came near to death, in this case death by sickness, but death nevertheless. Then, in the participial and the purpose clause he connects the Philippians in the closest way with this act of Epaphroditus': he risked his life as their representative in the public service to which they had commissioned him to help Paul. This very participle παραβολευσάμενος (the variant is only an attempted correction of this very rare word) has recently been found in a second-century inscription: "having risked his life" (M.-M. 480).

Τὸ ὑστέρημα, "that in which one comes behind" or falls short, denotes the absence of the Philippians. Epaphroditus "filled this up," i. e., he consented to step in, to act as their ἀπόστολος and λειτουργός (see v. 25), as their representative and official servant in this work of Christ. Since they were absent and far from Rome, the Philippians could assist Paul in his work only by a volunteer who would go in their place and thus "fill their absence." We may regard ὑμῶν as a possessive or as an objective genitive: the ὑστέρημα was *theirs,* it left *them* out. "Of the official (public) service toward me" is the genitive after a term of want, lacking, or coming short. Paul has already (v. 25) called

Epaphroditus: *"your* commissioner and *public officer";*
and now he says that he filled *"your* absence in this
public office toward me." When he came he was
Paul's public official assistant, not one selected by Paul
but a representative of the Philippians, selected by
them.

Every term is delicate, and the combination is
exquisite. They were only unavoidably absent, that
was the only coming behind. It pertained only to them
(objective genitive is probably best). Epaphroditus
filled it up completely (aorist). It pertained to the
great official public service, to nothing less. The Philippians had it at heart as a congregation, had sent this
their own representative. This service was, of course,
for others, but Paul puts in "toward me," Epaphroditus was to be *his* assistant. Just as μου and ὑμῶν in
v. 25 bind Paul and the Philippians together, so again,
in reverse order, ὑμῶν and πρὸς ἐμέ bind them and him
together.

But note that, while Paul is so close to the end of
his trial that he scarcely needs Epaphroditus, and when
the latter fell sick had little service from him and
considerable anxiety instead, he, nevertheless, honors
Epaphroditus as fully being his official assistant and
asks the same honor for him from the Philippians.
Not so much the amount done but the will counts.
This brother *had* ventured his life. That it was by
way of sickness and not by way of persecution, did
not change the fact. Paul, one nobleman, recognizes
and honors another.

CHAPTER III

Paul Adds a Warning against Judaizers and Points to his own Example

1) The supposition that Paul intended to close his epistle with τὸ λοιπόν, but that something else flashed into his mind at the moment so that he began again and then made another attempt to close with another τὸ λοιπόν in 4:8, is not tenable. Paul certainly intended to write 4:10, etc., as the final part of his letter. Please note that already in Paul's time τὸ λοιπόν began to be little more that οὖν in force (R. 1146) and that it has come to be this in modern Greek. So the expression may occur more than once in a piece of writing and not necessarily only as marking the conclusion. Here this adverbial accusative introduces the warning against the Judaizers and concludes the admonition against pagan adversaries begun in 1:27-30. That is why τὸ λοιπόν is quite in place, and why it is untenable to deny that there is a connection between this chapter and the preceding. In fact, even 4:8, 9 is not a conclusion but rather the summary and last positive admonition.

Furthermore, my brethren, rejoice in the Lord! To be writing the same things to you for me (is) **not sluggish but for you** (it is) **safe.**

The call to the affectionately addressed "my brethren" to rejoice in connection with the Lord to whom they belong with heart and soul, is the preamble to what follows, which, however, is not merely the brief direct warning against the Judaizers but far more the glorious position of the Philippians in contrast to these errorists (v. 3), which is illustrated at length by using Paul himself as an example (v. 4-14), whom the Philippians are to follow (v. 15, etc.). So this is the proper note to strike by way of preamble even as joy rings through the entire epistle. This is not an afterthought but a carefully thought-out, integral part of the letter.

"The same things" refers to what follows and not to the call to rejoice. These "same things" are frequently taken to be warnings that were written to the Philippians in previous letters, namely letters which thanked them for remittances for Paul's support, in which letters he also repeatedly warned against the Judaizers. But we have already seen that, besides the gift just sent Paul, only two other gifts had been sent while Paul was in Thessalonica (4:16). The multiplication of these gifts is unnecessary. "The same things" refers to 1:27-30. There he warns the Philippians to stand firm against opponents; now he issues the same warning against another set of opponents. Today some would say, "The same old polemics over again!"

Μέν and δέ balance: thus to repeat "for me (is) not sluggish," or sluggishness as though my mind is lazy and can harp only on one string. These things are, to be sure, practically the same things. But to repeat them as I do, "for you (it is) safe" or a safe thing, the word "safe" is to be taken in an active sense, tending to make you safe. "Not sluggish" is a litotes. Paul is diligent and very active in repeating warnings and fortifying them. Standing on Zion's towers, he is no dumb dog (Isa. 56:10), he does not fail to blow the trumpet, no blood of any poor victim will be required at his hand (Ezek. 33:2-6). Paul is pure from the blood of all men (Acts 20:26). Here is the interpretation of "for you — safe," the answer to those who balk at "the same things" when they hear the least polemics. This double statement is the narrower part of the preamble.

2) Now the direct warning. **Beware of the dogs! Beware of the base workers! Beware of the Mutilation!**

Concise, crushing! Like Tennyson's: "Break — break — break!" (R. 1178), with great rhetorical effect (R. 1100). This is the entire warning, all the rest is offered in substantiation. Βλέπετε is frequently used in the sense of "look out for," "beware of." We may imitate the Greek direct object: "Beware the dogs!" The verb indicates that these "dogs," etc., were not as yet present in Philippi but that they might appear at any time. They had invaded the Galatian churches and had done great damage in Corinth. These Judaizers established no congregations of their own, they bored into sound congregations that had been built up by others. See their arrogant tyranny in II Cor. 11:20.

There is no need to seek for the connotation of "the dogs" and to think of insolence, shamelessness, roaming tendencies, barking at people, etc. "Dogs" was the Jewish designation for all Gentiles; Paul hurls it back at the Judaizers: *they* are "the dogs" in the true sense of the word. In the Orient the dogs were ownerless, roamed the streets and acted as scavengers, and were filthy in this sense. In Matt. 15:26, 27 the point of Jesus' answer is lost when "dogs" is understood in this sense. Jesus used the word κυνάρια, the diminutive, "little pet dogs" that were owned by the family, kept in the house, allowed under the dining table (see the author's interpretation). Yes, Paul called errorists rather harsh names. He followed Jesus in this respect: "ravening wolves" (Matt. 7:15), Paul: "grievous wolves" (Acts 20:29). These are not wrong, passionate names but terribly true ones. They are a little unpopular today. The *Expositor's Greek New Testament* (Kennedy) refers to Luther "who, in prospect of death, could not depart without wishing for

his followers not only the blessing of God but also
hatred of the pope."

"Dogs" is figurative, "base workers" is literal.
They were exceedingly energetic like the Pharisees
from whom they sprang, who compassed land and sea
to make one convert and made him thereby twofold
the child of hell (Matt. 23:15). Fanatic errorists are
marked by this energy which is the very opposite of
gospel zeal (Jesus, John 2:17; Paul, II Cor. 11:26, 27).
Κακός == "base," i. e., morally base in all their energy.
This adjective describes these men and their personal
moral character and not merely their fruits. This is
a fact on which to reflect, for this is their regular
characterization in Scripture.

"The Mutilation" is the abstract for the concrete,
κατατομή in *annominatio* with the following περιτομή (R.
1201). These words are similar in sound, opposite in
sense, and deadly in effect: "the Mutilation — the
Circumcision." The former is here not applied to all
Jews as circumcised individuals but only to the Judaizers who mixed the law with the gospel and made
physical circumcision necessary for all believers in
Christ. Our versions try to keep the similarity in
sound: "Concision — Circumcision," but the former
does not convey the point clearly enough. By their
insistence on circumcision for believers in Christ these
Judaizers were "the Mutilation," this being their true
name for the cutting which *they* did. What Christ
had abrogated they demanded as essential; what now
counted as nothing (Gal. 6:15) they counted as everything. To yield to them was to fall from grace, to let
Christ become of no effect (Gal. 5:3, 4).

What the three terms lack in length they more
than make up in force. Is the third sarcasm? What
else would sarcasm be? All three are definite (hence
the articles) and denote one well-known, dangerous
and vicious class. Those who think that they designate

three different classes cannot point these out. Pagan opponents are not mentioned after 1:28; "base workers" cannot be "base Christians" in general. All that follows is stated in opposition to Judaizers.

3) **For we on our part are the Circumcision, those worshipping God's Spirit and boasting in Christ Jesus and not resting confidence in flesh.**

Beware of the dogs, etc., "for" *we* are the very opposite and cannot have the least to do with them! This is the connection. "We" is decidedly emphatic; the articulated predicate "the Circumcision" is identical and interchangeable with the subject "we" (R. 769) and is amplified by the apposition which includes three participles that are united by one article (*οἱ*). These three balance the three terms used to designate the Judaizers. When Paul says to the Philippians: "*We* are the Circumcision," the opposite of "the Mutilation," this means the true spiritual Circumcision that is *not* handmade (see Eph. 2:11). "You" in v. 3, now changed to "we," includes also Paul and Timothy (1:1), in other words, all true Christians; the Judaizers are excluded. The abstract term is again used to indicate a concrete class.

"We" cannot be restricted to Paul and his assistants in the work of the gospel. The participial additions do not admit such a restriction. The epistle thus far has not touched on this restricted group. The view that in the following Paul speaks of himself as being physically circumcised is answered by the fact that two assistants of his, Titus and Luke, were not circumcised.

What makes Paul, Timothy, and the Philippians "the Circumcision," the true succession of the Israel of God (Gal. 6:16), who must beware of the Judaizers lest they, too, fall from grace and lose Christ (Gal. 5:4)? This that they are "the ones worshipping the Spirit of God," etc. Meyer terms this the *Erfahrungs-*

grund. Christians know from their own experience who and what they are, yet they know this in the way which Jesus indicates in John 7:17 when he includes the doctrine which makes them what they are. In Scriptural literature λατρεύω is used only in the religious sense to indicate the service we owe to God, which is obligatory for all of us and not only for persons in office, to indicate which latter the word λειτουργῶ is used (the noun in 2:17).

The correct reading is "God's Spirit" and not the dative "God" (A. V.). But the dative "God's Spirit" is not instrumental, the means "by" which *we* worship (R. V.). If that were the force, the very inferior reading πνεύματι Θεῷ would be preferable: worship God with (our) spirit (compare A. V.), John 4:24: "in spirit and truth." The Scriptures never say that *we* use the Holy Spirit as a means for worship or for anything else. On the other hand, we challenge the statement that the Scriptures never present the Holy Spirit as the object of our worship; this is sometimes extended to include also our Lord Jesus Christ. This claim is Arian. Right here Paul writes: "We are the ones worshipping God's Spirit."

Next, *we* are "the ones boasting in Christ Jesus"; ἐν names the cause of our happy pride and exaltation, "Christ Jesus," office and person, all that he is, has done, and will yet do for us. Finally, "the ones having and ever continuing to trust not in flesh" but, as the two preceding participles show, in God's Spirit and in Christ Jesus and what *they* do for us.

What do those called "the dogs" know about the worship of "God's Spirit"; "base workers" about "Christ Jesus" and his real work; "the Mutilation" besides "flesh" which they mutilate, to which neither God's Spirit nor Christ Jesus impels them? These three contradict the Judaistic three. Moreover, "God's Spirit" and "Christ Jesus" are properly named because

through them alone and not through "flesh" the Father
works our salvation.

4) This verse should be construed with the preceding: "We are . . . the ones resting confidence
not in flesh" **although I for my part possessing confidence even in flesh.**

Bengel is right: *having* but not *using*. Πεποίθησις,
"confidence," is here used objectively, not to indicate
feeling, but the objective reason or cause that might
produce such a feeling whether it actually does so or
not. The participial construction is continued from
v. 3: Paul is one of those worshipping the Spirit,
glorifying in Christ, not resting confidence in flesh
although *he especially* (ἐγώ, emphatic) possesses everything in the way of flesh that inspires the Judaizers
with their confidence and, if Paul would permit it,
would so inspire also him. Among all the Christians
who do *not* (οὐ, clear-cut, decisive negative when it is,
as here, used with the participle, v. 3) put their confidence in flesh Paul stands pre-eminently as one who
actually has reason for the Judaistic mistaken confidence. On καιπέρ, "although," as stating an emphatic
opposite point see R. 1154.

5) A new sentence begins. **If any other person
thinks of resting confidence in flesh, I for my part —**
(even) **more!** — i. e., I on my part have more reason
to think so than any other man. "In regard to flesh,"
i. e., anything of that kind (no article is used with
the three phrases), Paul challenges any Judaizer to
excel him. Of course, this is only "flesh" and not
"flesh" in the purely ethical sense, namely our depraved
human nature, but rather in the physical and Judaistic sense, prerogatives of Jewish birth and of Jewish
religious standing and attainments, as the following
shows. This emphatically repeated phrase "in (such
a thing as) flesh" already makes plain to every Christian reader what folly it is for any man to rest his con-

fidence in such a vacuous thing, however much he might possess of it.

Now there comes the catalog of the "flesh" prerogatives which Paul actually "has," in which he excels any Judaizer, on which, if he were a fool as they are, he might rest his confidence instead of resting it exclusively on Christ Jesus. All the items are appositional extensions of ἐγώ: **"I (even) more" — as to circumcision an eighth-day-one; out of Israel's stock, Benjamin's tribe; a Hebrew out of Hebrews; as touching law, a Pharisee; as touching zeal, a persecutor of the church; as touching righteousness in connection with law, one come to be blameless.**

The Greek has the adjective "an eighth-day-one" with the dative of relation "as to circumcision." Circumcision is named first because this was the chief thing for which the Judaizers contended. Well, Paul had it; nor did he get it later on in life like the many proselytes of the Jews or like Judaizing proselytes and like converts made by Judaizers. Paul was circumcised exactly on the eighth day according to the law.

Secondly, he was of genuine Israelite stock, namely of Benjamin's tribe, which tribe, together with that of Juda, constituted the real Jews after the loss of the ten tribes and after the Babylonian captivity. Paul was not a leftover from any of the ten tribes. Since he was a Benjaminite, his father named him after the one king, Israel's first, who had been furnished by this tribe: Saul.

Thirdly, Paul was a pure-blooded Hebrew, "a Hebrew out of Hebrews," no ancester on either side being of other blood. The word Hebrew means "one from beyond the river (Euphrates)" who returned to Palestine from there after the Babylonian captivity; then it also means one who speaks the Aramaic dialect. Paul's Hebraic extraction was the genuinely purest and best in Jewish eyes.

Already in these three physical "flesh" excellencies many and many a Judaizer was outclassed by Paul. But he climbs higher and higher until he leaves every Judaizer behind. This list is cumulative.

He names three more "flesh" prerogatives, the very highest in all Jewish and Judaistic eyes, these are marked by κατά which denotes measure or norm. Measured by "law," Paul was "a Pharisee," a *pharush*, a "separatist," the strictest Jewish sect that stood for completest observance of law (Acts 26:5) and was revered as such by all Jews. Paul was even the son of a Pharisee (Acts 23:6), a most genuine article of this type. How many Judaizers could say this of their Jewish past?

6) Measured by "zeal," i. e., zeal for Pharisaic observance of law, Paul had been "a persecutor of the church," this innovating body of Christians who were abrogating the law and following Jesus, who had been crucified as one accursed of God according to the Jewish estimate (see on "death of a cross," 2:8). We know how Paul outdid himself in this "zeal" which was so meritorious in Jewish eyes. With their "zeal" the Judaizers only proselyted the Christians. What was that compared to Paul's old record? Here he leaves them all behind. Gal. 1:14.

The most important item is kept for the last. Measured by the standard of "righteousness," namely "that in connection with law," the old Jewish standard which the Judaizers were upholding with might and main, Paul was "one become blameless," faultless. Δικαιοσύνη is forensic as always; but here the judges who pronounce the verdict: "Righteous because blameless!" are the Jews and the Judaizers. That is the verdict and the quality Paul had actually reached (aorist participle). How many of either class, Jews or Judaizers, could truthfully say the same?

The anarthrous νόμος = "law" in its quality as law. While the Jewish law is referred to, "*the* law" would be an inexact translation, compare "blameless" in Luke 1:6; Phil. 2:15. Paul scored 100 per cent in regard to all six items. The first three without will or act of his own, the other three by his will and his acts; the first was character derived, the last, character personally attained.

7) **But what things were for me gains, these I have considered because of Christ loss.**

They "were" at one time in Paul's blind Jewish eyes "gains," the Judaizers still regarded them thus, they "*were*" but *are* that no longer (significant tense). Ἅτινα = what things of this kind (Paul has not mentioned all of them) and because they are of such a kind. "These," because they are what they are, "I have considered" for a long time and continue to do so (extensive perfect) "loss" or damage. They were, as Paul at last discovered, fallacious gains, gains which robbed him and only damaged his soul. No Judaizers can make him think otherwise at this late day. He had invested in absolutely worthless stock; nobody could ever sell him any more of this kind. Why? "Because of Christ," which sums up the great reason in briefest form: "because he is the one and only gain."

8) **Yea, also I still consider everything to be loss because of the surpassingness of the knowledge of Christ Jesus, my Lord, because of whom I suffered the loss of all these things (and still consider them dung) that I might get to gain Christ and get to be found in connection with him as not having any righteousness of my own, that** (derived) **out of law, but the one** (obtained) **by means of faith in Christ, the righteousness** (derived) **from God on the basis of this faith:** (namely) **to get to know him and the power of his resurrection and fellowship of his suf-**

**ferings in being conformed to his death, if somehow
I may get to arrive at the rising up from the dead.**

This second ἀλλά is climacteric (R. 1186): "Yea."
This is enhanced by the following participles, a sample
of the old witchery of the Greek particles (R. 1143), five
of them being combined: "yea, indeed, therefore, at
least, even" (R., *W. P.*), a combination that is impossible to our cold English which has never had such delicate touches and knows nothing of such exquisite shad-
ing of thought.

Paul repeats with emphasis the thought expressed
in v. 7 and brings out the vital points. No one can
persuade us that Paul intends to convey no difference
between the perfect tense ἥγημαι, "I have considered"
(v. 7), and the two presents ἡγοῦμαι, which emphasize
and mean: "I still continue to consider." When different tenses of the same verb occur side by side, the difference is intentional. Here this difference even ob-
trudes itself: what Paul has done (ἥγημαι, v. 7) he emphatically "also" (καί) continues to do (ἡγοῦμαι), and no
Judaizer shall ever change him. In v. 7 he says "such
things" (ἅτινα), now he says "everything" (πάντα) he
considers to be loss and nothing but loss for the reason
assigned. But now he expands this reason from "because of Christ" to the full, emphatic "because of the
surpassingness of the knowledge of Christ Jesus, my
Lord."

The substantivized neuter participle τὸ ὑπερέχον is
equivalent to an abstract noun. At one time Paul sur-
passed all the young men of his age in Pharisaic zeal
and false Jewish merit, Gal. 1:14; now he has found a
far different "surpassingness," the true one, one that
bestows upon him "the surpassingness of the knowledge of Christ Jesus, my Lord." He now uses the full
confessional name and not merely the terse "Christ"
which he used in v. 7. He now writes "the knowledge,"
γνῶσις (the verb occurs in v. 10; both words indicate,

not the mere relation of the object to the subject as in
intellectual knowing, but of the subject to the blessed
object as in heart knowledge, C.-K. 388). "Everything" fades into worthlessness before this knowledge
which makes "Christ Jesus, my Lord," Paul's inward
possession, Christ's person and his work, his Lordship
full of grace and glory. John 17:3: "This is life eternal that they may *know* . . . Jesus Christ whom thou
hast sent."

Now he states the loss and the gain, but the loss
that is the surpassing gain. Δι' ὅν is emphatic: "*he* the
one because of whom I was made to lose all these
things" that in my folly I at one time considered such
great gain, τὰ πάντα, the article of previous mention
(πάντα). The passive is significant. Paul did not of
himself give up his Jewish excellencies, somebody made
him lose them; we need not ask who. Ever since that
time (Acts 9:4, etc.) Paul has considered these things
as loss (perfect tense, v. 7) "and still goes on considering them (now he uses a still stronger term) as
manure." We let the linguists debate the derivation of
σκύβαλον and the meaning as to whether this is dung,
manure, or just rubbish that is swept out. See M.-M.
579, the singular being found in a papyrus with the
meaning "rotten hay," the whole of it being decayed
and no better than "dung" (manure). The connotation is that all Paul's Jewish excellencies were for him
made and are now by him ever considered a stinking
mess.

In the purpose clause: "in order that I may gain
Christ and be found in connection with him," etc., some
puzzle about the aorist subjunctives. They seem to be
future to "I still consider." On that supposition various explanations are offered, all of which in some way
operate with a future gaining of Christ, etc., and think
that this must ever be renewed (but these are aorists),
that the final gaining has not yet been attained, etc.

The construction is plainly *ad sensum* with the ἵνα clause being dependent on the divine act by which Paul was made to suffer the blessed loss.

One ought to note that these strong final aorists cannot depend on Paul's subjective considering. Moreover, through to v. 10 all the aorists are ingressive. The little insertion "and still consider dung" is merely thrown in to repeat "and still consider everything to be loss," the only new point being "dung." So we have this: "I was made to suffer loss of all these things (and still consider them dung) in order that (by that loss) I should get to gain Christ and get to be found in connection with him," etc. Instanter with this loss (historical aorist of fact) the purpose was accomplished: Paul got the gain, was found, etc. That is why he ever since considered as he had, and why he declares he still so considers.

"Get to gain Christ" is again terse and concentrated like "loss because of Christ" (v. 7) ; in fact, they go together. As the latter is expanded and expounded in v. 8, so the former is elucidated in v. 9, καί being epexegetical.

9) One gets to gain Christ, not as one acquires those Jewish and Judaistic gains, by natural birth and by personal zeal and work, but by divine agency, "without any merit or worthiness of our own" (Luther). Hence we have another aorist passive: "and get to be found in connection with him." We gain Christ when by his grace God connects us with him, and when you and I are found thus connected by God. "In him" is the same phrase that is used scores of times; ἐν = "in connection with," it is neither mystical, mysterious, nor anything that is beyond the ordinary reader. The connection is ever and always made by faith.

Here it is fully elucidated: "found in connection with him as (or by) not having any righteousness of my own," having been made to suffer the loss of any such righteousness as v. 8 states. Note the strong ἐμήν and not μού, and the absence of the article. "Any righteousness of my own" would be "that (derived) out of law" of some kind (again no article) whether Jewish or some other. Ἐκ indicates source. To get any righteousness of one's own out of anything in the way of law would have to be done by perfectly fulfilling such law, a thing that is impossible for born sinners. The Jews and the Judaizers had only an imaginary righteousness out of their law, the one God took from Paul by this very law in Acts 9:5 and stripped him clean. This is the negative part of having gotten to be found (ingressive) in Christ.

The positive is the very opposite: "but (as or by having) the one (obtained) by means of faith in Christ (objective genitive), the righteousness (derived) out of (or from) God (himself) on the basis of faith." The commentary is found in Rom. 1:17: "God's righteousness" as revealed by him in the gospel, "out of faith," "for faith"; in Rom. 3:21: published and attested by the Old Testament: "God's righteousness through faith in Jesus Christ for all the believers." As in these passages in Romans "faith" is mentioned twice, so here in Philippians.

This is the genuine righteousness — Paul emphatically repeats the word — for it is "out of God" and not "my own." We get to have it as ours "by means of faith," add through the gospel, the opposite of any law. "Gratis, by his grace" (Rom. 1:23), hence by means of faith alone. It is the quality of righteousness that is produced by the divine verdict which pronounces the sinner righteous "on the basis of his faith," this very "faith in Christ" who expiated our curse on the cross (2:8; Gal. 3:13). This verdict is pronounced on believers only (Rom. 3:22), the verdict pronounced on all others is damnation (Mark 16:16; John 3:18b). It is pronounced in the instant of faith and recorded everywhere in Scripture (Rom. 3:21). This faith which is so essential as the means for having God's righteousness and as the basis for the verdict involved in it is kindled by God himself and is never without its contents, "Christ."

10) The infinitive with τοῦ is epexegetical whether it is considered final (continuing the idea of ἵνα in v. 8) or consecutive to the ἵνα clause: "in order to — or so as to get to know him," etc. In either case it is ingressive. The construction is: "I suffered the loss of all things . . . in order to gain Christ and to be found in him . . . (namely) to know him and the power of his resurrection and fellowship of his suffering in being conformed to his death." Τοῦ γνῶναι does not express a further purpose, one beyond that expressed by ἵνα. Paul would then have used a second ἵνα. He would have written in the same way if he had intended to have two parallel purposes. Here the infinitive expounds what the ἵνα clause contains. The great purpose of the loss that snatched everything away from Paul was in that very instant to make him gain Christ and in that instant to be found in him as having the true righteousness; and this means that then and there, in that very instant, Paul got to know Christ, the power of his resurrection, etc. Mark the four aorists and do not make the last one ("get to know") a durative, continuous, progressive present.

This answers those who have the infinitive depend on this or that intervening subordinate point. We need not refute them in detail.

"To get to know him" = "the surpassingness of the knowledge of Christ Jesus, my Lord," in v. 8. What we have said on the latter regarding γνῶσις and γνῶναι applies also here: Paul got to know, not merely intellectually (relation of the object "Christ" to the subject, οἶδα), but in a personal, saving way (relation of the subject to the object, γινώσκω), *cum affectu et effectu.*

Paul is restating God's great purpose as it was actually accomplished at the time of his conversion as recorded in Acts 9. Jesus appeared to him; that is how Paul "got to know *him.*" Jesus appeared to him in the blinding glory of heaven; that is how Paul "got to know his resurrection and the power of it." Jesus said: "I will show him how great things he must suffer for my name's sake" (Acts 9:16); that is how Paul "got to know the fellowship of his sufferings." So much strained interpretation fades away when this connection with Acts 9 is seen.

There, on the road to Damascus, at one blow went everything that Paul had built up in the way of a righteousness of his own; there (and through Ananias) he was put into connection with Christ and with the righteousness from God through faith in Christ, on the basis of this faith, ἐπὶ τῇ πίστει, v. 9. And all this means that there Paul truly got to know Christ. The infinitive is clearly epexegetical. The aorist designates the purpose achieved by God so that we may also call it result; it makes no difference as long as we let it remain epexegetical.

We now see that "him" (get to know *him"*) is expounded by the double addition: "and (epexegetical) the power of his resurrection and fellowship of his sufferings." This is what Paul got to know near Damascus regarding Christ. He himself saw the risen Lord, saw him in all the power of his resurrection. This is "the surpassingness" of the knowledge Paul there got (v. 8). This power of Christ's resurrection became Paul's personal, blessed *gnosis.* He was made to know Christ Jesus as "his Lord" (v. 8), for Jesus appeared to Paul to bring him to contrition and to faith, not to damn him with his omnipotence.

"The power of his resurrection" means that by the resurrection he was made both Lord and Christ (Acts 2:36), exalted as Prince and Savior to give repent-

ance to Israel and forgiveness of sins (Acts 5:31),
made unto us wisdom and *righteousness* and sanctification and ransoming (I Cor. 1:30). "The power of his
resurrection" is the seal of his redemption. God accepted his ransom by raising Christ and by glorifying
him so that all who by faith embrace this Christ who
died and rose again for our justification (Rom. 4:24,
25) are justified by God, have "the righteousness from
God on the basis of faith" (v. 9). This is "the surpassingness of the knowledge of Christ Jesus, *my
Lord.*"

There is only one article: "the power — and fellowship." Some texts have two. Some commentators
desire two because they find "power" and "fellowship"
too diverse to be combined under one article. Some
even divide into three objects: "get to know 1) him,
2) the power of his resurrection, 3) the fellowship of
his sufferings." We have only one object: "him."
This one is unfolded by epexegetical καί and means:
him according to his power as Savior and our fellowship with his sufferings. Paul's confession: "Christ
Jesus, *my Lord,*" sums it up. Acts 9:16 applies to Paul
as regards these sufferings. Read Matt. 5:11, 12;
20:22; John 15:19-21; Rom. 8:17; II Cor. 1:5; 4:10;
Col. 1:24; Phil. 1:29; I Pet. 4:13. These passages
and others are the Scripture's commentary. Also
Paul's own addition "in being conformed to his death."
The fact that Paul expected eventually to die a martyr's death we have noted in 2:17. He was not certain;
but he certainly lived with death at his elbow many a
time.

This participation in Christ's sufferings is not a
participation in their expiatory quality as all the passages show. It is due to the world's hate, due to its
hate of our Lord which is extended to us because of
our connection with him. The plural refers to all the
sufferings of Christ and not only to the final ones; they

climaxed in his death. The present durative passive participle is construed like the one in v. 9 ("as or by not having") : "as or by being conformed."

The participle contains μορφή (see 2:6). We are not merely receiving the σχῆμα or outward fashion but the real form that fits the essence, so closely are we connected with Christ who is "formed" in us (Gal. 4:19). Outward resemblance is not referred to but something inward and far deeper. It should now be clear that "the power of Christ's resurrection" and "fellowship with his sufferings, conforming to his death," are not diverse, each to have its own article on that account, but a unit that is properly placed under one article. Christ's resurrection, sufferings, and death ever go together, and thus Paul got to know as a joint thing the power of his resurrection and fellowship of his sufferings: his *power* as justifying and saving us, Paul's *fellowship* in being conformed to this Christ.

11) The durative participle is in distinct contrast to the preceding aorists (four of them). Being made to conform runs through Paul's entire life to his very death (whether he suffers martyrdom or not). It is essential to note this in order to understand what follows. The four aorists place us at Damascus, at the time of Paul's conversion, the durative participle carries us to Paul's death. Paul thinks of that death: "if somehow (in any way) I may get to arrive at the rising up, the one from the dead." He has combined Christ's resurrection, sufferings, and death; he has spoken of his participation in Christ's sufferings and of conformation with Christ's death. So now, as is done in other passages (Rom. 8:17; I Pet. 4:13), he adds the coming glory of his resurrection.

We have εἰ πως with the subjunctive which is akin to an indirect question and hence is used with the subjunctive and expresses expectation (see B.-D. 375).

The verb might be the future indicative, but we do not think that it is so here, for in v. 12 we have the same εἰ with a subjunctive. The subjunctive is still more certain because this "if" is a part of God's purpose in getting Paul to gain Christ and to be found in him, etc. (v. 8, etc.), in getting him to know Christ, etc., and in more and more conforming him to Christ's death (v. 10). The expected end of all this realized purpose is: "if somehow I may get to arrive,'' etc. The aorist "get to arrive" at last also conveys the proper sense. Neither εἰ nor its addition intends to express doubt; B.-D. is right, it expresses expectation. Paul confidently expects that "somehow" the conformation God is working out will attain its goal and make him arrive at last at the blessed resurrection from the dead.

The only uncertainty is in the "somehow." Will it be by a martyr's death, his blood being poured out in a libation (2:17) or by a non-violent death (such as John suffered)? Will Paul, who had been a prisoner for four long years, at last die in prison or die in free apostolic activity? Some say that Paul speaks with modesty, that he still distrusts his sinful nature, and the like. These ideas are well meant, but they misunderstand the Greek εἰ πως and overlook the divine agent in "was made to suffer loss" (v. 8), this agent appearing again in "being made conform." These passives are genuine in the sense of 1:6: "He who began in you a good work will bring it to its goal up to Christ's day." In 1:6 Paul says, "I am confident of it"; here his "if" says, "I am expecting it."

Only here the word ἐξανάστασις is used, and the question is asked why Paul does not write the common ἀνάστασις as he does in v. 10. Some fanciful answers are given on the basis of ἐκ and on misconceptions of the resurrection. Paul apparently uses the double compound regarding his own resurrection from the dead because this is not identical with Christ's resurrection.

In v. 10 we have: "the power of his resurrection,"
Christ arose by his own power. Paul's is "a rising up"
that is effected by Christ. Remember how often Jesus
said: *"I* will raise him up at the last day!"* (John
6:39, 40, 44, 54) and not: *"He* will arise." Of the
temple of his own body Jesus said: "I will raise it up"
(John 2:19). "From the dead" (ἐκ νεκρῶν) means:
"from death." Paul will arrive at this blessed goal
when he dies. His body will sleep in peace until Christ
awakes it from sleep at the last day.

Paul is not speaking of a spiritual resurrection.
Misinterpretation of Rev. 20:5 posits two physical
resurrections with a great interval between them and
introduces this thought into our passage. John 5:28,
29: "the *hour* is coming" is divided into two widely
separated hours. The questions: "Did Paul expect
to die before the Parousia? Did he not expect to live
until the Parousia?" are answered in I Thess. 4:13-17.
How could he know? No more than you can. If he
had either experience, the expectation here expressed
would be fulfilled.

12) God is still at work conforming Paul to
Christ's death, and Paul is yet to get to arrive at the
resurrection from the dead. So Paul writes: **Not
that I did already get hold of or have already been
made complete. No, I am continuing pursuit if also
I may get to capture, since also I got captured by
Christ Jesus. Brethren, I on my part am not yet
reckoning myself to have captured. One thing, yes,
— forgetting the things behind and stretching out
goalward to those in front, I continue pursuit for the
prize of the lofty calling of God in Christ Jesus.**

We supply nothing; "not that" is common also in
English. Paul is not warding off a misunderstanding,
he has written nothing that needs what follows as a
correction. He is simply elaborating his blessed condition now that he has gotten rid of the false Jewish

righteousness and has been put into possession of God's
true righteousness.

Here we have another study in tenses. Robertson
has said well that there are sermons in Greek tenses.
Paul's meaning is expressed by the verbs plus their
tenses. "Not that I did already get hold of," aorist:
that I have already gotten to that point. Paul has
been a Christian for years; yet at no point during
those years, not even in the recent past, could he say,
"I am done!" Some ask, "Got hold of *what?*" and then
supply some object, perhaps reaching down even into
v. 14, "the prize." But the aorist past act as such is
the whole point. This is strictly punctiliar and *not* a
constative, summary aorist as R., *W. P.,* states.

"Or" is conjunctive and not disjunctive. It presents
the same thought with a different word, yes, and with
a different voice: "or have already been made complete." "To get hold of" is an act of Paul's, and *he* has
to take, grasp, get hold of. The Christian is filled
with life, with a new will, with spiritual power and
ability. He must not only use it constantly, but the
great moment comes when the final grasp must be
made. Yet ever and always activity and passivity are
combined. That is also the case in this final act of
which Paul speaks. God will do the act of completing
(1:6). Hence the passive: "Not that — I have already been made complete," i. e., by God. Now the
tense is the perfect: "have been made complete" so
that I stand as such, so that God is through and can
look at me like a contractor who has finished a building.
God's task regarding Paul is not yet finished.

Take the two verbs together also as to their tenses.
The time will come when Paul can say, Ἔλαβον, "I did
get hold!" and when God can say, Τετέλεσται (as in
John 19:30), "It has been finished!" or Paul, Τετελείωμαι,
"I have been finished!" namely by God and his grace.

But "no" (δέ), not yet can either be said by Paul.

He must still say: "I am continuing pursuit!" I am
still chasing, a durative present. The verbs are so
diverse that no one object can be supplied, Paul himself
prevents it by the diversity. "I am continuing pursuit
if also I may get to capture, since also I got captured
by Christ Jesus," "if also," as in 2:17 (R. 1026),
leaving no doubt worth considering. The relative
phrase = "because" or "since," see the discussion of it
in Rom. 5:12; II Cor. 5:4. Ἔλαβον is now turned into
the stronger καταλάβω, and this is joined to the passive
κατελήφθην, simplex and compounds, which it is difficult
to reproduce in English, it is something like: "I did
not already get *hold of* — if I may get to *hold down* —
since also I got *held down* by Christ Jesus."

Εἰ has the subjunctive just as in v. 11 and with the
same expectancy. Paul is steadily pursuing in expectation of making the capture with finality (aorist), and
this rests on the fact that at Damascus he got captured
by Christ. Again there is the significant combination
of active and passive, but now "got captured" by
Christ is the historical aorist and lies in the far past
(Damascus), and "may get to capture" lies in the
future (as a subjunctive). Both are strictly punctiliar
and indicate momentary acts: all in an instant Paul
got captured; all in an instant, when the time comes,
he will get to capture. Our versions misunderstand
the relative phrase and make it: "that for which."
Pursuing and capturing match; but see the paradox:
the one who got captured does steady pursuing so that
he may eventually also get to capture.

13) Paul repeats and elucidates by doing so.
Some think that Paul is referring to the Philippians
and is aiming at them by his pointed ἐγὼ ἐμαυτόν and is
implying that in Philippi some imagined that they
were through and could rest on their oars. We do not
agree. This strong "I on my part — my own self,"
which is even placed side by side for the purpose of

greater emphasis, is opposed to a wrong estimate of Paul. Was he not the revered apostle of Christ, who had suffered so exceedingly much in his apostleship, who had borne four long years of imprisonment? Surely, the Philippian brethren might think him a saint who was entirely finished and complete, who might well admonish others but no longer himself needed admonition. Paul cuts off such thoughts. It is well that, like John, the other saintly apostle (I John 1:8-10), he has done so. Lesser men have persuaded themselves that they have attained perfection in this life, have strenuously preached their perfectionism with great damage to themselves and to others. Here is the antidote, another is offered in Rom. 7:14-25. The first of Luther's famous 95 Theses is true: "The whole Christian life is a continuous repentance."

"Brethren" sounds as if Paul means: "Please, brethren, do not think of me that *I* have such a high opinion about *myself.*" "I am not (some texts: not yet) reckoning myself to have captured," I could not dream of doing such a thing; nor must any one of you think of me as already having made the capture. The perfect active κατειληφέναι implies that, having made the capture, Paul may sit at ease since he has made it, sit so now.

"One thing, yes (δέ) — forgetting the things behind and stretching out goalward (κατὰ σκοπόν, this goal being in sight) for those in front, I continue pursuit toward the prize of the lofty calling of God in connection with Christ Jesus." We supply nothing with ἓν δέ, not even a copula, much less: "but one thing I do" (our versions). What this "one thing" is Paul states directly and balances the participles with μέν — δέ. It is asked what "the things behind" are which he forgets, whether they are those enumerated in v. 4-6, his old Jewish prerogatives and attainments, or all that lies behind him in his Christian life. Undoubtedly the

former. This is not an absolute forgetting, for he
has just recalled these things once more; the participle
is the durative present. This is the forgetting of
constant discarding.

The other things, namely that he had been captured
by Christ, had been set on the road toward the blessed
resurrection from the dead to travel along the path
of fellowship with Christ's suffering in conformity
with his death, Paul could in no way "forget" or dismiss from his heart. These were ever the moving
power in his life. In fact, forgetting the Jewish ideas
of righteousness is only the negative for ever remembering the Christian reality of righteousness by faith
in Christ. "Stretching out goalward to those (things)
in front" = eager to meet these things. The things
in front are not yet "the prize" itself but all that lies
goalward in Paul's life until his death. He has
mentioned "fellowship with the sufferings of Christ
by being conformed to his death" (v. 10). Like a
runner on a race track Paul rushes into each one of
the sufferings that lie before him on that track, ever
stretching out goalward, goalward.

14) Thus he continues pursuit "for the prize of
the lofty calling of God in connection with Christ
Jesus." He has already named this βραβεῖον or "prize"
in v. 11: "may arrive at the raising up from the
dead." This is, of course, eternal blessedness, but the
whole of it, pertaining to the body as well as to the
soul. "Prize" is derived from the Greek word for
umpire, the βραβεύς who bestows the prize at the end
of the race, who is here Jesus who promised: "I will
raise him up at the last day."

The genitive "of the lofty calling" is stated objectively, for this is "the calling" of every believer. "Of
my lofty calling" might be understood with reference
to Paul's exceptional apostolic calling. "The calling"
(κλῆσις) is active, "of God" states who called. In the

epistles this is always the successful gospel call which
is actually followed by the power of grace in faith. The
adverb "above" is used as an adjective. The purpose
in adding this is not to indicate that this calling comes
from on high, i. e., is divine, for this thought lies in the
genitive "of God," who certainly is "above." This
call is "high or lofty" because of the goal, the heavenly
blessedness to which it calls us. It is improper to add
inadequate ideas such as that "the goal ever moves forward as we press on yet is never out of sight." Who
ever heard of a goal doing that? The goal is always
stationary and fixed; σκοπός names it as a mark that is
seen, toward which the runner stretches with all his
might.

We do not understand how anyone can say "in
Christ Jesus" is to be construed with the distant verb
"I continue pursuit"; it belongs where Paul placed it:
"the calling of God in Christ Jesus," God's calling is
in connection with Christ. To say that this is self-evident and need not be said forgets the fact that it is
just as self-evident that our pursuing is in connection
with Christ. Some self-evident things, nevertheless,
need be said. The true Christian's high calling comes
to him "in connection with Christ Jesus," and because
of that it is the very opposite of all Judaism and Judaistic schemes of life that are based on law and works.
Our call connects with him who died and rose again,
who is the fount of gospel grace, the opposite of works
of law.

And right here is the place to touch that most vital
and distinctive point in our calling. *We* did not set up
the prize; *we* did not even call ourselves to run for it.
All this is of God and of Christ. Nor does our running
create the prize or even earn it. The prize is pure
grace, even our call is nothing but pure grace like the
new life by which we are able to run and the running
itself to which grace moves us. Paul reached the prize

when he died. Then he arrived at the resurrection. His body fell asleep in order to be awakened by Christ as his sure promise states.

15) In v. 2 we have the sharp warning against the Judaizers. In v. 3 Paul and the Philippians are described as being the very opposite of the Judaizers. In v. 4-8 Paul, more than any Judaizer, had discarded it all for Christ. In v. 9-14 Paul who has the divine righteousness runs for the goal of eternal blessedness in the resurrection. Thus Paul has used his own striking case, he being a former wonderful Jew, to substantiate and fully elucidate his warning. Paul had had far more than any Judaizers could even pretend to have. Had he tried to combine it or any part of it with the gospel and with Christ as the Judaizers demanded wherever they appeared? God himself had destroyed all of it for Paul when he called him in Christ, had shown Paul that it was all stinking dung, that Christ was everything, namely righteousness by faith in Christ alone, a life in conformity with Christ's suffering, the goal the resurrection granted by Christ. Now Paul reverts to the "we" of v. 3 in a brief exhortation that includes himself.

Accordingly, let us, as many as are mature, keep minding this thing; and if on some point you are differently minded, this, too, God will reveal to you. Only to what you have attained, with the same keep in line!

Τέλειοι is the predicate to ὅσοι, the copula being omitted, and states who "we" in the verb suffix are. The word means "mature," those who have reached an end, here, as in passages like I Cor. 4:12; 14:20; Eph. 4:13, spiritual growth and maturity. A glance at M.-M. 629 shows how common the word is in this sense, and how a technical meaning like that found in the pagan mystery cults certainly did not influence Paul in his use of this adjective. Masonry uses various terms in its rituals, but this certainly does not mean that, when Christian preachers use these words, they are drawing them from such rituals.

It is fancy when we are told that "mature" should be put between quotation marks because the Philippians used the word regarding a certain class of their own number, who claimed a sort of perfection, Paul referring to this peculiar use. Even a certain irony is supposed to lurk in this quoting of the term. Paul uses the word in the same way in which he uses it elsewhere: "mature Christians" who are no longer "babes" that need to be nursed. Paul places himself among the mature.

No play on words is intended between τέλειοι and τετελείωμαι in v. 12 although they are derived from the same root. They are placed too far apart from each other for this. The verb denies regarding Paul that God has brought him to a certain finished stage (the one indicated in the context) while the adjective asserts that Paul and most of his readers have attained a finished stage (a different one from that mentioned in v. 12). That this is the stage of perfect holiness, as the perfectionists claim, is excluded already by the double denial in v. 12. Paul plus many Philippians had, indeed, reached spiritual maturity. To be sure, like every congregation, they had among them children, young people, and new, immature converts, all needing the mature members to guide and to help them. Paul is now addressing the mature.

Τοῦτο is not adverbial as we see also in 2:6; not: "Let us be *thus* minded!" but: *"This thing* let us keep minding!"　The hortative subjunctive means more than "keep thinking" as does the imperative in 2:6; it includes thought plus conduct. But what is "this thing" that Paul and all the mature Christians must ever keep minding? To say it is the "one thing" mentioned in v. 13 is well enough; but if this is understood so as to exclude the rest of Paul's exposition in v. 2-14, the idea is mistaken, for by "one thing" in v. 13, as Paul describes it in v. 13, 14, he includes all that he says in v. 2-14. No one can forget the things behind, stretch out goalward to those in front, and keep in pursuit of the prize of the lofty calling unless he heeds all that Paul has said. Οὖν reverts to all of it, and the whole of it, Paul says, let us keep minding. That is why he wrote all of it down for his readers. To be sure, they had not all been Jews like Paul, their life's history had run a different course; but the same danger (v. 2) threatened them, and in order to keep safe they had ever to mind "this thing" that Paul so clearly sets forth on the basis of his own soul's history.

We decline to make καί a kind of apodosis: "This let us keep minding, *and then* (or: *and so*), if on some point you are differently minded, this, too, God will reveal to you." This creates confusion in wording as well as in thought. Καὶ εἰ regards the supposition as improbable, as an unlikely, extreme case (R. 1026, where the difference between this expression and εἰ καί is shown) : "and if" as I really have no reason to suppose, as is barely possible. Why is this so unlikely? Because all these are "mature" Christians. Yet suppose that it should after all happen that "on some point (adverbial τί because an adverb follows) you are differently minded," what then? Why, "also this God will reveal to you," i. e., in due time he will correct the slight mistake. "With καὶ εἰ the truth of the principle sentence is stoutly affirmed in the face of this one objection" (R. 1026).

What is this point of some kind or "some respect" (τί) in which the mature Philippians might be differently minded than Paul? It is evidently some minor matter or respect. Paul himself does not specify, for he himself cannot guess. If we care to guess we might think of the ugly titles Paul bestows on the Judaizers

in v. 2, or of some of the Jewish prerogatives Paul lists
as having been his own.   The Philippians had as yet
had no personal experience with such Judaizers as Paul
has had it, they might thus judge them less severely
although Paul scarcely thinks so.   So also the Philippians, the greater number of whom were former Gentiles, had never had so violent an experience as Paul
had had when all his Jewish glory was turned into
dung for him.   They might thus be differently minded
in one or the other respect regarding Paul's experience
and its exact meaning for them although Paul scarcely
thinks so.

When Paul says, "This, too (even this), God will
reveal to you," he is not turning them over to God
because he himself does not know what else to do.   Nor
may we think of an immediate revelation.   Καί, "even"
or "also" implies that God had revealed to these mature
Christians all that had brought them to their maturity,
all their knowledge of Christ and his righteousness,
and all their earnest, zealous Christian life; and God
had done this by the Spirit who works through the
Scripture Word (the Old Testament in this case) and
through Christ's apostles (John 16:13, 14), the doctrine and the instruction which spread all the truth and
make it a power in the hearts of Christians.   Paul says
that God will thus enlighten the Philippians on even
any minor point that may yet be left and that is not
fully clear to them either in itself or in its value for
them.   In fact, in this very epistle Paul is presenting
anew to the Philippians a good deal of God's revelation
which ever penetrates our hearts more deeply.   Our
constant experience is that even we mature Christians
see many a point more clearly as time and our own
personal experience go on.

16) The conjunction πλήν concludes by lifting out
the essential point (R. 1187) of this matter: "Only to
what you have attained" in having become mature (the

Greek uses the aorist "did attain"). "With the same,"
Paul says, "(ever) keep in line," that is all you have
to do. This is the imperative use of the infinitive (R.
1092, 944; B.-D. 389) which is frequently found in the
inscriptions and in the papyri and needs no further
explanation except that the infinitive leaves the command impersonal. The thought is the same as that
expressed in Gal. 6:16: "as many as are keeping in
line with *this canon*" or rule (the one stated in Gal.
6:15). Στοιχεῖν = to stand and march like a soldier,
each in his place in rank and file.

Paul by no means says that being minded differently in some respect is a matter of indifference just
so we keep to the main thing, faith in Christ. He is
not an indifferentist regarding even the least point.
He is the soundest unionist that ever lived, who united
in the completest inner union of heart and life all whom
he taught. The Philippians, lined up and ever keeping
in line with all that by God's grace and revelation they
have thus far attained, will by this very means attain
also one mind in any minor matter that may still need
one-mindedness. Perfect oneness in the Word (revelation), with one heart and one spirit, is the prayer of
Jesus (John 17:17-21) and the preachment of all his
apostles. Paul's effort is a completely united front
against the errorists of his day.

Paul Impresses his Warning with a Personal Appeal and with the Resurrection Glory

17) The terse exhortation consisting of only two
words found in v. 15a: "this thing let us keep minding," is certainly not the entire exhortation that corresponds to the long elaboration regarding himself
which Paul presents in v. 4-14. He completes the exhortation in v. 17. Thus he also reverts to the Judaizers and their following, who were mentioned briefly in
v. 2 (v. 18, 19), and once more, as in v. 3, contrasts

himself and the Philippians with these enemies of the gospel (v. 20, 21), but now, not, as in v. 3, according to their present Christian character and life but, as in v. 11-14 (where he speaks only of himself), according to their coming resurrection glory. So closely is this paragraph connected with the contents of the one preceding (v. 1-15) that it is impossible to separate the two and to make the one deal with Judaizers and the other deal with pagan libertinists.

Be joint imitators of me, brethren, and watch those walking so as you have us as an example! "Be," not "become." The sense is "ever be" as you now are, and not, "get to be" as you have not yet been hitherto. The word Paul uses is "joint imitators," i. e., all of you joined together in imitating me (σύν associative). The idea is that they are to aid and support each other in imitating Paul. In what respect they are to imitate him need not be stated after all that Paul has said about himself in the preceding. Such a statement would be necessary if Paul were now turning to pagan libertinism. "Brethren" not only aids the appeal, it also conveys the idea that the Philippians are to imitate him as being a brother jointly with them.

The idea of self-exaltation when Paul asks the Philippians to imitate him personally disappears when he adds: "And watch those walking so as you have us as an example." Paul does not say, "And watch those who walk so as I walk," and make himself the only example, one for these persons as well as for the Philippians. No; Paul is only one of the whole number who are to serve as an example. It is incorrect to say that "do you keep watching" includes all the Philippians, and that "those walking" are an entirely different group. This idea overlooks *"joint* imitators." In Philippi there were many who walked so as to serve as an example together with Paul. All these imitate each other and are to keep on doing this, Paul himself

being one of them. They are not to be imitated merely
by those who are not yet fit to be imitated. They are
not to serve as dummy models. Themselves active imitators, their very imitating is to be imitated, by each
one of themselves as well as by all others. The Philippians have a most intensive and stimulating model.
"Joint imitators" is found only here, Plato has the
verb. In Rom. 16:17, because of the context, σκοπεῖν has
the meaning "to watch" so as to beware of; here the
context indicates "to watch" so as to copy, cf., σκοπόν
in v. 14. Τύπον, "type," is the impression left by a blow
as when a die is struck, metaphorically "an example."

18) **For many are walking, of whom I told you
often and now tell you even weeping, the enemies of
the cross of Christ, whose end** (is) **perdition, whose
god the belly, and** (whose) **glory in their shame —
they minding the earthly things.**

This is the special reason for the admonition given
in v. 17. These "many" are the horrible example over
against which Paul places the perfect one. Paul says
he has kept telling the Philippians about these enemies
of the cross of Christ, which he says also in v. 1 when
he writes "the same things" to them. The accusative
"the enemies of the cross" is in this case merely by
attraction to the relative οὕς; the nominative οἱ φρονοῦντες
at the end of the statement in v. 19 escapes the attraction because of the intervening genitive of the relatives. The Greek is perfectly regular.

Who are these "many"? Whom does Paul's description fit? Some answer: Epicurean antinomian
libertinists and not Judaizers and their following. This
answer is based chiefly on the statement that the god
of these errorists is "their belly." Rom.16:18 is cited
in support because "belly" is also found there. But
Romans 16 is thereby misinterpreted (see this passage
in extenso.) This interpretation ignores all the points
interspersed throughout this paragraph and in v. 1-15.

If with v. 17 Paul turns to an entirely opposite class
of errorists, how is it to be explained that he does not
indicate this change? Why look only at "the belly"
and ignore the rest?

When Paul first came to Philippi he had every reason even at that time to warn against Judaizers, for
such errorists had brought about the convention in
Jerusalem (Acts 15), and this convention itself had
sent its resolution to all the Gentile churches. When
the congregation at Philippi was founded, no libertinists had appeared. Much is made of being strictly
historical. History excludes "many" libertinists. The
few times that Paul was at Philippi are ample to justify the imperfect ἔλεγον and the adverb "often" as pertaining to the Judaistic danger; historically considered, libertinism could not have been Paul's subject of
constant warning.

The view that Judaizers dealt with doctrine and
not with life is as untenable as that libertinists dealt
with life and not with doctrine. All living is the outcome of the teaching one believes. Paul says: "Many
are walking," but this includes the doctrine that produced this conduct. Paul does not locate these "many"
or any of them in Philippi. Thus far Philippi had
escaped direct contact with such men as we have already noted; but the danger was that also Philippi
might be invaded, the very word "many" involves such
a danger.

It breaks Paul's heart to know that many of these
errorists are abroad, disturbing the church; tears come
to his eyes as he now characterizes them anew. Verse
2 is full of indignation, v. 18 is full of pain. "The enemies of the cross of Christ" is exact, for the Judaizers
claimed to believe in Christ Jesus (Acts 15:5) and also
in his cross; but their legalism nullified the atoning and
the justifying effects of the cross (Gal. 5:2, 4). The
worst enemies of "the cross" are not those who object

to a crucified Savior but those who deny that the cross
and the sacrifice of Christ alone justify and save the
sinner. These Judaizers made Jesus himself a Judaizer. Had Jesus not been circumcised; had he not kept
the Mosaic law; had he not died on the cross for that;
must we not follow this example of his to be saved? So
they probably argued. The cross is still nullified. It
is used to make Jesus a noble martyr, an example
for us.

19) "The end of whom — perdition" states the
plain, terrible fact. "Perdition" = everlasting ruin.
Mark 16:16b. The Judaistic faith in Christ failed to
trust in the very thing which gives us the σωτηρία,
eternal salvation. In this connection read Matt. 7:22,
23; Paul merely repeats its substance. "Whose god —
their belly" = Rom. 16:18: "Such are not serving as
slaves our Lord Jesus Christ but their own belly."
They emancipate themselves from absolute obedience
to Christ and his will and his Word, he is no longer
their God although they shout: "Lord, Lord!" (Matt.
7:22); they obey their "belly" as their "god." In both
passages Paul states it drastically, for "belly" is figurative for their lower and their lowest nature. In Rom.
16:19 Paul defines "belly" by τὸ κακόν, "that which is
base"; here he adds "their shame (disgrace)" and "the
earthly things." These items go together.

This reference to "belly" makes some sure that
libertinists are referred to. They draw on First
Corinthians for illustrations of laxity in morals. Libertinists serve their belly and the appetites of the
belly. In Romans, however, this thought would call for
διακονέω whereas Paul writes δουλεύω even as he here
writes ὁ θεός, "the god" before whom one bows as a
slave. Every error is false emancipation from Christ
and his Word and his will, the Judaistic error eminently so; every error thus enslaves us to our own
lower nature, lets that dictate as "god." Error is

not merely intellectual. The intellect is only its tool.
Its source is "the flesh," the depravity in us. Its
coarsest part is "the belly." Even in its physical sense
the word applies to these Judaizers who made the
belly their god by demanding only kosher food. Read
Matt. 15:17; Col. 2:20-23. Paul does not confine "the
belly" to this narrow, physical sphere even as this
is only a part of the larger one which is indicated by
what precedes and what follows.

For he adds, not as a third feature with another
ὧν, but as being a part of the second: whose god the
belly "and (thus) their glory in their shame." The
things their fleshly belly nature dictates to them, in
obedience to which they see "their glory," are in
reality nothing but their shame and disgrace. Ewald
makes αἰσχύνη their *Schamteil*, the circumcised *membrum vile;* but we hesitate to make the abstract
"shame" so concrete.

Paul's great glory is the cross (Gal. 6:14). Everything Judaistic is to him dung (v. 8), yea, everything
else in the world is crucified for him, and he for it
(Gal. 6:14). To Christ and to his cross alone he
looked up in obedience as a slave, there he found his
glory. Simpler, and thus the final elucidation is:
"they (ever) minding the earthly things," all these
are by "the belly" summarized as being basely earthly.
So the spiritual things might be called "the spirit."
We have Rom. 8:5 constrasting the two mindings, the
word referring both to what our thought demands and
our conduct carries out.

20) In v. 18 "for" supports the admonition given
in v. 17 by pointing to what the Judaizers and their
following are; in v. 20 "for" does this by pointing to
what "we" are in contrast with them. It is the same
contrast as that indicated in v. 2 and 3 and not one
between an entirely different class of errorists and us.

For our commonwealth exists in (the) heavens from which also we expect as a Savior the Lord Jesus Christ who will change the fashion of the body of our lowliness conform to the body of his glory in accord with the working of his being able also to subject to himself all the things (that exist).

The contrast with the Judaizers and their following does not present a list of opposite items which match those stated in v. 18, 19. Paul's contrast is summarized in the vital one of the vast difference obtaining between "those minding the earthly things" over against whom we stand whose "commonwealth exists in heaven." This enables him to bring in the resurrection, at which he in v. 11 says he wants to arrive and in v. 14 calls "the prize of the lofty calling of God in Christ Jesus." For the Judaizers "the end is perdition," for true believers the Savior who will transform our bodies. So plainly does Paul link together v. 11-14 with v. 20, 21 that we cannot think of two sets of errorists. What v. 11-14 contain is also most grandly elaborated in these two closing verses. The whole chapter is a perfect unit.

The note on πολιτεύεσθε given in 1:27 and the reason for this verb may serve for πολίτευμα, the noun, which is used for the same reason. A "commonwealth" stands against those who do not belong to it, especially against those who would invade it. This commonwealth stands against "the enemies of the cross of Christ," for its very head is Christ, and all who are his ἐχθροί or personal enemies must be regarded as such by Christ's true believers. The suffix -μα does not fit the abstract idea "citizenship" (R. V.); it fits rather the idea of result, "a commonwealth" which is actually constituted of citizens. Among the examples collected by M.-M. 525, etc., we find one that is useful: the Phrygians had set up a "commonwealth" in Alexandria. But this example only helps, for the true Christians set up no commonwealth here on earth, their great commonwealth exists in heaven, they are strangers and pilgrims here. Their great business is never to mind the earthly things but to mind the heavenly.

That has nothing to do with Epicurean libertinism, sensual, fleshly pleasures, but, as the context shows (v. 4-6), with *religious* earthly things. Get Paul's full blast against the errorists and the errors they seek to spread in the church. His is no high intellectualism. Paul sees vile dogs (v. 2), a belly god (v. 19), stinking dung (v. 8), utter shame (v. 19) and thus perdition. Not only do the true Christians shun and abhor all of it, their whole "commonwealth" to which they belong, into which they yearn to enter, is in heaven. M.-M rightly object to the rendering: "We are a colony of heaven"; but the reason should not be that this reverses the relation between the colony and the mother city, we are not a bit of heaven here on earth, heaven has not colonized earth with a few angels. The whole state (πολίτευμα) to which we belong is "*in* heaven" and not on earth. John 18:36 is not a parallel passage.

"From which" is best referred to the commonwealth (singular) and not to the heavens (plural) although our versions translate "whence," and R. 714 accepts the clash in number. In the sentence, "We are expecting as Savior (predicative) the Lord Jesus Christ," the word "Savior" is scarcely used in the way in which this title was accorded the Roman emperors. In this connection nothing points to a contrast with men who were called "saviors." C.-K. 1035 notes that the imperial title "Savior" had no more than the pale meaning of *Nothelfer*, who was not much of a helper at that. We must go to the Old Testament for the idea of the Greek Σωτήρ, "divine Deliverer." Nor is this title derived from the mystery cults which flowered in the pagan world at a rather later time.

21) The relative clause states in what sense "Savior" is here used: he who brings us the final salvation by raising our bodies from the dead and glorifying them, "who will change the fashion of the body of our lowliness conform to the body of his glory." This will occur at the Parousia. The statement is so worded as to include also those who are alive at the time of Christ's coming (I Thess. 4:15-17).

Paul uses both terms, the one derived from σχῆμα and the one derived from μορφή, as he does in 2:7, 8: "form of a slave — fashion as man," but he now has them in reverse order: "change the fashion — conform." Σχῆμα is the fashion or appearance, μορφή the form corresponding to the very being itself. In v. 10 Paul describes our body as "the body of our lowliness" (qualifying genitive); it is the body in t⁀e "fellowship of his sufferings being *conformed* to his death." Conformed to his death, it shall at last be *"conform* (predicate adjective) to the body of his glory" (qualifying genitive). So completely shall its fashion be changed that its very form shall be like Christ's glorified body.

"Body — body," and yet in the face of this passage and of many others the resurrection of the body is denied. Rom. 8:17, 18 is restated here save that the double mention of "body" places the main point beyond question. Add I Cor. 15:52-54, "corruption" shall be turned into "incorruption," "mortality" into "immortality." But Paul now adds the conformity with "the body of his glory," our body shall have glory that is similar to the glory of Christ's body. His body shines as the sun in divine glory and effulgence, our bodies shall shine as the stars in created glory. This expectation and this hope the Judaizers give up by clinging to "the earthly things," their glory being their shame, their god the belly. Paul is in pursuit of this heavenly prize, stretching to arrive at the raising up from the dead, the dung of all his Jewish earthly prerogatives and attainments being left behind and forgotten, and the Philippians are to keep imitating him and all others that are like him.

Does anyone ask how the Lord Jesus Christ as Savior shall do all this with the body of our lowliness? The answer is: "in accord with the working of his being able also (or: even) to subdue to himself all the things," τὰ πάντα, all that exist (definite). Whether we make αὐτῷ the simple pronoun "to him" or give it the rough breathing αὑτῷ and make it reflexive "to himself," makes no difference, either is correct, the grammarians vary. The infinitive is the qualifying or descriptive genitive used as a noun, B.-D. 400, 2 finds consecutive force in it: *Kraft, dass er kann,* "energy *so that* he is able." He who is able, who has the power to subdue all the universe to himself, he will with his omnipotence raise up our dead body in glory. This will be the final miracle.

Ask all you please how our body whose dust has perhaps been scattered far and wide as they threw the ashes of John Huss into the river, or which has been devoured by wild animals or by fish in the sea, how this body can possibly be restored again — omnipotence will restore it. Philosophizing tries to make it easier for the omnipotent Lord and Savior by letting him conserve only a germ and bring that forth; or by dispensing even with the germ and letting the Lord create another entire body so that he does not need to restore "the body of this lowliness," or by letting him dispense altogether with the body and leaving the souls of the blessed bodiless like the angels. But all these ideas are untenable.

4:1) **And so, my brethren beloved and longed for, joy and crown of mine, thus keep standing firm in the Lord, beloved!**

This is the concluding appeal of the entire third chapter, which forms a unit, and not only of 3:17-21.

Ὥστε is like 2:12. No other congregation does Paul address as he does the Philippians in this verse. He repeats "beloved," he adds "longed for" and then unarticulated and with predicative force: "joy and crown of mine." Paul lets all his love, all his joy in the Philippians, all his pride in them, speak out at once. They had never been anything but joy for him, hence joy, joy runs through this epistle.

"Crown of mine" recalls 2:16. He had not run in vain, they had been given him as the victor's crown. I Thess. 2:19, 20 is similar to this. "Thus keep standing" = thus as chapter 3 sets forth, the verb is used also in 1:27. "In the Lord," in union with him, is especially effective after v. 20: "the Lord Jesus Christ as Savior" who will do all that v. 20, 21 say. "Stand" or "stand firmly" includes all of it. Let no errorists move you in the slightest degree! It is the one thing we all need. Some even drift of their own accord; some are swayed by every new wind of doctrine. The Lord help us to stand!

CHAPTER IV

The Little Case of Euodia and Syntyche

2) Much has been read into these two simple verses, and most of it is rather fanciful. Some treat these two sentences as if they were intended to be a charade, each name having some hidden meaning.

Euodia I admonish, and Syntyche I admonish — Paul treats them exactly alike — **to keep minding the same thing in the Lord.** We decline to preface this statement with "Beloved" by drawing this address from v. 1 to v. 2 as though Paul were informing the whole "beloved" congregation of the fact that he is admonishing these two members in their midst. Will the letter, when it is read, not show this without an address? Paul constantly uses the verb παρακαλῶ in the sense of "I admonish" and not in the sense of "I beseech" (A. V.). Zahn, *Introduction* I, 562, rightly calls the allegorizings of the two names "fantastic conceits." These are two women of Philippi and not two peculiar parties. They bore rather common names: twenty-three or twenty-four other Euodias have been found, twenty-five Syntyches; Zahn thinks that further search may yield even double these numbers.

All that we know about these two women is contained in the relative clause in v. 3, and all efforts to extract more is love's labor lost. The two women once worked together with Paul in bringing the gospel forward, and it seems they had advanced the cause of the gospel since that time. We thus gather that they were both energetic. The supposition that they were deaconesses or that they held some office cannot be substantiated. Why they both needed the admonition "to keep minding the same thing," they and the Philippians knew, we do not. All that we note is that both women were equally at fault.

The brevity of Paul's statement shows that this case is quite minor and incidental. Paul had received knowledge of it through Epaphroditus (2:25, etc:). These two energetic women were not pulling together. This is not an unusual occurrence when energetic personalities are engaged in the same cause. No doctrine was involved but only what each woman considered the better or the best way of furthering the work of the church, and this as to certain details. All that can safely be assumed is that the disagreement was not one of a day or a week but of long standing, otherwise Paul would have passed it by.

It was not a good thing for these two to differ as they did. It was not a good example for the other members to witness. It did not increase the joint efficiency of the two and the benefit the congregation should have had from their efforts. When one horse pulls and the other lags, and when this is reversed at the next effort, the wagon does not move as it does when both throw themselves into the harness with the same mind.

Paul teaches us a bit of practical theology by the way in which he handles this case. He applies brief, gentle admonition to the women themselves, and he asks one of the esteemed members in the congregation to lend aid. Paul does not address the women directly, which means that he treats their case objectively. Paul does not scold them, either jointly or separately. Paul avoids negative, "don'ts." "Mind the same thing in the Lord!" is the proper admonition. Are they not both "in the Lord"? Do they not both intend to mind whatever they mind "in the Lord"? Then, surely, they both should equally mind "the same thing," i. e., have the same thing in their thoughts and in their efforts. It is so simple, so natural, and should be so easy. Paul feeds no little spark of dissent in order to bring on a flame; he gently quenches the spark itself.

These two are women, and the Philippian church began with a woman convert. In fact, some have advanced the thought that one of these women was Lydia, the term "Lydia" being regarded, not as her personal name, but as one that was derived from her former country Lydia, she thus being called "the Lydian." But Acts 16:14 says that her "name" was Lydia, and Horace repeatedly uses this as a woman's name as do other writers. Whether Lydia was still in Philippi no one knows. Zahn offers no proof for thinking she was one of these two. Lightfoot tells us with a good deal of evidence that women generally played prominent parts in Macedonia. But look at the names of women mentioned in Rom. 16:3 etc.; we find them in the Gospels; also "honorable women" in Acts 13:50 and 17:12. The church has always had many intelligent and zealous women. Macedonia as a country deserves no special credit in this respect.

3) **Yes, I request also thee, genuine Syzygus, be of assistance to them, who are such as strove with me together also with Clement and my other fellow workers whose names** (are) **in the Book of life.**

"Yes" = I do even this, namely "request also thee," etc. "Also thee" means "thee" especially and thus in a way requests also others who may be able to lend assistance. Is it possible that after two personal names (Euodia and Syntyche) and before a third (Clement) Paul should *not* write the personal name of the one whom he even addresses directly and personally, that Paul should designate this one person of the four only by a descriptive term, "true yokefellow"? To ask the question seems to us already to answer it. Where did Paul ever call an assistant of his or of anybody else a σύζυγος? They are his συνεργοί as in this very verse. But the name "Syzygus" cannot be duplicated

from books, inscriptions, etc.; hence it is claimed that
it cannot be a proper name here. The usual answer
given is too mild, namely that this is not convincing.
We must say more. Since when has the canon been
established that, unless at least *two* persons are found
in ancient writings with the *same* name, *one* person
alone cannot have such a name? Let someone go
through the list of ancient names and report to us how
many lack duplication. The result should be interesting.

Would the mere appellation "genuine yokefellow"
suggest to this unnamed person and to the rest of the
Philippians the person to whom Paul refers? Was
there only one man in the Philippian church who was
a "genuine yokefellow," and were all the Philippians
cognizant of this strange fact? Such questions
answer themselves.

Those commentators who do not regard Syzygus
as a proper noun differ widely in regard to the identity
of the person addressed "genuine yokefellow." Here
are some of their suggestions.

(1) Paul's wife. We are told that he did not take
her along on his journeys, in substantiation of which
I Cor. 9:5 is quoted, although Paul is now not on a
journey and has been a prisoner for four years. Moreover, the adjective "genuine," γνήσιε, is masculine; if
it were the feminine γνησία it would mean "legitimate
wife" and might imply that Paul also had one or more
concubines!

(2) Lydia, despite the masculine adjective.

(3) Christ.

(4) Paul's brother who is thought to reside in
Philippi.

(5) Timothy, despite the fact he is the co-writer
of this epistle (1:1).

(6) Γνήσιος is taken to be an Arminian proper
noun, the Greek word for "Chenisi" or "Khenesis."

(7) Silas.

(8) The husband or the brother of one of the two women.

(9) Epaphroditus. This is the suggestion of Victorinus which was adopted by Grotius and others, among whom we find Lightfoot, von Hofmann, and Zahn. Zahn thinks that Epaphroditus is sitting at Paul's side, is perhaps serving as Paul's scribe, and that Paul at this moment is addressing him with the vocative "genuine yokefellow."

Since duplication of proper names has been called for by some of these commentators, we feel entitled to apply their canon to themselves. Let them show us another letter that is intended for persons living at a distance in which the writer addresses a friend sitting at his side at the moment of the writing, who is perhaps himself doing the writing! Zahn points to Col. 4:17; but Archippus was in Colosse, Paul is not addressing him, he is addressing the Colossians.

It is unfair when Zahn mentions only Laurent as supporting the view that Syzygus is a proper name; many others who have never heard of Laurent support this as being the only tenable view. It is again unfair when Zahn (*Introduction* I, 538) places *between* the idea that the name means Chenisi (Khenesis) and the idea that it means Christ — two impossibilities! — the idea that Syzygus is itself a proper name, thereby leaving the impression that this is likewise an impossible idea.

When Paul writes "genuine Syzygus" he plays on the beautiful meaning of this man's name. One whose own personal name is Σύζυγος, "Yoked together," may well demonstrate the propriety of his name by helping to yoke these two women together, henceforth to pull together and to work hand in hand for the congregation. So a "Frederick" may be told to act as a *genuine*

"Peacemaker" or a woman named "Grace" to do a gracious deed. Even the tone in which Paul refers to the etymological meaning of this brother's name accords with the kindly way in which Paul treats the case of these two women. A little assistance will be good for them from one whose very name points to what they both need in the way of assistance.

Most significant in this direction is the relative clause that is introduced with αἵτινες (qualitative and causal) : "they being such as," "because they are such as," etc. When Paul worked in Philippi, either on the occasion of his first visit or when he went from Ephesus to Corinth and spent some time in Macedonia, these two women had shown themselves not only of a type to be *yoked* up with Paul but actually "to *strive* strenuously together with him in the gospel" (i. e., in the missionary work). Nor were they the only ones; Paul mentions Clement as another and names him, no doubt, because of his equally energetic cooperation. There was, in fact, a whole company of this type; Paul calls them "the rest of my fellow workers."

Note the first point: all these acted σύν, i. e., in finest cooperation, and now it ought surely to be an easy matter for these two women again to cooperate thus, especially if someone gives them a little assistance (note σύν even in the imperative). Then note also the second most beautiful point: the strongest one of the three terms used refers to these two women and to Clement. Of these alone he says that, like athletes, they *strove* together (σύν) with him; regarding the others of this type he uses the lesser word, they *worked* together (σύν) with him. So also of the one brother he asks only that he take hold together (σύν) with the two women, i. e., that he assist them. Thus we see why Paul plays on his name *Syzygus*, which contains these three σύν in a double way, namely in its

prefix σύν and in its root "yoke," the yoke harnessing
two to pull together.

John's delicate sense of propriety has been noted
in John 11:5 where he mentions not only the two
sisters as being loved by Jesus but also Lazarus. We
have the same delicacy here when Paul adds Clement
and the rest to the two women who strove together
with Paul. When Paul says of the other fellow workers
that "their names are in the Book of life," he uses
Old Testament language (Exod. 32:32; Ps. 69:28;
Dan. 12:1) that is copied in Rev. 3:5 (13:8 negative;
also Jer. 17:13) for praising them. Superficially considered, this seems to lift the fellow workers above
Euodia, Syntyche, and Clement; but in reality it does
not, for if those who *worked* with Paul are thus
praised, shall not those who *strove* jointly with him
have equal praise?

All God's children are written in the Book of life.
The Scriptures speak of blotting out of the Book of
life when one ceases to be a child of God. Thus the
expression Book of life may be used with reference to
our justification: when we are justified, our names
are written in the Book of life. Yet Rev. 13:8 goes
back to eternity: "from the foundation of the world."
So we may refer the expression also to our eternal
election (Eph. 1:4), but always as making Christ
"the true Book of life" (*C. Tr.* 1067, 13). "Thus the
entire Holy Trinity, God Father, Son, and Holy Ghost,
directs all men to Christ, as to the Book of life, in
whom they should seek the eternal election of the
Father. For this has been decided by the Father from
eternity, that whom he would save he would save
through Christ, as he himself says, John 14:6: 'No
man cometh unto the Father but by me.' And again,
John 10:9: 'I am the door; by me, if any man enter
in, he shall be saved.' " *C. Tr.* 1085, 66. "Therefore,
whoever would be saved should not trouble or harass

himself with thoughts concerning the secret counsel of God, as to whether he also is elected and ordained to eternal life, with which miserable thought Satan usually attacks and annoys godly hearts. But they should hear Christ, who is the Book of life, and of God's eternal election of all God's children to eternal life: He testifies to all men without distinction that it is God's will 'that all men should come to him' who labor and are heavy laden with sin, in order that he may give them rest and save them, Matt. 11:28" (1085, 70). "Moreover, this doctrine gives no one a cause either for despondency or for a shameless, dissolute life, namely when men are taught that they must seek eternal election in Christ and his holy gospel, as in the Book of life, which excludes no penitent sinner, but beckons and calls all the poor, heavy-laden, and troubled sinners to repentance and the knowledge of their sins and to faith in Christ and promises the Holy Ghost for purification and renewal," etc. (1093, 89).

The καί before Clement and the feminine αἵτινες have been made the reason for separating the phrase "together also with Clement," etc., from the relative clause and for construing this phrase with the main clause: "I request also thee, genuine Syzygus — together both with Clement and the rest of the workers," etc. The punctuation of our versions leaves this point in doubt. The idea that all these people are to help the two women in minding the same thing (even if some of them were women) is untenable. Too many cooks spoil the broth; nor does this assistance need such a host of assistants. No ordinary reader would refer the μετά phrase back to the vocative. Kennedy names no less than five writers who use καί just as Paul does here: "together also with," etc. By referring the phrase back one loses the effect of the σύν in "strove jointly with me in company with Clement and the rest of the workers," namely that Euodia and Syntyche

are *now* not pulling together whereas *at one time* they
pulled together so strenuously with Paul, with Clement,
and with the other fellow workers.

The claim that this Clement is *Clemens Romanus*
of a later day, and that thus Paul did not write this
letter, needs no refutation. We know no more about
this Clement than we know about Euodia and Syntyche; no more than is said here. "Whose names are
in the Book of life (Life's Book)" does not imply that
Clement and the rest of the workers were dead when
Paul wrote.

Verses 2, 3 are a beautiful text for any meeting
of Christian women.

Paul Summarizes the Whole Christian Spirit and Life

4) Verses 4-9 are added without a connective and
present a lovely picture of the temper, the quality, and
the motivation of all true Christian hearts. This is the
substantial conclusion of the epistle, leaving only Paul's
thanks for the gift the Philippians had sent him.
Euodia and Syntyche (v. 2) are, of course, also to show
this spirit toward each other, but it is to fill the entire
congregation both for its own sake and for all with
whom it comes in contact.

**Rejoice in the Lord alway! Again I will say,
Rejoice!** The purest, highest, truest joy is to fill the
Christian life like sunshine. Paul wrote this as a
prisoner, as one who had been conformed to the death
of Christ. Nothing is ever to dim our spiritual joy.
Paul is not dwelling on the source of this joy, on all
the streams of grace and blessings that produce this
rejoicing. He is rather picturing the life that is
animated by the joy with which it shines. In 3:1 he
calls on us "to rejoice in the Lord" even while we
beware of errorists, knowing that we have the true
righteousness and the hope of the blessed resurrection

(3:9-11, 20, 21). Here he adds "alway," no matter what the circumstances of our life may be. Our sun of grace is "always" shining.

Paul repeats: "Again I will say, Rejoice!" The future is volitive: he will decidedly say this again. It is such a blessed thing to do. But the imperative "rejoice" is thus repeated, for the whole stress is on this activity of the heart. Add Eph. 5:19, 20 regarding how we are to give expression to this joy with songs on our lips and constant thanksgiving in our hearts to God for everything. No; the Christian life is not gloomy, it is the happiest life in the world. All its joy is genuine, not a bit of it is artificial like all the joys of the world. This epistle sparkles with joy, for its very subject and its occasion call for the sweet admonition to rejoice with true joy.

5) **Your yieldingness, let it get to be known to all men!** Ever filled with joy and happiness in all heavenly blessings that are ours, anything like rigorousness must be foreign to us, sweet gentleness, considerateness, *Lindigkeit* (Luther's beautiful rendering) must ever emanate from us so that all men with whom we come in contact may get to realize, feel, and appreciate it (ingressive and effective aorist). Does this exclude people like those mentioned in 3:2? The question is evaded when it is remarked that Judaizers had not yet appeared in Philippi. Why should these or even pagan persecuters be excluded? Many will not appreciate this gentleness; but oh, the victories it has won among the worst enemies! Paul knows of no exception when he writes "all men."

The neuter τὸ ἐπιεικές = the abstract ἐπείκεια and is often used by Paul and by the author of Hebrews and in the higher type of the Koine (B.-D. 263, 2; R. 763). Would that we had a good English equivalent for this noble term! We lack one, hence the A. V. offers "your moderation," the R. V. "your forbearance," margin

"gentleness," Matthew Arnold "your sweet reason-
ableness." Yet each of these touches only one side of
the Greek concept. When we are preaching we should
know just what is meant so that we may at least
describe with exactness. Trench is a good teacher:
the derivation is from εἴκω, ἔοικα, Latin *cedo*, hence the
meaning is "yielding," not insisting on one's legal
rights as these are often inserted into moral wrongs
by making the *summum jus* the *summa injuria*. The
word always refers to the treatment of others while
"meekness" is an inner quality. Many angles converge
in "yieldingness" such as *clementia, aequitas, modestia*.
Even the Latin lacks a real equivalent. God and Christ
exhibit what is meant. God deals so leniently with
men, he remembers that we are dust, he withholds
justice so long. Christ is gentle, kind, patient, more
than only fair. Only our perverted reason would think
that "yieldingness" might include a yielding of truth
to error, of right to wrong, of virtue to vice and crime.

Kennedy quotes W. Pater's *Marius the Epicurean*,
which describes the spirit of the new Christian society
as it appeared to a pagan: "As if by way of a clue,
recognition of some immeasurable divine condescen-
sion manifest in a certain historic fact, its influence
was felt more especially at those points, which
demanded some sacrifice of one's self, for the weak,
for the aged, for little children, and even for the dead.
And then, for its constant outward token, its significant
manner or index, it issued in a certain debonair grace,
and a certain mystic attractiveness, a courtesy, which
made Marius doubt whether that famed Greek blithe-
ness or gaiety or grace in the handling of life had been,
after all, an unrivaled success."

Yes, this is not the yieldingness of a slave or of an
inferior but of a superior in a noble and generous
spirit. The Christian keeps his high nobility, he con-
descends; he considers the weak and the needy and also

the pitifulness of the world's haughty and tyrannical. He has that purest and noblest grace which few are able to resist. All of this lies in this term *epieikeia*. Let it shine out from your joyous hearts!

Like a revealing flash the one statement: **The Lord (is) near!** shows what produces this "yieldingness." This is not the constant, invisible nearness of Christ; it is the nearness of his Parousia. No man knew the hour of his coming, every Christian lived as if he might come at any time. So we do to this day. Why, then, stress this word as though Paul were sure Christ would come before Paul died while pressing other statements of Paul's to make him contradict himself by saying that he would die before Christ came? Here the great point is the connection: we who live in constant expectation of the Parousia, of our resurrection (3:11), of our glorification (3:20, 21), we, filled with abounding joy, cannot but show this noble gentleness, this generous yielding to all men. Those who live for time alone, for this life alone, who ever mind only earthly things (3:19), they will act meanly, selfishly, rigorously, or with false, hollow gaiety, as Marius correctly estimated the blithe grace of the pagan Greek attitude toward life.

6) But what about our troubles in daily life, some of which are painful and depressing, indeed? Look at Paul, a prisoner while he is writing this. **Worry about nothing but in everything by means of your prayer and your petition together with thanksgiving let your askings be made known to God!**

Martha "was bothered about many things" (Luke 10:41). The verb means "to be of a divided mind," to be anxious, whether to seek this way out or that, to use this means or that. The Christian is never to worry thus about a single thing. I Pet. 5:7: "All your worry cast on him, seeing that he is taking care of you." Certainly, unless we can constantly get rid

of our worries before they worry us, joy would cease,
and that noble, gracious yieldingness would disappear.
But we need do no more than to let God know. The
scoffer will say, "Do you first have to inform God?"
God certainly knows even before we ask (Matt. 6:8);
but God bids us ask and promises to give us what we
ask. Those who, like the skeptic, refuse to ask simply
do not have (James 4:2).

Paul's exhortation is elaborate; he uses three
terms: "in everything" or "in every case" that may
worry you, "by means of your *prayer* and your *petition* (the articles have the force of the possessive) let
your *askings* (the things asked) be made known to
God." The datives denote means: "by means of prayer
and petition," the nominative is the subject: "askings."
Jesus, too, used three terms: ask — seek — knock.
We are to pray and not to shrink from *petitioning* and
to let τὰ αἰτήματα, the actual *things asked for*, be ever
and ever made known to God. Then no worry will
ever be able to arise. In what better hands can any
trouble of ours rest than in God's hands? Paul's very
words contain the assurance that God will attend to
all that we ask by either giving this to us or giving
us something better above what we ask or think. Our
prayer and our petition will naturally be accompanied
by (μετά) "thanksgiving," will thus be offered with
constant joy. Only the thankful heart is a joyful heart.
Without thankfulness for what God has already given
to us and done for us, how can we ask him for more?
The heartthrob of all true prayer is thankfulness.

**7) And the peace of God which exceeds all
understanding will guard your hearts and your
thoughts in Christ Jesus.**

The καί has consecutive force: "and so," R. 1183; it
states the blessed result of leaving everything in God's
hands by means of prayer with thanksgiving. "The

peace of God" (see 1:2) is to be taken objectively, the
condition of *shalom* when by God's act all is well with
us. "Of God" is to indicate source: God creates and
bestows this peace. The fact that the objective condition of well-being is referred to we see from the verb:
this peace "will guard" (voluntative and not merely
futuristic). Like a guard or sentry it will stand over
our hearts and thoughts lest anything disturb them.

The greatness of this peace assures its ability so
to guard us, for it is the peace "exceeding all understanding." The point of this attributive modifier is
often indistinctly apprehended or entirely misappre-
hended. Paul is not telling us that the peace of God,
either objectively or subjectively conceived, is beyond
our comprehension. The Scriptures tell us at length
how God has wrought peace in Christ Jesus, and all of
us upon whom this peace has been bestowed know its
sweetness from our own experience. What Paul says
is that this is the peace "exceeding all mind" in what
it is able to do for us regarding our hearts and our
thoughts. The Christian does not depend on his νοῦς,
his mind, to fend off worry from his heart and his
ιοήματα or thoughts. That is the best that worldly men
are able to do. We read much in the way of advice as
to how to manage the mind (νοῦς) so that it shall keep
the heart and the thoughts clear of worry. Paul points
the Christian to something that "exceeds all mind"
and all that mind can do in this regard. It is "the
peace of God" bestowed upon us as a gift in Christ
Jesus.

In the Scriptures the heart is the center of the
personality. There dwells the νοῦς which produces the
νοήματα, the thoughts, theoretical and practical reasonings with their purposes, plans of action, and personal
decisions. Heart, mind, and thoughts are constantly
subject to assaults which distress, harass, and worry

us. The νοῦς or mind bravely tries to hold the fort
but is ever a poor guard and protector. The peace of
God exceeds all mind in this function.

Turn to Psalm 73. There is the mind trying to
guard and protect itself. "Why does God allow me
to suffer so? Why does he allow the ungodly to flourish
and thrive?" In v. 16 and 22 the psalmist confesses
the inability of his own mind to protect itself from the
assaults of such thoughts. In v. 23, 24 he makes the
peace of God his refuge, where all his harassing
thoughts are answered and brought to rest.

"In Christ Jesus" is to be construed with the verb
and thus also with its two objects just as in Eph. 1:4,
for the action is "in connection with Christ Jesus," and
the objects of that action cannot be in some other connection. As far as the feeling of peace (subjective)
is concerned, we need scarcely say a word. Where
the actual state of peace exists with its great guarding effects, how can the feeling of peace, the enjoyment
of it, be absent? If the feeling ever declines, this
divine guard will revive it. All we need is prayer,
petition, asking, i. e., getting back under the protection
of our guard, then we shall feel safe and happy again
and shall joyfully offer thanksgiving.

8) **As for the rest, brethren, whatever things
are true, whatever things revered, whatever things
righteous, whatever things pure, whatever things
lovely, whatever things of good report, if anything
(is) excellence, and if anything praise, with these
things reckon! What things you both learned and
received as well as heard and saw in me, these things
practice! And the God of this peace will be with
you.**

Τὸ λοιπόν has nothing to do with the adverbial
accusative occurring in 3:1 and does not resume it. It
connects most closely with v. 4-7: no worry but prayer
and "for the rest" these two, that you reckon in your

thoughts with the right things (v. 8) and that you
practice them by deeds (v. 9). This close connection
is put beyond question by the mention of "peace" in
v. 9b which corresponds to its mention in v. 7.

Paul's list has six items in one series. All six
designate the same things. True things are at the
same time revered, righteous, pure, etc. So each predicate applies to every item in the list. The indefinite
and comprehensive "whatever" includes everything
"true," etc. All of these things Paul turns first in
one way and then in another and shows them now
from this side as being "true," now from another as
being "revered," now from a third as being "righteous," and so on.

Six is not a rhetorical number. In symbolical
connections it denotes one short of the sacred seven,
i. e., the antichristian group (in Rev. 13:18: $6 \times 10 \times$
10 plus 6×10 plus $6 = 666$, the number of the beast).
Our passage has no symbolism. So we ask whether
this $6 = 3 + 3$ or $2 + 2 + 2$ or $4 + 2$ or $2 + 4$? We
note that two "if" follow. Also the two: "lovely" and
"of good report," go together. We thus regard this
list as being made up of three pairs: true things are
revered — as righteous they are pure — as lovely they
are of good report. In other words, Paul has a rhetorical three, each of which is a pair. All are thus
"virtue" and as such are also "praise." "Whatever"
regards them as a mass; "anything" considers any
and every one singly. All this is typically Pauline
rhetorical formulation and worthy of appreciation
as such.

Some eliminate doctrine and restrict the list to
conduct. True, these things refer to conduct yet not
as though conduct could ever be divorced from doctrine. These things are taught and are received as
being taught (v. 9); in 2:1-4 our lowly-mindedness is
to rest on the great doctrine concerning Christ's self-

humiliation. If we only remember that "doctrine" is simply a statement of a fact or of a set of facts we shall not divorce doctrine from conduct, for the latter is only the expression of the former in our daily lives.

"Whatsoever things are true," spiritually true and real, not lying, false, fictitious, imaginary — reckon with these! True things in doctrine and in life count, for they are bound to assert themselves as being true in the end. All false things will be unmasked as being false in the end, and those who carry them out in their lives, thinking them to be true, will go down in dismay when they find that they are not true at all. It is not a true thing that God does not care what we believe and how we act in consequence. This is a damnable, destructive lie. So we may go on with doctrine after doctrine and with the life it supports. Only the true stands now and forever.

All true things are σεμνά, i. e., they may show their face anywhere at any time and be "respected," honored, and "revered" as true. Only liars sneer at them, refuse to answer, respect, honor them, and by so doing seal their own doom. The opposite of "things revered" are "things worthy of scorn." Derived from σέβομαι, the word connotes what is divinely august and thus worthy of worshipful reverence.

"Righteous" and "pure" throw another light on these things. The divine Judge declares them right in all his verdicts. The opposite are things that this Judge condemns in all his verdicts. In order to receive the verdict "righteous" or "right" these things must naturally be "pure," without stain of error or sin. The opposite is "unclean," a term that is applied to the demons and not only to what they do. There is no restriction to sex as some suppose, just as "true" means vastly more than veracity in speech. Such restrictive reading of the terms divides them whereas they are not to be separated.

Being true, etc., they are certainly also "lovely"
so that the heart should incline toward them (πρός)
in affection (φιλεῖν) and embrace them. The opposite
is what one should despise, hate, and thrust away.
Those who divide the items think of lovable personal
bearing toward others, our manners should be pleasing. But more is implied. We ourselves are to love
and to embrace these things.

"Lovely things" will naturally be spoken of accordingly, will be "of good report," *ansprechend,* appealing,
not "high-toned," for the opposite is δύσφημα, "of ill
report." In II Cor. 6:8 Paul says of himself: "through
ill report and good report." Evil men slander us and
our doctrine and our life, but this is not a stain on us
but on such men themselves.

Paul now individualizes: "if anything (is) excellence, and if praise," (speaking of it as put in the
way in which it deserves to be mentioned). Both
terms are, of course, to be regarded from the Christian standpoint like the other items. Paul is not using
the terms employed by pagan, namely Stoic, moralists;
Christian exhortation does not need to borrow from
pagans, it is rich in its own linguistic right. The two
terms used here refer to personal possession ("excellence") and to Christian estimate ("praise").

'Αρετή, much used by secular writers but seldom
found in the New Testament, means *Tuechtigkeit,*
"efficient ability," and does not well lend itself to Christian thought. "Virtue" in its older English sense will
do but not in the usual sense as being the opposite of
"vice." C.-K. 163, etc., rightly states that our passage
is not to be restricted to moral virtues or to anything
specifically moral as little as the previous terms are.
"Excellence" includes faith as well as life and thus all
that also goes with faith. Its opposite must be just as
broad. Lightfoot's view is unacceptable: "Whatever
value may exist in (heathen) virtue" — none exists

there for the Christian. Deissmann's "splendor of God" is out of line, nor does "praise" mean the praise that is due to his splendor. The opposite of the effective excellence here referred to is spiritual worthlessness, either objective or subjective.

"These things keep reckoning with," not merely "think on" them (our versions) but ever take account of them as what they are and never appropriate any but these. To reckon with them is to treat them as being the genuine values.

9) To the reckoning, which is found in the enlightened mind, Paul thus adds: "These things keep practicing," namely in your lives. Paul uses two verbs, but he does so because they go together. Whoever reckons only with these things as being the only true, righteous ones, etc., will at the same time practice them. Carrying them in his heart and his mind, he will use none others in his faith and his life. Again we should not narrow to what we call "morality"; John 6:40 makes our seeing the Son and believing him most essential. The whole activity of faith is included in πράσσετε, all our receiving and embracing and not only our producing and our good works.

Now Paul defines "these things" in a new way, in one that is concrete and personal: "What things you both learned and received as well as heard and saw in me." These things have been exemplified in Paul's own person (ἐν = in the case or person of, R. 587) and have been personally communicated to the Philippians. We do not correlate twice: "both learned as well as received, both heard as well as saw." For learning and receiving is the one act, hearing and seeing the other, "in me" is to be construed only with the second. Paul had taught them these things in their true value, and they had learned and received them, made them their own. Paul had ever exemplified these things in his own person (faith and life), and they

had heard this from many sources, heard what Paul
was before he came to Philippi, heard what he was
after he left Philippi even as they are now hearing it
in the epistle, they had also seen it right in Philippi
every time he was in their midst. Paul lived what he
taught; he could say: "Be joint imitators of mine"
(3:17). Every preacher should be able to say this.
"Like priest, like people" should be raised from being
a fling at preachers to honest praise of them.

"And" is again consecutive (v. 7). "And so the
God of this peace (article of previous reference to
peace in v. 7) will be with you." Instead of "the
peace of God" Paul now has "the God of this peace,"
he himself who bestows this peace with its power will
be with you with this peace. No wonder this peace
will be so mighty in guarding and protecting their
very hearts and thoughts. It is plain that "this peace"
is as objective as God himself. Blessed, indeed, will all
Paul's readers be who heed these exhortations of his and
receive the fulfillment of the promises assured to them.

Paul Thanks the Philippians for the Gift They Sent Him by the Hand of Epaphroditus

10) This he reserves for the last. It is by no
means the real reason for writing this letter; regarding
that reason see the introduction. Paul had sent his
thanks at once when the companions of Epaphroditus
returned to Philippi. That is why: "I thank you!"
does not occur in this paragraph. After having properly sent his thanks Paul writes *about* this gift, states
what it means to him, namely beautiful fruit from the
Philippians that rejoices his heart. Paul has *not*
referred to the gift in the previous parts of the letter,
not even in 2:25, 30.

**Now I rejoiced in the Lord greatly that now at
last you were letting your being minded for my**

benefit bloom anew — since you, indeed, were minding but were having no opportunity.

Transitional δέ introduces the new subject. Robertson, *W. P.*, does not explain why the verb is a timeless aorist so that it may be translated with the English present: "I rejoice"; he may be trying to justify the translation of the R. V. This is a simple aorist of fact (A. V.) : Paul rejoiced when the gift was presented to him, and the aorist places his readers at the moment when that joy came to him because of the sweet surprise. In English we use the perfect to express actions that are recently past (R. 842, etc.) and we may do so here: "I have rejoiced greatly in the Lord." Here the word for joy is again found, the last time it occurs in this epistle. Its connection with the Lord is evident when we see the unselfish, spiritual quality of this joy. Here alone "greatly" is associated with rejoicing, and it lets us see how surprised and delighted Paul was when a handsome gift was so unexpectedly presented to him by the messengers from the Philippian church.

Ὅτι states the reason for this rejoicing: "that now at last you were letting bloom anew your being minded for my benefit," i. e., your mindfulness in my behalf. This makes the verb causative and transitive, the substantivized infinitive its object. Equally good is the intransitive: "that now at last you were blooming anew in regard to your being minded for my benefit," the infinitive being the adverbial of respect. See B.-P. 84. This verb is used in both ways. This point of grammar should not cause us to overlook the beauty of the expression. Like a flowering plant the Philippians were sending out new bloom as they did twice before in the same way (v. 15). The imperfect tense pictures the process, the bud starting, swelling, bursting into flower.

Here we again have φρονεῖν, the minding which takes interest, makes plans, and then proceeds to act. It is the proper word and is used several times in this letter (v. 2; 2:2, 5; 3:15, 19) and twice here. The subject of the infinitive is the same as that of the verb: "your minding." The durative present tense states that the Philippians have always had Paul in mind — a fine touch, indeed. We shall find the same delicacy running through the paragraph.

Tó is scarcely to be construed with the phrase alone: minding "the thing in behalf of me," although this verb governs the accusative; in the Greek this would be τά, the plural, also because τά could not be construed with the infinitive. The relative phrase is causal: "since," see *in extenso* on Rom. 5:12, and compare 3:12 and II Cor. 5:4. The classics would use the plural ἐφ᾽ οἷς. We need not discuss the efforts to have the phrase mean "in which," "upon which," etc. (R., *W. P.*, and others; "seeing that" in the R. V. margin is correct, not so "wherein" in the A. and R. V. texts).

Καί and δέ contrast: "since you also or indeed were minding but were having no opportunity." What the present infinitive implies is stated outright by the imperfect: the Philippians "were minding," i. e., all along had Paul in mind, wanted to do something for him but were not in a position to do anything. Paul does not say why they had no opportunity. We have, however, II Cor. 8:1-3 which mention the hard times that had struck the Macedonians and put them into great poverty. While that occurred about six years before this time, the tenses used by Paul justify the conclusion that these bad times continued, and that the situation had not improved until this time.

This explains ἤδε ποτέ, ποτέ indicating the indefinite past, ἤδη the immediate present: "now at last," i. e., so soon they flowered in their generosity after the long depression of the past. We likewise see the causal force of the relative clause. They were now at last flowering *because* they minded all along although they were all along unable to do anything. This is beautiful praise of the Philippians. Just as soon as they could they went into bloom *because* they had it in mind all along and had been prevented only from showing it. But some turn the praise into blame: Paul has been waiting with impatience for this last remittance from Philippi and is glad that they have now at last sent it. Paul then tries to soften the blame by adding that they thought of him but had no opportunity to forward their gift, but this still leaves the sting that, if they had tried hard enough, they would have found an opportunity and obviated this delay. We do not, of course, agree with this view.

11) **Not that I am speaking with regard to lack** (lacking, being short of means) as though this were the reason for Paul's joy at receiving the Philippians' gift. No; his joy is without this thought about himself and his personal circumstances; it lies entirely in the thought about the Philippians, about their flowering so promptly in their thoughtfulness regarding him the moment their circumstances improved somewhat.

"For" explains: **For I on my part learned,** (the English prefers: have learned) **in what circumstances I am, to be content. I know both to be made lowly, I know as well to abound; in everything and in all ways I have been initiated both to be filled and to be hungry, both to abound as well as to lack** (be behind, short of necessities).

The emphatic "I on my part" is not in contrast to other people but in reference to the statement just made that Paul is not referring to any lack in means when he expresses his joy because of the gift sent him. He has long since learned to be content in whatever circumstances ($\dot{\epsilon}\nu$ $o\tilde{\iota}s$, not masculine, Luther) he is.

The Stoics practiced the virtue of being "content" in all circumstances by letting no joy elate, no adversity depress them, and bearing everything "stoically" as we still say. The idea they had was to be self-sufficient. What a gulf between the pagan and the Christian conception! The pagan virtue is self-made, the Christian rests on God, on his provident love and care.

12) Paul specifies: "I know both to be made lowly (2:3), I know as well to abound." Καί — καί is "both — and (as well)"; the repetition of "I know" makes the two infinitives more emphatic and equal. It is incorrect to say that οἶδα = I know by experience when this is the meaning so often attributed to γινώσκω. The difference between these verbs is stated by C.-K. 388. Here only the relation of the two objects to Paul is stated and not his relation to them. The idea of experience lies in the infinitives. Paul is well acquainted with these opposite experiences: to be made very lowly — to abound in or to be amid plenty. The idea is that he knows how to adjust himself to either with equal contentment. I Thess. 6:6.

Paul explains still farther: "In everything and in all ways (as in Eph. 1:23: ἐν πᾶσι, in all ways, or in all respects, adverbial; not: in all things) I have been initiated both to be filled as well as to hunger, both to abound as well as to lack." The perfect tense implies that, once having been initiated, Paul remains so. We take issue with those who claim that Paul borrows this verb from the initiatory rites of the pagan mystery cults and refer the word μυστήριον, which is derived from this verb μύω, to the same source. Kennedy even inverts the usage of this verb by claiming that the technical sense came first and the general sense later. Scores of words prove the opposite. All sciences, for instance, take common words in their ordinary use and often attach a technical meaning to

them for technical purposes. Only at times, when no
common word is at hand, a brand-new one is coined,
which may then come into commoner use. This verb
and its noun "mystery" are beyond question such as
belong to the former. "To learn a secret" is as old as
women's gossip. I do *not* use the language of the
lodge every time I say "mystery," "secret," "I have
learned a secret or mystery," "I am let in on one," "I
am initiated." I am not talking like a Stoic when I use
"content" or "contentment" (I Tim. 6:6). Nor is Paul.

Now "both — as well as" are doubled, first with
the specific idea of being filled with plenty of food
and then also being in hunger for food; secondly, with
the broad abounding in all that one needs and in
being behind, short of what one really needs. Note
"in necessities" and "in (forced) fastings" (II Cor.
6:4, 5) ; "we both hunger, and thirst, and are naked"
(I Cor. 4:11), "in hunger and thirst, in fastings often,
in cold and nakedness"; compare Matt. 25:35, 36; Heb.
11:37b. Paul was ever in God's hands. If he was to
perish from want, it would be God's will.

13) He reaches out still farther. **For everything I am strong in connection with him who
empowers me.** Enduring want is among the least
of the matters that Paul faces. He does not regard it
such a great achievement to be content when he is
lacking necessities; he had much more that taxed his
strength. Πάντα is called a cognate accusative by R.
413; it seems to be an adverbial accusative: "as to
everything I am strong," "everything" with its natural
limitation to what the Lord may send. The participle
is the stronger, being derived from δύναμις, "power,"
while the verb is derived from the lesser ἰσχύς,
"strength." The ἐν is *not* instrumental but = "in connection with." Being connected with the Lord who
keeps empowering him, Paul always has the strength
for everything in his life and his work.

All that is stated about himself is not said boastfully, nor is it said in order to let the Philippians know that he could have done without their recent gift. It is said in order to put the gift and Paul's joy because of it on the true plane, not that of mere use that Paul could make of the gift toward filling his need, but of what the gift revealed about the givers themselves. I might say: "Thank you; I am glad for *the gift* and can surely use it!" Paul says: "I rejoice greatly over *you givers,* over what I see in you, beautiful flowering and fruit (v. 17)!" The spiritual mind moves on the higher plane. Then, too, Paul says all this about himself in order to instill a like spirit in his readers. He does not need to use the admonitory form, the Philippians will feel that they, too, should rise to this height. They had passed through hard times and might have to do so again. Some are always poor. Nor was poverty the only burden that needed strength from him who empowers us. This is a good text for hard times in the common meaning of the expression and also in its wider meaning.

14) After the digression with the import indicated Paul returns to the main point of what made him rejoice so greatly in regard to the gift. Πλήν has the same force it had in 3:16. **Only you did nobly in jointly fellowshipping my affliction.** Σύν in the participle means that the Philippians acted jointly in this matter. They all combined their efforts in fellowshipping Paul's affliction. See how beautifully Paul thus describes their gift: he regards it as their joint coming to share his affliction, his condition as a prisoner in behalf of the gospel. This is what their gift means to him, and by saying it he elevates the thought of his readers so that their gift will mean the same to them. For that is the real nobleness of their act. Καλῶς is more than: you did "well"; it is "excellently," "nobly." Paul's straightforward commendation is the best kind

of thanks. Yet note that it does not turn on the monetary value for Paul but on the spiritual value of the act of the givers in their relation to Paul.

15) This is not all that Paul is able to say. He vividly recalls the days, some ten years ago, when the Philippians had done the same thing. **Moreover, also you Philippians know that in the beginning of the gospel, when I left from Macedonia, not a single church fellowshipped me as regards an account of giving and receiving except you alone, (namely) that even in Thessalonica both once and again you sent for my need.**

"Moreover" adds this old item to the new one, and it is to the credit of the Philippians. "Also you Philippians know" means: as well as I know and will never forget. "Philippians" is not a vocative (R. V.) but an apposition (A. V.) "The beginning of the gospel" is like the caption of Mark's Gospel. Read together: "in the beginning of the gospel when I left from Macedonia." This marks the time. There is no need to debate as to whether this "beginning" refers to the standpoint of the readers, the beginning of gospel work in Europe, or includes Paul's previous work in Galatia. In either case "beginning" denotes not a day but a time. So also the clause "when I left from Macedonia" does not mean "when I *had* left" or "*after* I had left." It simply notes the time, and there is no need to insist on the imperfect: "when I was leaving."

Ὅτε = at the time when I left, before I got entirely away. For Thessalonica is located in Macedonia, and there the two gifts that were sent from Philippi reached Paul. That is why καί, "even" is added: "even in Thessalonica," before I actually got farther away. Two points are stressed: 1) the Philippian church had just been founded yet, infant church that it was, sent gifts to Paul; 2) it did this immediately, when Paul left Macedonia, while he was in Thessalonica, before

he got any farther away from Philippi. Not a single
other church ever fellowshipped Paul in this way "save
you (Philippians) only." None had this distinction
save this one. Credit to whom credit is due!

Because of its simple aorists some think that "when
I left from Macedonia" intends to point to II Cor. 11:9;
and this passage is then taken to mean that the Philippians sent a collection to Paul while he was in Corinth
whereas this passage states that "the brethren who
came from Macedonia" helped Paul who was at the
time without funds. Windisch goes to extremes and
thinks that Paul had ordered *mit Nachdruck* that a
general collection be taken in all the Macedonian
churches and be given to him! II Cor. 11:9 does not
mention a collection or a church but only some brethren
who helped Paul. It is unlikely that they came from
Philippi. This idea is unacceptable here where the
two gifts that were sent to Thessalonica *follow* (v. 16),
a gift that was sent to Corinth cannot *precede*.

Paul remains on the high plane: none "fellowshipped me." "Not a single church" omits reference to
individuals who acted as did those mentioned in II Cor.
11:9. But he now expresses himself in the technical
language of business: "as regards an account of giving
and receiving," i. e., as opening a ledger account with
credit and debit columns. Does this mean 1) an
account kept by Paul or 2) one kept by such a church
or 3) one kept by both? Opinions are divided. Yet the
subject is not Paul nor Paul plus a church; it is "not
a single church" that opened such an account save you
Philippians alone. No; Paul would not think of keeping a business account of what *he* gave and what *he*
received. The most that he ever said in this respect
is I Cor. 9:11; in v. 12 he adds that he used no such
power, in v. 18 that he preached the gospel gratis. A
man who works gratis keeps no ledger, for he has no
entries to make.

While Paul is praising the Philippians he is not
blaming the other churches for never having sent him
a gift; pay and regular support he always absolutely
refused; read the reason in I Cor. 9. The gifts sent
to him by the Philippians he could not refuse without
insulting and offending this church. Yet he neither
expected nor wanted even an occasional gift, his wealth
was his contentment.

16) Neither the ὅτι in v. 15 nor this one in v. 16 =
"because." Our versions think the latter should be
so translated ("for"), but we should then expect γάρ.
The clause is explicative: "except you only, (namely)
that even (already) in Thessalonica both once and
again you sent for my need." Καὶ ἅπαξ καὶ δίς = a
couple of times (B.-P. 311), meaning twice. "Both
— and" makes prominent the "one time" (ἅπαξ) and,
with the other gift coming, "two times" (δίς) : both
once, yes, even twice, cf. I Thess. 2:18 . Here we have
Paul's own word for it that he had received *two* gifts
from Philippi.

17) **Not that I am out for the gift but I am out
for the fruit, that which increases to your account.**
Paul is not making a complaint and does not want
a reader to think that he is. Such a thing is far from
his mind. R., *W. P.*, is right, this is not "nervous
anxiety to clear himself" of wanting a gift but "delicate courtesy." "*The* gift," like "*the* fruit," considers
both concrete and actual, hence the articles. In v. 15
Paul writes δόσις, "giving," the act; here δόμα, "gift,"
the thing given. R. 151. The two verbs = "to seek
after," to be intent on getting. "Fruit" continues the
idea of bloom mentioned in v. 10. Yet to say that
Paul is seeking after "the fruit" is still liable to be
misunderstood as though he wanted "the gift" as "the
fruit" for his own consumption; no, he does not want
the fruit for himself, he wants only "that fruit which,
of whatever it consists, grows to your account," "to

the account *of you*." This is again the commercial use of λόγος. Paul is seeking for one thing only, to make the credit side of the ledger of all his churches grow as large as possible. Christ will settle the account as he himself pictures it for us in Luke 19:15, etc.; Matt. 25:19, etc.

18) **Moreover, I duly have everything and abound; I have been filled by having received from Epaphroditus the things from you, an odor of sweet odor, a sacrifice acceptable, well-pleasing to God.**

The connection of thought is simple: Paul is not after the gift, but he is after what redounds to the credit of the Philippians; δέ, "moreover," as far as their gifts is concerned, it actually makes Paul feel rich and surely is to the credit of the Philippians. We have noted the mercantile terms Paul uses, for instance, λόγος, "account," just preceding. Ἀπέχω is another such term which was used by Jesus in the same way (Matt. 6:2, 5, 16). The papyri and the ostraca have it in the sense of: "I have received in full," as we give a receipt in full for moneys or goods received. As is the case regarding a few other verbs, ἀπό has the force of "duly." Yet Paul is not sending the Philippians a formal receipt. If he intended to do that he would stop with this statement: "Now I receipt in full for everything." Paul is only adopting this business term and uses it together with two other verbs, not in the sense of assuring the Philippians of a receipt in full, but to let them know how rich he feels. Epaphroditus, we are certain, had not come alone. We have seen that he was more than the bearer of the gift to Paul; the Philippians had sent *him* as a gift to be Paul's assistant in their place (see 2:25). The companions of Epaphroditus had returned to Philippi and had reported that the gift had been duly delivered to Paul. A formal receipt at this later writing would be out of place. But the language employed in receipts joined with other expressions that indicate Paul's feeling of being very rich are very much in place.

He has duly received everything — which may not have been only money — and so he "abounds" as one who has more than enough. Without a connective he adds: "I have been filled" like a vessel to the very brim, the perfect tense indicating that he continues to be full. The asyndeton indicates that this verb includes the two that precede, it is like an apposition. Hence the participle does not modify the three verbs; it modifies only the last.

Epaphroditus was the leader of the little party that brought the gift. The emphasis is, however, on the character of the gift "from you," namely that it is "an odor of sweet odor," etc., which recalls Eph. 5:2. Both words are derived from ὄζω, to emit an odor; our word "odor" is a derivative. The Hebrew *reach nichoach* = odor of soothing, the second noun being *ein Ersatz von "versoehnend," "angenehm"* (Ed. Koenig, *Woerterbuch* 276); it is used thus in Gen. 8:21 and repeatedly in Leviticus. The genitive may be adjectival: "a sweet-odored odor" ("a sweet-smelling savor," A. V. in Eph. 5:2; but "an odor of a sweet smell" in the A. V. of our passage). Incense was burned, so were the burnt sacrifices, and they emitted an odor, the true sweetness of which consisted in the spiritual condition of the persons bringing the sacrifice, cf., Lev. 26:31; Amos 5:21, 22; Ps. 5:16, 17.

Bringing out still more the thought that the gift of the Philippians is really an offering to God, Paul adds: "a sacrifice acceptable, well-pleasing to God." We need not say that θυσία drops the idea of a slaughter sacrifice. Since it is appositional to "odor," the thought centers on the odor of the sacrifice that was burned and thus sent up an odor. The entire designation is figurative: what the old Jewish sacrifices at the Temple were this gift of the Philippians is, it has the same sweet odor for God and is thus "acceptable, well-pleasing to God." Would that all our gifts deserved this characterization!

19) I have been filled by you, God will fill you. **Now my God will fill every need of yours according to his riches in glory in connection with Christ Jesus.** "*My* God" because Paul was the recipient of the gift which was in reality a sacrifice pleasing to God. The future is volitive: God *will* fill every need of those who are well-pleasing to him, he has said so: "Give, and it shall be given to you" (Luke 6:38; Prov. 19:17). The fact that God often employs the agency of men for this makes no difference. The idea that this promise refers to the coming Messianic kingdom is an undue restriction of its meaning. Like other promises of this character, this one, too, refers to the present life, to its bodily needs, and to its spiritual needs, to "every" one of them. In heaven we shall have no needs, and it is only rationalizing to contend that we shall have, for all of them will then be supplied. In v. 16 Paul mentions his own need which was certainly one of this life; so he now refers to the need of his readers which was also of this life. Paul cannot repay the Philippians, Paul's God will.

How bountifully! "According to his riches in glory in connection with Christ Jesus." We read this as it stands: the riches are in glory, and the glory is in Christ. Incredible, we are told, because Paul should then write: "according to the riches *of* his glory in Christ Jesus." Paul means, we are told: "God will fill your every need in glory," but then there is a debate as to whether ἐν is instrumental: "with glory," or modal, "in a glorious manner." The phrase is supposed to place the filling of every need into the glory of the hereafter although some add: not exclusively.

These contentions overlook the fact that, if Paul meant what they think he says, he would have written

the phrase where it ought to stand: "will fill your every
need in glory according to his riches," etc. Are not
God's riches *"in* glory" as well as "riches *of* his glory"?
And all this glory is the shining forth of his love and
his grace "in Christ Jesus." Paul wants all three
included in his κατά phrase which denotes the norm
and measure God will use when he fills every need of
the Philippians: God will use his great *riches,* the
riches that shine "in *glory,"* and this is the glory connected with *Christ Jesus,* our blessed Savior. It is
about as grand a way of expressing what norm God
will use as one can devise. What are our litte needs
here on earth when God uses this norm?

20) **Now to our God and Father the glory for
the eons of the eons! Amen.** This doxology marks
the end. To the glory which is God's own eternal
possession is added the glory we ascribe to him when
we know, praise, worship, and glorify him. This is
an exclamation. Since they follow the one article,
"God and Father" are considered a unit, "our" modifies
both. Regarding the εἰς phrase with its duplicated
plurals compare Gal. 1:5 where "amen" is also added.

The Conclusion

21) **Salute every saint in Christ Jesus!** This
is the usual way of sending greetings (see Rom. 16:3,
etc.), not: "I salute," but "do you salute," literally
"embrace" for me. The view that "in Christ Jesus"
does not modify "every saint" because "saint" already
includes connection with Christ, and that the phrase
is to be construed with the verb: "salute in Christ
Jesus," is answered by 1:1: "to all the saints in Christ
Jesus," where no verb is used. We do not know why
Paul greets no one in Philippi by name. See the full
discussion at the end of Ephesians where no greetings
whatever are sent.

There salute you the brethren with me. These
are the assistants of Paul. We do not know just who
they were. There is no difficulty regarding 2:20,
where Paul does not say that he has no one with him
but that he has no one who is equally minded with
Timothy.

22) **There salute you all the saints, especially
those from Caesar's household.** "All the saints" =
the congregations at Rome. In the first and original
congregation there were many "from Caesar's household." The reason that Paul is able to send greetings
from them "especially" is most likely due to the fact
that they had more easy access to Paul or more frequent access. These were neither members of Nero's
family nor praetorian soldiers (see 1:13).

"Those from Caesar's household" are the imperial
slaves who came into Nero's possession upon the death
of their former masters, Aristobulus and Narcissus.
See the author's exposition of Rom. 16:10, 11. In Rom.
16:3, etc., there is mentioned the *whole* original Roman
congregation to which Paul addressed Romans; here
this whole congregation sends greetings. Prominent
in it were the two groups of slaves who were now
belonging to Nero. But these slaves were not unedu-
cated, menial servants. Parables such as Luke 19:12
with its δοῦλοι, Matt. 25:14 with its "slaves," offer us
clearness on that matter. Great lords used many
slaves as managers of their estates, their finances, their
business. These were highly educated men who were
often abler than their lords. The emperor needed
many of them. How they became Christians, apparently before they came into Nero's possession (in
Rom. 16 Paul still names them after their former
masters), is an intriguing question; but they did.
Their membership in the Roman congregation explains,
at least in part, how Paul came to write a letter as
grand as Romans to this congregation.

The fact that these men of the emperor's own great household are especially mentioned as sending greetings reveals the truth that at this time, when Paul's case was up before the imperial court, they are in closer touch with him. At an earlier time, when Paul wrote Colossians, Philemon, and Ephesians, this was not the case. Naturally; for now the trial, so long awaited, was bringing not only Paul's own case but also the whole cause of the gospel to an issue. Who would now be more concerned than these slaves of Nero's own household?

From the original congregation in Rome, to whom Paul had addressed Romans from Corinth, we must distinguish the great mass of Jewish Christians whom Paul had converted during his stay of two years in Rome, see the author's exposition of Acts 28:17-31. These Jewish Christians remained together in their own synagogues. They were altogether too numerous to enter into the old congregation *en masse;* nor was there any reason that they should not remain in their own synagogues. At least three or four of the seven large synagogues in Rome were entirely Christianized. Paul's πάντες οἱ ἅγιοι perhaps included also these saints as well as those of the old Jewish and Gentile church. See also the author's introduction to Hebrews.

23) **The grace of the Lord Jesus Christ with your spirit!** Some texts read "with you all" (A. V.). "With your spirit" is thought to have been taken from Gal. 6:18; but why this should be done is not stated. Substantially there is no difference: if grace is with us, it is with our spirit. "Grace" (1:2) is the saving favor of the Lord plus all its gifts. It is always undeserved, unmerited, even in the case of "saints," whom the word itself thus reminds that they are still sinners. "Amen" at the end may be textually genuine although our R. V. does not think so.

The note at the end: "To the Philippians," appears in most of the important texts yet amounts to no more than the ancient title which was affixed by the copyists also to the outside of the manuscript roll. This title was expanded by some of the copyists: "To the Philippians written from Rome through Epaphroditus" (A. V.). "From Rome" is correct, but "through Epaphroditus" is only an ancient tradition. We do not know whether Paul employed Epaphroditus as his amanuensis for this letter. The fact that Epaphroditus carried the letter to Philippi is almost certain.

Soli Deo Gloria